YOUTH & CRIME

YOUTH & CRIME

Third Edition

John Muncie

Los Angeles | London | New Delhi
Singapore | Washington DC

First edition published 1999; second edition published 2004
Reprinted 1999, 2001, 2002, 2005, 2006

SAGE Publications Ltd
1 Oliver's Yard
55 City Road
London EC1Y 1SP

SAGE Publications Inc.
2455 Teller Road
Thousand Oaks, California 91320

SAGE Publications India Pvt Ltd
B 1/I 1 Mohan Cooperative Industrial Area
Mathura Road
New Delhi 110 044

SAGE Publications Asia-Pacific Pte Ltd
33 Pekin Street #02-01
Far East Square
Singapore 048763

British Library Cataloguing in Publication data

A catalogue record for this book is available from the
British Library

ISBN 978-1-84787-431-3
ISBN 978-1-84787-432-0

Library of Congress Control Number: 2008933575

Typeset by C&M Digitals (P) Ltd., Chennai, India
Printed in Great Britain by TJ International, Padstow, Cornwall
Printed on paper from sustainable resources

FOR ELLA

Contents

Detailed Contents

List of Boxes

Preface to the Third Edition

This book is designed to encourage the reader to adopt a critical understanding of the array of political talk, media stories, government initiatives and academic research about young people with which we are daily bombarded.

The first edition of *Youth & Crime* was completed in October 1998. At the time the UK was in the throes of a panic about 'superpredators' and persistent young offenders. The first secure training centre for 12 to 15 year olds had just opened and the entire structure of youth justice in England and Wales was in the process of radical reform as a result of the flagship legislation, the Crime and Disorder Act. The second edition of *Youth & Crime* was written in 2003 amidst another set of concerns about street crime and anti-social behaviour. The Anti-social Behaviour Act with its powers of dispersal and 'naming and shaming' had just received Royal Assent. Now, in the summer of 2008, it is 'hoodies', youth gangs and knife crime that head the law and order agenda. Another crackdown is promised with nationwide curfews, 'shock tactics', more police, increased 'pay back' sentencing powers and more prisons advocated as the means to mend 'our broken society'. Adult fear of, and obsession with, youth, crime and disorder are unrelenting. Over this decade a blizzard of new and old initiatives have been launched to tackle the 'youth problem' ranging from targeting teenage mothers and the 'at risk' yet to be born to ensuring that England and Wales have one of the highest rates of youth custody in Western Europe. Yet this constant media and political talk of national crisis has taken place against a backdrop of significant falls in the recorded youth crime rate and decreases in the numbers of violent crimes.

'Youth' and 'crime' are excessively politicized: terms of condemnation, rather than description. And this concern goes beyond the 'criminal' to include behaviour designated as 'pre-criminal', 'anti-social' and 'nuisance'. Governmental rhetoric also talks of the need to support and protect – as currently expressed through the 'Every Child Matters' agenda. As a result, all three editions of this book have never been (and cannot be) simply about crime as committed by young people. Youth crime must be placed in a broader context in which it is acknowledged that the most serious harms afflicting society are clearly not perpetuated by young people at all. Any serious analysis must also confront the issue of why certain aspects of young people's behaviour are singled out as particularly problematic and in what circumstances they are considered as deserving a criminal justice-based rather than a social welfare-based response. In this sense neither is the book simply about young people. It is just as much concerned to explore the nature of adult reaction – whether this is grounded in protection, anger, resentment, philanthropy, fear, vengeance, child hatred or ambivalence.

Structure of the book

Chapter 1 examines current parameters of the 'youth crime problem' as expressed through media representations, political discourses and statistical data. It now includes new material on youth gangs, drugs and street crime as well as updating those assessments of the extent of disorder as can be gleaned from police records, self report studies and victim surveys. Vitally, it reveals the constantly shifting parameters and meaning attached to the two key concepts: those of 'youth' and 'crime'.

Chapter 2 draws upon social history research to reveal how much of our current obsession is far from unprecedented and novel. Moreover, it shows how the identification of 'troublesome youths' is inseparable from the various policies that have been formulated for their control. The chapter provides an important reminder that while adult concern may be persistent, the precise means through which it is articulated is subject to continual dispute and change. One of the key insights from recent work in this area has been to underline the gender-specific nature of problem identification and policy response.

Chapter 3 looks at a diverse range of criminological theory – from anthropology, biology, psychology to sociology – which has attempted to discover the causes of youth crime. These theories – largely rooted in positivism – continue to make a significant impact not only on academic understandings but also on public perceptions and policy formulation. Of note has been a growing faith in theories that claim to be able to predict future delinquency by identifying the 'risk factors' embedded in our early lives.

Chapter 4 explores a different range of theories which are more concerned with the relationship between crime and how and why certain behaviours become criminalized while others do not. Radical criminology is primarily concerned with revealing how crime is selectively 'created' through relations of power and the capacity of state institutions to confer criminality on others. A newly emergent social harm perspective, for example, warns of any unreflective juxtaposition of the referents of 'youth' and 'crime' such that young people are constantly denied their place as legitimate citizens and many more serious harms go unchallenged.

Chapter 5 has been specially written for this edition. It reverses the logic of dominant representations of the 'youth problem' by not only drawing attention to the extent of youth victimization but also exposing the depth of abuse and violence to which some young people are routinely exposed in the home and in institutions. By going beyond the parameters of conventional youth criminology, the chapter also reveals the degree of national and international negligence and indifference to child harm as most vividly illustrated by child trafficking, child soldiering and child poverty which appear promulgated on a global scale.

Chapter 6 underlines the point that the 'problem of youth' is not simply one of 'criminal behaviour' by examining how youth lifestyles, in the form of subcultures, consumer groups and countercultures, have been, and continue to be, constituted as a 'threat'. The chapter draws extensively on the insights offered by a cultural criminology designed to reveal the links between youth marginality, the transgressive, media representations and processes of both commodification and criminalization.

Chapter 7 examines how youth is also a prime site of regulation; how social policies in employment, housing and welfare have become progressively submerged within criminal justice agendas. Traditional policy boundaries are now blurred in an interlinked series of interventions designed to reconstitute youth welfare through the zero tolerance policing of public space, the targeting of incivilities and the 'anti-social', the identification of dysfunctional families and the prevention of social exclusion through new moralities of inclusion. Issues of child protection and welfare have become merged with those of the 'anti-social' and the criminal.

Chapters 8 and 9 analyse the diverse and contested strategies that make up the complex of contemporary forms of youth justice. Traditionally the fault lines of youth justice have been generated by the twin concerns to have regard to the welfare of children while also holding them responsible for their actions. This welfare and justice debate has been made significantly more complex since the 1980s. Experiments in restorative justice, evidence-led practice, partnerships and adherence to principles of 'what works', seem to herald some new beginnings. However, the 'new' is also submerged within a persistent authoritarianism and populist punitiveness. What is it that seems continually to feed our punitive obsession so that we are more concerned to punish rather than to understand?

Chapter 10 has also been specially prepared for this edition and examines international developments, global trends and national and local configurations in youth justice policy and practice in the twenty-first century. This analysis not only allows some assessment of UK performance relative to other western countries and to international children's rights directives, but also considers how far a combination of neo-liberal economic pressures and neo-conservative political agendas is shaping youth justice and welfare policy around the (western) world.

In these ways the book outlines the parameters of a comprehensive *critical youth criminology*. Youth studies has traditionally been viewed as a minor field in both sociology and criminology, somewhat surprisingly for the latter, given that most of its research and theoretical output has been driven by studying the young as the 'most criminogenic age'. Conversely, youth leisure pursuits and questions of style have tended to remain in sociology and cultural studies. It has taken the emergence of a cultural criminology in the 1990s to begin to break down these disciplinary boundaries. Conversely again, social policy and criminology have traditionally been viewed as separate disciplines with barely any mutual exchange. The seeping criminalization of social policy and particularly the impact of theories of governance in conceptualizing how young people are constituted in time and space are, however, beginning to break down these barriers. It is also becoming increasingly apparent that our understanding of youth and crime has been historically trapped in Anglo-American conceptions and nation state specific prescriptions. Emergent international children's rights agendas and the flows of global capital and social policy necessitate moving beyond these familiar territorial boundaries. They also necessitate moving out of the confines of what is currently understood to be 'criminology'.

A teaching and learning resource

The book contains numerous devices to facilitate the teaching and learning of the complexity of youth and crime. The chapters have now been more explicitly designed to mirror a series of lectures, guiding the reader through key topics and debates. In each chapter you will find:

Chapter Overview

At the beginning of each chapter a brief bullet-pointed introduction is given to provide a flavour of the types of issues that will be addressed.

Key Terms

A list of those key terms particularly pertinent to each chapter is provided. These terms are subsequently emboldened when they are first encountered in the text itself. Each of these terms is also described in the glossary.

Cross-References

Every effort has been made to reveal how the issues raised within the ten separate chapters of this book are not hermetically sealed and self-contained. Extensive cross-referencing (indicated in bold type) has been included to illustrate, for example, how theory inflects policy and practice and how long-established disciplinary boundaries are being broken down.

Boxed 'Resources'

A special feature of this book is the inclusion of a variety of extracts from original sources and a number of tables, diagrams, summaries and graphs which are designed to present complex ideas, concepts, theories and data in a more accessible form.

Summary Section

Each chapter concludes with a summary of the main issues and debates that have been raised. They are designed as a reminder of the material discussed more fully in the chapter itself.

Study Questions

Again, at the end of each chapter, are included a number of study questions. These are intended to encourage further reflection on the issues raised. Some of these questions have been answered successfully by cohorts of Open University students as either course or examination questions so they may give you some idea of what could feasibly be asked of you after studying this and related materials.

Further Reading

This book can only ever have hoped to introduce you to the multitude of issues that are pertinent to the study of 'critical youth criminology'. There is no substitute for reading some of the original texts yourself. This section directs you to some of the best places to start this search. Full references to these and every other source referred to in this book can be found in the extensive reference list beginning on p. 407.

Web Resources

Researching this edition has been made immeasurably easier through access to numerous research articles, newspaper commentaries, international conventions and statistical data that are now available on-line. Placing such terms as youth and crime into a search engine is, however, likely to return over 3 million hits! This section at the end of each chapter lists some of the most useful websites to guide you in your studies.

Glossary

At the end of the book you will find a glossary of all the key terms that are listed at the head of, and emboldened in, each chapter. A quick glance through these will reveal the diversity of this book's subject matter, but they also provide a short 'definition' of each to begin the process of critical understanding. For further detail of particular concepts, you might consult a specialist dictionary or encyclopedia: the two most pertinent to this book are *The Sage Dictionary of Criminology* (Sage, 2006) and *The Dictionary of Youth Justice* (Willan, 2008).

Acknowledgements

In many respects this book is the culmination of over 25 years of researching and writing about criminology, youth crime and youth justice policy both for the Open University and beyond. In particular, this edition brings together and consolidates work done for dictionaries, journal articles, and chapters for edited collections over the past five years. Innumerable conversations with students and colleagues have made it possible to refine its presentation. The accessibility and scope of this edition have also been notably enhanced by the wise words of Natalie Aguilera at Sage and the panel of eight anonymous respondents who took the time to let me know how the previous edition might best be revised and improved.

The advice of Peter King, who kindly commented on Chapter 2, was invaluable. My thanks also to Barry Goldson who, as well as checking that Chapter 5 was in good order, has been a remarkably supportive fellow traveller amidst the travails of the 'new youth justice' over the past decade.

As ever, I am particularly grateful to Caroline Porter at Sage, who has given me the continual encouragement and the opportunity once more to try to clarify the core issues and debates.

I hope I have not let any of them down.

John Muncie
September 2008

1

Youth Crime

Representations, Discourses and Data

Overview

Chapter 1 examines:

- the concepts of 'crime', 'youth', 'criminalization' and 'social construction';
- how young people have come to be regarded as a threat;
- how the 'problem of youth' is frequently collapsed into the problem of crime and disorder;
- how young people are represented in media and political discourses;
- the reliability of statistical measures of youth offending;
- the gendered nature of offending;
- the relationship between gangs and violent crime;
- the relationship between drug use and criminality.

| **key terms** |

corporate crime; crime; criminalization; delinquency; demonization; deviance; discourse; folk devil; gang; hidden crime; moral panic; official statistics; protective factors; recording of crime; reporting of crime; representation; risk factors; self report studies; social constructionism; status offence; youth

---

This introductory chapter is designed to promote a critical understanding of the relationship between youth and crime. The equation of these two terms is widely employed and for many is accepted as common sense. Stories about youth and crime are a mainstay of most forms of media. Official crime statistics are readily and uncritically recited to substantiate a view that youth crime and disorder are now 'out of control'. But how far do the media reflect social reality and how much are they able to define it? How valid and reliable is statistical evidence? By asking these questions, the chapter draws attention to how the state of youth and the problem of crime come to be defined in particular circumscribed ways. Its critical starting-point is to view 'crime' and 'youth' as social constructions. Populist assumptions and dominant political **discourses** tend to treat social problems as phenomena about whose existence and seriousness we can all agree. The basis of **social constructionism** is that we should ask instead, who says this is a social problem? – and why do they say so? This approach affords a central role to the processes through which the meaning of social phenomena is constructed, produced and reproduced. It is based on the premise that social issues (such as crime, anti-social behaviour, disorder, delinquency – all terms commonly associated with young people) are not self-evident. Rather, their identification, as being worthy of primary media and political (as well as academic) concern, depends on certain individuals and/or organizations making 'truth claims' about the phenomena and being in a position to bring their claims to public awareness.

As a result, the chapter explores how certain negative images and notions of youth and crime are able to be institutionalized, sedimented or 'taken for granted' as facts and objective knowledges, while positive images of young people are relatively downplayed or ignored. It also pays attention to the ways in which these 'constructions' have been challenged, or can be contested, by empirical and theoretical research. In short, it provides an overview of the presences and absences routinely employed in discourses of the 'problem of youth'.

The Threat of Youth

1.1 There is no neutral English noun which can identify a period of **youth** with the same certainty and impersonality as 'child' or 'adult' (Springhall, 1983–84, p. 20). While 'child' and 'adult' are largely neutral terms connoting what is generally viewed as a normative period in life, 'youth' and 'adolescence' usually conjure up a number of emotive and troubling images. These range from notions of uncontrolled freedom, violence, irresponsibility, vulgarity, rebellion and dangerousness to those of deficiency, vulnerability, neglect, deprivation or immaturity. In 2008, the American magazine *Time* captured this mood by declaring that 'Britons are frightened of their own young' (Mayer, 2008). As such, 'youth' is largely defined in terms of what it is lacking; by what it is *not* rather than by what it is (Furlong and Cartmel, 1997, p. 41).

For young people, the terms '**crime**', '**deviance**' and '**delinquency**' collide to attract critical attention to a much wider set of 'problem' behaviours than is usually afforded to adults. For example, 'being incorrigible', running away from home, truancy and congregating in groups are usually only considered to be problematic when committed by young people. In the USA, they are commonly termed '**status offences**'. Common-sense understandings of crime also tend to rely on legal definitions and those behaviours and events that are specified in criminal law. They imply there is some underlying consensus about what constitutes criminality and what does not. But conceptions of crime clearly vary from place to place and change over time. Indeed, Wilkins (1964, p. 46) has claimed that 'there are no absolute standards. At some time or another, some form of society or another has defined almost all forms of behaviour that we now call "criminal" as desirable for the functioning of that form of society.' Moreover, many of the most harmful actions in terms of loss of life and property (think: illegal arms dealings, genocide, corporate fraud, state-sponsored torture, workplace death and injury, domestic violence, child abuse, and so on) either remain relatively hidden or are not recognized as 'crime' at all. The picture is further confused because many of the 'crimes' that we attribute to young people – vandalism, joyriding, mugging, hooliganism – are media-inspired terms and not specific offences recognized by the law.

This section explores how these troubling, and often contradictory, notions are 'resolved' in media and political discourses.

Innocents and Demons

On 12 February 1993, 16 video cameras in a shopping centre in Bootle, Merseyside, filmed two 10 year old boys abducting 2 year old James Bulger. He was found two days later battered to death near a railway line. This particular murder was to form a watershed in media and political responses to youth crime, and not simply because of its apparent brutality. It had at least three related consequences. First, it initiated a reconsideration of the social construction of 10 year olds as 'demons' rather than as 'innocents'. Second, it coalesced with, and helped to mobilize, adult fear and moral panic about the moral degeneracy of youth in general. Third, it recast child offenders as 'devils' (Fionda, 2005) and legitimized a series of tough law and order reforms which came to characterize the following decade and continue to do so. The reverberations are still being felt in a climate of 'child hate' and the denigration of a generation of 'undisciplined' and 'disrespectful' children as 'feral', 'evil' and 'barbarous thugs' (Scraton, 2007, Chapter 6).

The death of James Bulger triggered widespread moral outrage. It was also given widespread and sensational press coverage, both nationally and internationally. The story conformed perfectly to what Chibnall (1977) referred to as the five informal 'rules of relevancy' that govern how popular crime journalism decides what is *newsworthy*: that is how news is *selected* and how it is *presented*. These 'rules' are visible and spectacular acts, physical or sexual violence, graphic presentation, notions of individual pathology, and demands for a firm deterrent and retributive response.

In June 2001, the two boys convicted of the murder were released on parole. The tabloids had long condemned the fact that they had been held in secure units (rather than prison), where according to the *Sun* (9 January 2001) they had enjoyed a 'luxury life' of 'treats, trips and gifts'. When the High Court Judge, Lady Butler-Sloss granted them life-long anonymity to protect them from vigilantes, the *Daily Mail* (9 January 2001) declared this to be 'NO JUSTICE'. Since then the rumour mill has gone into overdrive. On the tenth anniversary of the murder, the *Sunday Mirror* (9 February 2003) had asked where the two boys might be now: 'ON HOLIDAY (ALL EXPENSES PAID, OF COURSE)', with round-the-clock protection by armed police, was the reply. Many seem to assume that the two boys have been relocated to Australia, although this has been consistently denied by both governments. Nevertheless, in 2006, police in Perth, Australia, were forced to make a public statement that a man accused of murdering an 8 year old school girl was *not* either Venables or Thompson (*The Age*, 28 June 2006). Successive email campaigns ('we have to do something to make them pay') have been launched to petition Butler-Sloss to reverse the anonymity ruling. The latest of these was in 2008, following a request for information made in the Queensland State parliament (*Courier Mail*, 4 May 2008).

The Bulger murder still seems capable of galvanizing a mistrust of youth in general and of raising interminable fears of a failing justice system, of child abduction and of 'stranger-danger' in particular (Brown, 2003, p. 52). However, the murder of children by strangers is rare; children are at far more risk from parents and carers (see **Chapter 5**). The murder of a child by other children is also rare. There have been only 27 such murders in the previous 250 years – most notably the case of 11 year old Mary Bell, who killed two small children in 1968. So the story of James Bulger was exceptional: indeed, 'unthinkable' (James and Jenks, 1996, p. 315). But being unusual and unexpected, it was automatically considered newsworthy. In Hall's (1978, p. 22) words, 'It's as if newspapers set out each day with the unspoken assumption that things in the world will be exactly as they left them yesterday. The bigger, the more unexpected, the more violent the change, the bigger the story.' This is what is new; this is what makes the news.

Franklin and Petley (1996) and Davis and Bourhill (1997) provided detailed assessments of the newspaper reportage of the trial of the two boys who were eventually convicted for the murder of James Bulger in November 1993. For all but the *Financial Times* and the *Morning Star* it was the front-page headline story. The *Daily Mail* carried 24 separate articles; the *Daily Express* an eight-page supplement. One of the *Daily Mail's* headlines 'THE EVIL AND THE INNOCENT' (25 November 1993) set the tone for some intensive media agonizing over 'HOW COULD IT HAPPEN?' However, it was the video footage from a security camera of James Bulger being led hand in hand by one of the 10 year olds out of the shopping centre that made the case famous. The blurred and shaky image was replayed endlessly on television. As Alison Young (1996, p. 112) argued, it invited feelings of helplessness and horror as we watched the boys slowly disappear from view with the voyeuristic knowledge that death was to follow. As such, the event 'always existed as much as an image of itself as it did in itself' (Young, 1996, p. 137).

A recurring theme in media **representation** of the case was the juxtaposition of childhood innocence and children as inherently evil. Innocence was easily imputed to James Bulger; he was the symbolic epitome of an ideal child. Normally, 10 year old children would also be media-idealized as innocent victims. But, as Hay (1995) argues, herein lies the crux of the event. We are forced to confront the uncomfortable notion that 10 year olds may not be innocent at all. As the *Sunday Times* (28 November 1993) put it: 'we will never be able to look at our children in the same way again ... Parents everywhere are asking themselves and their friends if the Mark of the Beast might not also be imprinted on their offspring.' And so it was that one of the preferred media explanations of 'why it happened' dwelt on the theme of 'evil'. The *Daily Mirror* (25 November 1993) described the 10 year olds as 'Freaks of Nature' with 'hearts of evil'. Elsewhere, terms such as 'boy brutes', 'monsters', 'animals' and the 'spawn of Satan' abounded. For many, the case demanded that *all* children be regarded as a threat and that childhood be redefined as a time of innate evil. As James and Jenks (1996) suggested, it was not just two children who eventually were put on trial, but the very nature of childhood itself.

Other popular explanations dwelt on an assumed decline in moral responsibility as a result of '1960s permissiveness'. The disintegration of the nuclear family, single parenting and the influence of media violence (particularly the film *Child's Play 3*, 1991) were all cited as key precipitating factors. William Golding's novel *The Lord of the Flies* (1954) was repeatedly referenced as 'evidence' of the horror and evil that are unleashed when children are free from the discipline of adults (*Guardian*, 16 February 1993; *Daily Mail*, 25 November 1993). As a result, any number of alternative 'readings' based on welfare, health, psychology, victimology, psychiatry, behavioural science or economics were subsumed by, or were ruled out in favour of, the law. Once the killing was coded as 'crime', it was the legal process and the assumption of individual responsibility which 'laid down the agenda for what could be reported and commented upon as "news"' (King, 1995, p. 173). To do otherwise would necessitate the questioning of some fundamental inequalities in society and how the state treats some of its most vulnerable and disadvantaged citizens. And such questions do not conform to the imperatives of newsworthiness (Muncie, 1984, p. 20).

The Prime Minister's initial reaction was simply that we should 'condemn a little more and understand a little less' and the Home Secretary opined that no excuses could be made for 'a section of the population who are essentially nasty pieces of work' (*The Times*, 22 February 1993). The two 10 year olds – Jon Venables and Robert Thompson – were tried as adults in the Crown Court and eventually sentenced to be detained for a minimum of eight years. This was raised to 10 years by the Lord Chief Justice and to 15 years by the Home Secretary (a decision subsequently declared to be illegal in July 1996). Much of this punitiveness was inspired by the *Sun* urging its readers to plead with the Home Secretary that the boys should be locked up for life. In 1999, the European Commission of Human Rights ruled that both their trial and their sentencing violated articles of the European Convention on Human Rights and the 'right to a fair trial'. Doubts had long been raised that the age of the defendants and the formality of the Crown court process precluded their full understanding and participation in the legal proceedings. It also ruled that sentencing decisions must be reserved for those independent of government. As a result the *Criminal Justice and Court Services Act 2000* removed such power from the Home Secretary and handed it to the courts.

The Bulger case also came to symbolize something much broader; it became a signifier for a generalized 'crisis' in childhood and a breakdown of moral and social order (James and Jenks, 1996; Davis and Bourhill, 1997). In a climate of general anxiety about crime, the exceptional murder of an infant by two boys, barely at the age of criminal responsibility themselves, was viewed as symptomatic of a prevailing youth crime wave, even though they bore no obvious relation to each other. As Hay (1995, p. 204) argues:

> One mediated event ... does not in and of itself constitute a moral panic. Through the process of discursive amplification, the 'event' is translated from a particular conjuncture that must be understood in its own terms, to an event which is seen as emblematic and symptomatic of broader processes – moral decay, social malaise and the destruction of the social fabric of the family and thus society itself. The shadow of such a threat only becomes identifiable by virtue of the event itself. Yet once the event is seen in this context, the nature of the submerged threat becomes immediately obvious and this in turn makes sense of a multitude of formerly unrelated, yet nonetheless individually troubling phenomena.

In the early 1990s, a raft of youth troubles – most notably truancy, drug taking, disturbances on housing estates in Oxford, Cardiff and Tyneside following police clampdowns on joyriding, and images of 'youth out of control' and 'one-boy crime waves' – had already raised levels of public concern. The Bulger case provided 'the strongest possible evidence to an already worried public that there was something new and terrifying about juvenile crime' (Newburn, 1996, p. 70). Individual TV images, such as that of an 11 year old in a balaclava mask being arrested after crashing a stolen car, galvanized politicians of all parties, the police, judges and magistrates to demand more effective measures to deal with young offenders. Indeed, just 10 days after the Bulger murder, the Home Secretary announced plans to establish a new network of secure training units for 12–15 year old offenders.

The Prime Minister also promised a crackdown on 'bail bandits', whereby those committing further offences while on bail (or if there was the slightest reason to believe they *might* reoffend), would be automatically remanded in custody ('I'LL LOCK UP YOUNG VILLAINS' – headline, *Daily Mail*, 22 February 1993). 'Truancy Watch' was launched in autumn 1993. Above all, a sense that the courts and law and order agencies had become impotent to deal effectively with offending was widely propagated and this mood persisted for much of the decade. In the run-up to the 1997 general election, a bewildering array of *additions* to the youth justice system in England and Wales were proposed, including curfews for children, the naming of young offenders in court, the shaming and public humiliation of offenders, parental control orders, fast-track punishment for 'persistent' offenders, the adoption of 'zero tolerance' campaigns to prosecute even the most petty and minor of offences, secure training centres for 12–15 year olds and the removal of the legal presumption of *doli incapax* for 10–13 year olds. Indeed, all of these measures were acted upon in the following decade. And between 1993 and 2003 the number of under-18 year olds held in secure institutions increased from some 1300 to over 3000 (see **Chapters 7, 8 and 9**).

The role of the media, and particularly the symbolic purchase of the Bulger case, no doubt played a part in this escalation of fears and change in political mood. By comparing the Bulger case with a similar murder in Norway in 1994, Franklin and Petley (1996) argued that the contemporary British press and judicial system were particularly 'punitive, harsh and unforgiving'. The initial sentence of Venables and Thompson was widely condemned as being too soft. Not only was the recommendation of eight years seen as too lenient but the conditions of their custodial confinement were viewed as akin to a 'holiday camp' (*Today*, 25 November 1993). In contrast, the language used by the Norwegian press and judiciary was more conciliatory. There the murder of a 5 year old by three 6 year olds was phrased in terms of a 'tragic accident', in which it served no purpose to simply apportion blame to those involved. Moreover, in most European countries, Venables and Thompson would have been considered much too young to be prosecuted at all. In England, the age of criminal responsibility is 10; across Europe it is usually 14 or above (see **Chapter 10**).

Comparison of the media and legal treatment of Venables and Thompson with that of two 8 year olds – Barrett and Bradley – in a similar murder case in Stockport in 1861 is also informative. Though also initially demonized, the jury in 1861 delivered a judgment of manslaughter and was widely supported for having done so. Barratt and Bradley were sent to a reformatory for five years with public support, rather than resentment, for the prospect of their rehabilitation (Rowbotham et al., 2003). Most pernicious, perhaps, was the way in which reaction to the death of James Bulger firmly located violence solely with youth. As Scraton (1997a, p. 164) concluded: 'What a terrible irony this represents given the apparently insatiable appetite that much of the adult, patriarchal world has for violence, brutality, war and destruction.'

In these ways the Bulger case came to signify something more than an isolated tragic event. It set in motion fears about juvenile crime in particular and a **demonization** of young people in general. Quite simply it was widely assumed that Demons had invaded the Innocents.

Youth in the News: Dangerous, Deficient and Vulnerable

Images of dangerousness are arguably the most familiar public appearance of youth encapsulated in the threat and danger of the mob or gang. It is a recurrent theme vividly illustrated by the headline 'LORD OF THE FLIES GANGS RULE ESTATES' (*Sunday Times*, 17 August 2003) as evidence of what can happen in areas of high child population density whether in Britain or (as was claimed in this article) Baghdad and Beirut. A sequence of moral panics about 'depraved youth' has been a dominant and recurring feature of media representations of young people. In 1950s Britain, for example, these fears were premised on the image of a teenager who had no respect for authority and lived in a world that was generally dismissive of anything adult. Teddy boys were Britain's first post-war teenage **folk devils**, popularized as violent, depraved and sex-crazed (see **Chapter 6**). In the 1960s, student revolt, drug usage, sexual permissiveness, football hooliganism, vandalism and truancy combined to amplify the level of public concern. In the 1970s, black youth, mugging, punks, violence in schools and groups of 'vicious young criminals' were the most potent symbols of a now 'rapidly deteriorating youth condition'. In the 1980s, the sight of thousands of young people rioting on the streets added a new dimension to this social preoccupation with youth disorder. In the 1990s, panics about joyriding, alcopops, Ecstasy, girl gangs and persistent offenders were the latest in a long history of despairing but 'respectable fears' (Pearson, 1983); to be joined by 'hoodies', 'boy racers', 'mini-moto riders', 'happy slappers', 'video-gamers', 'under-age binge drinkers', and 'feral yobs' in the first decade of the twenty-first century.

In contrast, some young people are portrayed not so much as depraved but as deprived, not necessarily of material wealth and power (though this is usually the case), but of moral standards, proper guidance, training and self-responsibility. Such 'deficiency' is characteristically viewed as part and parcel of the peculiarities of adolescence. Bizarre dress, 'blatant' sexuality, irresponsibility and moodiness are somewhat disparagingly passed off as 'just a phase they are going through' which will be 'grown out of'. As a result, young people are typically viewed as being at a 'vulnerable' stage: capable of being corrupted by all manner of 'evil' influences, unless their behaviour is tightly regulated and controlled. Such control is often justified in terms of giving young people 'protection' (from others and themselves). The notion that youth are a problem both to society *and* to themselves is a recurring theme in media and youth research (Wyn and White, 1997, p. 21).

Although the sources of 'youth' imagery are wide and varied (including personal experience, television news, radio, film, TV sitcoms, and so on), it is apparent that one of the key agencies that informs the public about young people is the national and local press. The first quantitative content analyses of British newspapers to focus specifically on young people was carried out in the late 1970s (Porteous and Colston, 1980). Throughout June 1979 Bradford University's Social Work Research Unit scanned eight national daily newspapers and two local (Yorkshire) papers. Any article that involved young people between 11 and 19 years was categorized according to size, location and content, and each was assigned an evaluation category (positive, negative, neutral). A total of 913 articles were analysed. The local *Bradford Telegraph and Argus* contained most stories (15 per cent of total), followed by the tabloids (between 10 per cent and 12 per cent of total), the broadsheets (between 7 per cent and 9 per cent of total), and the *Morning Star* (2 per cent of total). Stories relating to sporting events accounted for 11.4 per cent of this coverage and education 6.7 per cent, but most notably 34.9 per cent of all reports of youth were related to crime in one form or another. Of these, the most frequent categories were burglary, theft, vandalism and breach of the peace (9.2 per cent), murder (5.1 per cent) and sex crimes (2.3 per cent). Reporting was also frequent where adolescents were the victims of crime. The authors concluded that 'according to our daily press, a typical adolescent is a sporting youngster, criminally inclined, likely to be murdered or injured in an accident' (Porteous and Colston, 1980, p. 202). The 'positive' aspects of 'youthfulness' that were given coverage, were largely accounted for by the atypical careers of a small number of media celebrities and sporting personalities. A tripartite image of youth emerged: as either gifted, dangerous or innocent.

Twenty years later, the charity Children's Express monitored over 400 stories in local and national newspapers and found a similar degree of stereotyping. Young people were routinely parodied as 'victims', 'demons', 'cute', 'brilliant', 'brave' or as 'adult accessories' (Neustatter, 1998). In 2004, Porteous and Colston's study was replicated by MORI. Monitoring 17 newspapers which carried 603 youth-related articles during one week in August, they found that 71 per cent had a negative tone and a third of articles discussed young people in the context of violent crime or anti-social behaviour (see Box 1.1).

▌ Box 1.1 ▐

Newspaper articles about youth, by newspaper type, subject and tone

Base	Tabloids (281)	Broadsheets (159)	Locals (53)
Violence/Crime/ASB	35	26	33
Child abuse/ Neglect	12	17	8
Lifestyle	16	9	7
(Mental) Health	10	11	12
Accident	14	8	15
Education/Parenting	6	22	17
Achievement	8	6	9
Negative	82	50	71
Neutral	8	36	9
Positive	11	15	20

Source: www.ipsos-mori.com/polls/2004/young-people-now.shtml

Clarke (1984) concludes that the link between these separate and diverse images lies in their assumption of the *different* or *deviant* nature of *all* young people. So although the images of dangerousness, deprivation, vulnerability, and so on find their pinnacle in those singled out for media attention, the implications of such imagery carry over to inform adult reaction to the invisible mass. All young people are variously demonized by a persistent dominant imagery of 'being adolescent', of 'lack of control, of 'posing a threat' ('WHO'S AFRAID OF TEEN TERROR?': *Observer*, 1 August 1999; 'KNIFE TEENS RULE IN CITIES OF CRIME': *Sunday Mirror*, 27 January 2008).

Phil Cohen (1986, p. 6) has identified four major assumptions that lie behind most political, policy and professional reactions to the 'youth question' (see Box 1.2).

Box 1.2

Dominant representations of the youth question

1. Youth is a unitary category with certain psychological characteristics and social needs common to the age group.

2. Youth is an especially formative stage of development where attitudes and values become anchored to ideologies and remain fixed in this mould in later life.

3. The transition from childhood dependence to adult autonomy normally involves a rebellious phase which is itself part of a cultural tradition transmitted from one generation to the next.

4. Young people in industrial societies experience difficulty in making successful transitions and require professional help, advice and support to do so.

Source: Cohen (1986, p. 6).

These 'common senses' of a universal 'youth condition' continually resurface in political and media discourses as explanations of why young people can never be freed from moral, legal and social regulation. At one time feared, young people are at another time pitied for their vulnerability. They are simultaneously constituted as in need of control, and protection. They are the constant object of fascination. The adult gaze is fixed on youth as something both desirable and threatening. Desirable, because youthful energy remains a part of adult longing; desirable too because it is here that new styles and fashions are generated that are ripe for commercial exploitation. In this sense 'youth' is also a commodity. But a fear of youth is never far beneath the surface. Too much freedom is dangerous when unsupervised and unregulated. Above all, youth is treated as a key indicator of the state of the nation itself. Young people are the nation's future. To secure that future and to solve the problems of the present, 'youth' is a consistent referent. Young people have to carry this 'peculiar burden of representation' (Cohen, P., 1997a). Their condition is increasingly seen as being 'symptomatic of the health of the nation, or the future of the race, the welfare of the family, or the state of civilization as we know it'. Youth is 'the site of a singular nexus of contradictions' (Cohen, P., 1986, p. 54).

Crime in the News: Demonization and the Criminal 'Other' __

Various critical studies of media representations of youth and crime have identified a number of key and recurring processes:

- A distortion of the nature and incidence of crimes against the person. While personal violence accounts for only 6 per cent of all recorded crime, on average, British newspapers devote 64.5 per cent of their crime reporting to such cases (Williams and Dickinson, 1993, p. 40). Similarly, studies of the provincial press by Ditton and Duffy (1983) in Strathclyde and by Smith (1984) in Birmingham found that media reportage consistently and dramatically distorted the 'true' picture of crime. Surette (1998) refers to this as 'the law of opposites'.

- Definitions of youth crime are structured within particular explanations proffered by the 'primary definers' of politicians and law enforcement agencies (Hall et al., 1975). The credibility of their definitions is enhanced by their official and institutional standing such that a 'deviance-defining elite' is able authoritatively to set its own moral and legal agendas (Ericson, 1991, p. 223). Such agendas may be contested and, in certain circumstances, negotiated, but the organization of journalistic practice generally seeks out and promotes the views of those in authority (Schlesinger and Tumber, 1994, p. 20).

- Stereotypical images of offenders and their behaviour encourage understandings of events in terms of the simple dichotomies of good (the victim) and evil (the offender). Such stereotyping and dismissive labelling may be used to deny legitimacy to the actions of whole groups – they become defined as the nation's 'folk devils', as the 'criminal other' (Cohen, S., 1973a; Hall, 1978).

- In particular, *atypical* crime events (such as youth violence) are selected as newsworthy. But these are presented as *stereotypical* (symptomatic of a general youthful moral decadence) and contrasted with visions of the 'normal world' which are *overtypical* (adults as law-abiding) (Young, 1974).

- The media do not simply reflect reality, they define it in a particular way. They are not a window on the world but a prism subtly distorting and side-stepping 'reality' (Jewkes, 2004). To prolong an event's newsworthiness, other apparently similar (but unrelated) incidents are sought out (Hall, 1978). Public concern and fear are directed from a single incident and towards the possibility of 'crime waves' through which the whole of society appears threatened (Cohen, S., 1973a). The reaction to particular crime incidents at particular times, it is argued, has more to do with fears of social transformation than with any significant shifts in the actual behaviour of young people (Taylor, 1981a).

- This process is now commonly referred to as a **moral panic** in which clear boundaries are drawn between 'right' and 'wrong' and which need to be secured through retributive and deterrent responses towards offending (Goode and Ben-Yehuda, 1994). The term 'moral panic' was first used by Jock Young (1971, p. 182) to illustrate the process whereby an initial concern over drug taking in Notting Hill, London prompted the police to set up specialist drug squads, thereby ensuring that the 'problem' was *amplified* by increasing the number of drug-related arrests. A 'fantasy crime wave' was created (see **Chapter 5**).

- Crime news is a commodity. Its intrinsic 'market value' tends to override other news-making criteria, such as accuracy or relevance (McQuail, 1993, p. 253). As a result, it has been contended that public images of youth crime are 'popular' only in so far as they are the consequences of information provided by law enforcement sources with a vested interest in 'crime control' and by media sources with a vested interest in 'newsworthiness' (Muncie, 1984, p. 23). News values also militate against any balanced public knowledge of sentencing practices. The popular misconceptions that crime is always rising, that most crime is violent and that the courts routinely hand out unduly lenient sentences are all fuelled by a steady 'repetitive' stream of atypical and unrepresentative stories emanating from the media (Sanders and Lyon, 1995; Hough and Roberts, 1998). Nevertheless numerous researchers have concluded that there is no simple deterministic relationship between media reportage and the formation of public opinion. While media representations do have an effect, they are unlikely to be received passively, but rather interpreted by an 'active audience' (Roshier, 1973; Livingstone, 1996; Reiner, 2002).

- Since the late twentieth century it appears that there has been something of a shift from discrete panics to a perpetual period of moral crises in which the fact/fiction dichotomy has been dissolved. Crime-as-news has blended into crime-as-entertainment. 'Reality' TV, crime reconstructions, live newscasts and CCTV footage have fused 'facts' with institutional values and popular myths. Mass media and law enforcement agencies have become inextricably related in constituting the 'realities' of crime, justice and order (Osborne, 1995; Brown, 2003). It has become increasingly difficult to disentangle the real from the mediated (Jewkes, 2004).

Collectively, these processes may not determine public reaction, but they remain a key source of political sensitization. In political discourse young people tend to be a perennial source of anxiety. Law and order enthusiasts, for example, have persistently warned us of 'new' delinquent syndromes in which youth seems to delight in crudity, cruelty and violence. The characteristic perennial expression of this is that young people have suffered unduly from single parenting or from the degeneracy of parents and have developed into a dangerous and undisciplined mob. In 1961, the British Medical Association offered the following despairing analysis of British youth:

> Looked at in his worst light the adolescent can take on an alarming aspect: he has learned no definite moral standards from his parents, is contemptuous of the law, easily bored. He is vulnerable to the influence of TV programmes of a deplorably low standard ... [and] reading matter [which is] full of sex and violence. (Cited by Pearson, 1983, p. 17)

In the 1970s, Patricia Morgan, of the Institute of Economic Affairs, readily equated violence and destruction with youth, and talked of this 'new barbarism' as the major cause of urban breakdown and moral decline in Britain (Morgan, P., 1978, pp. 12–13). Government ministers foresaw the imminent destruction of society epitomized by Margaret Thatcher's denunciation of the football hooligan as the 'new enemy within'. Twenty years later, it seemed little had changed. The Chief Executive of the School Curriculum and Assessment Authority expressed his opinion that:

> a family breakdown, a 'synthetic pop culture' and a lack of identity among bewildered youngsters all contributed to a failure of a growing number of pupils ... some young people have little sense of their own worth. Some have little sense of basic values. Some have no sense of identity as members of a community. Some are unaware that they have responsibilities as well as rights. (*Daily Mail*, 20 September 1996, p. 25)

MPs have gone to some quite extraordinary lengths to lay claim to 'solutions' to the 'youth problem'. Some have called for a return to corporal punishment and the use of stocks to punish offenders (*The Times*, 14 March 1981). One Conservative MP contemplated flogging criminals live on television before or after the weekly National Lottery draw in order to humiliate and deter (*Independent*, 20 March 1995). In the 1990s, Digby Anderson, founder of the conservative Social Affairs Unit, reiterated a familiar concern that now the 'yobs and criminals' had been 'allowed to take over' (*Sunday Times*, 2 June 1996). Indeed from mid-1991 onwards, stories appeared regularly in the press about some young people who, it was argued, were so involved in crime that they seemed to account for much of the crime in the areas where they live (Newburn, 1996, p. 69) (see Box 1.3).

In popular and political discourse the 'problem of crime' is almost synonymous with 'youth crime'. By 1997, the *Sunday Times* (16 February) was talking of a 'persistent hard core' of 'superpredators': a term taken from American neo-conservative commentators. In the USA, the political scientist John DiIulio declared that 'this nation is threatened by large numbers of remorseless young predators' amidst dire predictions that crime was going to get much worse. In a similar vein in the late 1990s, John Ashcroft (later to become US Attorney General) declared 'we are living with a juvenile system that reprimands the crime victim for being at the wrong place at the wrong time and then turns round and hugs the juvenile terrorist' (cited by Gary Smith, 2002). Of course the 'superpredator bloodbath' failed to materialize but served to underline a transatlantic orthodoxy that the young are to be defined primarily as a problem, rather than representing any positive or creative possibilities for the future (Muncie, 1997; Waiton, 2001).

Box 1.3

The demonization of children

'ONE-BOY CRIME WAVE' (*Daily Mail*, 10 September 1992)

'RATBOY: A 14 YEAR OLD BECOMES A BYWORD FOR TROUBLE'
(*Independent*, 9 October 1993)

Alleged to have committed 55 offences by the time he was 14, one boy in north-east England first came to the notice of the police when he was 10, for burglary. After two cautions his parents volunteered him for local authority care, from which he absconded 37 times. In February 1993 he was found hiding in a ventilation duct. A local newspaper could not print his name, so invented the nickname Ratboy. Next day he was front-page national news. With the construction of images of sewers, of a hidden underworld and of secret tunnels running beneath the urban landscape, the boy became a symbol of all juvenile crime against which the police and courts were 'impotent' to act (despite the existence of local authority secure units). But in many other respects the boy did not live up to the prevailing stereotypes of dangerous and outcast youth. He did not come from a broken home; he was not violent; he did not grow up in some 'urban wasteland'; he became a 'symbol surrounded by clichés' (*Independent*, 9 October 1993). Again, in 1993, an 11 year old crashed a car through a fence. When he appeared on television in a black ski mask, he became Balaclava Boy. Spider Boy, Homing Pigeon Boy, Boomerang Boy and The Terror Triplets all followed until it was decided that in certain circumstances young offenders could be publicly named.

Source: Muncie, 2004, p. 28.

Such 'excessive' fears do, however, feed into political debate and policy formulation. For example, in 2002, the *Sun* launched its 'crusade against crime' with the headline 'ANARCHY IN THE UK' and seven subsequent pages detailing the failures of the justice system 'to smash crime with an iron fist' (*Sun*, 8 March 2002). It followed this with the assertion that 'our streets are ruled by muggers and yobs' (*Sun*, 18 March 2002). The newspaper was responding to the Metropolitan Police Commissioner's claim of undue delays in court procedures, excessive use of bail, and processes that favour defendants over victims. The campaign also reflected the Lord Chief Justice's call for a 'robust sentencing policy' for mobile phone thieves first made in January. It was also a response to the assertion that muggings had risen in London, particularly after September 11, 2001, when police were 'diverted from crime fighting to antiterrorism' (*Sunday Times*, 30 December 2001). By early 2002, the *Mirror* (21 February 2002) was already announcing that we are 'drowning in a tidal wave of violent crime'. The Home Secretary first responded by announcing an extension of electronic tagging of young offenders on bail (*Independent*, 27 February 2002). At the end of March, the Prime Minister made the unprecedented move of convening a taskforce with seven cabinet ministers to combat street crime. Meanwhile the *Mirror* (20 March 2002) ran with the headline 'VILE LAWLESS

TEENAGERS TERRORISING THE STREETS' and the *Daily Express* (25 March 2002) declared that 'KIDS OF FOUR TURN TO CRIME'. By April, a robbery reduction initiative based on the principles of zero tolerance and fast-track courts was in place in ten police areas. On 22 March 2002, the *Daily Express* argued 'AT LAST WE GET TOUGH ON YOBS' as on-the-spot fines for low-level offenders were introduced. One local authority began drawing up plans to impose curfews for under-15 year olds (*Guardian*, 26 March 2002). Docking child benefit from the parents of young offenders was proposed. Extra resources were released to finance over 2,000 new places in secure units and prisons (*Guardian*, 18 April 2002) and to pay for a more intensive policing of truants (*Guardian*, 26 April 2002). Further, the Home Secretary insisted that children as young as three should be monitored for signs of nascent criminality. In May a mother was jailed for 60 days for failing to ensure that her children attended school.

Debate continues over whether the year 2002 did in fact witness a 'tidal wave' of street crime associated with violence. The British Crime Survey reports that there was a 25 per cent fall in all crime and a 24 per cent fall in violence between 1997 and 2002/3. The risk of being a victim of crime was reduced to an all-time low. Police recording of violent crimes, however, increased by 2 per cent (Simmons and Dodd, 2003). This might suggest that the police recorded more crime when fewer offences were being committed. It is a process that fuels political expediency and media sensationalism as well as heightening public fear. In 2002, almost three-quarters of the public still believed the crime rate to be increasing (Simmons and Dodd, 2003). Repeated claims were being made that the justice system was too soft, particularly when the tabloids questioned the proposition 'TOUGH ON CRIME?' by devoting 11 pages to gruesome pictures and harrowing accounts of violence (*Daily Mirror*, 12 July 2002). In contrast, research on sentencing practices revealed magistrates and judges bowing to media and political pressure by bypassing fines in favour of community penalties; by jailing offenders who previously would have received community penalties; and by imposing longer sentences. As a result the number of under-18 year olds sentenced to detention increased from 4,000 in 1992 to 7,600 in 2001 (NACRO, 2003). Over the decade custodial rates increased by 71 per cent for adults, but by 90 per cent for young people (see **Chapter 9**).

Such punitiveness appears unrelenting. In 2003, the *Sun* (15 October) launched its 'Shop a Yob' campaign promising to name and shame the 'guilty', condemning the 'politically correct claptrap' of 'soft courts' and advocating the setting up of 'tough work camps' for the 'animals who make your lives a misery'. By 2007, the *Sun* (20 August) was once again declaring that there was ANARCHY IN THE UK in which an absence of police patrols had allowed 'yob gangs' armed with knives and 'fuelled by cheap booze' to rule 'our streets by fear'. The theme of 'anarchy' was readily turned to by the Conservative leader on the same day when launching an attack on government 'failure' to tackle 'family breakdown' (*Daily Mail*, 20 August 2007). More prison places, zero tolerance policing, more powers to 'exclude unruly pupils' and the 'common sense that with young people you need to hit them where it hurts – in their lifestyle and aspirations' were all advocated as means to 'mend our broken society' (Cameron speech, 22 August 2007). By March the next year the American magazine *Time* (26 March 2008) was faithfully reproducing the adage that 'the most important issue now facing Britain' is that of 'the scourge of feral youngsters'. And there appears to be little political resistance to such an idea. When the Secretary of State for Justice was asked what he might do to reduce the trend of demonizing young people, his response was unequivocal: 'these are not children; they are often large unpleasant thugs' (Hansard, 10 June 2008).

In promoting such views the media and politicians regularly claim they are simply responding to public opinion. The nature of populist punitiveness is, however, far from straightforward. 'Public opinion' is often presented as some undifferentiated and homogeneous entity and its divergences and complexities rarely fully acknowledged and understood. Public attitudes to crime and punishment often exhibit a degree of tolerance that is frequently lost when asking bald generalized statements about sentencing preferences. When presented with concrete descriptions of actual cases, the public tend to be less punitive. When given adequate information about the range of legal punishments available, the public are less likely to endorse the use of imprisonment (Hough and Roberts, 1998; 2004). The more detail that people are given about the circumstances of any given crime, and the more time they are given to reflect on appropriate penalties, the less likely they are of perceiving the courts as being 'too soft' (Gillespie and McLaughlin, 2003; Hancock, 2004).

The Extent of Offending

1.2 The 'true facts' of offending by young people (or any other group) have been, and will remain, unknowable. There are three main means by which crime rates have been estimated – recorded statistics, victim surveys and self report studies – but none can claim to provide an objective and incontrovertible picture. The problem arises because all quantitative data depend not only on which behaviours are perceived and *defined* as crime, but also on the *validity* of the various statistical measures and on the range of *interpretations* that can legitimately be made of any figures, no matter how they are produced (see Box 1.4).

Most obviously, changes in policing priorities, or changes in what the law counts as crime, or shifts in public tolerance will all affect statistical representations of the 'youth problem'. It might be tempting, then, to discard all such measures as 'worthless'. Yet they cannot be so readily dismissed. They provide valuable insights into self-, police and court definitions of crime and tell us much of the organizational capacities, constraints and priorities of the youth and criminal justice systems. They cannot, however, be expected to aid our understanding of an 'independent entity of crime' for, as Lea and Young (1984, p. 15) acknowledge, 'by its nature no such fact exists'.

Box 1.4

Press headline reaction to release of crime statistics 24/25 January 2008 (ranked by circulation)

30 GUN CRIMES COMMITTED A DAY (*The Sun*)

DRUG OFFENCES SOAR 21 PER CENT IN A SINGLE YEAR (*Daily Mail*)

HOME SECRETARY JACQUI SMITH SAYS CRIME FIGURES ARE 'EXCELLENT' (*Daily Mirror*)

GUN CRIME UP AS SMITH SAYS UK SAFER THAN EVER (*Daily Telegraph*)

GOVERNMENT ACCUSED OVER CRIME RISES (*Daily Express*)

GOVERNMENT ACCUSED OVER CRIME RISES (*Daily Star*)

FEWER ROBBERIES, ASSAULTS AND BURGLARIES, BUT CRIME AT GUNPOINT IS ON THE RISE (*The Times*)

CRIME FALLING EVER FASTER, BUT DRUG AND GUN OFFENCES INCREASE (*Guardian*)

RISK OF BECOMING VICTIM OF CRIME AT 27 YEAR LOW (*Independent*)

The Social Construction of Official Statistics

The main sources of data on the extent of offending in England and Wales are the annually and quarterly produced *Criminal Statistics* (based on crimes recorded by the police) and the *British Crime Survey* (BCS) (based on victim interviews). Following a review in 2001 these are now combined in the annual Home Office reports *Crime in England and Wales*. In Scotland, similar statistics appear in *Recorded Crime in Scotland* and the Scottish Executive Justice Department conducted its own victim surveys four times between 1993 and 2003. In 2004, these data sources were renamed the *Scottish Crime and Victimization Survey*.

The first National Crime Survey was carried out in 1972 in America. It surveyed a representative sample of the population and questioned them on their experience of being a victim of crime. The aim was to shed light on **hidden crime** by uncovering those crimes committed (and for which a victim was recognized) which were not reported to the police. Predictably, these early victimization surveys revealed that the extent of crime may be up to five times greater than that detailed in official statistics. The first British Crime Survey (BCS) was carried out in 1982 (Hough and Mayhew, 1983) and by 2000 had been repeated eight times. Since then it moved to an annual cycle with 40,000 interviews with those aged 16 and over conducted each year. Collectively these are the most commonly referred to sources of information on offending rates and patterns and are regularly used by politicians, the media and criminological researchers (see Box 1.5).

Box 1.5

Statistical pictures of youth offending

- The peak age of known offending is 17 or 18 for males and 15 for females, but adults account for more than 80 per cent of all detected crime.

- The number of indictable offences committed by young people under 18 dropped by 27 per cent between 1992 and 2004 (despite public perceptions to the contrary). Between 2003 and 2006 there was a 19 per cent rise.

- Theft and handling stolen goods account for just under a half of all youth crime. Violence against the person accounts for less than one-fifth of indictable offences.

- Adults are responsible for three times as many violent offences and five times as many sexual offences, than young people.

- Approximately 80 per cent of youth offenders are male.

- Black or black British young people are over-represented at all stages of the youth justice system.

- 33 per cent of males and 9 per cent of females born in 1953 had been convicted of an offence before the age of 46.

Source: Simmons and Dodd (2003); Bateman (2006); NACRO (2008).

However, **official statistics** often paint a controversial and contradictory picture. First, they imply that for much of the past two decades youth crime became less of a problem as crime rates generally fell, but they still maintain that 'youth' is the most criminogenic age. Public confidence has failed to reflect such a long-term downward trend. Second, they suggest that the 'crime problem' is a problem caused predominantly by males. Third, the majority of youth crime is made up largely of less serious property offences. Sexual offences and robbery are rare. Violent crime, though increasing, accounts for less than one-fifth of all indictable offences. Moreover, in 2004, 63 per cent of these were dealt with by reprimand and warnings, suggesting their less serious nature (NACRO, 2008). Finally, there is a widespread belief that whatever these figures do tell us, they represent the tip of an iceberg. Many other offences are not detected, others are not recorded by the police or a conviction is not secured. Indeed, the Audit Commission (1996, p. 14) argued that only 3 per cent of offences lead to arrest and action by the criminal justice system. If this is the case, then the official statistics provide a particularly skewed vision of the nature and extent of young offending.

The first and most paramount 'fact' about the *Criminal Statistics* is that they are both partial and socially constructed (Muncie, 2001, p. 25). This is so for a number of reasons, outlined below.

Public Reporting

The *Criminal Statistics* depend initially to a large degree on the **reporting of crime** to the police by the public. Although the police do detect some crime, in the main they rely on the general public or victims to bring crime to their notice (Bottomley and Pease, 1986, p. 34). Yet not all crimes are reported, for a variety of reasons: there may be ignorance that a crime has occurred (for example, computer fraud and many instances of corporate crime and state crime); there may be no obvious victim (for example, certain drug offences); the victim may be powerless (for example, child abuse); there may be distrust of the police (for example, by certain youth cultures); the offence may seem too trivial (for example, shoplifting); the offence may be considered to be youthful 'high spirits' (for example, brawls); or the victim may have no faith that the police will take the offence seriously (for example, racial harassment) (Jupp et al., 1999).

The 1996 British Crime Survey (which bases its data on reports from victims) found that the main reasons for not informing the police were that the incident was not considered serious or that the police would not be able to do much about it or would not be interested. Some felt that the incident was better dealt with privately without recourse to formal agencies. Vehicle vandalism, assault and minor theft had particularly low reporting rates. Burglary with loss and motor vehicle theft had almost 100 per cent reportage rates, presumably in order to meet insurance company requirements (Mirrlees-Black et al., 1996, pp. 24–6). This latter observation has caused many to query the validity of the assumption that crime is always on the increase. As Jenkins (1987, p. 25) perceptively argued: 'the total has about it an eerie, suspicious regularity. It advances relent-lessly in step with the proliferation of telephones, of police computers and of household insurance ... we could be victims of nothing more offensive than a wave of being middle class'.

Police Recording

Even when an incident is reported to the police, it will not count as crime unless the police *record* it as such. As Walker (1983, p. 286) noted, although the police have a statutory obligation to record crimes, considerable discretion remains about whether it is considered sufficiently serious to warrant their attention. The 1994 British Crime Survey estimated that 40 per cent of offences reported to the police were not recorded (Mayhew et al., 1994), while eight years later, the 2002/3 survey found it had increased markedly to 70 per cent (Simmons and Dodd, 2003).

Coleman and Moynihan (1996, p. 35) argue that the police **recording of crime** depends on three broader contexts: the political context at the time of the offence, the organizational context of policing priorities and the situational context of how the offence is reported and by whom. For example, in the 1950s when crime was not a political issue, there was little or no incentive for the police to record large numbers of offences. It had no financial (increased resource) implications and if there seemed little chance of a 'result', then such recording would only reflect poorly on subsequent clear-up rates. For many years Nottinghamshire, somewhat surprisingly, has had one of the highest crime rates in England and Wales, but this has been accounted for by the tendency of the

Nottingham police to record minor thefts and to record multiple and continuous offences as separate crimes (Farrington and Dowds, 1985). This particular recording policy was subsequently considered worthy of national implementation and a National Crime Recording Standard was introduced in 2002.

Similarly, how a reported offence is recorded by the police – as 'theft from a person' or 'robbery' or as 'attempted break-in' or 'criminal damage', for example – will affect the rate at which certain crimes are believed to being committed. Indeed, Farrington (1996), commenting on the statistical decline in juvenile crime since the 1980s, argues that this was illusory and simply reflected the police practice at the time to deal with many juvenile offenders informally. One of the clearest example of crime rates being affected by police targeting and recording occurred in 1932. Then, London's Commissioner of the Police ruled that all cases classified as 'suspected stolen' should be redesignated as either 'lost' or 'stolen'. The result was that recorded thefts increased by over 300 per cent in one year (Williams, 1994, p. 49)! Similarly, increases in the youth crime rate since 2004 have been largely accounted for by changes in police practices in order to meet government targets. This has led to disproportionate rises in 'sanction detection' for younger age groups, for girls and for lesser offences (NACRO, 2008). Previously these offenders and offences were more likely to have received an informal response.

Creating Crime Waves

Changes in law enforcement and in what the law counts as crime preclude much meaningful discussion over whether youth crime is forever rising (or indeed falling) (Muncie, 2001, p. 27). Pearson (1983, p. 216), for example, notes how successive pieces of welfare-inspired legislation governing the treatment of young people in the early twentieth century encouraged law enforcement agencies to proceed with cases they might previously have dealt with informally. The end result was more young people being dealt with in court, creating the impression of a 'crime wave' when all that had changed was the readiness of official agencies to intervene (see **Chapter 2.4**). Pearson (1983, p. 217) elaborates on this process by noting how after 1977, the distinction between minor and major criminal damage was abandoned in favour of a classification of all as 'known crimes'. This resulted in an apparent doubling of vandalism in one year: 'adding at a single stroke a sixth of a million indictable offences to the criminal records'. Similarly, Singer (1996) details how changes to juvenile offender law in New York in the late 1970s effectively *recriminalized* youth by redefining previous acts of delinquency as 'crimes' and delinquents as 'juvenile offenders'. In the wake of a media and political 'moral panic' about a 'crisis' in youth crime, the age of criminal responsibility was lowered, ensuring that juveniles were placed in New York's adult criminal justice system (see **Chapter 10**). Taylor (1998a) also notes how changes in police priorities and politics will effect what is recorded. He argues that increases in crime between 1914 and 1960 can be accounted for by senior police officers 'playing the crime card' in order to increase police numbers and powers. In the 1990s with the advent of performance indicators, 'cuffing' of cases was revealed as common practice as the police tried to improve clear-up and detection rates to politically acceptable levels (*Guardian*, 18 March 1999).

While victimization surveys are undoubtedly a more reliable means of measuring crime than police statistics, they too suffer from a range of methodological problems (Coleman and Moynihan, 1996, pp. 74–82). Inevitably they only measure criminal incidents where a victim can be identified or where a victim accepts such a status. 'Victimless' crimes such as some drug offences or consensual sexual acts will not be recognized and for crimes such as domestic violence there may be an unwillingness to accept a 'victim' status. For **corporate crime**, individual victimization is not only likely to be unknown, but its extent may be enormous. Other shortcomings include the lack of representativeness of the chosen samples, the problem of victims' memory recall and indeed whether respondents can always be relied upon to tell the truth. Moreover, questions relating to *youth* victimization have remained conspicuously absent from the BCS (to date it only included specific information on under-16s in 1992, though the Home Secretary has promised that this will be rectified) (see **Chapter 5**).

Self-evidently, changes in legislation and in the number of arrests and sentences do not represent actual changes in the level of crime, but changes in the capacity of the criminal justice system to process individual cases. More police and more prisons, coupled with the political will and resources to support law enforcement, have an infinite ability to increase the amount of recorded crime. As Christie (2000) argues, there is always an unlimited well of unrecorded crime/disorder/anti-social behaviour to be tapped and as techniques of mass surveillance increase and political priorities change, so too will more 'crime' be discovered. This again is likely to impact most strongly on young people: their offences usually occur in the most visible of public places – the street, the shopping mall, the football ground. In contrast many 'adult' crimes will remain hidden at work (pilfering), in the home (domestic violence), the corporate boardroom (fraud, embezzlement) or in the corridors of power (torture, illegal arms dealing). As such, increases in police resources will almost inevitably lead to a statistical rise in *certain kinds* of crime, just as prison building programmes will create more prisoners of the same kind. New legislation meanwhile remains capable of ensuring the **criminalization** of ever wider sections of the population. For example, Nick Cohen (2003) noted that since 1997, 661 new criminal offences had been created and hundreds of anti-crime initiatives had been launched. Between 1997 and 2007 there were more than 50 major Home Office bills (more than in the whole of the previous century). Many of these were directed at non-conformist and anti-social behaviour or that previously considered 'irritating' (see **Chapters 7 and 9**).

Box 1.6 outlines the various processes whereby an incident may, or may not be, eventually registered as an official crime statistic and reveals how 'official data are social products' (Box, 1981, p. 208).

Box 1.6

The social construction of youth crime

Event	Mitigating factors
Incident occurs	Visible or hidden?
	Recognized as crime?
	Changes in law over time?
Reported	Serious or trivial?
	Police able to act?
	Trust in police?
Recorded by police	Serious or trivial?
	Organizational priorities?
	Law and order directives?
	Status of complainant?
Arrest	Nature of evidence?
	Sufficient police resources and time?
	Possibility of a 'result'?
Charge/court/sentence	Legislation reform?
	Legal representation?
	Social status of offender?
	Previous convictions?
	Political climate of 'law and order'?

↓   ↓

The compilation of official criminal statistics are the end result of numerous intervening social variables. Data are partial, misleading and unreliable.

Self Reports and Hidden Crime

Given the doubts about the validity of official statistics, criminologists have increasingly turned to other measures. **Self report studies**, which ask people to list the crimes they have committed (whether they have been detected or not), were pioneered in the USA in the 1940s. Since then they have been widely used as a means not only to gain a more accurate picture of 'hidden crime' but also to shed light on why offending occurs and the degree to which it correlates with other social factors, such as gender, 'race' and socio-economic position. They have, in the main, been directed at young people.

Most self report studies conclude that young offending is far more widespread than the official statistics would have us believe. In a study of 1,400 London schoolboys, Belson (1975) reported that 98 per cent admitted having at some time kept something they found (legally, theft); 70 per cent had stolen from a shop and 88 per cent had stolen from school. Yet only 13 per cent had been caught by the police and only half of these were subsequently sent to court. Similarly, Rutter and Giller's (1983, p. 27) summary of youth self report research found that *inter alia* 82 per cent admitted breaking windows of empty houses, 70 per cent had stolen from a shop and that almost no one admitted no offences at all. Risk of prosecution ranged from 8 per cent (shoplifting) to 60 per cent (breaking and entering).

In 1992/3, Graham and Bowling (1995) interviewed a national sample of 1,721 young people aged 14–25 about their family life, school experiences, lifestyles and offending behaviour. Twenty-three offences were covered, ranging from shoplifting to serious assault. Similar to previous studies, they found offending to be widespread with over a half of males and a third of females admitting that they had committed an offence at some time. For a majority, however, these were restricted to no more than one or two minor property offences. A follow-up study in 1998/9 (Flood-Page et al., 2000) found little overall change, but with an increase in the population of 14–17 year olds admitting an offence. The Home Office now carries out such surveys on an annual basis under the auspices of the *Offending, Crime and Justice Survey* (for example, Wilson et al., 2006).

The prevalence of crime as an everyday part of young people's lives was also substantiated by research in Edinburgh (Anderson et al., 1994). On the basis of questionnaires completed by 1,150 11–15 year olds and 120 face-to-face interviews in 1990, this study found that two-thirds admitted to committing a crime in the previous nine months: the majority being rowdiness, fighting in the street or shoplifting. In a nationwide sample of 14,500 11–17 year olds in 2000/1 almost half reported having knowingly broken the law at some stage. A third of 14–15 year olds admitted shoplifting. Twenty per cent of 15–16 year old boys admitted attacking someone intending serious harm. The survey, on the other hand, also found that offending was infrequent and that most young people were law-abiding most of the time (Beinart et al., 2002). In the largest survey to date, Armstrong et al. (2005) collected self-reported data from over 30,000 young people, aged 7–16, in what were considered the *most* high deprivation, high crime areas in England and Wales. They found that 52 per cent reported involvement in offending in the last 12 months (55 per cent of boys and 49 per cent of girls). The most commonly reported types of offending were, however, vandalism, stealing and receiving stolen goods.

From studies such as these it is clear that a majority of people have broken laws and rules at some time in their lives. To this degree, transgression may be considered a typical, rather than abnormal, form of behaviour. It is, as Durkheim (1895/1964) argued, a normal and enduring feature of the social order (see **Chapter 3**). However, the major contribution of self report studies has been to seriously question widely held beliefs about the correlations of class position, 'race' and gender to criminality. Both Anderson et al. (1994) and Graham and Bowling (1995) found that middle-class children were just as likely to be involved in crime as working-class children. Indeed, a survey by the British Household Panel in 2001 based on interviews with 1,000 13–15 year olds found that those from higher-income families were *more* likely to commit vandalism, play truant and take illegal drugs (*Guardian*, 25 February 2001). The relationship between social class and offending that is reflected in the *criminal statistics* (and accepted by many criminological theories) is at best tenuous and probably non-existent. As Box (1981, p. 91) concludes: 'self report studies have on the whole failed to reveal the significant inter-class differences implied in official statistics ... Only if this single fact is kept in the forefront of the reader's consciousness can there be sustained a critical stance towards many sociological theories on delinquency.' This suggests strongly that official statistics reflect not patterns of offending but patterns of policing. As a result, the relative criminality of certain groups of young people has been exaggerated. For example, inner-city working-class youths face a greater risk of arrest than middle-class youths engaged in similar activities but in areas where the police presence is lower. Ethnic minority youths are statistically more likely to be stopped and searched by the police (Burke, 1996), but self report studies show that those of Indian, Pakistani and Bangladeshi origin have significantly *lower* rates of offending and that for African-Caribbeans the rate is no higher than for whites. Self report data also cast some doubt on the relative lack of offending by young women. Up to the age of 17, offending rates are not dissimilar to those of young men, but female offending then drops sharply, while male property offending increases (see Section 1.3 below). Graham and Bowling explain this differential by noting that those young women who have completed full-time education, left home, formed stable partnerships and had children are more likely to stop offending abruptly than those who have not. For males, however, passing these landmarks has no such effect: 'they tend to lag behind young women in virtually every area of social development' (Graham and Bowling, 1995, p. 56).

Despite these seemingly 'incontrovertible' findings, it would be misleading to take self report studies at face value. They too have a number of limitations. Most obviously they depend on the willingness of interviewees to admit their 'criminality' to researchers. Second, they are often administered by questionnaires which have notoriously high non-completion rates, particularly from ethnic minority groups. This in itself may result in highly skewed samples (Coleman and Moynihan, 1996, p. 59). Third, they tend to check offending against a relatively small list of 'standard' and sometimes trivial offences. Other areas of hidden crime such as domestic violence, child abuse and corporate crime are rarely (if ever) analysed. As a result the parameters of the 'crime problem' and assumptions about 'typical offenders' are not seriously challenged.

Patterns of Offending and Non-offending

1.3

Despite the shortcomings of official statistics, self reports and victim surveys, it remains widely assumed that age is a major indicator of involvement in crime. Because proportionately more ethnic minority and working-class youth and fewer female youth are dealt with by the youth justice system, it is also believed that the crime problem is predominantly a problem of young males from lower social class and ethnic minority communities. This focus has also encouraged research into 'risk prediction' and how criminal careers are formed and developed. In popular idiom, the 'truant of today' will eventually be the 'criminal of tomorrow'. And for a small number, offending will not be transient, but will be both frequent and persistent. This section provides a critical assessment of these 'taken-for-granted' notions.

Risk Prediction and Criminal Careers

The 'criminal career' approach suggests that offending is part of an extended continuum of anti-social behaviour that first arises in childhood, persists into adulthood and is then reproduced in successive generations. One of the most ambitious projects to investigate why delinquency begins and to assess how far criminality can be predicted is the ongoing Cambridge Study in Delinquent Development. In 1961, a sample of 411 working-class boys aged 8 was selected from six primary schools in Camberwell, London. Girls were not included. Twelve boys were from ethnic minorities. They were contacted again when aged 10, 14, 16, 18, 21, 25, 32, 46 and 48 to examine which of them had developed a 'delinquent way of life' and why some had continued a 'life of crime' into adulthood. About a fifth of the sample had been convicted of criminal offences as juveniles and over a third by the time they were 32. But half of the total convictions were attributed to only 23 young men – less than 6 per cent of the sample. Most of these 'chronic offenders' shared common childhood characteristics. They were more likely to have been rated as troublesome, impulsive and dishonest at primary school. They tended to come from poorer, larger families and were more likely to have criminal parents. They had also experienced harsh or erratic parental discipline (Farrington, 1994, 2003). Based on this data, Farrington has consistently identified various individual, family and environmental predictors ('**risk factors**' or 'profile') of future criminality. The most important *individual* factors are low intelligence, personality and impulsiveness. The strongest *family* factors are criminal or anti-social parents, poor parental supervision and disrupted families. The most notable *environmental* factors are peer association, areas of deprivation and high delinquency rate schools (Farrington and Welsh, 2007). On this basis, the Cambridge study contends that future 'chronic offenders' can be identified with reasonable accuracy at the age of 10. Moreover, Farrington (2000) maintains that similar longitudinal research, particularly in the USA and the UK, has established that the 'risk factor prevention paradigm' has global (western) reliability and strong practical application (see **Chapter 9**). The most significant – in policy terms – are individual and family factors (Farrington, 2007) (see Box 1.7).

Using the same sample, Farrington et al. (1996) also maintained that if children had a convicted parent by the time they were 10, then that was the 'best predictor' of their becoming criminal and anti-social themselves. Criminal behaviour, it was argued, was transmitted from parents to children: simply put, crime runs in the family.

Risk analysis has become more and more common since the 1990s as interest in crime prevention research has burgeoned. Something of a consensus around the precipitative factors of family conflict, truancy, drug use, irresponsible or lack of parenting, low intelligence, delinquent friends and community disorganization has emerged (Goldblatt and Lewis, 1998; Rutter et al., 1998; Flood-Page et al., 2000; Beinart et al., 2002; Youth Justice Board, 2005). The problem, however, remains of deciphering which of these numerous variables has more pertinence with some people at some times. The degree to which they interrelate and react remains uncertain. And while they may correlate with *recorded* offending, their applicability to all rule breaking – as self reports indicate – is at best tenuous. For example, Webster, MacDonald and Simpson's (2006) qualitative research of 185 young people (including girls) found that over 50 per cent who would be considered high risk on Farrington's measures (came from broken homes/were regular truants) had never offended at all. Other longitudinal research carried out by the University of Edinburgh has argued that the key risk factor propelling young people into and through the criminal justice system is not their 'dysfunctional families' but police perceptions of who appears respectable and who is not (McAra and McVie, 2007, and see **Chapter 9**).

A core problem with the 'risk factor prevention paradigm', therefore, is its presentation of specified individualized 'risks' as if they comprise uncontroversial facts, truths and scientific realities. Risk factor research may reveal some *correlations* with statistical records of offending but this should not be confused with having discovered the *causes* of such offending. It is a self-fulfilling and reductionist exercise in so far as it only measures offenders against a prescribed menu of factors derived from research with a narrow psycho-social focus. Its replication, then, is predictable, but not necessarily revealing. Such aggregate studies only tell us *what* factors are linked to (known) offending, not *how* and *why* such factors might be linked. Such quantitative data also necessarily 'miss' valuable data about perceptions of risk that could be gleaned from juvenile justice practitioners or young people themselves (Armstrong, 2004; Case, 2007). It applies *generalized* probabilities to individuals which are likely to produce substantial numbers of 'false positives': that is mis-labelling and inaccurate identification of putative offenders who are then subject to unwarranted degrees of intrusive intervention (Smith, 2006). It peripheralizes the significance of material and social-structural contexts. The Pittsburgh Youth Study, for example, concluded that a key 'risk factor' is the socio-economic status of particular neighbourhoods. Those with some of the lowest *individual* risk factors offended more frequently if living in the most deprived neighbourhoods (Wikström and Loeber, 2000). This places some doubt on the priority given to individual and family factors which have dominated mainstream criminology and deeply impacted on criminal justice policy (see **Chapters 4 and 9**).

Using an ethnographic, rather than statistical and personality measurement approach, Foster's (1990) study, which spanned the generations in one area of south-east London in the early 1980s, also found that parental attitudes to education, street life and crime were replicated (through subtle processes of parental reinforcement) by their children. Youth crime served as an apprenticeship to adult offending when, for example, techniques could be learnt to minimize the risks of detection and arrest. But all this occurred in a context whereby many of their illegal activities were not considered as crime: 'these were not criminal "careers", just ordinary people whose everyday world took for granted certain kinds of crime' (Foster, 1990, p. 165). As a result, while the Cambridge study is a good example of the degree to which various social and personality factors correlate statistically with 'known' offending, it fails to capture the broader context in which such offending takes place. It assumes that legal definitions of crime are shared by all communities. Foster's analysis shows clearly that this is not the case. The issue becomes not simply one of law breaking, but of conflicting cultural and moral values embedded in different material realities. Moreover, the Cambridge study substantiates public concern about lower-class criminality, but only because the range of other types of criminal activity typically associated with white-collar and corporate crime are not identified as problematic. For example, it has no application to understanding crimes of the powerful and state crime and serves only to identify the 'usual suspects' and to perpetuate an uncritical listing of the 'failings' of (some) white working-class male youth in industrialized western societies. It may be able to shed some light on the characteristics of those offenders who are recorded in the official statistics, but it tells us little about the extent, causes and meaning of offending *per se*.

From a different theoretical perspective, Craine and Coles (1995) used the concept of 'career' to explore how young people in inner-city Manchester coped with unemployment and social deprivation in the 1980s and the realization that the prospect of a traditional 'career' in the formal labour market had largely disappeared. The alternative 'careers' that were developed included market trading and social security fraud (working and claiming), 'fencing' stolen goods, unlicensed street trading, acting as 'lookouts', 'touting' and 'hustling'. As with Foster's (1990) informants, these 'edge of crime' activities were regarded as quite legitimate. For some this ethos may have heralded a progression to organized shoplifting, robbery and drug dealing whereby crime came to be a major means of earning a living. But, above all, the 'drift into crime did not involve a major moral dilemma for the young people concerned. Rather it was the result of a series of incremental choices to access the alternative opportunity structures around them' (Craine and Coles, 1995, p. 20). The picture of 'crime careers' painted by the Cambridge study is one of inadequate and morally damaged individuals. For Craine and Coles it is a matter of young people reacting rationally to the (lack of) opportunities available to them.

The question of risk has also been tackled from another angle: namely that intervention at an early age – particularly in the form of secure institutions – is unlikely to prevent re-offending and may only succeed in cementing 'criminal careers'. In Crowley's (1998) sample, more than half had spent time in institutional care. Bailey et al. (1994) found that of all those sent to a secure unit, 80 per cent had previously been in local authority care. Some 93 per cent had had previous psychological or psychiatric contact. Similarly, Boswell (1995) found that 91 per cent of all 10–17 year olds who had committed the most serious offences had experienced abuse or loss in their earlier life. Re-conviction rates on leaving the secure estate are also high. Most studies estimate this to be between 70 and 90 per cent (Goldson, 2006). This suggests that some types of intervention are not only inappropriate, but may also encourage those 'careers' that they are designed to treat or deter (see **Chapters 5 and 9**).

A Question of Gender?

Farrington (1996) contends that the **protective factors** that best serve to protect young people from offending include having a resilient temperament, an affectionate relationship with at least one parent, parents who provide effective and consistent discipline and parents who maintain a strong interest in their children's education. However, one of the strongest predictors of non-offending seems to be that of gender. Only one in six of all known young offenders is a young woman. In general their offending seems less serious, with theft and handling stolen goods by far the most common. Such data led Newburn and Stanko (1994, p. 1) to observe that 'the most significant fact about crime is that it is almost always committed by men'.

Nevertheless some reservations about the validity of such a bald statement should be noted. Gelsthorpe and Sharpe (2006), for example, note that, notwithstanding the questionable nature of statistical data, available evidence does suggest something of an increase in female youth offending since the 1970s. Self-report studies, for example, have suggested that although fewer girls than boys do break the law, the difference is not marked. Anne Campbell (1981, p. 22) noted that while official statistics in 1976 produced a ratio of male to female offending of 8.95:1, results from self reports of 16 year old schoolgirls showed a ratio of 1.33:1. She argued that when young women commit crime they follow the same pattern as young men in terms of which acts they commit. In contrast, Walklate's (1995, p. 6) review of the statistical data concludes that while 'men and women commit similar crimes albeit at different rates, women appear to commit the more serious crimes at a much lesser rate than men'. This is even more the case when the largely hidden crimes of domestic violence are taken into consideration. Moreover, as self report studies (Graham and Bowling, 1995; Flood-Page et al., 2000) found, the rate of offending for young women peaks earlier and recedes at an earlier age than that of young men. So although at ages 12–14 a similar proportion of boys and girls admit offending, by the age of 17, boys outnumber girls 3:1 and by the ages of 22–25 it is 11:1.

It is clear then that even though it would be misleading to view young women as non-offenders, significant gender-based differences in rates and frequency of offending still need to be explored. One explanation lies in shifts in the continuities of control in women's offending and non-offending lives. As Worrall (1999, p. 46) put it: 'The criminalization of a small group of girls, the welfarisation of a larger group and the socialisation of all girls are processes which form a "pyramid" of gendered social control.' By 2000, it seemed as if the shape of this pyramid was shifting towards criminalization. Fuelled by media-driven panics about a 'new breed' of girl gangs, the numbers of girls convicted of indictable offences rose, the use of diversionary measures (cautions, reprimands and warnings) decreased, and the numbers sentenced to immediate custody increased dramatically (by 365 per cent between 1993 and 2002) (Gelsthorpe and Sharpe, 2006). Much of this increase, particularly since 2003, however, may be the result of an increased presence in the night-time economy and a propensity to view young women as less in need of protection and more deserving of criminal control (*Guardian*, 9 May 2008).

Overall, men account for nearly nine out of every ten people found guilty of indictable offences and are responsible for 92 per cent of convicted cases of violence against the person. Statistics such as these have long been available, but it is only in the past few decades that it has seriously been suggested that the problem of crime may indeed be a 'problem of men'; or perhaps more precisely termed a problem of 'maverick masculinities'. This academic interest coincided with increasing public and political concern about the apparently growing anti-social behaviour of the young urban male which the Prime Minister referred to in 1994 as a 'yob culture' (see Box 1.8).

Box 1.8

Representations of the 'yob'

Yob is a species of young white working class male which if the British media is to be believed, is more common than ever before. The yob is foul mouthed, irresponsible, probably unemployed and violent. The yob hangs around council estates where he terrorises the local inhabitants, possibly in the company of his pit-bull terrier. He fathers children rather than cares for them. He is often drunk, probably uses drugs and is likely to be involved in crime, including domestic violence. He is the ultimate expression of macho values: mad, bad and dangerous to know … The yob is carrying the weight of masculinity which for a variety of reasons middle class society finds increasingly unacceptable and rhetorically dumps onto the men of the lower class. He is a classic scapegoat: lugging around the sins of our culture whilst the rest of us look sanctimoniously on.

Source: Ros Coward (1994) 'Whipping Boys', *Guardian Weekend*, p. 32.

The term captures many of the real and imaginary fears of crime and disorder, although it is unclear at what point shouting, swearing and drinking and so on turn from the irritating to the 'yobbish'. In the 1990s, images of the 'yob', as Coward (1994) contended, became to a degree legitimized by right-wing notions of a dangerous under-class (Murray, 1990) and by feminist critiques of masculinity (Campbell, 1993). For Murray, unmarried and unemployed men are akin to primitive beasts lacking any civilizing influence (see **Chapter 4.2**). For Beatrix Campbell, the 'threat' of masculinity is more complex. Her analysis of the various riots of 1991 in Britain's working-class housing estates drew attention to what was 'self-evident' but publicly rarely acknowledged: they were perpetuated in the main by young men. While public debate circulated between unmarried mothers failing to exercise control over their male offspring, and unemployment and urban deprivation creating legions of the dispossessed, Campbell (1993) stressed how the abandonment of certain communities by the state has not caused a crisis of masculinity, but unleashed it in extreme forms. Young men on council estates became engaged in a militaristic culture of crime: celebrating war and force as ways of sorting things out (Campbell, 1993, p. 323). Unemployment denied access to legitimate masculine status. Joyriding, drugs, ram raiding, burglary or rioting on the streets became the key means by which *young men* in economically deprived areas could assert themselves as men. In contrast, Campbell argued, *young women* responded to the same circumstances of deprivation by forging self help and constructive solidarities and provided vital means through which their communities could be sustained. Moreover, she contended that on the streets, and particularly in the context of car crime, joyriding and police chases, it is a similar display of masculinity that is being expressed by the perpetrators and the law enforcement agencies alike. Or as Connell (1995, and see **Chapter 4**) contends, violence and crime are key contexts in which a particular collective conception of masculinity is 'made'.

Nevertheless trying to find 'violent crime' predominantly in 'masculinity' remains a vexed issue. Coward (1994, p. 35), for example, notes how the equation has simply 'become a way of attacking the least powerful men in our society'. Indeed, demonizing the 'yob' can serve to hide the continuities between their behaviour and that of other men (Walklate, 1995, p. 179). Similarly, Stanko (1994) argues that the discourse of male violence is fixated on the predatory crimes of the street. Not only does this tend to overlook the fact that working-class male youth are likely to be both the perpetrators *and* victims of such crime, but it detracts from the hidden violence used by men against women in the home. A focus on *masculinity* denies that there may be many and varied masculinities (Connell, 1995). The key variable may indeed not be gender alone, but, as Segal (1990, p. 27) contends, how gender and class combine to reflect back the 'increased barbarism' created by the social divisions and inequalities of contemporary capitalism. The limitations of a 'doing gender' approach have also been commented upon by Walklate (2001, p. 73) when she argues: 'debate which proceeds under its umbrella strains to fit all kinds of criminal behaviour occurring in all kinds of contexts within its terms'. It is both simplistically universal and tautological.

Gangs, guns and knife crime

Although groups of youth have long attracted adult condemnation (see **Chapter 2**), the notion of the 'gang' is peculiar to the twentieth century and largely confined to America. The gang was first defined by Puffer (1912) as 'the play group' existing alongside the family and the neighbourhood. This interpretation was subsequently adopted by Thrasher (1927) in his influential study *The Gang: A Study of 1313 Gangs in Chicago*. Influenced by social ecology theory (see **Chapter 3.2**), Thrasher estimated that in the 1920s there were over 1,000 youth gangs operating within Chicago's 'zone of transition' alone. While it is clear that this included any number of loose-knit groups, Thrasher's work set the tone for much subsequent gang research in his argument that what begins as a form of play brings youth into conflict with their community and into an environment where a delinquent career progresses. The gang is organized around working-class territorial imperatives and is based on group solidarity and codes of conduct that are passed down through generations of boys on the streets. The gang provides an alternative refuge and source of belonging and support in otherwise socially disorganized (and largely immigrant) communities: 'a substitute for what society fails to give . . . it fills a gap and affords an escape' (Thrasher, 1927, p. 33). Whyte's (1943) similarly classic study of street corner boys in Boston reiterated many of these themes while stressing the importance of a structured (rather than disorganized) environment supportive of long-term mutual obligations. The gang, rather than being in conflict with its community, was viewed as an integral part of the local social order.

However, Campbell and Muncer (1989) argued that (notwithstanding the British media's continual use of the term) none of this much applied to Britain. Downes' (1966) classic study *The Delinquent Solution* had suggested that the idea of gangs existing in Britain (at least in the 1960s) was symptomatic of middle-class attempts to impute a structure and organization to working-class groups which they did not possess. The orthodoxy is that America owns the gang, while Britain has traditionally been the home of youth subcultures (see **Chapter 6**). Thirty years later, Bill Sanders, an American academic moved to Brixton, London, to test this proposition. He concluded that 'US style street gangs were not in Lambeth and that they never really have been' (Sanders, 2005, p. 3). One of a few British studies which did claim to have discovered the gang was Patrick's (1973) Glasgow research, but, as Campbell and Muncer argue, even though these groups of male youth may have been known by territorial names, they had little internal structure and failed to persist over time. In contrast, the contemporary and classic ethnographic studies of white, black, Chinese and Puerto Rican gangs in America (Thrasher, 1927; Whyte, W.F., 1943; Vigil, 1988; Jankowski, 1991) paint a picture of neighbourhood groups, organized largely along racial lines, with a strong sense of local territory, mutual obligations and, latterly, direct involvement in extortion, trafficking and the drugs trade. As such, Campbell and Muncer (1989) conclude that unlike British youth cultures, American gangs are typically alternative business enterprises and communities of identity. While this may be the case, American gang research in the 1990s has also warned of imputing any uniformity to the processes of gang formation and development. Huff (1996), for example, notes that none of the contemporary research on American gangs delivers clear or unequivocal messages. Gangs are diverse and take a wide variety of forms. Gangs may be joined for protection yet *intra* gang conflict is endemic. They may offer a sense of belonging but many lack stability of membership, cohesion and continuity. Gangs have long been popularly associated with crime, but entire gangs as collectives are rarely involved in its commission. Gang members are not uniformly delinquent. Most violence is internally directed. Gangs are firmly associated with youth, but the age spread of gang members also extends into the forties. There is little evidence that gangs evolve into adult criminal organizations. There may be 'drug crews', 'wilding groups', 'prison gangs', 'gutter punks', 'bikers', 'neo-nazi skinheads' and 'football hooligans' *ad infinitum*. But their differences confound any attempt at definition. Ball and Curry (1995, p. 227) were forced to conclude that most attempts to identify 'the gang' are little more than 'veiled expressions of bourgeois disapproval'.

Indeed, Katz (2000) argues that widely held perceptions of the American gang as rapidly increasing in number, increasingly violent and embedded in drug trafficking are largely driven by news coverage, police recording practices and a popular culture that widely assumes that, but for the existence of gangs, youth crime rates would be substantially lower. Comparing New York and Los Angeles, he contends that gangs, as an interpretive lens for understanding deviance in the American city, appear to rise and fall in relationship to anxieties focused on waves of foreign immigration (Katz, 2000, p. 180). Thus the preoccupation with gangs in New York in the 1950s – subsequently reflected in the play *West Side Story* – coincides with the immigration of Puerto Ricans after the Second World War. The 'gangs problem' in Southern California in the 1980s converges with coterminous initiatives to block immigrants' access to public services. The 'gang' provides a convenient symbol to attach to all forms of youth crime and violence.

These complex issues in definition and identification have, however, done little to prevent the constant search for the 'gang' in Britain. In 1998, Eurogang, a collaboration of European and American academics was established. From the late 1990s a proliferation of gang membership and gang-related crime has become widely assumed. Under the headline 'GANG MEMBERSHIP SPIRALS AMONG

UNDER 16s' (*Observer*, 8 September 2002), it was claimed that there were as many as 30,000 gang members in England and Wales clustered within London, Birmingham and Manchester. A year earlier the same newspaper (*Observer*, 15 April 2001) also announced that 'GIRLS LEAD THE PACK OF GANGLAND VIOLENCE'. Reality or myth? How far – as Katz might suggest – is contemporary concern with gang violence in the UK simply generative of fears, say, about immigration and asylum seekers?

Such questions were brought into a sharper focus during 2007. From January through to September, eight children and teenagers lost their lives in shootings while another 17 died through stabbings. The most infamous was the tragedy of 11 year old Rhys Jones in Liverpool in what appeared to be an 'accidental shooting' in a long-standing dispute between youths from estates in the Croxteth and Norris Green areas. Like the murder of James Bulger 14 years earlier, the *Sun* announced it as a 'pivotal moment' and the *Telegraph* declared that we were now 'CAUGHT IN THE CROSSFIRE OF GANGLAND BRITAIN' (*Telegraph*, 26 August 2007). The next day the *Telegraph* posed the familiar question: 'How could it have come to this? Surely these tribes of anarchic children murdering one another and terrorising whole adult communities into silence must be some entirely new phenomenon, unique in Britain's social history?'

A report for the Youth Justice Board (2007) was, however, more circumspect maintaining that 'while there are gangs that use serious violence and threats to assert control locally (often in competition with similar groups), these are more likely to involve young adults than 10 to 17-year-olds. While juvenile versions of these gangs may exist, these are relatively rare' (see Box 1.9).

Most information we have comes from Home Office projects into particular crime problems. For example, Bullock and Tilley's (2002) research into shootings and violent incidents in Manchester was part of a Targeted Policing Initiative and relied on police data for identifying gang members. The research identified four main gangs – Longsight Crew, Pit Bull Crew, Gooch and Doddington – in a small area of South Manchester – each largely made up of black or mixed race males but all were between the ages of 21 and 25. There were relatively few female members. Indeed, the idea of hyper-violent girl gangs so often depicted in the media has been widely dismissed as fanciful (Chesney-Lind et al., 1996; Batchelor, 2001). Conflict between the four gangs was endemic. The existence of such groups may be beyond dispute. Their permanency is, however, open to debate. Research conducted by Manchester University's school of law also found that while the police respond to gangs as clearly identifiable groups, in reality, they are forever changing, and are less criminally active and have less of a clear leadership than is commonly supposed (*Guardian*, 14 July 2008). At the time of the Rhys Jones shooting the government was also keen to point out that while firearms-related homicides might be increasing, these were not necessarily gang related and that the overall trend in gun crime was down. Gun crime is neither prolific nor widespread.

Further concern has been repeatedly voiced about knife crime. Between 1997 and 2006, the number of young people convicted of carrying a knife rose from 482

Groups, gangs and weapons

- Mislabelling of youth groups as gangs runs the risk of glamorizing them and may even encourage young people to become involved in more serious criminal behaviour.

- While evidence shows that most offending by young people is group related in some way, it is less clear is whether group offending by young people has increased in recent years, despite an increase in public perceptions of groups of young people as posing a problem.

- Most young people who had carried a knife claimed this was only for protection and that they had never actually used them.

- Young people who offended together were not necessarily tied exclusively to a particular group and they might also associate with non-criminal peers.

- Where group violence was anticipated, members might carry weapons, which included knives but might also be improvised, such as sticks and bottles. Few routinely carried a knife – not least because of the risk of being stopped and searched by the police.

- Despite claims that many knew how to obtain guns, with the exception of one gang member, there was little to suggest they had ever had possession of a gun, still less used it.

- The young men involved in group offending recognized that there was a certain kudos in claiming to be a gang. However, they tended to see most such claims as empty boasts, and they drew clear distinctions between their own group affiliation and gang membership. Real gangs were distinguished by transgressing certain norms they themselves adhered to, particularly with regard to their deliberate use of unacceptable levels of violence.

Source: Derived from Youth Justice Board (2007).

to 1265, but the extent of knife-related crime remains unknown. According to the British Crime Survey, knife-enabled crime (any crime involving a knife) remained stable at around 6–7 per cent of all crime, comprising 30 per cent of all homicides (Nicholas et al., 2007). A survey by the Metropolitan police in 2007 showed that knife crime dropped by 15.7 per cent over the previous two years, from 12,122 to 10,220 incidents (*Guardian*, 13 May 2008). Total murders in London were down in 2007 for the fifth year in succession, from 222 in 2003 to 160. Within that total, 'the numbers of teenagers killed rose – by 'over 50 per cent' as some reports put it – but this was an increase from 17 deaths to 26' (http://www.spiked-online.com/index.php?/site/article/5196/). The recording of deaths specifically by a knife (as distinct from any other sharp object) has never been classified separately. Year on year comparison is thus impossible. The official statistics, however, do tell us that the number of young people killed in violent crime is small and volatile: ranging in recent years from 44 in 1995 to 20 in 2005/06. Moreover four out of 10 child homicides are perpetrated by a parent (BBC News, 31 January 2008 and see **Chapter 5**). Knife carrying is thought to be largely driven by a concern for self-protection or to enhance status. At the end of 2007, new powers were enacted making it illegal to sell an imitation gun or a knife or an air rifle to anyone younger than 18 years old; in 2008, £5 million was devoted to targeting 'knife hot spots', the use of electronic metal detectors burgeoned and the police were given new powers to stop and search. The Prime Minister urged that there should be a 'presumption to prosecute' over-16 year olds carrying a knife. This was not enough for the leader of the Opposition. He sought a 'presumption to incarcerate' *anyone* caught carrying a knife without good reason (BBC News, 7 July 2008). What was given less attention was that both perpetrators and victims were most likely to be from the most disadvantaged neighbourhoods and that *if* youth knife crime is indeed increasing, it may also reflect a growing lack of young people's trust in the ability of adults to protect them.

This of course does not deny that lethal violence is a matter of concern. However, it calls into question the accuracy of media pronouncements such as 'AN EPIDEMIC OF DEADLY YOUTH VIOLENCE' (The *Sun*, 27 May 2008) and the convenient academic, political and popular concepts of the 'gun gang' or 'knife gang'. This problem is exacerbated in any attempt to distinguish the gang from crime firms, organized crime and alternative commercial practices. Fraud and the drug trade, as bootlegging has in the past, often represent a significant blurring of what constitutes legality and illegality (Hobbs, 1997).

Drugs: Crime and Criminalization

Tackling drug use has long formed the centrepiece of governmental strategies to control criminal and anti-social behaviour. Yet the use of drugs for experimental, recreational and social reasons appears to be widespread. Miller and Plant's (1996) survey of 7,722 15 and 16 year olds found that 94 per cent had drunk alcohol, a third had smoked cigarettes in the past 30 days and that 42 per cent had at some time used illicit drugs, mainly cannabis. In Graham and Bowling's (1995) self report study of 14–25 year olds, 45 per cent of young men and 26 per cent of young women admitted to illegal drug use at some time. The rate was significantly *higher* for white than ethnic minority populations. Similarly, data derived from successive British Crime Surveys estimated that around one in two young people has tried a prohibited drug at some point in their lives and 25 per cent in the last year (Ramsay and Percy, 1996; Ramsay and Spiller, 1997; Ramsey et al., 2001; Aust et al., 2002; Murphy and Roe, 2007).

Statistics such as these appear to suggest that half of the population have engaged in criminal activity, simply through their use of illegal substances. Moreover, in the 1990s, a number of media, probation and police sources came to argue that drug use was a significant factor in driving young people towards other forms of crime – most commonly expressed as a 'need' to thieve or rob in order to finance an 'expensive' drug habit. The National Association of Probation Officers claimed that nearly a half of all property crime and theft that had been cleared up had been committed to fund drug and alcohol dependence (cited by Matthews and Trickey, 1996, p. 3). A Home

Office study – the NEW-ADAM survey – initiated in response to requests from the Association of Chief Police Officers, found that 65 per cent of all people arrested in Britain tested positive for some illicit drug (Bennett et al., 2001). In these ways a drugs–crime connection has become widely assumed.

However, the BCS studies also reported that while illicit drug use amongst young people is widespread, it is an episodic rather than ongoing activity. The 2006/07 survey estimated that only 14 per cent of 16–24 year olds had taken illegal drugs in the previous month. The picture is also confused when measured against the use of particular *types* of illicit drug. The 2001/02 BCS survey found that by far the most common monthly use was cannabis (17 per cent), followed by Ecstacy (3 per cent), amphetamines (2 per cent), cocaine (2.1 per cent), amyl nitrate (1.5 per cent), LSD (0.3 per cent), solvents (0.2 per cent), with use of heroin and crack cocaine extremely rare (0.1 per cent) (Aust et al., 2002). Moreover, while some research studies have shown a relation between use of heroin or crack cocaine and acquisitive crime, in general there appears to be no direct causal relationship to support the popular perception that drug use invariably results in anti-social, criminal or violent behaviour. Seddon (2006) concludes that such assumptions are unhelpful and far too simplistic. Again, contrary to media depiction, there is also evidence that illegal drug use by young people may be declining. For example, the BCS reported that among 16–24 year olds use of any drug decreased from 31.8 per cent to 24.1 per cent between 1998 and 2006/07. Cannabis remains the most used, but now followed by cocaine and Ecstasy. Class A drug use has, however, remained stable over the past decade (Murphy and Roe, 2007).

Researchers have come to recognize that any reliable investigation of a drugs–crime connection must take into account the relevance of historical shifts in law enforcement, specific forms of drug use, local variations and subcultural factors. All of these tend to be missing from national surveys such as the BCS.

The idea of a 'drugs problem' is probably no more than a hundred years old. In the eighteenth century, opiates (opium, morphine and heroin) were freely available and widely used for pain relief. Opium was used – as laudanum – to calm distressed children, and explored for creative reasons by a succession of Romantic poets, notably Coleridge, Wordsworth and Thomas De Quincy. In the mid-nineteenth century Britain fought two major wars to compel the Chinese government to continue importing British opium grown in India (Porter, 1996). In the early 1900s cocaine use was marginal in Britain but it was widely used in the USA, where it was a primary ingredient of Coca-Cola. The origins of an overtly penal response to such drug use lie amidst a complex of imperialist, racist and political concerns. In the USA, the Harrison Narcotics Act of 1914, aimed at regulating and controlling opiates and cocaine, made it illegal for doctors to prescribe such narcotics to patients. It was largely designed to placate white fears of Chinese opium use and black cocaine use. As a result whole new *criminal* classes of addicts were constructed. The addict became not a medical problem, but a criminal one (Beirne and Messerschmidt, 1991, pp. 139–40). In turn, criminalization created a black market and a narcotics underworld. In Britain, the Dangerous Drugs Acts of 1920 and 1923 similarly initiated a 'criminal' model of addiction, even though the regulation of supply was left in the hands of doctors as well as the Home Office (Pearson, 1991).

The next wave of drug control legislation surfaced in the 1930s. This time, in the USA, it was directed at Mexicans with the 1937 Marijuana Tax Act being introduced not because of any medical evidence of marijuana's effects but because of racist attitudes towards those minorities who used it. In Britain, cannabis has been prohibited since 1928 and until 1971 was considered, legally, to be on a par with heroin. Current concern about its use originates from the mid-1950s, associated in the main with jazz and black music cultures. However, it was not until the 1960s that young people, in particular, were believed to be the major source of the nation's 'drug problem', epitomized by the use of cannabis, amphetamines and LSD in various bohemian and youth subcultures (see **Chapter 6**). As Porter (1996, p. 4) concludes:

> perception of a 'drugs problem' is quite modern; it has little to do with the substances involved and much to do with social crisis and the strategies of politicians, police and experts ... the formulation of theories of addiction and the pursuit of criminalization have together created a problem that will not easily go away.

Of all the illegal drugs currently in circulation, it is heroin that has received the lion's share of criminological research, although it should be remembered that cannabis remains the most widely used and accounts for over 90 per cent of all drug seizures. Various researchers (Parker and Newcombe, 1987; Pearson, 1987; Parker et al., 1988) noted a sharp increase in heroin use in particular cities in the north of England and Scotland during the 1980s. Research based in Merseyside suggested that there was a very close relationship between increases in theft and burglary between 1981 and 1986 and the presence of a large number of young, unemployed heroin users. Yet as Parker and Newcombe (1987) point out, most acquisitive crime continued to be committed by non-heroin users and most opiate-using offenders had committed crimes *before* beginning their heroin use. A causal relationship between heroin use and crime is thus far from established. Equally, Pearson (1987, p. 5) notes that the problem was highly scattered and localized, often concentrated in areas with high levels of unemployment and thus arguably reflective more of poverty and deprivation rather than of wilful criminality. By the 1990s fears of a heroin 'epidemic' were largely superseded by a new set of concerns about Ecstasy, amphetamines, and poly-drug use where a mix of drugs used in combination (alcohol, cannabis, Ecstasy, amphetamines) was believed to have become a 'normalized' practice (Measham et al., 1994). In such 'pick and mix' usage, clear distinctions between the legal and illegal have become eroded. All of this throws the drugs–crime debate into further disarray. Certainly both Parker, Measham and Aldridge's (1995) research in the north-west of England and Matthews and Trickey's (1996) research in Leicester suggest that amongst 13–16 year olds there is no direct link between drug use and crime. In the Leicester sample only six (of 758) respondents admitted that their drug use was financed by crime. Only a small minority had problems of drug dependency. As a result, most reviews of the literature in Britain and internationally conclude that only a small proportion of crime is drug-driven (Hough, 1996, and see Box 1.10).

Box 1.10

Young people, drugs and crime

- Around four million people use illicit drugs each year; about 45 per cent of those aged 16 to 24 have used drugs in their lifetime.

- Most illicit drug use is relatively controlled 'recreational' use of cannabis.

- Since 2003, cocaine has been the second most commonly used illicit drug after cannabis.

- The use of any illicit drug by young people decreased between 1998 and 2007.

- There is no persuasive evidence of any causal linkage between drug use and property crime. Most offenders who use drugs do not commit crime to finance their drug use.

- A very small proportion of users – estimated at 300,000 – have chaotic 'problematic' lifestyles involving dependent use of heroin, crack/cocaine and other drugs.

- An even smaller proportion of users – perhaps around 100,000 people – finance their use through crime.

- Problem drug-using offenders have particularly high rates of offending, but they also have high rates of a range of other problems, such as homelessness, unemployment, low educational attainment and disrupted family background.

- If appropriate drug treatment is given to this group, they reduce their offending levels.

- Police crackdowns have no impact on drug availability or on levels of crime.

Source: Derived from www.drugscope.org.uk/, accessed 2003/2008; Murphy and Roe (2007).

This is not to deny, however, that illicit use of drugs – particularly cannabis – has not become an increasingly normal aspect of some young people's recreation. The normative nature of drug usage is such that it can no longer be simply attached to particular youth cultures, but has transcended class and gender boundaries. As Parker (1996, p. 296) put it, 'perceptions of how to create and take "time out" are in transition in the UK'. As such, it is all the more anachronistic to pathologize drug usage as evidence of some delinquent or damaged personality (Perri, 6. et al., 1997).

The case for normalization has been most forcefully put by the north-west England longitudinal study of recreational drug users (Parker et al., 1998; Parker et al., 2002). This traced the changing attitudes to drug use of 465 young people from 1991 to 1995 and again in 2000. Various measures of normalization appear to have been met, particularly in acceptance, availability and use of cannabis. Not only did informal friendship networks make the drug readily available, but usage rates increased with age and had by the age of 22 become further accommodated into everyday lifestyles. As Parker et al. (2002, p. 959) explain:

> That so many otherwise law-abiding citizens have collectively socially recon-
> structed an illegal act, the supplying of controlled drugs, which carries severe

penalties is a good example of the interplay of the dimensions of normalisation; availability and access of drugs continues to grow but is only made possible by socio-cultural accommodation of 'sorting' by youth populations.

Further evidence of the normalization of cannabis might also be seen in the government's decision in 2002 to downgrade it to a C classification, with possession to be treated on a 'seize and warn' basis. But decriminalization and legalization were ruled out (*Guardian*, 11 July 2002) and the fragility of 'liberalization' was witnessed six years later when a B classification was once more advocated despite the Advisory Council on the Misuse of Drugs advising the contrary. The irony at that time was that two-year prison sentences for possession, and up to 14 years for supply were already in place. Moreover, since reclassification, cannabis consumption had markedly declined.

As a result, the political urgency to fight a 'war on drugs' still holds the potential to criminalize large numbers of the otherwise law-abiding. What criminal and social policy still fails to reflect is that for most young users drugs are *not* a problem; they do not interfere with other aspects of their lives; they are quite simply a rational lifestyle choice (Coffield and Gofton, 1994; Hammersley et al., 2002). Equally research on 'drug-related crime' will remain of limited value unless it begins to seriously address the geopolitical contexts of economic polarization, social exclusion, consumerism, drug production and trafficking in which conditions of supply and demand are maintained (Seddon, 2006).

▟ ■ Summary ▪

- In much media and political debate the terms 'teenage', 'adolescence', 'youth' and 'generation' have been trapped in a negative discourse to describe a condition which is considered both troubled and troublesome. These images in the main derive from a predominantly bio-psychological literature dating back to the first decade of the twentieth century but persist as a successful newsline for the press, television and radio and as a potential vote winner for politicians.

- Young people are trapped in official definitions and measurements of 'crime'. Legal definitions reflect only what is sanctioned by the criminal law and fail to recognize far more serious 'social harms' committed by adults and the powerful.

- The concepts of 'delinquency' and 'anti-social behaviour' extend the parameters of 'youth crime' to include a host of trivial 'nuisances' and 'misconducts'.

- Young people are widely perceived not to be rational and responsible enough to be fully empowered, but are deemed fully rational and responsible if they offend.

- The extent of youth crime is unknowable. There are no reliable statistical indices. To this extent what is known about young offending is a social construction – a product of particular social reactions and policing practices which become embedded as 'facts', not only in official statistics, but also in popular and political discourses.

- Youth regularly appear as the cornerstone of a number of key concerns about a disordered present. Are the streets safe? Are schools too permissive? Are parents failing to exercise proper control? Is television a corrupting influence? Are the courts too soft on young offenders? The 'problem of youth' is driven by adult mistrust, fear and intolerance.

■ study questions

1 What can be learned about youth crime by studying crime statistics?

2 Why do media, politicians and law enforcement agencies attach so much significance to the transgressions of young people?

3 In what ways can 'youth crime' be considered a social construction?

4 The 'youth crime problem' is an illusion, a trick to deflect our attention from more serious crimes and social harms. How far do you agree?

5 'The issue of youth crime is less to do with breaking the law and more to do with fears for the nation's future.' Discuss.

■ ■ Further Reading ■

One of the best critical commentaries on the construction of criminal statistics remains that of Coleman and Moynihan's *Understanding Crime Data* (1996). Disjuncture between statistical evidence and public opinion is revealed by Hough and Roberts (2004). There is still no single text which explores media representations of youth and crime, but the most accessible introduction to media and crime in general can be found in Jewkes (2004). Davis and Bourhill (1997) catalogue how the media were implicated in creating a 'crisis' about childhood in the 1990s. The breakthrough self report studies are those associated with the Youth Lifestyles Survey first conducted in 1992 (Graham and Bowling, 1995) and repeated with a larger sample in 1998 (Flood-Page et al., 2000). The Home Office now carries out an annual self report survey targeted at 10 to 25 year olds. Anyone seriously interested in youth drug use and the possibilities for reform can do no better than start with Parker, Aldridge and Measham's *Illegal Leisure* (1998). For a good introduction to gender and crime see Walklate's (2001) *Gender, Crime and Criminal Justice*, though this does not focus exclusively on young women. Sheila Brown's (1998; 2nd edition 2005) *Understanding Youth and Crime* does more than most to force us to acknowledge that 'youth crime' is a product not of absent fathers, single mothers, lack of discipline, and so on but of the production and consumption of partial knowledges.

http://www.homeoffice.gov.uk/rds/index.html
The main portal for criminal statistics, victim surveys and self reports in England and Wales.

http://www.scotland.gov.uk/Topics/Statistics/15730/9012
The main portal for crime and justice statistics in Scotland.

http://www.nacro.org.uk/data/resources/
The crime reduction charity organization NACRO (National Association for the Care and Resettlement of Offenders) occasionally produces briefings which synthesize statistical data on youth crime and youth justice.

http://www.umsl.edu/~ccj/eurogang/euroganghome.htm
A collaboration of US and European academics who have formed a 'thematic network for comparative and multi-method research on violent youth groups'.

http://www.drugscope.org.uk/
A useful site for current statistics on drug use and commentaries on contemporary policies.

http://www.ic.nhs.uk/statistics-and-data-collections/health-and-lifestyles-related-surveys/smoking-drinking-and-drug-use-among-young-people-in-england
An annual survey carried out on behalf of the NHS in participating schools across England to provide information on 11 to 15 year olds' smoking, drinking and drug use behaviours.

http://www.mediastudies.com/
A hub providing links to over a hundred international news, media studies sites, and other resources worldwide for students, and researchers.

http://www.iir.com/nygc/
The National Youth Gang Centre is part of a coordinated response to America's gang problem by the Office of Juvenile Justice and Delinquency Prevention and illustrates the centrality of concern about gangs (as opposed to youth cultures) in American law and order discourse.

http://www.spiked-online.com/
An on-line critical commentary on various current affairs including media and political campaigns against youth, anti-social behaviour, crime and violence.

2

Histories of Youth and Crime

Overview

Chapter 2 examines:

- the 'invention' of childhood;

- why juvenile delinquency emerged as a major social problem in the early nineteenth century;

- the relevance of the concepts of 'deprived' and 'depraved' for the treatment of boys and girls in trouble;

- the significance of 'adolescence' in understanding troubled and troublesome youth in the early twentieth century;

- the origins of 'hooliganism';

- the role of medico-psychological discourses in consolidating the 'youth problem' in the inter-war years.

key terms

adolescence; child-saving; dangerous classes; delinquency; depravation; deprivation; hooligan; idealist history; perishing classes; reformation; rescue; revisionist history; social crime; waywardness

Is youth crime a relatively new phenomenon? Is the situation far worse now than in the past? Can historical research shed any light on how best to treat young offenders? This chapter traces the origins and development of discourses of juvenile delinquency (in the context of changing policies and practices of youth justice primarily in England and Wales) from the early nineteenth century to the 1930s. This focus on history is informed not simply by a curiosity with the past, but because it guards against the impression that the 'youth problem' is either timeless or relatively recent. Similarly, it is only by placing crime (and the reaction to it) in precise socio-historical contexts that we are able truly to grasp the meaning and significance of our subject matter. However, any brief excursus into social history must bear two vital matters in mind. First, historical research is never a simple matter of telling facts in an unproblematic fashion. It is a profoundly political subject in its own right. Second, it is not possible simply to recall a single, uncontested history. This chapter deals with *competing* interpretations of youth crime and youth justice. While legislative and organizational landmarks might be placed quite accurately, the extent of crime and delinquency and the purpose of youth justice remain the subject of dispute and controversy.

Broadly speaking, a basic distinction between idealist and revisionist histories can be made. Until the 1970s most histories of youth crime and punishment told a story of reformers who struggled against the 'cruel and barbaric' practices of the past and initiated a movement towards 'more humane' methods of dealing with young offenders. This **idealist history** was constructed 'from above', concentrating almost exclusively on the reforming zeal of powerful and notable individuals. The history of youth crime was told as one of progress from cruelty to enlightenment in how the young criminal was treated. Contemporary assessments of the nature and extent of offending were largely taken for granted.

During the 1970s this version of events came to be questioned by revisionist accounts of historical change. In short, **revisionist history** was more intent on retelling the story of crime and reform in the context of changing socio-historical circumstances, economic interests, power relations and a strengthening of state power. Reform was analysed not so much in terms of benevolent progress, but as an insidious extension of centralized power and control. Above all, it was argued that it was impossible to view reform as a simple reaction to a growing problem of youth crime. Rather, it was only through the developing legal powers and institutions of juvenile justice that the 'problem' of childhood and youth could be constituted and defined. Notions of youth as either innocent or dangerous were only fully realized in those developments of criminal law and in the expansion of institutional interventions that characterized the early to mid nineteenth century. Revisionism also questioned the motives of the humanitarian reformers themselves, arguing that they were driven as much by self and class interest as they were by conscience. Above all, it is argued that it was only through the particular motives and moralities of the reformers that attention was drawn to new categories of youthful behaviour and the very concept of juvenile delinquency invented. The revisionist concern then is not so much with unearthing the causes and extent of youth crime, but with identifying the ways in which certain behaviours and groups of the population were subject to processes of criminalization – how some children and young people came to be considered as criminal.

This chapter tries to capture something of the spirit of these debates while remaining alive to the possibilities of a 'new revisionism' which neither condemns reform as overt repression nor celebrates it as a successful humanitarian crusade. In particular it focuses on the historical controversies of two particular moments: (i) the emergence of 'juvenile delinquency' as a discrete social problem in the early nineteenth century; and (ii) the significance of the concept of 'adolescence' in understanding youth crime in the early twentieth century. Throughout it is informed by Pearson's (1983, 1993–94) and Humphries' (1994) insistence that the identifying of young offending as particularly troublesome is nothing new. British social history – at least from the eighteenth century – is replete with 'respectable fears' in which the present is compared unfavourably with the past. A common and recurring complaint is that the behaviour of young people is worse than '20 or 30 years ago' or 'in my day' or 'before the war'. However, such assumptions fail to stand up to sustained historical scrutiny. Whether it be the 2000s (antisocial behaviour and street crime), the 1970s (football hooligans), the 1950s (teddy boys), the 1930s (immoral youth), the 1890s (street gangs), the 1860s (garrotters) or the 1830s (street arabs), young people's behaviour has consistently been singled out as symbolic of national moral decline and as indicative of some new and unprecedented problem in which things have 'gone too far' (see Box 2.1). In addressing the pressing problems of the day, it seems that the Victorians suffered from the amnesia that inflicts many contemporary readings of the present.

Box 2.1

A catalogue of complaints

- … people nationally are sick of kids making their life hell … It never happened in the 1950s. (Letter to provincial newspaper, 2005)

- We will never get reasonable behaviour among the young until we bring back National Service. Without decent standards to guide them, the young have become lawless. Before the war there was little lawlessness. We need to return to those days. (Newspaper editorial, 1985)

- Over the past 20 years or so, there has been a revulsion from authority and discipline. (Newspaper editorial, 1981)

- The adolescent has learned no definite moral standards from his parents, is contemptuous of the law, easily bored. (British Medical Association, 1961)

- There has been a decline in the disciplinary forces governing a child. Obedience and respect for law have decreased (*The Times*, 1952).

- The passing of parental authority, defiance of pre-war conventions, the absence of restraint, the wildness of extremes, the wholesale drift away from churches are but a few characteristics of after-war conditions. (Boys' club leader, 1932)

- Their vulgarity and silliness and the distorted, unreal, Americanized view of life must have a deteriorating effect and lead to the formation of false ideals. (Social commentator and advocate of boys' clubs, 1917)

- Our young people have no idea of discipline or subordination. (Chief Constable, 1904)

- The manners of children are deteriorating … the child of today is coarser, more vulgar, less refined than his parents were. (Howard Association, 1898)

- Insubordination to parental authority, leading to insubordination to all authority is very general. (Clergyman, 1849)

- Morals are getting much worse. When I was young my mother would have knocked me down for speaking improperly to her. (Newspaper editorial, 1843)

- They are links which have fallen off the chain of society which are going to decay and obstruct the whole machine. (Politician, 1788)

- I would there were no age between 10 and three-and-twenty, or that youth would sleep out the rest; for there is nothing in the between but getting wenches with child, wronging the ancientry, stealing, fighting. (*The Winter's Tale*, Act III, Scene III, c. 1610)

Source: Derived from Pearson, (1983, 1985, 1993–4); Wills (2007).

We are just as likely to find complaints about social change, permissive decline, the break-up of the family, 'disturbing' tendencies of modern life, sexual promiscuity, the deterioration of manners and growing numbers of irresponsible youth surfacing in the nineteenth century as we do in the present. Moreover each new complaint seems to gather strength from a prevailing assumption that 'nothing like this has had to be endured before'. As Pearson (1983, pp. 242–3) eloquently concludes:

> If this long, connected history of respectable fears tells us anything at all, then it is surely that street violence and disorder are a solidly entrenched feature of the social landscape. Hence they are going to be much more difficult to dislodge than if we imagined that they had suddenly appeared from nowhere ... it will help first to repossess the past if we are to understand the present and build the future.

The Social Construction of Childhood and Youth

2.1 A catalogue of complaints about youth behaviour may be traced back at least through two centuries, but childhood has not always been a time in the life cycle to which much importance was attached. Often the reverse was true. Infanticide or abandonment of the newborn was not uncommon in Europe as late as the eighteenth century, and the practice of disposing of illegitimate children continued into the nineteenth. Cultural beliefs partly determined who should or should not survive. Typically boys were considered of much greater value than girls and any child who was considered imperfect was likely to be subject to a premature death. Even when allowed to live at birth, a child's survival was often tenuous owing to high mortality rates among babies and young children.

This may in part explain why childhood received so little attention, to the extent, as the social historian Philippe Ariès (1962, p. 28) maintains, that the various languages of the Middle Ages and later did not possess words to distinguish infants from juveniles or juveniles from adults. Ariès' radical notion was that prior to the seventeenth century there was no conception of childhood, adolescence or youth. Unsurprisingly, his work has not gone unchallenged. For example, Pollock's (1983) study of diaries and autobiographies led her to conclude that there has been no time in which parental indifference predominated. Parents have always held an emotional attachment for their children. Some conception of childhood has always existed. Similarly deMause (1976) has maintained that childhood was not 'discovered' or 'invented' in the way that Ariès claimed but has always been afforded special status within the human life course. Nevertheless the defining contribution of Ariès was to challenge the orthodoxy that simply viewed childhood as a universal biological given. It remains the case that in pre-industrial societies children mingled with adults in everyday life, in work, in leisure and in sport to a far greater degree than they might do today. They did not live in a separate world or behave differently and were not subject to different codes of morality and propriety. So children were quite 'naturally' and 'happily' involved in any number of activities – drinking alcohol, manual work, gambling – that we might now define as inappropriate in order to safeguard their 'innocence' and morality (Empey, 1982, p. 33). As a result there could be no conception of childhood as a social problem in itself. Some children might be 'selected as problematic by particular value judgements' – but not to the extent that it demanded a legal response (Dingwall et al., 1984, p. 208).

The process of strictly distinguishing a period of childhood and a morality of childhood began in the late Middle Ages, largely from within the aristocracy and nobility. The most obvious influences came from Renaissance humanism and moralists of the Protestant Reformation (Cunningham, 1995). There were two important emphases. First, children gradually became seen as innocents and as objects of affection, especially within the family, but second, they were seen by moralists as rather odd creatures – fragile maybe, but also capable of bringing into the world a corrupt nature and evil disposition. These two images, described by Hendrick (1997, pp. 37–40) as the 'Romantic child' and the 'Evangelical child', collided in the view that children were in need of both protection *and* discipline/regulation. What was emerging was a modern concept of childhood in which a child was thought to require a moral and educational training before entering adult life. Moreover, given children's vulnerability, such training could not be undirected. Thus the moralists placed responsibility not only on the Church, but also on the family and the school to raise children in a proper fashion. By the eighteenth century a vision of the ideal child had been developed and widely projected – a child who was dependent, submissive to authority, obedient, modest, hard-working and chaste. If children did not meet such standards, then the fault lay primarily with parents and, second, with schools which had failed to exercise an appropriate measure of discipline.

Historical analyses have suggested that both this ideal concept and its practical implementation were formative influences in the origins of the nuclear family. During the Middle Ages, children were common property and, except for a few early years, were not necessarily raised by their own parents. However, by the seventeenth century, direct responsibility was placed on natural parents to provide a safe and disciplined upbringing. The irony in this development and the instigation of an ideology of parental responsibility was that, although not solely confined to aristocratic and bourgeois elites, such conceptions of childhood and family did not have much (if any) purchase upon the material conditions of life or the culture of the mass of the population. For them the necessity to make children economically active as soon as possible precluded any consideration of instigating prolonged periods of childhood training and dependency. There was then a clear class differentiation in conceptions of childhood (Thane, 1981, p. 9). Only the privileged classes could afford the 'luxury of childhood with its demands on material provision, time and emotion' (Jenks, 1996, p. 64). As a result, as late as the mid-nineteenth century the majority of children participated in acts which, if committed today, could not only result in their being defined as delinquent but could require their parents to be charged with negligence or contributing to their children's delinquency.

Much of this was the outcome of child labour being an economic necessity for many families. Children were viewed as a vital source of family income and were placed in work as soon as they could be economically active. Child labour from the ages of 4 or 5 was a long-established practice in the rural farms and fields, where children performed tasks including straw plaiting and preparing raw materials for such domestic industries as lace making. With the onslaught of the industrial revolution, the children of the poor formed the bulk of factory labour. In the late eighteenth century it has been estimated that, because of the high birth and death rates, 40 per cent of the population were under the age of 15 (Morris and McIsaac, 1978, p. 1). In particular they worked in the mines, traversing the narrower roadways and in the mills, where they crawled under machines to clear waste.

Such a situation remained unquestioned, not only by families who needed to maintain a level of income, but also by factory owners who were acutely aware of the benefit of maintaining such a cheap source of labour. In the first decades of the nineteenth century, 80 per cent of the workers in English cotton mills were children (Gillis, 1974, p. 56). Children were legally the property of their parents and were used by them as family assets. Among the poor, the labour of children was exploited; among the rich, their marriages were contrived, all to the economic advantage of their parents. This degree of complacency was bolstered by the law. Not until 1889 did cruelty to children by parents become a specific criminal offence. Children were also held to be adult if above the age of 7 and were held responsible for any misdemeanour. There was no special provision for young offenders. For example, on one day in 1814, five children between the ages of 8 and 12 were hanged for petty larceny (Pinchbeck and Hewitt, 1973, p. 352).

All of this lends credence to the notion that childhood and youth are not universal biological states, but social constructions in particular historical contexts. It is clear that for a majority of young people in the early nineteenth century, the modern concepts of 'childhood' or 'youth' had little or no bearing on their lives. However, while eighteenth-century conceptions of the child were at best ambiguous and class-specific, by the twentieth century 'childhood' had become recognized as a universal condition. This was made possible not only through changes in economic and social conditions, but by the establishment of identifiable age groups in law and in medical, psychological, educational and welfare discourses and policies. As a result, notions of 'childhood as constructed' continue to be highly influential in many criminological texts because they reveal connections between socio-economic transformations, adult perceptions and the ability to recognize 'delinquency'. They reveal how, as the concept of childhood expanded, it became possible to define certain behaviours as new and unique social problems.

Discovering Juvenile Delinquency

2.2 Most historians agree that particular expressions of youthful behaviour were first identified as a major social problem in the early nineteenth century, although they may disagree over whether the precise origins lay in the 1840s, the 1810s or earlier. A mixture of contemporary accounts, social surveys and empirical investigations first permitted a problem to be identified but they presupposed existing conceptions of how youth should behave, what relation should exist between different age groups and what should be the 'appropriate' role of the family. In the early nineteenth century, with the rapid growth of industrial capitalism, factory production and high-density urban populations, the condition of the labouring classes became the object of considerable middle-class concern – whether this was fear of their revolutionary potential, disgust at their morality or alarm at their impoverishment and criminal tendencies. The need to ensure a reliable, healthy and willing workforce to maintain factory production produced a wide range of reformist initiatives which have variously been interpreted as human-itarian in motive or repressive in intent. Many of these centred on the delineation of juvenile **delinquency** as a distinctive social problem, demanding special and immediate action.

Depravity, Destitution and Urbanization

In early nineteenth-century Britain it was commonplace for children to work in many industries including textiles, mining, agriculture, domestic service, docks and machinery and metals. The first attempts to restrain child labour came from landowners hostile to manufacturing, adult trade unionists seeking limitations of adult hours of work, or from middle-class intellectuals and humanitarians who were appalled at the exploitation and brutalization of young workers and the violence thereby done to the 'nature' of childhood itself (Thompson, 1963, p. 367; Hendrick, 1997, p. 40; Cunningham, 1995, pp. 138–45). As a result of such pressure, the *1819* and *1833 Factory Acts* stipulated that no child under the age of 9 was to be employed in the mills and factories, and hours were limited to eight per day for those under 13, and 12 hours for those under 18. This legislation marked the first step in acknowledging a 'universal' childhood. While the Acts were consistently contravened, where the law was upheld it indirectly compelled families with children to seek further employment in order to compensate for lost wages. And while parents were at work, children were left to their own devices or neglected. Similarly, the urban youth population often grew more rapidly than the now restricted work opportunities. A growing number of children, therefore, were fundamentally displaced and, within such adverse social and economic conditions, gravitated towards 'delinquent' activities and/or acquisitive forms of petty crime in order to survive. In Hendrick's (1997, pp. 40–5) terms, the 'Factory Child' was replaced by the 'Delinquent Child'.

Vagrancy and the sight of children eking out a living on the street (gambling, selling necklaces, matches, braces or boxes of dominoes) increasingly came to be viewed as a serious social problem. Mayhew's (1861) vivid descriptions of the rookeries in the East End of London catalogued the activities of such young 'preco-cious' traders, 'daring' thieves and 'loutish' vagabonds. Children attracted to the streets as a result of the 'brute' tyranny of parents, association with costermongers, orphan-hood or destitution, necessarily lived on the edge of crime. There was no clear demarcation between honest work and illegal trading for those existing on a subsistence level on the streets of Britain's newly industrialized cities. It was in such conditions that bands of young pickpockets and other 'artful dodgers' thrived, whose independence and street-wise lifestyle were anathema to the growing number of middle-class journalists and social commentators. Such observers tended to carry with them their own bourgeois conceptions of childhood and youth as a period of dependency and vulnerability. They expressed concern not simply about the need to control criminality, but about the need to tackle a 'premature precocity', symbolized by promiscuity, irreligion, pauperism and knowledge of 'the adult world and its pleasures' (see Box 2.2). In short, the problem was viewed as having as much a moral as a criminal character.

Box 2.2
London Labour and London Poor, 1861

Each year sees an increase of the numbers of street-children to a very considerable extent, and the exact nature of their position may be thus briefly depicted: what little *information* they receive is obtained from the worst class – from cheats, vagabonds, and rogues; what little *amusement* they indulge in, springs from sources the most poisonous – the most fatal to happiness and welfare; what little they know of a *home* is necessarily associated with much that is vile and base; their very means of existence, uncertain and precarious as it is, is to a great extent identified with petty chicanery, which is quickly communicated by one to the other; while their physical sufferings from cold, hunger, exposure to the weather, and other causes of a similar nature, are constant, and at times extremely severe. Thus every means by which a proper intelligence may be conveyed to their minds is either closed or at the least tainted, while every duct by which a bad description of knowledge may be infused is sedulously culti-vated and enlarged.

Source: Mayhew (1861, p. 479).

It was from similar concerns some 50 years earlier that the first public body to investigate youth crime – the *Society for Investigating the Causes of the Alarming Increase of Juvenile Delinquency in the Metropolis* – was established in 1815 (Muncie, 1984, p.34; Shore, 1999, p. 20). Whether or not the rate of crime was in fact increasing at the time is statistically unanswerable, as the Society's report contained no figures, but it is clear that it was contemporary conviction that this was the case. The Society's evidence was taken from interviewing children already incarcerated in prison, and it concluded that the main causes of delinquency were the 'improper conduct of parents', the 'want of education', the 'want of suitable employment' and 'violation of the Sabbath'. In addition, the report made much of the failures and criminalizing tendencies of existing legal procedure, police practices and penal regimes (see Box 2.3). The Society proposed a separate system of dealing with the young offender: one that depended on the 'mildness of persuasion' and the 'gentleness of reproof' rather than the infliction of bodily punishment. It was such beliefs that helped to encourage voluntary effort to provide institutions whose aim would be to reform, and not merely punish, delinquent youth.

Box 2.3

Report of Committee into Juvenile Delinquency, 1816

The want of employment – the prevalence of improvident marriages – the degrading tendencies of the poor laws – and the increased facilities for the consumption of spirituous liquors have doubtless contributed much to deteriorate the moral character and consequently to weaken the natural affections of the lower classes of society. To an evil so general and extensive it is impossible at once to apply a remedy. This alone can be found in measures which are calculated to raise the condition and promote the religious and moral improvement of the poor at large ... Dreadful is the situation of the young offender: he becomes the victim of circumstances over which he has no control. The laws of his country operate not to restrain, but to punish, him. The tendency of the police is to accelerate his career in crime. If when apprehended, he has not attained the full measure of guilt, the nature of his confinement is almost sure to complete it; and discharged, as he frequently is, pennyless, without friends, character or employment, he is driven, for a subsistence, to the renewal of depredations.

Source: Report of Committee into Juvenile Delinquency (1816, pp. 12–13, 25).

These concerns about juveniles were also indelibly tied to the growing fear of crime and disorder in general that captured the imagination of the early Victorians. The criminal statistics that began to be published annually from 1810 painted a disturbing picture of incremental rises year on year. Whether this measured 'real' crime or was merely a reflection of improved record keeping, system capacity and 'supply-side' policies is a problem that afflicts 'readings' of criminal statistics then as now (Weiner, 1990; Taylor, 1998b, and see **Chapter 1.2**). Nevertheless, although they did not distinguish between adults and juveniles, successive select committees between 1816 and 1828 were in no doubt that crime was being committed (not just in London but in the counties) at a much earlier age than formerly and that the principal cause was parental neglect. When such statistics were refined to include a wide range of factors, including age, it became possible to gain a more detailed account of the population that was being processed through the criminal courts. From 1834, when information on the age and education of offenders was first included, it became possible to claim that crime was increasing out of all proportion to population rises and that such increase was greatest among the young. As a result, a number of unofficial enquiries produced by magistrates, teachers and church officers (or indeed any professional whose occupation brought them into contact with the world of the working-class street) began to give specific consideration to delinquency as something separate from crime *per se*.

It is clear that in the early nineteenth century with the expansion of the criminal law, previous concerns over sin were being replaced with concerns over delinquency and crime – in particular property crimes and the defence of property. 'Crime' was gradually assuming its modern meaning:

> [a] vehicle for articulating mounting anxieties about issues which really had nothing to do with crime at all: social change and the stability of social hierarchy. These issues invested crime with new meanings, justified vastly accelerated action against it, and have determined attitudes to it ever since. (Gatrell, 1990, p. 249)

The rapid growth of towns seemed to promote moral dissolution: the crowding, fast pace and young population acting to 'dangerously stimulate the passions' (Weiner, 1990, p. 19). The working population, and especially the young, were believed to be in desperate need of 'moral guidance' and 'civilized order'.

Legislation, Prosecution and Criminalization

These fears were galvanized by dramatic images of gangs of 'naked, filthy, roaming, lawless and deserted children', believed to number more than 30,000 in London alone in 1848 (Lord Ashley, cited by Magarey, 1978, p. 16). But accurate estimations of the extent of 'delinquency' were impossible, not least because of its ill-defined nature. Nevertheless Susan Magarey (1978) contends that there was some justification for these growing fears, particularly in the newly recorded prison statistics of the 1830s. The number of under-17s imprisoned increased from some 9,500 in 1838 to around 14,000 in 1848. However, she finds that this rise is explicable less with reference to 'increased lawlessness' and more by changes in the position of children in relation to the criminal law and the subsequent criminalization of behaviour in relation to which previously there may have been no official action. First the presumption that the under-14s were *doli incapax* (incapable of evil) fell into disuse (see **Chapter 8.1**). Second, the *Vagrancy Act 1824* and the *Malicious Trespass Act 1827* considerably broadened legal conceptions of 'criminality' to include, for example, suspicion of being a thief, gambling on the street and scrumping apples from orchards and gardens. Previous nuisances were transformed into criminal offences. Third, the remit given to the Metropolitan Police in 1829 included apprehension of 'all loose, idle and disorderly persons not giving good account of themselves'. This alone made many more street children liable to arrest.

Magarey estimates that between 1838 and 1856 summary convictions for vagrancy accounted for more than 20 per cent of all juvenile convictions, while those for malicious trespass, larceny and being a known or reputed thief accounted for 30 per cent. She argues that 'at least half of the increasing numbers of juvenile prisoners were in prison as a result of the creation of new criminal offences, an extension of the powers of justices of the peace and a widespread readiness to treat children as young as 9 or 10 as fully responsible adults' (Magarey, 1978, p. 23). In these ways juvenile delinquency was 'legislated into existence'. Similarly, Shore (1999, p. 150) concludes that 'a lack of willingness to overlook the crimes of children combined with the decreasing use of acquittal verdicts implies a conscious inclination to draw children into the criminal justice system'. If not created, then policing and legislative action in the early to mid nineteenth century certainly accentuated the 'problem of delinquency'.

Rescue and Reformation

Legal recognition of the juvenile offender as being in some way different from the adult also emerged in the field of penal reform. Although the introduction of the penitentiary and the reform of the local prisons in the early nineteenth century did not entail any special differentiation on the basis of age, the emphases placed upon separation, classification and categorization highlighted age differentials and led to various conclusions being drawn about the position of the young. *The Society for the Improvement of Prison Discipline and the Reformation of Juvenile Offenders* (1817), for example, was convinced of the need to separate the juvenile from the hardened adult criminal in order to avoid the former's moral contamination. Similarly, the Society advocated the establishment of separate, highly controlled institutions in which young offenders could be reformed and reclaimed. May (1973, p. 12) argues that 'cellular isolation clearly revealed the mental and physical differences between children and adults' and she notes how this led prison inspectors to conclude that 'so marked is the distinction in the feeling and habit of manhood and youth that it is quite impractical to engraft any beneficial plan for the lengthened confinement of boys upon a system adapted to adults'. This sensitivity was also reflected in the transportation of young offenders to Australia. A sentence of transportation was frequently given to the young in place of a capital sentence and with the justification that it offered the possibility not simply of banishment but the hope of 'making a new start'. The early period of modern imprisonment permitted the apparently unique needs of the young to be recognized. Refinements in prisoner classification brought the particular case of the *young* offender to the fore.

In 1825, a separate convict hulk (prison ship) specifically designed for juveniles was introduced. In 1838, the first penal institution solely for juveniles was opened at Parkhurst. Yet as Weiner (1990, p. 132) notes, its regime was hardly less repressive than that afforded to adults. It was 'decidedly of a penal character' and its founder assured the Home Office that there was 'no reason to doubt that a strict system of penal discipline is quite compatible with the means requisite for the moral and religious improvement of the offender'. Prisoners were manacled and confined to their cells except for brief periods of exercise and religious instruction. Yet this severity was viewed as philanthropic, Parkhurst's governor claiming that 'every punishment is a weapon drawn from the armoury of truth and love ... and directed for their real happiness' (cited by Weiner 1990, p. 133). Parkhurst, however, did little to undermine the prevailing view that *all* offenders should be held fully responsible for their actions, and long before its conversion to a women's prison in 1864, its administration had ceased to speak of its role as one of **reformation** and **rescue**.

Pressure to develop separate institutions (other than prison) for young offenders was also mounting from voluntary organizations such as the Philanthropic

Society and the Society for the Suppression of Juvenile Vagrancy. As early as 1756 the Marine Society had established a system whereby delinquent children of criminal parents or those who had been deserted could avoid institutional confinement by being sent to sea. It was, as Radzinowicz and Hood (1990, p. 134) concluded, 'more a policy of sweeping the gutters, of flushing out, than of reintegrating the poor, the unemployed and the depraved into society'. By contrast, the *Philanthropic Society (for the Prevention of Crimes and the Reform of the Criminal Poor; by the Encouragement of Industry and the Culture of Good Morals, among those Children who are now trained up to Vicious Courses, Public Plunder, Infamy and Ruin)*, which had been founded in 1788 on the initiative of Robert Young, aimed to reform the depraved *and* the deprived. Accordingly, an asylum was established for 60 children to provide as far as possible a 'normal' home, with each child assigned to a local manufacturer for industrial instruction. This was complemented by daily prayers and compulsory attendance at church each Sunday. In 1792, further property was acquired in Southwark complete with its own dormitories and workshops: this was the first full-scale institution for delinquent and potentially delinquent children of both sexes. The early 'family system' was replaced by a 'house' master supervising groups of 45 children, and admissions were eventually to be restricted to those who had already been convicted of a criminal offence. By 1806, the asylum had three sections: the reform as a prison school for young delinquents; the manufactory for the employment of partially reclaimed delinquent boys; and the training school for girls (Pinchbeck and Hewitt, 1973, pp. 419–30). The distinguishing feature of such schools was the principle of self-instruction under surveillance, whereby discipline and order were viewed as the vehicles for self-improvement and beneficial activity. This has led such revisionist theorists as Michel Foucault (1977) to argue that discipline served as an education for similar degrees of order which were being demanded in the factories, workhouses, poorhouses and prisons across Europe. The schools were essentially a disciplinary machine for the arrangement and classification of bodies and the promotion and regulation of preferred activities. Classification of pupils and inmates provided a principle of order in itself, by setting standards to be followed and instituting schedules of reward and punishment (Rush, 1992). The separation of male and female delinquents was similarly designed to prepare children for future roles. At Southwark, girls were employed in making, mending and cleaning their own and the boys' clothes and keeping the house clean, while the boys were employed in shoemaking and ropemaking. Girls were sent out as menial servants for domestic labour, while boys were apprenticed to local employers.

Such a reformatory option in sentencing was at the time pretty much restricted to these institutions, but in the 1810s the London Refuge for the Destitute was also made available. As King's (2006) exhaustive research has revealed, this predated orthodox histories of the origins of state-sponsored reformatories by more than 40 years. Rather, a series of complex and informal alliances between philanthropists, 'liberal' judges and a government experimenting with ways of allaying new public fears about delinquency in the first decades of the nineteenth century created 'what appears to have been Europe's first centrally funded juvenile reformatory' (King, 2006, p. 154).

These early initiatives were, however, significantly augmented by the reformatory movement of the 1840s. Inspired by the establishment of the Mettray reformatory near Tours in France, which instituted a regime of strict self-denial, religious zeal and continual exercise for delinquents and vagrants, the Philanthropic Society established its own agricultural farm at Redhill in Surrey in 1849. Lauded as a great success, the cause was subsequently taken up by such philanthropists as Mary Carpenter, the daughter of a Unitarian minister. A forceful critic of penal regimes such as at Parkhurst, she was convinced that reformation depended on meeting the perceived needs of children for care and support as well as overt discipline. The causes of crime were seen to lie firmly in deficiencies in working-class family life, in the low moral condition of parents and in parental neglect. Preventing the contamination of youth and restoring their moral guardianship in the family were to serve as the principles for 'humanitarian' reform. In 1853, a British Parliamentary Select Committee advised that state-sponsored reformatories and industrial schools should move beyond a singular emphasis on punishing the young offender. Influenced by similar developments in America and Continental Europe, the rationales for institutional intervention were increasingly couched in terms of 'moral detriment', 'rescue from temptation' and 'training' for an 'industrial occupation'. While boys were typically considered to be 'at risk' of criminal offending, girls were viewed as especially vulnerable to moral and, in particular, sexual transgressions. A construction of childhood as an essentially innocent and dependent state, requiring nurture and discipline on the part of parents and other adults, led to the dispersal and expansion of interventions directed not only at the 'criminal' but also at the 'morally deviant':

> The child must be placed where the prevailing principle will be, as far as practicable, carried out – where he will be gradually restored to the true position of childhood … He must perceive by manifestations which he cannot mistake that this power, while controlling him, is guided by interest and love; he must have his own affections called forth by the obvious personal interest felt in his own individual well being by those around him, he must, in short, be placed in a family. (Carpenter, 1853, p. 298)

Carpenter's language was notably gender specific, but concern was directed as much at girls as boys. Carpenter herself argued that criminal women and girls were blatantly depraved – 'they are, as a class, even more morally degraded than men' (cited by Gelsthorpe, 1984, p. 2). And as Zedner (1991, p. 43) argues, in Victorian discourses about crime, female criminality was viewed as particularly abhorrent: not only transgressing legality and femininity but also being a source of moral contagion in itself. Criminal women were widely represented as 'utterly depraved and corrupted beyond repair'. One of the key aims of the reformatory movement was the control of female sexuality (Shore, 2002, p. 168).

Given a set of 'common-sense' presuppositions about the true nature of childhood, femininity and masculinity and the increasing accumulation of empirical data organized directly around these presuppositions, it is not surprising that a specific set of conclusions surrounding the nature and causes of delinquency was to emerge in Victorian society. A view of childhood as an essentially innocent and dependent state requiring nurture and discipline on the part of parents led to a certain definition of delinquency in particular, but also of youthful behaviour in general. It was not just criminal behaviour that was of concern to the nineteenth-century reformers. While there was a recognition that economic and social conditions connected with the criminal propensities of the young, this was subordinated to a consideration of the *moral* dimension of the problem. In the reformatories the 'rescue' of children was dependent on their understanding 'the value of labour' rather than learning specific industrial skills: 'The salutary fatigue of the body removes from the mind evil thoughts and renders it necessary to devote to repose the hours which in the towns are given to vicious pleasures' (Carpenter, 1853, p. 306). The terms that emerged to describe the problem were 'unnatural independence', 'deterioration', 'contamination' and 'parental neglect and irresponsibility'. Delinquency and youth behaviour in general became firmly associated with the conditions of working-class family life. Victorian concern also encompassed orphans, the illegitimate, the deserted, the independent young and anyone who failed to live up to middle-class assumptions of normal family life. As May (1973, p. 16) argues, the Victorian social investigators and reformers produced such damning reports of the conditions of existence for working-class children because the realities of slum childhood violated their sense and image of their own protected childhood. Concern was directed not only towards these children, but also towards the failings of parents – the apparent absence of supervision and control; the failure to imbue their children with proper moral habits. Such parental shortcomings were viewed as the root cause of what was seen as the 'progressive career of the delinquent child'. The roots of social disorder were tied directly to the family, working and moral life of the poorer classes (see Box 2.4).

Box 2.4

Juvenile depravity or destitution?

A large proportion of the population were found to be grovelling in the veriest debasement, yielding obedience only to the animal instincts; brooding in spiritual darkness in a day of gospel light, and as much shut off from participating in the blessings of Christian privilege as if they had been the inhabitants of another hemisphere.

Source: Submission to inquiry into juvenile depravity, London, 1849 (cited by Shore, 1999, p. 4)

(Continued)

Above all, reformist conceptions of childhood and interpretations of delinquency marked a major shift in how the troublesome young should be dealt with. They tended to relieve the young from full responsibility for their actions and emphasized the central role that family and family life should play in the creation of obedient and respectable citizens. When the family failed, the state had a duty to intervene – not simply to punish offending but to compel responsible behaviour on the part of parents. For the first time it became quite appropriate for the state to act *in loco parentis* – to intervene in working-class life in order to ensure that children were 'properly' educated, moralized and disciplined. In doing so it was believed that the chain that links the deprived child of today to the criminal of tomorrow would be broken (McLaughlin and Muncie, 1993, p. 160). It was not necessary for a child to have committed an offence for intervention and removal from home to be justified.

In the abiding concern for categorization, Carpenter labelled **the deprived** as the **'perishing' classes** and **the depraved** as the **'dangerous' classes**. Advocating industrial schools for the former and reformatories for the latter, her initiative was to gain legal status in the *1854 Youthful Offenders Act* and *1857 Industrial Schools Acts*. Under the 1854 Act, courts were allowed to sentence any child convicted of an indictable or summary offence to a reformatory for between two and five years; under the 1857 Act, children found begging or who had no visible means of subsistence and were deemed to be beyond parental control could be sent indefinitely to an industrial school. By 1860, there were 48 certified reformatories in England and Wales holding about 4,000 young offenders. The development of industrial schools was slower, but by the end of the century reformatories and industrial schools held more than 30,000 inmates. The state had come to assume the responsibility of parents for one in every 230 of the juvenile population (Radzinowicz and Hood, 1990, p. 181).

The reforming zeal was not without its critics. Traditional advocates of the principles of classical justice argued that age could not be taken as a sufficient index of responsibility and that *no* circumstances should preclude the necessity of punishment in dealing with offenders, whether juvenile or not. In contrast to the reformist discourse of welfare and treatment, May (1973, p. 25) notes a continuing and influential body of opinion that punishment should fit the crime and not be mitigated by personal circumstances; that juveniles should be treated as all other offenders; that 'the idea of pain might be instantly associated with crime in the minds of all evildoers'. Carpenter's proposals were thus subject to legislative compromise. Before entering a reformatory, a 14-day prison sentence had to be served. The maintenance of the reformatories was to be paid for partly by the state, but also through parental contribution. Moreover, the 1854 Act was only advisory and magistrates could continue to send juveniles to prison if they so decided. Stack (1992, p. 117) estimates that between 1856 and 1875 sentences to reformatory detention formed only 12.6 per cent of all child commitments to prison. The reformatory system was thus grafted on to the existing institutions of punishment and justice and did not replace them.

With the establishment of industrial schools, the issue of parental responsibility was more acute. Here parents were again required to contribute to the maintenance of their children and denied the right to bring their children up as they wished, even when no criminal offence had been committed. Such institutional intervention was legitimized in the name of care and protection, centring not so much on material as on moral care. There was a double incentive for parents to try to conform to the dominant morality and middle-class child-rearing practices: both the fear of losing their child and the burden of maintenance that attended such separation. Parents who failed to provide such care in effect signed away their rights to their children.

Such tensions between reclamation and punishment for the deprived and depraved alike have continued to impact on the rationale and practices of a separate system of justice for juveniles (see **Chapter 8**). But, significantly, it was only through the initiation of such disputes that the concept of the 'juvenile delinquent' achieved not only public and political recognition, but also its own legal status. The establishment of separate institutions – particularly from the 1810s onwards – gave the 'juvenile delinquent' a new legal status. The operation of the English legislature, penal and educational systems and the perceptions of social investigators had resulted in new distinctions between the child and the adult and were critical in cementing the idea of a *juvenile* offender (see Box 2.5).

Juvenile offenders, however, were not drawn equally from all sections of society. Most were working class and male and their 'crimes' were typically of minor – albeit regular – property theft. Stack (1992), working on data derived from judicial and prison statistics between 1856 and 1875, finds that almost all custodial sentences for juveniles were given for petty larceny and petty theft. Criminalization and punishment also appeared to be highly racialized. Significantly many more juvenile inmates were Irish than English. Irish children were roughly four times more likely to end up in prison and reformatories

Box 2.5

The making of the delinquent: key legislative and institutional landmarks

1756 Marine Society

1788 Philanthropic Society

1804 Establishment of London Refuge for the Destitute

1815 Society for Investigating the Alarming Increase in Juvenile Delinquency in the Metropolis

1820 Malicious Trespass Act

1825 Establishment of a prison ship (the hulk, *Euryalus*) for male juvenile convicts

1830 Society for Suppression of Juvenile Vagrancy

1838 Establishment of Parkhurst Prison for boys

1839 Establishment of Mettray reformatory in France

1847 Juvenile Offenders Act

1849 Establishment of Red Hill reformatory (the English Mettray)

1851 Publication of Carpenter's *Reformatory Schools for the Children of the Perishing and Dangerous Classes, and for Juvenile Offenders*

1852 Select Committee on Criminal and Destitute Juveniles

1854 Reformatory Schools Act

1857 Industrial Schools Act

1870 Elementary Education Act

1879 Summary Jurisdiction Act

1894 Prevention of Cruelty to Children Act

1908 Children's Act

1908 Crime Prevention Act

1933 Children and Young Persons Act

than their counterparts in the general population. As Green and Parton (1990, p. 24) argue, 'The Irish in particular were stigmatized as wild and uncivilized, little different in habits and appetites, according to the more xenophobic observers, from the pigs with which they sometimes shared a residence.' But in general the young urban poor were viewed almost as a 'separate race' in need of ever watchful surveillance and regulation. Similar to Magarey's (1978) analysis, Stack (1992, p. 129) argues that the three factors which 'encouraged' the increased prosecution of children were: the growing availability of formal methods of prosecution, the decline in informal means of chastisement and the expanded activity of the police. It was the very existence of the sentencing alternatives of reformatories and industrial schools that enabled 'juvenile delinquency' gradually to take on its modern meaning as a clearly identifiable and distinctive social problem. The first half of the nineteenth century constitutes a distinct watershed in ways in which the debate about youth, crime and punishment came to be packaged and institutionalized.

Pre-industrial Traces: Disorderly Youths _____

Something of a new orthodoxy emerged in the 1970s which challenged previous historiographies and the assumption that juvenile justice developed as a humanitarian response to a real and dramatic increase in youth crime. Though the term itself was coined in 1776, revisionist histories have largely accounted for the origins of *juvenile delinquency* as a creation of late eighteenth-early nineteenth-century processes of industrialization, urbanization and criminalization. As a regulatory discourse, the concept was only *fully* realized in law as a result of the heated debates about reformatories in the 1840s (Rush, 1992). The precise origins of juvenile delinquency, however, remain a matter of some debate. Radzinowicz and Hood's (1990, p. 133) contention that 'the concept of the young offender ... is a Victorian creation' has subsequently been revised by more detailed empirical research on the rate of juvenile prosecutions in the period 1790–1820. King and Noel (1993) acknowledge that between the mid seventeenth and the late eighteenth centuries, juvenile delinquency was rarely regarded as a distinct and serious problem. However, their analysis of records at the Old Bailey suggests that a sea change in offending and prosecution was in place well before the 'moments of discovery' believed by Magarey to be the 1820s and by May to be the 1840s. In particular, there was a marked shift in the peak age of offending, from between the ages of 20 and 21 in 1791–93 to between 17 and 19 by 1820–22. In addition, the numbers of offenders under 17 coming before the Old Bailey rose nearly fourfold (King and Noel, 1993, p. 22).

Was this then the period in which modern conceptions of juvenile delinquency first emerged? If so, in London at least, the 'problem' arrived long after urbanization and well before 'the city's economy was affected, by anything that could be termed an industrial revolution' (King and Noel, 1993, p. 28). King's (1998) subsequent study of court records across England also notes a rapid increase in crime rates between 1782 and 1793, but yet no significant panic about delinquency. To address these anomalies, King suggests that a complex of changing attitudes of magistrates and prison reformers, growing fears about the social consequences of economic change and financial incentives offered to detective and policing agencies need to be taken into account when considering the root causes of the juvenile 'crime wave' in the 1810s and 1820s. In congruence with previous researchers, he concludes that alarm about 'the problem of juvenile delinquency' had little to do with substantial changes in levels of criminal activity and more to do with changing attitudes to childhood and the poor and the reactions of those who wrote about, investigated and prosecuted crime. The authors of the report of the *Society for Investigating the Causes of the Alarming Increase of Juvenile Delinquency in the Metropolis* in 1815 were only the latest in a long tradition of social commentators who had berated youthful disorder, mischief, merriment and idleness as indicative of a decline in national morality.

In the seventeenth century a major focus of concern was the apprenticeship system. Established in 1563, the system placed young men and women at the age of puberty with masters who were responsible for teaching trade skills and industrious habits. Initially systems of 'indoor' apprenticeship provided strict controls over virtually every aspect of the young person's life: from the ownership of personal possessions to clothing and hair style. Described by Smith (1973) as an identifiable subculture with its own standards, heroes and sense of fraternity, 'indoor' apprenticeship gradually declined through the century as the demand for more flexible working patterns evolved. Freed from the omnipresent strict regulation of their masters, apprentices were routinely condemned as idle, violent and profligate. Carnivals, initiation rituals and traditional customs provided seasonal occasions for apprentices to engage in revelry and rowdy behaviour. For example, as Pearson (1983, p. 192) records, London apprentices devoted Shrove Tuesday to the wrecking of brothels, ostensibly to prevent their own temptation during Lent. As a result, a succession of new regulations and legal statutes were created to ban apprentices from visiting public houses and brothels, from attending tennis courts, bowling alleys and cock fights and from playing cards, dice and billiards (Smith, 1973, p. 151). Feast days, carnivals and traditional customs – May Day, maypoles, morris dancing, hobby horses, fertility rites – were condemned as relics of paganism, particularly their propensity to incite violence, disorder and debauchery. They were routinely censured as the source of 'all kinds of moral ruin' (Pearson, 1983, p. 196).

Davis (1971) records how festive life – masking, costuming, parades, farces, dancing, lighting fires, gaming and charivaris (a demonstration to humiliate some wrongdoer in the community) – persisted throughout Europe in the sixteenth century. Organized informally by friends, craft guilds or by 'fools' societies', Abbeys of Misrule regularly mocked the behaviour of local dignitaries and representatives of officialdom. They parodied their rulers in carnivals of mock justice. As one defender of the Feast of Fools proclaimed in 1444, 'Foolishness is our second nature and must freely spend itself at least once a year. Wine barrels burst if from time to time we do not open them and let in some air' (cited by Davis, 1971, p. 48). Above all, these events were led and orchestrated by groups of young, unmarried men. (Most men did not marry until their mid-20s, particularly in rural areas.) Such rituals of rebellion were not simply 'safety valves' but acted to define and maintain certain community values (especially with regard to marital fidelity) and provided avenues for criticizing the political order. In the violent revelry and rowdy charivaris of the sixteenth century it is thus possible to witness some of the characteristics of 'adolescence' or of youth subcultures that were to emerge some four centuries later (see **Chapter 6**). While the Abbeys of Misrule gradually died out as a result of official censure and the decline of traditional rural customs, vestiges of the carnival can still be glimpsed in the confrontations, chants, slogans and rituals of street cultures of the twentieth century (Presdee, 2000). And it raises the intriguing proposition that juvenile delinquency was only capable of being recognized as a distinct social problem when the 'foolish' ribaldry and revelry of young people could no longer be tolerated.

Further, Griffith (2002) maintains that historians' obsession with the origins of delinquency at the turn of the nineteenth century has made them blind to traces of the problem stretching back to at least the sixteenth century. Cunningham

(1995) too emphasizes that street children are a centuries-old problem. Griffith (2002) notes how age-specific offences, penalties and policing measures were prevalent in the houses of correction, in transportation and in discourses of youth reformation across Europe which preceded the semantic twist of 'juvenile delinquency' by some 200 years. Nevertheless the combination of juvenile-specific legislation and institutions in the early nineteenth century continues to mark out this period as a watershed in the definition and management of disorder. Juvenile delinquency may not have been 'invented' as such at this time, but it underwent a dramatic reconfiguration in terms that are now familiar to us today (Shore, 2000; Cox and Shore, 2002).

Troublesome Adolescence

2.3 The concept of **adolescence** gained pre-eminence in the late nineteenth and early twentieth centuries to describe a period of life between childhood and adulthood which had its own particular problems of emotional adjustment and physical development. The rapidly developing psycho-medical disciplines of social psychology and child psychology gave traditional concerns about young people 'both a more profound substance and a new legitimacy' (Hendrick, 1990, p. 11). Delinquency was viewed as a 'natural' attribute of adolescence and consequently Victorian assumptions of a causal relationship between working-class culture and delinquency came to be challenged (though rarely superseded) by theorizing that focused on the age of *all* young people.

The discovery of adolescence by psychologists also coincided with specific renewed anxieties about working-class youth. In the 1880s, amid the emergence of the 'boy labour market', dramatic increases in juvenile crime, the rise of socialism and threats to the British Empire and Britain's economic position, concern was expressed once more about undisciplined and independent working-class youth. The twin concerns running through the complaints were that the urban working-class family was not fulfilling its regulatory functions and that the wage-earning capability of working-class youth enabled them to buy freedom from parental control (Springhall, 1986). Manifestations of this lack of discipline and independence were to be found in the street-based leisure pursuits of working-class adolescents. For the reformers of the late nineteenth century, independence and unwholesome leisure pursuits (e.g. street gambling and football) would inevitably result in delinquency and criminality. It was in this period that the term 'hooliganism' first emerged. The reformers saw their task as being to re-establish control over working-class adolescents in order to enforce their dependency. Consequently, working-class youth and their families were subject to renewed interventions.

First, the moral crusades of youth organizations sought to impose the 'new norms of adolescence' and as a result the working class was subject to heavier policing. Youth clubs were set up to provide the discipline, regulation, guidance and improvement that working-class parents would/could not. Working-class girls also found themselves on the receiving end of specialist youth work because it was believed that too much independence from the family and home was socially undesirable (Dyhouse, 1981, p. 113). Second, the growing public concern about adolescence and its presumed direct connection with juvenile delinquency resulted in a number of important changes in the legal position of young people. A plethora of early twentieth-century legislation clarified the position of the child and the adolescent in criminal law. Probation was introduced in 1907, and the *1908 Prevention of Crime Act* inaugurated specialist detention centres – borstals – for young people. In the same year the *Children Act* introduced juvenile courts. The primary assumptions underpinning this legislation were that juveniles were less responsible than adults for their actions and should not be subject to the full majesty of the law. But, such legislation (as in the early nineteenth century) can be read as not simply humanitarian in intent. While separating juvenile from adult justice, it further cemented the notion that the troublesome young (once again) constituted an entirely *new* and *unprecedented* problem for the nation's future.

Inventing Adolescence

The invention of the *concept* of adolescence is usually attributed to Rousseau, writing in the 1760s. He likened adolescence to a second birth, and viewed it principally as a period of emotional turmoil, which led to various forms of moral degeneration, and most particularly sexual precocity. Rousseau's chief concern was that the young were becoming worldly-wise and sexually aware at too early an age. He proposed that the young should be 'protected' and segregated from adult life for as long as possible (Simmons and Wade, 1984, p. 17). Musgrove (1964, p. 43) thus argues that adolescence was *invented* at the same time as the steam engine. It was directly related to the prolonged education afforded to *upper-class* students and apprentices in the late eighteenth century. The debates among the parents of the gentry and the professional middle classes at this time were concerned with the relative merits of keeping predominantly male youth education in the home or moving it out into the hands of public schools. Despite strong pressures to the contrary, by the 1830s the public school system achieved ascendancy, giving to the young 'a status and importance which they had not hitherto enjoyed' (Musgrove, 1964, p. 64). However, this development was by no means uncontested: public schools had a reputation for generating insubordination and rebellion. In 1818, for example, riots at Winchester public school were finally dealt with by the military; and the last of the revolts by public school boys was not until 1851 at Marlborough. But by the mid-nineteenth century, the reform of the public schools was established to the extent that the numbers of middle-class pupils rose significantly. In the process, the state of adolescence was born. Nevertheless the development extended only as far down the social hierarchy as the new bourgeoisie of industrialists, bankers and merchants. Adolescence at this time was still irrelevant to the mass of the labouring poor. It was not until the late nineteenth century and the advent of compulsory state education to the age of 13 that the concept of adolescence began to affect the children of the working classes.

It was a concept that gradually became endowed with pathological connotations. Adolescents were viewed as relatively unrestrained by the discipline of family or labour. Adolescence was replete with 'negative' and 'troubling' connotations. As Gillis (1974, p. 114) notes, 'what were the historically evolved social norms of a particular class became enshrined in medical and psychological literature as the "natural" attributes of adolescence'. Consequently, by the turn of this century, youngsters of all classes were viewed as sharing certain characteristics *solely because of their age*. Although originally related to the adult desire to regulate the increased leisure and period of dependency of middle-class youth, the equation of pathology with a particular period of life enabled all youthful behaviour to be subject to adult supervision and control. This was all the more anachronistic because, as Thane (1981, p. 16) notes, the children of the labouring poor still shared very fully the life of adults until well into the twentieth century, since they had to work for survival. Rather than being dependent, working-class youth remained very independent. Their material position contradicted much of what was scientifically considered to be the 'natural' attributes of 'adolescence'. Youthful independence thus became defined as a problem. Working-class youths in particular were viewed as morally degenerate and in need of stricter control. The label of 'adolescence', therefore, not only secured the view that *all* young people were potentially troublesome, but also that those (working-class) youths who did not or could not conform to this new view of being young were further stigmatized as 'delinquent'.

By the first decades of the twentieth century the concept gained scientific credibility and subsequently informed and underpinned a diverse and expansive range of initiatives designed to control and redirect youthful behaviour. Many historical accounts (Davis, J., 1990, p. 60; Hendrick, 1990, p. 101) see the role of the American psychologist Granville Stanley Hall as pivotal. In his *Adolescence, Its Psychology and Its Relations to Physiology, Anthropology, Sociology, Sex, Crime, Religion and Education* (1905), Hall argued that each individual relives the development of the human race from early animal-like primitivism (childhood) through savagery (adolescence) to civilization (adulthood). Such argument was clearly influenced by the ideas of Darwin concerning the origin and evolution of the human species. In this individual recapitulation of evolutionary development, adolescence was viewed as particularly troublesome because it was a stage in which young people were being pulled in two opposite directions – back to the primitivism of childhood and forward to the rational and civilized state of adulthood. Adolescents were characterized as half animal, half human, and the struggle between these impulses directly caused a period of emotional 'storm and stress': adolescence (see Box 2.6).

Adolescent pathologies

[N]ormal children often pass through stages of passionate cruelty, laziness, lying, and thievery ... their vanity, slang, obscenity, contagious imitativeness, their absence of moral sense, disregard of property, and violence to each other, constitute them criminals in all essential respects, lacking only the strength and insight to make their crime dangerous to the communities in which they live ... Degenerate children are neurotic, irritable, vain, lacking in vigor, very fluctuating in mood, prone to show aberrant tendencies under stress, often sexually perverted at puberty, with extreme shyness or bravado, imitative, not well controlled, 'dashing about like a ship without a rudder, fairly well if the winds be fair and the sea be calm, but dependent on the elements for the character and the time of the final wreck.' Invention, poetry, music, artistic taste, philanthropy, intensity, and originality, are sometimes of a higher order among these persons, but desultory, half-finished work and shiftlessness are much more common ... They are apt to be self-conscious, egoistic, and morbidly conscious. They easily become victims of insomnia, neurasthenia, hypochondria, neuroticism, hysteria, or insanity. They offend against the proprieties of life and commit crime with less cause or provocation than other persons. While many of them are among the most gifted and attractive people in their community, the majority are otherwise, and possess an uncommon capacity for making fools of themselves, and of being a nuisance to their friends and of little use to the world.

Source: Hall (1905, pp. 334–6).

Hall also went on to equate the 'barbarity' of adolescence with increased criminality. Thus for Hall, 'adolescence is pre-eminently the criminal age', and 'criminals are like overgrown children' (Hall, 1905, pp. 325, 338). Although Hall's notions of evolution and adolescent development may appear as strange anachronisms of his time, his central premise that adolescence is marked by *pathological* storm and stress has continued to inform numerous psychological and psychoanalytical studies (see **Chapter 3.1**). His characterization of adolescence as a period of disturbance akin to sickness has been successfully popularized, such that it is widely accepted as 'common sense'.

The discovery of adolescence by psychologists and educational reformers coincided with public concerns about working-class youth gangs and the 'boy labour problem'. Generally, delinquency appeared all the more threatening because it could now be viewed as an attribute of 'natural' social and psychological growth and could only indirectly be related to social and economic conditions: 'A stage of life, adolescence, had replaced the poverty of the working class, as the perceived cause of delinquent behaviour by the 1900s' (Springhall, 1986, p. 27). Or as Gillis argued, the concept of 'adolescence' had served to redefine the independence and legitimate traditions of youth as delinquent:

> In reality the troubles of the children of the poor were deeply imbedded in the economic and demographic structure of society. The growing tendency to treat these as psychological and therefore as subject to clinical, rather than political or economic solution was at least as disturbing as the phenomenon itself. (Gillis, 1974, p. 131)

Nevertheless, Hendrick (1990, p. 120) argues that while the psychology of adolescence was to gain influence, it never superseded that of social class as the predominant object of the reformers' attention and concern. The debate between adolescence as 'natural' or 'socially constructed' is summarized in Box 2.7.

Box 2.7
The nature of adolescence

The biological approach to adolescence focuses on:	The social construction approach to adolescence focuses on:
adolescence caused by biological maturation	adolescence created by changes in methods of schooling and shifts in the economy
adolescence as universal	adolescence as specific to particular cultures and economic structures. Originally a concept of the upper classes
adolescence as pathological and problematic	adolescence as normal, given social constraints/conditions
adolescence as primarily a unitary category. Gender differences derive from biological differences. No class differentiation	adolescence as variable according to class, 'race' and gender
the legitimization of medical and psychiatric interventions to solve the problem of adolescence	changes in social conditions and social tolerance to alleviate the socially constructed problem of adolescence
adolescence: the key concept in understanding youth	adolescence: a term which obscures more than it reveals of young people's behaviour

'Hooliganism'

The word 'yob' derives from the late nineteenth century as backslang for 'boy'. It was widely used as a description for members of street gangs in the city slums. Most cities had well-known gangs – in Manchester the Ikey Boys and Scuttlers; in Birmingham the Peaky Blinders; in Glasgow the Redskins and the Beehive; and in London the Hooligans. The word **hooligan** first entered common English usage during the summer of 1898. It was a word, like the 'teddy boy', 'mod' or 'skinhead' terms of the 1950s and 1960s, which emerged from working-class popular culture in London. Sometimes associated with the name of a notorious Irish family of the time, the Houlehans, its precise origins remain unknown. But the word was to become notorious after a rowdy August bank holiday celebration in 1898, when hundreds of people were brought to court on charges of assault, drunkenness and attacks on policemen (Pearson, 1983, p. 73). The Hooligans wore bell-bottomed trousers, colourful neck scarves, leather belts and steel-capped boots; the Redskins had cropped hair and wore red headbands. They were akin to what we would now call 'youth cultures'. The gangs battled with each other for territorial supremacy: some were violently racist and anti-Semitic, but the main 'enemy' was the police. The issue was largely one of who 'owned' and controlled the streets (Cohen, P., 1979). In August 1898, the term 'hooligan' was picked up by the newspapers and used as a generic term to describe all trouble-some youths who might previously have been described as 'ruffians' or 'roughs' (Pearson, 1983, p. 75). It was a word that convinced 'respectable England' that it was suddenly engulfed by a new variety of crime.

In a report compiled by the Howard Association on Juvenile Offenders in 1898, the general impression given was that young people were becoming increasingly unruly, more vulgar and undisciplined. Magistrates and police believed themselves to be impotent in the face of what they considered to be a rising level of crimi-nality and violence. In Parliament, MPs advocated the punishments of whipping and birching, and 'from the late 1890s to the First World War there was a flood of accusations against youth' (Pearson, 1983, p. 55). Urban youth was condemned as growing up in a 'state of unrestrained liberty' and 'irresponsible freedom' (Bray, 1911, pp. 102–3) in which parental authority, discipline and subordination were absent. Youth was believed to be not only lacking in discipline but excessively affluent, accusations that were directed mainly at those young people employed in various kinds of street work – paper-sellers, van boys, flower-sellers, barrel organ boys, messengers, and so on (Pearson, 1983, pp. 57–8).

Anxiety about the visible presence of youth on the streets was not about youth in general, however, but about *working-class* youth. Concern was directed towards girls when it was considered that they lacked domestic and moral surveillance. This might arise when they were away from home, working as domestic servants, or when their own homes were thought to offer inadequate protection from the temptations and 'moral danger' of the street. It was still considered inappropriate for girls to spend their work or leisure time outside the confines of the domestic sphere. As a result, whenever girls 'showed signs of cherishing anything resem-bling autonomy' (Dyhouse, 1981, p. 138), they were likely to find themselves subject to official intervention. Typically penal welfare practice has defined girl delinquency as **waywardness** and underpinned by a strong desire to regulate female sexuality (Cox, 2003, p. 170).

Between 1890 and 1910 the publication of 'scientifically' collected national statistics of juvenile crime appeared to confirm that the problem was indeed growing. Using figures based on police court records in Oxford, Gillis (1975, p. 99) noted that the juvenile crime rate rose from a decennial average of 29.6 offences per year in the 1880s to 99.2 in the first decade of the twentieth century. However, Gillis discovered that much of this rise was accounted for by such non-indictable crimes as drunkenness, gambling, malicious mischief, loitering, begging and danger-ous play. This evidence suggests that the 'increase in crime' was due largely to efforts on the part of the police and the courts to control traditional working-class youth leisure pursuits and working practices. Forms of street activity that had formerly been considered acceptable came to be perceived as indicative of a new social problem. As a Westminster police court probation officer giving evidence to the National Council of Public Morals in 1917 argued:

> Our streets are now more rigidly supervised ... there is a large and increasing army of officials whose duty it is to watch over child life. In many cases it has seemed to me that the zeal of these officers was not always adequately tempered by human- ity and expediency. The practical result has been a systematic increase in the number of charges brought against children. (Cited by Springhall, 1986, p. 179)

As Pearson (1983, pp. 53–73) notes, a whole range of material and cultural innova- tions were transforming urban life in the late nineteenth century, such as football stadiums, 'penny dreadful' comics, bank holidays, the new unionism, the music hall, the fish and chip shop and the bicycle. Although we might now consider these as part and parcel of urban life, in the 1890s they were greeted as 'signs of an alarming development which threatened to destroy the "British way of life"' (Pearson, 1983, p. 62). All of these elements were considered to be inducements to depravity and crime. Music halls lowered moral standards, penny dreadfuls glorified criminality, football encouraged rowdyism and violence, on bank holidays seaside resorts were 'invaded' by the urban masses, and the increasing use of the bicycle caused a panic about 'hit and run' cyclists.

Stedman-Jones (1971) placed such 'respectable fears' in the context of a struc- tural decline in established industries, trade depression, shortage of working-class housing and a bourgeois fear of socialism at the turn of the century. The preoccu- pation with youth disorder was invariably associated with wider social tensions. The moral panic about youth at this time (and also in other historical periods) was the surface manifestation of a deeper concern revolving around the place and passivity of the British working class.

The 'Boy Labour Problem'

The state of the juvenile labour market was a special object of concern for social reformers and policy-makers at the turn of the century. The transition from school to work was viewed as 'haphazard', occupational mobility was 'excessive' and working-class boys in particular were condemned to 'blind alley' employment. Collectively these issues came to be known as creating the 'boy labour problem'. Industrial training was considered so woefully inadequate that after boys left school – usually between the ages of 10 and 14 – there was nothing but dead-end jobs for them, thus perpetuating a cycle of working-class poverty. The situation was exacerbated by the tendency of employers to take on low-paid juvenile labour in preference to adults. When young workers reached an age at which they would by law attract adult wages, they were commonly fired in order to make way for a new generation of juveniles. This practice not only deprived skilled adults of employment but also ensured that much of youth received no formal work train- ing and thus regularly faced unemployment when they were discharged.

This came to be a matter of concern in the Edwardian era when lack of regular work, 'blind alley' jobs and occupational mobility were considered to be the root causes of the two 'vices' of indiscipline and precocious independence which manifested themselves in 'unruly' youth leisure on the streets (see **Chapter 7.2** for a modern version of such concerns). In part, this reconceptualization of working-class youth as a 'problem' was only made possible by the instigation of compulsory state schooling in the 1870s. This helped to set a norm for childhood and youth as a time for dependency, supervision, guidance and training from which wage-earning schoolchildren, school-leavers and child street traders obviously deviated. As Springhall (1986, p. 96) and Hendrick (1990, p. 9) argue, the concern of educationalists and reformers to 'safeguard' young people's welfare and employment prospects helped to construct new definitions of what could be considered troublesome and wayward behaviour. According to the Fabian socialist Sidney Webb, giving evidence to the Poor Law Commission in 1910, the young worker was 'indisciplined, precocious in evil, earning at 17 or 18 more wages than suffice to keep him, independent of home control and yet unsteadied by a man's responsibilities' (cited by Hendrick, 1990, p. 121). The social commentator and reformer Reginald Bray was convinced that the working-class family was devoid of discipline and supervision because parents were fearful of exercising their authority lest their sons leave and take their earnings with them. As a result, he argued, 'city bred youth is growing up in a state of unrestrained liberty' (Bray, 1911, p. 101). The debates of the time dwelt on these two themes: the failure of the working-class home and the freedom that came with wage earning. Echoing some of the same concerns of reformers some 100 years earlier, young workers were viewed as 'premature adults', full of precocity and profanities and as anathema to adult sensibilities (see Box 2.8).

Box 2.8

Boy labour

The result is a species of man-child, in whom the natural instincts of boyhood are almost overwhelmed by the feverish anxiety to become a man. It is at this age that he begins, with disagreeable precocity, to imitate the habits of his elders – smoking daily an unwholesome number of cheap and nasty 'fags' ... adding to his vocabulary the wealth of coarse and profane expletives ... for his amusement a cheap theatre or music hall on Saturday night ... followed by a starch and buttonhole promenade in the Sunday evening, probably with a girl ... and a lively interest in any others he may happen to meet ... It is an odd material, hard to mould and baffling ... but the contradictions in it are after all only the inevitable result of premature face to face acquaintance with the hard facts of life.

Source: Urwick (1904, pp. xii–xiii).

The reformers' concern was multi-faceted. It included worries about employment and unemployment, youth promenading on the streets, leisure, education and general health. By comparing the 'worldly-wise' activities of working-class youth with the extended period of education offered to public school boys, images of working-class depravity and deprivation abounded. Moreover these coalesced with general fears about the nation's physical and moral health. By the 1900s, national efficiency became a key issue when the Boer War revealed an alarming proportion of volunteers as medically unfit. As John Davis (1990) has argued, the focus on youth at this time was not simply generated by fears of disorder, but by fears for racial preservation. Sidney Webb's description of undisciplined but also of 'weedy, narrow chested, stunted weaklings' (cited in Hendrick, 1990, p. 127) brought attention to the notion that young people were the nation's future. The 'boy labour problem' was just one element in a series of entangled debates about imperial security, social stability and the nation's assets that exercised the minds of early twentieth-century reformers and politicians. The newly identified 'adolescent' could be a source of national degeneration if left untutored, but was also capable of ennobling the race if educated, directed and organized in 'appropriate' ways.

Youth Organizations

It was in the context of the debates about 'adolescence', 'hooliganism' and 'boy labour' that numerous youth movements, clubs and organizations were formed. The urge to 'improve' working-class socialization and secure national unity underlay the Boys' Brigade, founded in Glasgow in 1883, and the Boy Scouts, founded in 1908. These were supplemented by university, church and school missions designed to provide healthy activities that would extend public school virtues of *esprit de corps* and 'muscular' Christianity to working-class youths in order to improve their 'character' (Springhall, 1986, p. 149). The intention was to organize youth leisure and, as a result, protect young people from the 'vices of the street'.

Such organizations were designed to preserve the idealism of youths and redirect their 'wayward tendencies', while simultaneously improving physical health and promoting an ideology of nationalism. Accordingly by the turn of the century, 'the model adolescent became the organized youth, dependent but secure from temptation, while the independent and precocious young were stigmatized as delinquent' (Gillis, 1975, p. 97). However, as Blanch (1979) notes, although the principles of organized youth were to apply to all, they were most popular with the middle classes and with children of skilled workers. The majority of youths were excluded from youth clubs and organizations because membership fees could not be met or, more pertinently, because the principles of such organizations were alien to the customs of the adult-centred, working-class family. The end result of this move to 'organize' youth was to highlight divisions within youth and make its delinquent element more visible and detectable. The more independent the youths, the more responsible they were for their own conduct and thus the more likely to be stigmatized as real or potential delinquents. It was a self-fulfilling prophecy. The historian John Gillis (1975, p. 122) noted:

The spread of secondary schools and youth organizations helped establish in the public mind what seemed to be a moral distinction between rough and respectable youth, for the school and athletic uniforms of the model adolescent produced their antithesis in the wide leather belts and bell-bottomed fustian trousers which were becoming the costume of many working youths at the turn of the century ... The contrasts between the military style of the Brigades and Scouts on the one hand and the costuming of corner boys and girls on the other served only to create in the public mind an awareness of differences within the youth population which because they no longer followed class boundaries in an obvious manner could be interpreted as moral in nature.

While the youth organizations were originally intended solely for boys, comparable movements were also established for girls to help them resist the temptations of sex, alcohol and undisciplined conduct. The Girls' Guildry was formed in Glasgow at the turn of the century as a combination of a senior Sunday school class, friendly club and female equivalent of the Boys' Brigade. Despite its aim to develop 'capacities of womanly helpfulness', the marching and military drill characteristic of their male counterparts were also adopted. Many condemned the Guildry for its encouragement of 'unladylike behaviour', and the Girl Guides (sister organization to the Boy Scouts) received a similar reception in the 1910s because of male prejudice against anything that could be seen as part of a general movement towards women's rights. It was not until it was acknowledged that women had played a vital role in the war effort of 1914–18 that organizations for girls gained in membership and credibility (Springhall, 1977, pp. 130–3). But the First World War also saw the first employment of women police officers to patrol military camps and munitions factories with the express purpose of 'protecting' young women from prostitution and 'controlling' large numbers of young female workers (Emsley, 1996, p. 35).

The ultimate aim of all such organizations was the elimination of working-class street cultures and the provision of a morally healthy alternative to such 'corrupt' influences as the music hall and the cinema. In the process the street and street corner leisure grew to be perceived as dangerous and were more rigorously policed. As Gillis (1975) and Weinberger (1993) concluded on examining prosecution data from Oxford and Manchester respectively, a combination of compulsory education, the regulation of street trading, increases in male and female youth independence and extended periods of leisure (coupled with the new notions of adolescence) resulted in a vast expansion of the means to monitor and regulate the presence of young people on the streets. In order to explore the statistical 'crime wave' of the 1900s, we thus need to move far beyond an examination of offending behaviour itself.

Child Saving

The concept of adolescence also had some immediate implications for juvenile justice policy. As delinquency was tied to a particular life stage that was both 'natural' and 'inevitable', adolescents were seen as less responsible for their behaviour. It then made little sense to subject young people to the full rigours of the law; rather their delinquencies could be treated and cured by special forms of intervention. But as Weiner (1990, p. 360) records, such a 'naturalization of delinquency' created two opposing tendencies: greater tolerance and heightened interventionism.

In many historical accounts of juvenile justice, the first decade of the twentieth century is lauded as a progressive milestone. In 1907, the *Probation Act* established community supervision as an alternative to prison and as a means to prevent re-offending through befriending, advising and assisting. In 1908, the *Children Act* established separate juvenile courts to hear criminal and care and protection cases, the imprisonment of children under 14 was abolished and special places of detention (remand homes) were set up to avoid any child being kept in prison, before trial. Imprisonment of 14–16 year olds was sanctioned only for those deemed 'so unruly' that reformatory detention would be unsuitable. Pinchbeck and Hewitt (1973, p. 144) refer to these developments as a 'Children's Charter' which provided 'a more comprehensive and child oriented legal system and more generous and liberal provisions for children in all walks of life'. Above all, the 1908 Act was viewed as the forerunner of a series of twentieth-century reforms in which humanitarianism and the welfare of the child are assumed to have become prominent in juvenile justice policy (see **Chapter 8**).

The juvenile courts were empowered to act upon both the criminal offender and the child who may have been found begging, vagrant, in association with reputed thieves or whose parents were considered 'unworthy'. The categories of criminal (the troublesome) and destitute (the troubled) were conflated. Morris and Giller's (1987) analysis, however, argues that the juvenile courts remained essentially criminal courts. The idea that the child was a wrongdoer prevailed and despite a range of available sentences – from fine, discharge and probation to committal to industrial school, whipping and imprisonment (if over 14) – the procedures for dealing with adults were usually thought to be the most appropriate for dealing with children. Although imprisonment for children under 14 ended, later in the same year the *Crime Prevention Act* set up specialized detention centres where rigid discipline and work training could be provided in a secure environment. The first of these was at Borstal in Kent, which gave its name to numerous similar establishments.

Platt's (1969) account of the origins of the juvenile court in America, however, argues that we need to look beyond the rhetoric of benevolence and the 'child-saver's' concern for 'salvation', 'innocence' and 'protection'. Rather, he notes how ideologies of welfare enabled constant and pervasive supervision and allowed the state to intervene directly into any element of working-class life that was deemed immoral or unruly. Troublesome adolescents could now be depicted by the new bodies of professional psychiatrists, social workers and philanthropists as 'sick' or 'pathological'. As a result young people were imprisoned 'for their own good', were exempted from full legal rights and were subjected to correctional programmes which required longer periods of incarceration. Platt (1969, p. 176) is thus able to argue that the **child-saving** movement was far from libertarian. It used such rhetoric to justify a vastly increased level of intervention which denied working-class youth any initiative, responsibility and autonomy. At root, the state's intention was to implement more and more extensive networks to enforce industrious habits and discipline.

Morris and Giller (1987, p. 32) are more circumspect, arguing that 'the social construction of childhood did prevent the economic exploitation of juveniles ... but most reforms were also implicitly or explicitly coercive ... humanitarianism and coercion are essentially two sides of the same coin'. Garland (1985, p. 262) probably best captures the nuances of Victorian and Edwardian reform when he argues that it was 'constructed around an eclectic series of disparate and contradictory forms and logics which may sometimes be strategically related, but are never singular or uniform'. It is in such terms that he accounts for a new 'penal-welfare complex' emerging in the period 1895–1914, in which classical conceptions of punishment and generalized deterrence were contested and disrupted by positivist conceptions of reclamation and individualized treatment. The end result was new means of 'normalizing', 'correcting' and 'segregating' young people, which in their complexity and interrelation could no longer be simply viewed as either humanitarian or repressive.

2.4 The Consolidation of the 'Youth Problem'

During the First World War the number of juvenile offenders is assumed to have risen once more. The press reported that gangs of hooligans were terrorizing communities and the Home Office warned of a juvenile crime epidemic. It is estimated that at least 12,500 more children and young people were appearing before magistrates in 1916 than in 1914. Now it was the absence of fathers sent to war, the independence of married women employed in munitions and lack of parental and school discipline that were the most widely cited causes (Springhall, 1986, pp. 179–80; Smith, D., 1990, pp. 122–5). The influence of the cinema was also believed to be encouraging new and dangerous trends of lawlessness either through imitating the new celluloid heroes and villains or by succumbing to the 'moral dangers of darkness' in the cinema itself. Charles Russell (1917, p. 6), a leading advocate of boys' clubs, warned that the cinema's 'vulgarity and silliness and the distorted, unreal, Americanized (in the worst sense) view of life presented must have a deteriorating effect and lead, at the best, to the formation of false ideals'. Juvenile crime was in large part viewed as resulting from the lack of opportunities for healthy recreation (Bailey, V., 1987, p. 12). These concerns also impacted on girls. In 1918, an MP worried that girls now 'dress themselves rather more flashily … one can hardly go down a street without seeing girls of 13, 14 or 15 with powder on their faces and rouge on their lips' (cited by Cox, 2003, p. 3). New definitions of socially acceptable behaviour for girls were accompanied by new welfare and control discourses designed to manage their 'emancipation' and produce 'respectable working women'. Girls may have made up a minority of cases in the juvenile court but were brought to court for similar offences as boys (typically petty theft) and most significantly by a wider range of agencies. They were more likely to be considered in 'moral danger' (for example, by running away from home and associating with men). Outside of the formal system thousands of girls were also 'policed privately in rescue homes, preventive homes, VD hostels and lock hospitals' (Cox, 2003, p. 7).

Oral histories of the period have, however, come to challenge these dominant images of adolescent depravity through which offending could be defined predominantly in moralistic terms. By recording the 'voices from below', Humphries' (1981) study of property theft from 1890 to 1940, for example, illustrates that minor thieving was viewed by some working-class parents and children as a customary right and essential for family survival. Taking coal from slag heaps, wood from timber yards, vegetables from fields and poaching rabbits were an integral and historical part of working-class culture and committed out of economic necessity. Class disadvantage, labour disputes, resistance to the property laws of the privileged, and severe economic hardship provided the context in which **social crime** was morally sanctioned in working-class communities. Rather than connoting family breakdown, juvenile delinquency was often inspired by motives of family duty. Successive legislation which criminalized such activities served to exacerbate the extent of the 'problem'.

In the 1920s, the growing problem of juvenile delinquency became an established topic for British academics. Earlier emphases on economic factors were slowly replaced by a focus on the psychological conditions produced in the home and family. The crime rate, though reduced after the war, started to rise again in the late 1920s, coinciding with the years of the Great Depression. Unemployment and the continuing practice of 'boy labour' were once again promoted as a key causative factor. The preferred solution now was to 'improve' home conditions and family life. The rising problem of crime may have coincided with high levels of unemployment, but the problem was laid firmly at the door of working-class families. Young people may have been without jobs, but according to a growing medico-psychological discourse, what they really required was a stable and protective home life. For example, Cyril Burt's *The Young Delinquent* (1925) arose from his work as an applied psychologist advising on the psychological difficulties of London children referred to him by magistrates. Using a definition of delinquency which spread from assault and theft to truancy, 'excessive bad temper' and 'excessive masturbation', he concluded that delinquency is 'nothing but an outstanding sample – dangerous perhaps and extreme, but none the less typical – of common childish naughtiness' (Burt, 1925, p. viii). The key factors, of some 170 considered, which propelled juveniles from 'naughtiness' to 'delinquency' were believed to be defective discipline, defective family relationships and particular types of temperament. Burt proposed that delinquency was multi-causal and complex, but that deficient personality coupled with broken homes were central. To tackle delinquency he advocated intervention by parents in the pre-school period, by teachers' reports at school and by supervision of school-leavers by after-care workers.

Such medico-psychological notions were not only to gain prominence in the emerging field of British positivist criminology (see **Chapter 3.1**), but remained influential at least up to the 1980s. Neglect and delinquency became conflated, such that the problem of juvenile crime was viewed as 'but one inseparable portion of the larger enterprise for child welfare' (Burt, 1925, p. 610).

In 1932, industrial schools and reformatories were amalgamated and reconstituted as approved schools. In deliberations before the 1933 *Children and Young Persons Act*, the Home Office Departmental Committee on the Treatment of the

Young Offender had argued that the juvenile court should have primary regard to the welfare of the child, whether that child was brought before the court for offending or welfare reasons (see Box 2.9).

Box 2.9

Neglect and delinquency

[N]eglect and delinquency often go hand in hand and experience shows that the young offender is only too often recruited from the ranks of those whose home life has been unsatisfactory. The legislature draws a distinction between the two classes, but in many cases the tendency to commit offences is only an outcome of the conditions of neglect, and there is little room for discrimination either in the character of the young person concerned or in the appropriate method of treatment. There are also young people who are the victims of cruelty or other offences committed by adults and whose natural guardianship having proved insufficient or unworthy of trust must be replaced ... there is little or no difference in the character and needs between the neglected and the delinquent child. It is often a mere accident whether he is brought before the court because he is wandering or beyond control or because he has committed some offence. Neglect leads to delinquency and delinquency is often the direct outcome of neglect.

Source: Report of the Departmental Committee on the Treatment of Young Offenders (Home Office, 1927, pp. 6, 71).

By the mid-1930s an earlier limited practice of having a specially selected *panel* of magistrates to hear juvenile cases was adopted as uniform for the whole country; restrictions were placed on the reporting of cases in newspapers; the age of criminal responsibility was raised from 7 to 10 (8 in Scotland); and above all magistrates were directed to take primary account of the 'welfare of the child'. In this, considerable responsibility was given to probation officers and social workers, recruited in the main from the Charity Organization Society: 'Regulation *within*, rather than removal *from*, the community was constructed as the dominant strategy for the delinquent' (Clarke, 1985a, p. 251).

However, while we might presume that such welfarism would lead to less formal means of intervention, in fact, the reverse was true. As Springhall (1986, p. 186) comments, there is 'abundant evidence' to show that the effect of the 1933 Act was not to divert youth from court, but to actively encourage formal intervention. Because of the Act's 'welfare' focus there was an increased willingness to prosecute in the name of 'being beyond control' or as 'being in need of care and protection'. The creation of child-centred interventions and the development of protective legislation brought many more delinquent and neglected children (particularly girls) into the judicial system (Cox, 2003, p.163). As one contemporary declared:

Experience shows ... that each time a new statute relating to the young has been put into effect, the immediate result is an apparent rise in the number of offences.

This 'rise' is not due to any 'wave' of crime among juveniles but to a desire on the part of those concerned with putting the law into motion, to make use of the new method of treatment. (Assistant Secretary at the Home Office, cited by Smithies, 1982, p. 172)

Such a view was, however, not shared by all. Retributionists drew different conclusions. For them the 1930s had witnessed a real rise in juvenile crime attributable (once again) to adolescent 'mischief', the want of organized leisure, lack of employment, the proliferation of consumer goods, the influence of American gangster movies and lack of parental control. As Smithies (1982, p. 177) also notes: 'The popular press had built up a picture of juvenile offenders as "wasp-waisted loungers, who ape the methods of their film heroes", breaking the law in gangs and with impunity. They need an "intensive police clean up" to deal with them.' In opposition to welfarism, stricter punishments, including use of the birch, were strongly advocated and implemented. In 1939, 50 birchings were inflicted on boys under the age of 14. In 1941, there were over 500 (Smithies, 1982, p. 175). Indeed, the 1933 Act had retained a clause – Section 53 – whereby those aged under 18 can, if convicted in a Crown Court for 'grave crimes', be detained for lengthy periods and in effect treated as if they were adults. Such powers remain today in the form of Sections 90–92 of the *Powers of Criminal Courts (Sentencing) Act 2000* (see **Chapter 9**). Corporal punishment was not abolished until 1948.

Such discourses and policy debates are, of course, now familiar to us, and serve as a telling reminder that whatever romantic images we may now hold about the inter-war years (or of earlier periods), these were certainly not voiced at the time. Images of youth as 'led astray' or as 'vicious hooligans' and ideas about welfare and punishment, treatment and control, 'moral danger' and wilful criminality continue to circulate around, and inform, the various contradictory policies and practices of contemporary youth justice. But what is clear is that having 'invented' the 'juvenile delinquent' in the early nineteenth century and the 'troublesome adolescent' in the early twentieth, increasing numbers of 'expert knowledges' (from social work, probation, child care, education, and so on) have come to do battle over their respective place in the control and supervision of the young. Typically they have sought legitimacy in the rhetorical narratives that youthful behaviour is 'always getting worse' and that the measures employed for their control are always becoming progressively 'more enlightened' (Wills, 2007). As we have seen, both notions are seriously misleading simplifications.

■ ■ Summary ■

- This chapter has traced the origins and development of delinquency and juvenile justice policy from the early nineteenth century to the 1930s. It has explored changing conceptions of the young offender and revealed that definitions and explanations of crime are inseparable from the various policies and practices that have been constructed for the ostensible reason of its control. As revisionist historians have argued, the precise definition of troublesome behaviour is frequently only realized through the very means by which it is believed such behaviour might best be regulated and constrained.

- Many authors have argued that the young offender was a Victorian creation. The reasons lie not simply in any growing visibility of juvenile waywardness, but in a complex of factors including: humanitarianism and control of child labour; religious zeal and need for moral guidance; bourgeois philanthropy and attempts to combat neglect; expansion of the scope and severity of the criminal law; fear of social disorder; fear of crime; and fear of moral destitution.

- 'Juvenile delinquency' is as much an index of adult perceptions as a description of youth behaviour. As a result, it is difficult to catch sight of the meaning and extent of young offending in any objective fashion. Instead we are forced to rely on the definitions and discourses created in the processes of political, social and legal intervention.

- What constitutes 'young offending' is in a constant process of (re)invention and (re)definition. In the early nineteenth century, the *juvenile delinquent* was created in the midst of wider concerns about unemployment, lack of discipline and moral degeneration. In the early twentieth century, the *troublesome adolescent* was invented in the midst of concerns for 'boy labour', 'wayward girls', street leisure and imperialism. In the mid-twentieth century, notions of the *troubled offender* were constructed, reflecting the increased presence of welfare agencies and professionals at the time. Social concern may be persistent and recurring but the disciplinary tactics, practices, issues and concepts through which it is articulated are subject to change.

- Hendrick (1997) notes how the eighteenth-century contradictory conceptions of childhood as inherently innocent (the Romantic child) or evil (the Evangelical child) have inspired a whole series of competing constructions of childhood, youth and delinquency. Young people have been relocated from mill, mine and factory into reformatories, schools, youth organizations, welfare agencies and the family. At each stage the nature of childhood has been defined differently (see Box 2.10).

- The chapter illustrates some of the difficulties involved in working with the nebulous concept of delinquency. Changes in police practices, legislation and shifts in public perception of crime make it difficult to produce a consistent definition of what actually constitutes delinquency and what its causes might be. We are left with a series of contradictory and competing discourses of which one of the most familiar is that of national decline and moral degeneration. Above all, it is clear that delinquency is not simply a crime problem.

- The repeated fear has been that youth are getting out of control. Often the solution is believed to lie in the past, harking back to some mythical 'golden age' of peace and tranquillity when young people 'knew their place'. But these notions do not allow us to see the issue with any clarity. The recurring fears directed at young people probably tell us more about adult concerns for morality, national security, unemployment, leisure, independence, imperialism, and so on than they do about the nature and extent of young offending.

Box 2.10

Competing constructions of childhood, 1800–1930

The Romantic child (from the eighteenth century) – the elitist portrayal of childhood as funda-mentally different to adulthood; a time of 'natural' and 'original' innocence.

The Evangelical child (from the early nineteenth century) – the contrary image of childhood as inherently corrupt and in need of overt control and moral guidance.

The Factory child (from the early nineteenth century) – child labour as an economic necessity for the working classes, but also the object of philanthropic reform.

The Delinquent child (from the mid-nineteenth century) – the separation of child from adult offenders and legal recognition of the difference of childhood.

The Schooled child (from the late nineteenth century) – childhood as a universal condition and defined as a state of dependence and ignorance in need of compulsory education.

The Psycho-medical child (from the early twentieth century) – childhood and adolescence as a time of emotional upheaval in need of constant psychological and medical monitoring in order to improve national efficiency. Delinquency redefined as 'subnormality'.

The Welfare child (from the early twentieth century) – children as vulnerable, in need of care and protection. Delinquency redefined as 'neglect' or 'lack of moral education'.

The Psychological child (from the mid-twentieth century) – childhood as imbued with its own psychological and psychiatric problems. Delinquency redefined as 'disturbance' or 'maladjustment' or 'pathological'.

Source: Derived from Hendrick, (1997).

study Questions

1 How far is the proposition that the 'juvenile delinquent was a Victorian creation' borne out by historical research?

2 Why was 'hooliganism' a cause for concern at the end of the nineteenth century?

3 Which is the greatest cause of youthful delinquency: unemployment, poverty or adolescence?

4 Is adolescence a biological fact or a socio-historical construction?

5 How different is a child considered 'deprived' from one considered 'depraved'? Should they be dealt with separately? What implications did this have for the polic-ing of girls?

Two of the most accessible and engaging introductions to the potential of social history research in (re)informing contemporary debates can be found in Wills' (2007) analysis of 'historical myth making in juvenile justice policy' and Pearson's *Hooligan: A History of Respectable Fears* (1983). Both trace some remarkable historical continuities in adult reaction to troublesome youth, marked in particular by misplaced views of 'reform as progress'. A useful overview of some of the most important social reconstructions of childhood since the end of the eighteenth century which illustrates the theme of histori-cal variability is provided by Hendrick (1997). Collectively, May (1973), Magarey (1978), King and Noel (1993) and King (1998) provide the debate about the origins of juvenile delinquency with a much needed historical substance. Chapters 2, 3 and 4 of King's (2006) *Crime and Law in England* are useful in breaking with some previous orthodoxies of the origins of delinquency and reformatory effort. His research focuses particular attention on the previ-ously overlooked period 1790–1825. Shore's *Artful Dodgers* (1999) does more than most to humanize the experiences of working-class children and offenders in the early nineteenth century by drawing on their own personal accounts. Part 2 of the edited collection by Muncie, Hughes and McLaughlin (2002) draws together many of these formative texts. Springhall's *Coming of Age* (1986) is a thoughtful overview of the period 1860–1960 which focuses on the impact of the concept of adolescence. Hendrick's (1990) focus is narrower, restricted to 1880–1920, but is important in placing the debates in the context of class, as well as age, relations. Bailey's (1987) *Delinquency and Citizenship* and latterly Cox's (2003) *Gender, Justice and Welfare* give sustained attention to the, other-wise neglected, period 1914–48. Dyhouse (1981), Zedner (1991), and Shore (2002) also reveal the extent to which gender divided Victorian and Edwardian society and they remind us that until relatively recently, most social histories have been written by men and solely about men and boys.

⁞ // Web Resources /

http://www.historyandpolicy.org/
A series of articles designed to illustrate the relevance of historical research for contemporary policy debates. Carries multiple themes, one of which is criminal justice and law reform.

http://www.oldbaileyonline.org/
A valuable resource which contains accounts of over 200,000 criminal trials between 1674 and 1913 and which are searchable by keywords, offences, verdicts and punishments.

http://www.learnhistory.org.uk/cpp/
Designed for secondary school students but includes a useful section, with illustrations, on crime, punishment and protest, 1450–2004.

http://www.britishorigins.com/BritishOrigins/gallery-employment/Childrens Employment.aspx
Government publication of 1842 which contains vivid and detailed description of the conditions of child employment in the early nineteenth century.

3

Explaining Youth Crime I: Positivist Criminologies

Overview

Chapter 3 examines:

- a diverse range of theoretical and empirical studies that have addressed the issue of why young people commit crime;

- theories of individual positivism that locate the causes of crime in the individual;

- theories of sociological positivism that locate the causes of crime in social organization and social structures;

- the endurance of positivism as a major strand in contemporary criminological theory and research;

- the limitations and problems of attempts to isolate specific causes of youth crime.

---

key terms

aetiology; anomie; cause–effect; correlational analysis; determinism; developmental criminology; differential association; essentialism; eugenics; extroversion; genetic determinism; maternal deprivation; positivism; social capital; social disorganization; somatotyping; status frustration; strain; zone in transition

---

Explanations of youth crime are various, diverse and contradictory. In popular and political idiom, poverty, inequality and unemployment have been cited as precipitating factors, but so too have affluence and a concomitant fear of 'premature independence'. Single parenting, lack of parental control, child abuse and broken homes provide another recurring set of causal images, but so do notions of inherent wickedness, lack of self-control, greed and wilful irresponsibility. In addition, low IQ, media violence, illegitimacy, 'bad blood', drugs, homelessness, 1960s permissiveness, moral decline, masculinity, truancy, deprivation, alienation and run-down housing estates have all been evoked at one time or another as the key to understanding youth crime. The list could be expanded indefinitely. But significantly, all of these motivational conditions do not just exist in popular discourse, but are grounded, albeit sometimes implicitly, in some biological, psychological or sociological theory of crime causation.

This chapter and Chapter 4 introduce some of the major criminological paradigms that have attempted to explain youth crime. In particular, this chapter focuses on the insights and modes of explanation offered by *positivist* and scientific criminologies. The origins of a scientific criminology are usually located in the late nineteenth century, when biological research (based on physiological and anthropological studies) attempted to explain crime with reference to hereditable disorders. In the early twentieth century this was complemented by psychological studies that purported that many criminals were of low intelligence and feebleminded. At this time academic criminology in Britain was largely the domain of doctors, psychologists and psychiatrists. It was not until the 1960s that British sociologists began to make a sustained impact, although influential work on the relationship between the inner city, subcultures and crime had already been carried out in the 1930s in Chicago, USA. Much of this work – whether grounded in psychology, biology or sociology – is positivist in nature because it attempts to isolate key causal variables, located in particular individuals or in particular social situations or social structures. Chapter 4, in contrast, examines how positivism came under attack in the 1960s by a variety of *radical* criminologies and has subsequently been reworked by a variety of *realist* criminologies since the 1980s. In the twenty-first century, mainstream theories of crime causation have been dominated by criminal career research, risk and prediction studies and the pursuit of 'scientific certainty'.

It would, however, be misleading to assume that criminologists have moved *en masse* from one explanation to another as the limitations of preceding theories were exposed. Each has a contemporary presence and relevance. Moreover, positivist accounts tend to remain paramount in media and popular discourses, whether they are expressed in terms of crime being caused by pathological individuals, inadequate parents or social deprivation. Even within positivism, the academic search for the causes of youth crime is a highly contested terrain and one that is frequently reflected in competing political discourses.

Individual Positivism

3.1 The key characteristic of **positivism** is the application of the methods of the natural sciences to the study of social behaviour. It has generally involved the search for '**cause–effect**' relations that can be measured in a way similar to which natural scientists observe and analyse relations between objects in the physical world. Positivism does not concern itself with the abstract and quantitative, but with the tangible and quantifiable. It is dominated by the search for 'facts'. Through gaining 'objective' knowledge about how behaviour is *determined* by physiological, psychological and environmental conditions, it is assumed that most social problems can be understood and treated through the 'positive application of science'.

This approach first emerged in the late nineteenth century and was a radical departure from the dominant understandings of crime, law and justice at the time. It is widely assumed that modern *scientific* criminology began with the advent of a criminal anthropology associated with the work of the Italian physician, Cesare Lombroso (1876, 1911). By studying the skulls and body shapes of executed criminals, Lombroso attempted to prove 'scientifically' that those who broke the law were physically different from those who did not (see Box 3.1).

Box 3.1

Lombroso and atavism

[M]any of the characteristics presented by savage races are very often found among born criminals. Such, for example, are: the slight development of the pilar system; low cranial capacity; retreating forehead; highly developed frontal sinuses; great frequency of Wormian bones; early closing of the cranial sutures; the simplicity of the sutures; the thickness of the bones of the skull; enormous development of the maxillaries ... greater pigmentation of the skin; tufted and crispy hair; and large ears ... To these we may add the lemurine appendix; anomalies of the ear; dental diastemata; great agility; relative insensibility to pain; dullness of the sense of touch; ... blunted affections; precocity as to sensual pleasures; greater resemblance between the sexes; incorrigibility of the woman; laziness; absence of remorse; impulsiveness; physiopsychic excitability.

Source: Lombroso (1911, p. 365).

His observations led him to conclude that:

- serious offenders were born to be criminal; such people had inherited certain physical characteristics – such as large jaws and strong canine teeth – which marked them out as criminogenic;

- criminality was biologically determined – individuals had no control over whether they were to become criminal;

- crime was generated by biological pathology and atavism. Physically, criminals were throwbacks to more primitive times when people were deemed to be 'savages'.

Such notions were in direct contrast to the prevailing judicial doctrine, which was grounded in principles of neo-classicism and which maintained that, with few exceptions, behaviour was a matter of free will and individual choice. People broke laws because they anticipated that the benefits would outweigh any loss. They acted largely out of hedonism, choosing behaviour that was pleasurable and avoiding that which would give pain. For much of the eighteenth and nineteenth centuries this meant that no defences of criminal acts could be entertained. And although strict adherence to such principles was gradually tempered by the recognition of mitigating factors such as age (see **Chapter 2.2**), the arrival of Lombroso's theory remained a significant challenge to the judicial orthodoxy. For, if criminality was determined by factors other than rational choice, then surely it made little sense to punish offenders. Rather, their condition should be treated.

By the early twentieth century the development of a criminological science – positivism – was to become influential, not only in physiology, but also in medicine, psychiatry, psychology and sociology. Offending came to be thought of as being determined by biological and cultural antecedents. It was no longer viewed as simply self-determining. A leading protagonist of the positive school, Enrico Ferri (1901, p. 161) argued:

> The illusion of a free human will (the only miraculous factor in the eternal ocean of cause and effect) leads to the assumption that one can choose freely between virtue and vice. How can you still believe in the existence of free will when modern psychology, armed with all the instruments of positive modern research ... demonstrates that every act of a human being is the result of an interaction between the personality and the environment of man?

By searching for the specific causes (or **aetiology**) of *criminal* behaviour as opposed to other behaviours, positive criminology assumes that criminality has a peculiar set of characteristics. Accordingly, most research of this type has tried to isolate key differences between criminals and non-criminals. Some theorists have focused on biological and psychological factors, thus locating the sources of crime primarily *within* the individual and bringing to the fore questions of individual pathology and abnormality. This approach is central to *individual positivism*. In contrast, *sociological positivism* (considered in Section 3.2 below) argues that the key causative factors lie in the social contexts *external* to the individual. Here crime is more a matter of social pathology. However, whether individual or sociological, a number of common threads run through all positivist modes of analysis (see Box 3.2).

Box 3.2
Characteristics of positivist criminologies

- Use of *scientific methodologies* in which quantifiable data (such as criminal statistics) are produced and can be tested by further empirical investigation and scrutiny.

- Emphasis on the study of *criminal behaviour*, rather than the creation of laws, the functions of legal systems or the operation of criminal justice systems.

- The assumption that criminality is different from normality and indicative of various *pathological states*, such as degeneracy, feeble-mindedness and frailty. Abandonment of rationality in the aetiology of crime.

- The attempt to establish 'cause and effect' relations scientifically and thus to increase the ability to *predict* criminality (when particular criminogenic factors can be identified).

- The assumption that, as criminals are abnormal, their behaviour is in violation of some widely held *consensus* in the rest of society.

- *Treatment* or neutralization of causes, when these become known, with the ultimate goal of eliminating anti-social behaviour. As behaviour is involuntary and not a matter of choice for the offender, punitive responses are misplaced.

Physiology

In the early twentieth century several attempts were made to isolate the key physiological characteristics of known criminals. Goring (1913) studied over 3,000 male prisoners in and around London and compared them with various control groups of non-prisoners. Using **correlational analysis** – a then new statistical procedure for quantifying the degree of association between variables – he found that the criminal tended to be shorter in height and weigh less. He explained such difference with reference to notions of 'inbreeding within a criminal class' which generated a lineage of mental deficiencies within certain families. Similarly, Hooton (1939) found that criminals were marked by smaller heads, shorter and broader noses, and sloping foreheads. Criminals were (akin to Lombroso's theory of atavism) viewed as biologically inferior and made up an incorrigible, inferior class.

Such correlations of body build and behavioural tendencies reached their most sophisticated expression in the work of Sheldon (1949). His analysis of **somatotyping** suggested that the shape of the body correlated with individual temperament and mental well-being. A person's somatotype is made up of three components: endomorph, ectomorph and mesomorph.

- *Mesomorphs* have well-developed muscles and athletic appearance. Body shape is hard and round. Personality is strong, active, aggressive and sometimes violent.

- *Ectomorphs* have small skeletons and weak muscles. Body shape is fragile and thin. Personality is introverted, hypersensitive and intellectual.

- *Endomorphs* have heavy builds and are slow moving. Body shape is soft and round. Personality is extrovert, friendly and sociable.

Analysing and comparing 200 boys in a reformatory with 4,000 students in Boston, USA, Sheldon concluded that most delinquents tended towards mesomorphy. Ectomorphs had the lowest criminal tendencies. Glueck and Glueck (1950), using large samples of delinquent and non-delinquent boys, found similarly that there were twice as many mesomorphs among delinquents than could have occurred by chance. Sixty per cent of delinquents were mesomorphic, while only 14 per cent were ectomorphic, compared with 40 per cent of non-delinquents. The Gluecks contended that strength and agility may enable boys to fill a delinquent role. Endomorphs were too clumsy, and ectomorphs too fragile, to be successful delinquents. On reviewing a number of such studies, Wilson and Herrnstein (1985, p. 89) felt confident in concluding that criminals do differ in physique from the population at large. Physique, however, does not cause crime, but it does correlate with temperaments which are impulsive and given to uninhibited self-gratification.

Such research into physiology is clearly controversial, particularly in Lombroso's case, where certain physical traits are considered to be reflective of a biological inferiority. With hindsight it is clear that his work was more informed by notions of racial and gender superiority at a time of Italian unification than it was by any scientific objective method (Valier, 2002, p. 17). By the early twentieth century, anthropology had totally ruled out the possibility of an evolutionary throwback to earlier, more primitive species. Psychology and psychiatry were demonstrating that the relationship between crime, epilepsy and mental disorder, for example, was far more 'complex and involved than Lombroso supposed' (Vold and Bernard, 1986, p. 38). Clearly the leap from skull type to criminality to atavism does not necessarily mean that one causes the other. As is common with such studies, it is not *causes* that are revealed but *correlations*. Being athletic in stature may be correlated with delinquency, but this does not mean that either is the cause of the other. Both are probably influenced by other factors, including the adequacy of nutrition, extent of manual labour and social class position. Similarly, what Hooton and Sheldon were measuring was not the characteristics of the criminal *per se* but of the identified and processed criminal, who is most likely to be of working-class origin. Above all, any association between body type and crime remains in need of explanation. Are mesomorphs biologically predisposed to crime or is their criminality simply more socially visible? Such questions continue to plague physiological research, but its assumptions have had a major impact on popular conceptions of crime. Bull and Green (1980) showed members of the public and the police ten photographs of men and asked to match them with any of eleven particular crimes. For crimes of robbery, gross indecency, fraud, soliciting, car theft and drug possession, respondents readily and consistently put a face to a crime. However, none of the photographed men had ever been convicted of any crime! Similarly, Ainsworth (2000) notes how visual stereotyping is constantly reinforced by employing the same actors to play criminal roles in film and drama. We remain deeply wedded to the idea that criminals not only act, but also look different to the 'normal population'.

Genetics and the 'Pathological Family'

The earliest attempts to isolate a genetic cause of criminality involved analyses of the family trees of known criminals. Of note were Dugdale's (1910) study of the Jukes and Goddard's (1927) study of the Kallikaks. Dugdale traced over 1,000 descendants of the Jukes – a New York family infamous for criminality and prostitution – and found 280 paupers, 60 thieves, 7 murderers, 140 criminals and 50 prostitutes. Goddard studied the descendants of Martin Kallikak, who had an illegitimate son by a woman of 'low birth' and subsequently married into a 'good' family. The relations of the illegitimate offspring contained substantially more criminal members than the latter. Both studies concluded that 'undesirable' hereditary characteristics were passed down through families. Criminal families tended to produce criminal children. Criminals were born, not made.

Goring (1913), though dismissive of physiological determinism, likewise argued that criminality was largely inherited and was linked to mental inferiority. His study of convicts discovered high correlations between the criminality of spouses, between parents and their children, and between brothers. He found that poverty, education and broken homes were poor correlates of crime, and so he was led to conclude that social conditions were insignificant explanations of criminality. He believed that criminality was passed down through inherited genes. Accordingly, in order to reduce crime, he recommended that people with such inherited characteristics should not be allowed to reproduce. This logic was fertile ground for the growth of **eugenics**, a doctrine concerned with 'improving' the genetic selection of the human race.

Most critical commentaries on **genetic determinism** – notwithstanding the question of its ethical position – have argued that it fails to recognize the potential effect of a wide range of environmental factors. Although Goring remained alive to such effects, the few social conditions he examined were subject to inadequate measures. The high correlation in the criminality of family members could just as easily be explained by reference to poor schooling, inadequate diet, unemployment, common residence or cultural transmission of criminal values. In other words, criminality is not necessarily an inherited trait, but can also be learnt or generated by a plethora of environmental factors (Vold and Bernard, 1986, p. 86).

Nevertheless, evidence from the Cambridge Study in Delinquent Development (see **Chapter 1.3**) continues to suggest that crime does indeed run in families. Farrington et al. (1996), for example, note that of 397 families, half of all convictions were concentrated in just 23. Convictions of one family member were strongly related to convictions of other family members. Three-quarters of convicted mothers and convicted fathers had a convicted child. While these correlations suggest that criminality may be transmitted in certain families, they do not, as the researchers acknowledge, allow us to distinguish the relative importance of genetic and environmental factors. Nevertheless Farrington et al. (1996, p. 61) conclude that 'while offending (specifically) cannot be genetically transmitted because it is a legally and socially defined construct, more fundamental characteristics that are linked to offending (e.g. intelligence, impulsivity, aggressiveness) could be genetically transmitted'.

More rigorous research directed at isolating 'a genetic factor' has been carried out with twins and adoptees. These have attempted to test two key propositions:

1 that identical (monozygotic or MZ) twins have more similar behaviour patterns than fraternal (dizygotic or DZ) twins;

2 that children's behaviour is more similar to that of their biological parents than to that of their adoptive parents.

If either proposition could be supported, then the case for biological determinism would be stronger. In a review of research carried out between 1929 and 1961, Mednick and Volavka (1980) noted that, overall, 60 per cent of MZ twins shared criminal behaviour patterns compared to 30 per cent of DZ twins. More recent work has found a lower, but still significant, level of association. Christiansen's (1977) study of 3,586 twin pairs in Denmark found a 52 per cent concordance for MZ groups and a 22 per cent concordance for the DZ groups. The evidence for the genetic transmission of some behaviour patterns thus appears quite strong. However, telling criticisms have also been made of this line of research. For example a tendency to treat identical twins more alike than fraternal twins may account for the greater concordance. Thus the connection between criminality and genetics may be made through environmental conditions, derived from the behaviour of parents or from twins' influence on each other's behaviour (Einstadter and Henry, 1995, pp. 94–5).

As a result, Mednick et al. (1987) proposed that the study of adoptions would be a better test of a relative genetic effect, particularly if it could be shown that the criminality of biological parent and child was similar even when the child had grown up in a completely different environment. Using data from over 14,000 cases of adoption in Denmark from 1924 to 1947, Mednick et al. concluded that some factor *is* transmitted by convicted parents to increase the likelihood that their children – even after adoption – will be convicted for criminal offences. However, the question of exactly *what* is inherited remains unanswered. Rutter and Giller (1983, p. 179) argue that the mysterious factor is unlikely to be criminality as such, but rather 'some aspect of personality functioning which predisposes to criminality'. Or as Beirne and Messerschmidt (1991, p. 484) conclude, if prospective parents are routinely informed about the criminal convictions of biological parents, this may trigger a labelling process and a self-fulfilling prophecy.

Nevertheless the evidence from twin and adoption studies has not ruled out the possibility that there is some genetic basis to some criminality and this type of research continues to attract research funding and publicity. In 1994, a new Centre for Social, Genetic and Development Psychiatry was opened at the Maudsley Hospital in south London to examine what role genetic structures play in determining patterns of behaviour (including crime). In 1995, a major conference discussed the possibility of isolating a criminal gene – the basis of which rested on the study of twins and adoptees (Ciba Foundation Symposium, 1996). One of the best-selling social science books of the 1990s, Herrnstein and Murray's *The Bell Curve* (1994), claimed that American blacks and Latinos are disproportionately poor, not because of discrimination, but because they are less intelligent. Further they suggested that IQ is mainly determined by inherited genes and that people with a low IQ are more likely to commit crime because they lack foresight and are unable to distinguish right from wrong. Such theory indeed remains attractive (to some) because it seems to provide *scientific* evidence which clearly differentiates 'us' from 'them' (see **Chapter 4.2**). Similarly, if certain people are inherently 'bad', then society is absolved of all responsibility. But as Einstadter and Henry (1995, p. 98) warn, such reasoning is also characteristic of totalitarian regimes 'whether in Nazi Germany or the former USSR and extending more recently to forced therapy in the United States'.

Further research has examined a wide range of biochemical factors in attempts to isolate an individual causal factor in the generation of deviant, anti-social, criminal or violent behaviour. These have included: hormone imbalances; testosterone, vitamin, adrenalin and blood sugar levels; allergies; slow brain-wave activity; lead pollution; epilepsy; and the operation of the autonomic nervous system. None of the research has, as yet, been able to establish any direct causal relationships. While some interesting associations have been discovered – for example, between male testosterone levels and verbal aggression, between vitamin B deficiency and hyperactivity, and between stimulation of the central portion of the brain (the limbic) and impulsive violence – it remains disputed that such biological conditions will automatically generate anti-social activities, which in turn will be translated into criminality. Indeed, most current research in this tradition would not claim that biological make-up *alone* can be used as a sufficient explanation of crime. Rather, some biological factors may generate criminality, but only when they interact with certain other psychological or social factors.

The tendency has grown for biology to be considered as but one element within *multiple factor* explanations (Wilson and Herrnstein, 1985). In terms that are consonant with those of classical (pre-positivist) criminology, they argue that individuals have the free will to choose criminal actions when they believe that the rewards will outweigh any negative consequences. Such a decision (freely made) is, however, influenced by inherited constitutional factors. Wilson and Herrnstein argue that low IQ, abnormal body type and an impulsive personality will predispose a person to make criminal decisions. Criminality for them is not a matter of nature versus nurture, but of nature *and* nurture. This approach is also a defining characteristic of *sociobiology*, developed in the 1970s and heralded by its advocates as a way forward in unifying the social and natural sciences. Generally, it is argued that some people carry with them the potential to be violent or anti-social and that environmental conditions can sometimes trigger anti-social responses. Sociobiologists view biology, environment and learning as mutually dependent factors. Jeffery argues, for example, that:

> We do not inherit behaviour any more than we inherit height or intelligence. We do inherit a capacity for interaction with the environment. Sociopathy and alcoholism are not inherited, but a biochemical preparedness for such behaviours is present in the brain which if given a certain type of environment will produce sociopathy or alcoholism. (Jeffery, 1978, p. 161)

Nevertheless it is acknowledged that the usual comparative controls of criminal and non-criminal are doubly misleading. Offenders in custody are not representative of criminals in general, but constitute a highly selected subset of those apprehended, charged and convicted. Control groups of the non-criminal are almost certain to include some individuals who have committed crimes but whose actions have remained undetected. Above all, the search for biological, physiological or genetic correlates of criminality is continually hampered because it is practically impossible to control for environmental and social influences and thus to be able to measure precisely the exact influence of a genetic effect. Nevertheless biochemical research has been given a significant boost through the Human Genome Project which reported in 2003 that it had 'cracked the code of life'. It is claimed that by sequencing and mapping human genes, doors will open not only to advancements in health care but also in law enforcement and criminal identification. Caspi et al. (2002), for example, claim to have identified a specific gene that triggers violence in some previously abused children. Similarly Viding et al.'s (2005) comparison of 7374 MZ and DZ twins found that, at the age of seven, the 'exhibiting of high levels of callous-unemotional traits … is under strong genetic influence', which in turn is related to high levels of anti-social behaviour. Once more the possibilities of a 'criminal gene' and 'gene therapy' (and fears of eugenics) are being debated. Such notions also have strong popular appeal. In 2007, an episode of the American forensic science TV drama – *CSI Miami* – was devoted to finding elements of DNA that were predictive of aggressive and violent actions. At its peak *CSI* (Crime Scene Investigation) had an audience of 30 to 40 million.

The Adolescent Personality

Another form of individual positivism – often termed 'the psychogenic school' – has shifted the focus of causal analysis away from biologically given 'constitutional' factors and towards more 'dynamic' mental processes and characteristics.

The earliest versions of this work were applications of the principles of Freudian psychoanalysis. Briefly, Freud, while not directly addressing the issue of crime causation, argued that all behaviour is the result of tensions existing between unconscious drives (the id) and conscious understandings of self, morality and the social order (the ego and superego). Crime is the symbolic expression of such psychic conflict, when the individual has failed to learn and develop adequate measures of self-control through which unconscious drives can be channelled into socially acceptable acts. The repression or inadequate control of the unconscious is usually related to a lack of intimate and trusting relationships in early childhood. Aichhorn (1925) concluded that delinquent children continue to 'act infantile' because they have failed to develop an ego and superego that would allow them to conform to prevailing social mores. In Freudian terms, the 'pleasure principle' has not been sufficiently controlled and adapted to the 'reality principle'.

Writers in the psychoanalytical tradition have been particularly influential in linking crime with the 'pathological' conditions of adolescence. Criminal behaviour is the result of a failure of psychological development in which the underlying latent delinquency of adolescence is allowed to govern behaviour. The earliest version of this argument was that of G. Stanley Hall (see **Chapter 2.3**) and his premise of an adolescent storm and stress (*Sturm und Drang*) has remained remarkably influential. In the 1950s, Anna Freud, for example, argued:

> Adolescence is by its nature an *interruption* of peaceful growth, and … the upholding of a steady equilibrium during the adolescent process is in itself *abnormal* … adolescence resembles in appearance a variety of other emotional upsets and structural *upheavals*. The adolescent manifestations come close to symptom formation of the *neurotic*, *psychotic*, or *dissocial* order and merge almost imperceptibly into … almost all the *mental illnesses*. (Freud, 1952, pp. 255–78, italics added)

In this way adolescence is viewed as a time of crisis in which the struggle between the forces of natural instinct and those of cultural constraints are acted out in behaviour patterns comparable to madness. The problem of adolescence derives from the conflict caused as instinctual drives are constrained by social learning and the demands of a *social* existence. Similarly, Eissler, writing in 1958, viewed adolescence as stormy and unpredictable behaviour marked by dramatic mood changes which manifest themselves as 'neurotic at one time and almost psychotic at another' (quoted by Rutter et al., 1976, p. 35).

Erikson (1968) went on to argue that adolescence is characterized by an 'identity crisis' in which the key task is to resolve a conflict between 'ego identity' and 'identity confusion'. Failure to achieve a positive resolution to such contradictions, he argued, will adversely affect development later in life. Although Erikson was at pains to show that such a crisis was predictable rather than unusual, he nevertheless uses the same medical terminology of 'symptoms', 'neuroses' and 'psychoses' to describe the adolescent condition. In this way the concept of adolescence is firmly associated with emotional disorder, impairment and pathology. It is an abnormal condition, reducible ultimately to universal biological determinants.

Applying such concepts to crime, Healy and Bronner (1936) compared two groups of children from a child guidance clinic and argued that the delinquent group showed greater signs of emotional disturbance. This was explained with reference to instability in family relationships and lack of affectional ties. Delinquency was viewed as a form of sublimation in which the delinquent attempted to meet basic needs that had not been met by the family. Similarly, Bowlby's (1946) study of *Forty-four Juvenile Thieves*, who were referred to a London child guidance clinic between 1936 and 1939, concluded that 'the prolonged separation of the child from his mother or foster-mother in the early years commonly leads to his becoming a persistent thief and an Affectionless Character'. Lack of affectional ties or **maternal deprivation** was viewed as the root cause of criminality.

Other psychoanalytic explanations for crime have focused on the inability to control pleasure-seeking drives, on parental permissiveness and on the acting out of feelings of oppression and helplessness. While such hypotheses continue to be highly influential both popularly and politically, they largely remain immune to objective scientific testing – a cornerstone of assessing the adequacy of any positivist criminological theory. This is because the reliance on unconscious factors, symbolic behaviours and the analyst's own interpretations of that behaviour place psycho-analysis beyond the boundaries of scientific demonstration.

Psychologists and psychiatrists have also attempted systematically to associate particular personality traits with criminal behaviour. Much of this has depended on the construction of performance tests, personality scales and measurements of intelligence. From these a wide range of traits have been singled out as indicative of delinquent and criminal propensities. They include extroversion, vivacity, defiance, resentfulness, suspicion, assertiveness, low IQ, excitability, impulsiveness and narcissism (for example, Glueck and Glueck, 1950). More narrowly focused, a review of 94 personality studies conducted between 1950 and 1965 by Waldo and Dinitz (1967) found that over 80 per cent of these studies reported statistically significant personality differences between criminals and non-criminals. The studies generally concluded that criminals were more 'psychopathic' than non-criminals. Similarly, Wilson and Herrnstein (1985, pp. 187–8) conclude that such personality traits as conflict with authority and low personal attachments (on a psychopathic deviate scale), bizarre thought and withdrawal (on a schizophrenia scale) and unproductive hyperactivity (on a hypomania scale) all correlate with criminal tendencies.

Another form of personality measurement was devised by Eysenck (1970). He focused on two basic dimensions: ***extroversion***, a continuum from extroversion to introversion along an E scale, and *neuroticism*, a continuum from unstable to stable along an N scale. He found that those having high NE personalities were the most likely also to have deviant characteristics. Eysenck attempted to explain such results by adopting a multi-factor approach which incorporated biological, individual and social levels of analysis. The basis of his theory was that through genetic endowment, some people are born with a particular structure of the cortex of the brain which affects their ability to learn from, or adapt to, environmental stimuli.

The extrovert was considered to be cortically under-aroused and sought to gain stimulation through impulsive behaviour. The introvert was considered to be cortically over-aroused and avoided stimulation through adopting a quiet, reserved demeanour. Eysenck argued further that extroverts condition less efficiently than introverts, thus affecting their ability to develop an effective conscience and behave in a socially acceptable manner (see Box 3.3).

Box 3.3

Eysenck and personality theory

- Children learn to control anti-social behaviour through the development of a conscience.

- A conscience is developed through conditioning whereby children are deterred from 'wrong' acts by disapproval and punishment, in which certain acts become associated with fear and anxiety.

- The effectiveness of conditioning depends mainly upon the child's personality in terms of E and N.

- The extrovert requires a higher level of stimulation than others, lacks inhibition, and engages in more 'risky' behaviour.

- High E and high N personalities have poor conditionability and are the least likely to learn self-control.

- Dramatic and impulsive behaviour, unhindered by conscience, means more potential crime.

- High N and high E personalities will be over-represented in offender populations.

Source: Derived from Eysenck (1970).

Eysenck's theory combines elements of biological determinism with social conditioning, and he argues that it is universally applicable, given that all personalities are made up of N and E factors. It also retains an environmental component. As Eysenck explains:

> The very notion of criminality or crime would be meaningless without a context of learning or social experience and, quite generally, of human interaction. What the figures have demonstrated is that heredity is a very strong predisposing factor as far as committing crimes is concerned. But the actual way in which the crime is carried out and whether or not the culprit is found and punished – these are obviously subject to the changing vicissitudes of everyday life. (Eysenck, 1970, p. 75)

During the 1970s Eysenck's theory generated a great deal of empirical research. The findings were somewhat inconsistent, but the general pattern to emerge was that offender populations did appear to be high on the N scale, but within the normal E range. The key element of Eysenck's theory – extroversion – thus appears to be subordinate to that of neuroticism – a factor regarded simply as intensifying behaviour of any kind. A direct correlation between extroversion and criminality remains unproven (Crookes, 1979). In response to such limitations, Eysenck added a third dimension of psychoticism (characterized by such personality traits as insensitivity, aggression, foolhardiness and lack of concern for others) but this has also shown mixed results, in particular missing a critical 'hedonism' factor (Burgess, 1972).

The Cambridge Study of Delinquent Development relied on devising a scale to measure 'anti-social' tendencies, based on attitudinal measures and such activities as smoking, loitering, tattooing, heavy drinking, gambling and promiscuous sex (West and Farrington, 1973, 1977). This **developmental criminology** found that those who scored high on anti-social attitudes and behaviours were more likely in the future to have criminal records than those who scored low. The authors concluded that a 'delinquent' way of life – particular attributes of personality and lifestyle – was clearly connected to officially recorded criminality. In exhaustive reviews of international research, concerned with family backgrounds, circumstances and attitudes, numerous risk factors including being the child of a teenage mother, impulsive personality, low intelligence and poor performance in school, harsh or erratic parental discipline and parental conflict, as well as peer group influences have been consistently identified as predictive of future offending (Farrington and Welsh, 2007, and see **Chapter 1.3**). Latterly Wikstrom's study of 1,957 14 to 15 year olds in Peterborough in 2000 combined personality (self-control, morality, dispositions) factors with family social position, lifestyles and community contexts. It found a 'strong interaction' between individual characteristics and high risk lifestyles (alcohol and drug use; association with delinquent peers in public spaces). These findings suggested three distinct groups of adolescent offenders: *propensity induced* (the maladjusted); *lifestyle dependent* (related to peer group pressure); and *situationally-limited* (well-adjusted individuals but who may nevertheless occasionally offend, dependent on situation). Such research provides a useful refinement of individual positivism but remains wedded to a familiar classification of young people into risk categories and risk propensities. Its originality lies in its insistence that it is not personality alone but the relation between individual factors and situational contexts that is important (Wikstrom and Butterworth, 2006).

Assessment

If we assume for the moment that all young people do go through a period of inner turmoil, is this caused by an unalterable biological law or by adjustments necessitated by particular environments, cultures and moments in history?

Margaret Mead's famous work *Coming of Age in Samoa* (1928) set out to contradict biological positivism in particular. If a culture could be discovered in which adolescents did not appear to suffer 'storm and stress', it was argued, then biological determinism could be declared invalid. Over a period of several months Mead studied the behaviour of 25 adolescent girls in three villages on the Manu'an island of Tau in Eastern Samoa. She reported that while social ranking by age existed, their adolescence was not characterized by any form of role confusion, conflict or rebellion. She concluded that the state of adolescence was not universal, but culturally variable. The stresses of adolescence were socially, rather than biologically, determined. For Mead, the adolescent anxieties so troubling middle-class America in the inter-war years were produced through young people being confronted with a wide range of occupational choice, extreme competitiveness, and conflicting standards of sexual morality, rather than being biologically inevitable.

This cultural determinist approach was criticized some 50 years later. Derek Freeman's visit to Samoa in the 1940s convinced him that Mead's analysis was full of inaccuracies. For, whereas Mead claimed that the behaviour of Samoan adolescents was untroubled and that adolescence was 'the age of maximum ease', Freeman (1983, p. 262) notes relatively high rates of delinquency in the 14–19 age group, characterized by rape and male aggression. Mead's book rapidly attracted popular attention largely due to her portrayal of Samoa as a paradise of adolescent free love and pre-marital sexuality. However, Freeman's observations again contradict such assertions. He discovered a cult of chastity in which high value was placed on female virginity prior to marriage and noted how the Samoan girl was strictly watched and guarded from the time of her first menstruation. What for Mead was unrestrained sexual promiscuity was for Freeman a custom of *moetotolo* (sleep crawling), whereby young men would compete to deflower any sexually mature virgin, and if a young man was successful he would claim her as his own. Such a practice usually involved a man sexually assaulting a sleeping woman through force or deceit in a manner which in the West we would describe as 'surreptitious rape' (Freeman, 1983, p. 244). Above all, Freeman claimed that any attempt to explain behaviour in purely cultural terms must be 'irremediably deficient'. Instead he argues for a synthesis of biological and cultural variables.

In addition, the pathological connotations of a universal and biologically based 'adolescent personality' have also been widely critiqued. For example, Fass's (1977) study of college youth in the 1920s reported that the young were essentially conformist, rather than hostile to parental attitudes, and she was struck by the absence of 'storm and stress' in young people's lives. Springhall (1983–84) suggested that one reason why some adolescents have problems of adjustment is simply because parents and teachers expect them to have such problems. In a 1970s survey, 80 per cent of teachers stated that adolescence was a time of great stress, while 60 per cent of adolescent pupils denied that they had ever felt miserable or depressed. Springhall concluded:

> The misleading images of the disturbed adolescent can be blamed, according to taste, on: unrepresentative sampling techniques, the threat presented to the adult by certain deviant forms of adolescent behaviour or on the role of the professional hand-wringers of the mass media in publicizing the sensational behaviour among the young ... The ordinary public can thus be forgiven for

holding a stereotyped version of adolescence as a social problem which requires to be dealt with either through separate institutions or by handing out heavier forms of punishment. (Springhall, 1983–84, p. 34)

In general, individual positivism assumes that all human behaviour is determined by biological, psychological or environmental factors, or a combination of these. What is noteworthy is that such theory focuses on individual motivations and provides us with very specific representations of the young criminal as either 'born bad', for example, through genetic inheritance, or 'made bad', for example, through inability to develop a conscience. The issue of crime causation is often alluded to, but in the spirit of developing vigorous scientific methods of analysis what emerges is a series of correlations rather than 'proven' causal relations.

Nevertheless individual positivism formed the bedrock of criminological studies for the first half of the twentieth century and has regained importance since the 1990s. For some, because of advances in our understanding of genetic structures, it offers a way forward in understanding criminality which is 'free' from a multitude of complicating social variables. For others, it is little more than a dangerous political gambit to segregate those deemed to be physically or emotionally unfit. Indeed, from within psychology, positivism has been attacked for its lack of attention to processes of human cognition and social learning in which individuals are viewed as capable of self-reflection and self-development, rather than as beings who simply act upon pre-given determinants. In addition, some sociologists have argued that there is 'meaning' in all social activity. Thus, while theorists, such as Eysenck, characterize deviant behaviour as pathological, it has also been argued that deviancy is a meaningful behaviour pattern which becomes undesirable only when judged and labelled by others (see **Chapter 4.1**).

Hollin (1989, pp. 60–1) points to two major limitations of theories that attempt to replicate principles of scientific **determinism**. First, the more that criminological research has developed, the more the number of variables thought to be important in crime has increased. Even if such variables were capable of adequate measurement, controlling for their relative effect is probably impossible. This leads to sampling variations between studies so that results are always difficult to replicate. We are thus left with a long list of correlations, which though interesting in themselves, shed no light on the question of causation. Second, psychological research continues to unearth more and more variables, but then attempts to explain crime with reference to existing psychological theory that is designed to account for some psychological abnormality. Thus criminal behaviour becomes a genetic defect, an extreme of personality development, a failure of family socialization, and so on. Finally, it is always worth questioning that if crime and delinquency are as widespread as self report studies indicate (see **Chapter 1.2**), what sense does it make to impute some biological or psychological disturbance (learnt or otherwise) to these forms of behaviour?

Nevertheless, theories based on individual positivism continue to have widespread popular and political appeal. Notions of adolescent disorder, parental neglect, 'bad blood' and psychopathology all have their root here. The search for the aetiology of crime by identifying a criminal type, a criminal gene or a criminal personality will continue because of a general reluctance to believe that youthful criminality is in any way 'normal'.

Sociological Positivism

3.2 Most of the explanations of crime that were examined in Section 3.1 focused on the characteristics of individual criminals and attempted to identify certain behavioural or physiological anomalies or abnormalities which distinguish the criminal from the non-criminal. The sources of crime were, in the main, found to lie *within* the individual. In contrast, sociological approaches stress the importance of social factors as causes of crime. Their broad aim is to account for the *distribution* of varying amounts of crime within given populations. This mode of analysis predates the work of Lombroso, and can be traced back to the work of the French statistician, Guerry, and the Belgian mathematician, Quetelet, in the 1830s. They analysed official statistics on variables such as suicide, educational level, crime rate and age and sex of offenders, within given geographic areas for specific time periods. Two general patterns emerged: types and the amount of crime varied from region to region, but within specific areas there was little variation from year to year. Because of this regularity it was proposed that criminal behaviour must be generated by something other than individual motivation. Quetelet (1842) found that the factors most strongly tied to criminal propensity were gender, occupation and religion, as well as age. Fluctuations in crime rates were explained with reference to changes in the social, political and economic structures of particular societies, while crime itself was viewed as a constant and inevitable feature of social organization. He argued:

> Society includes within itself the germs of all the crimes committed, and at the same time the necessary facilities for their development. It is the social state, in some measure, which prepares these crimes, and the criminal is merely the instrument to execute them. Every social state supposes, then, a certain number and a certain order of crimes, these being merely the necessary consequences of its organization. (Quetelet, 1842, p. 108)

Such an analysis was clearly associated with the emergence of a sociological form of positivism first developed by philosophers such as Comte and Saint-Simon in the mid-nineteenth century. Comte's insistence that society both predates and shapes the individual psychologically provided the foundation for *sociological positivism*. At the turn of the century its most influential advocate was Émile Durkheim (1895/1964). He argued, in a similar way to Quetelet, that in any given social context, the predictability of crime rates must mean they are social facts, and thus a normal phenomenon. Crime is rarely abnormal – it occurs in all societies, it is tied to the facts of collective life and its volume tends to increase as societies evolve from mechanical to more complex organic forms of organization. Above all, crime and punishment perform a useful function for society because they maintain social solidarity, through establishing moral boundaries and strengthening the shared consensus of a community's beliefs and values (see Box 3.4).

Box 3.4

Durkheim and the normality of crime

Crime is present not only in the majority of societies of one particular species but in all societies of all types. There is no society that is not confronted with the problem of criminality. Its form changes; the acts thus characterised are not the same everywhere; but, everywhere and always, there have been men who have behaved in such a way as to draw upon themselves penal repression … There is, then, no phenomenon that presents more indisputably all the symptoms of normality, since it appears closely connected with the conditions of all collective life. … Here we are, then, in the presence of a conclusion in appearance quite paradoxical. Let us make no mistake. To classify crime among the phenomena of normal sociology is not to say merely that it is an inevitable, although regrettable phenomenon, due to the incorrigible wickedness of men; it is to affirm that it is a factor in public health, an integral part of all healthy societies. This result is, at first glance, surprising enough to have puzzled even ourselves for a long time. Once this first surprise has been overcome, however, it is not difficult to find reasons explaining this normality and at the same time confirming it … In the first place crime is normal because a society exempt from it is utterly impossible … since there cannot be a society in which the individuals do not differ more or less from the collective type, it is also inevitable that, among these divergences, there are some with a criminal character. What confers this character upon them is not the intrinsic quality of a given act but that definition which the collective conscience lends them. If the collective conscience is stronger, if it has enough authority practically to suppress these divergences, it will also be more sensitive, more exacting; and, reacting against the slightest deviations with the energy it otherwise displays only against more considerable infractions, it will attribute to them the same gravity as formerly to crimes. In other words, it will designate them as criminal. Crime is, then, necessary; it is bound up with the fundamental conditions of all social life, and by that very fact it is useful, because these conditions of which it is a part are themselves indispensable to the normal evolution of morality and law.

Source: Durkheim (1895/1964: 65–73).

Many of these early sociologies of crime were at direct odds with the premises of individual positivism. However, although the level of analysis is different, the mode of analysis remains very much the same. Sociological positivism continues to view the individual as a body that is acted upon, and whose behaviour is determined, by external forces. Little or no role is given to the processes of choice, voluntarism or self-volition. While Durkheim argued that crime is a normal social fact, he also acknowledged that in given contexts its rate might be abnormal. Thus, crime is also regarded as some form of pathology: if not the abnormality of individuals, then dysfunctions in social systems. The study of crime remains in the tradition of scientism, **essentialism** and positivistic method: that is, it can be measured and evaluated by means of statistical methods and empirical data. It also assumes that there must be something about crime that differentiates it from normal behaviour. A consensus, or in Durkheim's terms a 'collective conscience', exists which marks out the criminal from the non-criminal. The role of social conflict between individuals and among competing groups is downplayed. Finally, as both individual and sociological positivism maintain that it is theoretically possible to specify causes, they also hold that it is theoretically possible to 'treat' or 'correct' the aberrant condition (see Box 3.5).

Box 3.5
Individual and sociological positivism compared

Individual positivism	Sociological positivism
Crime caused by individual abnormality or pathology	Crime caused by social pathology
Crime viewed as a biological, psychiatric, personality or learning deficiency	Crime viewed as a product of dysfunctions in social and economic conditions
Behaviour determined by constitutional, genetic or personality factors	Behaviour determined by social conditions and structures
Crime as a violation of the moral consensus surrounding legal codes	Crime as a violation of a collective conscience
Crime varies with temperament, personality and degree of 'adequate' socialization	Crime varies from region to region depending on economic and political milieux
Crime as an abnormal individual condition	Crime as normal: a social fact, but rates of crime are dysfunctional
Criminals can be treated via medicine, therapy and resocialization	Crime can be treated via programmes of social reform

Social Ecology and Criminal Areas

Social ecology explanations of crime have traditionally been influenced by human geography and biology. As Quetelet had observed, crime is always subject to uneven geographical distribution. Urban areas appear to have higher recorded crime rates than rural areas, and within cities there are presumed to be 'criminal areas' or 'hot spots' of crime. To explain these patterns of crime distribution, analogies were made between the ecology of plant life and human organization. Cities were viewed as akin to living and growing organisms. The analogy, as Downes and Rock (1995, p. 70), suggest, was attractive to 'sociologists who were searching for metaphors and principles to advance their own new and rather incoherent discipline … just as plants, insects and animals translate a physical terrain into a mosaic of distinct communities, so people become separated into a network of unlike communities which form an intelligible whole'. Such an approach allowed the prevalent paradigm of individual positivism to be challenged. Above all, it was claimed that because particular areas maintained a regular crime rate even when their populations completely changed, there must be something about particular places that sustains crime.

In the 1920s and 1930s, sociologists at the University of Chicago embarked on a systematic study of all aspects of their local urban environment. Park, a newspaper reporter turned sociologist, and Burgess, his collaborator, were especially influential. They noted that, like any ecological system, the development and organization of the city of Chicago were not random but patterned, and could be understood in terms of such social processes as invasion, conflict, accommodation and assimilation. They likened the city to a living and growing organism and viewed the functions of various areas of the city as fundamental to the survival of the whole. The city's characteristics, social change and distribution of people were studied by use of Burgess's concentric zone theory. The city was divided into five areas: zone 1, the central business district; zone 2, a transition from business to residences; zone 3, working-class homes; zone 4, middle-class homes; and zone 5, commuter suburbs. Zone 2 – the **zone in transition** – was a particular focus of study. Here the expansion of the business sector continually meant that residents were displaced. It became the least desirable living area. It was characterized by deteriorating housing stock, poverty, pawn shops, cheap theatres, restaurants, casual workers, new immigrants and a breakdown in the usual methods of social control.

Park and Burgess (1925) hypothesized that it was in zone 2 that crime and vice would flourish. Shaw (1929) set out to test this hypothesis by using juvenile and adult court and prison statistics to map the spatial distribution of the residences of delinquent youths and criminals throughout the city. Among his conclusions were the following:

- Rates of truancy, delinquency and adult crime varied inversely in proportion to the distance from the city centre. The closer to the centre of the city, the higher the rate of crime.

- Areas showing the highest rates of juvenile delinquency also had the highest rates of adult crime.

- The rates reflected differences in the make-up of different communities. High crime rates occurred in areas characterized by physical deterioration and declining populations.

- Relatively high rates of crime persisted in zone 2 despite the fact that the composition of the population in that area had changed significantly over 30 years.

These observations suggested that it was the nature of neighbourhoods, and *not* the nature of the individuals who lived there, that determined levels of criminality. As a result, this line of reasoning has been termed 'environmental determinism'.

The concentration of crime and delinquency in a zone of transition was viewed as indicative of processes of **social disorganization**. As industry and commerce invaded and transient populations entered such areas, community ties were destroyed and resistance to deviance lowered:

> In this state of social disorganization community resistance is low. Delinquency and criminal patterns arise and are transmitted socially just as any other cultural and social pattern is transmitted. In time these delinquent patterns become dominant and shape the attitudes and behaviour of persons living in the area. Thus the section becomes an area of delinquency. (Shaw, 1929, pp. 205–6)

This early work was clearly positivist in orientation. Subsequently Shaw and McKay (1942) developed the notion of a delinquency area into a *cultural transmission* theory of delinquency. This held that within transitional (zone 2) areas, particular forms of crime became a cultural norm: they were learnt and passed on through the generations. Shaw and McKay (1942, p. 436) proposed that:

> This tradition becomes meaningful to the child through the conduct, speech, gestures and attitudes of persons with whom he has contact. Of particular importance is the child's intimate association with gangs or other forms of delinquent and criminal organisation. Through his [*sic*] contacts with these groups and by virtue of his participation in their activities, he learns the techniques of stealing, becomes involved in binding relationships with his companions in delinquency and acquires the attitudes appropriate to his position as a member of such groups.

Originally such factors as overcrowding, slum housing and poverty were viewed as causal factors in themselves; now structural factors were relegated to the minor role of predisposing symptoms of the more significant processes of social and cultural transmission. A shift away from structural determinism (and thus away from positivist modes of analysis and understanding) was a key element of the Chicago School's later studies. Using detailed case studies of the 'career' of individual offenders, *appreciative studies* of the criminal's own perspective and attitudes were promoted in which the principles of positivism were rejected in the detailed study of interactional, learning and associational processes. A key influence was Sutherland's theory of **differential association**. His central hypothesis was that crime is not caused by personality or environment, but is the product of learning. It is learnt just as any other behaviour is learnt. From association with others, the potential delinquent or criminal learns definitions favourable to deviant behaviour. When these definitions exceed the frequency and intensity of definitions favourable to conformity, the chances of criminality are higher. The basic principles of differential association, first formulated in the 1930s, were subsequently detailed by Sutherland and Cressey (1970, pp. 77–9) (see Box 3.6).

Box 3.6

Sutherland and differential association

- Criminal behaviour is learned.

- Criminal behaviour is learned in interaction with other persons in a process of communication.

- The principal part of the learning of criminal behaviour occurs within intimate personal groups.

- When criminal behaviour is learned, the learning includes techniques of committing the crime and the specific direction of motives, rationalizations and attitudes conducive to crime.

- The specific direction of motives and drives is learned from definitions of the legal codes as favourable or unfavourable.

- A person becomes delinquent because of an excess of definitions favourable to violation of law over definitions unfavourable to violation of law.

- Differential associations may vary in frequency, duration, priority and intensity for each individual.

- The process of learning criminal behaviour by association with criminal and anti-criminal patterns involves all the mechanisms that are involved in any other learning.

- While criminal behaviour is an expression of general needs and values, it is not explained by those general needs and values since non-criminal behaviour is an expression of the same needs and values (for example, it is not the need for money that inspires crime, rather the learnt method that is used to acquire it).

Source: Sutherland and Cressey (1970, p. 77).

A key to understanding Sutherland's theory lies in his argument that learning does not necessarily have to occur through association with criminals, but rather with people who may not consistently support, or adhere to, strict legal codes. However, the theory does not explain why some people associate with those who approve of law violation while others in similar circumstances do not. A problem remains too of defining exactly *what kinds* of association favour such violations. Nevertheless, there have been numerous subsequent observations that appear to confirm the centrality of learning crime via association. Rutter and Giller's (1983, p. 249) review of the relevant positivist research finds that most delinquent acts are committed in the company of other children; an individual's delinquency is strongly associated with parental and familial criminality; children living in high-delinquency areas, or attending a high-delinquency school, are also likely to become delinquent themselves; and the probability of committing a specific delinquent act is statistically related to the prevalence of delinquency in one's peer group.

The Chicago School simultaneously developed two contradictory notions of crime causation. Individual behaviour was viewed as determined by social disorganization, but also as imbued with an element of freedom of action, particularly in the learning of patterns that were favourable to law violation. The two notions are theoretically incompatible (Taylor et al., 1973, p. 114). Above all, the normative learning of behaviours implies a level of social organization which the concept of *disorganization* tends to deny. Thus subsequent researchers, such as Matza (1964), abandoned the concept in favour of that of cultural *diversity* or *differential* social organization.

Nevertheless, the notion of a delinquent or criminal area remained influential in a number of British studies in the 1950s and 1960s. In particular, London, Birmingham and Liverpool (cities that seemed to replicate the turbulent and expanding Chicago of the 1920s) were subject to a similar environmental analysis in attempts to explain the relatively high incidence of recorded crime in inner-city working-class areas. For example, Terence Morris (1957) found that the areas of peak crime rates in Croydon were two of the inter-war council housing estates and two older residential areas noted for slum housing and physical deterioration. From this he argued two points:

1 The type of housing and the housing policies of local authorities were central in creating criminal areas.

2 The chances of becoming delinquent were related to the strength of delinquent influences in the local environment.

Further British area studies widened the focus to include the study of differential access to housing space, of policies concerning the allocation of publicly owned housing, and of the effects on people compelled to live in low-grade housing in 'rough' areas. The concepts of social *class* and differential access to *power* became central to understanding the continuing 'competitive struggle for space' (Rex and Moore, 1967; Damer, 1977; Gill, 1977).

The collaboration of some geographers and sociologists in the 1980s once more suggested that understandings of *space* and *place* should be included in any adequate theory of criminality. The problem faced by such an endeavour reflects the contradictions encountered by the Chicago studies. While it is clear that official crime rates are concentrated in particular areas, can it be unequivocally claimed that it is such places that create crime? Similarly, while the ethnographic study of criminal careers in specific localities has shed light on the importance of individual motivations and social interactions, this micro level of analysis often appeared blind to the effects of structural constraints. Nevertheless, versions of spatial analysis (Brantingham and Brantingham, 1984; Bottoms and Wiles, 1992) succeeded not only in substantiating that crime is spatially as well as socially defined, but that it is a natural and normal expression of social interaction given the organization of particular localized communities. It is how individuals recognize the role of space in their own biographies and how space mediates the relationship between individual and environment that creates different *opportunities* for crime. Interest in this area also burgeoned in the UK in the late 1990s as a result of attempts to regenerate certain 'deprived' and 'high crime' neighbourhoods through a combination of 'empowerment funds' and 'strategic partnerships'. The aim was to reduce crime and stimulate local economic enterprise not only by improving the physical environment but also by providing better access to health, education and housing resource. Such a policy tends to assume a direct link between crime and urban decline. However, Hancock's (2001) Merseyside study found that, contrary to governmental claims of equitable partnerships, local regeneration initiatives rarely addressed local needs. Rather 'regeneration' was more designed to attract 'outsiders' (as consumers and as labour) than to expand local employment opportunities. When 'renewal' takes the form of developing a night-time economy, for example, it may act to increase local fears and anxieties rather than secure their abatement. The relationship between urban regeneration and crime reduction is complex. To fully understand the role of social and spatial divisions in generating crime, fear and perceptions of safety, detailed and intimate knowledge of specific community cultural dynamics is clearly required (Nayak, 2003).

Anomie, Strain and Subcultures

The proposition that crime is a consequence of societies based on values of competitive individualism and structured by a high division of labour was first formulated by Durkheim (1895/1964). He argued that crime has a positive function in affirming the moral consciousness of society. It is also positive in challenging and effecting change in that consciousness: 'There is no occasion for self congratulation when the crime rate drops noticeably below the average level, for we may be certain that this apparent progress is associated with some social disorder'. (Durkheim, 1895/1964, p. 72). Crime is both an expression of individual freedom and a necessary and desirable precursor of social change. The rate at which individuals deviate from the norm is related to the degree of integration and cohesiveness by which society is governed at particular times. For example, the higher rate of suicides in times of economic crisis is explained by the lack of regulation in society at such times. Because society encourages individualism and unlimited aspirations, situations arise when such aspirations cannot be realistically achieved. Unless society imposes new regulations on aspirations, then a social state of **anomie** or normlessness will occur, resulting in personal crises and a higher tendency towards suicide:

> No living being can be happy or even exist unless his needs are sufficiently proportioned to his means. In other words if his needs require more than can be granted or even merely something of a different sort, they will be under continual friction and can only function painfully. (Durkheim, 1897/1952, p. 246)

In the 1930s, Merton elaborated on this theme of unobtainable or unrealistic aspirations to apply the concept of anomie beyond suicide to all forms of deviance. Following Durkheim, Merton (1938) argued that socially produced aspirations could exceed what is obtainable through available opportunities. But while Durkheim claimed that anomie resulted from a failure to regulate behaviour, Merton proposed that such a condition was generated from **strain** in the social structure that actively encouraged individuals to develop unrealistic aspirations. Anomie was viewed as dependent on the degree of divergence between cultural goals – through which success and status in society are defined – and institutionalized means – the acceptable methods of achieving such goals. For Merton, the cultural goal of American society – the American Dream of open and infinite opportunity for all – had come to overemphasize the ambition of monetary and material gain. The ideal that anyone, regardless of class origin, ethnicity or religion, could achieve material wealth stood uneasily against the essentially closed opportunity structure by which American society was in reality constrained. Such a situation produces a structurally induced strain in which the cardinal American virtue of ambition ultimately promotes the cardinal American vice of deviant behaviour (Merton, 1957, p. 200). Because aspirations are encouraged to be endless, but in reality are blocked by what the social structure makes possible, large sections of the American population find that they cannot achieve their goals through conventional means. In this way, intense pressure for deviation is produced.

Merton continued by analysing how such 'breakdowns in the cultural structure' are responded to by a series of *individual* adaptations. These are depicted not as individually perverse or destructive, but as reflections of the range of options available to people, given their position within the social structure. He identified five possible modes of adaptation – conformity, innovation, ritualism, retreatism and rebellion. About each he asks whether cultural goals and institutionalized means for their realization are accepted or rejected (see Box 3.7).

Box 3.7

Modes of adaptation to strain

	Culture Goals	Institutionalized Means
Conformity	+	+
Innovation	+	−
Ritualism	−	+
Retreatism	−	−
Rebellion	+/−	+/−

Notes: + = 'acceptance'
− = 'elimination'
+/− = 'rejection and substitution of new goals and standards'

Source: Merton (1938, p. 676)

- *Conformity* describes the acceptance of goals and means, and is the most frequently used adaptation.

- *Innovation* occurs when the value of attaining goals is accepted and acted out irrespective of the impropriety, immorality or illegality of the chosen means. For example, for those groups situated in lower echelons of the social hierarchy, the problems of poverty and restricted opportunity may be 'solved' by innovative and deviant adaptations. This situation may explain the higher rate of property crime in poor areas. Merton points out that poverty does not cause crime, but when combined with acceptance of cultural goals, the possibility of criminal behaviour is increased.

- *Ritualism* is explained as typically lower middle class, as opposed to innovation which is seen as typically working class. In ritualism, aspirations are abandoned in favour of strict adherence to institutionalized means – 'the perspective of the frightened employee, the zealously conformist bureaucrat' (Merton, 1957, p. 150). Such modes of 'playing it safe', however, remain deviant because of non-compliance with dominant cultural goals.

- *Retreatism* similarly involves a rejection of cultural goals, but here institutionalized means are also abandoned. Rather than coping with structural strains, the retreatist opts out altogether. Drug addicts, vagrants, alcoholics and psychotics are viewed as such highly individual deviants seeking their own rewards outside of the dominant value system.

- *Rebellion* involves not only a rejection of goals and means, but also the intention of altering the social structure from which such norms emanate. The non-conforming rebel challenges the status quo and attempts to institutionalize *new* goals and means for the rest of society.

In sum, Merton suggested that the very nature of American society generates crime and deviance. The more the cultural goal of material success is advocated, the more the power of institutionalized norms to regulate behaviour is diminished. Criminality becomes prevalent once certain modes of adaptation – particularly innovation – are practised successfully and observed by others. But for Merton such criminality is not simply deviant, because it is also generated by conformity to the widely accepted goal of pecuniary success (see Box 3.8).

Box 3.8

Merton and anomie

A high frequency of deviate behaviour is not generated simply by lack of opportunities or by pecuniary emphasis. A comparatively rigidified class structure, a feudalistic or caste order may limit such opportunities far beyond the point which obtains in our society today. It is only when a system of cultural values extols, virtually above all else, certain common symbols of success for the population at large while its social structure rigorously restricts or completely eliminates access to approved modes of acquiring these symbols for a considerable part of the same population that antisocial behaviour ensues on a considerable scale … Frustration and thwarted aspiration lead to the search for avenues of escape from a culturally induced intolerable situation; or unrelieved ambition may accentuate in illicit attempts to acquire the dominant values. The American stress on pecuniary success and ambitiousness for all thus invites exaggerated anxieties, hostilities, neuroses and antisocial behaviour.

Source: Merton (1938, p. 679).

The theory of anomie, as proposed by Durkheim and Merton, subsequently provided a platform for the development of *subcultural* theories of delinquent and criminal behaviour (see **Chapter 6**). Albert Cohen's (1955) research on delinquent boys and the subculture of the gang in Chicago, for example, accounted for their actions as lower-class adaptations to a dominant middle-class society which discriminated against them. However, Cohen noted that the Mertonian modes of adaptation to strain failed to account for the non-utilitarian, malicious and negative forms of their behaviour. Delinquents, he argued, usually steal items of minor value or are involved in acts of petty vandalism. How could this be explained within Merton's utilitarian framework in which all actions were viewed as a rational means to an end? Accordingly Cohen developed the notion of **status frustration** in preference to that of anomie. He viewed the gang as operating *collectively* within a different value system from that which, according to Merton, characterized the whole of American society. The development of specialized vocabulary, internal beliefs and innovative ways of dressing and acting, he argued, represented a total inversion of dominant values. Status frustration becomes visible in negative forms of behaviour whereby the dominant goals of ambition and achievement, deferred gratification and respect for property are rejected and reversed. By a process of *reaction formation*, dominant values are inverted to offer a collective solution to restricted opportunity in which 'the delinquent conduct is right by the standards of his subculture precisely because it is wrong by the norms of the larger culture' (Cohen, 1955, p. 28).

Similarly, Cloward and Ohlin (1961) explain working-class deviance as a collective, rather than an individual solution. In this version of strain theory, however, the problem for the delinquent is to achieve a high status position in terms of lower-class, rather than middle-class, criteria. By combining anomie and differential association theory, these authors were able to explain why one form of adaptation was preferred to another. The answer lay in the differential availability throughout the social structure of legitimate and illegitimate means to gain material and status success. Thus they argued that a *criminal subculture* develops mainly in lower-class neighbourhoods where the successful criminal is not only visible to young people, but is willing to associate with them. Although denied access to the conventional role models of people who have achieved success via legitimate means, these youths do have access to criminal success models. In more disorganized neighbourhoods access even to a criminal subculture is denied. In such situations a *conflict subculture* is more likely to arise in which the lack of legitimate and illegitimate opportunities for material success is solved by achieving status through fighting and violence.

Strain and subcultural theories have, in the main, been largely concerned to explain high rates of delinquency within the lower classes. They take the criminal law and statistical representations of offending rates as given. They propose that both the origins and development of juvenile delinquency are structurally determined, and as such also offer a *general* framework for understanding all crime by contending that the denial of legitimate opportunity acts as the major precipitative factor. In this regard they can be clearly located in a tradition of positivist and determinist modes of analysis. However, subsequent studies, based in particular on self reports, have found that most people from all social classes commit acts for which they could be adjudicated criminal or delinquent. Strain theory is thus said to be both class- and gender-biased. In ignoring both the ubiquity of crime, and its white-collar variants, it cements the notion that lawlessness is exclusively a lower-class and male phenomenon (Lilly et al., 1989, p. 76).

The degree to which behaviour is determined by structure and class position has also been questioned. Matza's (1964) research found that individual members of a gang were only partially committed to subcultural norms. Rather than forming a subculture which stands in antithesis to the dominant order, he argues, the delinquent 'drifts' in and out of deviant activity. This is made possible because there is no consensus in society – no set of basic and core values – but a plurality in which the conventional and the delinquent continually overlap and interrelate. Instead of viewing delinquent acts as a direct expression of delinquent norms and thus system determined, Matza was more concerned to illustrate how their diversity was dependent on particular individuals and situations. This line of enquiry was ultimately to provide a critique of all positivist modes of thought, not just its strain theory variant, in its insistence that *pluralism* rather than consensus and *interaction* rather than determinism provided more adequate means of studying social behaviour (see **Chapter 4.1**).

Nevertheless, traces of strain and anomie theory can be found in numerous subsequent American and British analyses. Adopting a Marxist perspective, Greenberg (1977), for example, argues that the high rate of property crime among youth in America is a response to the disjuncture of the desire to participate in the consumer society and being prevented from securing legitimate funds to enable such participation. From a labelling perspective, Stanley Cohen (1973a) writing of the mods and rockers in 1960s Britain, claims that in part they were driven by 'desperation' because of their exclusion from the leisure goals of mass teenage culture. In Lea and Young's (1984) left realist perspective, youth crime is viewed as a response to the 'relative deprivation', and 'perceptions of injustice' engendered when expectations are not met by real opportunities (see **Chapter 4.2**). In Agnew's (1992) 'revised' and social psychological strain theory it is stressed that when the theory is expanded to focus on all *negative relationships* which may generate anger, despair or resentment – that is, relationships in which individuals are not treated equitably or as they might wish to be – then it has the potential to explain a broad and diverse range of delinquencies from theft and aggression to drug use. Researching the experiences of youth homelessness and street crime in Canada, Hagan and McCarthy (1998) propose an integration of strain with a **social capital** theory of crime in order to explore how unemployed and disrupted families provide a limited 'social capital' for their children and how this subsequently impacts on their success or failure to reach cultural goals. So while the functionalist and essentialist nature of Mertonian strain theory has been widely criticized, the notion that crime may be generated by unequal and restricted opportunities continues to inform some radical and realist 'readings' of youth crime (see **Chapter 4**).

Assessment

Compared to individual positivism, sociological theories appear less interested in crime as a specific pattern of behaviour and more in *probabilistic* accounts of variations in crime rates given particular social, geographical and economic circumstances. They focus on general patterns of criminality rather than on individual motivations.

Nevertheless, early versions of sociological criminology continued to harbour major positivist principles. The concern remained to isolate key causal variables, such as anomie, social disorganization and criminal area, and to infer that such conditions *determined* rates of criminality. Crime remained a violation of a social order that was considered to be based on a consensus of legal and moral codes. As Laurie Taylor (1971, p. 148) has remarked, 'it is as though individuals in society are playing a gigantic fruit machine, but the machine is rigged and only some players are consistently rewarded ... nobody appears to ask who put the machine there in the first place and who takes the profits'. Little room was given to the contrary positions that crime may be a freely chosen course of action and that it may be due to *different* forms of socialization, rather than lack of socialization.

Many of the basic principles of positivism came to be questioned during the 1940s, particularly from within the 'appreciative' strand of the Chicago School (see Box 3.9).

Box 3.9

Critiques of positivism

- It denies the role of human consciousness and meaning in social activity.

- It presents an overdetermined view of human action.

- It assumes that there is an underlying consensus in society, of which crime is a key violation.

- It ignores the presence and relevance of competing value systems, cultural diversity or structural conflict.

- It equates crime with undersocialization or social disorganization rather than accepting the validity of different forms of social organization.

- It exaggerates the difference between the criminal and the non-criminal; fails to recognise ubiquity of crime and different forms across the social spectrum.

- It contains serious methodological difficulties in isolating a specific cause; particularly if cause and correlation are conflated.

Such critiques suggested that non-positivist forms of analysis may offer more fruitful lines of enquiry. The relevance of space, place and economic constraints may remain acknowledged, but their relation to crime is not asserted as determining. Moreover, in such seminal works as Matza's *Delinquency and Drift* (1964), young people are not only (re)bestowed with a degree of free will, but positivism's search for motivational and socio-economic causes of crime is placed in doubt. The main questions of positivism – 'Who is deviant?', 'Why do they do it?' – ignore that crime is not only *action*, but also *infraction*. Actions only become 'crime' when they are defined as such by legal and other institutions.

While positivism retains popular and political appeal in both its individual and sociological variants, it is by no means universally accepted. Some would argue that the use of the scientific method remains superior to conjecture or polemic, but such methodology carries no automatic guarantee of uncovering the 'truth'. Inaccurate assumptions, misinterpretations, misapplication of findings and inadequate measures for testing can all conspire to produce not only misleading but also dangerous conclusions. Assumptions are likely to be made about exactly which factors, from a myriad of the potentially relevant, are worthy of study. In this, the selection of particular variables will depend on *a priori* assumptions the scientist holds about the nature of human behaviour. There is also the potential misuse to which some theories can be put. As McCaghy pointed out:

> Since there are several possible theories concerning the fundamental nature of man, it should not be surprising that since the advent of positivism every human appendage has been measured, every emotion plumbed, every social influence probed and every bodily fluid scrutinized. As a further result of such theories, social environments have been engineered, parts of the brain removed, families counselled, organs lopped off and many sorts of chemicals injected into the human system. All this has been done in the apparently limitless search for answers to the question of why some ignore or disobey others' concepts of right-eous behaviour. (McCaghy, 1976, p. 9)

Nevertheless despite a failure to keep its promise of scientific certainty, it would be dangerous to dismiss the continuing appeal positivism holds for political, popular and (some) academic audiences. Yet it must also be acknowledged that this endeavour, focused as it is on trying to unravel what causes disaffected teenage boys, in particular, to engage in delinquent behaviour has fundamentally restricted the criminological imagination for over a century (Brown, 2005). This 'youth criminology' has typically reproduced the following propositions as universal criminological 'truths' (Braithwaite, 1989, pp. 44–50):

1 Crime is committed disproportionately by males.

2 Crime is committed disproportionately by 15–25 year olds.

3 Crime is committed disproportionately by unmarried people.

4 Crime is committed disproportionately by people living in large cities.

5 Crime is committed disproportionately by people who have experienced high residential mobility and who live in areas characterized by high residential mobility.

6 Young people who are strongly attached to their school are less likely to engage in crime.

7 Young people who have high educational and occupational aspirations are less likely to engage in crime.

8   Young people who perform poorly at school are more likely to engage in crime.

9   Young people who are strongly attached to their parents are less likely to engage in crime.

10 Young people who have friendships with criminals are more likely to engage in crime themselves.

11 People who believe strongly in the importance of complying with the law are less likely to violate the law.

12 Being at the bottom of the class structure increases rates of offending for all types of crime (apart from white-collar crime).

13 Crime rates have been increasing in most countries since the Second World War.

Such 'conclusions' are continually reproduced, but only because of a failure to look beyond the official statistics of recorded crime or beyond legal definitions of crime (see **Chapter 4.3**). It is indeed the case, as Sumner (1994, p. 137) eloquently concluded, that 'a sizeable chunk of criminology today [still] remains locked in the emotional-conceptual-political prison within which Lombroso did a long sentence'.

▓ ■ Summary ■

- Positivism has formed the bedrock of most criminological research over the past century. The belief that it is possible to distinguish criminal traits and circumstances from those of the 'law-abiding' (and thereby be able to respond effectively) remains one of the most enduring political and scientific aspirations.

- This chapter has reviewed a wide variety of criminological theory which has attempted to find the causes of youth crime in a range of biological, personality and environmental conditions. Despite their obvious differences, in the main they all share the basic assumption that criminality is a behavioural problem and that people are propelled into crime by circumstances over which they have no control. This is the defining characteristics of positivist criminology: that crime is *caused* either by individual 'pathologies' and/or by precipitative social and economic conditions.

- The chapter has not been designed to provide answers to the many issues and debates about what causes young people to commit crime, but to compare different theories and suggest ways in which they can be subject to critical enquiry. The simple desire to discover the 'facts' of youth crime causation is far from a straightforward exercise. This is partly because, even within positivism, there is no *one* criminology but a variety of competing positions. Box 3.10 provides a summary of some of the major theories and theorists which occupy this field.

Box 3.10

Positivist theories of youth crime

Theory	Explanation of crime	Key theorists
Somatotyping	Mesomorphic body type	Sheldon (1949)
Genetics	Heredity	Mednick, et al. (1987)
Bio-social	Multi-risk factors, including genetics, lack of discipline, personality, low IQ, family background	Wilson and Herrnstein (1985) Farrington (1996)
Personality	Extroversion/psychopathology, affectionless character/ psychosocial disorder	Bowlby (1946) Eysenck (1964/1970) Rutter and Smith (1995)
Anomie and strain	Disjunction between high aspirations and restricted opportunities/status frustration	Merton (1938, 1957) Cohen (1955) Cloward and Ohlin (1961)
Social ecology	Breakdown of urban communities	Shaw and McKay (1942)
Differential association	Beyond positivism? Learnt through exposure to an excess of influences favourable to violations of the law	Sutherland (1939)

- Although positivism is capable of revealing *correlations* between offending and such factors as age, personality, peer groups, urban space, and so on, it can never unequivocally state that any *one* factor is the chief causative agency.

- No one theory can, or should, be expected to be capable of accounting for all forms of youthful offending. The category of 'youth crime' covers a wide variety of behaviours and activities – from petty theft to violence – and in itself is subject to changing legal, moral and social definition. Indeed, most of the theories we have considered focus not on all forms of youth misbehaviour and legal transgression but on those that have come to the notice of official agencies and are recorded in the criminal statistics. Because such statistics consistently reveal strong correlations between offending and young, male and low-income sections of the population, it is to these groups that most academic research (and public outrage) are directed.

- While these associations undoubtedly have some validity (and many criminological theories take them for granted), they do allow statistical indices to set the research and policy agendas. In contrast, self report studies have revealed that not only is young offending more widespread, but that it is not simply the province of working-class urban males who have 'failed families' or who have 'failed' at school or who live in 'failing' neighbourhoods.

- Positivist approaches lay claim to truth, accuracy and rationality, but their fundamental approach to understanding behaviour ignores a wide range of cognitive processes, situational contingencies, accidents and mistakes which are not amenable to quantitative and scientific measurement.

- As will be discussed in Chapter 4, crime is not simply a behavioural problem. It is also a means of stigmatizing what is considered to be 'undesirable' and of legitimating the control of particular sections of the population while ignoring the legal, social and moral transgressions of those considered to be 'the normal law abiding majority'.

study questions

1 How far is youth crime determined by constitutional factors such as physiology and genetics?

2 How far is youth crime determined by the 'pathological' conditions of adolescence?

3 How far is youth crime determined by social factors, such as 'strains' in the urban environment and economic deprivation?

4 Is youth crime normal or pathological?

5 How can the argument be sustained that 'young people are propelled into crime through circumstances beyond their control'?

Further Reading

There are now numerous textbook introductions to criminology in general such as the American-based Beirne and Messerschmidt (1991; 3rd edition, 2000) and the UK-based Newburn (2007), Carrabine et al. (2004) and Hale et al. (2005) which all include accessible outlines of key criminological theories. But for a thorough understanding of the divergences and disputes in positivist theories of youth crime (and in criminology in general), all of the original authors cited in Box 3.10 deserve attention.

One of the most comprehensive and accessible theoretical reviews is Einstadter and Henry's (1995; 2nd edition, 2006) *Criminological Theory*. Tierney's *Criminology: Theory and Context* (1996; 2nd edition, 2006) is an introductory text focusing on historical shifts and resonances. Downes and Rock's *Understanding Deviance* (1982; 5th edition, 2007), White and Haines' *Crime and Criminology* (2000; 3rd edition, 2004) and Hopkins Burke's *Introduction to Criminological Theory* (2001; 2nd edition, 2005) clearly illustrate theoretical diversity. Valier's *Theories of Crime and Punishment* (2002) is a more advanced critical and appreciative text which explores the social and cultural contexts from which principal theories of crime – from the eighteenth century to the present – have emerged. All include specific chapters devoted to a critical examination of positivist knowledges.

On youth and crime specifically, Rutter et al.'s (1998) *Anti-Social Behaviour by Young People* (largely an update of Rutter and Giller, 1983) reviews numerous theories and indeed restricts itself to those that are largely positivist in nature. Farrington (2007) is the leading contemporary exponent of positivist and predictive 'knowledges'.

Some of the best critiques of positivism in general remain that of Matza (1964) in his *Delinquency and Drift* and Chapter 2 of Taylor et al.'s *The New Criminology* (1973).

http://www.crimetheory.com
An American site with brief introductions to some of the early criminological theories and theorists and including full text of some of the classics such as Beccaria's *On Crime and Punishment*.

http://en.wikipedia.org/wiki/Criminology
Another brief introduction to some of the major positivist and orthodox criminological paradigms.

http://www.emiledurkheim.com/
This site provides a comprehensive bibliography and access to online materials by, and about, Émile Durkheim, considered by many to be 'the father of sociology'.

http://www.museocriminologico.it/.htm
The website of the criminological museum in Rome which holds exhibits and details the work of the Italian School of criminology including Lombroso.

http://www.internetjournalofcriminology.com/
A free online journal carrying a wide range of scholarly articles on criminology, including youth and crime.

http://www.britsoccrim.org/
The British Society of Criminology with links to various resources including selected proceedings from the society's annual conferences.

http://www.asc41.com/
The American Society of Criminology.

http://www.anzsoc.org/
The Australian and New Zealand Society of Criminology.

http://www.crimsociety.wlu.ca/
The Canadian Society of Criminology.

http://www.esc-eurocrim.org
The European Society of Criminology.

http://wcr.sonoma.edu/
The Western Society of Criminology based in Sacramento, California, and including access to their on-line journal.

4

Explaining Youth Crime II: Radical and Realist Criminologies

Overview

Chapter 4 examines:

- the emergence of radical criminologies in the 1960s and 1970s;

- crime as a social construction and the relationship between crime and social control;

- the distinction between 'crime' and 'criminalization';

- the relevance of gender in constructions of youth crime;

- the appropriation of the crime debate by 'realist' criminologies in the 1980s and 1990s;

- problems inherent in any attempt to discover the 'cause' of youth crime;

- the relationship between crime and social harm.

| **key terms** |

abolitionism; classical Marxism; critical criminology; deviancy amplification; drift; folk devil; hegemonic masculinity; interactionism; labelling; left realism; modernity; moral panic; postmodernism; pyrrhic defeat; racialization; rational choice; relative deprivation; right realism; social harm; underclass

---

This chapter explores how the 'positivist orthodoxy' discussed in Chapter 3 was subsequently challenged by a range of radical criminologies first emerging in the 1960s and reworked by realist criminologies which surfaced in the 1980s and 1990s.

Radical criminologies were marked by a deep scepticism of any theory that proposed that crime was 'caused' in a simple cause–effect fashion. Although adopting diverse research agendas from analyses of labelling and moral panics to structural conflict and gender issues, they were more concerned to explore processes of criminalization – how crime was 'created' through the power to define certain behaviour as illegal.

Realist criminologies can be considered as products of the 1980s and 1990s and are epitomized by the attempts of some sections of the right to reintroduce notions of individual moral culpability into the 'crime debate' and by some sections of the left to reintroduce notions of social causation.

The chapter concludes by examining a number of key problems in any attempt to unearth the causes of youth crime. Most significantly, it asks why it is, after over one hundred years of academic endeavour, no one 'cause' is deemed irrefutable. Why is it that we seem to be left with a never-ending series of disputes and debates? Why does the 'youth problem' seem to lie beyond criminological resolution? The limitations of criminology as an academic discipline, when its subject matter is pre-determined by criminal law, are exposed with reference to the challenges posed by postmodern and social harm perspectives.

Radical Criminologies

4.1 The term 'radical criminology' can be used as a convenient umbrella term under which a number of diverse theories (whose chief characteristic is one of anti-positivism) can be drawn together. This section examines how interactionism, labelling, Marxism, critical criminology and gender studies have shifted the object of enquiry away from explanations of why a pathological few transgress legal codes, towards an analysis that focuses more on the activities of competing interest groups and how processes of law creation and enforcement are implicated in the causation of the (young) criminal. In the USA, this 'radical turn' was most associated with a group of radical scholars based on the West coast; in Britain it was a foundational inspiration for the National Deviancy Conference (see Box 4.1).

Box 4.1
The National Deviancy Conference (NDC)

The NDC was formed in July 1968, a radical breakaway from a criminological establishment that was then graphically represented by the Home Office-sponsored criminology conferences being held at the Cambridge Institute of Criminology. The NDC was critical of the medico-psychological assumptions and positivist tendencies of mainstream criminology which it saw as primarily acting to support repressive state practices. It was a 'heady mixture of well-meaning liberalism, romantic anarchism and New Left style Marxism'.

Its founding members were Kit Carson, Stan Cohen, David Downes, Mary McIntosh, Paul Rock, Ian Taylor, and Jock Young.

The group proceeded to organize numerous conferences between 1968 and 1979 but just as significantly sought to provide financial support and a forum for campaign groups around social justice and criminal justice, such as the Claimants' Union, the Preservation of the Rights of Prisoners (PROP), Radical Alternatives to Prison (RAP), Case Con (a forum for radical social work) and People not Psychiatry.

It was subsequently influential in the establishment of the European Group for the Study of Deviance and Social Control which held its first meeting in Florence, Italy, in 1972.

Source: Derived from Cohen (1988); van Swaaningen (1997); Young (2002).

The first traces of anti-positivism were found in the 1930s within an interactionist school of sociology. In contrast to positivism, **interactionism** presented a view of the world which emphasized the flexibility of individual responses to social situations. Rather than viewing behaviour as determined by 'external' forces, interactionism was more concerned with questions of human choice, voluntarism and the variability of meaning in everyday life. It owed much to a philosophy of 'subjective realism' and echoed the appreciative strand of the 1930s Chicago School of Sociology (see **Chapter 3.2**). For example, George Herbert Mead (1934) argued that 'the self' is a social construct and that the way in which individuals act and regard themselves is in part a consequence of the way others see and react to them. This shifted the focus away from macro social structures and their determining effect, to the meso and micro personal interactions that make up social life. Human action was deemed voluntarist, forever changing and adaptive to social conditions. In this conception of human nature it made no sense to depict the social order as consensual. Rather, that order comprised a set of fluid relationships embracing conflict, domination, exploitation and disagreement, as well as co-operation and consensus.

Nor did it make much sense to argue that criminality is *caused*. If criminals were as different from the law-abiding as positivists assumed, then individual criminality would be a more permanent and all-pervasive phenomenon. In *Delinquency and Drift*, Matza (1964) argued forcefully that delinquency is transient and intermittent. Juvenile delinquents are not that different from other juveniles. Conformist values and non-conformist values often intersect and propagate similar desires, such as for hedonism, fun and excitement. The delinquent is committed neither to the mainstream nor to a delinquent culture, but chooses to **drift** between one or the another 'in a limbo between convention and crime responding in turn to the demands of each, flirting now with one, now with the other, but postponing commitment, evading decision' (Matza, 1964, p. 28). Moreover delinquents are able to move freely between delinquency and conformity, by adopting various rationalizations to justify their behaviour. According to Sykes and Matza (1957), these techniques of neutralization include:

- denial of responsibility (I didn't mean it);

- denial of injury (I didn't really cause any harm);

- denial of victim (he deserved it);

- condemnation of condemners (they always pick on us);

- appeal to higher loyalties (you've got to help your mates).

In these ways positivism's rigid separation of the criminal and non-criminal, and its insistence that criminality is not chosen but determined by external pressures, were called into question. Matza argued that most delinquents 'grow out of' crime precisely because they are never seriously committed to it in the first place.

Interactionism was also a crucial reference point for a *pluralist* conception of crime and deviance. Deviance could no longer be viewed simply as a pathological act that violated consensual norms, but was something created in the *process* of social interaction, in which some people who commit deviant acts come to be known as deviants whereas others do not. In one of the earliest formulations, Frank Tannenbaum (1938) argued that deviance was created through a process of social interaction. While a majority commit deviant acts, only a minority come to be known as deviant. The known deviant is then targeted, identified, defined and treated as such even though their behaviour may be no different to those who have not been so identified. As a result, certain people 'become deviant' through the imposition of social judgements on their behaviour: they *become* the essence of what is being complained of.

In short, interactionism opened up a new line of critical enquiry by posing definitional rather than behavioural questions – 'Who defines another as deviant?'; 'How does that person react to such designation?' Rules and regulations cannot be accepted as 'givens' but are sites of negotiation and dispute. In addressing such issues, it was necessary not only to begin to study how rules/laws were created, but also to ask in whose interests they were enforced. As a result the subject matter of criminology was considerably expanded to incorporate theories of power, social order and the state and processes of social control and resistance. The meaning of 'crime' itself became politicized.

Labelling and Moral Panics

The **labelling** perspective is distinctive because it begins from the assumption that no act is intrinsically criminal. What counts as crime and deviance is forever problematic because deviance only arises from the imposition of social judgements on others' behaviour. Such judgements are established by the powerful through the formulation of laws and their interpretation and enforcement by police, courts and other controlling institutions. But these formulations and interpretations are by no means constant: they change according to historical contingencies and individual discretion. Thus exactly what constitutes 'crime' and 'deviance' is subject to historical and social variability. Neither can be 'objectively' defined because their existence always depends on a series of negotiated transactions between rule makers/enforcers and rule violators (see Box 4.2).

▌Box 4.2
Principles of labelling

Deviance is not a property *inherent in* certain forms of behaviour; it is a property *conferred upon* these forms by the audiences which directly or indirectly witness them. Sociologically, then, the critical variable in the study of deviance is the social *audience*, rather than the individual *person*.
Kai T. Erikson (1962, p. 308)

Deviance may be conceived as a process by which the members of a group, community, or society (1) interpret behavior as deviant, (2) define persons who so behave as a certain kind of deviant and (3) accord them the treatment considered appropriate to such deviants.
John Kitsuse (1962, p. 248)

Deviance is *not* a quality of the act the person commits, but rather a consequence of the application by others of rules and sanctions to an 'offender'. The deviant is one to whom that label has successfully been applied; deviant behaviour is behaviour that people so label.
Howard Becker (1963, p. 9)

This is a large turn away from older sociology which tended to rest heavily upon the idea that deviance leads to social control. I have come to believe that the reverse idea, i.e., social control leads to deviance, is equally tenable and the potentially richer premise for studying deviance in modern society.
Edwin Lemert (1967, p. v)

The twin concepts of 'label' and 'career' are central to labelling in explaining how deviance is first constructed and subsequently cemented in future behaviour. Lemert (1967) distinguished between primary deviance – isolated, relatively insignificant rule breaking (e.g. petty theft, classroom misbehaviour) – and secondary deviance – the construction of a deviant identity as a result of social reaction to the initial act. In making this distinction, Lemert emphasized, first, that deviance is a process, and, second, that social control is not simply a response to deviant activity, but plays an active and propelling role in its creation and promotion. This proposition that *social control causes deviance* effectively stood the premises of positivist criminologies on their head. Labelling also raised a number of questions about how the labelled react to their newfound status and change their lifestyle to accord with their new identity. A number of studies were published in the 1960s and 1970s which attempted to reveal the process of *becoming* a marijuana smoker, a juvenile delinquent, a prostitute, a homosexual, and so on. In each, it was the application of a stigmatizing label that was considered pivotal in informing future behaviour patterns. Lemert (1951), for example, argued that while most youths commit some delinquent acts, only a few are eventually labelled as delinquent. Official reactions (condemnation, treatment, punishment) to this few do not deter or reform but initiate processes that push the labelled delinquent towards further delinquent conduct. If there is no official reaction, delinquent behaviour may dissipate or at least will not accelerate, because the notion of a delinquent 'career' will not be established.

The implications of attaching a particular label to certain behaviours are evident in Stanley Cohen's (1968; 1973c) analyses of 'vandalism'. Vandalism is not a legal category but a label attached to certain incidents of property damage, defacement or destruction. Conjuring up images of 'barbarity', 'ignorance' and 'ruthlessness', it is differentially applied, denying 'meaning' to certain actions while turning a blind eye to others. As Cohen (1968, p. 17) remarked:

> Painting 'Fink College is the Best' on a wall is not vandalism, painting 'Stop Making Bombs' is. Destroying property during rags is 'youthful exuberance' and after all 'for a good cause', but destroying property during a political demonstration is 'thoughtless hooliganism'.

By categorizing 'vandalism' into five main types – acquisitive, tactical, vindictive, play and malicious – Cohen (1973c) provides meaning and sense for behaviours that are commonly condemned as 'meaningless' or 'senseless' (see Box 4.3).

Pearson (1975) also directs our attention to another form of 'vandalism' – that indirectly performed by planners and architects. Following observations in a Cardiff park, he noted how juvenile vandalism became more frequent when the park was closed and rescheduled for office development. As he rightly questioned: 'Just who are the vandals in the park?' Such critical readings of media labels in the 1960s and 1970s not only granted 'meaning' to criminality and 'humanized' the deviant (Muncie and Fitzgerald, 1981), but enabled alternative definitions of crime to be promoted. For example, as environmental protection groups have increasingly asked: which is the more serious, dumping toxic waste in the sea or breaking windows in derelict factories? And why is one routinely labelled as criminal damage, while the other is not?

Box 4.3

Making sense of vandalism

- *Acquisitive vandalism*, Cohen argues, is in some respects akin to petty theft. Damage is done in the course of acquiring money or property such as stripping lead, removing street signs and looting coin boxes.

- *Tactical vandalism* is a conscious tactic used to advance some end other than acquiring money or property through the use of slogans and graffiti of a political nature.

- *Vindictive vandalism* is a form of revenge against persons or institutions believed to be the source of personal grievance. Much school vandalism is of this type.

- *Play vandalism* is motivated by curiosity and the spirit of competition and skill. The fact that property may be destroyed is often minor or incidental.

- *Malicious vandalism* is the category that most closely corresponds to dominant media and public images of apparently mindless and wanton destruction. But Cohen contends that such actions can also be explained by reference to a variety of subjective feelings – boredom, despair, failure and frustration – and that they can be rendered intelligible through understanding the context in which they occur.

Source: Derived from Cohen (1973c).

Above all, labelling denies that criminality is driven by any peculiar motivation or that criminals are a species apart. Rather, crime is ordinary, natural and widespread and requires no more special an explanation than for any other everyday activity. What needs an explanation is the complex process by which moral entrepreneurs and agencies of social control are able to realize the public identification of certain people as criminal; how social reaction and labelling of certain acts act to produce and reproduce a recognizable 'crime problem'. One of the characteristic ways in which the non-conformity of some sections of society is 'demonized' is through the generation of moral panics and perceptions of 'crime waves'.

The term **moral panic** was first used by Jock Young in his study of 'drug-takers' published in 1971. But it was only from the following year when it appeared in the title of Stanley Cohen's book *Folk Devils and Moral Panics: The Creation of the Mods and Rockers* that it became ubiquitous in criminology and the sociology of deviance. A third edition containing the original text with a new introduction was published exactly 30 years later. Cohen (1967; 1973a) had argued that relatively minor incidents between groups of youth over a bank holiday weekend were exaggerated by media reportage and magnified by subsequent police and judicial targeting. Their deviance was amplified through social reaction which in turn produced an actual amplification in real levels of deviancy as the mods and rockers took on aspects of their new publicly defined personas. Wilkins (1964) had referred to such processes as a **deviancy amplification** spiral. Such youthful 'rowdyism' was of course by no means new (Pearson, 1983; and see **Chapter 2**) but it was to receive front page outrage in the national press. The media spoke of a 'day of terror'; of youngsters who 'beat up an entire town'; of a town being invaded by a mob 'hell-bent on destruction'. Youths were presented as being engaged in a confrontation between easily recognizable rival gangs – 'mods' or 'rockers'. Cohen's research, on the other hand, found no evidence of any structured gangs. The typical offence throughout was not assault or malicious damage, but threatening behaviour. A few days after the event a journalist was forced to admit that the affair had been 'a little over-reported'.

Cohen argued that this over-reporting set in train a series of interrelated responses. First, it initiated a wider public concern which obliged the police to step up their surveillance of the two groups. Second, an emphasis on the antagonism between the groups, and their stylistic differences, encouraged the youths to place themselves in one of the opposing camps. Third, continuing disturbances attracted more news coverage, increased police activity and further public concern. Exploring the socio-economic background to these events Cohen argued that the mid-1960s was the time of a supposedly new permissiveness, a rise in working-class youth spending power, the onslaught of a new consumerism, and decline of traditional working-class communities. Public anxiety, uncertainty and anomie circulating around these social changes were 'resolved' by identifying certain social groups as scapegoats or **folk devils**. They became the visual symbols of what was wrong with society. The more intractable and structural problems to do with deprivation and restricted opportunities were passed by in a developing climate of pervasive social control.

In *Policing the Crisis*, Hall et al. (1978) reused the concept of moral panic in identifying a series of concerns about permissiveness, vandals, student radicals, football hooligans, and so on, culminating in 1972–73 with the moral panic of 'mugging'. Hall et al. showed how the news media, working with images from the New York ghetto, defined the incidence of street robberies by youth in Britain's inner cities as an outbreak of a new and dangerous kind of violent crime. What was previously known as 'snatching' or 'getting rolled' – or in the nineteenth century as 'garrotting' – was now defined as 'mugging'. This label was employed to justify not only a new category of crime, but also punitive sentencing and an image of a generalized breakdown of law and order in society. Also, as the panic developed, mugging became defined almost exclusively as a problem with black youth – they became the primary folk devils. The notion of moral panic was central to both studies in explaining how particular sections of youth (working-class/black) become identified as worthy of police and judicial attention. The implications of such identification were, however, extended by Hall et al. For them, a moral panic is the first link in a spiral of events leading to the maintenance of law in society by legitimized rule through coercion and the general exercise of authority. The enunciation of authoritarian policies, if repeated often enough, is able to form the terrain of any debate concerned with issues of law and order. As Hall succinctly put it in writing about football hooliganism: 'the tendency is increased to deal with any problem, first by simplifying its causes, second by stigmatizing those involved, third by whipping up public feeling and fourth by stamping hard on it from above' (Hall, 1978, p. 34) (see Box 4.4).

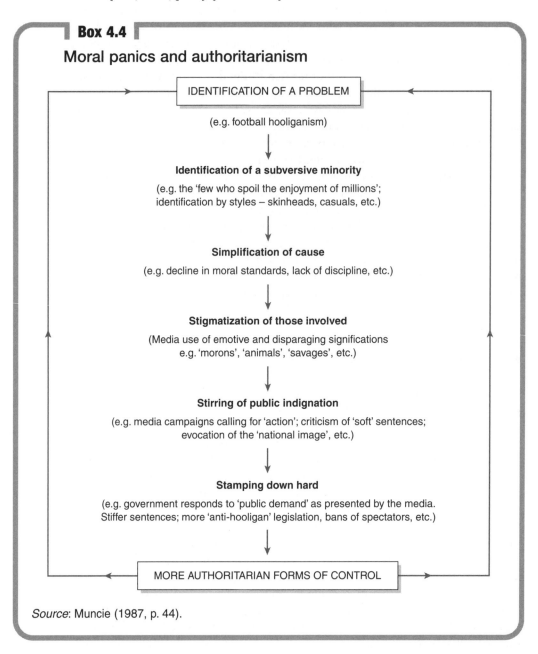

Box 4.4

Moral panics and authoritarianism

IDENTIFICATION OF A PROBLEM

(e.g. football hooliganism)

Identification of a subversive minority

(e.g. the 'few who spoil the enjoyment of millions';
identification by styles – skinheads, casuals, etc.)

Simplification of cause

(e.g. decline in moral standards, lack of discipline, etc.)

Stigmatization of those involved

(Media use of emotive and disparaging significations
e.g. 'morons', 'animals', 'savages', etc.)

Stirring of public indignation

(e.g. media campaigns calling for 'action'; criticism of 'soft' sentences;
evocation of the 'national image', etc.)

Stamping down hard

(e.g. government responds to 'public demand' as presented by the media.
Stiffer sentences; more 'anti-hooligan' legislation, bans of spectators, etc.)

MORE AUTHORITARIAN FORMS OF CONTROL

Source: Muncie (1987, p. 44).

Subsequently, as Cohen (2002) records, the concept has been used in a wide variety of forms to explore reactions not only to unruly working-class youth but also school violence, drugs, single parenting, permissiveness, paedophilia, satanic abuse, asylum seekers, and so on. Its use now appears ubiquitous, often ungrounded and employed as much by the media themselves as by radical scholars. Goode and Ben-Yehuda (1994) attempted a more precise definition by noting the five key characteristics of: concern, hostility, consensus, disproportionality and volatility. They concluded that moral panics serve as a mechanism for simultaneously strengthening and redrawing society's moral boundaries – the line between morality and immorality. When a society's moral boundaries are sharp, clear and secure and the central values are strongly held by nearly everyone, moral panics rarely grip its members. However, when the moral boundaries are fuzzy and shifting and often seem to be contested, moral panics are far more likely to take hold.

Nevertheless the concept has been critiqued for a lack of any precise theoretical grounding (Plummer, 1979); for being a polemical rather than an analytical concept (Waddington, 1986); for ignoring the reality of crime (Lea and Young, 1984) and for simplifying complex processes of media representation, public perception and pressure group contestation (McRobbie and Thornton, 1995). Left realism (see Section 4.2 below) maintained that crime and the fear of crime should be taken seriously and not dismissed as 'just' an expression of media over-reaction or panic (see Box 4.5).

Box 4.5

Limitations of labelling

- Failure to address why people commit criminal acts in the first place. For positivists, its premises lacked empirical evidence and were un-testable.

- By concentrating on 'victimless' crimes such as drug taking, homosexuality, and so on, labelling appeared to insufficiently recognize the fundamental deviance attached to other 'serious crimes' such as domestic violence, murder, rape and institutional violence. For some it was simply indefensible to claim that 'no act is intrinsically criminal'.

- A complex of motivations may underlie the development of deviant careers, of which social reaction might play a relatively small part.

- Labelling may have rejected the determinism of psychological, biological and social factors as causes of crime, but seemed to have had simply replaced them with the determinism of social reaction. In both cases, the deviant was depicted as 'driven' rather than acting voluntarily.

- Labelling has been most commonly applied to explain escalations in expressive forms of deviancy. In 'humanizing deviance', it has been accused of over-romanticizing deviant behaviour with labelling theorists acting as voyeuristic 'zookeepers of deviancy'.

- As a result of the above, labelling is viewed by many as a 'sensitizing concept' and not meeting the requirements for a fully worked up criminological theory.

McRobbie and Thornton (1995) were also persuasive in their argument that moral panic, rather than necessarily being an unwanted label designed to denigrate youth cultural pursuits, has become something to be actively pursued by youth themselves.

Indeed, the growing prevalence of niche media, lobbies, pressure groups and commercial interests has made it virtually impossible to talk of discrete moral panics (or discrete youth cultures) as in Cohen's original use of the term. Rather we appear enmeshed in an endless debate about deviance, difference, and diversity in a climate of permanent public unease and fear (Feeley and Simon, 2007, and see **Chapter 6**).

Classical Marxism, Critical Criminology and Processes of Criminalization

Labelling clearly opened up the area of analysis of how deviance was identified and processed by the defining agencies, and how conformity to social rules and norms was secured. However, these relations are not simply subjective encounters, but social processes set in objective historical conditions. Control agencies have an institutional location and function within a particular structure of power. To apply the insights of labelling to concrete situations, it was necessary to consider the issue of social control within a broader analysis of social structure or the state. It was necessary to explore how the abstract notion of social control connected to the maintenance of social order in particular types of social formation (see **Chapter 7.1**). Such analysis required a general model of society and the state to which crime and deviance could be related. In this context the insights of Marxist analyses of crime and the law in capitalist societies have been drawn upon (Marx, 1859, 1865; Marx and Engels, 1848).

One of the core elements of **classical Marxism** is that all social phenomena are explainable in terms of each society's means of production or economic relations. In a capitalist economy, the private ownership of the means of production and control over the exchange of wealth creates both structural inequality and structural conflict. In this respect classical Marxism clearly challenges positivist conceptions of the social order as consensual. However, it also retains a view of human action as grounded in degrees of determinism. The exploitation of the proletariat by the bourgeoisie is viewed as endemic. Deviance can be seen as an expression of a struggle in which the economically powerless attempt to cope with the exploitation and poverty imposed upon them. While Marx wrote little on crime *per se*, a number of influential propositions have been derived from his general analysis. First, that crime is not caused by moral or biological defects, but by fundamental conflicts in the social order. Second, that crime is an inevitable feature of existing capitalist societies because it is an expression of basic social inequalities. Third, that working-class crime results from the demoralization caused by labour exploitation, material misery and appalling conditions at home and in the factories. Fourth, that in certain respects such crimes as theft, arson and sabotage may be considered a form of primitive rebellion – a protest or rebellion against bourgeois forms of property ownership and control. Finally, Marx stressed that the extent and forms of crime could only be understood in the context of specific class relations and the nature of the state and law associated with particular modes of production.

The Dutch academic, Bonger (1916), was the first systematically to apply a theory of social order based on the notion of structural conflict to the topic of crime. His argument is encapsulated in the following propositions:

- Notions of immorality and criminality are socially and historically variable.

- The criminal law exists to protect the interests of the powerful.

- Capitalism is held together by coercive exploitation rather than co-operative consensus.

- Capitalism encourages egoism and greed. In the pursuit of such 'pleasures' both proletariat and bourgeoisie become prone to crime as their sense of responsibility towards each other is diminished.

- Poverty prompts crime to the extent that it creates a desperate need for food and other necessities.

- Crime also results when there is a perceived opportunity to gain an advantage through illegal means and/or when opportunities to achieve pleasure are closed off by a biased legal system.

For Bonger, the competitive and individualist tendencies of capitalism actively encourage an unbridled egoism in which acts of criminality are likely to flourish. Significantly, he recognized that crime was not confined to the working classes. The bourgeoisie was also criminogenic because of the opportunities for crime that accompanied their power and because of a lack of morality within capitalist modes of production. The higher rate of recorded criminality in the working classes was viewed as a product of inequitable economic relationships in a context of general poverty.

It was not until some 60 years later that subsequent researchers (e.g. Quinney, 1970; Chambliss, 1975) more fully developed the notion that modes of economic production impact on all social relations in which particular notions of 'crime' are constructed (see Box 4.6).

Box 4.6

Crime, class, capitalism and conflict

- Acts are defined as criminal because it is in the interest of the ruling class to define them as such.

- The ruling class will violate laws with impunity while members of the subject classes will be punished.

- Criminal behaviour is a consequence of the repression and brutalization of capitalism.

- Crime diverts the working class's attention from the exploitation they experience; it contains their resistance.

- Crime will persist in capitalist societies because of the fundamental tendency of such societies to promote inequality and class conflict.

Source: Derived from Chambliss (1975).

The proposition that patterns of crime are intimately connected to modes of economic production has been taken up in a number of ways. For example, Spitzer (1975) argued that deviants and criminals are 'constructed' when certain groups create problems for those who rule. In other words, those who call into question the social conditions under which capitalist production takes place (for instance, the bohemian or New Age traveller who refuses to perform routine wage labour) or those who fail to comply with processes of socialization for production roles (e.g. those who refuse to be schooled) or those who adopt deviant patterns of consumption (e.g. those who use alcohol/drugs for escape) are likely to find themselves criminalized. Similarly, Greenberg (1977) 'appropriated Marxian theory for criminology' by identifying a number of *structural* sources of youth crime. The most significant of these were exclusion from work, extended schooling, dependence on peers for approval, and obstacles to the acquisition of legitimate sources of funds. In consumer societies, young people face considerable pressure to turn to illegitimate means to finance their leisure. Youth property crimes serve as an alternative to work. Similarly, interpersonal violence, committed largely by males, is viewed as symptomatic of masculine status anxiety. Exclusion from the labour market, inability to achieve traditional cultural expectations, and structural constraints on status attainment all combine to generate male criminality.

In these ways, classical Marxism has been developed to promote a more complex analysis of why certain behaviours are criminalized by the state while others are not, and how a capitalist economic system itself is capable of generating certain patterns of crime (Beirne and Messerschmidt, 1991, p. 498). For example, in Britain, Taylor, Walton and Young, writing under the auspices of *The New Criminology* (1973), attempted to fuse such Marxist principles with the insights gained from interactionism and labelling. They sought to synthesize an interactionist approach to deviance, focusing on its meaning for the individuals involved, with a structural approach grounded in the analysis of political economy, class relations and state practices (see Box 4.7).

Box 4.7

Constituent elements of a 'fully social theory of deviance'

- *The wider origins of the deviant act* (the economic and political contingencies of advanced industrial society).

- *The immediate origins of the deviant act* (the interpretation and meaning given to deviance by individuals).

- *The actual act* (the rationality of individual acts and the social dynamics surrounding them).

- *The immediate origins of social reaction* (the contingencies and conditions crucial to the decision to act against the deviant).

- *The wider origins of deviant reaction* (the political and ideological concerns of the state).

- *The outcome of social reaction on the deviant's further action* (the conscious decisions made by an individual to respond to sanctions).

- *The nature of the deviant process as a whole* (the necessity to integrate all elements of the deviant process while being alive to the conditions of social determination and self-determination).

Source: Derived from Taylor et al. (1973, pp. 270–8).

However, *The New Criminology* was not only an attempt to develop the parameters of an adequate criminological theory; it was also designed to promote a form of radical politics. Its insistence that inequalities and divisions in material production and ownership are intrinsically related to the social factors producing crime, brought notions of the possibility of a crime-free society to the fore: a society based on principles of socialist diversity and tolerance. The intention, then, was also to construct the parameters of a radical praxis.

This politicization of criminology was indeed a logical extension of the critical questioning of social science and its role in research, teaching and policy-making that had emerged in the 1960s. Becker (1967) brought such questioning directly into criminology and the sociology of deviance by asking social scientists: 'Whose side are you on?' Social science in general, and individual positivism in particular, were charged with lending the state a spurious legitimacy and functioning as little more than a justification for oppressive power. What such a critique managed to achieve was a radical reconstitution of criminology as part of a more comprehensive sociology of the state and political economy, in which questions of political and social control took precedence over behavioural and correctional issues. By the mid-1970s such reflections on the construction of crime became pivotal in the formulation of a **critical criminology** (Taylor et al., 1975; Hall and Scraton, 1981).

Jeffrey Reiman (1979/2007), for example, argued that the label of 'crime' seems reserved for the 'dangerous actions of the poor' in general and the actions of working-class young males in particular. In his classic text *The Rich Get Richer and the Poor Get Prison* he noted how numerous serious harms such as avoidable deaths and injury in the workplace, medical malpractice, pollution and poverty never enter dominant discourses of crime. The particular ways in which 'the crime problem' is articulated and acted upon by the agencies of criminal justice tend to reproduce structures of class, race and gender discrimination. The aim of criminal justice, he argues, is not to reduce crime or to achieve justice but to construct a public image of the perpetual threat of crime from particular sections of society. To do this, a significant and particular population defined as 'criminal' must be maintained. And to do this, criminal justice must be designed to fail to reduce crime. Reiman refers to this 'upside-down' idea of criminal justice as **pyrrhic defeat** theory in which criminal justice serves the powerful, not by its success but by its very failure. The public is continually presented with a partial and distorted image that crime is largely the actions of the poor. More dangerous acts committed by the powerful are ignored or not defined as criminal. The image conveyed is that the real danger comes from below rather than from above. Criminal justice must be seen to fight (some) crime but never enough to reduce or eliminate it. This helps to explain why criminal justice regularly produces the same 'problem populations' and also why it often appears to be in perpetual crisis. The ideological fiction of criminal justice benefits the economically powerful by helping to keep their own crimes hidden while legitimizing inequalities in wealth through the criminalization and control of the powerless.

Howard Parker's (1974) classic ethnographic research on juvenile theft in an inner-city area of Liverpool adopted a theoretical framework that attempted to capture a dialogue between micro and macro structural variables. In his *View from the Boys*, Parker records how he spent three years 'hanging out' with the lads of 'Roundhouse'. According to the official crime statistics, 'Roundhouse' was the most 'delinquent' area of Liverpool. However, Parker found that delinquency was neither a core part of the Boys' activities, nor the aspect of their behaviour which cemented the group together. Rather they were a loose-knit peer group who had experienced the problems associated with having few educational qualifications in a high unemployment area. Collectively they had turned to a highly instrumental form of delinquency – stealing 'catseyes' (car radios) as a solution to their lack of money. Such theft was important mainly because it provided resources for leisure. 'Roundhouse' was in general a 'condoning community' towards most kinds of delinquency. Theft was regarded as acceptable, if it was from people outside of the local area. The Boys only 'became delinquent' in the eyes of outsiders, social workers, the police and the courts – the 'Authority Conspiracy'. Accordingly, the Boys' commitment to the dominant social order was ambiguous. Moral restraint tended to be community bound, extending beyond only in relation to their fear of authority. Parker concluded that the Boys' involvement in theft was not the 'real problem' at all. Rather these were accommodative and rational solutions arrived at by some working-class youth faced with the constraints of a particular social and economic context.

The clearest example of how critical criminology could be applied to 'youth crime' in a specific historical period was Hall et al.'s (1978) analysis of mugging and the crisis of hegemony in the British state in the 1970s. As we have seen, their work made clear how crime can be defined differently at particular historical moments. This has little to do with actual events, but reveals how the state uses 'crime' to prepare the ground for a general exercise of legal constraint and political control. Condemning crime as a product of 1960s permissiveness, the British state was able to construct public unease about historically recurring street crimes – now labelled as muggings – into popular mobilization of fear and anxiety which were drawn upon to legitimize the construction of an 'exceptional' form of 'authoritarian state'. In an increasingly divided society, the 'young black mugger' became one of the few symbolic sources of unity. The state, faced by a crisis of hegemony brought on by Britain's postcolonial economic decline and reflected in industrial disputes, attempted to regain its legitimacy by defining the crisis as one of lack of respect for the rule of law. The crisis was deflected on to youth, crime and particularly 'race'. The crime debate not only became politicized, but was also significantly subject to **racialization**: a specific section of society was construed as a 'type' by referring to a limited number of their physical or cultural attributes (Solomos, 1988).

Critical criminology also made significant contributions to understanding aspects of youth crime through its impact on youth subcultural and social history research. In particular, it reasserted the centrality of class analysis and modes of resistance in the study of youth subcultures (see **Chapter 6**). In its insistence that crime can only be analysed within its precise socio-historical setting, it also encouraged numerous revisionist histories of how the 'youth problem' is socially constructed in particular historical periods (see **Chapter 2**). Critical criminology, in myriad forms, continues to flourish. Its opposition to those cultures of control, scientism, patriarchy, positivism and correctionalism associated with orthodox criminology remains vital in understanding and challenging how power is exercised, knowledge legitimated and social order maintained (Carrington and Hogg, 2002; Hillyard et al., 2004; Barton et al., 2007; Scraton, 2007) (see Box 4.8).

Box 4.8

Characteristics of critical criminologies

- Human action is voluntaristic (to different degrees), rather than determined (or in some formulations, voluntary in determining contexts).

- Social order is pluralistic or conflictual, rather than consensual.

- Economic policies lead to immiseration and force people to consider turning to crime as a viable survival strategy.

- Criminalization strategies are class, race and gender control strategies that are consciously used to depoliticize political resistance and to control economically and politically marginalized neighbourhoods and groups.

- Moral panics about crime being out of control are used to deflect attention away from inherent structural conflicts.

- Orthodox crime control strategies are incapable of tackling the crimes of the powerful and state crimes.

- Legal categories which claim to be race/gender neutral are riddled with white, male assumptions of what constitutes normal or reasonable behaviour.

- 'Mainstream' criminology requires exposure as a criminology of the state.

- The criminological agenda should be expanded to include those social harms ignored or underplayed in dominant discourse such as gendered and racialized violence, poverty, war, crimes of the powerful, environmental crime, state-sanctioned violence and crimes against humanity.

Feminist Perspectives and Gender Studies

The vast majority of criminological theories – positivist and radical – have traditionally focused on *male* offenders, *male* juvenile delinquents and *male* prison populations. The issues of gender and crime and women and crime remained absent from much criminological discourse until the 1970s. Female deviance was largely perceived as relatively insignificant, given women's under-representation in the official crime statistics. If explained at all, it was with reference to biological difference. Male deviance was accounted for with reference to a host of individual, social and economic factors but very rarely with reference to men's gendered position (see **Chapter 1.3**).

A critical feminist criminology (Klein, 1973; Smart, 1976; Leonard, 1982) first took the form of a critique of the *neglect* and *distortion* of women's experiences that characterized the criminological enterprise. It was noted how such concepts as anomie, strain and subculture had only been applied to male populations. But the exposure of criminology as the criminology of men also marked the starting point of feminist attempts to find alternative ways of conceptualizing the social world. As Leonard (1982, p. 11) asked: 'Why is crime so rampant among men...? What does this imply about the traditional role of men or about our society?'

First, *liberal feminists* (Oakley, 1972) noted how *role theory* may be used to explain differential rates of criminality. Here it is argued that women are socialized to different roles and are subject to more forms of social control than men. The protection and supervision of women and their training to be non-aggressive, dependent and restrained highlight the way in which women are purportedly less predisposed to delinquency. Such an approach challenged traditional notions of sex roles as 'natural' and revealed how gender differences are socially constructed. It also revealed how criminality and masculinity may be linked because the sorts of acts associated with each (aggression, status achievement) have much in common. As Oakley (1972, p. 72) concluded, 'the dividing line between what is masculine and what is criminal may at times be a thin one'.

Second, *radical feminists* (Millett, 1970) argued that crime is intimately related to structures of masculine power and privilege. Patriarchal societies are based on sets of social relationships through which men maintain power over children and women. The power attributed to men is realized in sexual violence and is often condoned by the state. Thus rape, domestic violence and sexual harassment are not so much a problem of male deviance as a problem of dominant notions of acceptable *masculinity*. In short, much criminality (and the subjugation of women) can be accounted for as a problem of patriarchal society which encourages aggression for men and passivity for women.

Third, *socialist feminism* (Rowbotham, 1973) combined insights from Marxist analyses of class and capitalism, and radical feminists' analysis of patriarchy to produce accounts that prioritized neither class nor gender. It is the *interaction* of these relations that structures crime in any given society at any given time. Criminality is the product of the unequal distribution of power in both the market and the home.

These three perspectives decisively demonstrated that not only has criminology traditionally ignored female crime, but also that there is no single feminist criminology. While liberal feminism emphasizes gender role socialization, it has been criticized for lacking a structural explanation of the origin of those roles (Smart, 1976, p. 69). Nor does it explain why a considerable number of women do commit crime, if their socialization into conformity is as effective as assumed. Similarly, the assumption within radical feminism that all women are universally subjugated to male power within the monolith of patriarchy has been critiqued for its essentialism and reductionism. It imputes a single and unitary male personality (Messerschmidt, 1993). In contrast, socialist feminism has come under attack for simply grafting 'gender' on to an uncritical reading of Marxism, for failing to recognize the structuring context of 'race' and for propagating a determinist analysis from which notions of human action or intent remain absent (Carlen, 1992).

Such points of dispute within feminism and between feminism and criminology have led some writers to adopt an explicitly 'anti-criminological' position. Brown

(1986), for example, argues that feminists working within criminology have by necessity uncritically adopted some of its key referents such as 'crime' and 'deviance' and that this has often led to 'unwanted consequences and obstacles to thinking and empirical analysis'. She maintains that awareness of feminist issues or the recording of discriminatory practices do not in themselves amount to a 'feminist analytical project'. Above all, 'in its wish to restore women to their place in criminology or to demonstrate their exclusion from it, feminist criminology has failed to be sufficiently critical of the discipline itself' (Brown, 1986, pp. 366–7). Acceptance of its empirical referents has meant that it has remained 'trapped in essentialist categories obstructing the production of new knowledge' (Carlen, 1992, p. 53). Smart (1990, p. 70) similarly states that 'the core enterprise of criminology is problematic, that feminists' attempts to alter criminology have only succeeded in revitalizing a problematic enterprise'. In this view the problem of criminology, in whatever form, is that by definition it always returns to notions of 'crime' and will be forever drawn to state-defined, 'scientific' analyses and solutions:

> The thing that criminology cannot do is deconstruct crime. It cannot locate rape or child sexual abuse in the domain of sexuality, or theft in the domain of economic activity, or drug use in the domain of health. To do so would be to abandon criminology to sociology; but more importantly it would involve abandoning the idea of a unified problem which requires a unified response. (Smart, 1990, p. 77)

For Smart, the alliance of feminism and criminology is likely to be more damaging for the former, and beneficial only to the latter. Since the 1970s feminism has developed into a broadly based scholarship and political practice addressing questions of philosophy, representations and political engagement. It no longer needs to work through, or be attached to, more restrictive disciplines, such as criminology. Equally, Cain (1989, 1990) notes how feminist criminologists have been increasingly forced to 'transgress criminology, to break out of it'. This involves a distancing from dominant and limiting discourses, recognizing their internal inconsistencies and facilitating moves for women outside or beyond them with impunity. This, by necessity, is a gender-specific exercise:

> Studying women as women and comparing different groups of women, rather than women and men, takes off the blinkers of the male-as-yardstick and male commonsense, so that *new* thoughts can come into the social and criminological worlds. (Cain, 1990, p. 9)

Yet Cain (1990, p. 12) suggests that a 'transgressive criminology' must also tackle the questions of 'what in the social construction of maleness is so profoundly criminogenic: why do males so disproportionately turn out to be criminals?' As we have noted, some critical criminologists (Greenberg, 1977) had begun to frame their explanations of youth crime in terms of a 'masculine status anxiety' induced by exclusion from the labour market, but the question of exactly how masculinity was constituted remained unanswered. In the 1990s, a small but growing literature emerged to 'take masculinity seriously'. The key figure here is the Australian academic Bob Connell (1987, 1995). His chief insight was to recognize 'multiple masculinities': black as well as white, homosexual or heterosexual, working class as well as middle class and that all are subject to change, contingency and open to challenge. Connell (1995, p. 77) accepts that a **hegemonic masculinity** based on a dominant ideal of heterosexual power and authority currently stands at the head of a gender hierarchy among men, but that it is always contested by a series of alternative, subordinate forms, notably from gay men. Male power, then, is not absolute, but historically variable and a contested terrain of social practice.

In his work *Masculinities and Crime*, Messerschmidt (1993, Chapter 4) applies this analysis of diverse and contested masculinities to youth crime. Different forms of crime by young men are patterned through various interpretations of masculinity generated by 'structures of labor and power in class and race relations'. Crime provides a means of 'doing masculinity' when other resources are unavailable. Where class and 'race' position combine to reduce conventional opportunities for the accomplishment of hegemonic masculinity, then crime can provide a ready replacement (Messerschmidt, 1993, p. 88). But crime takes different forms according to how different class and ethnic groups come to define their masculinities. So he argues that for white middle-class youth, 'crime' takes the form of vandalism, minor theft and alcohol consumption. For white working-class youth, masculinity is constructed around physical aggression and, for some, hostility to all groups considered inferior in a racist and heterosexist society. Lower working-class racial minorities find their masculinity in the street gang. While the white middle class may envisage a future in mental labour and the white working class in manual labour, both of these routes are perceived as closed to ethnic minority youth. Crime, such as robbery, provides the opportunity to accomplish a particular form of masculinity based on toughness and physical power. In these ways Messerschmidt (1993, p. 117) argues that 'unique forms of masculinity' are situationally accomplished through engaging in different forms of crime. But each represents an attempt to meet the 'cultural ideals of hegemonic masculinity' that are denied to young people elsewhere, whether it be in the home, at school or in work (see **Chapter 1.3**).

While these analyses clearly provide some important insights into the variable relationships between gender (and class and 'race') and crime, they continue to prioritize structural determinants. As Jefferson (1997, 2002) remarks, they tell us little of why only a particular minority of men from a given 'race' or class background come to accomplish their masculinity in a crime option while a majority do not. He suggests that future enquiry should not restrict itself to the issue of structural constraints but should also encompass a theory of subjectivity – a psycho-social criminology – capable of reworking 'the fragile, contingent and contradictory character of masculinity (and femininity) without losing sight of the social' (Jefferson, 1997, p. 536). As both Katz (1988) and Presdee (1994, 2000) have noted, criminological knowledge has consistently failed to recognize the subjective gratifications involved in 'doing masculinity' and 'doing crime'. Unless we also understand the pleasures to be derived from the 'drama of crime' we will never have a complete picture of youthful criminality (see **Chapter 6.5**).

Assessment

Within the broad classification of 'radical criminology' there is a diverse range of theories which contest the behavioural questions posed by positivist criminologies. Crime is to be found less in individual characteristics and environmental conditions and more in relations of power and selective processes of criminalization. In labelling, this is expressed in terms of a 'society' that creates rules. Within Marxism and critical criminology, it is expressed in terms of 'a capitalist state' that has the power to criminalize those behaviours that are deemed 'threatening'. In some feminist perspectives, it is expressed in the social construction of 'hegemonic masculinities' within patriarchal societies. All such notions have shifted the criminological agenda away from popular ideas about causation. As a result they have been critiqued for addressing 'political interpretations to the detriment of posing or answering empirical questions' (Rutter and Giller, 1983, p. 264). In tandem they have come under fire for an apparent lack of political pragmatism and a failure to be policy prescriptive. For example, the pursuit of structural change and a tolerance of diversity may smack of a utopianism which is incapable of giving practical help to those on the receiving end of repressive control systems or to those members of the working class who suffer most the effects of everyday criminal actions (Tierney, 1996, pp. 284–5). Tendencies to romanticize the deviant (via ethnographic and subcultural studies – see **Chapter 6**) may seriously underestimate the damaging consequences of some youth crime. To this extent Young (1986), adopting a left realist position, argued that a focus on criminalization and moral panics fails to 'take crime seriously': not only by ignoring causal explanations, but also allowing the right to dictate the terms of the 'law and order' debate (see Section 4.2 below).

Radical feminist theory has also been critiqued for its view that social classes are subordinate to gender inequalities and for assuming a universal female subjugation. Explanations of male violence against women have also been treated in biological terms or as simply a reflection of masculine power and deviance. Above all, the unreflective use of such terms as 'patriarchy' and 'capitalism' has been critiqued as reductionist in its characterization of male/class power as universal. Historical changes in, and various forms of, patriarchy and capitalism tend not to be accounted for (Beirne and Messerschmidt, 1991, p. 526). Or as Walklate (2001, p. 75) puts it, the key questions of how and when masculinity and/or social class become the key variable in committing crime, remain unanswered.

Nevertheless, in the current climate of authoritarian 'law and order' politics, the need for a critical criminological imagination appears more urgent than ever.

Realist Criminologies

4.2 These formative developments within critical criminology occurred during the 1970s and 1980s at a time when, as De Haan (1990, p. 20) noted, 'a wave of law and order' was 'washing over the western world'. Against a backcloth of increases in rates of recorded crime, industrial unrest and urban disorders, conservative politicians depicted crime as the outcome of a broader decline in moral values. In Britain and the United States 'law and order' was a key electoral issue in the 1980s, which fuelled and fed off a growing public concern for, and fear of, crime. Both Reaganism and Thatcherism's rise to power were built on an appeal to the logic of social authoritarianism, in which free market economics, reduced state welfare intervention and increased state punitive intervention were paramount. The most manifest outcome of such economic and political doctrines was long-term unemployment, economic marginalization of certain groups and attempts to reduce crime by strengthening the deterrent impact of the criminal justice system. Within this context, police powers were extended, tougher sentencing options were given to the courts and the use of imprisonment expanded, such that by the 1990s the United States could claim the highest incarceration rate in the world and Britain the highest in Europe.

On both sides of the Atlantic, the rhetoric of the radical right presented a popularly received picture that criminality was a matter of choice – a course of action freely chosen by pathological individuals with no self-control who, without coercive control, threatened the very moral fabric of society. The dominant public/political debate about crime came to be focused almost exclusively on images of youth violence and lawlessness in which it made no sense to treat or rehabilitate offenders; rather, the emphasis was firmly on securing the means for their vindictive punishment. New right 'realist' criminologists in the USA, such as the political scientist and government advisor James Q. Wilson, writing in the mid-1970s, departed from the prevailing liberal consensus by simply claiming that crime emanates from wicked, evil people who are insufficiently deterred from their actions by a criminal justice system deemed to be chaotic and ineffective. In this view, the only remedy lay in capital punishment and the strengthening of penal sanctions.

This almost wholesale capture of the political terrain of law and order by the 'new right' forced sections of the left to rethink their position. In particular, the self-styled school of **left realism** gradually dissociated itself from the 'new' and critical criminologies and attempted to formulate alternative law and order policies in which the problem of crime would be 'taken seriously' and accountable programmes of crime control would be implemented. Politically, this necessitated the forging of alliances with centrist Labour or Democratic parties and the overcoming of any latent reluctance to become engaged in day-to-day issues of crime and criminal justice policy.

'Realist' criminologies, whether of the right or the left, are primarily concerned with developing responses to a perceived intensity in the public's fear of crime. They concentrate more on those crimes that are at the centre of public and media concern, namely youth crime, street crime, violence and burglary, than on crimes of the powerful or those crimes perpetrated by the state itself. Similarly, they are more concerned with developing defensible measures of crime control (see **Chapter 9**) than with exploring issues concerned with the power to criminalize. The urge to 'become real' represents a significant move away from radical criminologies and a selective reworking of some aspects of positivist criminologies.

The 'New Right': Freedom and Discipline

The term 'new right' escapes easy definition. Broadly speaking, it refers to the merging of a number of schools of thought whose primary analytic orientation was to the concepts of individual freedom, self-responsibility and justice (Tame, 1991, p. 127). These concepts have, however, been activated in a variety of intellectual movements including Christian fundamentalism, economic liberalism, traditional conservatism, racism, fascism and indeed any expression of anti-socialism. Belsey (1986, p. 173) usefully picks out two, seemingly contradictory, ideologies around which the 'new right' can be defined, namely neo-liberalism and neo-conservatism. However, while neo-liberalism emphasizes *laissez-faire* market economics in which the individual is to be protected through freedom of choice and minimal state interference, neo-conservatism stresses the need for strong government and social authoritarianism in order to create a disciplined and hierarchical society in which individual needs are subordinate to those of the 'nation'.

Within criminology this paradox of freedom and discipline has been reflected in the politically influential work of Hayek (1983), van den Haag (1975), Wilson (1975) and Gottfredson and Hirschi (1990). Hayek's conception of the social order, for example, while clouded in the rhetoric of individual freedom, assumes that 'civilization' rests on the restraining and taming of primordial instincts. Such 'bad' instincts, however, are deemed to be not those of egoism or aggression, but of altruism and solidarity. It is the latter that need to be kept in check in order to maintain individual freedom and choice within a market-based economy. The problem for Hayek is that 'primitive' instincts such as demands for social justice, welfare or egalitarianism continually threaten to disrupt the efficient running of a capitalist society. Because of this inherent instability, the 'spontaneous' market order also requires a strong state to uphold it. Similarly, van den Haag's work on the role of punishment is characterized by a defence of the efficacy of deterrence and a reaffirmation of the existence of individual free will and responsibility. He argues that the 'paramount duty of governments is to provide a legal order in which citizens can be secure in their liberties' (van den Haag, 1975, p. 3) and that such liberty fundamentally rests on the meting out of retributive punishment to those who threaten it. Lamenting a 'worldwide decline in punishment and therewith of respect for law' (1975, p. 155), van den Haag argues for an increase in penalties in which 'social authority' once more finds its nerve to support capital punishment: 'When murder no longer forfeits the murderer's life (though it will interfere with his freedom), respect for life itself is diminished, as the price for taking it is. Life becomes cheaper as we become kinder to those who wantonly take it' (van den Haag, 1975, p. 213). He advocated a series of sanctions ranging from fine through prison, exile and banishment to the death penalty, in which the task is 'not to dream up an order that can do without punishment, but rather to consider how punishment can be just and effective' (van den Haag, 1975, p. 265). Crucially, effectiveness rests on devising a series of threats that will reinforce resistance to temptation and deter most people from crime for most of the time. Temptation is not the sole property of criminals; rather:

> They are like us. Worse, we are like them. Potentially we could all be or become criminals. Which is why deterrence is necessary. The population cannot be neatly split into two disconnected groups – potential offenders and untempted citizens. Beginning with Adam, people have been temptable even though most people do not commit crimes. They do not, not because they are healthy, but because they are deterrable and deterred when credible threats are made. (Van den Haag, 1975, pp. 118–19)

Within this logic, questions of the causes of crime are sidestepped, in favour of an almost sole focus on techniques of crime control. Van den Haag (1975, p. 77), for example, argues that theories of crime causation may be fascinating, but none promises to 'tell much that can be applied to crime control now' or suggests 'modification of its instruments such as punishment'. Similarly, Wilson (1975, pp. 233, 235) dismissed the search for the causes of crime as utopian:

> Though intellectually rewarding, from a practical point of view it is a mistake to think about crime in terms of its causes and then to search for ways of alleviating those causes. We must think instead of what it is feasible for a government or a community to do ... Wicked people exist. Nothing avails except to set them apart from innocent people.

Indeed, Wilson's work *Thinking about Crime* is in part devoted to establishing the failures of positivist criminologies: arguing that individual positivism tended to promote causal variables that were difficult to isolate and that sociological positivism was simply wrong. He firmly concluded that poverty is not related to crime because the most dramatic increase in recorded crime occurred during the period of post-war economic growth and relative prosperity in the United States. Criminality is simply accounted for by the existence of 'lower class' people who 'attach little importance to the opinion of others'; are 'preoccupied with the daily struggle for survival'; and are 'inclined to uninhibited, expressive conduct' (Wilson, 1975, pp. 41–2). In a later work, *Crime and Human Nature*, Wilson and Herrnstein (1985) concluded a lengthy survey of causal and correlational factors by arguing that 'personality traits' such as impulsiveness and lack of regard for others are key factors in criminality, particularly when these traits are found in 'discordant families'. They stress that criminality rests on choice; a choice, however, that is mediated by the perceived consequences of the costs and benefits of such action. The criminal, as described by Wilson and Herrnstein (1985, p. 61), is a person without a conscience, but who is capable of reacting to a variety of influences in which 'the larger the ratio of the rewards (material and non material) of non crime to the rewards (material and non material) of crime, the weaker the tendency to commit crimes'.

This attempt to merge aspects of positivism with an essentially free will conception of human nature has been questioned by Gottfredson and Hirschi (1990). They contend that the key factor underlying criminal behaviour is lack of *self-control*.

The concept suggests that 'people differ in the extent to which they are restrained from criminal acts', whereas the concept of criminality suggests that 'people differ in the extent to which they are compelled to crime'. The 'offender' is 'impulsive, insensitive, physical (as opposed to mental), risk-taking, short sighted and non-verbal' (Gottfredson and Hirschi, 1990, pp. 88, 90). Crime may not be an automatic consequence of low self-control, but this is viewed as its primary distinguishing feature. In turn, self-control derives from factors affecting calculation of the consequences of one's acts and, most crucially, on effective socialization. Thus, the major 'causes' of low self-control, it is argued, are ineffective child rearing, poor parental supervision and discipline, working mothers and broken families: in short, a lack of self-control in the home (see **Chapter 3.1**).

These realist propositions have arguably come to dominate mainstream criminology in the twenty-first century. Attention has shifted towards the *circumstances* surrounding the commission of different criminal acts rather than attempting to understand or deal with the offender. **Rational choice** theory, for example, is based on the premise that most offenders are reasoning and normal rather than pathological. Crime is understood as rational action performed by ordinary people but also acting under particular pressures and exposed to specific opportunities and situational inducements. Crime rates have increased in advanced industrial societies because opportunities have increased. For a crime to occur, two events must coincide: the opportunity for the commission of the criminal act must present itself; and the individual must decide that the gains to be had from taking the opportunity outweigh both the chances of being caught and the penalty should s/he be apprehended (Clarke, R., 1992; Felson, 1998). However, contemporary neo-conservative theorizing on crime not only rests on the doctrines of free will and rational action but is also heavily informed by notions of moral culture, moral decline and parental permissiveness. Its formative ideas are listed in Box 4.9.

Box 4.9

Characteristics of neo-conservatism

- The search for the causes of crime in terms of predisposing social factors (deprivation, unemployment, poverty) is misguided because improvements in social conditions in the 1950s and 1960s did not herald a decrease in crime, but rather an increase.

- Crime, essentially, has biological roots which are not amenable to individual treatment or social engineering. Wicked people exist; nothing avails but to set them apart from the innocent. Thus it is impractical to try and 'cure' crime.

- Individuals commit crime through rational choice. Lack of self-control and a lack of individual responsibility are at the root of all criminal responsibility.

- Crime is a symptom of declining moral standards epitomized by 1960s permissiveness, welfare dependence, liberal methods of child-rearing, family breakdown, illegitimacy, single parenting and the lack of effective means of discipline. Collectively these factors have been instrumental in the development of a dependent, demoralized and dangerous 'underclass'.

While these 'new realists' obviously differ in theoretical sophistication and are not ideologically homogeneous, Platt and Takagi (1977) argue that they have a unity of interest and purpose in that:

- they focus almost exclusively on those crimes that are either specific to, or concentrated within, the working class (e.g. street crime);

- they are basically uninterested in the causes of crime, except to divorce it from questions of political economy;

- they concentrate on questions of control and deterrence to the detriment of questions of social justice.

An Underclass?

The new and reinvigorated themes of neo-conservative criminology first found a ready market in Britain in the 1980s when Conservative politicians and ideologues were mounting a vigorous moral campaign against various forms of deviance. And these themes continued to underpin part of the reforming agenda associated with successive Labour administrations since 1997. Thatcher made crime a primary election issue in 1979 by attaching it to a general concern to re-establish 'Victorian values' and overturn the supposedly permissive culture of the 1960s. Left-wing and liberal theory and policy were denounced not only for a failure to respond to public concerns, but because of their role in accelerating a process of 'demoralization' (Davies, 1987) rooted largely in their indifference to 'family disintegration' (Dennis, 1993). A critique of critical criminology was mounted, denouncing its support for civil liberties, welfare rights and organized labour and condemning progressive trends in social policy as evidence of a monolithic political correctness (Morgan, P., 1978; Dennis and Erdos, 1992). In moral and political terms, such ideology has been translated into critiques of welfare dependency, illegitimacy and single parenting as central to the formation of a 'criminogenic' underclass. These themes have indeed proved just as attractive to Labour, as they always have to Conservative politicians (Muncie, 2000b).

The term **underclass** was first used by Myrdal (1964) to describe the unemployed, but it was not until some 20 years later that it entered the public domain through the work of a New York journalist, Ken Auletta (1982). He argued that a sizeable number of North America's poor never assimilate into society, but remain trapped in an underclass characterized by dependency on state benefits, denial of the work ethic, failed morality and rejection of family norms. This group also contains those individuals who commit most traditional street crime and are the most likely to be involved in urban riots. While the term remains poorly defined, it has been used by both left and right to describe those sections of society who are not engaged in gainful productive work. For some observers on the right, 'the underclass' is young and homeless. For others it almost invariably refers to those sections of the black population who are welfare dependent. Illegitimate births, crime, child abuse, drug dependency, single mothers, promiscuity and begging have all been cited as its key features. In contrast, for some of those on the left, the 'underclass' is a pejorative label to describe those who have been systematically excluded from the labour market. They point out that a succession of such labels has been consistently attached to the poorest members of society in order to mark them out as either politically danger- ous or as marginal outsiders – from the 'undeserving poor', 'dangerous classes' and 'social outcasts' of the nineteenth century to the 'culture of poverty', 'scroungers' and 'work-shy' of the twentieth (Mann, 1991). Broadly speaking, the right focus on the pathology and culture of the underclass (promoting an ideology of 'idle, thieving bastards': Bagguley and Mann, 1992), while the left emphasize industrial decline, recession, political marginalization and deprivation.

The chief protagonist on the right is the American, Charles Murray. In his influ- ential work *Losing Ground* (1984), he argued that much of the federal welfare system should be abolished because it encourages state dependency and fecklessness. In particular, welfare benefits have enabled young mothers to live independently of fathers, so increasing numbers of young people have grown up without viable male role models. This culture is then passed on to the next generation. Young men, who by nature are 'essentially barbarians' until they are civilized by marriage, turn to drugs and crime and a vicious circle is created. For Murray, it is not poverty or unemployment that creates an underclass, but the 'affluence' and independence afforded to young women through their welfare entitlement. In the USA, the underclass debate has focused almost exclusively on crime, 'race' and youth. In 1990, Murray applied his argument to the situation in Britain and claimed that increasing rates of illegitimacy, violent crime and drop-out from the labour force were clear signs that an underclass was in emergence. (see Box 4.10)

Box 4.10

Murray and the underclass

[W]hen large numbers of young men don't work, the communities around them break down, just as they break down when large numbers of young unmarried women have babies … Supporting a family is a central means for a man to prove to himself that he is a *mensch*. Men who do not support families find other ways to prove that they are men, which tend to take various destructive forms. As many have commented through the centuries, young males are essentially barbarians for whom marriage – meaning not just the wedding vows but the act of taking responsibility for a wife and children – is an indispensable civilising force. Young men who don't work don't make good marriage material. Often they don't get married at all; when they do they haven't the ability to fill their traditional role. In either case, too many of them remain barbarians.

Source: Murray (1990, p. 37).

In subsequent analyses Murray (1994, 2000) focused more directly on illegiti- macy. His tone was also more apocalyptic. The restoration of the two-parent family, through marriage, he argued, was the only way to ensure the survival of 'free institutions and a civil society'. Noting an increasing rate of illegitimacy throughout British society, especially in the working classes, he conjures up a future vision of segregation between 'New Victorians' (characterized by a levelling off of illegitimacy among the upper middle classes) and the 'New Rabble' (characterized by increasing rates of illegitimacy among the working classes). Affluent, well-educated sections of the population will edge back towards traditional morality; poorer sections will continue to degenerate into an underclass characterized by more violence, more crime, more widespread drug addiction, fewer marriages and more unemployment. The breakdown of the family results in a breakdown of the socialization of the young which is then reflected in a higher propensity for violent behaviour.

As before, Murray's solution to this 'crisis' was resort to the prison and a reduction in welfare benefit levels for single, unmarried mothers in order to encourage their avoidance of pregnancy. In Britain, this analysis was largely shared by such self-styled 'ethical socialists' as Norman Dennis and George Erdos. They argued that children from 'fatherless families' would grow up without appropriate role models and supervision and would thus reduce their own chances of becoming competent parents. For Dennis and Erdos (1992), it is 'common sense' that family breakdown and rising crime will go hand in hand. Such a vision has percolated through to both Conservative and Labour policy-makers in the UK. Single parenting has often been cited as a chief cause of moral decline and rising lawlessness; and withholding welfare support and compulsory parenting programmes as a route to their solution (see **Chapter 7.4**). In 2007 (in response to gun crime), the Leader of the Conservatives claimed:

> The problem lies within families and communities – and so does the solution ... Children learn their morals, no less than their manners, from their parents. And that means both parents – including fathers. We urgently need to reform the law, and the rules around child maintenance, to compel men to stand by their families.

The Labour Home Secretary agreed: 'We have to use a whole array of methods to tackle it, from police and prisons right through to demanding family responsibility' (*Guardian*, 16 February 2007). There appears almost universal political consensus that the root cause of youth crime lies in a breakdown of morality associated with dysfunctional families and a feckless underclass.

Left Realism: Relative Deprivation

The emergence of a left realist criminology in Britain in the 1980s can be viewed as both a product of, and a reaction to, the dominant 'law and order' political climate at the time. Initially, it promoted itself by advancing a virulent attack on critical criminology (in particular for what it viewed as its *left idealist* tendencies). Lea and Young in their pivotal work, *What Is to Be Done about Law and Order?* (1984, p. 266), for example, condemned the left's 'myopia about crime' and for simply 'turning their back on the problem'. Accusing the left of adopting crude reductionist arguments (crime caused by poverty; criminal law as the direct expression of a ruling class); and of underestimating and romanticizing the nature of working-class youth crime (as relatively minor, as primitive rebellion, as constructed through state-engineered moral panics), Young (1975, 1979, 1986) argued that the political arena was left wide open to Conservative campaigns for law and order. In contrast he argued for the development of a left *realist* theory and praxis:

> The central tenet of left realism is to reflect the reality of crime, that is in its origins, its nature and its impact. This involves a rejection of tendencies to romanticize crime or to pathologize it, to analyse solely from the point of view of the administration of crime or the criminal actor, to underestimate crime or to exaggerate it ... most importantly it is realism which informs our notion of practice: in answering what can be done about the problems of crime and social control. (Young, 1986, p. 21)

From the first murmurings of discontent with the original formulations of a critical criminology by two of its originators (Young, 1975; Taylor, 1981b), left realism developed the following propositions:

1 *Crime is a real problem.* Left realism tried to avoid the over-dramatization of crime by the right and the minimization of its impact by the left. By contrast, it argued that it 'takes crime seriously'. Thus working-class crime (street crime, burglary, personal violence) is viewed as a problem of the first order. 'Street crime is the most transparent of all injustices' (Lea and Young, 1984, p. 75). It noted that most crime is intra-class and intra-racial; committed by relatively disadvantaged perpetrators on similarly relatively disadvantaged victims. The task of the left, it was argued, was to accept this reality, try to understand it and do something about it, rather than deny it.

2 *Crime has specific causes.* Left realism was critical of both the right and the left for their abandonment of the search for the causes of crime: a neglect that facilitated the rise of utilitarian forms of crime control and punishment. Left realism continues to maintain that crime can best be explained with reference to the processes of *relative deprivation* and *marginalization.* When such access is denied, young people are pushed to the margins of society, as peripheral to the economic process of production and consumption and to the political process of democratic representation. Left realism suggests that one adaptation to marginalization (and to the feeling of relative rather than absolute deprivation) is the emergence of a criminal subculture. While rejecting any direct causal link between deprivation and crime, Lea and Young (1984, p. 81) stress that is the *perception* of injustice derived from deprivation that is central. Thus the notion of a **relative deprivation** (derived from anomie theory and Runciman, 1966) is utilized to explore the contradictions involved when expectations are not met by real opportunities. This situation explains the growth of street crime and disorder amongst the most relatively deprived section of the working class, namely young, inner-city, Afro-Caribbean males.

3   *Fear of crime reflects social reality.* Again in contrast to critical criminology's insistence that most crime is by and large a minor problem and that the media and other state agencies exaggerate its seriousness for wider political gain, realism maintains that criminology should begin its analysis from problems as people experience them. For example, as the Islington Crime Survey (Jones et al., 1986) found that 36 per cent of local residents saw crime as a major problem; that 56 per cent worried about being burgled, that 46 per cent had been a victim of street robbery and that a third of women avoided going out at night for fear of sexual harassment, then these should be the proper and central concerns of criminologists.

4   *The need for an accurate victimology.* The major empirical base for realism is the local victim survey because, it was argued, this provides an accurate reflection of people's concerns and a realistic picture of the nature and extent of crime (in contrast to officially recorded statistics or national surveys, for example). Realism argues that criminology has traditionally ignored the victim, or, even worse, has preferred to view the offender as victim. The survey provides a means by which public attitudes to crime and policing can be measured and thus a basis for developing a social policy that is responsive to the voice of the 'consumer'.

5   *The need for effective means of crime control.* Lea and Young (1984, Chapter 5) are particularly critical of the police and their failure to 'clear up' much of the crime in the inner cities. This is viewed as a reflection of a loss of public confidence, a decline in consensus policing and subsequent discriminatory policing which further aggravates the crime problem. The political solution offered by left realism is greater democratic control and community accountability of the police. Such developments would restore public confidence, increase willingness to report crime and thus aid police efficiency and community protection. Coupled with the advocacy of alternatives to custody, victim restitution schemes and the minimal use of the penal sanction, the realists argued for reduced central state intervention and its replacement by localized interagency and community-based forms of crime prevention and control.

6   *The need to merge theory and political practice.* The key rationale for the development of a left realism was to 'combat the tendency of a divided and disillusioned public to move to the right' (Lea and Young, 1984, p. 272). Thus it initially aligned itself with the British Labour Party in an effort to overcome the right's monopoly on matters of law and order and to construct an alternative social democratic set of criminal justice policies which it hoped might be taken seriously by parliamentary bodies (see **Chapter 9.1**).

Latterly, Young (1992, p. 27) attempted to draw these elements together by referring to a 'square of crime' in which the interactions and relationships between police and other agencies of crime control, the public, the offender and the victim must be accounted for. This implies a fourfold aetiology of crime. It includes, but moves beyond, the traditional focuses on the causes of offending, to the factors that make victims vulnerable, the social conditions that affect public perceptions of control and tolerance, and the social forces that propel the formal agencies, such as the police. The four parts of the square, it is maintained, must be explained with reference to the micro level of interaction, the meso level of control agency administration and bureaucracy and the macro level of the economic and political domains. In this way it is argued that realism is not a denunciation of *The New Criminology* but is its more sophisticated version: a version that avoids partial explanation and reductionism and which is comprehensive and pragmatic enough to explore and respond to the 'complex reality of crime as it is experienced in everyday life' (Matthews, 1987a, p. 380).

This agenda touched a nerve in many of those on the left, and has been taken up, with various degrees of enthusiasm, by academics in other Western countries. In the United States the work of Currie (1985) mirrored that of left realism in so far as it was designed to provide a pragmatic counter to the criminologies of the 'new right'. This version differs to the extent that crime is considered endemic in a society built on principles of competition, conflict and individualism. To attack the roots of the crime problem, 'we must build a society that is less unequal, less depriving, less insecure, less disruptive of family and community ties and less corrosive of co-operative values' (Currie, 1985, p. 225). In short, an effective crime control strategy lies outside of the criminal justice system and in the fields of education, training and employment, through which fundamental economic, cultural and political practices can be challenged. Brown and Hogg (1992) and McQueen (1990) have similarly attempted to assess the relevance of realism in an Australian context, but they conclude that it represents more of a politically strategic response to the dominance of the 'new right' in Britain and USA, than it does a fully worked out 'theory' in its own right. In Canada, MacLean's generally sympathetic account also acknowledges that left realism is the product of a 'specific political configuration' and that there are some 'important theoretical and ideological biases inherent in the discourse' which are 'deserving of sceptical scrutiny' (MacLean, 1991, p. 246). In particular, left realism appears to be driven by popular conceptions of 'crime' and fails to acknowledge that the issue of what actually constitutes a criminal occurrence is far from settled (see Section 4.3 below).

Indeed, it has been claimed that the import of 'realism' (whether left or right) necessarily narrows the crime debate to a focus on those visible intra-class (and youthful) crimes of the street. Accordingly, other (non-youth) crimes such as fraud, embezzlement and corporate crime tend to be overlooked. Although this may be the case, there are certain crucial differences between left and **right realism**. While both are critical of utopianism and claim to be rational responses to increased levels of public fear of crime, left realism insists that neo-liberalism and neo-conservatism are part of the problem and not its solution (see Box 4.11). As Young (1990, p. 10) maintains, realism argues for the minimum use of coercive sanctions, the decriminalization of certain (e.g. drug) offences, and 'that only socialist intervention will fundamentally reduce the causes of crime rooted as they are in social inequality'.

Box 4.11

Right and left realism compared

Right realism	Left realism
Rejection of utopianism in favour of neo-conservatism	Rejection of utopianism in favour of democratic socialism
Acceptance of legal definitions of 'crime'	Acceptance of legal definitions of 'crime'
Primary focus on 'crime' as represented by official statistics.	Primary focus on 'crime' as perceived by victims.
Fear of crime as rational	Fear of crime as rational
Reworking of genetic and individualistic theories	Reworking of subcultural, anomie and structural conflict theories
Crime caused by lack of self-control	Crime caused by relative deprivation, social injustice and marginalization
Prioritizing order (rather than justice) via deterrent and retributive means of crime control	Prioritizing social justice via programmes of crime prevention

Source: Derived from Young (1990).

Assessment

Realist criminologies encompass a plethora of notions of crime causation as evidenced in the divergent approaches taken by neo-conservatism and left realism. While the former combines elements of free will, genetics and social control theory and marks something of a return to the principles of individual causation, the latter combines elements of anomie (relative deprivation) and subcultural theory and marks something of a return to the principles of social causation. Both accept that crime is becoming more of a problem and stress the urgent need to address that problem with feasible and effective measures of crime control.

The neo-conservative account of crime causation, however, does not address why individuals choose to commit particular types of crime rather than others. It is simply assumed that innate propensities have been unleashed by weakened social bonds. Also the claim that coercion is essential for the maintenance of social order is not demonstrated. Coercion may lead to greater injustice and the further separation of 'criminals' from 'non-criminals'. It does not aid reintegration. Reducing welfare benefits in order to break the 'dependency culture' of an underclass encourages a widening of income differentials and the raising of social tensions which may also eventually be expressed in rising levels of crime (Brake and Hale, 1992, p. 115). Further, Macdonald and Marsh (2005) argue that conservative theories of the underclass are misinformed because they fail to acknowledge that individuals can and do react quite differently to similar events. It is then quite wrong to talk of a 'static underclass', particularly in the context of disadvantaged young people who typically find themselves embroiled in fluid, complex and changing life experiences.

Much of the left realist agenda has also come under critical scrutiny, in particular for its abandonment of critical criminology and its seeming return instead to the 'citadels of the old criminology' (Cohen, 1988, p. 9). Indeed, in its attempt to revive an aetiology of crime, it draws extensively on American subcultural theory of the 1950s (see **Chapter 3.2**). In particular, the utilization of such theory to assert the existence of a specifically *black* youth criminal subculture came under virulent attack for its racist connotations (Ginsberg, 1985; Gilroy, 1987a). More generally, the primary focus on 'crime' as perceived by victims tends to ignore, or at best underplay, the more damaging consequences of corporate crime, white-collar crime and crimes of the powerful. The realist agenda then does little to challenge political and media-driven definitions of what constitutes 'serious crime' and fails to capture the harm caused, for example, by workplace injury, occupation-related diseases and environmental pollution (Pearce and Tombs, 1992). Much of this stems from a theoretical orientation grounded in the notion of relative deprivation, rather than class/gender/'race' exploitation.

Left realism's programme for social reform, based on proposals for enhanced police accountability and community-based crime prevention, has been condemned as 'simplistic' and 'naive'. As Sim et al. (1987, p. 54) argue, 'their policy prescriptions have become no more than "constructive criticism" welcomed by the police and incorporated as an integral part of social democratic politics'. Similarly, Jefferson et al. (1992) have questioned the 'realism' involved in the narrow focus on individual victims of crime in which working-class street and property crime remain the key components of the 'crime problem'. The key issue for the left, they argue, should remain the way in which crime is activated by the new right to justify coercive and authoritarian state practices, and latterly the way in which the 'victim of crime' has been reconstructed as a *consumer* of police, and other agency, service. Realism's commitment to a community-based crime prevention policy renders its position very similar to the early 1990s notion of the 'new right' that crime is 'caused' by a lack of vigilance on the part of the 'active citizen'. Politically, then, there is some merging and co-option of the concerns of left realism by the right. This view – that left realism has failed to challenge right-wing ideology, but by accepting some of its key premises has become a part of it – has indeed been latterly accepted by some of its originators who, in particular, have noted how much of its agenda has been usurped by an authoritarian New Labour since the late 1990s (Young, 2003). While left realism continues to be a serious and politically committed project to tackle the issue of intra-class and intra-racial crime, the problem remains of how far the theoretical gains made by critical criminology have been jettisoned in the search for a social democratic law and order politics (Carrington and Hogg, 2002).

Beyond Criminology?

4.3 If criminology has been traditionally conceived as the scientific study of the causes of crime, then it is clear that the paradigm of critical criminology has moved far beyond the original remit. Critical criminologies are as much an examination of political economy and state formations as anything we might like to call crime. Feminist criminologies have shifted the study of crime into addressing questions of patriarchy and gender roles. These avenues of enquiry are able to move beyond the issue of crime causation because they do not take the concept of 'crime' for granted. 'Crime' is not something that can simply be described with reference to what is, or is not, circumscribed by the law. 'Crime' is not simply law-breaking behaviour, but is something constructed through the processes of interaction, social reaction and power. Not only has a hundred years of positivist criminology, with its persistent problem of distinguishing cause from correlate, been unable to isolate a specific cause, but the whole endeavour, it is argued, is doomed to failure, because 'crime' refers not to a unified phenomenon, but to a diverse multitude of behaviour patterns. If one accepts Hester and Eglin's (1992, p. 269) proposition 'that "crime" is a status accorded to some acts and not to others, at some times and in some places and not others, and that those acts are engaged in to some degree by most people at least some of the time', then it is highly questionable whether it warrants any special explanation at all. However, such a view is inimical to new right and left realist (as well as positivist) criminologies. For the latter 'crime', and particularly 'youth crime', remain a major social problem about which something needs to be done. This impasse in itself accounts for the current fragmented, diverse and contradictory nature of criminology. Criminology appears united only in its fascination with its key referent – 'crime' – but is racked by internal debate and controversy because what actually constitutes 'crime' is forever changing and open to dispute.

Modernity and Postmodernism

This chapter and Chapter 3 have introduced a number of theoretical approaches which, despite their obvious and clear divergences, are all grounded in rationalistic and meta theories about the relationship between individual behaviour, cultural values and social structure. Despite their points of difference, all the approaches we have considered assume that social reality is ultimately 'knowable' and 'understandable' when the 'correct' terms of reference, concepts and mode of research are employed.

These attempts to make sense of the social are characteristic of modes of thought typical of **modernity**. Modernism attempts to use the rational knowledge of science, law and technology to construct the social into an essentially ordered totality and is underpinned by faith in the 'master narratives' of progress, self-advancement and emancipation (Morrison, 1995, p. 453). Such fundamental premises have, however, been called into question through the challenge of **postmodernism.** For example, a postmodern perspective views the modernist project of developing objective and scientific means to understand the social as misguided and redundant. The questions it asks are unanswerable; the answers it formulates are too dogmatic (Einstadter and Henry, 1995, p. 289). Postmodernism views the world as replete with an unlimited number of models of order, each generated by relatively autonomous and localized sets of practices which are incapable of being explained by any 'scientific' theory. Whereas modernism strives for universality and the overcoming of relativism in theory and practice, postmodernism accepts relativity as a lasting feature of the world. Postmodernism challenges us to accept that we live in a world of contradictions and inconsistencies, which is not amenable to objective modes of thought. Assumptions about the 'real' and the 'virtual' (and how they might be distinguished) are less readily sustained. More knowledge produces less certainty and less ontological security (Valier, 2002, p. 175). Modernist theory (of which criminology is but one example) simply serves to impose a pre-defined meaning and structure on the disordered social; if anything, it moves us further from the truth, rather than helping us to understand it. Grand theorizing is rejected by postmodernism in favour of a pluralist and appreciative relativism. As Bauman (1993, p. 245) explains:

> What the post-modern mind is aware of is that there are problems in human and social life with no good solutions, twisted trajectories that cannot be straightened up, ambivalences that are more than linguistic blunders yelling to be corrected, doubts which cannot be legislated out of existence, moral agonies which no reason-dictated recipes can soothe, let alone cure. The post-modern mind does not expect any more to find the all-embracing, total and ultimate formula of life without ambiguity, risk, danger and error, and is deeply suspicious of any voice that promises otherwise. The post-modern mind is aware that each local, specialised and focused treatment, effective or not when measured by its ostensive target, spoils as much as, if not more than it repairs. The post-modern mind is reconciled to the idea that the messiness of the human predicament is here to stay.

As a result, postmodernism implies an abandonment of the concepts of 'crime' and 'youth' and the construction of a new language and mode of thought to designate and explore objects of censure and codes of conduct (Hulsman, 1986; De Haan, 1990; Smart, 1990; Sumner, 1994; Brown, 2005). Henry and Milovanovic (1994, 1996) insist that crime will only stop being a problem once the justice system, media and criminologists stop focusing attention on it. A postmodern imagination should indeed alert us to the many ways in which 'youth crime' is 'problematic' – not only in its effects, but in its formulation and the ways in which it is so readily framed and understood. We may better capture 'youth crime' not by searching for causes, but by using narratives and accounts derived from young people themselves. It is only through a reframing of 'youth' and 'crime' which either removes 'youth' as the key referent or repositions them as legitimate citizens, that dominant (adult) discourses will be overcome (Brown, 1998, p. 119). This uncertainty and doubt should not necessarily be a reason for nihilistic despair. Morrison (1995, p. 475) affirms, 'doubt is essential to creation' and provides the impetus for 'continual (re)construction'. But exactly what is to be 'reconstructed' often remains unspecified. Intellectual scepticism may be preferable to dogma, but, if ungrounded, can simply produce inertia and political inaction. The continuing problem for radical criminology is to know when detachment or commitment should be prioritized and how (if at all) they can ever be combined (Cohen, 1998).

From Crime to Social Harm

In the 1960s and 1970s the then newly emergent critical criminology maintained that if criminology restricted itself to legal definitions of crime and to questions of cause/remedy it would merely continue to be an adjunct of the state or at best a think tank to develop policy and advance the interests of particular political constituents. Critical criminology insisted that crime cannot be identified by simply focusing on known offenders. These are but one particular element of the 'problem of crime' and only capable of identification following a series of social constructions involving the power to formulate particular criminal laws, police targeting, court room discretion, media representations and so on. Rather, criminology should direct attention to processes of criminalization: how certain harmful acts/events come to be defined and recognized as 'crime' while others do not. Since then two major initiatives have been:

1 To broaden the subject matter of criminology away from a sole reliance on those injurious acts defined as such by the criminal law – theft, burglary, criminal damage, and so on – in order to establish that a vast range of *harms* – sexism, racism, imperialism, pollution, state atrocities, economic exploitation, and so on – could and should be included as the focal concern of an area of study called criminology (Schwendinger and Schwendinger, 1970).

2 To recognize that 'what is crime' rests crucially on the power to define and the power to police certain 'transgressions' while ignoring or giving little attention to others. The key problematic for criminology then becomes not crime or criminal behaviour, but social order and how that order is produced and struggled over (Muncie, 2001)

In the 1980s and 1990s, an important body of deconstructionist knowledge – originating in no small measure from a European school of **abolitionism** – attempted to move beyond the essentialist signifiers of 'crime', 'criminality' and 'criminal justice' in order to facilitate the production of new critical insights and alternative visions of justice (Steinert, 1986; Bianchi, 1986; De Haan, 1990; van Swaaningen, 1997). Abolitionists established that if our concern with crime (and youth) is driven by fears for social stability, and personal safety, then we would be well advised to look beyond 'crime' to discover where the most dangerous threats and risks to our person and property lie. For example poverty, malnutrition, pollution, medical negligence, breaches of workplace health and safety laws, corporate corruption, state violence, genocide, human rights violations, and so on all carry with them more widespread and damaging consequences than most of the behaviours and incidents that currently make up the 'youth problem' (Muncie, 2000a). The contention is that the criminological gaze should extend beyond its typical focus on relatively powerless young people and give equal, if not more, attention to the serious harms committed by powerful adults.

Latterly many of these themes have been developed within an explicit **social harm** perspective (Tifft, 1995; Henry and Milovanowicz, 1996; Hillyard et al., 2004; Hillyard and Tombs, 2007). In particular, it is argued that the concept of social harm, utilized instead of the narrow definition of crime, allows for the innovation of policy around wider considerations of responsibility for economic and geographical inequalities and forces acknowledgement of the role of government and corporations in their perpetration. In a harm-based discourse the concept of 'crime' remains important only in so far as it alerts us to relations of power embedded in social orders which generate a whole series of social problems for their populations but of which only a selected few are considered worthy of criminal sanction. A conception of crime without a conception of power is meaningless. The power to render certain harmful acts visible and define them as 'crime', while maintaining the invisibility of others (or defining them as beyond criminal sanction) lies at the heart of the problem of working within notions of 'the problem of crime'. The social harm perspective is particularly illuminating for the study of youth and crime because it forces recognition that a host of state- and corporate-initiated damaging events are far more endemic and can be more devastating than those that make up the 'youth problem'. Moreover, much of the political and media concern over youth crime focuses on the exceptional or on recreational drug use, vandalism, brawls, antisocial behaviour, and so on which by comparison would not seem to score as high on a scale of serious persistent harm. Despite this, it is often a large number of 'minor' events that take up much of the time and preoccupation of law enforcement agencies and the youth justice system (see **Chapter 9**). A focus on youth crime then typically not only deflects attention away from more pressing harms but in many respects it acts to exclude them from debates over law and order. By focusing on how the 'problem of youth crime' is constructed through statistical measures and by media, political and public discourses (and by revealing the significant absences in those discourses), it becomes possible to recognize that we are not simply dealing with a problem of youthful transgression, but with problems of the definition, representation and political reaction (or nonreaction) to a much wider set of harms (see **Chapter 1**).

A social harm perspective is in its infancy and more work needs to be done to define its parameters in order to avoid the same historical and cultural contingencies that inflict the concept of crime (Hillyard and Tombs, 2007). What also remains unclear is how far the recoding of crime as harm is capable of replacing legal definitions. Nevertheless a harm perspective serves as a telling reminder that if we are to fully appreciate the complexity of youth offending we will certainly need to move beyond the limited horizons of state-centred criminology.

▓ ■ Summary ▓

- An overview of radical and realist theories of crime is given in Box 4.12. Not all of these theories are directed explicitly towards explaining *youth* crime, but all are of relevance. It is noteworthy in itself that a majority of criminological theories have either explicitly or implicitly used 'youth' as a key referent in formulating their notions of 'causation' or 'criminalization'.

- Rather than refocusing on the illusive search for the *causes* of crime, radical and critical criminologies have sought to illustrate how crime is socially constructed through the capacity and ability of state institutions and the political economy of advanced capitalism to define and confer criminality on others. This 'radical turn' began with the advent of interactionist and labelling paradigms of the 1960s.

- The *New Criminology* claimed that the key subject of criminology should not be crime and deviance as behaviours, but a critical understanding of the state and social order. To understand youth crime, we need also to examine how, why and when the state assumes the power to criminalize. In part, this relied on a reworking of the theoretical premises of Marxism.

- These radical visions surfaced against a political backdrop of neo-conservative law and order politics. By capitalizing on the fear of crime, the notion of endemic criminality was instilled in communities and enabled the public/political debate to be dominated by images of violent crime, youth lawlessness and a declining morality which required authoritarian control.

- With empirical support from a series of victim surveys carried out during the 1980s, left realism also claimed that the problem of crime was indeed growing and that in particular property and street crimes were real issues that needed to be addressed. Its solution however lay in the advocacy of social justice and social crime prevention programmes.

- A key failing of positivist and the early radical criminologies was the absence of any discussion or critical analysis of gender relations and women and crime. Never was it made explicit that the problem of crime may also be one of men, masculinities and patriarchal social relations. Since the mid-1970s, however, a burgeoning literature has demonstrated how criminology is driven by male assumptions and interests, how criminalized women are seen as doubly deviant, and how assumptions about appropriate gender roles mean that women are judged less on the nature of their offence and more on their 'deviant' lifestyle.

- A postmodern position claims that such 'unifiers' as 'crime', 'criminology' and 'youth' trap any investigation in essentialist categories that obstruct the production of new knowledge. Postmodernism argues against the construction of 'master narratives', claiming that such totalizing accounts lose sight of the multiplicity and diversity of modern power relations. By implication it argues that the *causes* of youth crime have been, and will remain, 'unknowable': that is, its complexities preclude definitive analysis particularly when that analysis is grounded in modernist concerns for capitalism, unemployment, patriarchy, the underclass, permissiveness and so on.

Box 4.12

Radical and realist theories of youth crime

Theory	Explanation of crime	Key theorists
Neutralization	'Moral holiday'/removal of inhibitions/drift	Sykes and Matza (1957) Matza (1964)
Labelling	Stigma attached to social reaction (moral panic) cements deviant careers. Social control causes crime	Becker (1963) Cohen (1973a) Lemert (1967)
Classical Marxism	Capitalism produces alienation and brutalizing socio-economic conditions	Bonger (1916)
'New criminology'	Lack of tolerance	Taylor et al. (1973)
Critical criminology	Certain populations criminalized through denial of opportunity, social exclusion and crises in hegemony	Chambliss (1975) Hall et al. (1978) Greenberg (1977) Scraton (1987)
Feminist	Patriarchal society encourages 'maverick masculinities'	Smart (1976) Messerschmidt (1993)
Social control	Absence of control (by parents/schools) allows ever present criminal inclinations to be realized. Cultural permissiveness	Gottfredson and Hirschi (1990) Wilson and Herrnstein (1985) Wilson (1975)
Underclass	Illegitimacy, single parenting, welfare dependency	Murray (1990)
Left realism	Relative deprivation	Lea and Young (1984)
Postmodernism	Causal statements impossible to make	Henry and Milovanovic (1996)
Social harm	Crime as a state constructed category	Hillyard et al. (2004)

study questions

1 What contribution have radical criminologies made to the youth crime debate?

2 What is the difference between the social causation and the social construction of youth crime?

3   Do realist criminologies add anything particularly new to the youth crime debate or are they simply reworkings of older, positivist theories?

4   Why have some theorists argued that the search for 'a cause' is a misdirected and fruitless activity?

5   'Criminological research is invariably drawn into the political domain.' How far do its agendas and priorities simply reflect prevailing socio-economic and political conditions? How can the supposed truism of criminology – that crime is predominantly an activity of the young – be challenged?

■ ■ Further Reading ■

For an informed overview of the diverse and various strands of radicalism and realism, all of the key texts cited in Box 4.12 deserve some attention.

Matza's *Delinquency and Drift* (1964) was republished with a new introduction in 1990 and remains a key challenge to positivist notions of causation. Becker's (1963) analysis of marijuana smoking is the classic text on labelling. Hall et al.'s *Policing the Crisis* (1978) shows how labelling can be developed within a critical paradigm to provide some enlightened understanding of how and why particular 'youth crimes' (mugging) are constructed in particular socio-economic conjunctures. One of the best ethnographic studies of this period remains Parker's Liverpool-based *View from the Boys* (1974). For a contrary view of how the study of youth crime can be developed by studying young women using theories that transgress criminology, see Cain's edited collection, *Growing Up Good* (1989). On the relevance of gender, and masculinity in particular, Messerschmidt (1993) is the most useful place to start. The classic left realist text is Lea and Young's *What Is to Be Done about Law and Order?* (1984), while Murray's (1990) increasingly influential analysis of the underclass captures many of the elements of right realism. A critique of both can be found in Scraton (1987). Chapter 12 of Einstadter and Henry (1995) provides an accessible summary of the types of issue that would be involved in deconstructing 'youth crime' from a postmodern perspective, while the edited volumes on contemporary critical criminology by Carrington and Hogg (2002), Hillyard et al. (2004) and Barton et al. (2007) continue to reveal the necessity of critical analysis, theoretical innovation and political intervention.

Anyone not yet convinced of the fictions of crime and crime control should read Reiman's (2007) *The Rich Get Richer and the Poor Get Prison*, now in its eighth edition.

∴ // Web Resources /

http://critcrim.org/
The critical criminology division of the American Society of Criminology with access to their regular newsletters.

http://www.europeangroup.org/
Site of the European Group for the study of deviancy and social control first established as a forum for critical analysis in 1972.

http://home.earthlink.net/~hsbecker/
Howard Becker's home page.

http://www.statewatch.org/
An important body monitoring state power and civil liberties in Europe. Regularly comments on youth justice policy such as the compulsory fingerprinting of children and the legality of anti-social behaviour initiatives. Retains thousands of articles on its database.

http://www.aei.org/
American Enterprise Institute: a highly influential neo-conservative think tank with commentaries on public policy.

http://www.ecln.org/
European Civil Liberties Network launched in 2005.

5

Youth Victimology

Overview

Chapter 5 examines:

- children and young people as victims of crime;

- the relationship between offending and victimization;

- the abuse of children in their homes;

- the abuse of children in institutional settings, such as care homes and custodial centres;

- the exploitation of children internationally in relation to child trafficking, forced labour and recruitment in armed conflicts;

- the partiality of victimological (and criminological) discourse.

| | **key terms** | |

abuse; child soldiers; child trafficking; demonization; exploitation; victim blaming; victim survey; victimization; violence

Historically the core concern of criminology has been with exploring the motivations for offending and of formulating 'appropriate' criminal justice-based responses. Much of criminology has been articulated around the construction of urban working class youth as a 'social problem'. It was not until the 1940s that attention began to be given to the victim or, more accurately at that time, to a concern to address the relationship between the victim and the offender. Over the next half-century, victimology grew into a vibrant global discipline in its own right and victim issues have been recognized as central to policy-makers and policy reform. Victim support, counselling, reparation, mediation, and so on are now commonplace. It would, however, be misleading to view victimology as some homogenous field of study. Mawby and Walklate (1994) have identified three main perspectives. *Positivist* victimology has been largely concerned to develop and refine quantitative measures of victimization, first, with reference to recorded crime statistics and latterly through victimization surveys. Typically this perspective has constructed victim typologies and explored the relationship between offending and victimization or more particularly the extent to which victims contribute to their own victimization. This **victim-blaming** approach focuses on the effects of victim precipitation and victim lifestyle. It also concentrates on trying to differentiate victim from non-victim behaviour. At core it is individual behaviour that determines levels of risk. Typically this positivist concern focuses overwhelmingly on the 'visible victim' and on conventional interpersonal crime (see **Chapter 3**). Victims of state and corporate crime, for example, have remained absent. By way of comparison, a *radical* victimology emerged during the 1970s which attempted to contextualize victimization within its precise political and socio-economic contexts. In particular, it extended the definition and identity of the victimized to include all those enduring rights violations, oppression and exploitation, including at the hands of the powerful, the state and its agencies. This perspective was subsequently developed by variants of *critical* victimology. Advocates of left realism had drawn attention to disparities in risk of victimization in terms of geographical location, class, 'race' and gender (see **Chapter 4.2**). Critical victimology continues with such line of argument but asks who comes to be defined as a victim?; how is the victim constituted?; what are the implications of having such a constitution? Informed by a fusion of radical criminology, feminism and left realism, Mawby and Walklate (1994) articulated a view of victimization as structural powerlessness, recognizing that the impact of criminal victimization is mediated and rendered more complex by factors such as age, sex, and race. In these ways the ambit of victimology has the potential to be significantly expanded. But alongside such developments has also emerged debate over what counts as victimology and challenge to use of the term 'victim' and the circumstances in which such a term is applied. In these ways reliance on the victimization survey has been eschewed (Walklate, 2007).

Despite these expansive and expanding agendas the specific issue of *youth* victimization has been given scant attention. The predominant representations of youth do not 'sit easily within a victim discourse' (Brown, 1998, p. 116). It is only in the past decade that anything approaching a specific critical youth victimology could be said to be emergent (Brown, 1998; Muncie, 2003b; Francis, 2007). Even so it remains embryonic. A defining characteristic is the intention not only to reverse the conventional criminological logic by revealing offences against (rather than committed by) young people, but also to expose the extent of familial and institutional abuse and violence and reveal the range of social harms to which young people are routinely exposed through state negligence or indifference. This chapter extends this focus by also examining child victimization on a global scale, as most dramatically illustrated by child trafficking, child soldiering and all manner of indifferences to child welfare and child powerlessness which appear promulgated by adults and governments of whatever political persuasion.

Victimization

5.1 The concept of victimization can refer both to the interactional processes whereby certain people acquire 'victim status' and to the age, gender, class and ethnic differentials in patterns of becoming a victim. The two are not necessarily consistent. For example, Christie (1986) has noted how political and media constructions of the 'ideal victim' generally focus on those perceived as vulnerable, defenceless and worthy of compassion. Elderly women and very young children are the most likely to conform to this notion of 'legitimate' victim status. On the other hand, survey data have consistently revealed that young people are more likely to be victimized than older people; the economically marginalized more than the wealthy; ethnic minorities more than white populations; and men more than women (at least in regard to street crime). In reality it is young working-class males who are the 'typical victims' but they are the least liable to be identified as vulnerable to victimization. In this sense there exists a *hierarchy of victimization* in which some abusive and violent events (for example, child abduction) appear guaranteed to receive extensive media and political attention while others are relatively ignored (for example, child labour).

The concept of victimization is also typically employed in a narrow fashion referring only to victims of crimes as recognized in the criminal law. By moving beyond legal definitions, critical criminology allows us to appreciate a broader range of harms and injuries through which children and young people are routinely 'victimized' (see **Chapter 4.3**). For example, acknowledging governmental culpability in the continuance of child poverty in rich nations suggests that the state itself can be a significant agency in the perpetration of child harm (see **Chapter 10**). Similarly the indiscriminate targeting of groups of children through curfews and dispersal zones suggests an age-specific victimization and criminalization of behaviours which would be ignored if practised by adults (see **Chapter 7**). The role of the media in consistent negative reporting and demonization can also be viewed as tantamount to an insidious ongoing 'victimization' of childhood and youth (see **Chapter 1**).

The Victimization Survey

The vast majority of survey research on youth and crime has focused exclusively on young people as offenders rather than as victims of crime. The first attempt to reverse this priority was Mawby's (1979) study of 11–15 year olds in two Sheffield schools. He found that 40 per cent had had something stolen from their person and that 25 per cent had suffered a physical assault. Overall 67 per cent said that they had been a crime victim. Nevertheless it was not until the 1990s that the issue was given much sustained attention. Anderson et al.'s (1994) pioneering **victim survey** work in Edinburgh established that criminal acts are committed against young people with 'alarming frequency'. They found that over a period of nine months half of their sample had been victims of assault, threatening behaviour or theft (Anderson et al., 1994, p. 39). Moreover some 52 per cent of young women and 36 per cent of young men recalled that they had suffered from adult harassment, ranging from being 'stared at', to importuning and indecent exposure. While for males such offences decreased as they grew older, for females they increased to the extent that 30 per cent of 14–15 year olds had experienced 'touching' or 'flashing' (Anderson et al., 1994, p. 59). In a follow-up study in Glasgow (Hartless et al., 1995), high levels of victimization were again found to be common, with 82 per cent of a sample of 208 12–14 year olds recalling they had been victimized in the previous year. Sixty-eight per cent of young women had been sexually harassed, while two-thirds of young men had suffered from assault *and* theft. In comparison, on average, a quarter of the sample admitted that they themselves had committed an offence, leading the authors to conclude that young people are 'more sinned against than sinning'. Similarly, Brown's (1998, p. 92) research in Teesside, which compared rates of youth and adult victimization, found that 'young people endured levels of victimization which would not be tolerated by adults'. Moreover, all three studies concluded that whatever the known rates of victimization, young people were often reluctant to report offences committed against them.

Specific questions about youth victimization have only once been included in the British Crime Survey: that of 1992 (though the Home Secretary announced in 2008 that under-16 year olds would be included in future sweeps). From a sample of 1,350, in just six months a third of 12–15 year olds claimed that they had been assaulted at least once, a fifth had had property stolen, a fifth had been harassed by people their own age and a fifth harassed by an adult. Again it was notable that the risks of theft and assault were substantially higher than for the adult population, but that few incidents were reported to the police (Aye Maung, 1995).

In the first decade of the twenty-first century the number of child victimization surveys has burgeoned. The MORI Youth Survey (2002) of 5,000 school children revealed that 35 per cent had been physically attacked, 45 per cent threatened, 34 per cent racially abused and 34 per cent suffered from theft in school alone. A survey for the Howard League (press release, 11 April 2002) of 11–15 year olds found that only 4 per cent believed they had never been a victim of crime. The 2003 report on Crime in England and Wales which collated BCS and police statistics (Simmons and Dodd, 2003) confirmed that young men aged 16–24 were most at risk of violent crime. The Crime and Justice Survey (Wood, 2005) found that 10–25 year olds were the most likely to have been the victims of personal crime (for example, assault, robbery, theft from the person) in the previous 12 months. About a third of this age group had experienced one or more personal crimes. The prevalence of personal crime was considerably lower among the 26–65 age group (see Box 5.1).

Deakin's (2006) analysis of data collected from 2,420 children as part of The Children and Young People's Safety Survey explored the extent of harassment, bullying and threatening behaviour endured by 9–16 year olds. This extended understanding of victimization by going beyond what may be defined in criminal law as 'criminal'. Unsurprisingly, high levels of victimization were recorded ranging from almost 80 per cent reporting being harassed to almost a quarter reporting theft. Significantly it unearthed diverse forms of victimization with boys more likely to have experienced assaults and girls suffering from various forms of 'sexual intrusion'. Those aged 12 to 13 appeared to be most at risk of victimization. But in common with many other surveys it found that while children expressed most fear from 'stranger danger', by far the most likely perpetrators were those known to the victim, including other children.

Box 5.1

The victimization of young people: findings from the Crime and Justice Survey 2003

- Over 35 per cent of young people aged 10 to 15 had experienced at least one personal crime in the previous 12 months. This was about the same level as for those aged 16 to 25 (32 per cent) and well above those aged 26 to 65 (14 per cent).

- Theft from the person was highest for 18 and 19 year olds (12 per cent), while robbery was most common for 16–19 year olds with 6 per cent being a victim of robbery in the last 12 months. Those aged 10 to 11 years were more likely to experience other thefts of personal property, such as thefts from changing rooms (16 per cent).

- Money was the main target of thefts (28 per cent of victims), while mobile phones were the target for 25 per cent of victims followed by stationery (20 per cent) and bicycles (11 per cent).

- 21 per cent of 10 to 15 year olds experienced assaults compared to 19 per cent for 16 to 25 year olds. Older adults were far less likely to have been victims of assault (7 per cent).

- Among 10 to 17 year olds, 19 per cent said they had been victims of bullying. Those aged 10 to 11 were significantly more likely to be victims within this group (27 per cent compared with 9 per cent of 16 to 17 year olds). Females were also more likely to experience bullying (21 per cent) than males (17 per cent).

- 60 per cent of 10 to 15 year olds who experienced violence in the previous 12 months did so on more than one occasion. 19 per cent had experienced 5 or more violent incidents in the previous 12 months.

- Those young people that had committed an offence themselves were more likely to be victims. Other underlying risk factors were the presence of anti-social behaviour in their local area, being male and committing anti-social behaviour.

- There was no difference in the level of overall personal crime victimization between young people in different ethnic groups. Within specific types of crime, white young people were more likely to have been victims of assault than black and minority ethnic young people but were less likely to have been victims of robbery.

Source: Adapted from Wood (2005).

A report by the Howard League in 2007 seemed to confirm that being a victim of crime had become the norm for most children in Britain. This suggested that government figures on child victimization, such as provided by the 2003 Crime and Justice Survey, were serious underestimations. The Howard League Survey found that 95 per cent of 10 to 15 year olds had experienced crime at least once. Of more than 3,000 children surveyed, almost three-quarters had been assaulted over the previous year, and two-thirds had been victims of theft. More than half had had their property deliberately damaged, while others reported a proliferation of threats and verbal abuse (see Box 5.2).

Box 5.2

Key findings of *Children as Victims: Child-Sized Crimes in a Child-Sized World*

- 95 per cent of children surveyed had been a victim of crime on at least one occasion.

- Many children had been victims of theft: 49 per cent had had property stolen from them at school, and 18 per cent between school and home.

- 57 per cent had property deliberately damaged.

- A majority of children had experienced bullying or assaults, with 46 per cent stating they had been called racist names, and 56 per cent threatened on at least one occasion. Nearly three-quarters of children in the survey had been assaulted.

- Children predominantly reported their victimization to family members and friends. Only a third reported incidents to the police or teachers.

- Children had a fear of crime and wanted safe places to play. They told us they felt vulnerable and scared. They felt adults demonized them as the perpetrators of crime when they should be viewed as the victims of crime.

- Children had very clear ideas on crime prevention. Their ideas included examples of more local activities, for example: building more child-friendly cafés; skate parks; and youth clubs – to keep children busy.

- Children demonstrated to us that they had a clear idea of justice and fairness. They had views about acceptable standards of behaviour, with the problematic behaviour, seen as 'anti-social' by some, being regarded as 'anti-civil behaviour' in young people's eyes – and thus being accepted as part of their growing up process and something they have to deal with on a daily basis.

- The majority of incidents of victimization in this report were low-level crimes taking place in schools and playgrounds.

Source: Derived from Howard League (2007).

The Howard League Survey helped to address various key issues. First, that the demonization of young people as perpetrators of crime has led to a wanton neglect of the extent of their victimization. Second, that adults are likely to dismiss much of this behaviour as 'children behaving as children' whereas for children in a 'child-sized world' these instances clearly do matter. Third, as most incidences occurred in and around school, it is clear that the very institutions where children should feel safest are where they experience some of the highest levels of vulnerability and fear.

Another characteristic commonly associated with victimization is ethnic background, though such surveys as Wood's (2005) found no clear correlation. Nevertheless racially motivated violence (as reported to the police) increased by 250 per cent between 1989 and 1996, marking the UK as having one of the highest levels of such incidents in Western Europe (Human Rights Watch, 1997). Between 1997/8 and 2001/2 there was a fivefold increase in reported racial incidents in England and Wales (Webster, 2007). All ethnic minority groups are more likely than whites to be victims of both household and person offences. Asians are most at risk, being particularly vulnerable to vandalism of their houses and cars and to serious threats. African-Caribbeans are most at risk of assaults and acquisitive crime (Fitzgerald and Hale, 1996; Percy, 1998). The murder of the black teenager Stephen Lawrence in 1993 and the unrelenting campaign by his family to expose police and judicial racism catapulted racial violence and hate crime to the forefront of issues to be addressed by law enforcement and community safety agencies in the late 1990s. Six years after the murder, the Macpherson Report confirmed what black and Asian communities already knew about or suspected about police ambivalence, institutional racism and lack of accountability. But the report lacked an acknowledgement of the long history of violent racism in Britain. It dwelt on the failures of policing rather than on the daily experience of racist violence, threat and intimidation. Although survey research has burgeoned since the early 1980s, statistical snapshots of particular events are incapable of grasping the incessant and enduring process of victimization (Bowling, 1999).

In the USA, in response to a limited public recognition of the issue of youth victimization (which rarely stretched further than anger and concern at exceptional incidents such as school shootings), the National Center for Victims of Crime and the National Council on Crime and Delinquency combined in 2002 to establish the *Teen Crime Project*. Its aim was to raise national awareness that teenagers are twice as likely to be victims of violent crime than adults; that African American youth are five times more likely to be killed by a gun than whites; that almost as many girls reported being raped as boys reported being robbed; and that American Indian teenagers were more likely than any other group to be a victim of violent crime (Wordes and Nunez, 2002). These local and national surveys have also been supplemented by international surveys constructed specifically to try to overcome variations in offence definition and police recording practices in different jurisdictions. However, as with the British Crime Survey, they have not usually included those aged under the age of 16. Nevertheless the findings are of interest. On average, for 13 of the industrialized countries that participated in the 2000 International Crime Victimization Survey (ICVS), 22 per cent of the population aged 16 and older declared themselves to be victims of at least one of 11 named offences in the previous year. Victimization rates were highest in Australia and England and Wales; lowest in Japan and Northern Ireland. Between 1989, the first time the ICVS was conducted, and 2000, victimization rates remained fairly stable. However, the fifth sweep of ICVS published in 2007 recorded, on average, that victimization rates had fallen to an estimated 16 per cent of the population. The countries with the highest scores were then Ireland, England and Wales, New Zealand and Iceland. Lowest overall victimization rates were found in Spain, Japan, Hungary and Portugal. Most of the countries about which trend data were available did show a distinct downward trend in the level of victimization since the mid-1990s. The fall was most pronounced in property crimes such as vehicle-related crimes (bicycle theft, thefts from cars and joyriding) and burglary. In most countries, crime levels in 2004 appeared to be back at the level of the late 1980s (Van Dijk et al., 2007).

Victimization and Offending

The 2003 Crime and Justice Survey (Wood, 2005) had found that those young people that had committed an offence were more likely to become victims themselves. Indeed it has become increasingly common for victimological research to concentrate on the relationship between delinquent activity and risk of victimization. This suggests (in terms similar to some earlier 'victim blaming' discourse) that victims and offenders are from the same populations and that victimization is related to particular 'risky' lifestyles. The implication is that frequently it is something of an accident whether those involved, say, in altercations in school, street, pubs or clubs, end up being classified as either the 'victim' or the 'offender'.

Part of this research trajectory was stimulated by left realist criminology and the local victimization survey (see **Chapter 4.2**) which argued that most crime is committed *and* suffered by the poorest and least resourced urban communities. The notion that the offender and the victim are effectively one and the same has been substantiated by American research focussing on adolescent delinquent lifestyles. In particular, exponents of routine activity theory have argued that young single males are more likely to engage in social activities that puts them at risk of being a victim. Victims of crime, it is argued, are much more likely than non-victims to be involved in deviant behaviours (Lauritsen et al., 1991). Similarly Esbensen and Huizinga (1991) argued that offence activity increases the risk of personal victimization; that is victimization is an artefact of the victims' own behavioural patterns. There is also a correlation between offender 'risk factors' (such as single parent families, low levels of parental supervision, areas of social disorganization) and risk of victimization. The higher the involvement in delinquency, the greater the risk of victimization. Smith's (2004) findings from the Edinburgh Study of Youth Transitions and Crime and based on a sample of 4,300 young people also called into question the saliency of placing the study of victims and offenders in separate compartments. It showed that the likelihood of delinquency increases as victimization is repeated. In other words a 'causal link' may also run from victimization to offending. This might be partly accounted for by retaliation or because the victimized may be drawn to offenders for their own protection but also that **victimization** (abuse, neglect, maltreatment) in childhood might cause trauma which adversely affects personal development and increases the likelihood that the 'childhood victim' will be come an 'adult offender' (Falshaw et al., 1996; Falshaw, 2005). Harassment by adults has also been reported as strongly correlated to future rates of delinquency (Smith, 2004). There may indeed be multiple reciprocal *pathways* that can lead young people from and between one 'status' and the other. Research for Victim Support noted a frequent absence of any clear boundary between the two. Young people themselves argued that there was often no such thing as offender or victim but just losers or winners in any given incident. The study found that many young people regarded both the terms 'victim' and 'offender' to be unhelpful: the former signifying weakness; the latter replete with negative connotations. Both labels were regarded by young people as stigmatizing and disempowering (Owen and Sweeting, 2007).

Victimization surveys do provide some useful insight into the (previously hidden) extent of victimization of young people. However, their almost wholesale subsequent focus on the relationship between offending and victimization has only helped to secure some familiar storylines of 'feral youth' 'preying on each other'. As a result, the extent of youth powerlessness has been obscured. Such research of course also fails to move much beyond conventional interpersonal offences. Dominant definitions of what constitutes 'serious crime' are not challenged. We are left with the usual offences, the usual suspects and the usual victims. Surveys, by their quantitative nature, typically fail to contextualize the experiences of young people either in personal biography or in broader socio-economic or political contexts (see Box 5.3).

Box 5.3

Limitations of victimization surveys

- Surveys do not assess the full reality of offending, risk and harm. They are largely restricted to 'conventional crime'; a partiality repeated in lifestyle models of victimization and offending (white-collar offences are absent).

- Surveys do not usually include those under 16 years of age and do not focus on the most victimized groups or the most victimized localities, particularly young people who live in 'high crime' areas constrained by the relation between class and ethnicity in housing and labour markets.

- Their significance is limited by respondents' memory, their willingness to accept a 'victim status', and their credibility (exaggeration or withholding information).

- The results of victimization studies are co-determined by the framework of the survey instrument (typically, the questionnaire) and questions can reflect more the agenda of those financing and carrying out the research than faithfully recording the experiences of young people themselves.

- Many offences remain especially hidden. They may not be communicated either to the police or to the victimization study. This applies particularly to offences involving family members, relatives, friends, acquaintances, and neighbours.

- Surveys, particularly longitudinal surveys, provide a picture of whether victimization is increasing or decreasing but do not address questions of why, where, to whom or to what we should look for an explanation.

Source: Derived from Francis (2007), Walklate (2007), Webster (2007).

On reviewing much of the then available research, Furlong and Cartmel (1997, p. 93) argued:

> In many respects, the concentration on young people as the perpetrators of crimes has left us blind to the extent to which young people are victims … while adults express concerns about 'lawless' youth, many crimes are also committed against young people by adults.

Similarly, Brown (1998, p. 96) concluded that 'young people have to *earn* their status as victims, whereas they are eagerly *ascribed* their status as offenders'. Most significantly, from the viewpoint of a radical or critical victimology, even in those studies that have begun to record high levels of child victimization they typically still ignore the abuse and violence endured by young people in familial, institutional and state settings.

Abuse and Violence

5.2 Historically child **abuse** research has been located outside of the criminological agenda and subsumed within considerations of social policy, psychology, health, medicine, social work and child care. Here children have been typically constructed as innocent victims, not of crime, but of injury and harm at the hand of 'dysfunctional' or 'pathological' parents or relatives.

Domestic

What is remarkable about the emergent discourses of youth victimization is that even they fail to note one of its more alarming facets. Significantly the British Crime Survey, for example, has not asked about experience of youth victimization and **violence** in the home. More than 10 per cent of the 600 homicides in Britain each year are perpetrated by parents against their children. Children under 1 year old are more at risk of being murdered than any other age group, with 46 deaths per million of population compared with a national average of 16 per million. Parents are the principal suspects in 78 per cent of all child homicides (NSPCC, 2003). However, of 492 cases between 1997 and 2000 where children under 10 had been killed by parents and carers, only 27 per cent ended in conviction. Even then the conviction was more likely to be for child cruelty than for murder or manslaughter.

The extent of domestic child abuse remains largely unknown although research by the NSPCC (2002) estimated that 1 in 10 young adults have suffered serious abuse or neglect during childhood and it noted that over 600 children are added to child protection registers every week. UNICEF (2006) has estimated that up to 275 million children worldwide are routinely exposed to domestic violence including over 900,000 in the UK (see Box 5.4).

While child abuse was recognized as long ago as the late nineteenth century, it has generally been clouded in a discourse of cruelty and neglect or subsumed within a more general concern about juvenile delinquency. Within criminology little has been done to expose the routine of violence – from slapping to serious assault – endured by young people in their own homes. The corporal punishment of children is widespread and often justified in the name of discipline and delinquency prevention. Ironically, studies in the USA, such as Straus (1994), have revealed that greater use of corporal punishment correlates not with a decrease but with *increased* rates of street violence, depression and alcohol abuse. Attempts to outlaw corporal punishment in Britain have always floundered because of accusations of 'nanny state' interference.

Box 5.4

Domestic violence

For too many children, home is far from a safe haven. Every year, hundreds of millions of children are exposed to domestic violence at home, and this has a powerful and profound impact on their lives and hopes for the future. These children not only watch one parent violently assaulting another, they often hear the distressing sounds of violence, or may be aware of it from many telltale signs. 'Me and my sister are scared' says one nine-year-old girl who lives in a violent home in the United Kingdom. 'Our parents fight a lot and we fear they might split up. They fight when we're upstairs. They don't think we know what's going on, but we do.'

Violence in the home is one of the most pervasive human rights challenges of our time. It remains a largely hidden problem that few countries, communities or families openly confront. Violence in the home is not limited by geography, ethnicity, or status; it is a global phenomenon.

Source: UNICEF (2006).

New Labour has banned child-minders from using corporal punishment but not parents, on the grounds that it constitutes 'reasonable chastisement'. Since Sweden banned smacking a decade ago, child deaths at the hands of parents have fallen to zero. In Britain it is running at one a week (*Observer*, 4 May 2003). There appears something of an epidemic of routine violence inflicted by adults on children. Moreover debate circulates more on how much violence is reasonable rather than whether it is acceptable at all. This duplicity makes it extremely difficult to get a clear picture of the extent of abuse. It also makes it difficult to construct any convincing argument that might persuade children that violence is culturally unacceptable.

Susan Creighton (2004) of the NSPCC Research Department uses the analogy of an iceberg to illustrate the hidden dimensions of abuse ranging from where abuse is recorded (level 1) to a total lack of recognition (level 5) (see Box 5.5). In 2003, there were just 775 convictions for child abuse in England and Wales.

The UNICEF (2006) international report *Behind Closed Doors* suggested that up to 7.2 per cent of children in Britain are affected by domestic violence, compared to 2 per cent in Denmark, 2.4 per cent in Sweden, and 6 per cent in France. It concluded that young people who grow up with violence are more likely to be abused themselves and may suffer the same behavioural problems as direct victims.

In the child sexual abuse investigations of the 1980s in Cleveland, Orkney and Rochdale, blame was passed from parents to social workers for unnecessarily removing children from their families. Notions of family sanctity and privacy have always precluded widespread use of criminal prosecutions. A psychological, medical or welfare focus obscures the fact that criminal offences have been committed. Child victims continue to be marginalized by use of the term 'abuse' rather than 'assault' (Morgan and Zedner, 1992, p. 20). Further ambivalence is created by a prevailing political concern that the publicizing of child abuse and

Box 5.5

The hidden dimensions of child abuse

Layer 1: those children whose abuse is recorded in the criminal statistics of a country. For example, in 2002/03 there were 4,109 reported offences of *'cruelty to or neglect of children'* and 1,880 of *'gross indecency with a child under the age of 14'* in England and Wales.

Layer 2: those children who are officially recorded as being in need of protection from abuse, e.g. children on Child Protection Registers in England or substantiated child abuse cases in the USA. For example, 32,809 were added to the child protection registers in England and Wales in 2002/03.

Layer 3: those children who have been reported to child protection agencies by the general public, or other professionals such as teachers or doctors, but who have not been registered. For example, there were 570,220 referrals concerning child maltreatment to social services departments in England during the year ending 31st March 2003.

Layer 4: abused or neglected children who are recognized as such by relatives or neighbours, but are not reported to any professional agency.

Layer 5: those children who have not been recognized as abused or neglected by anyone, including the victims and perpetrator. By definition there are no figures for layers 4 and 5.

Source: Adapted from Creighton (2004).

children's rights is likely not only to undermine respect for authority and self-discipline but also to threaten family life itself. Despite moments of apparent visibility the issue of child victimization remains peripheral to mainstream law and order debates and absent from most criminological agendas (Saraga, 2001). Attempts to legislate against child abuse have never approached the 'constant stream of law and order legislation for youth crime' (Brown, 1998, p. 86).

Occasional cases threaten to break this mould. Eight-year-old Victoria Climbié arrived in the UK from the Ivory Coast in 1999. The following year she died at the hands of her great-aunt and her partner in conditions of neglect, hypothermia and deliberate torture. The subsequent inquiry (Laming, 2003) concluded that a wide range of social welfare services had failed in their duty to provide protection. The reverberations from this case eventually impacted on the construction of the *Every Child Matters* agenda and the subsequent 2004 *Children Act* (see **Chapter 7.4**). It stood apart, at least in media terms, from other child murders in its degree of violence and in its connotations of race and citizenship. However, as Brown (2005, p. 114) recalls, it did not lead to any great public outcry about child murder, adult power or the extent of child abuse in general but was again narrowly focussed on issues of policy, practice and the failures of welfare systems: 'ultimately this murder, as with many others like it, is placed firmly within a discourse of the failure of welfare agencies to deliver effectively; within a discourse of child abuse and protection'.

In addition, Morgan and Zedner (1992) draw attention to the fact that young people not only suffer from physical and sexual abuse and bullying but are witness to numerous and prolonged instances of parental violence in the home. Children are often 'indirect victims'. Over a third of households burgled each year include children who may be traumatized as a result, but are rarely considered to be victims themselves. Interviews with the relevant professional and voluntary agencies reveal not only a very low awareness about the effects of crime on children, but because of an overwhelming concern solely with sexual abuse, none of the welfare agencies consider it their responsibility to provide child victims with support and advice (Zedner, 1994). The NSPCC survey of the strategies developed by Crime and Disorder partnerships in England and Wales found that over half did not refer to child protection or the safety of young people at all. Even those that did tended to equate safety solely with reducing young offending: 'it is disappointing that the vast majority of partnerships prioritise dealing with young people only as perpetrators of crime and anti-social behaviour' (Mason, 2001, p. 17).

Institutional

Just as alarming is the growing number of revelations about the extensive abuse of children who have been in the *care* of local authorities and the prison service. In the language of social work, young people who are in the care of local authorities are known as 'looked-after children'. Over the past decade there have been between 7,000 and 11,000 young people in residential care at any one time in England, Scotland and Wales. Their treatment has long been a cause for concern, with allegations of systematic violence by residential staff regularly surfacing since the 1980s. Significantly such victimization, even when proved, has tended again to be clouded in terms of 'abuse', 'mistreatment' and 'lack of service delivery' rather than criminal violence (Muncie, 2003b). Any resultant inquiries have either been hidden from public view or at best restricted to identifying a small number of individuals who have taken advantage of the powerless. The main policy response has been to tighten checks on applicants for residential posts, rather than to overhaul residential care policies (Corby, 1997).

The issue first came to a head in 2000 with the publication of *Lost in Care* – the Waterhouse Report into abuse at children's homes in North Wales. Following allegations of sexual abuse in similar homes in Leicestershire, Islington, Dumfries, Buckinghamshire, Northumbria and Cheshire, the Waterhouse tribunal of inquiry was established in 1996. It uncovered widespread and organized abuse of boys and girls in North Wales between 1974 and 1990. Although by 1996, 12 people had already been convicted, Clwyd County Council had refused to publish 14 prior reports partly for fear of compensation claims. Waterhouse eventually heard 259 complaints, named 200 workers in more than

40 homes and found evidence not only of daily physical assault but also of gross sexual exploitation and emotional abuse. It attributed at least 12 deaths, by suicide or in suspicious circumstances, to the experience of being 'in care'. Such criminal violence, it was concluded, was the result of a catalogue of failure by those – at all levels – who were supposedly responsible for delivering children's services (*ChildRight* 2000, no. 164, pp. 3–5).

Further evidence of systematic abuse of children has surfaced from investigations into Roman Catholic seminaries, orphanages and schools. In 2001, the Nolan Report on paedophile priests in England and Wales recalled that between 1995 and 1999 21 priests had been convicted for child abuse. In the USA, the John Jay Report commissioned by the US Conference of Catholic Bishops found accusations against over 4,000 priests between 1950 and 2002. In Ireland, the report of the Ferns Inquiry 2004 identified more than 100 allegations of child sexual abuse, made between 1962 and 2002, against 21 priests. In all countries, however, there has been a notable failure of the Roman Catholic Church to immediately respond to the complaints; the more typical response has been to move priests from church to church in order to conceal evidence. In the USA billions of dollars have been paid in compensation.

A further inquiry into allegations of institutional violence in council-run care homes in Lancashire was launched in 2000. At that time it joined at least 22 other similar inquiries being conducted elsewhere in England and Wales. In 2006, police began investigating allegations of systematic abuse and violence (including rape and flogging) of 11 to 15 year old boys and girls at Haut de la Garenne, a former children's home in Jersey. The investigation was made public in 2007 and took a dramatic turn with the discovery of bone fragments from at least 5 children in 2008 (though it subsequently transpired that the bones probably pre dated the 1940s so could not be related to the current allegations of abuse) and of possible punishment rooms in the home's cellar. By then over 100 people had made allegations of abuse: there were at least 140 alleged victims and 40 suspects (by July 2008, three had been charged). The allegations spanned a period from the 1960s to the early 2000s. As the investigation continued it was clear that numerous previous complaints had not been followed up, suggesting an institutional wall of silence. The Health Minister Senator Syvret alleged that there had been a culture of secrecy which extended to the very top of Jersey society. The Jersey police subsequently announced that corrupt police officers, politicians and a leading businessman were attempting to discredit the investigation.

Such institutional violence is not restricted to children's homes. Goldson (2008a), for example, argues that in young offender institutions and secure training centers officially sanctioned policies and practices are tantamount to 'institutionalised child abuse'. Moreover, those responsible are frequently able to neutralize accountability, evade responsibility and operate with impunity. The vulnerabilities of children in custody are often compounded by the very experience of detention itself. Child prisoners are routinely exposed to various forms of 'bullying', including: sexual abuse; verbal abuse; psychological abuse; extortion and theft; as well as physical assault. In 2006, a major independent inquiry led by Lord Carlile (2006) exposed problematic yet routine practices in custodial facilities holding children in England and Wales including: the use of physical restraint, solitary confinement and strip searching. Between April 2000 and February 2002, 296 children sustained injuries resulting from 'restraint' in prisons. His report recognized that such treatment would be considered 'abusive' in other settings. Yet two years later in 2008 the Chief Inspector of Prisons still found herself having to call for the closure of the Oakfield secure training centre in Milton Keynes because of its 'staggeringly high level of use of force by staff' (*Guardian*, 17 March 2008). Between 1990 and 2005, 29 children died in penal institutions in England and Wales (Goldson and Coles, 2005). Typically, official discourse overlooks the fact that child prisoners are routinely drawn from some of the most disadvantaged, damaged and distressed families, neighbourhoods and communities. Poverty, family discord, previous experience of 'care' institutions, emotional, physical and sexual abuse, self-harm, and a pressing sense of distress are defining characteristics of children in custody (see Box 5.6).

Box 5.6

In the Care of the State?: Case study

Anthony Redding was sent to Young Offender Institution Brinsford in January 2001, having been sentenced to four months for car-related offences. His parents had moved him from school after he had been systematically targeted by bullies. The prison service knew what to expect. Anthony had struggled with prior experience of custody and he had seriously self-harmed. The Youth Offending Service had notified the court of his previous self-harming behaviour. As soon as the second sentence was imposed Anthony attempted to hang himself while in the cellular escort vehicle that took him to prison. He was placed under 'suicide watch'. He consistently expressed high levels of anxiety. Despite this he was soon moved to 'normal location' and placed in a shared prison cell. On February 14 Anthony was found hanging from the bars of his cell. Just three weeks after being sentenced back to prison, 16 year old Anthony Redding was pronounced dead.

Source: Abbreviated from Goldson and Coles (2005, p. 48).

In the UK, research has revealed that approximately half of children held in custody at any given time have been, or remain, involved with Social Services Departments and other welfare agencies and a significant proportion have biographies scarred by adult abuse and violation (see **Chapter 9.3**). Yet even in comparison to such cases as Victoria Climbié, the death of children in custody has rarely been considered newsworthy or demanding of formal governmental inquiry. As Drakeford and Butler (2007) have argued, youth justice in general and child incarceration in particular appear characterized by a *lack* of ability to be a source of 'scandal generation'. The child offender is cast as undeserving of public sympathy and child deaths in custody are met with, at best, ambivalence. More generally, the relative powerlessness of young people has always placed them at potential risk of adult victimization. Such a risk is exacerbated at times when the vulnerability of youth is subjugated to that of 'threat'. Ironically, seeking their protection and/or regulation often ensures that they are placed in those same family and institutional settings that are a key source of their victimization.

Exploitation

5.3 As Goldson (2008a) records, in 1990 the 'World Summit on Children' assembled in New York, to declare that the 'well being of children requires political action at the highest level', and that upholding children's rights was to be a priority commitment. The United Nations Convention on the Rights of the Child (UNCRC) is seen to embody such commitment, stating, for example, that governments: 'shall take *all* appropriate legislative, administrative, social and educational measures to protect the child from *all* forms of physical or mental violence, injury or abuse, neglect or negligent treatment, maltreatment or exploitation'. However, despite the almost universal ratification of the UNCRC, in virtually all nation states and in contradiction to human rights obligations and children's developmental needs, the **exploitation** of, and violence against, children appear to be socially approved (see **Chapter 10**). It is often legal and is frequently state-authorized. In February 2003, Paulo Sergio Pinheiro was appointed to direct the 'United Nations Secretary-General's Study on Violence Against Children'. Informed by consultations with government departments, international human rights agencies, civil society organizations, research institutions and children and young people themselves, this was the first comprehensive global study to reveal the extent of violence against children in multiple settings. These 'places of danger' included home and family, schools and educational settings, care and justice systems, work and community. The final report was presented to the United Nations General Assembly in 2006 (United Nations General Assembly, 2006; Pinheiro, 2006) (see Box 5.7).

Box 5.7

World report on violence against children

1. No violence against children is justifiable; all violence against children is preventable. Yet the in-depth study on violence against children (the Study) confirms that such violence exists in every country of the world, cutting across culture, class, education, income and ethnic origin. In every region, in contradiction to human rights obligations and children's developmental needs, violence against children is socially approved, and is frequently legal and State-authorized.

2. The Study should mark a turning point – an end to adult justification of violence against children, whether accepted as 'tradition' or disguised as 'discipline'. There can be no compromise in challenging violence against children. Children's uniqueness – their potential and vulnerability, their dependence on adults – makes it imperative that they have more, not less, protection from violence.

Source: United Nations General Assembly (Pinheiro Report) (2006, p. 5).

The study noted that some forms of violence, including the organized sexual exploitation and trafficking of children; the excesses of child labour; and the impact of war on children, have begun to be taken seriously internationally. However, the impact of routine everyday violence continues to be ignored or condoned. On 27 November 2007, the Third Committee of the UN General Assembly approved a resolution on the rights of the child which included a commitment to eliminate all violence against children.

In general, the concentration on young people as the perpetrators of crime has always negated consideration of the extent of their relative powerlessness. This continually places children at potential risk of adult victimization. Nowhere is this more evident than in modern 'child slavery' and in the recruitment of 'child soldiers'.

Child Slavery and Trafficking

Trafficking was first defined in international law through the *United Nations Protocol to Prevent, Suppress and Punish Trafficking in Persons, Especially Women and Children* in 2000. Known as the 'Palermo Protocol' this stipulates that

> Trafficking in persons shall mean the recruitment, transportation, transfer, harbouring or receipt of persons, by means of the threat or use of force or other forms of coercion, of abduction, of fraud, of deception, of the abuse of power or of a position of vulnerability, or of the giving or receiving of payments or benefits to achieve the consent of a person having control over another person, for the purpose of exploitation. Exploitation shall include, at a minimum, the exploitation of the prostitution of others or other forms of sexual exploitation, forced labour or services, slavery or practices similar to slavery, servitude or the removal of organs.

The United Nations General Assembly Report (2006, p. 21) acknowledged that trafficking in human beings, including children, within countries and across international borders has become a major international concern. Estimates of its extent are inevitably imprecise but it is widely assumed that about half of all trafficking involves children, amounting (in 2002) to at least 1.2 million child victims. It has multiple causes and contexts arising from the interaction of poverty, labour, migration, conflict, or political unrest. The report noted that it can involve myriad forms including abduction or deception by recruiters in their transactions with children, their parents or other carers, sexual violence and being held captive while waiting for 'work' placement. In addition, most victims are trafficked into violent situations: prostitution, forced marriage, and domestic or agricultural work in conditions of slavery, servitude or debt bondage.

According to Save the Children UK (2007), around the world, 218 million children aged 5–17 work as child labourers, are forced to endure long hours for no or little pay and are left vulnerable to 'extreme harm, violence and rape'. Children are treated as commodities to be lent, sold, humiliated and abused across *all* continents (see Box 5.8).

Box 5.8
Modern child slavery

Child trafficking

- 1.2 million children and babies are trafficked every year, including into Western Europe, the Americas and the Caribbean, and the number is increasing.

Child prostitution

- At any one time across the world, around 1.8 million children are being abused through prostitution, child pornography and sex tourism.
- In the UK there are 5,000 child prostitutes. 75 per cent of them are girls.

Child labour

- Millions of children are forced to work away their childhood to pay off debt, or simply the interest on it.
- One million children are risking their lives in mines and quarries in more than 50 African, Asian and South American countries.
- More than 132 million children under 15 are trapped working in agriculture, often exposed to pesticides, heavy machinery, machetes and axes.

Child soldiers

- More than 300,000 children are involved in armed conflict, including government armies. Boys and girls in at least 13 countries are actively being recruited as child soldiers or as army 'wives'.

Forced child marriage

- Child marriage, which often includes mail order and internet brides, is one of the most widespread – yet hidden – forms of slavery. Girls as young as four are forced to live and have sex with their husband, and are often kept trapped indoors.

Domestic slavery

- Millions of children across the world, some as young as six, are forced to work up to 15 hour days as domestic workers. Many are beaten, starved and sexually abused.

Source: Derived from Save the Children UK (2007).

While the two hundredth anniversary of the abolition of slavery was being celebrated in 2007, modern child slavery appeared to be burgeoning. A combination of poverty, globalized economics and demand for cheap compliant labour has ensured that child slavery is now a worldwide industry. Save the Children UK (2007) estimated that human trafficking creates profits of $32 billion annually. It is 'low risk, high reward' capitalism. A report for the Joseph Rowntree Foundation on contemporary slavery in the UK (Craig et al., 2007) estimated that more than 5,000 children were being forced to work as 'sex slaves' in the UK, with Britain being a major transit point for the movement of child slaves around the world. In addition, some, possibly many, UK-based companies rely on people working in slavery to produce goods which they sell, though complex subcontracting often obscures such involvement. What this suggests is that profits from trafficking are not just reaped by organized criminal networks but by legal businesses or joint ventures between the two. Trafficking benefits important sectors of western European economies (Ruggiero, 1997).

A report produced for the Home Office by the Child Exploitation and Online Protection Centre (CEOPC), established in 2006, found that from 330 cases of suspected or confirmed victims of **child trafficking** into the UK, most were 14–17 year old girls from China and Africa forced to work as domestic servants or in the sex industry (*Guardian*, 12 June 2007). Typically, however, the governmental response has been directed more to law enforcement and tightening migration controls than to protecting children's rights. The emphasis is on criminal networks and traffickers rather than on victims. A UNICEF report on trafficked children in the UK found that, even if identified, their care and protection are inconsistent and in some regions completely absent. Of the 330 children identified by the CEOPC, 183 had subsequently 'gone missing' from social services care. A year later records from 16 local authorities around England's ports and airports estimated that 408 children (officially recorded as unaccompanied asylum seekers) had disappeared from safe houses between 2004 and 2007 (*Guardian*, 23 April 2008). The UK Government's determination to maintain strict immigration control has long informed its approach to child trafficking. For 17 years – until 2008 – it filed a reservation to the UN Convention on the Rights of the Child, stating that the UK will not be bound by the Convention in matters concerning children under immigration control, and therefore accepted no responsibility for upholding their rights (UNICEF, 2007a).

Children and Armed Conflict

Child soldiering is a unique and severe manifestation of trafficking in persons that involves the recruitment of children through force, fraud, or coercion to be exploited for their labour in conflict areas. Government forces, as well as paramilitary organizations, and rebel groups all recruit and utilize **child soldiers**. According to Human Rights Watch in 2006 (http://humanrightswatch.org/campaigns/crp/facts.htm, accessed 2007) more than 300,000 children under 18 are being exploited in over 30 armed conflicts worldwide. While the majority of child soldiers are between the ages of 15 and 18, some are as young as 7 or 8 years of age. Thousands fight and are killed at the behest of the political motivations of adults.

As Honwana (2006) established in her ethnographic study in Mozambique and Angola, children are uniquely vulnerable to the effects of war and military recruitment. They are more prone to manipulation and can be drawn into violence that they are too young to resist or understand. Technological advances in weaponry and the proliferation of lightweight automatic weapons have contributed to the increased use of child soldiers. Many children join armed groups because of economic or social pressure, or because they believe that it is their only access to food, protection or security. Others are forcibly recruited, or abducted. Once recruited, child soldiers may serve as spies or gunrunners or given work as guards, cooks, cleaners and servants. Many are pressed into combat, where they may be forced to the front lines or sent into minefields ahead of older troops. Particularly damaging is the impact of war on girls who routinely experience sexual abuse, rape and enslavement that are designed to demoralize, humiliate and immobilize an enemy. Girls who have been severely abused or have become mothers while in the armed forces are often subsequently disowned. For Honwana, (2006) it is this gendered and sexualized dimension of warfare that typically remains hidden, though it is a fundamental and pervasive feature of armed conflicts. Above all the concept of 'child soldier' forces us to move beyond clear demarcations between child and adult, between innocence and guilt, between civilian and combatant and between perpetrator and victim. Child soldiers 'epitomise the condition of simultaneously having multifaceted identities and utterly lacking a permanent, stable and socially defined place. In this way they occupy a world of their own' (Honwana, 2006, p. 4). Children are sometimes forced to commit atrocities against their own family or neighbours. Such practices help ensure that communities remain permanently fractured. Without community support they remain at continual risk of re-recruitment. Collectively these processes amount to one of the most extreme forms of institutionalized child abuse imaginable (Kimmel and Roby, 2007).

Since the early 1990s there has been growing concern amongst governments, non-governmental organizations (NGOs), and the United Nations about the effect of armed conflict on children. This awareness is due in no small part to the work of Graca Machel. In her path-breaking 1996 report for the United Nations, she noted that around the world 'millions of children are caught up in conflicts in which they are not merely bystanders, but targets'. In the past decade an estimated 2 million children have been killed and a further 5 million disabled. More than a million have been orphaned. Some die as part of a calculated genocide. Still others suffer the effects of sexual violence or the multiple deprivations of armed conflict that expose them to hunger and disease as well as exploitation as combatants (see Box 5.9).

Box 5.9

The moral vacuum of child soldiering

[M]ore and more of the world is being sucked into a desolate moral vacuum. This is a space devoid of the most basic human values; a space in which children are slaughtered, raped, and maimed; a space in which children are exploited as soldiers; a space in which children are starved and exposed to extreme brutality. Such unregulated terror and violence speak of deliberate victimization. There are few further depths to which humanity can sink ... war violates every right of a child, the right to life, the right to be with family and community, the right to health, the right to the development of the personality and the right to be nurtured and protected.

Source: United Nations (the Machel Report) (1996).

In 2000, the United Nations adopted an Optional Protocol to the Convention on the Rights of the Child (OP-CAC) on the involvement of children in armed conflict. The protocol prohibits the forced recruitment of children under the age of 18 and prohibits their use in hostilities. To date, it has been ratified by more than 110 countries. However, 10 State Parties to the OP-CAC continue the voluntary recruitment of 16 year old children, including the UK, Canada, Ireland, Serbia and Montenegro. In at least 60 other countries 17 years is the official minimum age for voluntary recruitment, including Australia, Austria, Germany, Jordan, the Netherlands and the United States. These countries have been responsible for weakening the protocol by insisting that a lower age of 16 be set for *voluntary non-combatant* recruits. This exception allows indirect and 'persuasive' measures to be taken to induce military recruitment. Indeed, the UK has the lowest recruitment and deployment age in Europe and is the only country to have routinely sent under-18s into armed conflict. In 2003, the UK ratified the OP-CAC but reserves the right to deploy under-18s in exceptional circumstances of 'genuine military need'. Between June 2003 and July 2005 15 soldiers were 'inadvertently deployed' to Iraq before their 18th birthday (*Guardian*, 8 May 2007).

It is of course easy to relegate the issue of child soldiering to developing non-western countries. However, as Peters (2005) notes, three detainees believed to be between the ages of 13 and 15 have been held as 'illegal combatants' by the USA at Guantanamo Bay. They were released in January 2004. Nevertheless the US Department of Defence acknowledged that an unspecified number of children, aged 16 and 17, remained at Guantanamo Bay, not separated from adult detainees and without education or rehabilitation assistance. In addition, we should acknowledge that the UK is the second largest arms exporter in the world (after the USA) and has a policy of actively promoting arms exports, seemingly at any cost. In 1998, the UK licensed military exports to 30 of the 40 most repressive regimes in the world. In 2007, the UK government approved arms exports to 19 of the 20 countries it had identified as 'countries of concern' for abusing human rights. These countries included Saudi Arabia, Israel, China, Russia and Colombia. British weapons are being used in most of the world's current conflicts. Open export licenses – where there is no limit on arms sales – have been approved to a number of countries with poor human rights records, including Egypt, Nigeria, Sri Lanka, and Turkey (*Guardian*, 21 May 2007).

Significantly, these issues in global violence and international children's rights have largely remained absent, not just from victimological, but also criminological, discourse.

■ ■ Summary ■

- Victimology, as the study of victims and victimization, emerged in the late 1940s and was primarily concerned then with exploring the part victims played in precipitating their own victimization. This 'victim blaming' was roundly dismissed in the 1970s particularly by feminist criminologists and through the study of physical and sexual violence against women. Positivist victimology continues to dominate the field. Mainly through the tool of the victimization survey, it weds victimization to the criminal law and aspires to the discovery of 'scientifically reliable facts'.

- Radical criminology emerging in the 1970s extended the conception of 'victim' to include human rights violations. Critical victimology of the 1990s combined aspects of radical victimology and left realism to place the 'victim' in relation to structures of socio-political power and also to provide a critical reading of victim advocacy.

- The issue of victimization has increased in visibility in the past 30 years as a subject of media interest, as an academic sub-discipline and in informing aspects of criminal justice reform. However, the specific issue of youth victimization remained largely overlooked. A series of victimization surveys carried out in the 2000s has begun to bring aspects of child and youth victimization to the fore, both academically and politically, but it remains the case that the attribution of 'offender' is more readily applied than that of 'victim'.

- There is a long history of research into child abuse and parental violence. However, this issue has been firmly located in a social work, health, psychology and medicine literature. It has yet to emerge as a *core* concern of criminology.

- The radical/critical tradition focuses attention on all forms of human suffering and not just those recognized by criminal law and criminal justice systems. Indeed, many aspects of child care and juvenile justice are themselves viewed as directly implicated in the widespread abuse and violence endured by children and young people.

- Such violence is most apparent when considering the exploitation of children worldwide. Despite the efforts of the United Nations, NGOs and individual governments, violence against children (as graphically illustrated in child slavery and child soldiering) appears endemic and institutionalized. But in criminology children and young people remain an absent victim voice. Discussion of children's rights violations will rarely be found in any criminological, let alone victimological, text. Historically, victimology (and criminology) have been limited to studying processes internal to the nation state. It is, however, no longer possible to justify such a remit. The growing importance of international agreements, globalized market economics and international communications means that 'common-sense' understandings of who are the 'victims' and who are the 'perpetrators' have to be subjected to continual critical inquiry.

 ■ study Questions ▬▬▬▬▬▬▬▬▬▬▬▬▬

1   Why has the child victim been absent from criminological discourse until relatively recently?

2   How would you distinguish between positivist, radical and critical victimologies?

3   What are the limitations of the victimization survey?

4   How and why do children and young people frequently find themselves subjected to violence and abuse in familial and institutional settings?

5   Why is an understanding of global socio-economic and political contexts important in explanations of child victimization?

There are no texts which are specifically devoted to exploring the nature and extent of youth victimization. However, Jo Goodey's (2005) *Victims and Victimology: Research, Policy and Practice* is a good introductory text to victimology in general and Mawby and Walklate's (1994) *Critical Victimology* is the clearest expression of the limitations of positivist victimology in general and the victimization survey in particular. The pioneering study of youth victimization on the streets was Anderson et al.'s (1994) Edinburgh research. Its discovery of widespread victimization was one of the first to call into question the usual ways of understanding the 'youth problem'. Chapter 5 of Brown's (2005) *Understanding Youth and Crime* provides an assessment of the nature and extent of violence and abuse experienced in familial and institutional settings as well as a critical evaluation of inherent limitations in governmental response. There is little academic work on the extent of child exploitation worldwide but the reports by the United Nations and UNICEF are informative. The United Nations General Assembly (2006) *Report of the Independent Expert for the United Nations on Violence against Children* (derived from Pinheiro's (2006) *World Report on Violence against Children*) is a devastating expose of adult violence and indifference to children's humanity and dignity.

: // **Web Resources** /

http://www.nspcc.org.uk/
The site of the National Society for the Protection of Children focussing on child abuse and child protection.

http://www.unicef.org/protection/index_exploitation.html
The United Nations Children's Fund site for the protection of children from violence, abuse and exploitation, including links to the UN's ongoing global survey of violence against children.

http://www.childtrafficking.org/
Hosted by the UNICEF Innocenti Research Center based in Florence, Italy, this site is dedicated to the protection of children and advocacy of child rights. The site allows access to many of its publications including analyses and recommendations to combat child trafficking worldwide.

http://www.un.org/children/conflict/
Office of the UN Special Representative of the Secretary-General for Children and Armed Conflict.

http://www.renewal.net/Documents/RNET/Research/Youthvictimizationliterature. pdf
A 2003 report by NACRO on the extent of child victimization in Britain.

http://www.violencestudy.org/IMG/pdf/English-2-2.pdf
The 2006 report of the independent expert for the United Nations study on violence against children.

http://www.essex.ac.uk/armedcon/
The children and armed conflict unit based at the University of Essex has up-to-date information on how children continue to be affected by armed conflict around the world.

6

Youth Cultures, Cultural Studies and Cultural Criminology

Overview

Chapter 6 examines:

- the meaning of 'youth culture', 'youth subculture', 'counterculture', 'club culture'; and 'neo-tribe';

- a range of youth styles that have emerged (particularly in the UK) since the 1950s and which have attracted adult censure and legal sanction;

- the relationship between youth leisure and (a) processes of consumerism and (b) processes of criminalization;

- strengths and weaknesses of British subcultural theory;

- the constituent elements of cultural criminology.

| **key terms**

bricolage; carnival; club cultures; consumerism; counterculture; cultural criminology; defusion/diffusion; difference; edgework; ethnographic research; hegemony; homology; imaginary solutions; moral panic; neo-tribe; night-time economy; resistance; semiology; style; subculture; transgression

---

Unsupervised leisure has almost always been considered a major source of trouble and as posing a threat to young people's moral development. During the sixteenth and seventeenth centuries carnivals were accused of promoting sexual promiscuity and popular ballads were denounced as bawdy and as glorifying criminality. By the nineteenth century, theatre, music halls, dances, penny dreadfuls, street football, gambling and other forms of popular entertainment were all subject to intense campaigns to halt their supposed contamination of youth. In the twentieth century another 'dangerous enemy' was discovered in the new medium of the Hollywood cinema (see **Chapter 2**). This chapter looks, in some detail, at how youth leisure pursuits from the 1950s on have been subject to adult censure, moral panic and regulation. A dominant theme – summarized in Sections 6.2 and 6.3 – is how far 'spectacular' youth subcultures – such as teddy boys, mods, skinheads, punks, hippies, beats and Rastafarians – are inherently deviant and oppositional or simply sites of consumerism and commercial appropriation.

In the tradition of radical youth studies established by the Centre for Contemporary Cultural Studies at the University of Birmingham in the 1970s, subcultures were first perceived as sites of resistance to adult authority. Section 6.4 offers a critique of this literature by noting how it has been challenged notably by post-subcultural studies and cultural criminology. A long-standing problem has been the degree to which 'outsider' academics can 'speak for' young people and how far (if at all) the followers of youth styles would recognize and place themselves in the theoretical ascriptions of structure, culture, subculture and resistance that were on offer. What has emerged is a level of analysis that is more flexible, more plural and more attuned to a complex array of subjectivities. Some researchers are wary of assigning any specific meaning, fixed structural position or invariable cultural significance to subcultural practice. Increasingly the boundaries between 'culture and crime'; 'resistance and commercialism'; 'opposition and collusion'; 'production and consumption'; and 'subculture and mainstream' have become blurred or dissolved. With the burgeoning of a remarkable diversity and transnationalization of youth styles since the 1990s, the insights initially drawn from the study of local, class-based subcultures in the 1970s have been called into question.

While much of this research is usually to be found in cultural studies and sociology, the chapter also reflects on how elements of a cultural criminology, with a heritage including the National Deviancy Conferences of the 1970s and interactionism (see Chapter 4.1) now devote a not inconsiderable part of their energy to studying the convergence of cultural and criminal dynamics so that fresh insights can be made into the meaning of rule breaking and how non-conformist styles have been (and continue to be) subjected to criminalization.

Subcultural Theory and Analysis

6.1 A Youth Culture?

In 1942, the American sociologist Talcott Parsons coined the term 'youth culture' to isolate the supposedly unique and highly distinctive behaviour patterns that were thought to be emerging amongst American 'adolescents'. For Parsons, youth culture emphasized values of hedonism, leisure, consumption and irresponsibility, rather than productive work. He saw the function of youth culture as one of providing a period when young people can break away from dependence on their families and develop a level of autonomy. Youth culture, however, was also seen as having dysfunctional qualities. Youth was viewed as a unitary adolescent **subculture** which transcended all other cultural attachments to home, neighbourhood or class. As a result young people were placed in an antagonistic relationship to the social order and were the source of major social problems (Parsons, 1942). Such analysis was indicative of a corresponding trend in much sociological enquiry both in America and Britain in the immediate post-war period which declared an end to poverty and heralded the emergence of a new classless society. Youth culture was seen as a classless phenomenon.

In Britain, the first influential sociological study of 'youth culture' was Abrams' *The Teenage Consumer*, published in 1959. This book, an empirical survey of a new consumer group, purported to reveal a new culture defined in terms of leisure – milk bars, fashion, clothes, cosmetics, hair styles, rock 'n' roll, films, magazines, dancing and dance halls. It implied a 'classless culture' but Abrams' research also revealed – in some contradiction – that the consumer habits of youth were dominated by the interests of working-class males. One of the earliest challenges to the 'classless teenage consumer' thesis was Willmott's study of *Adolescent Boys of East London*, published in 1966. Following a sample of 246 boys in Bethnal Green, Wilmott discovered that the new teenage leisure culture did not replace existing class-based cultures, but existed alongside them. Despite the fact that the boys had easy access to the growing number of discotheques, beat clubs and boutiques of the West End, they were more likely to use the resources of their locality. He found little sign of what was being referred to as 'the generation gap', as most boys remained with their families and regularly attended school with little or no hostility to their teachers. Willmott's study was important for various reasons. First, it demonstrated that the term 'youth culture' implied an unfounded homogeneity. Second, it revealed a marked continuity between youth and adult life. Third, it brought analysis of class divisions into the centre of youth studies.

To varying degrees, Downes's study of corner boy culture in Stepney and Poplar in 1966, Hargreaves' analysis of a secondary modern boys' school in 1967 and Sugarman's study of London schoolboys in 1967 all began to question the class-lessness thesis and offer demonstrations of the centrality of class inequalities in structuring both the work and leisure opportunities available to young people. Similarly, Murdock and McCron (1976, p. 24) reiterated the importance of class divisions, but argued that the concern should not be simply one of 'substituting class for age ... but of examining the relations between class and age and more particularly the way in which age acts as a mediation of class'.

Such reasoning was overlooked by many commentators of the counterculture of the late 1960s, who – probably more than most – helped the term 'youth culture' to gain widespread currency. The upsurge of cultural and political radicalism among students and 'drop-outs' in America and Europe in the years 1967–69 convinced such authors as Marcuse (1972) that class and class conflict were now largely redundant. As the problems facing Western society were analysed in terms of a repressive tolerance in which individual creativity had been suppressed (rather than by reference to poverty, social deprivation and class inequalities), the initial salvation of society was seen to rest with non-conformist youth. Roszak (1971) also made great claims for the unification of young people, for with them lay his vision of a viable revolutionary force which would be able to attack the problems of modern 'technocracy' and could trans-form 'the very sense men have of reality'. However, in Britain at least, the counterculture tended to reside within a small minority of the youth popula-tion, taken primarily from disaffiliated sections of the middle class. Their 'revolution' was couched largely in the class-specific goals of individualism, self expression and self-discovery.

As a result, Brake (1980, p. 8) notes that the concept of *a* youth culture glosses over the existence of 'a complex kaleidoscope of several adolescent and youthful subcultures appealing to different age and class groups, involving different life-styles'. Such class-based analysis, which achieved academic ascendancy in the 1970s, also highlighted how different groups of youth found different solutions to the problems they faced: problems that emanated not only from their respective localized economic and class positions, but also from gender and 'race' relations.

Although young people may share certain material and social disadvantage simply by virtue of their age (lower rates of pay; prohibitions on property ownership, drinking, driving and marriage; subjugation to adult authority), their claims to resources and power are significantly determined by their class, gender, ethnicity and geographical location.

Subcultural Resistance

The complex relationship between economic structures, class, culture, leisure, generation and subculture was first examined in detail by the Centre for Contemporary Cultural Studies at the University of Birmingham (the 'Birmingham School') in 1975 (Hall and Jefferson, 1976). On the one hand, the meaning of subcultural style was examined through various ethnographic and semiological analyses; on the other, the political implications of deviance were explored through investigations of the structural and class position of various subcultures and their propensity to engender '**moral panics**'.

The analysis of the Birmingham School stemmed directly from Phil Cohen's research (1972) on a succession of working-class youth subcultures in the East End of London during the 1960s. Changes in the mid-1950s in housing, employment and income, it was argued, had caught a majority of the working class in the middle of two contradictory ideologies: the new ideology of 'spectacular consumption' and affluence on the one hand, and the traditional ideology of work and pride in a job well done on the other. Post-war developments in the local economy served to undermine the solidarity, loyalties and traditions of working-class life. Automated techniques in manufacturing made traditional pride in craftsmanship impossible. The social space of the pub, the corner shop and the street was destroyed by high-rise flats. The changes that accompanied 'affluence', then, also threatened the very structure of working-class life. This predicament was registered most deeply in and on young men as they were forced to travel out of the community to work, or to move away permanently. Those that remained tried – in the form of subcultures – to retrieve those socially cohesive elements that had been destroyed in the parent culture. The subcultural styles of the young reflected and acted on these contradictions between traditional working-class puritanism and the new hedonism of consumption. Youth styles were viewed by Cohen as a 'generational solution' to contradictions facing the working class as a whole.

The Birmingham School refined this approach by drawing on the work of the Marxist author Gramsci (1971). They located subcultures not just in relation to their parent cultures, but also in relation to structures of class conflict. The British working class, it was argued, has developed its own historical cultures and the relations between these and the dominant culture are always negotiable. Working-class culture is always in a position to win 'space', for the hegemony of the dominant culture is never completed. It is always in the process of being contested and fought over. Subcultures contest this space through their 'focal concerns' and in the moments of originality created by the formation of deviant subcultural styles. As a result, working-class youth subcultures were considered oppositional because of their attempts to 'resist' dominant culture. It is significant that the Birmingham School's major publication was called *Resistance through Rituals* (Hall and Jefferson, 1976). Both Phil Cohen (1972) and Hall and Jefferson (1976) suggested that subcultures offered imaginary solutions – enacted through style and leisure – which allowed an expression of identity and self-image to counter or deny the contradictions and subordination faced in most other aspects of their lives. It was in this sense that the Birmingham School maintained that subcultural styles had not only creative, but also political, potential (see Box 6.1).

Box 6.1

Clarke and Jefferson on the political significance of subcultures

In terms of its political content then, we would characterise youth culture as being involved in a struggle fundamental to the social order – that of the control of meaning. Here one can see the significance of the media's stereotyping and thereby redefining of youth cultures. It is an attempt by the dominant culture to reaffirm its own view of society as the only correct one. It is significant that in this struggle for the control of meaning one of the most frequent adjectives used to describe disapproval of behaviour by the young is 'meaningless' …We wish to emphasize that this attempt to define and express one's own situation and to break with dominant cultural representations is a very real political struggle, both for those attempting to do it, and for those of us attempting to analyse and understand such phenomena from a distance.

Source: Clarke and Jefferson (1973, p. 9).

A Matter of Style

While it was recognized that the analysis of style cannot be made in isolation from a subculture's class position and practices, some authors gave privileged attention to a separate line of enquiry concerned primarily with how subcultures selectively appropriated symbolic objects and attached meaning to them. Clarke (1976), for example, used the cultural anthropologist Lévi-Strauss's (1966) concept of **bricolage** to explain how particular objects can be used by subcultures in such a way as to transform or subvert their original meaning. What was involved in this analysis was a *reading* of subcultural style to signify or denote something beyond its surface appearance. Objects are borrowed from the world of consumer commodities and, as they are incorporated into the focal concerns of subcultures, their meaning is reworked. This appropriation of style allowed subcultures to express their opposition obliquely or ironically. For Hebdige, subcultural styles acted as symbolic violations of the social order. Youth styles were not random, but constituted the basis for 'semiotic guerrilla warfare' (see Box 6.2).

Box 6.2

Hebdige on the significance of style

'[H]umble objects' can be magically appropriated, stolen by subordinate groups and made to carry 'secret' meanings which express in code a form of resistance to the order which guarantees their continued subordination. Style in subculture is then pregnant with significance. Its transformations go 'against nature' interrupting the process of 'normalization'. As such they are gestures, movements towards a speech which offends the 'silent majority', which challenges the principle of unity and cohesion, which contradicts the myth of consensus.

Source: Hebdige (1979, p. 18).

Hebdige borrowed another term from Lévi-Strauss: **homology**. Contrary to popular depictions of subcultures as lawless, Hebdige illustrated how different elements of style cohered into a meaningful whole (Hebdige, 1979, pp. 113–17). He argued, for example, that there was a homological relation between the spiked hair, the amphetamines, the spitting, the trashy cut-up clothes and the raw and basic music of the punk subculture of the late 1970s. Punk styles fitted together because of their generalized 'anarchy' and refusal to cohere around a stable and permanent set of central values. Similarly, Willis (1978) and Clarke (1976, p. 179) argued that there existed a homology between the intense activism, physical prowess and love of machines of motorbike boys and their preference for rock 'n' roll music, just as there was a homology between the structurelessness, self-introspection and loose group affiliation of hippies and their choice of underground or progressive rock music.

The twin concepts of 'bricolage' and 'homology' were used to explore how subcultures can alter and subvert normal expectations within a framework of meanings that is both coherent and meaningful. Through **semiology** and semiotic techniques of analysis, Hebdige was able to view style as a signifier of a unified subcultural practice, rather than as a series of distinct cultural expressions. However, in this concentration on the minutiae of subcultural activities, style is drawn some steps away from its followers' material existence. Whereas for Clarke it is class that was the key to discovering subcultural resistance, Hebdige selected **style** as the main variable in understanding how such resistance is eventually realized. The former attempted to relate a set of cultural phenomena to the question of class formations and the construction of hegemony. The latter tried to establish the autonomy of the signifying practices of subcultures from any simple reduction to the interests of any single class. In both accounts, however, it was young people's use of leisure and style which offered possibilities for subcultural **resistance**.

These analyses of youth subcultures and styles had, by the early 1980s, established the parameters within which a radical vision of youth cultures was contained (see Box 6.3). Recognizing the significance of style was also a key

Box 6.3

Key elements of British subcultural theory

- Situating youthful behaviour in its precise social, economic and historical context.

- Locating youth subcultures within the class structure and class conflict of post-war Britain.

- Explaining youth style as meaningful and in particular decoding its oppositional qualities.

- Examining youth cultures as social processes involved in an ongoing struggle for the 'control of meaning' with other class cultures, dominant culture and the consumer industries.

feature of a cultural criminology that emerged some 20 years later. Ferrell (1996, 1997), for example, argues that hip hop graffiti writing exists essentially as a 'crime of style' for both its practitioners and the authorities attempting to stop it. Style – particular ways of dressing, talking, walking, and so on – is the connecting thread between cultural practice and deviant/criminal identity: as symbols of resistance, indicators of difference and as targets for criminalization (see Section 6.5).

Subcultures and Resistance

6.2 This section offers a brief history of youth subcultures and styles in Britain from the 1950s to the end of the 1970s. It begins by examining how British subcultural analysis was applied to a succession of predominantly working-class, white youth cultures – teddy boys, mods, skinheads, punks – and black youth cultures – rude boys and Rastafarians – in terms that emphasized modes of *resistance*. Section 6.3 goes on to look at how the concept of counter-culture has been employed to capture the more overt forms of political *dissent* of the beats, CND, 'new left' and hippies of the 1950s and 1960s, the New Age travellers, saboteurs and eco-warriors of the 1980s and 1990s, and the anti-global capitalism movements of the 1990s and 2000s.

Teddy Boys

In the decade 1945–55 British social history was shaped above all by the memory and aftermath of the Second World War. But by the mid-1950s Britain was supposedly riding on a wave of affluence and full employment and was claiming the coming of a classless society. However, the post-war years also saw the 'planning blight' and consequent break-up of many working-class neighbourhoods. It is against this background that the 'utterly unexpected' rise of the teddy boys has been explained (Fyvel, 1961).

The teddy boy subculture (like a majority of British working-class youth subcultures) was specifically the creation of working-class districts in London.

In a period of 'full employment', it was such sections of the population traditionally lacking in power and status who were most likely to find themselves excluded. In the wake of the new affluence and increasing availability of consumer goods, it was the teds who discovered that there remained a general lack of public provision for leisure for the under-20s. They made the local 'caff' and the street their 'home'. Identity of self and group was maintained initially by adherence to certain styles of dress – the dandified cut of Edwardian clothes – and later through music – rock 'n' roll.

Although the teds, like all other subcultures, attracted a relative minority of youth, it has been argued that the 'nihilist ted spirit' did affect a great many and indeed it was from the rock 'n' roll mania of 1956 that the American term 'teenage culture' was imported into Britain (Melly, 1972). The teds responded to their lack of status and 'cultural space' by reaffirming and defending working-class values and defined their particular and separate stance by their choice of dress and music. Their hair, by military, or perhaps more pertinent, by National Service (1947–60) standards, was excessively long and was generally worn with sideburns, a great deal of Brylcreem, some form of quiff at the front and variations of the DA (duck's arse) at the back. Their preferred drug was alcohol. Their clothes were a bastardization of a pseudo-Edwardian style, ironically originally created by Savile Row in the early 1950s for young upper-class men-about-town. It consisted of long 'drape' jackets with velvet collars, tight 'drainpipe' trousers, bootlace ties and thick crêpe-soled shoes. For Jefferson (1976), such style represented an arrogant yet half-conscious parody of the upper classes and also an attempt to glorify the masculinity and slickness of the Hollywood criminal hero. The term 'Teddy Boy' first appeared in print in March 1954 when it was clear that they could no longer be simply referred to as the 'hooligans', 'spivs' or 'cosh boys' of the past (Rock and Cohen, 1970, p. 94).

Imported from America, rock 'n' roll marked an abrupt shift in musical style. Although it was derivative of black blues and white country styles, Melly (1972, p. 36) argues that it was 'a contemporary incitement to mindless fucking and arbitrary vandalism: screw and smash music'. It represented a blatant attack on parental sexual taboo and, for the underprivileged young, became one of the few means whereby self-autonomy could be expressed. At the showing of the rock 'n' roll film *Blackboard Jungle*, in London in 1956, Britain witnessed its first 'rock riot' (Hebdige, 1988, p. 30). Later, Bill Haley's British performances and the first showings of the Elvis Presley films were to be greeted with 'mass hysteria'. Notions of delinquency and 'the teenager' converged. When the adult world wanted order in the cinemas, coffee bars and streets, the teds responded by jiving in the aisles, razoring cinema seats and attacking 'intruders' in their 'territories'. They were assured of a hostile political and media reaction. The *Reynold News* (1 May 1954) described them as a 'grave social evil'; they were demonized as the end result of the importation of an un-British (American) degenerate culture into Britain (Pearson, 1983, p. 19).

However, recording, publishing and film companies gradually realized that there existed a huge market for such interests. The films *The Wild One* (1954), starring Marlon Brando, and *Rebel without a Cause* (1955), starring James Dean, became cult movies in their celebration of teenage lawlessness. The teddy boys' style too began filtering upwards and outwards from south London and underwent significant change. Leather jackets replaced the drapes, and motorcycles allowed greater freedom and mobility. The 'rocker' style emerged. Coupled with skiffle, the possibility of semi-amateur music-making by and for youth became a reality. It was from these origins that in 1957 a group in Liverpool was formed which over the next five years was to evolve into the Beatles.

Mods

From the late 1950s onwards, British society was being interpreted by many political commentators and sociologists in terms of a 'post-war affluence'. Despite contrary empirical evidence of the persistence of class structures and differential opportunities (Westergaard, 1965), working-class youths of the early 1960s were caught up in the desire to share the fruits of the 'new affluence'. The use of the term 'mod' reflected such contradictions by referring both to the image of a consumer-based 'swinging' London and also to a particular subcultural 'solution'. It was the province of upwardly mobile, working-class youths who had 'made it good' through art school and the commercialization of style – the Beatles, Mary Quant, David Bailey, Jean Shrimpton, Twiggy – and, more precisely, those who found the lower middle-class, non-manual occupations to which they had aspired just as stultifying as the manual jobs they had left behind.

As a subculture, the mods originated from East London and working-class estates in the suburbs of the capital. Typically they were engaged in semi-skilled manual work or basic white-collar jobs (van boy, messenger, clerk, office boy, and so on). Partly a reflection of their relative affluence and partly an attempt to emulate the cool and slick style of their West Indian neighbours (the 'shades' and pork pie hats and Jamaican bluebeat music), the mod style was characterized by short hair, smart Italian designed suits and an almost narcissistic obsession with neat appearance. Their preferred drug was amphetamine (speed). Mods were the epitome of the conspicuous consumer, whether in clothes, scooters, music or amphetamines. But for Hebdige (1976a) they were never passive consumers. The scooter and clothes were transformed into symbols of solidarity while 'speed' enabled a total commitment to all-night dancing in the clubs and discos. The style they created has thus been 'read' as constituting a parody of the consumer society in which they were situated (Hebdige, 1979).

If the mods were something of an apolitical or 'imaginary' reaction against the ideology of classlessness, then they equally reacted against the music and style of the previous decade. Rock 'n' roll and the descendants of the teds – the rockers – were dismissed as boorish, out of date and crude. In part this explains the conflicts on the beaches at Margate, Brighton and Hastings in 1964. Whether open hatred and violence were continually prevalent between mods and rockers remains open to debate. Certainly Stan Cohen (1973a) offers a convincing argument that our understanding of this phenomenon has been more than tainted by selective and sensational media reporting (see **Chapter 4.1**).

By 1966, the mod 'movement' in both its middle-class commercial (symbolized by Carnaby Street) and working-class subcultural variants was beginning to wane because of pressures from the media, the market and its own internal contradictions. These two elements of 'mod' never really merged into one and in the following years were to separate further with the coming of the skinheads and the hippies.

Skinheads

Skinheads probably first appeared in sections of the unskilled working-class community from the East End of London in early 1968. For Mungham and Pearson (1976), they represented both a 'caricature and [a] reassertion of solid, male, working-class toughness'. This was exemplified in cropped hair, braces, half-mast trousers and Doc Marten 'bovver boots'. Their association with violence, football hooliganism, and 'Paki' and 'queer' bashing has been viewed as an attempt to recover the cohesiveness of working-class communities and to retain some control over their territory – albeit in its most reactionary form (Hebdige, 1981, p. 40). Despite this, in line with their hard mod ancestors, the skinheads also tried to emulate the sharp 'rude boy' of an Afro-Caribbean youth subculture. But in general they explored avenues dominated by working-class chauvinism, the pub, alcohol, football and the street. Those who most obviously had dismissed such values – the middle-class hippies – became legitimate targets for their aggression. According to radical deviancy theorists, skinhead culture remained an affirmation of white working-class values (Clarke, 1976; Hebdige, 1981). It filled the gap opened up by the decline of working-class politics and culture – a gap which was defended by a developed sense of 'community' and 'territoriality'. As Ian Taylor (1971) noted, such allegiances were frequently centred on the local football team, where traditionally working-class values of collectivity, physical toughness and local rivalry could be acted out.

As the style spread outwards from the inner-city areas, it evaporated into groups known as crombies (derived from the crombie coat), smooth-heads and casuals, and the way was open again for consumerism to capitalize on style. Taylor and Wall (1976), for example, emphasized the role consumerism played in taking elements of the skinhead style, fusing it with remnants of the hippie underground and, perhaps for the first time, providing a style (later to be known as 'glam rock') which, they argued, conveyed a sense of classlessness within a now universal manufactured culture. But derivatives of skinhead style have never disappeared. It continually resurfaces – through Oi music, through football hooliganism, through the British National Party and neo-Nazi/white supremacist groups particularly in Germany and America and at the harder edge of working-class culture in general.

Punks

The 1960s were a time of relative affluence compared with the 1970s. By the mid-1970s mass unemployment and fascism, coupled with high inflation, had returned.

It was against this background that punk rock, or as Marsh (1977) termed it, 'dole queue rock' developed.

The formation of a subculture in 1976 was intrinsically tied to the creation of a 'new' musical style. As in the past, the initiating centre was London, the punks gathering in a shop called Sex and a rock club called the Roxy. In contrast to the skinheads, who created something of a fetishism of their class position, the punks were nihilistic and saw themselves as true outsiders – the blank generation (Hebdige, 1979, p. 120). They saw 'no future' in their own or society's life, and could rely on 'no heroes' from the rock culture of the past. Plastic bin liners, lavatory chains, zips, safety pins, dyed hair, ripped T-shirts, Nazi paraphernalia and defiled school uniforms were valued precisely because of their perversity, abnormality and lack of value: as glamorized in the use of rubber wear, fishnet stockings, bondage suits and the 'dirty raincoat'. Punk seemed to disrupt every pre-existing style, to reduce everything to absurdity. Its music was basic and direct. Everyone could play the guitar. Everyone could write and produce 'fanzines'. Everyone could invent styles of dance or dress. Essentially nothing mattered, as long as it was unacceptable to the 'others'. It amounted to a do-it-yourself culture (Burchill and Parsons, 1978).

Wilful desecration was epitomized by the names of the groups that emerged in 1976 (the Sex Pistols, the Clash, the Damned), their stage names (Poly Styrene, Sid Vicious, Rat Scabies, Johnny Rotten) and their songs ('Belsen Was a Gas', 'Pretty Vacant', 'I Wanna Be Sick on You', and 'Anarchy in the UK'). The Sex Pistols' first album was seized under the 1959 Obscene Publications Act because it had the word 'bollocks' in its title (Cloonan, 1995, p. 351). Punk also drew on influences from art school and conceptual art. In contrast to Marsh's concept of 'dole-queue rock', Frith (1978) argued that punks had connections with middle-class hippies, student anarchists and the avant-garde. Indeed, punks were essentially a stratified subculture: in one sense they contained reflections of all major post-war subcultures, but represented in chaotic and distorted form (Hebdige, 1979). Punk too may provide us with an example of the divergence of subcultural politics from subcultural style. Some of the lyrics of punk music – speaking of high-rise flats, dole queues and white riots – appealed to working-class experience, while others were content to display symbols of revolt without translating them into political action. Punk's political heart was similarity split between the 'cosmetic rage' of anarchism and the stand taken against the National Front by the organization of Rock against Racism concerts and Anti-Nazi League rallies. The difficulty of distinguishing a unified subculture was clear as early as 1977 when once more 'subversive' subcultural style was being fully catered for by the record and leisure industries. Indeed, by March 1978 Frith could describe punk as 'just another form of pop', as dedicated as all other subcultures to orderly consumption.

Rude Boys and Rastafarians

The thesis of the Birmingham School – that subcultural style is evidence of 'resistance' and developed as a response to economic equality – was also applied to the situation of black youth. Indeed, such uniquely black styles as Rastafarianism, reggae and the rude boy have been viewed by Hebdige (1979) as key elements informing some white subcultural practices – both as a means of establishing their own separateness (for example, the mods) or as a vehicle for reaction (for example, the teds). Dominant images of 'youth' and 'black culture' also share many characteristics. Both are routinely demonized as lazy, hedonistic and dangerous (Young, 1971).

In the mid-1960s Afro-Caribbean youth in Britain began to develop a style based on the 'rude boy' subculture of West Kingston, Jamaica. Rudies were 'hustlers' who lived by dope dealing, pimping and gambling. In Britain a style evolved based on self-assurance, coolness, 'sharp' clothes and ska music (Hebdige, 1976b). Inevitably, this combination of style, 'race' and petty criminality brought them into conflict with the police. For Sivanandan (1976), the development of these forms of black consciousness among 'rebellious black youth' must be placed first in the context of Britain's historical involvement in colonialism and slave trading. As a result of slavery, black people have been living in Britain since the seventeenth century and have consistently faced racism and prejudice. For example, in Britain's first 'race riot' in 1919, a black seaman was killed following white riots in the Cardiff, Liverpool and Bristol docks. Second, while the main period of black immigration to Britain in the 1950s was sponsored as a result of a chronic domestic labour shortage, the black population routinely occupied jobs in the low-status and low-paid service sector. Because such work was only to be found in already overcrowded urban conurbations, black immigrants also came to occupy some of the worst housing in the country. As a result, Sivanandan (1976) has argued, the black population came to constitute a sub-proletariat, separate and different to the indigenous workforce.

The second generation of blacks (British born) then grew up in a situation of social and educational disadvantage, exacerbated not only by growing unemployment but also by a recurring white racism which now manifested itself in the 'race riots' of 1958 in Notting Hill and Nottingham (in which the teds played no small part). As Hall et al. (1978, p. 347) argued, 'race' is the 'principal modality' through which blacks 'comprehend, handle and then begin to resist the exploitation which is an objective feature of their class situation'. 'Race' raises a level of consciousness of structured subordination which is lacking in white working-class youth. The 'resistance' of the 'rude boy' thus occurred in the context of a 'colony' culture: a defensive cultural space enabling the formation of alternative and more explicitly 'oppositional' lifestyles. Moreover the symbolic purchase of the Caribbean and Africa allowed black youth in general to develop styles and a language which were in antithesis to mainstream white sensibilities. As Hall et al. (1978, p. 351) recall:

> Here began the 'colonisation' of certain streets, neighbourhoods, cafes and pubs, the growth of revivalist churches … the shebeen and the Saturday night blues party, the construction of the sound systems, the black record shops selling blues, ska and soul – the birth of the 'native quarter' at the heart of the English city.

Behind the swagger, the cool and the hustling of the 'rude boy' lay the more visionary figure of the Rastafarian (Hebdige, 1976b, p. 143). The Rastafarian movement has religious overtones based largely on a reading of Christianity that draws on biblical metaphors to develop a political message. In contrast to the 'rude boy', property, alcohol and gambling are condemned as elements of Babylon (white colonial capitalism) while ganja (marijuana) is believed to be sacred. The Ethiopian colours of red, green and gold, along with long, uncut hair worn in dreadlocks, became vital symbols for black youth in promoting a positive evaluation of being black (Cashmore, 1979).

By the late 1960s, rudies were adopting a Rasta style largely because it provided a way forward from the image of the individual rebel and spoke more explicitly of the development of a black cultural consciousness and the possibility of collective resistance. This was one form of black youths' response to their increasingly strained relations with the British police and the development of Powellism and British Nationalism (see Box 6.4).

Box 6.4

'Race' and resistance

Between the late 1960s and the 1970s, the seeds of cultural resistance have not only sprouted in Britain's 'Harlems' up and down the country they have blossomed – but now in a distinctively Afro-Caribbean form ... The revival among 'colony' blacks of the apocalyptic religio-politics of Rastafarianism, the sounds of Anglo-Caribbean 'colony' music and the 'hard' style of the Jamaican 'Rude Boy' combined to provide a vocabulary and syntax of rebellion much more closely attuned to the material existence as well as to the emergent consciousness of those condemned to the drifting life of the streets. In and through the revivalist imagery of the 'dreadlocks', the music of the dispossessed and the insistent, driving beat of the reggae sound systems came the hope of deliverance from 'Babylon' ... It is the ideological point of origin of a new social movement amongst blacks, the seeds of an unorganised political rebellion. The extent of police supervision of the 'colonies', the arbitrariness and brutality of the hassling of young blacks, the mounting public anxieties and moral panic about 'young immigrants' and crime ... serve only to reinforce the impression, both inside and outside the colony that, in some as yet undefined way, a 'political' battleground is being staked out.

Source: Hall et al. (1978, pp. 357–8).

It is against this background that Hall et al. explain the crisis about mugging in the early 1970s, when a historically recurring form of street crime suddenly became defined as a 'black crime'. The period too is important in marking a fundamental politicization of the 'crime problem': a time when 'black youth' became synonymous with images of urban disorder (Solomos, 1988, p. 96; and see **Chapter 4.1**).

Yet as Hebdige (1979, p. 44) argues, the sights and sounds of 'the colony' spilt over to inform many of the predominantly white, working-class youth cultures. Black styles were 'a crucial determining factor in the evolution of each youth cultural form'. Elements of the 'rude boy' style were adopted by both mod and skinhead. In 1979, ska music was revived by the Coventry-based Two Tone record label promoting such bands as the Specials, Madness, Selecter and the

Beat. In the Anti-Nazi League demonstrations and Rock against Racism concerts of the late 1970s, reggae and punk rock often shared the same stage. As Gilroy and Lawrence (1988, p. 148) argued, 'through reggae, the Rastafarian discourse of "equal rights and justice" provided a political analysis of "police and thieves" for young whites'. Hebdige (1979, p. 45) goes so far as to argue that rather than being culturally distinct, 'black' and 'white' are in continual exchange such that a 'phantom history of race relations' can be read in the succession of post-war British youth cultures. And as Gilroy and Lawrence (1988, p. 127) astutely note, 'it is no accident that moral panics about youth should have occurred at precisely the point where Black cultural forms became incorporated into the subcultures of White, working class youth'.

Countercultures and Dissent

6.3 The 1960s also witnessed an upsurge in political and cultural protest emanating from middle-class and bohemian subcultures. Unlike the 'imaginary' nature of protest and resistance present in working-class subcultures, sections of middle-class youth have characteristically indicated their own disaffiliation and disillusionment by way of political organizations, liberation movements and alternative lifestyles. As a result there is a dominant tendency to view their activities as *counter*cultural rather than simply subcultural (Yinger, 1960). Clarke et al. (1976), however, remind us to be careful in its use. They note that many of its 'radical' notions have been incorporated into the values of dominant culture or indeed owe their existence to those very dominant values which they supposedly counter. In this way the meaning of **counterculture** may be best captured as a crisis *within* dominant culture, rather than as a conspiracy *against* dominant culture.

The Beats, CND and the New Left

Before the teds and rock 'n' roll's arrival in 1953, a section of middle-class youth – the beats – were already indicating their disaffection with post-war society. Pessimistic of technological materialism and for future 'progress', the beats lived out the present to the fullest in the style of Woody Guthrie and Dean Moriarty, Kerouac's hero of a life *On the Road* (1957). The American beat scene was best captured in Polsky's (1971) empirical study carried out in Greenwich Village, New York, in 1960. It was a scene characterized by anti-politicism rather than apoliticism, by work avoidance rather than inability to work, and by the belief that voluntary poverty was an intellectual gain.

Although the movement was predominantly American, the visual symbols of beat were exported to Britain. Jazz, poetry and marijuana were its hallmarks. The beat subculture in Britain eventually became one element of a humanist and intellectual rejection of industrialism which found its feet in the Campaign for Nuclear Disarmament (CND). Between 1953 and 1957 the dangers of atomic fallout were dominant in the minds of those campaigning for the abolition of nuclear tests. In

1958, the CND organized a protest march to the atomic weapon research centre at Aldermaston and was influential in attracting large numbers of youths to the peace movement. As Parkin (1968) recalls, nominal support for CND was a commonly accepted feature of this youth culture. It was a vehicle for protest outside class-based politics; accordingly, humanitarian and moral issues, which were marginal to traditional analyses of class politics, became central.

However, CND was far from politically united. It had two important groups of intellectuals – the older generation such as Bertrand Russell, A.J.P. Taylor and J.B. Priestley, who saw CND as providing a moral leadership to the rest of the world, and the 'Angry Young Men', those dramatists and novelists of the late 1950s, such as John Osborne, who were more concerned with the problems of being working class in a so-called middle-class social democracy. There was some discord too over the most appropriate forms of protest: whether they should follow constitutional methods or advocate non-violent civil disobedience. By the early 1960s, the anti-bomb movement went into decline and was not revived until the early 1980s when US Cruise missiles began to arrive in Britain.

CND, however, had also helped give birth to a movement known as the 'new left'. During the late 1950s and early 1960s the *New Left Review* group constituted the most important theoretical body of dissent in British youth politics. Born from a merger of ex-British Communist Party members (known as revisionists) with university intellectuals, the 'new left' advocated a socialism based not on the Leninist model of centralized political parties, but on a new libertarianism involving Trotskyite principles. After its peak period of influence in the days of the Aldermaston marches, the 'new left' also entered a period of decline. What was to emerge some five years later was a very different protest style, deriving its impetus from the American and European student revolts and from a countercultural 'underground'.

Hippies

The term 'hippie' covers a wide range of bohemian, drug, student and radical subcultures. As with the beats, there was a hard core of artistic-literary intelligentsia; as with the CND movement, there was a strong contingent of anti-war pacifists and radicals. Indeed, the hippie counterculture in Britain was something of a hybrid of CND's liberal humanitarianism and the beats' retreatism. The hippie, like the beat, was deeply critical of the growing dominance of technology and bureaucracy in both capitalist and socialist societies. However, the hippies' withdrawal was not necessarily one of self-imposed poverty; it attempted to create a 'new and distinct' way of life which, they hoped, would convert others by example. Nor was the culture manifestly politically orientated. It had no party, no leadership and no manifesto, but lived by its unwritten demands to the rest of society: to seek love rather than violence, and to express oneself freely without fear of social sanctions. Above all, the hippies' alternative lifestyle was aimed at revolutionizing society through peaceful means. As Abbie

Hoffman (1968, p. 14) proclaimed, 'Revolution is in your head. You are the Revolution. Do your thing.' For Yablonsky (1968), it was a para-society existing casually beneath the surface – neither subcultural nor countercultural but an attempt to resonate with a deeper reality of cosmic consciousness. It is largely accepted that this particular brand of bohemianism was born in the early 1960s on the West Coast of America, and particularly in the Haight Ashbury district of San Francisco (Wolfe, 1969).

The 'colony' brought with it some of the trappings of the beat subculture. Of note was the use of drugs to explore the limits of imagination and self-expression. A lifestyle developed based on the use of marijuana and particularly lysergic acid diethylamide (LSD or 'Acid') which, because of its hallucinogenic effects, enabled the user to 'trip' through a multitude of distorted ideas, images and actions in rapid succession. The dedicated believed that such an experience enabled reality to become clearer, to be seen free from all preconceptions. The cult was notably spread by Timothy Leary who founded the so-called International Federation for Inner Freedom in 1962 and coined the phrase 'tune in, turn on and drop out' and by Ken Kesey and his group of 'Merry Pranksters'. If Leary's interest was partly scientific and partly tied to religious awakening, Kesey's contribution was to make the acid experience spectacular, wild and playful.

At the beginning of 1967 San Francisco was the setting for the first 'Human Be-In' and by the summer had attracted 100,000 young people into the district. Soon the media discovered the Haight and invented the term 'hippie'. Hippies were soon to attract sympathy for their ideas of love and peace, but were mistrusted for their anti-work, pro-drug and permissive ethos. Drug abuse and permissive morality were to become the main focus for moral panics in the later 1960s. In Britain, LSD was made illegal in September 1966. Regional drug squads were formed in March 1967. Later that year the Rolling Stones were arrested for possession of marijuana. From 1967 to 1969, the offices of the underground newspaper *IT* (*International Times*) were raided by police and its editors imprisoned or fined on charges of obscenity or conspiracy to corrupt public morals (Stansill and Mairowitz, 1971). The underground music clubs, UFO and Middle Earth, were eventually closed after police raids. And in October 1970 the infamous *OZ* obscenity trial began after raids on its offices in June. *OZ*, an underground magazine, was fined £1,000 plus court costs. Prison sentences imposed on its editors, Neville, Dennis and Anderson, were dropped only after a lengthy appeal (Palmer, 1971).

'Permissiveness' was assured of an adverse and hostile social reaction. Drug law enforcement in particular developed dramatically throughout the 1960s. There was a marked increase in convictions for possession of marijuana in Britain – from 235 in 1960, to 4,863 in 1969 and 11,111 in 1973. As the 'drug problem' expanded, it took on the appearance of being especially a youth problem. Marijuana remained a vital element in creating a 'moral panic' about youth, even though every major official inquiry from the American La Guardia Report of 1944 to the British Wootton Report of 1969 recommended greater liberality in the treatment of users. The panic culminated in 1971 when the Misuse of Drugs Act was passed. This gave police greater powers to search and hold suspects, and penalties for possession were increased to a maximum of six months' imprisonment or a £400 fine for first offenders.

Political Activists and Anarchism

1968 was a watershed year when bohemian disenchantment was adopted by many student bodies in universities throughout Europe and America as a basis for building a radical political movement. Their contemporary origins lay in the free speech movement and protest at Berkeley, California, in September 1964 when the university authorities tried to ban all political activity on the campus. In the spring of 1965 the movement was fuelled by Lyndon Johnson's order for heavy bombing to start in North Vietnam. The three issues of American imperialism in Vietnam, black civil rights and educational control were to inform the spate of university sit-ins, marches and demonstrations of 1968, in which the 'strange agglomeration' of black militants, students, drop-outs, draft dodgers, mystical hippies and women's liberationists seemed to be momentarily united. In Europe the radical student was particularly motivated by the takeover of the Sorbonne in May by a student/worker alliance and the formulation of an ideology of situationism which emphasized the importance of developing the revolution in everyday life. Reverberations from Paris were felt most in Britain at the London School of Economics and the Hornsey Art College, where students demanded more autonomy in the organization of university education. Similarly, in March and October the Vietnam Solidarity Campaign organized demonstrations outside the American Embassy in Grosvenor Square, London.

At the turn of the decade, the first phase of the counterculture, based on drugs, student activism and mysticism, was superseded by anarchist political action. The Youth International Party (the Yippies) of America first became widely known in Britain when a group of 20, led by the American Jerry Rubin, disrupted ITV's Saturday night *David Frost Show* in November 1970 (Rubin, 1970). Rubin was quickly deported. A month later the Angry Brigade came to public attention. Like the Yippies, the Angry Brigade was not an organized group but loosely influenced by French situationism, the Weathermen and Black Panthers in America and the European Red Army Faction and Baader-Meinhof Group. As early as 1968 bombs were planted at targets connected with the American, British and Spanish governments and at the close of 1970 a bomb damaged a BBC van outside the Albert Hall on the morning of the annual Miss World contest. Explosions at the homes of the Attorney-General, the Commissioner of the Metropolitan Police and the Home Secretary, Robert Carr, in 1971 eventually broke the news silence (Vague, 1997).

The 1960s counterculture was a loose affiliation of many disparate radical and libertarian groups. Nevertheless, elements of this 'new radicalism' remained the dominant force in youth culture style until the early 1970s. The counterculture's contribution to youth cultural styles was indeed enormous. Because it encouraged a diverse range of 'alternatives' from Eastern mysticism to Third World revolution, it was able to draw on a multitude of romantic images and symbols (Hall, 1969). Similarly, because the personal and political were fused, all countercultural styles were able to retain an image of being progressive and radical. In music, the acid rock of the San Francisco bands, the progressive and electronic rock of the English Pink Floyd, together with blues and folk revivals, notably from Bob Dylan, achieved ascendancy in music charts worldwide. In fashion, the East was alluded to in the marketing of caftans, incense, Afghan coats and sandals. North American Indian styles – body painting, beads, long hair, headbands – were similarly appropriated in the romanticizing of a simple, primitive and tribal past (Neville, 1971).

Nevertheless this bohemian 'revolution' was shot through with its own contradictions. While condemning materialism and capitalist enterprise, hippiedom gave birth to numerous small capitalist businesses in T-shirts, pop art, posters, underground newspapers, drug-related paraphernalia and mail order records (think Virgin). Preaching equality, its sexual 'revolution' was also couched in male terms. By the early 1970s, feminists had largely dissociated themselves from the 'global' counterculture and established their own organizations and modes of political action.

DIY Culture: New Age, Sabs and Eco-warriors

During much of the 1970s, middle-class and student radicalism appeared to collapse. However, as McKay (1996) catalogues, it is possible to trace a recurring set of youth and marginal 'cultures of resistance' from the late 1960s to the present. From the hippie of the 1960s through anarcho punk of the 1970s to the New Age travellers of the 1980s, McKay detects a persistent disillusionment with modernist and rationalist politics and values. Typically such disillusionment has been expressed in retreatism, the occult, mysticism, self-sufficiency, grassroots direct action, free festivals and fairs. For example, the annual pilgrimage to Stonehenge to celebrate the midsummer solstice continued unabated from the 1970s to the 1990s despite regular over-reactive policing. 'Peace convoys' continued to travel from festival to festival throughout the summer months in a search of rural authenticity and the utopics of the countryside (Hetherington, 1998). In 1987, thousands gathered at Glastonbury Tor and at other ancient sites throughout Britain (and worldwide) to celebrate the 'harmonic convergence' – a spiritual and planetary realignment predicted in Mayan, Aztec and Hopi writings to be the birth of a 'New Age' (McKay, 1996, p. 51).

By the mid-1980s New Age travellers had come to occupy centre-stage as the new 'folk devils' of British society. When several hundred travellers attempted to hold a free festival in the 'contested space' of Stonehenge in June 1985, English Heritage and the National Trust took out injunctions. Riot police forced the travellers into a field and destroyed many of their vehicles. In the so-called 'Battle of the Bean Field', clubs and batons were freely used by the police. Some 420 travellers were arrested; their children taken into care. Twenty-four later sued for wrongful arrest, but lost in court. It may have appeared as if a renewed culture of grassroots environmentalism, spirituality, disenchantment with established institutions and a sense of being outside of society (homeless and jobless), had once more come to an end.

However, in subsequent years, defiance of materialism, urbanism, consumerism, capitalism and cultural orthodoxy spread out to an amorphous cross-section of marginalized, dispossessed and disillusioned youth. A 'loose network of loose networks' (McKay, 1996, p. 11) was created. Direct action, pleasure, idealism, creativity, plagiarism, narcissism, indulgence and a simultaneous rejection and embracing of new technologies combined to produce an intuitive liberal anarchism (McKay, 1998). In numerous protests against road building through ancient sites (Solsbury Hill, Twyford Down, Newbury) or the transportation of live animals (Coventry, Shoreham, Brightlingsea), middle-class adult protest emerged alongside that of the radical young. There was a sense of harking back to the English Civil War, to the Diggers and the Levellers, and of reclaiming the land for the 'common people'. New Age philosophy was thus instrumental in reawakening new social protest movements – movements that challenged orthodox politics, deliberately lacked traditional leadership patterns and relied on non-violent, but direct forms of action. It was a politics, as Rutherford (1997, p. 124) records, that was 'simultaneously here and not here – ephemeral, transient, disorganized'.

Animal rights movements, poll tax demonstrators, eco-warriors, squatters, new environmentalists, hunt saboteurs and anti-road protesters may indeed appear diverse and disparate groups, but by the mid-1990s many were united in protest against the *1994 Criminal Justice and Public Order Act (CJA)*. This law effectively attempted to outlaw a way of life. Large gatherings and convoys and camps of more than six vehicles were declared illegal and a new provision of 'aggravated trespass' was aimed at curbing many forms of environmental action, particularly hunt sabotage (see Box 6.5). In October 1994, 100,000 travellers, anarchists, ravers and environmentalists gathered at Hyde Park, London, to protest.

Box 6.5

Public order provisions of the *Criminal Justice and Public Order Act 1994*

- Extension of police powers to direct trespassers to leave land and to seize their vehicles. Failure to comply with such directions carries a maximum penalty of three months' imprisonment (sections 61–2).

- New police powers to prevent and stop raves if the playing of amplified music would 'cause serious distress to the inhabitants of the locality'. Maximum penalty three months' imprisonment (sections 63–7).

- A new offence of aggravated and mass trespass carrying a maximum sentence of three months' imprisonment (sections 68–71).

- New criminal sanctions against squatters who fail to leave premises within 24 hours' notice (sections 75–6).

- New powers for local authorities to move on illegal campers and removal of duty of local authorities to provide sites for gypsies (sections 77–80).

The Act also introduced secure training orders for 12–14 year olds, doubled the maximum sentence of detention for 15–17 year olds, allowed juveniles charged with a serious offence to be identified in court and provided for an area-by-area introduction of curfew orders enforced by electronic monitoring.

In the first few months after the Act over 90 arrests were made, but by the mid 1990s over 200 anti-CJA, 'Right to Party' and 'Reclaim the Streets' groups had been formed and anti-road protests, tree-sitting and disruption of hunt meetings still appeared to be rife: culminating in the treetop and tunnel protest at Manchester Airport in 1997. As Gartside (1997, p. 200) argued, these apparently new, disorganized, ad hoc and carnivalesque forms of protest seemed to destroy traditional conceptions of what constituted radical politics. The old adages of 'left' and 'right' no longer seemed to apply. But the combination of middle-class romanticism, anarchism, tribalism, mysticism, paganism, anti-rationalism, direct action, utopianism and 'opting out' also had clear resonances with the counterculture of some 25 years previously.

Anti-Capitalism and Global Justice

If America's military adventures in Vietnam were a major catalyst for worldwide demonstration and protest in the 1960s; at the end of the 1990s it was the activities of the World Trade Organization (WTO), the World Bank (WB) and the International Monetary Fund (IMF).

The anti-capitalist movement in many ways attempted to fill a political void following the collapse of communism, and the related increasingly global reach of western neo-liberal economics and multinational corporations (Burbach et al., 1997). Neo-liberal principles of freedom in investment, capital flow and trade underpin a new global economy. Profit for the few is pursued relentlessly without regard to the human and environmental costs. Nation states seem unwilling or unable to counter this realignment of power. The gap between rich and poor is increasing. Orthodox politics are moribund. Such readings of global economics and the possibilities of protest informed a growing number of loose coalitions of anti-capitalist movements at the turn of the twentieth century. These included *People's Global Action*, formed in Mexico to protest against the North American Free Trade Agreement; the environmental pressure groups *Friends of the Earth* and *Greenpeace*; *Earth First!*, a direct action ecology movement; *Globalize Resistance*, a coalition of socialists, anarchists, trade unionists and students; *Reclaim the Streets* and *Critical Mass*, best known for campaigns against road building; *Ya Basta!* (Enough!), and *Ruckus Society*, a US-based organization to train activists in the skill of non-violent civil disobedience, not to mention any number of human rights activists, representatives of indigenous peoples, asylum organizations and environmentalists (Bircham and Charlton, 2001).

London held its first Carnival Against Capitalism in June 1999 (an event predictably depicted by the media as hijacked by violent anarchists) but most analyses of these new anti-capitalist movements begin with Seattle, 30 November 1999 (Harman, 2000). Here 50,000 workers and students converged to force the closing of the second ministerial conference of the World Trade Organization. Protesters held workshops, occupied streets and blockaded the entrance to WTO meetings. The police response was to impose curfews and employ concussion grenades, plastic bullets and teargas. In April 2000, 30,000 protested at the annual meeting of the World Bank in Washington. In September 20,000 demonstrated at the annual WB/IMF summit in Prague. In April 2001, 80,000 were at the Summit of the Americas in Quebec and many thousands more at the G8 summit in Genoa in July (see Box 6.6).

(see Box 6.6)

Box 6.6

Global justice: a chronology of protest and criminalization

January 1994	Occupation of the state capital in Chaipas, Southern Mexico, by the Zapatista National Liberation Army in protest at the signing of the North American Free Trade Area. People's Global Action is formed.
April 1994	Critical Mass begins its London cycling campaign.
May 1996	Reclaim the Streets (RTS) occupies a stretch of motorway in West London.
May 1998	First RTS 'global party' with street parties held simultaneously in 17 cities around the world.
June 1999	'Carnival against capitalism' in City of London. Mass arrests and 150 injured.
November 1999	The 'Battle for Seattle'. Paramilitary policing and hundreds of arrests
April 2000	Protest at a IMF/WB meeting in Washington DC. Voluntary mass arrest of 600.
May 2000	Mass protest in central London. The biggest police operation in the capital for 30 years. 30 arrests.
April 2001	Disruption of Summit of the Americas meeting in Quebec City ratifying the Free Trade Area of the Americas. 400 arrests.
May 2001	Demonstrations worldwide. In London, police detain thousands of peaceful protesters for up to eight hours around Oxford Street.
June 2001	Three shot outside European Union summit in Gothenburg.
July 2001	Protester shot dead by Italian police at G8 summit in Genoa. 93 injured, police arrest protesters in hospital.
June 2003	Tanks, jeeps and helicopters used to protect G8 summit in Evian. British activist suing police for attempted manslaughter.
September 2003	Korean farmer commits suicide at demonstration against WTO summit in Cancun, Mexico. Anti-terrorism powers invoked by police at demonstration at International Arms Fair in London.
July 2005	G8 protest, Gleneagles, Scotland. 358 arrests.
August 2007	Camp for Climate Action, London Heathrow.

The global justice movement continues to demonstrate sporadically on issues such as Third World debt, global warming, genetically modified foods and the economic reasons for war. The common theme is one of self-determination and opposition to the global expansion of corporate power. It comprises thousands of movements intricately linked via the internet – this medium in itself allowing for fluid mobilization without bureaucracy, hierarchy and leadership. The activist network, *Plane Stupid*, was formed in 2005 and in 2008 campaigners scaled the roof of the House of Commons to protest against the building of a third runway at Heathrow Airport. In

Britain, the first Camp for Climate Change was set up outside the Drax power station in Yorkshire in 2006. The following year the target was Heathrow. The protesters there faced the combined powers of the *Harassment Act 1997*, the *Terrorism Acts 2000 and 2006* and the *2005 Serious Organised Crime and Police Act*. The latter had created an offence of trying to persuade any person not to do something that they are entitled or required to do if that persuasion is deemed to be causing 'alarm' or 'distress'. Alarm and distress were not defined. There were 58 arrests.

Post-Subcultural Studies

6.4 The Invisible Girl

In the analysis of youth cultures and subcultures, research (at least up to the 1970s) spoke overwhelmingly of *male* youth cultural forms. The significance of culture, class and community, which became well-established parameters in recognizing boys' leisure pursuits, was long ignored in discussions of girls (Dorn and South, 1982). Youth cultures have traditionally been defined in male terms. If part of youth culture's ability to evoke adult puritanical hostility lies in its explicit male sexuality, Angela McRobbie (1980) argues, this should not be misconstrued as any movement towards sexual liberation on its part. All aspects of youth culture – from working-class subcultures, black youth cultures and countercultures to the consumer industries – confirm traditional definitions of masculinity and femininity. Thus, while Frith and McRobbie (1978) noted that women and girls were by no means excluded from some youth cultures, as musical performers they were packaged largely to arouse male sexual fantasy and as consumers they were reduced to a state of non-intellectualism and political passivity. McRobbie and Garber (1976) also argued that because of their different structural position within the home, girls were pushed by male dominance to the periphery of social activity. What such studies concluded is that 'youth culture' is a demonstration of the extent of the victory of those who hold class and sexual power and an affirmation of their ability to retain such power. As McRobbie (1980, p. 41) noted in analysing the 'temporary flights' of the teds, mods or rockers, it was ignored that 'it is monstrously more difficult for women to escape (even temporarily) and that these symbolic flights have often been at the expense of women (especially mothers) and girls'. Moreover boys' peer-group consciousness and pleasure frequently seem to rest on a 'collective disregard for women and the sexual exploitation of girls'. Yet, most of the 1970s studies of youth cultures failed to adopt a critical attitude to the overt sexism of their subjects and unwittingly reinforced stereotypical images of women as passive, dependent and subordinate.

One of the first serious critiques of the Birmingham School's class-based work came from McRobbie's (1978) ethnographic study of 14 and 15 year old working-class girls in Birmingham. She focused on how 'resistance' was generated not through subcultures but through the 'more mundane' contempt for middle-class 'swots' in school and the flaunting of precocious womanhood. Her concept of a 'bedroom culture' was formulated as a means of addressing the different ways that girls organize their cultural lives and to account for their relative absence from the street. Young women's leisure is widely assumed (at least up to the 1990s) to have typically occupied the 'invisible space' of the home. In one of a very few assessments of McRobbie's original notions, Lincoln (2004) maintained that in the 1990s the bedroom remained one of the few spaces for privacy and autonomy and highlighted its continuing importance as a 'cultural space in the social worlds of teenage girls' (p. 106).

Conservatism, Consumerism and Conformity

Subcultural theory decoded style and consumption largely in terms only of opposition and resistance. The more conservative and reactionary aspects of subcultural style and practice – epitomized by the rise of youth wings within such fascist organizations as the National Front, the British Movement, Column 88 and Viking Youth in the late 1970s – were largely ignored (Cohen, S., 1980, p. xii). Subcultural theory might have explained such behaviour as a rational reaction to the 'invasion' of working-class territory, but such analysis tended also to move such problems as 'mugging', 'Paki-bashing' and 'queer-bashing' away from the personal responsibility of the individuals involved. As a result, subcultural theory was widely critiqued as 'idealist' and 'romanticist' (Young, 1986).

The terms 'magical', 'symbolic' and 'imaginary' may have allowed subcultural theory to infer a potentially infinite range of meanings from subcultural action, but while these analyses were certainly imaginative, they also appeared free-floating, unstructured and ambiguous. It was never clear when or how one symbolic interpretation was more adequate than another. This problem was further exacerbated by the concepts of 'bricolage' and 'homology' (see Section 6.1). British subcultural theory often appeared content to find meanings (magical solution, recovery of community, resistance) quite independent of intent and awareness. The danger indeed, as Cohen (1980, p. xiv) argued, was one of getting lost in the 'forest of symbols'.

Most obviously too, subcultural 'revolt' was limited by its interaction with the consumer and entertainment industries and the subsequent defusing of oppositional symbols. Melly (1972, p. 107) called this the 'castration via trivialisation syndrome' in which 'what starts as revolt finishes as style – as mannerism'. Subcultures may have provided fresh meanings to existing styles or create new styles themselves, but their **diffusion** also implies **defusion**, as resistance ultimately becomes dependent on marketing and commercial enterprise. In concentrating on moments of authenticity, subcultural theory neglected to view subcultures as also being continually engaged with processes of commercialism and trivialization; as only offering fleeting escapes from the problems of marginalization and powerlessness. Thornton (1995, p. 9) goes further and argues that notions of 'authenticity' are illusory and that the essence of subcultures also lies in how 'media and businesses are integral to the authentication of cultural practices ... commercial culture and popular culture are not only inextricable in practice but also in theory'.

Similarly, subcultural theory had difficulty in accounting for the processes whereby non-deviant styles were created and gained widespread popularity. While many young people 'follow fashion', they are not necessarily committed to non-conformist lifestyles (Muncie, 1984, p. 103). Most young people accept and use whatever styles are on offer from the consumer and entertainment industries. The major interests of youth reflect and correspond to those of the dominant value system and are by no means deviant or in opposition (Murdock and McCron, 1976). Thirty years after the pioneering work of the Birmingham School, the cultural landscape has also dramatically changed,

> not least because the desire to consume is so universal and pervasive, confronting us at every turn, bombarding us with an unprecedented array of aspirational messages ... people respond less to the inequalities of capitalism by turning inward ... rather the market has redirected our gaze outward. (Hayward, 2004, p. 8)

In a twenty-first century world seemingly awash with ontological insecurity and perpetual risk and in which the old 'sureties' of class consciousness appear to have disappeared, **consumerism** fills the void, providing a quick but 'temporary fix' (Hayward, 2004, p. 197).

Numerous ethnographic studies have also queried the resistance of youth cultural style and practice. The first of these was Willis's (1977) classic ethnographic study of boys in a Midlands comprehensive school in the 1970s. Here he detailed their opposition to authority and conformity in which the lads specialized in a 'caged resentment which always stops just short of outright confrontation'. Their counter-school culture, involving the disruption of lessons and the subversion of school work, was experienced by them as resistance, but ironically contained the seeds of their own downfall. An anti-school culture of chauvinism, solidarity, masculinity and toughness inadvertently prepared them for a life of manual labour. Their symbolic resistance to authority never developed any real power, but instead reinforced the power relations involved in the labour process. The boys colluded in their own domination. Rejecting educational qualifications in preference for 'mucking about' and 'skiving', these working-class 'lads' prepared themselves for a life of resisting boredom by time-wasting on the shop floor. Resistance at school ultimately led to exploitation in the workplace.

Hollands (1995) studied the meaning of youth leisure pursuits for young people themselves (as opposed to the spectacular/deviant/sensational) through analysis of the **night-tim**e economy in North-East England. Here he argued that the primary purpose of 'going out' was not to get drunk, to find a sexual partner, to rave or to cause trouble (as the media might presume) but the rather more mundane (and obvious?), namely, to socialize with friends. 'Going out' provides a space for the construction of identities. It is not simply about hedonism (let alone revolt) but about regaining 'community' through companionship. Winlow and Hall's (2006) qualitative (but less optimistic) study of young adults' experience of the night-time economy was also based in North-East England. Rather than signs of fulfilment, dissent or resistance, these researchers encountered more of a materially based 'tight connection' between alcohol consumption, competitive individualism and rising rates of violence: in short, an often reactionary and apolitical embracing of consumerism underpinned by a climate of social division, anxiety and hostile interpersonal competition (see Box 6.7).

Post-Subcultural Style

Punk's disruption of previous subcultural styles had some peculiar consequences for subcultural style since the 1980s. Hebdige (1979, p. 26) argued that because punk contained 'distorted reflections of all the major post-war subcultures' it indirectly led to their revival – at least in stylistic, if not in authentic subcultural terms. During the 1980s a diverse array of teds, scooter boys, suedeheads, bikers, punks, glam revivalists, new romantics, Goths, Rastas and long-haired 'crusties' seemed to coexist on the streets of Britain's inner cities. Brake (1990, p. 224) argued convincingly that youth cultures in the 1980s came to be dominated by and replaced by style to be 'consumed by the privileged elite amongst youth'. Or as McRobbie (1994, p. 159) put it 'things were never the same after punk'. Although there remains a continuing concern for youth as a source of social and political anxiety, youth leisure has evolved into a *mélange* and proliferation of styles that defy any straightforward class-, gender- or 'race'-based analysis. 'Young people no longer depend on subcultural affirmation for the construction of their identities (if indeed they ever did) but construct lifestyles that are as adaptable and as flexible as the world around them' (Miles, 2000, pp. 159–60; see also Bennett and Kahn-Harris, 2004).

One of the first traces of such a 'revisionist' cultural analysis of youth can be found in subsequent work produced by the originators of the Birmingham School themselves. In a report prepared for the Sports Council in the late 1970s on the cultural significance of pool, kung fu, discos and skateboarding, a shift from the strictly subcultural to broader notions of youth cultural consumption seemed to force an acknowledgement that:

a fad or fashion within youth culture may be subject to a *range of determinants*, carry a number of *contradictory meanings* and have *variously commercial or autonomously cultural roots* ... each particular phenomenon needs to be understood in its own *individual complexity*, yet can potentially reveal consistent processes and interrelationships. (CCCS, 1980, p. 10, italics added)

What such a statement seemed to suggest was that youth cultures could be the site of multiple, not simply class-based, meanings. Similarly, Gary Clarke (1990, p. 93) noted that by the 1980s the very diversity of youth styles 'makes a mockery of subcultural analysis' and an 'absolute distinction between subcultures and "straights" increasingly difficult to maintain'. Condemning the Birmingham School as 'essentialist', he argued that more attention should be given to how 'commercial' and 'subcultural' styles make sense to young people themselves. For McRobbie (1980), this necessarily means that such concepts as populism, leisure and pleasure be given as much critical attention as the established triad of class, sex and 'race'.

Such a project has subsequently been realized in a number of ways. In *The Language of Youth Subcultures*, Widdicombe and Wooffitt (1995) draw upon discourse analysis to illustrate how language is used to construct self-identities and negotiate the meanings of subcultural involvement. What emerges from their 'conversations' with young people is not a set of 'explanations' (as sought by the social scientist) but a series of 'resources for discursive social action'. As perceived by young people themselves, subcultures are viewed as 'variable commodities' imbued with 'multiple meanings'. Indeed, there is no unitary or fixed meaning to be discovered. Thus the 'nihilism and anarchy' of punk or the 'anti-establishment values' of the hippie are ascriptions imposed by academic analysis and form only one element in how these subcultures and leisure are actively 'lived' by those involved (see Box 6.8).

Box 6.8

The significance of youth leisure

Paul Willis's *Common Culture* (1990) is a detailed account of the particularities of youth leisure which cannot easily or desirably be generalized. He argues that through leisure, 'young people are all the time expressing or attempting to express something about their actual or potential cultural significance' (p. 1). It may be individual or collective, but through language, dress, imagination and 'drama', young people achieve a symbolic creativity in which their identities are forged, remade, lived with and experimented with. Thus it makes little sense to talk of subcultures as in some way authentic, and commercial cultures as imposed and inevitably conservative. Market categories and boundaries are continually being reworked and redrawn, so that it is impossible to predict future developments with any certainty. Moreover the market is an arena that young people are increasingly taking over and transforming for themselves.

Source: Muncie (2004, p. 190).

Youth and consumption were also the subject of Thornton's (1995) analysis of **club cultures**. Again in contrast to the Birmingham School, she argued that the analytical divide between mainstream media and subcultural practice, in which the former is invariably viewed as reactionary (or manufactured) and the latter innovative (or authentic), is a gross oversimplification. Instead the two exist in symbiosis:

> Contrary to youth subcultural ideologies, 'subcultures' do not germinate from a seed and grow by force of their own energy into mysterious 'movements' only to be belatedly digested by the media. Rather, media and other culture industries are there and effective right from the start ... The Birmingham tradition tended to study previously labelled social types – 'Mods', 'Rockers', 'Skinheads', 'Punks' but gave no systematic attention to the effects of various media's labelling processes. Instead they described the rich and resistant meanings of youth music, clothing, rituals and argot in a miraculously media-free moment when an uncontaminated homology could be found. (Thornton, 1995, pp. 117, 119)

The moral panics associated with youth cultures are not simply generated from outside, nor are they evidence of paranoid adult overreaction. Youth may resent 'the mass mediation of their culture but relish the attention conferred by media condemnation ... moral panics can be seen as a culmination and fulfilment of youth cultural agendas in so far as negative newspaper and broadcast news coverage baptise transgression' (Thornton, 1995, p. 129). In this way media outrage becomes a part of subcultural practice, self-identity and longevity: it legitimates and authenticates youth cultures as different, radical and deviant; it becomes 'the essence of their resistance' (Thornton, 1995, p. 137).

Cultural Exchange and Hybrid Identities

The difficulty of isolating authentic subcultural practice untainted by commercial appropriation has also been raised by numerous studies of patterns of cultural exchange and crossover between African-American, Asian, Caribbean and white cultural and musical styles. In *There Ain't No Black in the Union Jack* (1987b) Paul Gilroy argues that black styles, music, dress, dance, fashion and language are continually being made and remade in the context of new *diasporas* (patterns of dispersal) created by post-colonial migrations. People who have been dispersed from their homelands may retain strong links with their origins and traditions, but are also obliged to come to terms with the new cultures they inhabit without completely assimilating to them. Such people belong to *cultures of hybridity* belonging at one and the same time to several 'homes' but to no one particular 'home'. As Gilroy (1987b, p. 155) claimed, 'The assimilation of blacks is not a process of acculturation, but of cultural syncretism.' Accordingly black expressive cultures and self-identities are frequently the result of a fusion of different cultural traditions. Or as Hall (1992, p. 310) puts it:

Everywhere cultural identities are emerging which are not fixed but poised, *in transition*, between different positions; which draw on different cultural traditions at the same time; and which are the product of those complicated cross-overs and cultural mixes which are increasingly common in a globalized world.

It is in these terms that Gilroy's *The Black Atlantic* (1993) casts doubt on notions of some 'pure' or 'unified' black culture and notes how by the 1990s, black culture, especially in its musical forms, came to exist as a set of open-ended structures allowing a seemingly endless series of permutations and cultural meanings. In particular, derivatives of reggae – hip-hop and rap music – are described in terms of a 'doubleness' existing 'simultaneously inside and outside the conventions, assumptions and aesthetic rules which distinguish and periodize modernity' (Gilroy, 1993, p. 73). The case of 'gangsta rap' is emblematic (see Box 6.9).

Box 6.9

'Gangsta Rap'

The origins of rap are reputedly in Jamaica, where, in the late 1960s, DJs (rather than musicians) began 'sampling' pieces of previously recorded tracks, playing them repeatedly, or backwards, often with another track playing simultaneously, and adding their own voice or conversation to them. In the 1970s, it 'swept through' the black neighbourhoods of New York and New Jersey (Cashmore, 1997, p. 155). By the early 1980s it had spread to Los Angeles and in 1986 a rap entitled 'Boyz N the Hood' was recorded by NWA (Niggaz wit' Attitude) – a group consisting of Ice Cube, Easy E, Dr Dre, MC Ren and DJ Yella. This music spoke explicitly of street cultures, gang feuds, black militancy, cop killing, drug dealing and sexual violence. It frequently applauded sadism, misogyny and machismo. Following the release of their first album in 1988, NWA and their song 'Fuck tha Police' were targeted by the FBI for incitement of cop hatred and racial violence. Gangsta rap was widely condemned by US presidents, churches, women's groups and mainstream African-American organizations. Rivalry between LA and New York rappers was reputed to be the source of numerous murders.

In the UK, NWA's 1991 album *Efil 4 Zaggin* (Niggaz 4 Life inverted) was seized under the 1959 Obscene Publications Act (Cloonan, 1995, p. 357). Ten years later So Solid Crew were banned from performing live for allegedly glorifying gun violence. In 2003, the Culture Minister blamed the killing of two black young women on the 'hateful lyrics' of 'boasting macho idiot rappers'. The Home Secretary responded by announcing minimum five-year prison sentences for carrying any illegal weapons. Yet by the early 1990s gangsta rap had already become a multimillion-dollar international industry. The music may have been defiantly black but it also had a huge white following. These contradictions and crossovers have led Rose (1994) to argue that rap is 'a style nobody can deal with': authentic yet commercial (Cashmore, 1997); liberatory (Lipsitz, 1994) yet revolutionary conservative (Gilroy, 1993); confirming white stereotypes of a black criminal 'other', yet symptomatic of the violence, sexism and misogyny of white patriarchal society (hooks, 1994, pp. 115–24).

Source: Muncie (2004, p. 192).

Rap music has indeed been adopted and adapted around the world, creating new permutations (such as the peculiarly British jungle and drum 'n' 'bass as well as numerous crossovers with acid house and rave). Local levels of significance also continually produce diverse and fluid meanings which cannot be reduced to global market considerations (Bennett, 2000; Carrington and Wilson, 2002).

One such notable permutation in Britain has been the fusion of reggae and hip-hop with bhangra. It was long assumed in Britain that family and informal social controls over 'Asian' youth have been such that distinctive youth styles have never developed. Brake (1980, p. 128), for example, argued that Asian communities were more likely to draw exclusively upon their own historical, cultural and religious traditions and languages, but he also warned that 'as these fail to resolve contradictions, youth subculture will probably arise as a symbol of emancipation from the older generation'. By the mid-1980s there was some evidence that this might be the case. Images of a disaffected South Asian youth first emerged in the early 1980s following disturbances in Bradford and Southall, and achieved national prominence after conflicts with the police in Bradford in 1995 and with the National Front in Oldham, Bradford and Burnley in the summer of 2001. As Malek (1997, p. 141) notes, the contradictory and mythical representations of young South Asians as either assimilated into British society or as violently antagonistic to it dominate public debate, but neither 'captures the complexity of what it means to be young, South Asian and living in Britain'. Part of the problem is that white ethnocentrism and racism are incapable of recognizing differences within and between 'South Asian' communities and have generally promulgated essentialist notions of 'Asian traits' (Webster, 1997). 'South Asian' youth culture is discussed in terms of diasporic and globalized cultural formations in which Hindi films, 'indie' music, bhangra and a pick 'n' mix orientation to drug use have helped to forge a distinctively 'British Asian' set of identities. For example, bhangra, as performed by such artistes as Apache Indian and Bally Sagoo, reveals not only a borrowing of Caribbean sound systems and the soul and hip-hop of black America but also a fusion of Punjabi folk music with reggae. It is a blend which seems to defy unreflective talk about ethnic authenticity. In 1996, Bally Sagoo's 'Dil Cheez' became the first ever song with full Hindi lyrics to enter the top 20 in Britain. It is probably no coincidence that at this very moment of cultural ascendancy, sections of 'South Asian' youth were also being demonized as harbingers of an 'Asian criminality' reputedly linked to organized crime and drug dealing. Islamic fundamentalism and Asian masculinity have increasingly come to be associated with the 'criminal other', promoting – particularly since 9/11 – a criminalization of difference (Goodey, 2001).

However, some analysts have come to question cultural studies' new focus on **difference**, hybridity, fusions and migrancy. As Ashwani Sharma (1996) argues, these concepts can also act to deny the particularities and authenticities of 'South Asian' youth cultures and to promote a vision of British multiculturalism which has little basis in reality. The notion of 'hybridity' carries a tendency to erase the 'workings of highly differentiated global capitalism and racism' and leaves 'the subaltern subjects of the "Third World" having no position or location to speak from' (Sharma, 1996, p. 25). Or as Malek (1997, p. 149) concludes, 'the cross cultural locations negotiated by migrant populations are not void of the racial and cultural hierarchies constructed by western racisms'.

As a result, a new level of complexity has emerged in the analysis of cultural exchange and hybrid identities. While the categories of 'black', 'Afro-Caribbean' and 'Asian' have been critiqued as a means by which caricatures and stereotypes are maintained and the fluidity, diversity and variety of cultural identities disregarded (Said, 1991), the shift towards viewing 'race' as a social construction has tended to downplay the relevance of continuing racialized forms of power, domination and subordination. In all the talk of 'new ethnicities' (Hall, 1988) and 'the complex internal cultural segmentation [that] has cut through so-called Black British Identity' (Hall, 1997, p. 7), there is a danger that 'the valency of "Black" as a political positionality, that strategically unites disparate groups against increasingly organised and vicious manifestations of Euro-racism', will be lost (Sharma et al., 1996, p. 7). The processes of cultural exchange and globalization can be interpreted as polarizing some ethnic identities while simultaneously widening the number of potential hybrid subcultural identities.

Quite clearly, these modes of analysis – despite their internal disputes – allow for more complex and critical analyses of subcultural diversity and processes of resistance. Significantly, in the main, they originated from the early 1980s as a reaction against the essentialism and over-determinism of the 'Birmingham School' (Clarke, G., 1990; Griffin, 1993, Chapter 5). This critique coalesced with the collapse of the 'meta-narrative' or 'single order' means of explanation characteristic of much social science, whether Parsons's functionalism of the 1940s or the Birmingham School's neo-Marxism of the 1970s. As Scott (1990, p. 4) argued, 'increasing awareness of the complexity of social relations *vis-à-vis* single, coherent, but basically simple, explanatory systems has quite fundamentally altered social theory's conception of its role, and of what it can and cannot be expected to achieve'. So in place of 'grand theory', there has emerged a range of 'revisionist' and postmodern analyses which are more attuned to the ethnographic than the structural; to diversity and fluidity rather than determinism; to lifestyle rather than subcultural research; to different subjectivities rather than 'knowable' objective conditions; and to processes of 'becoming' rather than states of 'being' A more slippery language of 'lifestyles', 'youthscapes', 'taste cultures' and '**neo-tribes**' is preferred to that of hermetically sealed subcultures (Nayak, 2003; Bennett and Kahn-Harris, 2004; Muggleton and Weinzierl, 2003). These forms of analysis claim to offer fresh insights into the shift from the apparently local, class-based youth subcultures of the 1960s to the transnationalization and hybridity of contemporary youth styles (see Box 6.10).

Box 6.10

From subcultures to cultural hybridity

Subculture	Dominant drug/music/style associations
	Differentiated and 'authentic' subcultures 1950s–1970s
Beats	Marijuana; Jazz; college bohemian
Teddy boys	Alcohol; rock 'n' roll; Edwardian
Mods	Amphetamines; soul; Italianate; scooters
Rockers	Alcohol; rock 'n' roll; leathers; motor bikes
Skinheads	Alcohol/amphetamines; ska; working class; boots 'n' braces
Hippies	LSD; underground rock/progressive rock/folk; North American Indian/ Eastern
Rude Boys	Marijuana; ska; Jamaican street cool
Rastas	Marijuana; reggae/dub; dreadlocks
	Punk and post-punk derivative cultures 1970s–1980s
Punk	Amphetamines; punk; DIY pastiche
Metal heads	Alcohol; heavy metal; denim
New romantics	Amphetamines; post-punk/retro glam rock; polysexual/ androgyny
Goths	Poly drug; Death rock/industrial music; dark aesthetic, menace and mystique
	Diverse hybrid and transnational dance cultures 1980s–2000s
Acid House/Rave Hip hop/rap	Ecstasy/poly drug; post-northern soul/Balearic/garage/techno/trance/ ambient/R'n'B/Gangsta rap/jungle/drum 'n' bass/speed garage/hardcore/ bhangra; casual; USA black street culture

Nevertheless, as Hollands (2002), Nayak (2003) and Winlow and Hall (2006) also remind us, in all the 'new' talk of 'lifestyle', 'identities', 'subjectivity' and 'consumer choice', it is vital not to lose sight of ongoing inequalities/ divisions/fragmentations of 'race', gender, class and locality in a burgeoning climate of consumer capitalism. These continue to provide important structuring contexts for youth leisure, consumption and conformity.

Cultural Criminology: Explorations in Transgression

6.5 Emerging from these critiques, analyses of style and leisure matured in the late 1980s. As criminologists became more attuned to the fluid dynamics of representation, place, image and style, it became possible to sketch out the parameters of a distinctive **cultural criminology** (Ferrell and Sanders, 1995). Its heritage is multifold. It includes the foundational work of interactionism, critical criinology and the Birmingham School but is also deeply inflected with the intellectual insights of postmodernism (see **Chapters 4.1 and 4.3**). Akin to interactionism, cultural criminology is geared to exploring the multitude of interactions involving the media, the public, rule breakers and control agents through which meanings of crime are collectively constructed and contested. Drawing on anarchist, neo-Marxist and feminist insights, cultural criminology is embedded in critiques of social injustice. Of central influence is the Birmingham School's attention to cultural dynamics and everyday politics and in particular a recognition of the meaning and significance of style. All of this is underpinned by postmodern concerns to be alive to contingencies, hybridities and the way meaning is continually constructed and reconstructed through the discursive connections between subculture, media and crime control. As Ferrell (1999, p. 397) put it:

> [T]he study of crime necessitates not simply the examination of individual criminals and criminal events, not even the straightforward examination of media coverage of criminals and criminal events, but rather a journey into the spectacle and carnival of crime, a walk down an infinite hall of mirrors where images created and consumed by criminals, criminal subcultures, control agents, media institutions and audiences bounce endlessly one off the other.

Cultural criminology then engages with, if not synthesizes, a disparate series of old and new criminologies. Above all, it is concerned with unravelling the complex cultural processes through which 'crime' attains meaning. Vital to this is **ethnographic research**: that is a biographical immersion into the cultural and experiential realities of particular events themselves (Ferrell et al., 2004). So it is no surprise that one of its most challenging features remains that of recognizing the participatory pleasure and sheer fun of engaging in criminal(ized) behaviours. Cultural criminology advocates a criminology attuned to the emotions of excitement, humour and desire; to the adrenalin rush of crossing boundaries; to the exhilarations of 'living on the edge'; to the emancipatory power of **transgression**; and to the liberatory potential of the carnivalesque (see Box 6.11). In essence, it encourages cultural studies to recognize 'culture as crime', that is how certain cultural activities – art, music, dance, sex – are also increasingly sites of criminalization; while also imploring criminology to recognize 'crime as culture', that is how style and pleasure reside in the continually contested interplay between subcultural, media and political constructs of 'crime' (Ferrell, 1999, pp. 403–6).

Below, these intersections of crime and culture are exemplified in the notions of 'style as crime' as applied to the rave and club cultures of the 1980s and 1990s; and to the pleasures of rule breaking as applied to the analysis of the carnival in everyday life.

Style as Crime: Acid House, Rave and Club Cultures

From modest beginnings on the Spanish Balearic island of Ibiza in 1985, rave has been described as the most 'spectacular' and 'enduring' British youth movement of the twentieth century (Collin, 1997). Rave is essentially a combination of dancing at mass all-night events, synthesized techno music with a heavy repetitive beat and use of the Class A controlled drug, Ecstasy (MDMA). The all-night, open-air nightclub hedonism of Ibiza was brought to Britain by a handful of DJs interested in popularizing the intense and collective energy that was generated by acid house music. Initially restricted to such underground clubs as the Hácienda in Manchester and Future, Shoom, Spectrum and The Trip in London, large-scale warehouse acid parties first occurred on the outskirts of London during the second 'Summer of Love' in 1988. In June 1989, over 8,000 young people gathered in a disused aircraft hangar at White Waltham airfield, Berkshire, making history as the largest-ever unlicensed party. By 1992, 20,000–40,000 were to gather over eight days at the Castle-morton Common 'Mega-rave' in Worcestershire, marking a significant festival/traveller/rave crossover (McKay, 1996, p. 120).

Acid house took its name not from the drug LSD but from a musical form based on a 'house' dance style, pioneered in gay clubs in Chicago. Its key characteristic was a heavy four–four beat between 120 and 170 beats per minute. It was delivered through huge sound systems and a vast array of lighting and electronic effects including lasers, smoke machines, strobes, video screens, globes and fireworks. To participate in such parties required a certain degree of affluence – access to a telephone to learn of the latest clandestine venue, a car to travel there and money for the entry fee. Yet it also represented a curiously egalitarian reaction to the final days of Thatcherism. There were no stars or music heroes and while previous youth cultures were characterized by clear-cut boundaries of class position and related music or dress codes (or at least this is how they were 'read'), acid house and the warehouse parties seemed to merge all of these into one homogeneous whole. In particular, the Manchester (Madchester) rave scene drew on an earlier

Northern Soul scene, all-night dances, African-American music, baggy clothes and amphetamines, and seemed impervious to analyses that insisted that innovation be decoded in terms of resistance (Redhead, 1990).

Rave culture may have smacked of rebellion in that most parties were theoretically illegal and involved numerous circumnavigations of the laws of entertainment, licensing, public order and noise. But it was also a highly organized and commercial endeavour. Tickets sold a day or two before the event gave no indication of the venue. Instead a telephone number was given for further information on the day so that all the sound and light equipment could be set up (on a country estate, in farmers' fields, on airfields, in grain silos, in disused warehouses or wherever) before the police or local residents were alerted. If one venue became impossible, the whole party would simply move to another. Often these were located in the vicinity of the London orbital motorway – dubbed the Magic Roundabout – in order to facilitate ease of access. As Presdee (2000, p. 114) put it:

> Their culture, rather than being a search for the 'authentic' as in modern culture, is an endless search for the 'inauthentic'; that is, a culture that is empty of the authority and the imperatives that come with authenticity. It is this perceived 'emptiness as protest' that prompts panic from 'adult' society.

During the summer of 1989, warehouse parties were also becoming subject to greater police and legal control. By the end of the year a former council youth leader became the first person in Britain to be imprisoned for organizing such parties: he was jailed for ten years on a charge of conspiracy to manage premises where drugs were known to be available. In just two and a half months in 1989–90 the police monitored 249 parties, stopped 44, raided 20 and arrested 267 people on public order and other offences. At one party in Leeds in July 1990 over 800 were arrested by police in riot gear.

In the imagination of the popular press, acid house parties were synonymous with the drug Ecstasy. Described by users as producing rushed feelings of happiness, exhilaration and the 'illusion of an endless present', it also works on the brain in such a way that repetitive rhythmical activity becomes intensified (Keane, 1997). It is reputed to have been patented in Germany in 1914 as an appetite suppressant or for psycho-therapeutic purposes and its use was prohibited as early as 1977. While it is arguable whether the first warehouse parties were indeed full of drug users, by the 1990s it was clear that drug taking had become an integral part of many youth lifestyles (see **Chapter 1.3**). The drug information charities Lifeline and Release estimated that some half a million people a week were taking Ecstasy and attending raves at clubs and parties. Ninety-seven per cent of dance-goers had tried an illegal drug at some time and for 28 per cent this had led to problems with the police (Release, 1997, pp. 10, 25). Depictions of drug use as abnormal and unusual became harder to sustain (Hammersley et al., 2002). A 1994 unpublished Home Office report admitted that the elimination of drug use was an unattainable goal (*Guardian*, 1 August 1994). By 2000 the Police Federation were advocating the downgrading of Ecstasy from a Class A to a Class C drug (*Guardian*, 17 February 2000).

Some time in the early 1990s the commercialization of the dance party movement and the clampdown on unlicensed parties returned acid house and rave to the clubs. First, the Entertainments (Acid House) Increased Penalty Act of 1990 made holding unlicensed 'underground' parties illegal. Second, the 1994 Criminal Justice and Public Order Act outlawed any large gatherings featuring music with 'sounds wholly or predominantly characterized by the emission of a succession of repetitive beats'. Such criminalization was circumvented by entertainment industry entrepreneurs providing permanent venues which were able to meet strict licensing and health and safety regulations. Like all youth cultures before, the 'safe' aspects of acid house and rave were defused by commercial diffusion. Acid house music and its multitude of derivatives – techno, hardcore, garage, trance and ambient – all came to feature in the popular music bestselling charts. It also became a global phenomenon, with raves organized worldwide from San Francisco to Goa in India and Ko Pha-Ngan in Thailand.

In its apparent crossing not only of class but also of national boundaries, rave confounded the neo-Marxist analyses of youth subcultures put forward by the Birmingham School in the 1970s. The multitude of different dance cultures appeared as neither simply oppositional nor commercial; neither authentic nor manufactured; neither marginal nor mainstream. Rave culture has thus been viewed by some from a postmodern and cultural criminology perspective as something disparate and diffuse: as a 'sea of youth styles' continually (recirculating) in the pursuit of 'hedonism in hard times' (Redhead, 1993, p. 4). Nevertheless, Sarah Thornton (1995, p. 25), while admitting that rave 'may have involved large numbers of people and they may have trespassed on new territories', argued that it retained distinct demographics – 'chiefly white, working class, heterosexual and dominated by the lads'. Similarly, Angela McRobbie noted that young women appeared to be less involved in the cultural production of rave than their male counterparts, but she also detected in rave changing modes of femininity and masculinity. As dance is a key rationale for rave, it 'gives girls a new-found confidence and a prominence' and because the drug Ecstasy encourages an atmosphere of unity, traditional laddish aggro tends to be replaced by more sensuous and less threatening displays of masculinity (McRobbie, 1994, pp. 168–9).

In these ways the phenomenon of rave appeared to disrupt many of the traditional assumptions and expectations about subcultures that circulated around youth cultural studies (Bennett, 1999). In contrast to the Birmingham School, what seemed to be required was a 'revisionist' analysis that was capable of, on the one hand, recognizing 'different youthful subjectivities' and on the other accounting for an increasing globalization of youth culture made possible by the internet, satellite communications and the transnational marketing and cultural exchange of musical forms and cultural vocabulary. By the early 1990s, for the first time it became possible to talk of a 'global' dimension to many youth styles and cultures (Osgerby, 1998, p. 200). The phenomenon of rave also clearly illustrates how certain musical and cultural styles, when viewed as oppositional and threatening, activate 'criminalizing crusades' against large numbers of young people. Yet all attempts to regulate leisure, pleasure and desire only succeed in producing yet more transformations of the carnivalesque. Indeed, 2006 was widely claimed to be the year when the illegal rave party reappeared. Raoul Vaneigem (2001, p. 35) expressed the sentiment clearly enough by claiming there is always a world of pleasure to win 'and nothing to lose but boredom'.

Seizing Pleasure: Edgework and the Politics of Carnival ____

While much of criminology is content to construe crime as rational action inspired by opportunity and lack of control, cultural criminology points to a wide range of crime – from writing graffiti, joyriding and vandalism to murder – that is clearly expressive rather than simply instrumental. Cultural criminology stresses the existential motives for breaking rules, taking risks and challenging authority. That this recognition of the pleasure of crime has only begun to be seriously interrogated in the last decade is something of a surprise given that any cursory glance at television programme listings, the contents of mass circulation newspapers or bookshop shelves instantly confirms the extent to which audiences perceive crime not just as a social problem but as a major source of amusement and diversion. Cultural criminology challenges us to accept that the pleasures of creating harm, doing wrong and breaking boundaries is also part of the equation.

The starting point is Jack Katz's (1988) seminal work on the 'seductions of crime'. Here he maintains that individual emotions, such as excitement, are central to the criminal event. Deviance offers a means of 'self-transcendence': a way of overcoming the mundanity, banality and predictability of everyday life. Katz applies this analysis to shoplifting, robbery and murder but it surely has clear resonance in a whole series of criminal(ized) activities such as vandalism, car theft, drug use, joyriding, fire starting, car racing, hooliganism, gang fights, and so on that we usually associate with youth. Each speaks of the thrill of 'taking it to the limit'; of gaining moments of control; and of being seduced by the existential pleasures of transgressive acts.

Lyng's (1990) work on voluntary risk taking continued this theme by introducing the concept of **edgework**; a term borrowed from Hunter S. Thompson's journalistic descriptions of his anarchic – usually drug-induced – experiences. While not specifically addressing youthful deviant behaviours, Lyng's analysis of edgework in high-risk and dangerous 'extreme' activities such as sky diving, hang gliding, car racing, test piloting and fire fighting, had clear resonances for anyone interested in the expressive aspects of crime. 'Edgework' neatly captures the spontaneous creative and intrinsically rewarding aspects of self-actualization that are otherwise thwarted in a highly regimented, trivialized and degraded world of labour. Edgework provides an illusion of control in an alluring space of 'experiential anarchy in which the individual moves beyond the realm of established social patterns to the very fringes of ordered reality' (Lyng, 1990, p. 882).

Drawing on the insights of 'seduction' and 'edgework', O'Malley and Mugford (1994) have argued that a new phenomenology of pleasure is needed if we are to recognize 'crime' as *transgression* from the impermissible and as *transcendence* from the mundane. Moreover the notion of 'escape from the routine' provides one explanation for many forms of urban youth crime: as attempts to achieve some control within an otherwise insecure and alienating world. Transgression offers a mode of being in which individuals take control through a 'controlled loss of control' (Hayward, 2002, p. 87). In turn, the 'grasping of such moments' inevitably interacts with cultures of crime control. As Ferrell's (1996, 1998, 2001) ethnographic excursions into the Denver hip-hop scene, street busking, BASE jumping and gutter punks have established, when such activities become progressively more policed, outlawed and criminalized, the more 'edgy excitement' they are capable of providing, and the more the pleasure of insubordination can be realized.

These intersections of culture, crime and control are also the subject of Presdee's (2000) analysis of crime as **carnival**. Rules are transgressed because they are there; risk is a challenge, not a deterrent. Increases in control provoke further transgression rather than conformity. Presdee explores the paradox that as the state attempts to impose a greater regulation over the minutiae of everyday life, it produces not only a greater compliant rationality but also higher degrees of resistant emotionality. The pursuit of pleasure becomes in itself antagonistic to the state. Presdee neatly captures this entwining of regulation and pleasure through the notion of 'crime as carnival'. Carnival is a site where the pleasure of playing at the boundaries is clearly catered for. Festive excess, the mocking of powerful and 'irrational' behaviour, have long been temporarily legitimated in the moment of carnival. Now as the possibility of such moments recedes (and with them sources of joy, humour and celebration), as the consumer industries commodify pleasure and as the state attempts to stamp down on the 'anti-social', the spirit of carnival is expressed in numerous on the edge and spontaneous activities such as SM, raving, joyriding, computer hacking, Reclaim the Streets parties, recreational drug use and extreme sports. But not being part of the project of scientific rationalism renders such activities as 'irrational' and the resulting behaviour becomes rapidly criminalized: 'in other words everyday life is subjected to a creeping criminalization process where the carnival of crime becomes a necessity in our lives' (Presdee, 2000, p. 160).

It is this sense of a spiralling process of regulation ... consumerism ... transgression ... pleasure ... criminalization ... that cultural criminology offers. It may be accused of an excessive 'zookeeping' of the (male) deviant (O'Brien, 2005), but yet it is a mode of analysis that does more than most to open up the transgressive immediacy of youth lifestyles to an otherwise blinded criminological gaze. For Young (2002, p. 271), it once more offers an opportunity for critical criminology to keep in mind 'the urgency of opposition, yet with an eye for irony imbued as always with a sense of fun'.

- A routine element of popular notions of 'problem youth' is concern over unsupervised leisure and 'spectacular' subcultures. The 'deviant' qualities of British subcultures are to be found less in criminal or delinquent behaviour and more in non-conformist lifestyles. As a result, much of the research into this area has traditionally emanated from cultural studies, rather than from criminology *per se*.

- Cultural criminology marks a significant emergent paradigm in investigating the convergence (and contestation) of cultures, crimes and crime control. Not only does it fuse cultural studies and critical criminology but through its preferred concepts of transgression, edgework and carnival, it is able to unravel the complex circuitry through which the meaning of crime is constructed, lived, enforced and resisted.

- The terms in which academics have tried to make sense of youth cultures have shifted markedly over the past 50 years. In the 1950s, the dominant discourse was of a homogeneous *youth culture* which was believed to transcend all other social divisions. In the 1960s, this was substantiated by notions of a *youth counterculture*. Such visions were first critiqued by the Centre for Contemporary Cultural Studies in Birmingham ('the Birmingham School'), in the 1970s, who identified a series of *youth subcultures*, differentiated by their respective class positions. In the 1980s, feminist researchers pointedly argued that class-based analyses ignored or misrepresented gender divisions in subcultural formation. Coupled with a growing acknowledgement of the importance of black youth cultures, by the 1990s, radical youth studies had moved to a more complex position capable of recognizing *hybridity*, *difference* and *diversity* in all youth cultural practices. Ethnographic studies alive to flexible subjectivities have come to challenge theories based to differing degrees on the principles of structural determinism. Class, gender and 'race' have all weakened as predictors of style and identity *on their own*.

- Media appropriation and saturation have made it difficult to draw distinct lines under moments of subcultural authenticity or consumerist manufacture. To a significant degree, style has replaced youth culture. Youth culture, in the pursuit of self-gratification and identity construction through consumerism, might be inevitably politically reactionary. Nevertheless, the 'deviant' and the 'different' continue to evoke adult condemnation. Non-conformity remains subject to criminalization. The 'threat' of youth continues to maintain a high public profile – even if it seems notoriety is achieved as much through the political concern to impose more forms of rigid regulation, dependency and control as because of any 'new' and 'more alarming' behaviour patterns of young people themselves.

^ ■ **study ?uestions** ■■■■■■■■■■■■■■■■

1 Why should unsupervised youth leisure be considered a social problem?

2 How far are youth cultures able to challenge dominant culture?

3 Has the concept of youth subculture outlived its usefulness?

4 How useful are the twin concepts of *resistance* and *dissent* in explaining contemporary youthful behaviour?

5 How does cultural criminology re-use the concepts of 'crime' and 'culture' to provide fresh insights into the meaning of youthful transgression?

■ ■ Further Reading ■

The key texts in cultural criminology are Ferrell and Sanders' (1995) and Ferrell, Hayward, Morrison and Presdee's (2004) edited collections. Mike Presdee has produced an eminently readable text on the *Carnival of Crime* (2000). Ferrell (1999) provides a good exposition of cultural criminology's theoretical and methodological underpinnings while acknowledging its heritage in 1970s British subcultural theory. Here the original key text is the Centre for Contemporary Cultural Studies' collection of working papers published in summer 1975 and reissued by Hutchinson as *Resistance through Rituals* (Hall and Jefferson, 1976). The significance of style, particularly within punk, is given more detailed attention by Dick Hebdige in *Subculture: The Meaning of Style* (1979). Steve Redhead's analysis of acid house and rave in *Rave Off* (1993) remains one of the few serious attempts to explore the politics of 1990s youth culture. Thornton's *Club Cultures* (1995) provides a convincing argument for viewing processes of subcultural authenticity and manufacture as inseparable. McKay's edited collection *DIY Culture* (1998) is a useful overview of cultural politics and lifestyle politics in the 1990s. Bennett and Kahn-Harris' collection *After Subculture* (2004) critically examines the continuing value of subcultural theory in making sense of contemporary youth 'lifestyles' and 'scenes'. Winlow and Hall's (2006) study of youth nightlife is an important antidote to over-romanticized readings of youth leisure in a twenty-first century characterized by uncertain labour markets, consumerism and insecurity. Gelder and Thornton's (1997) edited collection *The Subcultures Reader* (2nd edition by Gelder, 2005) reproduces many of the key traditional and contemporary 'readings' of subcultures.

∶ // Web Resources∟

http://en.wikipedia.org/wiki/List_of_youth_subcultures
Provides a list and description of some 80 youth cultural and musical styles and is a useful reminder (whatever its current accuracy) of the constantly changing nature of contemporary subcultural forms.

http://www.urban75.com/Action/
News and information site for direct action, demos and campaigns against war, climate change and capitalism.

http://www.culturalcriminology.org/
The site of the cultural criminology group based at the University of Kent, UK.

http://www.globaljusticemovement.net/
Portal for the promotion of campaigns for peace and economic, environmental and social justice.

http://www.indymedia.org/en/index.shtml
A collective of independent media organizations and journalists offering grassroots, non-corporate news coverage.

7

Youth and Social Policy: Control, Regulation and Governance

Overview

Chapter 7 examines:

- the ways in which the everyday lives of young people are subject to particular forms of social regulation;

- various 'sites' of youth regulation including housing, welfare benefits, training schemes, parenting programmes and the policing of public space;

- the relationship between criminal justice and social policy;

- the politics of social control and notions of a disciplinary or carceral society;

- how the concept of 'social control' has been utilized in various criminological theories;

- the policy implications of discourses of 'social exclusion' and 'social inclusion';

- new modes of youth governance in the twenty-first century.

---

key terms

'anti-social' control; carceral society; dispersal of discipline; governmentality; marginal-ization; risk society; social control; social exclusion; social inclusion; state control; transcarceration; zero tolerance

---

This chapter explores the control and regulatory effects of welfare and social policy in the UK. Social policy has traditionally been viewed as an ostensibly progressive series of social arrangements concerned with the distribution of resources in order to meet individual and social needs. Yet, since the nineteenth century, social welfare provision has also contained rationales of regulation and discipline. Nevertheless while problems of control and order have always lain at the heart of discussions of youth justice and penal policy, it was only from the late 1950s that any sustained attempt was made to apply such concepts to the appar-ently benign implementation of social policies in such areas as health, education, housing and employment. One of the earliest contributions was Saville's (1957) Marxist thesis that the welfare state arose largely out of capitalist self interest: in order to increase social stability, secure a compliant workforce and ensure the financial gain of the few. Any progressive elements were portrayed as a series of concessions, just sufficient to blunt working-class resistance to the structures of their exploitation and powerlessness. Such lines of argument have been signifi-cantly developed since the 1960s. For some radical criminologists, a major concern has been to examine how the 'exceptional' and 'exclusionary' interventions of criminal justice intersect with the continuum of 'everyday' and 'inclusionary' interventions to be found in education, social work, employment and leisure.

This chapter assesses the ways in which the everyday lives of young people are regulated by examining developments in youth training, welfare entitlement, housing policy, family policy and policing from the 1980s to the present. While **Chapters 8 and 9** examine the relationship between young people and formal agencies of control, this chapter looks at the different ways in which social policy and policing establish a structuring context in which 'what it means to be young' has become more tightly defined and increasingly regulated. Indeed, criminal responsibility is one of the first 'rights' that are afforded to children in the UK (see Box 7.1).

Box 7.1

Becoming an adult: regulations, rights and responsibilities

Age	Regulation, Rights and Responsibilities
5	drink alcohol in private (placed under review in 2008)
8	be held responsible for a crime in Scotland
10	be held responsible for a crime in England, Wales and Northern Ireland
	be taken into the 'protective custody' of 'intensive fostering'
	be sent to secure unit for 'grave' offences
12	be held in a secure training centre
	own a pet
13	have a part-time job (with conditions)
15	be sent to a young offender institution
16	pay taxes
	consent to sexual intercourse
	have a homosexual relationship (lowered from 18 in 2000)
	leave home/marry with parents' consent
	leave school (to be raised to 18 by 2015)
	seek full-time employment
	drive a moped
	buy aerosol paint (introduced in 2003)
	join the army
	buy a lottery ticket
17	drive a car
	pilot a plane
	emigrate
18	vote in elections (to be reduced to 16?)
	serve on a jury
	buy a knife or razor blade (raised from 16 (except in Scotland) in 2006)
	buy alcohol
	buy tobacco (raised from 16 in 2007)
	marry without parents' consent

(Continued)

	be tried in a magistrates' court
	buy fireworks and sparklers (raised from 16 in 1997)
	bet in a betting shop
	entitled to lower rate of national minimum wage
	get a tattoo
	buy an airgun or replica guns (raised from 13 in 2003 and from 17 in 2006)
21	adopt a child
	become an MP
22	entitled to adult rate of national minimum wage

Social policy development since the 1980s has been dominated by the neo-liberal objectives of economy (reducing public expenditure), efficiency (reliance on market forces) and effectiveness (enhancing consumer choice). Yet it has also been influenced by a neo-conservative authoritarianism in which the imperatives of order and control have dominated. The contradictions have played themselves out in the identification of social exclusion as both the cause and product of crime. Work and family morality have been identified as the key targets in tackling the causes of crime. As a result, an eclectic series of concerns – from truancy, poverty, homelessness, worklessness to teenage pregnancy – and legitimating rationales – self-help, empowerment, responsibility – have been identified, in the process, drawing social policy and criminal justice agendas closer together in the business of overt and covert social control.

Theorizing Control, Regulation and Governance

7.1 The term **social control** is notoriously difficult to pin down. In functionalist sociology the concept appears as a neutral term to describe a variety of social processes – from infant socialization to incarceration – that induce social order, and to explain how conformity is maintained in pluralist democracies. Within interactionism the focus is somewhat narrower, but similarly concludes that the key to social integration lies in the realm of informal and primary socialization. Such benign readings of 'social control' as a functional necessity and as essentially apolitical were mirrored in traditional positivist criminology whose key concern, at least up to the 1950s, remained one of developing 'scientific', pragmatic and institutionally based policies for the individualized control of offenders (see **Chapter 3**). As Cohen and Scull (1983, pp. 5–6) recall, the standard definition of 'social control' is rooted in a social psychological perspective and is used as a term first simply to describe all the means and processes through which social conformity is achieved and, second, to construct a hierarchy of such means ranging from primary socialization, through informal mechanisms (such as peer group pressure) to formal methods associated with the police and the legal system. Within all such readings it is widely assumed that a consensus exists in society; that primary socialization is largely successful in achieving a widespread and uncontested conformity; and that external agencies are only called upon to 'mop up' those deviants who have suffered a failure or lack of adequate socialization.

It was not until the late 1960s that an alternative view of social control, as organized repression, came to the fore. Generated by the protest movements in America (civil rights, Vietnam, counterculture) and the emerging utopian and personal politics of the 'new left', arguments concerning the essential consensual nature of society became harder to sustain (see **Chapter 6**). In particular, labelling contended that the identification of the deviant and the criminal was an intrinsically political process through which, for example, capitalist institutions and the ruling classes were able to impose their will on the exploited and the powerless (see **Chapter 4.1**). In this formulation, social control was conceptualized not simply as a reactive exercise, but as an active force in the identification and creation of the deviant. As Chunn and Gavigan (1988, p. 109) noted, 'the concept of "social control" as "doing good" had become the concept of "social control" as "doing bad"'. Such a premise did indeed become influential in critical readings of a wide range of purportedly reformist and welfare-related practices. For example, a key concern of the National Deviancy Conference was to reveal the coercive – but often hidden – aspects of control entailed in the professional practices of youth training, social work, law, probation, medicine, schooling, psychiatry, and so on. The intrusion of the state into the private and familial; the capacity for behaviour to be continually subjected to surveillance, monitoring and regulation; and the spectre of mind control – all these constructed a powerful portrayal of a one-dimensional society (Marcuse, 1964) in the image of George Orwell's *Nineteen Eighty-Four* (1949) and Aldous Huxley's *Brave New World* (1932).

Moving the concept of social control from its benign underpinnings, this *control culture* approach maintained that social control, whether weak or strong, informal or formal, remained all-pervasive. There was very little that remained that could not be seen as an instrument of social control (Stedman-Jones, 1977). The key neglected issue – particularly within labelling – was how and why such control operated differently in different social contexts. Lacking any precise definition and consistent use, the concept was aptly described by Cohen (1985, p. 2) as 'Mickey Mouse' and by Lowman et al. (1987, p. 4) as 'a skeleton key opening so many doors that its analytic power has been drained ... a spectral category which becomes all things to all theorists'.

From Social Control to State Control

In the 1970s, the answer to such ambiguities lay in situating particular processes of social control in their precise socio-structural and historical settings. The emerging Marxist criminology and sociology of law, for example, placed a theory of the state centre-stage in the analysis of how control was exercised (see **Chapter 4.1**). Hall et al. (1978, p. 195), for example, found the control culture approach to be ahistorical and too imprecise for an adequate understanding of processes of conformity, legitimation and, most significantly, opposition, in the class-structured democracies of 'late capitalism'. It did not locate centres of power historically and thus was unable to account for moments of shift and change; it failed to differentiate between different types of state and political regime; and did not specify the type of social formation which requires a particular form of legal order. Above all, it adopted a predominantly coercive view of power and legal relations. Simply substituting coercion for the functionalist notion of consensus failed to identify how the exercise of power was often legitimized. The complex combination of processes of social regulation and civil liberties; of naked force and willing consent; and of resistance and deference was, quite simply, lost in a perspective that caricatured all police, social workers, teachers, philanthropists and reformers as unconscious agents of socio-cultural repression (Hall and Scraton, 1981, p. 470). As a result, Hall et al. (1978, p. 195) argued for the abandonment of the term 'social control' (except for 'general descriptive purposes') and its subjugation to that of **state control**. This, they argued, would enable recognition that the production of consent is achieved not simply through coercive measures, but through state leadership, direction, education and tutelage. Chunn and Gavigan (1988, p. 120) reached a similar conclusion, again by stressing the ahistorical nature of 'social control' and by arguing that critical scholars should be searching for alternative concepts that are 'attentive to the dynamic complexity of history, struggle and change'.

Feminist research has also alerted us to significant gender-based differences in the operation of both social and state control (Heidensohn, 1985). Disobedient or runaway young women and the 'unfit' teenage mother are far more likely to be candidates for intervention than disobedient, runaway or sexually active heterosexual young men. Moreover many social and employment policies have traditionally tended to be predicated on assumptions of female dependency and male independence. Systems of social control impact differently on different subject populations. A state-centred perspective may be able to recognize how 'social control' produces (rather than simply prohibits) certain behaviours, but on its own is unable to capture the nuances of control afforded by a 'gendered lens' (Walklate, 1995). In addition, some feminist authors have argued that the extension of control in some areas, rather than being dangerous, is urgently required in order to protect women from male domestic and street violence. As Smart (1989) argues, the law can be used not simply for disciplinary purposes, but also as a means to pursue a discourse of 'rights'.

Foucault on the Carceral Society

Following the work of Foucault (1977), the term 'social control' was resurrected as a means through which analytical justice could be done to the complex and contradictory means by which order is achieved in democratic societies. Foucault's critique of 'power as state centred' and the shift towards acknowledging the role of processes of diffuse societal power (or the 'microphysics of power') significantly broadened the concept of social control to include not only state and institutional practices but also the realms of discursive construction, ideology and the production of meaning.

Foucault refers to a continuous *disciplinary discourse*, in which no one source is given privileged attention, which informed and was intertwined with all forms of social control in the late eighteenth century. The reform of prisoners, confinement of the insane and supervision of industrial workers, as well as the training and education of children, all formed part of an emerging **carceral society**, in which it was not only deviance or crime that was controlled, but also every irregularity or the least departure from the norm (see Box 7.2).

■ Box 7.2 ▐

The disciplinary society

[I]t was no longer the offence, the attack on common interest, it was the departure from the norm, the anomaly; it was this that haunted the school, the court, the asylum or the prison ... [I]t is not on the fringes of society and through successive exiles that criminality is born, but by means of ever more closely placed insertions, under ever more insistent surveillance, by an accumulation of disciplinary coercion. In short the carceral archipelago assures in the depth of the social body, the formation of delinquency on the basis of subtle illegalities, the overlapping of the latter by the former and the establishment of a specified criminality ... By operating at every level of the social body and by mingling ceaselessly the art of rectifying and the right to punish, the universality of the carceral lowers the level from which it becomes natural and acceptable to be punished.

Source: Foucault (1977, pp. 299, 301, 303).

The carceral discourse, it is argued, is so pervasive that ultimately it affects our very vision of the world: it enters the human soul. The power of the prison, and in particular the juvenile reformatory (see **Chapter 2.2**) in the 1840s, is less explicable in terms of penal philosophy, or as a success or a failure, than it is by the 'power of normalization' that operates simultaneously and to varying degrees in the school, the hospital and the factory. This power emanates not simply from the state or a mode of production but, for Foucault, from forms of knowledge that inform all social relations. The emergence of the reformatory was but one reflection of the diffusion of new forms of knowledge grounded in positivism and the human sciences which first began to surface in the late eighteenth century. The aim was to produce a new kind of individual subjected to habits, rules, orders and an authority that is 'exercised continually around him, and upon him, and which he must allow to function automatically in him' (Foucault, 1977, p. 129). Foucault's initial investigation of penal reform became a means of exploring the wider theme of how domination is achieved and how individuals are socially constructed in the modern world. It is because of this broad canvas, on which images of regulation, discipline, surveillance, consent, normalization and coercion are constructed, that Foucault's work remains influential in historical and contemporary readings of social control. For example, it has enabled criminology to study the way in which various welfare state institutions are deeply implicated in the 'regulation of life'. But it also allows for a greater sensitivity to the interrelations of social structure with processes of power, knowledge and governance. It is at once attuned to processes of domination *and* enablement; of constraint *and* resistance (Lacombe, 1996).

Donzelot (1979), for example, has argued that from the mid-nineteenth century onwards 'expert knowledges', whether emanating from welfare agencies, the school or the juvenile court, have continuously devised remedies for the 'aberrant' which have penetrated deep into the everyday life of the urban working classes. Psychologists, paediatricians, social workers, teachers and health visitors formed a 'tutelary complex' to 'watch over' not only the young but also their families. This was achieved not by overtly coercive means but by persuading the family of its social responsibility to others and to its own members. Familial autonomy, or government *by* the family, was replaced by government *through* the family. The aim was to govern society by delegating legitimacy to professionals empowered to nurture individuals into social citizenship. Such programmes had as much to do with the governance of particular moral and social orders as they had explicitly to do with crime and disorder. Every departure from the norm comes under scrutiny to be monitored and regulated not simply through formal criminal justice legislation but through an ever-expanding range of familial and social policy interventions. Moreover as these interventions can act anywhere along a disciplinary/enabling continuum, they are difficult to characterize as either one or the other. Rather they are progressively internalized such that citizens come to unreflectively make and remake their own conceptions of themselves within a disciplinary discourse.

Box 7.3

Foucault's *Discipline and Punish*

- The punitive techniques of supervision and surveillance first formulated in the prison have penetrated the whole of society.

- Punishment is aimed not at the body, but towards training the human soul.

- Such techniques are directed not only towards offenders, but to all departures from the norm.

- Disciplinary networks become natural, legitimate and 'normalized' elements of the social landscape.

- Social control becomes diffuse, hidden and dispersed.

- Social control is exercised not simply through the state but through power-knowledge strategies. As a result, control may be pervasive but is always contingent. It produces resistance as well as subjugation.

Foucault and Donzelot's work clearly avoids any ready identification with 'grand' theoretical paradigms and more readily escapes the critique of essentialism so often directed at general theory. Indeed, Garland (1990, p. 154) concludes that, as a result, there is now 'a much greater sensitivity to the nuances of penal measures and to what they can tell us about the regulatory means through which we are governed and the forms of subjectivity (or objectivity) into which offenders are pressed'. Terms such as 'regulation', 'knowledge', 'normalization', 'governmentality' and 'discipline' have come to hold a central place in this 'revisionist' literature of social control. The key elements of Foucault's argument are summarized in Box 7.3.

Cohen on the Dispersal of Discipline

Stanley Cohen's (1979, 1985, 1987) **dispersal of discipline** thesis reworks that of Foucault to contend that as control mechanisms are dispersed from custody into the community, they penetrate more deeply into the social fabric. A blurring of boundaries between the deviant and non-deviant, the public and the private occurs. A 'punitive archipelago' is expanded as new resources, technology and professional interests are applied to a growing number of 'clients' and 'consumers'. Entrepreneurs are drawn into the control enterprise in search of profits. Communities are mobilized to act as voluntary control agents in their own right. But, throughout, the growing invisibility and diversification of the state's role do not mean it has withered away. The prison remains at the core of the system. The rhetoric of community control continues to camouflage what is really going on: 'The price paid by ordinary people is to become either active participants or passive receivers in the business of social control' (Cohen, 1985, p. 233). The end result of drawing law and order agendas into social policy for youth has meant that any progressive elements have become obscured by ambivalence and ambiguity (see Box 7.4). Alternatives to prison (such as community supervision) and crime prevention (rather than law enforcement) policies have failed to reduce the reach of criminal justice and have drawn more young people into the mesh of formal controls (see **Chapter 9**). Such reforms have also been supported for non-progressive reasons, as, for example, 'solutions' to the fiscal crises of the state, rather than as determined responses to youth marginalization or exclusion.

Lowman et al. (1987, p. 9) argue that these developments can best be captured in the concept of **transcarceration**. They argue that as the old institutions of control remain and the new are created, we are now confronted with

[a] peno-judicial, mental health, welfare and tutelage complex ... [F]or delinquents, deviants and dependants this means that their careers are likely to be characterized by institutional mobility as they are pushed from one section of the help–control complex to another. For control agents, this means that control will essentially have no locus and the control mandate will increasingly entail the 'fitting together' of subsystems.

Box 7.4

The outcomes of 'community control'

- The weak, pathetic and sick are subject to too little 'control'. Neglected and deprived of help, treatment and services, they are left to suffer silently or to be exploited by commercial interests.

- The petty or 'potential' delinquents are subject to more intrusive and disguised control in the name of diversion or prevention.

- The hardcore, serious criminals are subject to further degradation. As the soft end of the system appears more and more benign, so the hard core criminals appear more hopeless and become easy targets for policies such as selective incapacitation.

- The powerful remain free to carry out their depredations with impunity.

- The ordinary population are subjected to further and more subtle involvement in the business of social control. Everyday life becomes 'controllized' by Crime Prevention through Environmental Design, informers, new systems of surveillance of public space, and databanks. Whole populations are made the object of preventive social control before any deviant act can take place.

Source: Adapted from Cohen (1987, pp. 363–4).

In congruence with Foucault's thesis, this formulation of control continues to acknowledge its versatility: infiltrating many levels of discourse and 'arenas of action' and serving and constituting a diversity of interests. Of particular note is how, by the 1990s, much of this control became privatized – that is, removed from direct state control and activated by communities, voluntary agencies and private security companies. It is in this context that Cohen (1994, p. 74) can begin talking of social control as a commodity: as something to be purchased and sold.

Rose on Governance

To make sense of these shifts in crime control and social regulation, numerous authors have increasingly turned to the concept of 'governance'. Derived from Foucault's (1991) brief writings on 'governmentality', 'governance' (though often used in an eclectic fashion) draws attention to the numerous means through which power is exercised, and how particular 'mentalities' of governing are constructed, both within *and* beyond the state. Governance means something more than state government. Foucault suggested that, rather than framing investigations of regulation and control in terms of the state or politics, it would be more productive to investigate the formation and transformation of rationalities, discourses, proposals, strategies and technologies in order to explore, in his terms, 'the conduct of conduct'

(Dean, 1999). **Governmentality** theory challenges reductionist analyses by focusing on how particular modes of power depend on specific ways of thinking (rationalities of power) and of acting (technologies of power) (Garland, 1997). It is less concerned, for example, with how law is *imposed* and more with the *tactic* of using particular knowledges to arrange things in such a way that populations accept being governed and begin to govern themselves. It implies that power is not simply achieved through sovereign state dominance, but through myriad institutions, procedures, reflections and calculations in which citizens are 'made up' and come to realize themselves. Governing is viewed as heterogeneous in thought and action – captured to a certain extent in the various words available to describe and enact it: education, control, influence, regulation, administration, management, therapy, reformation, guidance (Rose, 1999). Recognition of this *dispersal* of governance has opened a door to examining how youth crime is 'governed', not simply by the police and formal control agents, but also by the 'rationalities' employed by the likes of the insurance industry, employers, potential victims, head teachers, shopping-centre managers, cognitive psychologists, parenting counsellors, and so on (see Box 7.5).

Box 7.5

The 'conduct of conduct'

The investigations of government that interest me here are those which try to gain a purchase on the forces that traverse the multitudes of encounters where conduct is subject to government: prisons, clinics, schoolrooms and bedrooms, factories and offices, airports and military organizations, the market place and shopping mall, sexual relations and much more … They focus upon the various incarnations of what one might term 'the will to govern' as it is enacted in a multitude of programmes, strategies, tactics, devices, calculations, negotiations, intrigues, persuasions and seductions aimed at the conduct of the conduct of individuals, groups, populations – and indeed oneself.

Source: Rose (1999, p. 5).

In this analysis the state is relocated as one element in 'multiple circuits of power' connecting a diversity of authorities, forces and complex assemblages. The subjects of government are not simply 'members of a flock to be shepherded, as children to be nurtured and tutored' but are 'citizens with rights, rational, calculating individuals whose preferences are to be acted upon' (Rose, 2000, p. 323).

How can this help us to understand the regulation of young people? Rose (1989, p. 121) contends that it allows us to realize how childhood has, over the past 200 years, become 'the most intensively governed sector of personal existence'. The continual casting of children in a double bind of in need of support and control has enabled virtually every aspect of their lives to be subject to inspection, surveillance and regulation. In criminology in general, and youth studies in particular, governance theory has also typically been employed in the context of exploring new forms of governance. Crawford

(1997) argues that attempts to control crime through partnerships of statutory, commercial and voluntary organizations imply a new *process of governing* through negotiation and bargaining, rather than command and coercion. The devolution and privatization of functions previously undertaken by statutory agencies suggest that a fragmentation of power into a plurality of competing agencies with none being able to exercise overall control. The idea of 'joined-up' government to attack multi-faceted and complex problems such as youth offending through multi-agency partnerships employing a broad spectrum of social policy interventions represents a significant break with some forms of centralized power. Governance theory then draws attention to the 'ways of thinking' that underpin processes of new manageri-alism; where governance is achieved 'at a distance'; where a language of risks and rewards has transformed that of care and control; and where partnerships, commu-nities and families have been 'empowered' and 'responsibilized' to take an active role in their own self-government, but where some citizens may also have been 'abandoned' (Clarke, 2005) (see **Chapters 8 and 9**).

Such analysis helps us to make sense of many of the policy reforms of the past two decades. They express a preference for free market solutions, 'best value' competition, deregulation, privatization and workfare (where any benefit entitlement is conditional upon acceptance of work) in a climate where risks are to be calculated and outputs are to be managed through continual performance measures and where policy is justi-fied through recourse to 'scientific' evaluations of 'what works' (see Box 7.6). Above all a multiplicity of modes of governance is created: authoritarian at one time, welfarist at another; delivering discourses of responsibility as well as rights; and driven by a deeply imbued moralization as well as pragmatism (Stenson, 2000; Muncie and Hughes, 2002).

Box 7.6

New modes of governance

- Replacing the command and control structures of government by 'governing at a distance'.

- Building partnerships and networks across the public, private and voluntary sectors to achieve 'joined-up' governance.

- Devolving responsibility for government to individuals, families and communities.

- Creating the 'active citizen' and 'negotiated self governance'.

- Opening up decision-making to greater public participation and the individual desire to govern their own conduct with freedom.

- Involving civil society in the process of governance.

- Privatizing the state sector.

- Promoting the role of government as steerer and co-ordinator rather than as controller.

- Regulating devolved governance through fiscal accounting, audit and evaluation research.

Source: Derived from Newman (2001, p. 24) and Muncie and Hughes (2002, p. 3).

Governance theory, to date, has mainly been concerned with unravelling the processes through which we are governed, but it also marks a significant theoretical step in understanding the detailed nuances and contradictions of reform. Foucault and Cohen clearly broadened the traditional subject matter of the criminology of youth by blurring the boundaries of social policy and criminological knowledges. Their strength lay in identifying major trends in 'the disciplinary' and 'the carceral'. Governance theory goes further by also alerting us to the 'heterogeneity, contestability and mobility in practices for the government of conduct' (Rose, 2000, p. 323). Rights-based social movements, local initiatives and the intrinsic spaces for resistance opened by the commitment to self-governance all suggest possible avenues for a reconstitution of 'social' modes of government. Such authors as Hughes (2007) and Young (2007) have come to argue (albeit in different ways) that the inclusionary principles, values and ideals that inform some social policies should not be abandoned, but resurrected within agendas of social justice, rather than criminal justice. For them, new imaginaries of public safety, transformative politics, mutual aid and social justice remain the preferable goals. For Stan Cohen (1987), it also meant moving away from discourses of crime and criminal justice: 'the further away we move from the discourse of criminal justice, the more likely are we to find the conditions for realizing those values … [T]o be realistic about law and order must mean to be unrealistic (that is imaginative) about the possibilities of order without law' (Cohen, 1987, p. 374).

Youth Training and the Labour Market

7.2 Research into the relationship between education, training, entry to the labour market and unemployment has tended to view the process as an orthodox linear *transition* from school to work and has failed to recognize its social control implications. Any deviation from an 'ideal' progression from full-time education to full-time employment is perceived in negative terms: as a 'broken' transition, as a 'failure' of certain young people to adjust to the demands of the labour market. Such concern is of course by no means new. The vagaries of the youth labour market vexed many a Victorian reformer and the problems of dead-end jobs, prolonged unemployment, 'wasted potential' and 'idle hands' were uppermost in the minds of the founders of the welfare state after the Second World War. During times of relatively full employment the transition from school to work has been viewed as non-problematic. But, as Coles (1995) has argued, the traditional 'careers' of young people – leaving school and finding employment, leaving families of origin and forming their own, and leaving the family home and living independently – rest crucially not only on personal decisions, but also on prevailing social and economic contexts. In the 1970s most young people seemed to manage these transitions with relative ease. A majority left school at 16 and within six months 90 per cent had secured employment (Coles, 1995, p. 30). By 1980, this picture had changed dramatically.

Youth Unemployment

Triggered by economic recession and a restructuring of the labour market which reduced the demand for young unskilled labour, the numbers of unemployed school leavers rose dramatically from the mid-1970s. In September 1973, there were 14,000 school leavers (under-18s) without a job. By July 1980, this figure had risen to 368,000. This almost 26-fold increase took place despite higher numbers of young people avoiding the labour market by going into higher and further education.

Ever since 1975 when youth unemployment first became a major political issue, governments have poured resources into various job creation, work experience and training schemes. In 1976, the then Prime Minister James Callaghan set the tone by blaming young people for not having the skills that the economy required of them. He further blamed education for not teaching students what was required of them by the business community. The bulk of subsequent reforms were initially directed towards 16 year old school-leavers. This was not unsurprising. In the early 1980s nearly 50 per cent of Britain's 16 year olds still left school to find work. In July 1983, over half of these were either unemployed or on a government-sponsored training scheme. Numerous programmes were established in the next 20 years, the most notable being the 1978 Youth Opportunities Programme (YOP) and the 1983 Youth Training Scheme (YTS) (a 12-month training programme directed at *all* 16 and 17 year old school-leavers) which in 1990 became known simply as Youth Training (YT) and subsequently as Skillseekers. All such schemes have met robust criticism.

The basic premise of such programmes was that youth unemployment had risen because of a sudden failure of youth to be suitable candidates for employment. In effect they promoted a 'blame the victim' ideology (see **Chapter 5**). Youth employment was presented as a problem of faulty supply rather than demand; a failure of the educational system rather than market economies; a personal problem of joblessness due to lack of motivation, experience or skill, rather than of precarious labour markets (Cohen, P., 1982, p. 45). The primary fallacy lay in the premise that a programme of vocational preparation would enable the young to be better equipped to compete for jobs, without actually expanding real job opportunities. As Stafford (1982, p. 77) warned, this form of integrating youth into the labour market would depend on their willingness to accept any alternative to the dole. As such it would be 'precarious and rests on a promise which must surely turn sour'. Similarly, Finn (1987, p. 190) concluded that the aim of youth training was essentially contradictory: 'to produce a generation of young people who are basically skilled and willing to work, but who can also maintain these qualities in suspended animation through any periods of unemployment'.

By 1988 the option of the dole was removed when the Conservative government abolished income support benefit for all 16 and 17 year olds, other than for a small majority who could plead 'severe hardship'. By now 16 year olds were faced with a limited range of options: to continue with schooling or further education; to accept a place on a government-sponsored training scheme; or, if unemployed, to stay dependent on their families. As a result it has been widely acknowledged that 'adolescence' was formally extended, with any possibility of independence removed for the vast majority (Furlong and Cartmel, 1997, p. 43). In 1989, 18 per cent of minimum-age school leavers entered the labour market; by 1994, this had been reduced to 9 per cent. Conversely the proportion of 16 year olds in full-time or part-time education rose to 80 per cent (*Observer*, 23 July 1995).

Those entering the labour market in the 1980s also faced a series of additional hazards. Since the nineteenth century a political consensus had ensured that young people were given some protection from market exploitation, but in the 1980s market deregulation meant that restrictions on hours and conditions of work and rates of pay were removed. The problem of youth unemployment, it was claimed, was one of young people being too expensive to employ. As Roberts (1995, p. 15) records, Young Workers' Schemes offered subsidies to employers only on condition that they hire young people at rates of pay below the average for the age group. In 1986, the protection of Wages Councils was also removed. The jobs available to 16 year olds increasingly became low paid and insecure. Those entering youth training fared little better. This 'route' rapidly contracted in the 1990s as educational participation grew. Despite government claims that YT was designed to improve skills and subsequent employability, the schemes were consistently critiqued by young people themselves as 'slave labour' with employers operating 'try-out schemes' in which young people's work performance was assessed and only the best retained (Coffield et al., 1986). For many, YT was also an exercise in 'warehousing' in which no long-term career benefits were forthcoming (Banks et al., 1992). Mizen's (1995) equally critical, empirical study of school leavers and trainees' experiences and accounts in Coventry painted a picture of YT 'more as an extension of pre-existing forms of discipline and control than as the beginning of a new and welcome chapter in the lives of many working class young people'. It was received by young people with a (realistic) combination of resistance, denial and ambivalence (Mizen, 1995, pp. 197–202). The experience of training was fragmented and stratified by class, gender and 'race'. The most disadvantaged and those from ethnic minorities tended to be concentrated in schemes with low rates of subsequent employment. The promised new opportunities failed to materialize, with the vast majority of schemes reinforcing and reproducing gender stereotypes in their provision of 'suitable' work for young men and women (Griffin, 1985; Cockburn, 1987; Wallace, 1987). Box 7.7 summarizes this parlous state of the labour market for young people in the 1990s.

One of the most palpable consequences of a contracting and deregulated youth labour market was the expansion of what Furlong and Cartmel (1997, p. 17) described as 'an army of reluctant conscripts to post-compulsory education'. A range of vocational courses (BTEC, NVQ and GNVQ) have been introduced in schools and colleges of further education, though arguably these have been mainly directed at lower-attaining, working-class pupils and have little affected the traditional academic routes followed by the middle classes. Moreover the 'careers' of young people in further education often remained precarious. About a third of those starting a full-time post-16 course left early or failed the relevant examinations. The concepts of 'career' and 'transition' seemed particularly irrelevant

Box 7.7

Youth labour markets in the 1980s and 1990s

- Shift from manufacturing to service sector.

- Decline in demand for unqualified 16 year old school leavers.

- Growth in part-time, temporary, low-paid and lower tier employment.

- Engagement with 'fiddly jobs' (the marginal economy) as a survival strategy.

- Deregulation of markets prioritizes increased training, flexibility and low labour cost.

- Decline in trade union membership and influence – reinforced by legislation.

- Restricted access to income support and unemployment benefits.

- From 1989 an increase in unemployment – disproportionately for young men and blacks.

- Growth in numbers remaining in full-time education and/or training.

- Complex maze of 'transitions' and multiple routes from school to work – 'transitions' extended, fragmented, fractured and individualized.

- Maintenance of regional-, class-, gender- and 'race' -based structures of opportunity and disadvantage.

- Conditions of uncertainty, risk and disaffection exacerbated.

Source: Derived from Furlong and Cartmel (1997; 2007, Chapter 3).

for such young people. Instead their lives were characterized by a *mélange* of training courses, part-time, low-paid work (as low as 33 pence per hour – *Guardian*, 11 February 1998) and unemployment. Here the sensitizing concepts of 'drift', 'normalized dislocation' and 'structured aimlessness' may better capture a sense of youth's uncertain futures in an unstable market, than those of 'transition' or 'marginalization' (Fergusson et al., 2000). Indeed, as Brinkley (1997) records, the free market logic of deregulation did not help young people back into work, despite their being cheaper to employ. Demand in industrialized economies for skilled workers meant that the young – especially those without qualifications – were left behind. Between 1979 and 1997, 31 changes were made to how youth unemployment figures were officially arrived at. But using data from Department of Employment Labour Force Surveys, Brinkley suggests that in 1996 the unemployment rate for under-25s was 14.8 per cent; almost twice the national average. Unemployment has always hit the young hardest, particularly so for ethnic minorities. Thus while, in 1995, 15 per cent of white 16–25 year olds were estimated to be unemployed, this compared quite favourably to the 51 per cent of Afro-Caribbean young men, 41 per cent of Afro-Caribbean young women, 34 per cent of Pakistani/Bangladeshi young men and 30 per cent of Indian young men

(*Runnymede Bulletin*, No. 292, February 1996, pp. 6–7). But these estimates also missed a sizeable number of the population. Wilkinson's (1995) Sunderland-based study found that between 5 and 10 per cent of 16 and 17 year olds were neither in education, employment or training (NEET), nor did they have any access to income support. Officially, they did not exist. This could amount to some 100,000 young people nationally who occupied what Williamson (1997) controversially, but perceptively, called 'Status-Zero'.

It was in this context that New Labour announced a range of 'welfare to work' initiatives prior to the 1997 election. In 1998, the New Deal for Young People effectively abolished youth unemployment at a stroke by compelling those not in work to take up the education, training or subsidized work options. However, it was still estimated that half a million 16–24 year olds (around 10 per cent) were unemployed in 2006. Numbers had reduced by a quarter over the decade but young adult unemployment rates remained three times as high as those for older workers (www.poverty.org.uk).

The New Deal for Young People

The New Deal for Young People (NDYP) was introduced nationally in April 1998 after being piloted for just four months. It was part of a broader 'welfare to work' initiative aimed at encouraging lone parents back to work, maintaining commitment to a work ethic, reducing levels of state dependency, compelling claimants to work in return for benefits, tackling social exclusion and encouraging individual responsibility. The NDYP, according to the Department of Work and Pensions, is here to stay as a key element in preventing 'a life on benefit' (*Guardian*, 26 March 2003). But does it offer anything more than the failed programmes of the past?

The New Deal is aimed at unemployed 18–24 year olds who have been claiming Jobseeker's Allowance for six months or more. In 1997, New Labour made their electoral claim that by 2002 the NDYP would get 250,000 young people off benefit and into work, education and training. To do so, young people first enter a Gateway period where for four months they receive support and guidance from a personal advisor initially designed to help find any (unsubsidized) employment. If this fails, there are five New Deal options: subsidized employment, full-time education and training, work in the voluntary sector, work with an Environment Task Force or self-employment. 'A life on benefit' is not an option. The New Deal is mandatory. Sanctions, in the form of cutting benefits, are applied to those who fail to cooperate. For some this smacks of US-inspired workfare, where almost all benefit entitlement is entirely conditional upon the acceptance of work (Fergusson, 2002). As such, while NDYP may hold inclusionary and developmental claims, its underlying rationale remains one of discipline. It is a continuation of the 'welfare bad; work good' ethic. No effort is made to address structural problems of inequality and lack of opportunity in precarious youth labour markets (Webster et al., 2004). Explanations of unemployment remain fixed in a skills-deficit model (Jeffs and Spence, 2000; Tonge, 1999; Hyland and Mussan, 2001). The talk is not of full employment but of 'individual employability'

(Mizen, 2003). The continuing significance of NDYP lies not in finding employment for the young unemployed working class but in promoting the neo-liberal ethos of withdrawing universal public support in favour of free market determinants and of institutionalizing low paid work (Mizen, 2006).

The success or otherwise of the NDYP has been subject to numerous official evaluations. Their findings are at best ambiguous. New Labour met its target of removing a quarter of a million from benefit as early as 2000. By the end of 2001 it was estimated that around 40 per cent of participants had found unsubsidized jobs. But a further 30 per cent had left for unknown destinations. The impact of NDYP was believed to have in reality reduced youth unemployment by some 35,000 while only creating some 15,000 new jobs (NAO, 2002). As with previous employment initiatives, job creation relies on demands in local economies rather than as something amenable to state engineering. Many participants would have found work anyway. Percy-Smith and Weil (2002) maintain that there is little evidence to suggest that the scheme has produced any tangible benefits in job security, conditions and future prospects. All that has been created is an endless roundabout of multiple moves in and out of training, paid work, unemployment, voluntary work: an intensifying of 'churning', frustration and instability (Fergusson, 2002: Webster et al., 2004). Further, the element of 'compulsory inclusion' treats lack of commitment as a 'punishable offence rather than an opportunity for learning' and only ensures integration into a world of inequalities and labour exploitation (Percy-Smith and Weil, 2002, p. 125). Much of this seems borne out by participants' perspectives. Ritchie (2000), for example, reports that nearly two-thirds leave NDYP in the initial Gateway period in order to avoid any of the compulsory (and unattractive) placement options. Avoiding sanctions inevitably means accepting low-paid, low-quality, short-term jobs (which in turn of course keeps wage inflation low). Kalra et al. (2001) report that non-participation and drop-out are driven by poor experiences of the programme and the sense that it would not deliver a decent job, particularly for minority ethnic young people.

The political rationale for youth training and employment schemes lies elsewhere than in the creation of jobs. Indeed, NDYP has been expressly identified as an anti-crime as much as an economic policy (Straw, 1998, p. 12). Yet, if NDYP is a vehicle for crime reduction then non-participation is likely to be interpreted as placing young people 'at risk'. This logic has also informed a raft of 'inclusionary' measures aimed at a younger 13–19 age group. Notable is the Connexions initiative of 2001. This is a universal service of advice and guidance but geared to that 9 per cent of 16–18 year olds not in education, employment, or training (NEET). Significantly, Connexions is about providing mentors in schools and colleges drawn from a range of agencies, but whose chief preoccupations are those of inducting young people into the labour market and monitoring those 'at risk' of becoming disconnected from the education/training/work complex. It involves establishing a database on all 13–19 year olds with information flowing from one agency to another. For Garrett (2002), it amounts to a 'new regime of virtual control'. The issuing of a Connexions Card to 2.4 million young people effectively allows their levels of 'participation' to be continually tracked and monitored. In

2007, the Children, Schools and Families Secretary looked forward to abolishing the 16 to 18 year old 'NEET culture' by introducing new laws requiring *all* young people to stay in education or training until the age of 18. This is to be implemented by 2015. Much of this of course easily resonates with the themes of 'active citizenship', 'governing at a distance', 'joined-up governance', 'individual responsibility' and 'state steering' to be found in New Labour's Third Way modes of governance (see Section 7.1 above).

Above all, historically, the young and unemployed working classes have been understood as both a potential threat to the social order and, partly as a consequence, in need of special provision from, and direction by, that same social order if they are to assume their role as the next generation of adult workers. Youth training has always been a vocational fallacy. It has always been a means through which working-class identities can be reworked and remade; providing a cultural, rather than vocational, apprenticeship in working-class expectations of work (Hollands, 1990). In this context, training policies display a Janus face, where what is altruistically proclaimed to be meeting 'needs' also acts to constrain and remake working-class identities. The social order consequences of youth unemployment is one underlying factor in this succession of educational and training initiatives. The fear is never far from the surface that if young people fail to gain experience of a market-based work ethic at an early age, then they will never acquire the 'appropriate' attitudes necessary for the establishment of a flexible, disciplined and compliant citizenship. It is a discourse that has become cemented in the insistence that waged work is the prime route through which young people can be rescued from 'passive dependency' and social exclusion. And that non-compliance must be met with harsher penalties.

Homelessness and the Housing Market

7.3 Measuring the extent of youth homelessness is largely guesswork. In the mid-1990s voluntary organizations estimated that between 150,000 and 250,000 young people became homeless every year (*Guardian*, 16 September 1996). Such estimates are usually based on enquiries or agency referrals to campaigning organizations such as Shelter. Official estimates based on local authority housing department records put the figure substantially lower. This is largely because a number of criteria have to be met before a person is officially *accepted* as homeless. For example, they must show that they are not intentionally homeless and that they have a 'priority need', such as being at risk of sexual or financial exploitation. Both estimates are likely to greatly underestimate the extent of homelessness among women and black youth who for different reasons tend to seek temporary accommodation with friends. The issue is also clouded by the lack of a precise definition of homelessness. It may, or may not, include any of the following: sleeping rough, newly arrived migrants, runaways, people in hostel/bed and breakfast accommodation, people with temporary and insecure tenures, squatters, travellers, people leaving care or prison, and people in involuntarily shared or unsatisfactory accommodation. Nevertheless it is widely regarded that the issue – once a key concern of nineteenth-century reformers – only resurfaced in many Western industrial countries in the 1970s and 1980s. In media and political discourse the issue has characteristically been phrased in behavioural terms for which the young homeless themselves must take responsibility. As Margaret Thatcher opined in 1988: 'There is a number of young people who choose voluntarily to leave home and I do not think we can be expected – no matter how many there are – to provide units for them' (Hansard, 7 June 1988, vol. 134). In contrast, a number of structural arguments have been forwarded which suggest that homelessness has been generated by changes in housing, social security and local taxation, as well as labour market policies. 'Young runaways' were an express target of New Labour's Social Exclusion Unit, which claimed that 5,000 children a year survived by stealing, begging, drug dealing and prostitution (SEU, 2002).

The Withdrawal and Reconstitution of State Welfare

A key cause of youth homelessness has always been a lack of affordable accommodation. In the 1980s access to such accommodation was further limited as a result of Conservative policy which severely reduced council house building from 125,000 in 1969 to 8,000 in 1991 (Hutson and Liddiard, 1994, p. 47). This decline was compounded by the 1980 Housing Act which instituted a 'right to buy' policy for existing council house tenants, thus removing 1.5 million residences from the social housing sector. Restrictions were also placed upon local authorities to use no more than 25 per cent of the revenue from sales to provide accommodation for the homeless. The end result has been a decline in publicly rented housing from 32 per cent to under 22 per cent of the total housing stock. Privately rented housing also fell by a half to less than 8 per cent of the total stock. Young people found themselves excluded from local authority housing (being deemed 'low priority') and from private rentals (due to cost, declining supply, unemployment and a fall in real incomes). While an expanding gap between demand and supply came to be widely recognized, the Conservative government was content to let the voluntary sector and housing associations fill this space, yet by 1991 the latter accounted for just over 3 per cent of the housing market (Hutson and Liddiard, 1994, p. 50). The commitment was clearly one of forcing young people to stay at home. The scale of the problem was provided by an opinion poll commissioned by Shelter in 1987. Twenty-four per cent of 15–25 year olds were found to have personally experienced difficulty in finding housing. A third of these were still living with their parents. As Killeen (1992, p. 192) argued: 'this stressful situation could apply to as many as 1.5 million young people in Britain. Youth homelessness is one of the consequences which occurs when families can no longer tolerate this stress.'

The 'crisis' has been exacerbated by consistently restricting young people's access to benefits. In 1985 limits were placed on payments for board and lodgings, following a media campaign against young unemployed who were living on the 'Costa del Dole' in seaside towns. Claimants could claim full board allowances only for short periods and no longer than eight weeks. They were then required to leave the area and not return to claim benefit for six months. In 1988 – following the *1986 Social Security Act* – a new era of 'repressive disciplinary welfare' (Carlen, 1996, p. 44) was initiated with abolition of all benefits for most 16 and 17 year olds and a gradated level of benefit introduced for those under 25. *Age*, rather than *need* became the chief determinant of benefit entitlement. Before the Social Security Act, housing benefit to pay for rent, household rates and water rates was available in full for the unemployed with no income. From 1988, however, all claimants had to pay at least 20 per cent of their rates (subsequently the poll tax, the community charge and then Council Tax) from their income benefit. As Hutson and Liddiard (1994, p. 55) explain, because those under 25 were already on lower benefit rates, these young people found they were required to pay a larger proportion of their income on rent than their older contemporaries. The result was failure to meet rent costs and frequent eviction. And the knock-on effect of having to pay part of the community charge was that increasing numbers failed to register as electors for fear that this would make them more easily traceable. In fact more than a million potential first-time voters did not register in 1992 and 2.5 million, or 40 per cent of 18–24 year olds, did not vote in that election: 'The consequences of this trend in terms of future participation in democratic processes are not difficult to predict' (Killeen, 1992, p. 194). In addition, supplementary benefit, housing benefit and income support have gradually been removed for those in further and higher education. Dependency on loans and/or families has been institutionalized (see Box 7.8).

Since 1997 New Labour reconstituted the issue of homelessness as one element in an array of 'risk factors' of social exclusion. 'Rough sleepers' were targeted as a key area for intervention – along with truancy and teenage pregnancy – in the 2001 report *Preventing Social Exclusion*. The Rough Sleepers Unit of 1999–2002 was specifically designed to act on routes into homelessness (such as young people leaving care) through 'joined-up' working with health, employment and education programmes. The main policy recommendations tended to remain at this level of providing integrated support and advice agencies. The lack of affordable housing, high rents, the impact of benefit policies and shortage of social housing were rarely officially alluded to (Kemp and Rugg, 2001). The 2002 *Homeless Act* did, however, require all local authorities to develop and publish strategies of how they intended to *prevent* homelessness; though again certain conditions such as 'priority need', 'local connection' and 'unintentionally homeless' had to be met. While 16 and 17 year olds are accepted as 'priority need', being the subject of an anti-social behaviour order, for example, may be deemed to have contravened the 'unintentionality' condition. All of these reforms continue to be legitimized in the name of tackling a so-called 'dependency culture' which, it is argued, inflates the costs of social security and actively supports a permanently out-of-work underclass (see Chapter 4.2).

| Box 7.8 |

The withdrawal and reconstitution of state welfare

1983	Unemployed 16–17 year olds living at home lose contribution to board
1984	Extended to 18–20 year olds
1985	Limits on length of time under-25 year olds living away from home can receive financial assistance towards board and lodging
1986	Young people's wages removed from Wages Council regulations
1987	No supplementary benefits for students during short vacation
1988	Income support withdrawn from most 16 and 17 year olds and reduced for those under 26
	Changes to housing benefit rules lead to relatively higher cost of rent for some under-25s in employment or on a training allowance
	Discretionary Social Fund replaces Exceptional Needs payments
	Compulsory payment of at least 20 per cent of Community Charge
1989	Employment Act repeals restrictions on hours of work for 16–18 year olds
1990	Students lose housing benefit. Student loans introduced
1991	No income support for students in long vacation
1996	Jobseeker's allowance replaces unemployment benefit
1996	Housing benefit for under-25s reduced to cover cost of a room in shared accommodation only: the 'single room rent' rule
1997	All benefits dependent on adherence to 'Welfare to Work' principles
	Social Exclusion Unit established
1998	Introduction of tuition fees for students
	National minimum wage introduced, but excludes 16–18 year olds
	Introduction of New Deal for Young People (NDYP) in 18–25 age group
	Withdrawal of jobseeker's allowance for those failing to take NDYP options
1999	NDYP benefit sanctions increased
	Rough Sleepers Unit established
	Piloting of Education Maintenance Allowances (EMA) to encourage 16–19 year olds to stay in full-time education/training: contingent on signing a 'learning agreement'
2001	Establishment of Connexions service to guide and track progress of all 13–19 year olds
2004	National roll out of EMAs
2006	Introduction of University 'top up' tuition fees
2008	Raising of school leaving age to 17 by 2013 and to 18 by 2015

Criminalization, Survivalism and Risk

Reviewing shifts in policy up to the mid-1990s, Carlen concludes that there is now 'a much strengthened disciplining of pauperised and redundant youth *independently of the criminal justice and/or penal systems*' (1996, pp. 46–7, italics in original) and that when young people are 'outwith the protection of employment, family and welfare they are most likely to adopt one of the transient lifestyles which may well bring them into conflict with the law'. Such a possibility has become a reality. A ready connection between homelessness and crime – shoplifting, petty theft, begging, prostitution, drug taking – is widely assumed, so that the homeless are more likely to be criminalized through police harassment and extra police surveillance. For 'homeless' travellers and squatters the *1994 Criminal Justice and Public Order Act* effectively limited their ability to live within the law. In 1994, John Major, then Prime Minister, launched an attack on 'offensive beggars' – claiming that 'it is not acceptable to be out on the street' and 'there is no justification for it these days' (*Guardian*, 28 May 1994). He urged more rigorous application of the law – begging is an offence under the *1824 Vagrancy Act* and sleeping rough is punishable by a £200 fine. A year later the then Shadow Home Secretary, Jack Straw, echoed such sentiments by calling for the streets to be cleared of the 'aggressive begging of winos, addicts and squeegee merchants' (*Guardian*, 5 September 1995). As part of a crackdown on 'anti-social' behaviour, in 2003 David Blunkett, Home Secretary, announced that begging would be a recordable offence (*Sunday Times*, 26 January 2003; *Guardian*, 13 March 2003). Reflecting the multiple agendas of social exclusion, youth homelessness is increasingly officially researched and understood in the context of other problems such as drug use (Wincup et al., 2003). Beggars face the prospect of being viewed solely as a criminal nuisance rather than as victims. Ironically, criminalization is known to further increase the risk of homelessness. If apprehended, lack of a fixed address ensures that the homeless are less likely to be given bail and more likely to be remanded in custody. On release, a known criminal record makes the chances of accessing rented or hostel accommodation that much more difficult. A third of young people leaving custody are likely to be homeless or at risk of being so. Criminalizing the young homeless only ensures that a vicious circle ensues (Hutson and Liddiard, 1994, p. 66).

In contrast to such authoritarian 'solutions' based on images of a 'feckless criminal and dangerous underclass', Carlen's (1996) interviews with 150 homeless young people in Manchester, Birmingham, Stoke-on-Trent and rural Shropshire led her to argue that the real issue was not one of homelessness, but an **anti-social control** characterized by the denial of citizenship rights to those who already face destitution (see Box 7.9).

Taken collectively, these shifts in employment, welfare and housing policy have created a situation in which young people have to negotiate a set of risks unknown to previous generations. Furlong and Cartmel (1997, 2007) draw on Beck's (1992) and Giddens's (1991) notion of a late modern **risk society**, to explore this changing context. They suggest that while Western industrial societies are undergoing a dramatic transformation in which the old and predictable structures of labour markets and welfare systems are being dismantled, some old structures of inequality remain. While risks have clearly increased, they continue to be distributed in a way that reflects established social divisions of class, gender and 'race'. Although the 'collective foundations of social life have become more obscure, they continue to provide powerful frameworks which constrain young people's experiences and life chances' (Furlong and Cartmel, 1997, p. 109).

Carlen on youth homelessness

Young homeless people do not constitute an underclass with moral values different to those held by any other cross-section of society – though their struggles to survive unpromising childhoods may have made them cynical about the extent to which those moral values have ever had (or ever will have) any political effects.

Young homeless people are a threat to society not because of their minor lawbreaking activities but because the economic, ideological and political conditions of their existence are indicative of the widening gap between the moral pretensions of liberal democratic societies and the shabby life chances on offer to the children of the already poor.

The crimes of 'outcast youth' in general should be understood neither in relation to motivational factors, nor in relation to social control, but in relation to 'anti-social' controls which, having deliberately excluded certain young people from citizen rights and citizen duties, in turn furnish the state with further justifications for abrogation of its own obligations to a youth citizenry denied.

Source: Carlen (1996, p. 124).

Exclusion, Reintegration and Inclusion

7.4 Tony Blair first coined the 'realist' slogan 'Tough on Crime, Tough on the Causes of Crime' in January 1993 in an attempt to wrestle the law and order agenda away from the Conservatives. This seemed to imply that anti-crime policies would have to be based on a number of social and economic, as well as legal, measures if they were to be effective. The following decade indeed witnessed a succession of initiatives – some old, some new – in an effort to prevent the onset of offending. These have included:

- proactive policing of public space;
- zero tolerance policing of incivilities;
- the targeting of 'dysfunctional' families;
- expansion of CCTV surveillance and population monitoring;
- 'positive activity' programmes and youth inclusion projects;
- the ethos of *Every Child Matters*.

All of this can be considered to have significantly blurred the boundaries between traditional social policy and criminal justice agendas.

Policing Public Space

Public space, and particularly the street, have always provided one of the main arenas for youth leisure. Public space provides one of the few sites in which young people can 'hang out' relatively free of direct adult supervision. Yet it is on the streets that troubling aspects of their behaviour are at their most visible and where crucial elements of the relationship between young people and the police are forged. As Corrigan's (1976, 1979) conversations with 'the boys' from Sunderland revealed, alternative sites for leisure are rejected because they 'are not open to the boys as real choices'. The cinema, disco, dance hall and clubs were frequently too expensive. Home was constrained by parents. Youth clubs were bypassed because of the need for compliance with their rules and regulations. As Loader (1996, p. 50) put it, 'the routine use of public space is not altogether a meaningful choice. Rather it is one consequence of an age-based exclusion from both autonomous private spaces and cultural resources of various kinds.' As a result, certain local places and spaces – the street corner, the city centre, the shopping mall, the precinct – take on a special significance, cementing a sense of collective *safety*, independence, territory and identity (McAra and McVie, 2005). Empirical studies in Belfast (Jenkins, 1983), Sunderland (Callaghan, 1992), Manchester and Sheffield (Taylor et al., 1996), Edinburgh (Loader, 1996) Brighton (Measor and Squires, 2000) and North-East England (Nayak, 2003) have all demonstrated the centrality of localized existences in framing the 'cognitive maps' of young people.

In popular and political discourse much is made of the street as a site of territorial rivalries and conflict, but for Corrigan's 'boys', their main street activity was 'doing nothing'. 'Doing nothing' though may be interpreted by external observers as 'loitering with intent'. It is an apparent lack of productive activity that inspires a hostile reaction. The boys' experience of leisure was likely to attract the attention of the police at some time. This was how they got into trouble:

> The boys see trouble as something connected purely with the police, or other social control agents; one cannot get into trouble without the presence of one of these groups. At no stage do they perceive it as doing wrong or breaking rules ... What wrongs are they doing if they just walk around the streets and the police harass them? The reasons for the harassment lie with the police, and *not* inside any rule that the boys are breaking, since for the boys the streets are a 'natural' meeting place. (Corrigan, 1979, p. 139)

Similarly, Loader's (1996, p. 78) interviews with police officers in Edinburgh showed that one of their most prominent views was that young people hanging about in groups were either directly or indirectly involved in criminal behaviour. Their objection was largely to the 'collective use of public space irrespective of whether or not others find it unsettling'. The issue here is essentially the historically recurring concern of 'who controls the streets', in which the imaginary connection between a 'dangerous' place (the street) and a 'dangerous' time (youth) is constructed and maintained (Cohen, P., 1979, p. 128). In the Brighton study (Measor and Squires, 2000), the act of congregating, gathering or hanging out in public places was essentially for the purposes of socializing, to do the things adults did when they got together – eat, drink, talk, flirt. Despite the fears expressed by welfare professionals and local inhabitants, these authors argued that such gatherings may be noisy but are largely harmless. They are as much the province of girls as of boys; of high achievers as well as the 'excluded'. These are not 'youth out of control' but moments of socialization afforded by the relative freedom of the street. Similarly McAra and McVie's (2005) exhaustive study of children's experience of policing in Edinburgh found that 'police working rules' based on assumptions about suspicious dress and appearance serve to construct a population of young people who are viewed as innately criminal and deserving of continual scrutiny: 'the policing of children may serve to sustain and reproduce the very problems that the system ostensibly attempts to contain or eradicate' (p. 28). Such selective and targeted policing has also almost certainly been compounded by the contraction of spaces deemed to be 'public'. Young people, for example, using shopping centres as a meeting place are, quite literally, rendered 'out of place'. From the point of view of 'consumption', unemployed and dispossessed youth are 'virtually worthless' and need to be moved on (White, 1990 and see Box 7.10).

Box 7.10

Surveillance

The planning and design of urban space have increasingly been informed by wider concerns for population control and surveillance. In 2003, plans were announced to close certain alleyways and footpaths on the grounds that they encourage anti-social behaviour (*Guardian*, 7 May 2003). The CCTV camera, along with gates, locks and alarms, have become a familiar sight in many public areas and are becoming so on housing estates and in rural villages. By 2008 there were believed to be over 4 million cameras across the country giving the UK the highest density of 'eyes on the street' in the world and marking it out as an 'endemic surveillance' society alongside Russia, USA and Singapore. Pioneering research on three such schemes by Norris and Armstrong (1999) found that those targeted for surveillance were disproportionately young, male and black. They were targeted not because of their involvement in crime but for 'no obvious reason' and on the basis of 'categorical suspicion' alone. Areas of commerce and affluent neighbourhoods are relying on a fortress mentality of gated communities and private armed response patrols to insulate themselves from the 'outside' and from 'outsiders'. New technologies of surveillance are rendering certain sections of the population both literally 'out of time and out of place'. They also fuel the demand for ever more sophisticated means of profiling, monitoring and tracking entire populations through smartcards, mobile phone alerts, eyescans, facial recognition, and so on (McLaughlin and Muncie, 1999). In 2006, police loaded the three-millionth genetic profile onto the UK's national DNA database including some 24,000 10 to 18 years olds who had never been cautioned, charged or convicted for any offence. Some 37 per cent of black men were on the database compared to 9 per cent of white men (*Sunday Times*, 22 January 2006). By 2008, there were 4.5 million DNA records including those of 150,000 children under the age of 16 (*Daily Telegraph*, 18 March 2008).

Source: Adapted from Muncie (2004, p. 233).

Despite these perpetual concerns, detailed qualitative studies of youth–police encounters are (somewhat surprisingly) relatively rare. Most are American. A report to the US Department of Justice in 2007 found that those in the 18 to 24 age group had the highest percentage of contact with police (29.3 per cent) compared to those aged 65 or older who had the lowest (8.3 per cent). American research on police–juvenile interactions conducted in the 1960s and 1970s reported that the majority of encounters resulted from a complainant's request for police assistance. However, 20 years later further research based on a study of police patrols in Indiana and Florida suggested that the police themselves were now initiating about a half of their encounters with juveniles as a result of giving greater attention to less serious quality-of-life ('broken windows') offences (Worden and Myers, 1999). In the Edinburgh study, 44 per cent of a sample of over 1,000 11–15 year olds had been 'moved on or told off', 13 per cent had been stopped and searched and 10 per cent had been arrested or detained in a police station in the previous nine months. Police/youth relations also appear to be highly racialized and gendered. African-Caribbean youth appear especially vulnerable to 'pro-active' policing. Currently in the UK, black young people are up to six times as likely, and Asian youth twice as likely, to be stopped and searched than white youth. Further, when black young people come into contact with the police, whether as victims or witnesses, their perceptions and experiences of the police tend to be worse than for white young people (Webster, 2006). It is also a highly gendered relation. In one of a very few ethnographic studies, research in St Louis, USA, found that while African American young *men* routinely describe being subject to aggressive policing and being treated as a suspect regardless of their involvement in delinquency, young *women* typically describe being stopped for curfew violations and being sexually harassed (Brunson and Miller, 2006).

The evolution of police cautioning programmes in the UK provides a telling example of recent shifts towards more proactive and interventionist forms of policing young people. From the early 1970s until the mid-1990s the delivery of a juvenile caution was one of the major means the police used to deal with young offenders. Inspired by a 'protective' and 'treatment' logic that young people's behaviour should be challenged but that formal proceedings were more likely to do harm than good, cautioning (in the form of a verbal admonishment usually with parents and a social worker present) was promoted as a key means of ensuring pre-court diversion. In 1970, 35 per cent of under-17 year olds arrested were cautioned; increasing to 50 per cent by 1979. Home Office circular 14/1985 furthered the process by encouraging the police to use 'no further action' or 'informal warnings'. By the 1990s, about 60 per cent of young offenders were being dealt with informally although there were wide and fluctuating regional variations. There is little doubt that the police discretion to *informally* caution made a significant impact on reducing court appearances and protecting young people from the stigma of a criminal record (as well as reducing police paperwork). However, this policy was to prove short-lived. Some critiqued the process because of its potential to administer a punishment without any judicial hearing; others argued that it simply widened the net by targeting the minor 'pre-delinquent' (Pratt, 1986). But the most influential governmental critique of cautioning was eventually to emerge in the White Paper – 'No More Excuses' – which preceded the 1998 *Crime and Disorder Act*. It claimed that police cautioning (whether informal or formal) was applied too readily, inconsistently and haphazardly. Moreover it was argued that there was often little or no follow-up so that youth were allowed to 'flout the law with impunity'. The interventionist (rather than diversionary) principles of the 1998 Act saw the replacement of cautions by reprimands (on first offence) and final warnings (on second offence). The latter drew in particular from the experience of 'caution plus' approaches and place the police under a statutory duty to refer the young person to a youth offending team (YOT) for standardized risk assessment and with the expectation of some eventual 'programme of intervention'. In 2005, the Youth Justice Board for England and Wales set a target for all YOTs to include intervention in at least 80 per cent of final warnings. This removed large parts of police discretion and effectively abolished informal action. The result, however, has not been a decline, but a rise in the number of prosecutions. In 2004, the Audit Commission reported that too many minor youth offences were being brought to court, taking up time and expense. The current evidence suggests that the formalization of early intervention, particularly through final warnings, has indeed led to a net widening where more children and young people are being prosecuted for trivial offences and with a subsequent related impact on the rate of custodial sentencing (see **Chapter 9**). Between 2003 and 2006 there was a 25 per cent increase in the numbers of 10 to 14 year olds receiving reprimands, final warnings or conviction: a rise NACRO (2008) has explained with reference to a greater willingness of the police to criminalize minor misdemeanours in order to meet government targets of increasing detections from 1.02 million in 2002 to 1.25 million in 2007/08 (see **Chapter 1**). In 2008 new initiatives were announced giving police greater powers to stop and search without having to state a reason and encouraging the police to actively harass groups of young people on the streets. This included 'frame and shame' operations (pioneered by Essex police in Basildon) to film and repeatedly follow and stop 'persistently badly behaving youths' (*Guardian*, 8 May 2008); and 'voluntary' curfews (pioneered by Devon and Cornwall police in Redruth) targeted at under-16 year olds during the school summer holidays but backed up by parenting and anti-social behaviour orders (*The Times*, 9 July 2008).

Zero Tolerance, Curfews and Dispersal Zones

Zero tolerance refers to intensive community policing strategies that were introduced in New York in 1994. The strategy is based on the principle that by clamping down on minor street offences and incivilities – begging, under-age smoking and drinking, unlicensed street vending, public urination, graffiti writing – and by arresting aggressive beggars, fare dodgers, squeegee merchants, hustlers, abusive drunks and litter louts, many of the more serious offences will be curtailed. In part, **zero tolerance** is based on Wilson and Kelling's (1982) right realist 'broken windows' theory which claims that if climates of disorder are allowed to develop, then more serious crime will follow in their wake. Merely leaving a broken window unrepaired, they argued, will quickly encourage outbreaks of vandalism. Failure to combat vandalism will see an escalation in the seriousness of crimes. In practice, zero tolerance was the brainchild of William Bratton, Police Commissioner of the NYPD, who reorganized New York policing strategies by making each precinct commander accountable for monitoring and reducing *signs of* crime, as well as crime itself (Dennis, 1997). Primary emphasis was placed on crime prevention and disorder reduction.

It was heralded as a great success, particularly in reducing the number of firearms offences and rates of murder. New York, once synonymous with urban violence, fell to the 144th most dangerous in an FBI comparison of crime in America's 189 largest cities. Even though the precise reasons for such a decline remain disputed – over the same period many American cities witnessed a fall in their crime rates without the introduction of zero tolerance; and it was also part of a longer trend in the decline of violent offences associated with the trade in crack cocaine – the idea of creating environments which discourage offending and incivility was imported into Britain in 1995 as part of New Labour's campaigning agenda. In Britain, the concept was also appropriated from the 'presumption to arrest' policies advocated by anti-domestic violence initiatives. Limited experiments in zero tolerance policing were first pursued by the police in King's Cross, London; Middlesbrough; Hartlepool; Birmingham; Shoreham; and Glasgow in 1996. In Glasgow, for instance, Operation Spotlight was specifically targeted at after-hours revellers, groups of youths on the streets and truants. As a result, charges for drinking alcohol in public places increased by 2,240 per cent, dropping litter by 320 per cent and urinating on the street by 140 per cent. Whatever its success or otherwise, 'zero tolerance' and 'broken windows' have become powerful policy narratives, but arguably doing more to impress public audiences than rigidly framing particular policing objectives (Newburn and Jones, 2007).

'Giving the concept of zero tolerance teeth': this is how a Home Office source first described such proposals to impose curfews, exclusion zones and other restrictions on vandals, persistent offenders and drug dealers (*Sunday Times*, 22 June 1997). What was novel about the renewed interest in curfews in 1997 was their application to children under the age of 10 and on the *presumption*, rather than committal, of crime. Again the notion has American origins. San Diego first introduced a juvenile curfew in 1947, but it was only in the 1980s and 1990s that the policy took off as politicians sought to 'act tough' on crime. By 1995, juvenile curfews were routinely used in at least 146 of America's 200 largest cities. Typically aimed at those 17 and under, they usually run from 10.30 p.m. to 6.30 a.m. but a growing number also operate during school hours. President Clinton, in 1996 pre-election mode, advocated curfews for all teenagers by 8 p.m. on school nights on the grounds that it would help people to be better parents. Violators can be fined, or can face community service and probation, or their parents can be fined. Again the policy has been lauded as a great success. In Phoenix, for example, juvenile crime was believed to have dropped by 26 per cent since a curfew was introduced in 1993; in Dallas serious offences fell by 42 per cent; while New Orleans claimed a 29 per cent fall in auto theft and 26 per cent fewer murders.

However, curfews are notoriously difficult to enforce and are likely to be implemented in a highly selective way in which all manner of myths and stereotypes about 'troublesome' people and places are likely to come into play. Nevertheless, in October 1997, Strathclyde Police became the first in Britain to 'pilot' a dusk to dawn curfew on under-16 year olds on three estates in Hamilton, east of Glasgow. They were empowered to escort children home or to the local police station if they had no 'reasonable excuse' to be on the streets – playing football, meeting friends – after 8 p.m. It was legitimized as a caring service to protect children and address public fears of harassment (*Guardian*, 4 October 1997). But its main impact appears to have been one of raising unnecessary fears among the elderly population and increasing parental insecurity about the safety of their children (*Guardian*, 11 April 1998; Waiton, 2001). On the grounds of civil liberties, Jeffs and Smith (1996, p. 11) argue that curfews are discriminatory and fundamentally wrong: 'Wrong because they criminalize perfectly legal and acceptable behaviour on the grounds of age ... to select young people and criminalize them for doing what the rest of the population can freely do is doubly discriminatory.' Or as Ferrell (1997, p. 27) put it, 'curfews protect symbolic constructions of adult authority by patrolling the cultural and temporal space of kids ... they work to unravel the nocturnal cultures and alternative spaces that kids have built around coffee houses, raves, music and style'. In so doing, positive communication between the generations is lost.

The 2003 *Antisocial Behaviour Act* introduced a further range of enforcement-led interventions including Parenting Contracts, Fixed Penalty Notices and Dispersal Orders. The latter operate in designated dispersal zones when authorized by the local authority and the police on the basis that a member of the public '*might be* intimidated, harassed, alarmed or distressed'. If two or more people, together in a public place, fail to disperse under the instruction of a police officer they commit a criminal offence and face possible detention. Under-16 year olds, if unaccompanied by an adult, can be escorted home by the police. (For further discussion of anti-social behaviour legislation, see **Chapter 9**). Between 2004 and 2006 over 1,000 areas were so designated in England and Wales with a further 6 in Scotland. Most were directed at young people (see Box 7.11).

The legality of one such zone in Richmond was successfully challenged by a 15 year old in 2005. This, however, should be viewed against the increasing use of ultrasonic devices to disperse young people – their sound being reputably only audible to those under the age of 25. The manufacturers have been quite clear of their purpose:

> *The Mosquito* ultrasonic teenage deterrent is the solution to the eternal problem of unwanted gatherings of youths and teenagers in shopping malls, around shops and anywhere else they are causing problems. The presence of these teenagers discourages genuine shoppers and customers from coming into your shop, affecting your turnover and profits. Antisocial behaviour has become the biggest threat to private property over the last decade and there has been no effective deterrent until now. (Cited by Walsh, 2008 pp. 122–3).

Box 7.11

Dispersal zones

- Most commonly used in relation to groups of young people.

- Can antagonize and alienate young people who frequently feel unfairly stigmatized for being in public spaces.

- Compliance more likely when accompanied by respect and procedural justice.

- Uncertainty about the value in removing under-16 year olds to their homes. Many police chose not to use the power.

- Reinforces a view of view of young people as a risk to others, obscuring the extent to which they are 'at risk' themselves.

- Generates displacement, shifting problems to other area.

- Provides short-term relief for local communities but invariably fails to address wider causes of troublesome behaviour.

- A 'sticking plaster over local problems'.

- Confusion over criteria for dispersal.

Source: Derived from Crawford and Lister (2007).

Parenting Deficits and Family Remoralization

'Parental responsibility' became something of a watchword in many aspects of British social policy in the 1980s and 1990s (Allen, 1990). While notions of 'good' and 'bad' parenting have informed much of youth justice reform since the nineteenth century, an image of wilfully negligent parents colluding with or even encouraging misbehaviour was popularized by the Conservatives in the 1980s as the inevitable result of a 1960s permissive culture. The breakdown of the nuclear family unit, high divorce rates and increases in single parenting, it was argued, were the root causes of moral decay epitomized by increased crime rates, homelessness and drug taking. In addition, excessive welfare dependency had encouraged families to rely on state benefits rather than on each other, and in this process children's moral development had been eroded (Murray, 1990; Dennis and Erdos, 1992 and see **Chapter 4.2**). On coming to power Tony Blair continued this theme:

> We cannot say we want a strong and secure society when we ignore its very foundations: family life. This is not about preaching to individuals about their private lives. It is addressing a huge social problem ... Nearly 100,000 teenage pregnancies every year; elderly parents with whom families cannot cope; children growing up without role models they can respect and learn from; more and deeper

poverty; more crime; more truancy; more neglect of educational opportunities, and above all more unhappiness. Every area of this government's policy will be scrutinized to see how it affects family life. Every policy examined, every initiative tested, every avenue explored to see how we strengthen our families. (*Guardian*, 1 October 1997)

Six years later it was reiterated that 'strong families are the centre of peaceful and safe communities. Respect is all-important and this is missing in families that behave dysfunctionally' (Home Office, 2003a, p. 8).

In these ways family rhetoric appears to have an enduring political and emotional appeal but built around traditional images of a 'safe haven' of conjugal, heterosexual parents with an employed male breadwinner. It is single parenting, teenage mothers, 'broken homes' and absent fathers that are identified as the key harbingers of social disorder (Day Sclater and Piper, 2000). One of Labour's key formative influences in defining a 'Third Way', Etzioni's communitarian agenda, also emphasizes that the root cause of crime lies within the home and that it is in the domestic sphere that the shoring up of our moral foundations should begin (Etzioni, 1995, p. 11). It is such a communitarianism which speaks of parental responsibility and moral obligation that continually resurfaces in the reforming agenda of the twenty-first century (Hughes, 1996, p. 21).

Successive governments have introduced a series of legal measures to enforce parents to bring up their children 'responsibly' (and penalize those that do not) but these initiatives have gathered pace in the last decade (Mooney, 2003) (see Box 7.12).

A centrepiece was the introduction of parenting orders in 1998. These enabled the juvenile court to require parents of every convicted juvenile offender to attend parenting classes and to ensure their children attend school or avoids associating with specified people in specified places. In 2003, further powers were introduced to fine parents who failed to comply with a parenting order. The conclusion is clear: all parents are to *blame* for their children's behaviour (Arthur, 2005). From a slow start, between 2003 and 2006 over 4,000 parenting contracts and 1,138 parenting orders were issued but with wide geographic variation. The only evaluation study was generally positive but also revealed the level of desperation of some parents who voluntarily joined parenting and counselling classes in the absence of any other means of support (Ghate and Ramella, 2002). It is clear that in many cases parenting skills and advice are not avoided but are highly sought after. This seriously calls into question the continuance of governmental rhetoric and policy based on compulsion and punitiveness. Inevitably such powers are also targeted on some of the most deprived neighbourhoods in the UK. But acknowledgement of the typical material contexts of poverty, economic hardship and inadequate housing is lost in the use of punitive means to tackle issues of family support and failures in welfare and educational services (Goldson and Jamieson, 2002; Rodger, 2006; Garrett, 2007). By 2007, for example, 133 parents had been imprisoned for their child's truancy.

Box 7.12

Enforcing responsible parenting

1933   *Children and Young Persons Act* establishes the juvenile court to act *in loco parentis* even if no crime had been committed.

1982   *Criminal Justice Act* orders parents to pay juvenile offenders' fines.

1991   *Criminal Justice Act* empowers courts to bind over parents to care for and control their children.

1994   Extends bind over provisions to ensure compliance with a community sentence.

1998   Parenting order compels parents to attend counselling and guidance classes.

2001   New offence of aggravated truancy created, carrying maximum 3 month prison sentence for parents 'condoning truancy'.

2002   Mother in Oxfordshire given a 60-day jail sentence for failing to ensure her daughters attended school.

2002   Plan announced for head teachers to issue fixed penalty fines for failing parents.

2003   *Anti Social Behaviour Act* gives parenting contracts the force of law and allows inclusion of a compulsory 'residential element'.

2005   Plans announced to invest £1.25 million to ensure failing parents are given 'intensive rehabilitation'.

2006   Respect Action Plan advocates extension of parenting contracts and parenting orders to allow schools to participate in their application.

2006   *Police and Justice Act* allows local authorities and landlords to apply for parenting orders.

2007   National Parenting Academy established.

2007   'Intensive care sin bins' established for 'disruptive families'.

2007   Plans announced to identify unborn babies 'at risk' of later offending and to give intensive support from midwives and health visitors until the child is 2 years old.

2007   New offence announced of 'failing to ensure a child is found in a public place without reasonable justification'.

2008   A £218 million expansion of Family Intervention Projects announced to sign up 1000 of the 'worst behaved children' to good behaviour contracts.

2008   Advice given to parents at what age they should allow children to drink alcohol at home.

2008   Plans announced for doctors and schools to identify children 'at risk' of offending and provide 'non-negotiable' intensive mentoring and training.

Tackling Social Exclusion

On coming to power in 1997, the first New Labour administration placed considerable rhetorical emphasis on the significance of securing social justice for children in general, and on 'tackling' child poverty in particular. It announced its 'historic aim' to reduce child poverty by a quarter by 2004/05, halve it by 2010 and eradicate it completely by 2020. This presented, and continues to present, a formidable challenge. In 1979, 10 per cent (1.4 million) of all children in the UK were living in poverty (defined as below 50 per cent of mean income after housing costs). The annual statistics on poor households showed that in 2005, 3.4 million children continued to live in poverty – 300,000 more than the target set in 1999 (*The Independent*, 8 March 2006). But, by 2008, the corresponding figures had risen to 33 per cent (3.8 million) (http://www.endchildpoverty.org.uk/). Moreover it is clear that being in paid employment is no guarantee of moving out of the poverty trap. Six in ten poor households have someone in work: 10 per cent more than in 1997 (*Guardian*, 3 January 2008). In the mid-1990s the Commission on Social Justice had observed that: 'Britain is not a good place in which to be a child' (cited in Goldson and Muncie, 2006) and it is clear that this remains so for a significant number of children. A report by UNICEF in 2007 placed the UK at the bottom of 'child well being' rankings across 21 'rich' countries (see **Chapter 10**).

Social exclusion is a relatively new term in British social policy. It has been officially defined as 'what can happen when people or areas suffer from a combination of linked problems such as unemployment, poor skills, low incomes, poor housing, high crime, bad health and family breakdown' (Social Exclusion Unit, 2001, p. 1.1). Young (2007, p. 18) sets out five key principles which underpin this thesis (Box 7.13).

The Social Exclusion Unit (SEU) had by 2002 identified and reported on five issues: neighbourhood renewal; rough sleeping; teenage pregnancy; school exclusion and truancy; and young people not in education/training/employment. Clearly it was not just crime, but youth and 'disorder', which was driving this agenda. The discovery that child poverty had trebled between 1979 and 1995, that Britain had more children growing up in unemployed households than anywhere else in Europe, that it had the highest teenage pregnancy rate, and that 80 per cent of rough sleepers used drugs, encouraged something of a move to a holistic approach to tackling the 'problem of youth'. The SEU was – along with the Children and Young Persons Unit established in 2000 – designed to co-ordinate policy-making across government, businesses, voluntary agencies, schools and communities. A plethora of initiatives have followed including: *Sure Start* to encourage young parents back into work through provision of nursery places; *Quality Protects* to provide sex education for those in care; *Positive Activities for Young People* (PAYP) and *Splash Schemes* to provide leisure activities for those 'at risk' during school holidays; *Education Action Zones* to reduce truancy; *Neighbourhood Renewal Funds* to improve local services; *Youth Inclusion Projects*, targeting 'high-risk' 13–16 year olds, as well as the *New Deal* and *Connexions* (see Section 7.2 above) and numerous advice and mentoring schemes which in turn all

Box 7.13

The social exclusion thesis

1   THE BINARY: that society can be divided into an inclusive and largely satisfied majority and an excluded and despondent minority.

2   MORAL EXCLUSION: that there exists a vast majority with virtuous conduct and stable family structures and a minority who are welfare-dependent, dysfunctional and criminogenic.

3   SPATIAL EXCLUSION: that the excluded are isolated from the included by barriers which are rarely crossed.

4   DYSFUNCTIONAL UNDERCLASS: that a residuum exists which is dysfunctional to itself and to society at large.

5   WORK AND REDEMPTION: that the provision of work will transform the underclass: changing their attitudes, habits, hedonism, dysfunctionality and criminal tendencies and transport them into the ranks of the contented.

Source: Abbreviated from Young (2007, p. 18).

connect with the work of crime reduction partnerships and the Youth Justice Board (see **Chapter 8**). All of this is directed at a perceived excluded underclass believed to be responsible for most crime (see **Chapter 4.2**). They have all been justified as 'ways of helping to tackle the roots of juvenile crime' (Home Office, 1997c, p. 10). Needless to say, some have been widely condemned by those on the right for rewarding troublemaking and in the case of PAYP, of providing a 'perverse incentive to offend' (*Sunday Times*, 10 August 2003).

In 2003 and 2005, two White Papers – *Every Child Matters: Change for Children* and *Youth Matters* – were published. Both promised a radical transformation in support services in which it was claimed that support would be available 'for *every* child, whatever their *background* or their *circumstances*'. *Every Child Matters* promoted the five key principles of: Be healthy; Stay safe; Enjoy and achieve; Make a positive contribution; and Achieve economic well-being (see Box 7.14). In the *Youth Matters* paper such opportunities and support were made contingent on accepting responsibilities. A balance is sought between *support* and demanding *responsibility* in return. The key initiative was the granting of 'opportunity cards' to provide discounts on 'constructive' activities but which can be withdrawn if a youth's behaviour is deemed 'unacceptable'. Similarly, the 2006 Social Exclusion Task Force paper *Reaching Out* was clear that 'opportunity and support' are contingent on individuals taking responsibility themselves and with 'clear consequences if those responsibilities are not met'.

At first sight these initiatives do seem to reveal some long-term, enlightened and structural responses to youth **marginalization**. Pitts (2001, p. 147), however, argues that they only offer a partial understanding and only deal with superficial aspects of the economic and political problems that lie at the heart of social exclusion.

Box 7.14

Every Child Matters

Our aim is to ensure that every child has the chance to fulfil their potential by reducing levels of educational failure, ill health, substance misuse, teenage pregnancy, abuse and neglect, crime and anti-social behaviour among children and young people.

When we consulted children, young people and families, they wanted the Government to set out a positive vision of the outcomes we want to achieve. The five outcomes which mattered most to children and young people were:

- **being healthy**: enjoying good physical and mental health and living a healthy lifestyle

- **staying safe**: being protected from harm and neglect

- **enjoying and achieving**: getting the most out of life and developing the skills for adulthood

- **making a positive contribution**: being involved with the community and society and not engaging in anti-social or offending behaviour

- **economic well-being**: not being prevented by economic disadvantage from achieving their full potential in life.

The Government has built the foundations for improving these outcomes through Sure Start, raising school standards, and progress made towards eradicating child poverty.

Source: http://www.everychildmatters.gov.uk/

First, the dynamics of exclusion result from market *forces* which generate economic insecurity and from market *values* which promote individual adaptations rather than fundamental reform. For Young (1999), we have witnessed a shift over the past half century from an inclusive society based on incorporation and full citizenship to a society organized around the material and cultural ramifications of *exclusivity*. Unless real opportunities are opened up through the advancement of a 'radical meritocracy', he argues, then little will be achieved either to facilitate inclusion or dismantle the structures of exclusion. Or as Currie (1985, p. 225) has argued, in order to tackle the roots of the crime problem 'we must build a society that is less unequal, less depriving, less insecure and less corrosive of cooperative values'.

Second, the very concept of 'exclusion' promotes a view of inequality as something peripheral; existing only at the margins of society. Attempts to reintegrate 'the excluded' fail to acknowledge that their inclusion would only be to a world dominated by market exploitation, discrimination and a widening gap between rich and poor. As Levitas (1996, p. 7) put it: it is a discourse unable to address the question of unpaid work in society (work done principally by women) or of low paid work and completely erases from view the inequality between those owning the bulk of productive property and the working population, as well as obscuring the inequalities among workers. Further, Young (2007) argues that constructions of inclusion/exclusion reinforce false ascriptions both to the 'otherness' of the 'excluded' and the 'normality' of the 'included'. The social exclusion discourse implies minimal reform. It stresses that it is the responsibility of individuals to accept the structures of their own dominance. It centres a puritanical work ethic as the route to inclusion, denying other forms of reciprocity and solidarity. It allows a benevolent view of society to be maintained even while levels of inequality multiply (Levitas, 1998).

Third, social exclusion *individualizes* social problems as personal failure to take up the opportunities on offer. The issue is then transformed from one of social justice into how risks can best be managed (Gray, 2007). The problem is defined as inadequate management rather than structural inequality; response becomes managerial rather than transformative (McLaughlin et al., 2001; Young and Matthews, 2003).

Finally, inclusionary policies are also frequently underpinned by coercive measures. Forcing young people into an insecure labour market on poverty wages, for example, may indeed be viewed as *promoting* exclusion rather than moving to its abatement. Targeting 'at risk' populations may simply exacerbate negative perceptions of particular areas or groups and accelerate their criminalization. Above all the talk is of economic and moral inclusion. The issue of *political* inclusion, through which communities might be empowered and full citizenship achieved, is largely overlooked (Percy-Smith, J., 2000). Indeed, exclusionary processes may stem more from an 'overclass' intent on protecting their own political and economic interests than from an 'underclass' in whose name the SEU sought to govern. The SEU was disbanded in 2006 and its work – persistently critiqued as 'failing to deliver' – transferred to a smaller taskforce in the Cabinet Office focussing on the 'most severely excluded'.

Criminalizing Social Policy?

As detailed in this chapter social policy has never been solely about an altruistic provision of welfare support or new educational and employment opportunities. It has also been underpinned by regulatory and disciplinary logics. For example, Pearson (1983, p. 239) noted in his historical analysis of hooliganism (see **Chapter 2**) that 'too often matters of vital public importance – jobs, homes, schools – are swallowed up in the maw of "law and order" discourse, and publicly addressed as if the only important consideration was whether these social deficiencies might lead to crime, vandalism and hooliganism'. However, the explicit notion of the *criminalization* of social policy did not emerge until the late 1980s in the context a study of multi-agency crime prevention partnerships which sought the collaboration of probation, social work, health, housing, recreation, education, employment and police in the 'fight against crime'. As a result, Blagg et al. (1988) argued that the welfarist values of social policy agencies were in danger of being merged with (or buried beneath) those of crime control. A decade later various commentators (Gilling and Barton, 1997; Crawford, 1997) noted that the issues of crime prevention and community safety were becoming major drivers of social policy decisions. What were once domain issues of social welfare, such as anti-unemployment and anti-poverty programmes, were increasingly being redefined in terms of their potential contribution to crime control. Through broad and loose definitions of crime prevention, disadvantage has been turned into a problem for targeted family intervention, policing and criminal law.

Such analysis is all the more pertinent to unravelling the trajectories of youth policy and youth justice since the first New Labour administration of 1997. A major preoccupation with the family, parenting, youth employment, social exclusion and anti-social behaviour has formed a central element of British social policy over the past two decades. These agendas, driven by a rhetoric of tackling the causes of crime, have drawn numerous aspects of social policy – housing, income support, race relations, family support, employment and nursery provision – into an expanding remit of crime control. In crucial respects it has become harder to disentangle social policy and welfare from youth and criminal justice. It is clear that any number of inclusionary and exclusionary practices can be legitimated within the general rubric of 'crime reduction, crime prevention and community safety'. Complex inter-related problems of child poverty, urban degeneration and social inequality are increasingly responded to through disciplinary techniques. Reform in these areas may be primarily legitimated in the name of opportunities, support and community empowerment, but it also raises the prospect that 'social deficiencies are being redefined as "crime problems" which need to be controlled and managed rather than addressed in themselves' (Crawford, 1997, p. 230).

The tendency is for all aspects of social policy to become governed by an overriding concern for crime and disorder management. Youth workers, for example, have been redefined as adjuncts of the criminal justice system (Stenson and Factor, 1994, p. 1). A problem for much social inclusion work, therefore, is that their operations are simply grafted onto the operations of the criminal justice system, rather than remaining independent with no formalized connections to the police, courts or corrections. Targeted government funding for, say, urban regeneration or family support or for welfare services in general, appears increasingly dependent on 'evidence' that they will impact on rates of crime. Access to resources is dependent on prior assessments of 'risk'. Early intervention, driven by the urgency to 'nip crime in the bud', intensifies the processes of scrutiny and surveillance to which children and families are subjected (see further **Chapter 9.1**).

A myopic focus on troublesome behaviour clearly devalues notions of positive and creative citizenship. As Muncie et al. (1995) claimed, the benefits of a preventive approach based on principles of social inclusion ultimately require a commitment to long-term change which cannot simply be measured by a reduction in the costs of crime and crime control, or by managing 'risks', but by improving the quality of life for all young people. Similarly, numerous commentators (Pitts, 2001; Hill and Wright, 2003; Gray, 2007) have called for a renewed political commitment to forge routes to social justice based on tolerance, mutual respect, empowerment and entitlement, rather than criminalization.

Intensive schooling, employer-led training, the reduction of welfare, parental rehabilitation, crackdowns on teenage nuisance, the resort to the rule of law: all of these attest to the conditions of being young, becoming 'a much more arduous state to be' (Mizen, 2004, p. 183). While there have been important shifts in discourse and practices over the past two decades, the dominant terms of the political debate over 'the youth problem' have not been disrupted, but extended. Intervening in all aspects of young people's lives has come to be an expected and essential requirement. Given the dangers and potentials of 'youth' – and the limited discourses of depravity and deficiency in which they are caught – the 'doing nothing' option has been rendered unthinkable.

■ ■ **Summary** ■

- Social policy for young people is generally constructed around three competing discourses: young people as *either* the producers of 'trouble' for others *or* as vulnerable and in need of protection *or* as deficient and in need of supervision and training.

- Anxieties concerning youth are realized in a growing multitude of welfare, educational, employment, crime prevention and policing programmes which serve to control and shape young people's lives by lengthening the period of family dependency and by moulding petty details of the domestic lives of their parents. In this way discipline is dispersed.

- State agencies act to tighten conceptions of 'normality' (as in youth training), but in other arenas state intervention is withdrawn (as in welfare support). Such withdrawal is legitimized by 'multi-agency partnership' and 'community responsibility'. The state has initiated ways of acting at a distance, of activating 'private' agencies and co-ordinating sectors of social policy to reorder all aspects of youths' everyday lives.

- Economic contingencies provide the parameters in which any social reform is entertained (e.g. housing policy, youth labour markets). Youth is generally perceived as lasting longer. Pathways to adulthood are broken, non-linear and individualized.

- Class/gender/'race' relations are reproduced through systems of discipline and surveillance (e.g. in employment policy, routine policing).

- Certain languages and classifications legitimize institutional practice and are exemplars of power in their own right (e.g. 'individualized risk', 'social exclusion' and 'blaming the victim' discourses).

- Social policy has its own propensity to create conditions of exclusion and 'risk' (e.g. housing and homelessness; labour market and unemployment) in which alternative survivalist 'careers' may be initiated.

- It is indisputable that since the 1970s more areas of young people's lives have been subject to surveillance, monitoring and institutionalized regulation. Governance has moved from a reactive to a proactive pre-emptive force – identifying the 'anti-social', anticipating disorder and criminalizing 'nuisance'.

■ study Questions

1 How has social policy reform in Britain in the past three decades affected young people?

2 Did New Labour's emphasis on social exclusion represent a break from or a continuation of past failures?

3 How do employment, welfare and housing policies encourage a protracted adolescence?

4 In what ways can it be argued that social policy and policing do not alleviate or control crime, but actively create it?

5 What is the evidence for the 'criminalization of social policy' or the 'socialization of criminal justice policy'?

■ ■ Further Reading ■

There is no existing work which *explicitly* draws on theories of social control and governance to explore the regulatory practices embedded in social policy for young people, but Mizen's *The Changing State of Youth* (2004) is an authoritative overview of how recent reforms in education, training, work, social security and youth justice continue to centre 'youth' in the political management of capitalist societies. For an empirical overview of how various youth policies in the 1990s (education, training, housing and criminal justice) fermented poverty and disaffection amongst the young, see Williamson (1993). Coles' *Youth and Social Policy* (1995) and Furlong and Cartmel's *Young People and Social Change* (1997; 2nd edition, 2007) cover much the same ground and in more detail, the former working with the concept of 'career', the latter with the concept of 'risk'. See Taylor (1999, Chapter 3) for an insightful analysis of how the material outcomes of market societies regulate the social circumstances and behaviours of the young. For the most incisive critical analyses of the concept of social exclusion, see Young's *The Exclusive Society* (1999), Young's *The Vertigo of Late Modernity* (2007) and Levitas's (1998) *The Inclusive Society?*

For those interested in sociologies of social control, the 'dispersal of discipline' thesis and theories of governance, Foucault's *Discipline and Punish* (1977) and Cohen's *Visions of Social Control* (1985) are the obvious places to start.

The journal *Youth and Policy* provides a useful critical analysis of most of the relevant issues.

: // Web Resources /

http://www.cabinetoffice.gov.uk/social_exclusion_task_force/
Formerly the Social Exclusion Unit, provides access to their publications dating back to 1997.

http://www.everychildmatters.gov.uk/
Government site to facilitate the 'joining up' of children's services across education, youth justice, social care, health, training and culture.

http://www.cypnow.co.uk/
A daily news update on all matters relating to children and young people including health, education, childcare, youth work and youth justice.

http://www.poverty.org.uk/
The UK site for statistics on poverty and social exclusion.

http://www.jrf.org.uk/child-poverty/
Details research on child poverty carried out by the Joseph Rowntree Foundation.

http://www.cpag.org.uk/
Site of the Child Poverty Action Group campaigning for the abolition of child poverty in the UK.

http://www.nch.org.uk/
Site of the NCH action for children, a charity which supports children and young people affected by poverty, disability, abuse or neglect.

http://www.childrenslegalcentre.com/
The Children's Legal Centre is a charitable organization established in 1981 and based at the University of Essex, UK. It is home to the monthly journal, *Childright*.

8

Youth Justice Strategies I: Welfare and Justice

Chapter 8 examines:

- major developments in youth justice (focusing initially on England and Wales and Scotland) from the 1960s to the present;

- the impact of welfare-based initiatives in delivering a separate justice system – based on need – for juveniles and young people;

- the impact of justice-based initiatives in delivering due process and diversion but also retribution for juveniles and young people;

- the nature, and limitations, of the welfare vs. justice debate;

- the interrelationship between political ideologies and reform of the youth justice system;

- corporatism and managerialism as a 'third model' of youth justice;

- the reconstitution of child welfare in the twenty-first century.

---

key terms

'adulteration'; bifurcation; corporatism; diversionary strategies; *doli incapax;* intermediate treatment; justice model; managerialism; net widening; rehabilitation; reparation; repressive welfare; retribution; welfare model

---

From the early nineteenth century, when the troubled and troublesome among the youth population were first thought to require a different response to that afforded to adults, the history of youth justice in England and Wales has been riddled with ambiguity and unintended consequences. In the 1830s, a liberal approach to young offenders first took the form of establishing specialized prisons for the young (such as that at Parkhurst on the Isle of Wight). The dominant strategy was one of *punishment,* but in segregated institutions where the 'vulnerable' young would not be contaminated by contact with older and more experienced offenders. By the 1850s, however, this approach was challenged by the reforming zeal of philanthropists and 'child savers'. In that era, young people were believed to be in need of treatment within moral re-education programmes designed to both deter and prevent offending. 'Justice' was offered to young people in the form of reformatories, which in the twentieth century evolved into approved schools and latterly community homes. Intervention was couched in a language of care directed not only towards the offender, but also towards those thought likely to offend – the orphan, the vagrant, the runaway, the independent and those with a 'deviant' street lifestyle. The emergent strategy was one of *treatment* within institutions (see **Chapter 2**).

A century later this 'progressive' approach to young offenders once more took a significant turn. Institutions were criticized as stigmatizing, dehumanizing, expensive, brutalizing and as criminogenic rather than rehabilitative agencies. 'Justice' for juveniles was now to be offered through the abolition of custody and the establishment of a range of treatment units located in the community. The care and control of young offenders were to be handed over to social service professionals. Intervention was couched in the language of *welfare* rather than correction and expanded to include younger and less or non-delinquent populations. By the 1980s, however, with the re-emergence of a justice-based philosophy, support for the rehabilitative ideal was relegated to the search for the most efficient ways of delivering *punishment in the community*. Initially this appeared to be successful. From the mid-1980s, the numbers sent to custody were dramatically reduced, while informal cautioning and the use of intensive supervision burgeoned. However, 'justice' took a decisively retributive turn in the early 1990s when custody was once more promoted with the slogan 'Prison Works'. The dominant strategy became that of *punishing all young offenders*, whether in community or institutional settings.

By the late 1990s, youth justice discourse had shifted once again. The incoming Labour government placed youth justice reform at the top of its agenda. It attempted to overcome, or bypass, the philosophical disputes of welfare/justice by reformulating the purpose of youth justice in England and Wales to that of '*preventing* offending by children and young people' in which there would be 'no more excuses' (see **Chapter 9**). While this chapter and Chapter 9 recall these policy shifts (and the debates and disputes that circulated around them) in something of a chronological fashion, they also stress how multiple youth justice strategies have, in some form, always coexisted and continue to do so. What follows then is predominantly a history of political and professional debate, in which the diverse and competing discourses of welfare, justice and corporatism (this chapter) and those of prevention, early intervention, risk management and punishment (Chapter 9) have come to do battle over their respective places in the governance of the 'delinquent body'.

Welfare

8.1 The key formal principle underlying all work with young offenders is the ensuring of their general welfare. *The Children and Young Persons Act 1933* established that all courts should have primary regard to the 'welfare of the child'; a requirement that is still in force today. This ruling was reinforced by the *1989 Children Act's* stipulation that a child's welfare shall be paramount. Similarly, the UN Convention on the Rights of the Child requires that in all legal actions concerning those under the age of 18, the 'best interests' of the child shall prevail (Association of County Councils et al.,

1996, p. 13). Further, in 2003 and 2005, two major policy programmes – *Every Child Matters: Change for Children* and *Youth Matters* – were launched, both of which emphasized the importance of safeguarding the welfare of *all* children and young people (see **Chapter 7**).

While the principle of welfare in youth justice has proved to be consistently controversial, since the early nineteenth century most young offender legislation has been promoted and instituted on the basis that young people should be protected from the full weight of the criminal law. It is widely assumed that under a certain age young people are *doli incapax* (incapable of evil) and cannot be held fully responsible for their actions.

Doli Incapax

The age of criminal responsibility differs across the UK, standing at 8 in Scotland and 10 in England, Wales and Northern Ireland. It differs even more markedly across Europe where children up to the age of 14, 16 and 18 are deemed to lack full criminal responsibility and as a result tend to be dealt with in civil tribunals rather than criminal courts (see **Chapter 10**). In England and Wales, while the under-10s cannot be found guilty of a criminal offence, for many years the law also presumed that those under 14 were also incapable of criminal intent. To prosecute this age group the prosecution had to show that offenders were aware that their actions were 'seriously wrong' and not merely mischievous. During the mid-1990s, however, the presumption of *doli incapax*, which had been enshrined in law since the fourteenth century, came under attack from both the left and right. Undoubtedly reacting to the Bulger tragedy (see **Chapter 1**), the doctrine was first placed under review by a Conservative government following a High Court ruling in 1994 that it was 'unreal, contrary to commonsense and a serious disservice to the law'. Three years later, the Labour Home Secretary announced that the ruling would be abolished in the *Crime and Disorder Act 1998* in order to 'help convict young offenders who are ruining the lives of many communities', on the basis that 'children aged between 10 and 13 were plainly capable of differentiating between right and wrong' (*Guardian*, 21 May 1996; 4 March 1997). This was in direct contradiction to United Nations recommendations – first made in 1995 and repeated in 2002 – that the UK give serious consideration to *raising* the age of criminal responsibility and thus bring the UK countries in line with much of Europe. Somewhat perversely, the *Crime and Disorder Act 1998* moved in the opposite direction. It gave no specific direction to the courts or to the newly established youth offending teams that child welfare should be of primary consideration. Instead it presented this retreat from child protection and erosion of children's rights as 'common sense' and as an enabling new opportunity and, even more paradoxically, as a measure of welfare protection (see Box 8.1). Such processes have been referred to as ones of 'adultification' or '**adulteration**' (Fionda, 1998).

Box 8.1

No More Excuses

The government believes that in presuming that children of this age generally do not know the difference between naughtiness and serious wrongdoing, the notion of *doli incapax* is contrary to common sense. The practical difficulties which the presumption presents for the prosecution can stop some children who should be prosecuted and punished for their offences from being convicted or from even coming to court. This is not in the interests of justice, of victims or of the young people themselves. If children are prosecuted where appropriate, interventions can be made to *help* prevent any further offending ... Children need protection as appropriate from the full rigour of the criminal law. The United Kingdom is committed to protecting the welfare of children and young people who come into contact with the criminal justice process. The government does not accept that there is any conflict between protecting the welfare of the young offender and preventing that individual from offending again. Preventing offending promotes the welfare of the individual young offender and protects the public.

Source: Home Office (1997d, para 4.4 and 2.2).

The abolition of *doli incapax* removed an important principle which (in theory at least) had acted to protect children from the full rigour of the criminal law. As Bandalli (2000, p. 94) argues, it reflects a steady erosion of the special consideration afforded to children, extends the remit of the criminal law to address all manner of problems which young people have to face, and is 'symbolic of the state's limited vision in understanding children, the nature of childhood or the true meaning of an appropriate criminal law response'.

Welfare Legislation

The argument that first surfaced in the nineteenth century that age and the neglect and vice of parents should be taken into account when adjudicating on juveniles opened the way for a plethora of welfare-inspired legislation in the twentieth century. As Clarke (1975, p. 12) argued, it created a hole in the principles of traditional punitive justice 'through which subsequent armies of psychiatrists and social workers have run and thoroughly confused the law's focus on criminal responsibility'. While the goal of 'delivering welfare' through the 'personal influence' of 'professionals' – as established by the *1933 Children and Young Persons Act* – was heralded as an important victory for the welfare lobby, it was to provide the juvenile justice system with a fundamental contradiction which is still being grappled with today. The two philosophies of criminal justice and welfare remain incompatible, because while the former stresses full criminal responsibility, the latter stresses welfare, treatment and **rehabilitation** to meet the *needs* of each individual child. The defining of what constitutes 'need' was, and remains, problematic. Welfarism, it seems, is just as capable of drawing more young people into the net of juvenile justice as it is of affording them care and protection. Moreover, the very existence of a system legitimized by 'welfare' is always likely to come under attack from those seeking a more retributive and punitive response to young offending.

By the 1950s, these disputes and contradictions were reflected in a system whose remit stretched from dealing with the neglected by way of some form of welfare assistance, such as receiving children into local authority care, to providing attendance centres (run by local authorities and the police) and to establishing detention centres (run by the prison service) expressly designed to 'retrain' the offender through hard labour and punitive military drill (empowered by the *Criminal Justice Act 1948*). Such confusion was to become most prominent in the spate of committees, recommendations and Acts concerned with the control and treatment of juveniles that characterized the 1960s. These culminated in the highly controversial *1969 Children and Young Persons Act* in England and Wales and the *1968 Social Work Act* in Scotland. Both advocated a rise in the age of criminal responsibility and sought alternatives to detention by way of treatment, non-criminal care proceedings and care orders. It was one element in the Labour Party's vision of a society based on full employment, prosperity, expanded educational opportunities and an enlarged welfare state which would overcome social inequalities and thereby remove a major cause of young offending (Pitts, 1988, p. 3). The prevailing political view of the late 1960s, as reflected in the 1968 White Paper *Children in Trouble*, was that young offending was largely trivial and transient in nature and above all was so commonplace that the full weight of the law was unjustified and counterproductive (see Box 8.2).

Box 8.2

Children in Trouble

Juvenile delinquency has no single cause manifestation or cure. Its origins are many, and the range of behaviour which it covers is equally wide. At some points it merges imperceptibly with behaviour which does not contravene the law. A child's behaviour is influenced by genetic, emotional and intellectual factors, his maturity and his family, school, neighbourhood and wider social setting. It is probably a minority of children who grow up without ever behaving in ways which may be contrary to the law. Frequently such behaviour is no more than an incident in the pattern of a child's normal development ... The social consequences of juvenile delinquency range from minor nuisance to considerable damage and suffering for the community. An important object of the criminal law is to protect society against such consequences: but the community also recognises the importance of caring for those who are too young to protect themselves. Over recent years these two quite distinct grounds for action by society have been moving steadily closer together. It has become increasingly clear that social control of harmful behaviour by the young, and social measures to help and protect the young are not distinct and separate processes. The aims of protecting society from juvenile delinquency and of helping children in trouble to grow up into mature and law abiding persons are complementary and not contradictory.

Source: Home Office (1968, pp. 3–4).

Reflecting such a philosophy, the White Paper advocated a range of interventions to deal with offenders through systems of supervision, treatment and social welfare in the community rather than punishment in custodial institutions. In Scotland, the Kilbrandon Report described delinquency as a 'symptom of personal or environmental difficulties' (cited by Morris and McIsaac, 1978, p. 26). Young offending was seen as an indication of maladjustment, immaturity or damaged personality: conditions which could be treated in much the same way as an illness or disease. Here the abolition of the juvenile court and its replacement by a welfare tribunal was advocated. Central to both was the increased involvement of local authority social workers. Their role was to prevent delinquency by intervening in the family life of the 'pre-delinquent', to provide assessment of a child's needs, and to promote non-custodial disposals. A significant reduction in the number of young people appearing before the courts was envisaged, with offenders, in the main, being dealt with under care and protection proceedings or informally. The perceived need was to divert young people from court and custodial processing. When court action was unavoidable, civil proceedings leading to care orders implemented by local authorities were to replace criminal proceedings. Attendance centres and detention centres were to be phased out in favour of either community-based **intermediate treatment** (IT) schemes, which would offer supervised activities, guidance and counselling or residential care in local authority-run community homes with education. Magistrates were no longer to be involved in detailed decisions about appropriate treatment; again this was to be the province of social workers and social service professionals (Morris and McIsaac, 1978, p. 25).

These proposals – which were to inform much of the *Children and Young Persons Act 1969* and the *Social Work (Scotland) Act 1968* – were quite explicitly based on a social welfare approach to young offenders. Authority and discretion were notably shifted out of the hands of the police, magistrates and prison department and into the hands of the local authorities and the Department of Health and Social Security. As Thorpe et al. declared, 'the hour of the "child-savers" had finally arrived' (1980, p. 6). However, in England and Wales during the 1970s vital elements of the *Children and Young Persons Act 1969* were never implemented. The Act had consistently attracted criticism during its White Paper stages for being too welfare-minded and permissive (Bottoms, 1974). The new Conservative government elected in 1970 almost immediately declared it would not implement those sections of the Act that were intended to raise the age of criminal responsibility from 10 to 14 years and to replace criminal with care proceedings. The Conservatives essentially objected to state intervention in criminal matters through a welfare rather than a judicial body. Likewise magistrates and the police responded to the undermining of their key positions in the justice system by becoming more punitively minded and declining the opportunity to use community-based services on a large scale. Above all, rather than replacing the old structures of juvenile justice, the new welfarist principles were grafted on to them. The treatment–punishment continuum was merely extended. Intermediate treatment was introduced but detention centres and attendance centres were not phased out. Community homes with education (CHEs) arrived but retained the character of the old approved schools. Care proceedings were made in criminal cases but, as it was still possible to take criminal proceedings against children under 14, the former were used only occasionally (Thorpe et al., 1980, p. 22). When care orders were used, they were largely targeted at young women, on the grounds of 'moral danger' and for 'status offences' – running away from home, staying out late at night, and so on – which would not be punishable by law if committed by an adult and rarely considered as 'serious' if committed by boys.

In practice, traditional principles of punitive justice were never seriously undermined by the 1969 Act. These remained largely intact, with welfarist principles merely being added to the range of interventions and disposals available to the court. The new welfare elements of the system were generally employed with a younger age group of, for example, low school-achievers, 'wayward girls' and truants from 'problem' families designated as 'pre-delinquent' (the social workers' domain), while the courts continued their old policy of punishing offenders (the magistrates' domain). Although ideologically opposed, 'the two systems have in effect become vertically integrated and an additional population of customer-clients has been identified in order to ensure that they both have plenty of work to do' (Thorpe et al., 1980, pp. 22–3).

Children's Hearings

In Scotland, a different outcome was reached from the welfare/punishment debates of the 1960s. The sheriffs, probation officers and police associations gave way to the advocates of reform largely because Kilbrandon's brand of welfarism was grounded in notions of social education which appealed to a strong Scottish identity with educational processes (Whyte, 2000). The *1968 Social Work (Scotland) Act* established new social work departments, gave local authorities a general duty to promote social welfare for children in need and, most significantly, established the children's hearings system (which came into operation in 1971) (see Box 8.3).

On its inception a majority of the grounds for referral were for offences. However, by the 1990s, non-offence grounds made up about a third, reflecting a rise in the number of girls referred for care and protection reasons. Reporters are endowed with considerable discretionary power. Initially they did seem to have been influential in reducing the numbers facing processing and adjudication. Between 1969 and 1973 a reduction of 39 per cent was achieved, whereas in England and Wales the numbers considered by the juvenile court increased by 4 per cent (Morris and McIsaac, 1978). However, rates of referral increased in the 1990s (McGhee et al., 1996, p. 62); the most common reason for referral being non-attendance at school (Scottish Consortium, 2000). In a review of the hearing's more positive features, Dickie (1979, p. 68) concluded:

Box 8.3

Children's hearings in Scotland

Children's hearings are not a criminal court but a welfare tribunal serviced by lay people from the local community. They deal with those from birth to age 16 deemed in need of care and protection and those from age 8 to 16 on offence grounds. Most offenders aged 16 to 18 are dealt with in the adult system. Cases can be initially referred to a reporter from a range of bodies including education authorities, social work departments, the police and procurators-fiscal, but most typically the police. The role of the reporter is to sift referrals and decide on a future course of action. The grounds for referral to a children's hearing, as established by the Children (Scotland) Act 1995, include:

- being beyond the control of parents;

- falling into bad associations and being exposed to moral danger;

- lack of parental care, causing suffering or ill health;

- having committed an offence;

- having been the victim of a sex or cruelty offence;

- living in a household where there is, or is likely to be, the perpetrator of such an offence;

- having failed to attend school regularly;

- misuse of alcohol or any drug.

When a case reaches a hearing it is deliberated upon by three lay members of a panel, the parents or guardians of the child, and social work representatives in the presence of the child. Since 2002, legal representation may be provided if a recommendation of secure accommodation is to be considered or when the case is legally complex. Legal aid is not available for representation at the hearing. Safeguarders may be appointed but rarely are so. The hearing cannot proceed unless all parties understand *and* accept the grounds for referral. The hearing does not determine guilt or innocence (it can only proceed if guilt is admitted) and is solely concerned with deciding on future courses of action. The main disposals available to the panel are residential and non-residential supervision.

The system encourages communication and collaboration between the relevant professions and permits a flexibility in the provision of services appropriate to the child's changing needs. Above all, perhaps, is its capacity to focus on the interests of the individual child and to tackle problems in a manner which encourages the family to participate and retain its self respect ... a system which has such inherently strong welfare values must appeal to social workers.

The hearings system is based on the principle that those who offend and those who are considered in need of care and protection have similar backgrounds and that as a result any attempt to assist young people from re-offending must take account of their social welfare needs. Early critiques, however, maintained that paternalistic discretionary decision-making, indeterminate intervention and lack of accountability hardly acted in the child's best interests and only served to institutionalize greater levels of social control. It is also worth remembering that while over 15,000 children might be referred to a hearing each year, there is also a minority whose offences are considered so 'serious' that the hearings system is bypassed and referred directly to the adult Sheriff and High Court system (Gill, 1985). In 1995, 213 and, in 1997, 148 under-16s were charged in an adult criminal court (Whyte, 2000). In this respect Scottish welfarism is reserved for less serious offences and some routes into adult justice have remained unchallenged. Moreover, the hearings system only deals with those up to the age of 16. While in Scotland there are almost no penal options for those under the age of 16, there remains a continuing presence of custodial institutions for older children whose regimes are far removed from the promotion of welfarism. In 1985, the only custodial centre for young people, at Glenochil, Alloa, came under criticism following a sequence of suicides unparalleled in the custody of young people. As in England, some of Scotland's most punitive systems still appear to be reserved for its young. Prior experience of the hearings system may lead to especially severe interventions in the adult system (Waterhouse et al., 2000). And welfarism always remains prey to shifts in the broader political climate. As McGhee et al. (1996, pp. 68–9) noted, during the 1990s there was something of a shift from notions of a 'child's best interest' to that of 'public protection':

> Nearly 25 years later the gap Kilbrandon tried to close between the needs of children in trouble with the law and children in need of care is beginning to open ... [T]his change in outlook is reflected both in the United Kingdom and abroad and is likely to pose a serious challenge to the philosophy which lies behind the Children's Hearings System. Increased public pressure to make children accountable for wrongdoing, plus a growing concentration on the needs of victims, have contributed to the public focus shifting from the welfare of the child to offending behaviour and its consequences.

Indeed, since 1995, Scottish youth justice has been seriously challenged and transformed by political and managerial imperatives which lay greater emphasis on offender accountability than general welfare needs (McAra, 2006). In 2003, amidst a panic about a newly identified group of persistent offenders, the Scottish Executive decided to experiment with re-establishing youth courts for 16 and 17 year olds. Pilot youth courts were established in Hamilton and Airdrie. This would ostensibly overcome the anomaly that Scotland is the only country in Europe to routinely deal with 16 and 17 year olds in adult criminal courts, but it is notable that it was this particular shift that was entertained rather than extend the remit of the hearings system (Audit Scotland, 2002; Scottish Executive, 2003; Piacentini and Walters, 2006). In addition, in 2003, plans were announced to give the hearings new powers to electronically tag under-16 year olds and to force their parents to take responsibility for their offending. *The Anti-Social Behaviour Act 2004* introduced parenting orders for the first time in Scotland. The Scottish Communities Minister clouded these authoritarian shifts in a welfarist discourse by claiming that 'We are not helping young people at all if we don't try to deal with their behaviour' (*Guardian*, 23 June

2003). As in England, Scotland it seems, is witnessing a dramatic repoliticization of youth justice. McAra (2006) refers to this as the 'detartanization' of a welfare-based ethos which had given youth justice in Scotland its particularly distinctive, robust and stable identity.

'In a Child's Best Interests?'

Welfare in youth justice is predicated on the assumption that all intervention should be directed to meeting the *needs* of young people, rather than responding to their *deeds*. Historically it has tended to see little differentiation between offending and non-offending troublesome behaviour: both are symptomatic of a wider deprivation, whether material neglect, lack of moral guidance or a 'parenting deficit'. As a result it is capable of drawing many more young people into its remit than if it were simply concerned with matters of guilt or innocence. Remarking on the impact of the *1933 Children and Young Persons Act*, Springhall (1986, p. 186) argues that there is 'abundant evidence' to show that rather than diverting youth from court, it actively encouraged them to court. Because of the 'welfare' focus of the Act, there was a greater willingness to prosecute on the assumption that care and treatment would follow. Similarly, because delinquency is ill defined, there is little or no control over who might be considered deserving of intervention.

The persistent critique of welfarism (which gathered pace in the 1970s) is that its rhetoric of benevolence and humanitarianism often blinds us to its denial of legal rights, its discretionary and non-accountable procedures and its ability to impose greater intervention than would be merited on the basis of conduct alone. As Hudson (1987, p. 152) put it: 'identifying needs amounts to listing reasons for intervention', often drawing young people into the justice system at an earlier age and for relatively innocuous offences. In particular, welfarism seems to encourage greater intervention into the lives of young women and very young children on the grounds of 'moral danger' and on the presumption that they are 'at risk'. 'Wayward girls', for example, may find themselves committed into the residential care of the local authority, and thence into stigmatizing institutions, without having committed an offence at all (Gelsthorpe, 1984, p. 2). A summary of the key assumptions of the welfare model is given in Box 8.4.

Box 8.4
Assumptions of welfarism

- Delinquent, dependent and neglected children are all products of an adverse environment which at its worst is characterized by multiple deprivation. Social, economic and physical disadvantage, including poor parental care, are all relevant considerations.

- Delinquency is a pathological condition, a presenting symptom of some deeper maladjustment out of the control of the individual concerned.

- Since people have no control over the multiplicity of causal factors dictating their delinquency they cannot be considered responsible for their actions or be held accountable for them. Considerations of guilt or innocence are, therefore, irrelevant and punishment is not only inappropriate but is contrary to the rules of natural justice.

- All children in trouble (both offenders and non-offenders) are basically the same and can be effectively dealt with through a single unified system designed to identify and meet the needs of children.

- The needs or underlying disorders, of which delinquency is symptomatic, are capable of identification and hence prevention, treatment and control are possible.

- Informality is necessary if children's needs are to be accurately determined and their best interests served. Strict rules of procedure or standards of proof not only hinder the identification of need but are unnecessary in proceedings conducted in the child's best interests.

- Inasmuch as need is highly individualized, flexibility of response is vital. Wide discretion is necessary in the determination and variation of treatment measures.

- Voluntary treatment is possible and is not punishment. Treatment has no harmful side effects.

- Child welfare is paramount, though considerations of public protection cannot be ignored. In any event, a system designed to meet the needs of the child will in turn protect the community and serve the best interests of society.

- Prevention of neglect and alleviation of disadvantage will lead to prevention of delinquency.

Source: Adapted from Black Committee Report (1979), cited by Stewart and Tutt (1987, p. 91).

Justice

8.2 During the 1970s, faith in social work's ability to diagnose the causes of delinquency and to treat these with non-punitive methods came to be questioned. Discretional social work judgements were viewed as a form of arbitrary power. Many young people, it was argued, were subjected to apparently non-accountable state procedures and their liberty was often unjustifiably denied (Davies, 1982, p. 33). Social work involvement not only preserved explanations of individual pathology, but also undermined a young person's right to natural justice. It may also have placed young people in *double jeopardy* – sentenced for their background as well as for their offence – and unintentionally accelerated movement up the sentencing tariff. Based on the experience of the 1970s, in which the numbers of custodial sentences increased dramatically, a new justice-based approach argued that a return to notions of due process and just deserts was called for.

The Opposition to Welfare

The critique of welfare had three main elements, which came from markedly divergent political positions. From the right, welfare and rehabilitative systems were condemned as evidence that the justice system had (once again) become too 'soft on crime'. Second, radical social workers argued that the 'need for treatment' acted as a spurious justification for placing considerable restrictions on the liberty of young people, particularly young women, which were out of proportion either to the seriousness of the offence or to the realities of being 'at risk'. Third, civil libertarians and liberal lawyers maintained that welfarism denied young people access to full legal rights and that their 'cause' would be better served by restoring due process to the heart of the justice system.

Political Opposition

In England and Wales, during the 1970s, the numbers sent to youth custody increased dramatically. This was in direct contradiction to the intentions of the 1969 Act. The recommitment to custody was based on the three main factors. First was the popular belief that the 1970s had witnessed a rapid growth in juvenile crime, characterized by a hard core of 'vicious young criminals'. The second factor was a tendency on the part of magistrates to give custodial sentences for almost all types of offence, particularly if the offender was already subject to a welfare-based care or supervision order. The third factor was the role of welfarism in drawing juveniles into the system at an increasingly early age.

Rather than acting as a check on custodial sentencing, these developments collectively accelerated the rate at which a young person moved through the sentencing tariff. A 1981 Department of Health and Social Security report concluded that the number of juveniles sent to borstal and detention centres increased fivefold between 1965 and 1980. Less than a fifth of this rise could be attributed to increased offending; instead, it was believed to reflect a growing tendency on the part of the courts to be more punitive (DHSS, 1981). The intermediate treatment schemes introduced by the *1969 Children and Young Persons Act* in England and Wales initially acted less as an alternative to custody and more as a means of drawing younger and 'pre-delinquent' children into the 'net' of the youth justice system. For Cohen (1985, p. 37) and Austin and Krisberg (1981) the real effect was **net widening** and an increase in the reach and intensity of state control (see Box 8.5).

Box 8.5

Net widening

- Expanding the remit of the youth justice system draws more people into its reach (*net widening*).

- Levels of intervention, involving individualized treatment and indeterminate sentencing, intensify (*net strengthening*).

- Institutions are not replaced or radically altered, but supplemented by new forms of intervention (*different nets*).

In addition, as Bottoms (1974) argued, it is important to recognize that the 1969 Act was never implemented in full, being opposed by the 1970–74 Conservative government, the magistracy, the police and some sections of the probation service on the grounds that it undermined 'the due process of law'. The underlying social welfare philosophy of the Act was quashed. While the legislation stressed the importance of fitting appropriate care and treatment to each individual child, the values held by the police and magistracy tended to stress punishment to fit the crime. Much of this resurgent authoritarianism coalesced with a highly politicized debate about the supposed criminality of black youth and their involvement in such street crimes as 'mugging' (Hall et al., 1978). At the time Landau and Nathan's (1983) study of the Metropolitan Police area, for example, showed that for some offences – violence, burglary, public order – black youths were more likely to be charged immediately rather than have their cases referred to a juvenile liaison bureau for a decision about whether to caution or not. In the early 1980s African-Caribbeans made up about 5 per cent of the population in London, but 17 per cent of the people arrested (Smith and Gray, 1983). In court, black youth were less likely to be given non-custodial sentences and received longer custodial sentences despite having fewer previous convictions. As a result, in the borstals and detention centres of the south of England, black youth often constituted over a third of the inmates (Kettle, 1982, p. 535).

While magistrates were committed to incarcerating the young offender, social workers extended their preventive work with the families of the 'pre-delinquent'. Ironically, this development meant many more children were under surveillance, the market for the courts was widened and more offenders were placed in care for relatively trivial offences. In practice, preventive work meant that children were being sent to institutions at a younger age. As in the past, new institutions which were supposed to reform youth instead created new categories of delinquency. As Thorpe et al. remarked, the liberalism of the 1969 Act produced a judicial backlash in which popular wisdom about juvenile justice and its actual practice became totally estranged:

> The tragedy that has occurred since can be best described as a situation in which the worst of all possible worlds came into existence – people have been persistently led to believe that the juvenile criminal justice system has become softer and softer, while the reality has been that it has become harder and harder. (Thorpe et al., 1980, p. 8)

Welfare and Young Women

Such arguments appeared all the more pertinent when applied to the situation of young women. Young women and girls were frequently brought into court for offences that might be dealt with informally or ignored if committed by adults or young men. Often their offences were (and remain) related to behaviour regarded as sexually deviant and promiscuous or to a perceived need for their 'protection'. Here a moral evaluation of what constitutes 'need' is much greater. While cultural codes of masculinity, toughness and sexual predation are the norm for young men, there is little or no conception of 'normal' exuberant delinquency for young women. When young women appear before the court, they are likely to be viewed as 'abnormal' – breaking not only the law, but also the 'rules' of how they should behave. Because of the statistically exceptional nature of their criminality, female delinquency tends also to be seen as a perversion of, or rebellion against, 'natural' feminine roles. As Hudson (1988, p. 40) argued, a predominantly treatment- and welfare-focused paradigm adjudicated as much on questions of femininity as it did on matters of guilt or innocence:

> [W]hen white male youth commit criminal offences they are not usually seen as intrinsically challenging normative expectations about behaviour for young and adult men ... rarely is there any suggestion that male delinquency is incongruent with masculinity ... Young women, however, are predominantly judged according to their management of family, sexual and interpersonal relationships ... [T]hey are subject to a double penalty: firstly because they have broken the law and secondly because they have defied social codes which prescribe passivity for women. (Hudson, A., 1988, pp. 39–40)

The end result of such gender-specific modes of social control was that young women were drawn into the justice system for reasons wholly unrelated to the commission of offences (Casburn, 1979); they were less likely to be fined and more often placed on supervision or taken into care than young men (May, 1977); and they were more likely to be committed to approved schools on 'care, protection and control' rather than 'offence' grounds (Shacklady Smith, 1978). They endure a **repressive welfare**. As Harris and Webb (1987, p. 154) concluded,

> [W]hether the overt intent of the courts and the experts is to monitor girls' behaviour or whether such monitoring is rather the effect of an almost complete dearth of ideas as to what is to be done, the effect of these processes is a disproportionate exercise of power over girls.

'Nothing Works'

The critique of the gender-specific nature of youth justice coalesced with a critique of welfare and rehabilitation in general. In Britain, Clarke and Sinclair (1974, p. 58) argued that 'there is now little reason to believe that any one of the widely used methods of treating offenders is much better at preventing reconviction than any other'. They questioned the notion that delinquency and crime were symptoms of individual pathology and instead advocated interventions based on the assumption that crime was a *rational* action performed by ordinary people acting under particular pressures and exposed to specific opportunities (see **Chapter 4.2**). Crime, it was argued, could best be controlled by making targets harder (e.g. through improved security measures) than by trying to identify and tackle any presumed underlying causes. The most devastating critique of welfare, however, came from Martinson's (1974) analysis of 231 studies of treatment programmes in the USA. He concluded that 'with few and isolated exceptions the rehabilitative efforts that have been reported so far have had no appreciable effect on recidivism' (Martinson, 1974, p. 25). This conclusion was widely received as 'nothing works': that it was a waste of time and money to devote energy to the rehabilitative treatment of (young) offenders. It prompted a collapse of faith in correctionalism, initially in relation to prison-based 'treatment programmes' but subsequently expanded to include all manner of probation interventions and community corrections. Doubt was cast over the efficacy of many fundamental aspects of 'welfare-based' juvenile justice.

'Back to Justice'

Finally, liberal lawyers and civil libertarians maintained that welfare, rather than being benevolent, was an insidious form of control. Young offenders were considered to need protection not only from punitive justice, but also from welfare's 'humanitarianism' (Cohen, S., 1985 and see Box 8.6).

Box 8.6

Critiques of welfare-based interventions

Under English law the child enjoys very few of the rights taken for granted by adults under the principles of natural justice. The law's reference to the child's 'best interests' reflects the benevolent paternalism of its approach. Essentially as far as the courts are concerned, the 'best interests' principle empowers social workers, psychologists, psychiatrists and others to define on the basis of their opinions what is good for the child . . . [The law] does not require that the experts should substantiate their opinions or prove to the court that any course of action they propose will be more effective in promoting the best interests of the child than those taken by the parent or by the child acting on his own behalf . . . a child may find that his/her arguments against being committed to care are perceived as evidence of their need for treatment, as a sign, for example, that they have 'authority problems'. (Taylor et al., 1979, pp. 22–3, commenting on English juvenile courts)

Euphemisms are frequently used to disguise the true state of affairs, to pretend that things are other than they are. Courts become tribunals, probation becomes supervision and approved schools are renamed residential establishments. But few are deceived by these verbal devices. (Morris, 1974, p. 364, commenting on Scottish children's hearings)

Underlying this critique was a scepticism about the value of treatment, welfare and therapy and their ability to provide justice for children. For example, the introduction of compulsory treatment measures denied other values such as individual liberty, natural justice, due process and fairness. In Scotland, the Kilbrandon Report made extensive use of such medical terms as 'symptom' and 'diagnosis' and compared its own recommendations to those of medical practice. In doing so it was assumed that the causes of delinquency lay primarily within the individual and his or her family. The 'problem' was defined in terms of pathology and maladjustment (emanating from individual positivism – see **Chapter 3.1**) rather than, for example, as arising out of social, economic and political conditions (such as unemployment, 'irrelevant' school-ing, urban deprivation, lack of recreational facilities). As a result, juvenile justice in Scotland in particular became dominated by the jargon and practices of the child-saving ideology – 'at risk', 'prevention', 'disturbance', 'deprivation', 'personality disor-der', 'treatment', 'cure' – which acted to reconstitute a child's identity as deviant and pathological. Such 'character assassinations', it was argued, legitimized greater incur-sion into young people's lives than could be provided by simply concentrating on the circumstances of the act of misconduct (Morris et al., 1980).

The Justice Model

In the wake of these wide-ranging criticisms of welfarism, a new justice-based model of corrections emerged. Its leading proponent in America, Von Hirsch (1976), proposed that the following principles be reinstated at the centre of criminal justice practice:

- proportionality of punishment to crime, or the offender is handed a sentence that is in accordance with what the act deserves;

- determinacy of sentencing and an end to indeterminate, treatment-oriented sentences;

- an end to judicial, professional and administrative discretion;

- an end to disparities in sentencing;

- equity and protection of rights through due process.

Advocates of 'back to justice' argued that determinate sentences based on the seriousness of the offence, rather than on the 'needs' of individual offenders, would be seen as fair and just by young people themselves. A greater use of cautions by the police for minor offences would, they argued, help to keep young people out of the courts. When in court, closer control over social workers' social inquiry reports would ensure that intermediate treatment (IT), care orders or other forms of welfare intervention would be used only in the most serious of cases. In this way most offenders would either not be prosecuted at all or at least would not be subject to social work surveillance. The role of social work, it was maintained, would be to offer supervision schemes only in those cases when custody was being suggested. Social work should only be involved at the 'heavy end' of offences. Above all, a greater promotion of community-based interventions by government and social service departments should be promoted.

Leading proponents of this philosophy, such as Morris et al. (1980) and Taylor et al. (1979), maintained that a social work understanding of delinquency, given its dominant grounding in psychoanalytical theories, does not necessarily lead to the more equitable exercise of justice. They condemned the fact that since the *1908 Children Act*, the fate of juvenile offenders had increasingly become dictated by the discretionary and arbitrary powers of individual social workers and magistrates. Children's rights, they argued, would be better upheld by returning to the principles of equality before the law. In some respects such arguments marked a return to early nineteenth-century principles of viewing the juvenile as a young adult. The approach, however, was complemented by proposals for law reform which would decriminalize such juvenile crimes as drinks and drugs offences, homosexual or heterosexual behaviour under the age of consent, and remove the force of law from misdemeanours such as truancy and running away from home. In this way it became possible to raise the issue of the 'rule of the law' as a progressive demand. Taylor et al. (1979), for example, argued for the right to legal representation and legal aid in the juvenile court and for it to be accepted that the proceedings were injurious. Rather than viewing the reforms of the past century as progressive, they argued that they had consistently served to erode the rights of children. For example, the child's 'best interests' were usually determined by such 'experts' as social workers, psychologists and psychiatrists by way of social inquiry reports. In court these assumed an authority greater than the definitions of 'best interest' made by the parent or by the child acting on his or her own behalf. Moreover such reports were not automatically available to the child, the parents or the child's lawyers. Any adult appearing before a court expects to know beforehand the full case to be answered. In the juvenile court this right was not always deemed to be in the child's 'best interests'.

The 'back to justice' approach thus advocated reform of both the English and Scottish systems of youth justice whereby the court's role as an administrator of *justice* would be reinstated. The assumptions of the **justice model** are outlined in Box 8.7.

Box 8.7

Assumptions of the justice model

- Delinquency is a matter of opportunity and choice – other factors may combine to bring a child to the point of delinquency, but unless there is evidence to the contrary, the act as such is a manifestation of the rational decision to that effect.

- In so far as people are responsible for their actions they should also be accountable. This is qualified in respect of children by the doctrine of criminal responsibility as originally evolved under common law and now endorsed by statute.

- Proof of commission of an offence should be the sole justification for intervention and the sole basis of punishment.

- Sanctions and controls are valid responses to deviant behaviour both as an expression of society's disapproval and as an individual and general deterrent to future similar behaviour.

- Behaviour attracting legal intervention and associated sanctions available under the law should be specifically defined to avoid uncertainty.

- The power to interfere with a person's freedom and in particular that of a child should be subject to the most rigorous standard of proof which traditionally is found in a court of law. Individual rights are most effectively safeguarded under the judicial process.

- There should be equality before the law; like cases should be treated alike.

- There should be proportionality between the seriousness of the delinquent or criminal behaviour warranting intervention and the community's response; between the offence and the sentence given.

Source: Adapted from Black Committee Report (1979), cited by Stewart and Tutt (1987, p. 92).

Progressive Justice: Diversion and Decarceration

The practical result of a resurgence of legalism and 'back to justice' in the 1980s was predictably complex and contradictory. On the one hand, it seemed to play into a retributivist discourse intent on making all offenders responsible for their actions and seeking their punitive just deserts; on the other, it opened the door to such notions as 'minimum intervention', 'maximum diversion', 'due process' and dealing with offences rather than offenders in which the reach of juvenile justice was to be reduced rather than increased.

In 1979, the Conservatives launched a strong attack on delinquency in the run-up to the general election and throughout the early 1980s condemned the 'soft' way that 'dangerous young thugs' were dealt with. Through the liberal use of terms such as 'wickedness' and 'evil', delinquency once more became a moral issue. Much of this approach rested on many Conservatives blaming the supposed permissiveness of the *Children and Young Persons Act 1969* and liberal child-rearing practices of the 1960s for the increase in delinquency (Morgan, P., 1978). Margaret Thatcher, the incoming Prime Minister, attacked those who had created a 'culture of excuses' and promised that her government would 're-establish a code of conduct that condemns crime plainly and without exception' (Riddell, 1989, p. 171). The search for individual or social causes of crime – personality, unemployment, deprivation, lack of opportunity – was to be abandoned. The rhetoric of treatment and rehabilitation was to be replaced by the rhetoric of punishment and **retribution**. Welfarism was to be replaced by the rule of law. The language of 'rights' was appropriated by one of self-responsibility and obligation (Anderson, 1992, p. xviii). Hall (1980) captured this mood by arguing that Britain was in the throes of a 'deep and decisive movement towards a more disciplinary, authoritarian kind of society' in which a 'regression to stone-age morality' was being realized in 'a blind spasm of control'. In October 1979, it was announced that new 'short, sharp, shock' regimes would be introduced into detention centres. In 1982, a new Criminal Justice Act gave magistrates powers to sentence directly to youth custody centres (previously they were limited to making recommendations to the Crown Court for borstal training). Those parts of the 1969 Act which had advocated a phasing out of custody were officially abandoned. It seemed as if there was going to be a considerable increase in the number of juveniles 'tasting porridge' (McLaughlin and Muncie, 1993, p. 176, and see **Chapter 9.3**).

However, contrary to the 'net widening' and 'net strengthening' predictions of many commentators, both the youth crime rate and the youth custody rate declined dramatically during the course of the 1980s. Indeed, the mid to late 1980s has been heralded as a 'successful revolution' in criminal – particularly juvenile – justice policy (Allen, 1991), or at least as 'a delicately balanced consensus' in which all elements of the youth justice system (for different reasons) appeared to support the principles of diversion, decriminalization and decarceration rather than the 'futile and counterproductive' outcomes of custody (Goldson, 1997b). According to Home Office criminal statistics, the numbers of young people aged 17 or under convicted or cautioned decreased from 204,600 in 1983 to 129,500 in 1993. The number of young offenders sentenced to immediate custody was also significantly reduced. In 1983, a total of 13,500 14 to 17 year old males were sentenced to immediate custody for indictable offences compared to 3,300 in 1993. This represented a fall from some 15 per cent of all court dispositions to 11 per cent (see Muncie, 1999b, p. 281).

The precise reasons for these dramatic reductions (and largely unexpected given that the political climate was dominated by Thatcherism) remain in debate. However, a number of key elements can be noted:

- *Demographic change.* There was a 19 per cent fall in the overall juvenile population in this period.

- *Diversion.* One of the foundational elements of youth justice has always been that young people should be protected from the full rigours of adult justice. This has meant that a range of **diversionary strategies** has always retained some presence in the form of:

  - *Diversion from crime* – typically this involves various methods of crime prevention which can range from target hardening and early intervention to skills training and education.

  - *Diversion from prosecution* – from the early 1970s to the mid-1990s the police increasingly adopted a system of cautioning minor offenders through formal and informal warnings rather than seeking prosecution.

  - *Diversion from custody* – while alternatives to adult prisons have existed since the mid-nineteenth century, the notion of custody, in any form, being harmful and counterproductive regained prominence in the mid-1980s. Community-based programmes were increasingly promoted as viable alternatives to custody.

- *Experiments in decarceration.* The epitome of diversion was the decision in Massachusetts, USA, to abolish institutions for juvenile delinquents in 1970. Jerome Miller, Head of the Department of Youth Services, adopted a strategy of closing all the state's youth training schools (akin to the English borstal) prior to establishing any community-based alternatives. Enlisting government and media support, the Department was able to portray juvenile institutions as destructive places, and by speeding up parole and through a number of novel administrative devices, all such schools were closed by 1975 (Miller, 1998). This commitment to decarceration survived, despite political pressure, until the early 1980s. Since then, however, it is generally acknowledged that slippage has occurred due to an increasing use of secure units and transference of juvenile cases to the adult courts (Rutherford,

1986, pp. 67–107). Nevertheless the Massachusetts experiment revealed to many policy-makers and practitioners that decarceration was not an impossible goal.

- *Cautioning*. Attempts to divert offenders from court, encouraged by the *1969 Children and Young Persons Act*, first took the form of juvenile liaison panels in which the police, together with social workers and teachers, decided whether or not to prosecute apprehended youths (Hudson, 1987, p. 145). Other schemes were entirely police-run and developed cautioning rather than prosecution for first-time or minor offenders. Nationally in 1970, 35 per cent of those under 17 were cautioned, but by 1979 this had increased to 50 per cent (Gelsthorpe and Morris, 1994, p. 968). By the 1990s about 60 per cent of young offenders were dealt with in this way, although there were wide and fluctuating regional variations. Home Office circular 14/1985 furthered this process by encouraging the police to use 'no further action' or 'informal warnings' instead of any formal action (until a reversal of the policy in 1994). This again seemed to have a major diversionary effect. In Northamptonshire, for example, in 1985, 86 per cent of juveniles who came to the notice of the police were either prosecuted or formally cautioned; but by 1989 this had been reduced to 30 per cent (Hughes et al., 1998). A recurring criticism of cautioning has been its potential to administer a punishment, particularly in caution-plus schemes which combine a warning with **reparation** such as gardening and house cleaning, without any judicial hearing (Ditchfield, 1976). However, in the late 1980s at least they did seem capable of significantly reducing prosecutions (see **Chapter 7.4**).

- *Legislative restrictions on custody*. The 1982 *Criminal Justice Act* may have extended magistrates' custodial powers but it also built in a series of conditions that had to be met before this could happen. First, the use of 'criminal' care orders was significantly curtailed. As a result there was a massive contraction of the residential care sector with the number of young people in community homes with education (CHEs) declining from 7,500 in 1975 to 2,800 in 1984 and the numbers of CHEs falling from 125 to 60. By the late 1980s the use of care orders in criminal cases had become so insignificant that it was repealed. It no longer became possible to commit offenders to residential care on the grounds that they were in 'need' of welfare. Courts were also required to specify the criteria under which custody was being recommended. Legal representation for juveniles was introduced. Community service orders were made available for 16 year olds. The *1988 Criminal Justice Act* further tightened the criteria before custody was to be considered. The *1991 Criminal Justice Act* cemented this process by arguing that prison was 'an expensive way of making bad people worse' and by establishing a proliferation of 'community sentences' within the broader philosophy of 'punishment in the community' (Home Office, 1990, para 2.7, and see **Chapter 9.3**).

- *Intensive intermediate treatment.* In 1983, the Department of Health and Social Security's Intermediate Treatment (IT) Initiative financed the establishment of 110 *intensive* schemes in 62 local authority areas explicitly to provide alternatives to custody (Rutherford, 1989, 1992). Intermediate treatment practitioners were required to evolve 'new justice-based styles of working' which focused less on the emotional and social needs of juveniles and more on the nature of the offence. IT was to be restricted to those who were at serious risk of custody. Through such means it was hoped that magistrates would be persuaded that IT was no longer a 'soft option' but a 'high tariff' disposal. As McLaughlin and Muncie (1993, p. 178) have recorded, a strong 'alternatives to custody' ethos was developed within many social work departments and supported by the campaign groups of NACRO, the Children's Society and the Association for Juvenile Justice. Many agreed with the criticisms of the welfare approach and the coercive role that social workers played previously and developed a justice-based approach as self-styled *youth justice* workers (Rutherford, 1989, p. 29). Social services departments began to construct their policies premised on the notions of minimum intervention, maximum diversion and underpinned by justice as opposed to welfare principles. By the mid-1990s, Martin (1997) was able to catalogue over 150 diversionary community programmes operating in England and Wales designed to address offending behaviour through victim awareness, anger management, drug awareness and positive leisure schemes.

- *Multi-agency collaboration.* A new localized *systems* approach emerged to operate these programmes drawing on social services, probation, the police, education, local authorities and numerous voluntary and charitable bodies. Youth justice teams came to be committed to creating 'custody-free zones' in their areas. Of crucial importance was the fact that this approach had the full backing of the Magistrates' Association. Hence those working in the juvenile justice system began to act in tandem: a stark contrast to the inter-agency conflicts and rivalries which were characteristic of the 1970s and early 1980s.

- *Expense and effectiveness.* In 1990–91, it was estimated that keeping an offender in custody for three weeks was more expensive than 12 months of supervision or community service. In addition, 83 per cent of young men and 60 per cent of young women leaving youth custody were reconvicted within two years; the reconviction rate of those participating in community-based schemes was assumed to be substantially lower. NACRO's (1993) monitoring of the Intermediate Treatment Initiative indeed found reconviction rates of between 45 and 55 per cent, and even though subsequent research funded by the Home Office and the Department of Health could find no clear evidence to suggest that community penalties held more than a modest advantage over custody in preventing reoffending (Lloyd et al., 1994; Bottoms, 1995), a major stimulus to community-based corrections had been born.

As a result of all of these factors, it appeared as if justice-based principles of proportionality in sentencing or 'just deserts' was capable of providing a more visible, consistent and accountable decision-making process which, despite the law and order rhetoric, was also able to make a significant impact on the numbers of young people entering and going through formal adjudication. It is precisely these 'successes' that were condemned as evidence of an 'excuse culture' by the incoming Labour government of 1997 (see **Chapter 9**).

Institutional Injustices

It is notable that the 'benefits' of the 'progressive practices' of the 1980s were not shared by all. Numerous studies in the 1980s found that African-Caribbean youth, in particular, were dealt with more harshly than whites at every stage of the judicial process – from arrest to sentencing. In 1987, 9.8 per cent of the under-18s received into custody were from ethnic minorities compared to their representation in the general population of no more than 5 per cent (Children's Society, 1989, p. 10). Whether such disparity occurs because of direct discrimination has remained stubbornly immune to statistical verification. As Asquith (1983) suggested, formal justice may simply reflect a wide range of legal *and* non-legal factors associated with criminality. So the over-representation of black youths may be explained by such factors as *age* (on average the African-Caribbean population is younger than the white and thus a higher proportion falls within the peak age of offending), *employment status* (African-Caribbean unemployment rates are consistently higher than for whites or Asians), *homelessness* (which may influence decisions about whether to grant bail) and *court of trial* (African-Caribbeans tend to plead not guilty and fail to benefit from a 'discount' afforded to those who plead guilty). Arguably, it is the accumulation of such factors – the 'multiplier effect' (Goldson and Chigwada-Bailey, 1999) – which acts to discriminate against young blacks, rather than overt judicial racism (see Box 8.8).

Hood's (1992) study of four Crown Courts (where all offenders can be committed for sentence for 'serious crimes') concludes that while discrimination clearly occurs, because sentencing disparities cannot be accounted for by crime rates or by previous criminal records, it is not systematic. Disparities in sentencing were most marked for offences of medium seriousness, where, arguably, judicial discretion is at its highest, and also varied markedly between different courts and judges. A decade later further research conducted by Feilzer and Hood (2004) for the Youth Justice Board focussed specifically on the new youth justice processes as implemented by New Labour but similarly found a higher proportion of prosecutions involving black males, a greater proportion remanded in custody and a 'much higher probability' of a longer prison sentence. All of this suggests that formal justice is not immune to producing discriminatory outcomes.

In general, the justice model has not been immune from criticism. Clarke (1985b) argued that the staking out of 'justice' as a strategy for reform is always

Box 8.8

'Race', youth and criminal justice

- Members of the Black and Minority Ethnic (BME) community in England are seven times more likely than their white counterparts to be stopped and searched, three and a half times more likely to be arrested, and six times more likely to be in prison.

- Once arrested, they are less likely to be cautioned than whites, and more likely to be prosecuted (Landau and Nathan, 1983; CRE, 1992; Goldson and Chigwada-Bailey, 1999).

- African-Caribbeans are more likely to be charged with indictable-only offences (Hood, 1992).

- African-Caribbeans are more likely to be remanded in custody, awaiting trial, rather than released on bail (Shallice and Gordon, 1990; Hood, 1992; Goldson and Peters, 2000).

- African-Caribbeans are subsequently more likely to be acquitted, either because they tend to be tried in Crown Court (where acquittals are higher), or because they tend to plead not guilty, or because they are more likely than whites to have been charged with crimes of which they are innocent (Walker, 1988).

- If found guilty, African-Caribbeans are more likely to be given a custodial sentence and for longer periods than whites (Hudson, 1989). They are also less likely to receive probation (Brown and Hullin, 1992).

Source: Developed from Fitzgerald (1993), Bowling and Phillips (2002), Ministry of Justice (2007) and Webster (2007).

liable to allow proponents of law and order to recruit the arguments of 'natural justice' for their own ends, even though the former is more concerned with retribution and the latter with judicial equality and consistency. And Goldson (1997b), commenting on the 1980s, concluded that 'the "justice" that prevailed was permeated with institutional injustices'. Within 'back to justice' and 'due process' strategies, the continuing social basis of law (and its interpretation and implementation) remained hidden by a liberal rhetoric of equality and rights (see Box 8.9).

As 'back to justice' entered the 1990s, early warnings of its possible appropriation by those more interested in retribution did indeed seem to be more than credible. The period 1991–93 may well go down in the chronicles of youth justice as yet another watershed when the public, media and political gaze fixed on the perennial issue of juvenile crime and delivered a familiar series of knee-jerk and draconian responses. This time, it was renewed images of the 'repeat' or 'persistent' young offender and the atypicality of the Bulger tragedy which provided the rationale for another U-turn in youth justice policy (see **Chapter 1.1**). By 1993 the Home Secretary's notion that 'prison works' was to lead to a further reinvention of the young offender and a corresponding increase in the use of youth custody over the next two decades (see **Chapter 9.3**).

Box 8.9

Critiques of justice-based interventions

Policies which ignore the social and economic realities in which children find themselves, while promoting greater equality and justice within formal systems of control, may not only ignore, but may compound the structural and material inequalities which have been historically associated with criminal behaviour. (Asquith, 1983, p. 17)

By disclaiming any reformative function of the law, by accepting that the most that can be done is punish fairly according to present definitions of crime and seriousness, the justice model colludes with establishment definitions of what are real problems. By abstracting crime from its social context, by abstracting individuals from their collectivities, by abstracting the administration of criminal justice from the wider field of political struggle, the justice model thus inextricably allies itself with the use of the legal system as an important part of the apparatus of repression. (Hudson, 1987, p. 166)

Rather than arguing about the relative merits of 'justice' and 'welfare' we ought perhaps to take a step backwards and survey the framework which effectively supports them both. The beads may be of different colours and situated at opposite ends. But they are on the same thread. (Thorpe et al., 1980, p. 106)

Beyond Welfare and Justice

8.3 Corporatism and Managerialism

As early as the late 1980s, some commentators had begun to argue that it made little sense to talk of youth justice in terms of offering either welfare and/or justice. Pratt (1989), for example, detected a newly developing **corporatism** which tried to remove itself from wider philosophical arguments of welfare, justice and punishment and seek to implement policy that would lead to diversion from court and custody and promote system effectiveness. It was characterized by administrative decision-making, greater sentencing diversity, the construction of sentencing 'packages', centralization of authority and co-ordination of policy, and inter-agency co-operation (Pratt, 1989, p. 245; Parker et al., 1987). The aim was not necessarily to deliver 'welfare' or 'justice' but rather to develop the most cost-effective and efficient way of *managing* the delinquent population. In the process the issue of offending came to be defined more in technical terms. Political/moral debates about the causes of offending and the purpose of intervention tended to be sidelined (Pitts, 1992, p. 142). Youth justice was subject to **bifurcation**: the hard core were still locked up, while an expanding range of statutory and voluntary community-based agencies tailor-made non-custodial sentences which, it was hoped, would be stringent enough to persuade magistrates not to take the (more expensive) custodial option (see Box 8.10).

Box 8.10

The third model of youth justice

	Welfare	Justice	Corporatism
Characteristics	Informality Individualized/indeterminate sentencing	Due process Determinate sentencing	Administrative decision-making Diversion from court/custody
Key agency	Social work	Law	Inter-agency structure
Core task	Diagnosis	Punishment	Systems intervention
Objectives	Respond to individual needs	Respect individual rights	Implement policy

Source: Adapted from Pratt (1989, p. 52).

By the 1990s, such corporate, multi-agency strategies were to become subsumed within a much broader process of public sector managerialization. This, as Clarke and Newman (1997) have catalogued, has generally involved the redefinition of political, economic and social issues as problems to be managed rather than necessarily resolved. When the Conservatives came to power in 1979, management was identified as the key means through which the public sector could be rid of staid bureaucratic structures and entrenched professional interests and transformed into a dynamic series of organizations able to deliver 'value for money'. The neo-Taylorist vision of rationalized inputs and outputs, being employed to reduce the costs of public services, became embedded in the drive to impose the three Es of *economy*, *efficiency* and *effectiveness* on all aspects of public provision. Social issues were depoliticized. Policy choices were transformed into a series of managerial decisions. Evaluations of public sector performance came to be dominated by notions of productivity, task remits and quantifiable outputs.

While the full impact of such managerial missions came relatively late to youth and criminal justice, by the 1990s the 'mean and lean' and 'more for less' mentalities gradually opened up law and order to a series of investigations from the Public Accounts Committee, the National Audit Office and the Audit Commission. Their recommendations have overwhelmingly been in support of subjugating professional skills and autonomy to management ideals of 'what works', of attaching resources to certifiable 'successful' outcomes and of devolving responsibility for law and order from a central state to a series of semi-autonomous local partnerships, voluntary agencies and privatized bodies. It is an agenda that has increasingly crossed party-political boundaries precisely because it *appears* apolitical. The removal of such 'transformative' issues as individual need, diagnosis, rehabilitation, reformation, due process and penal purpose and their replacement by actuarialism and techniques of classification, risk assessment and resource management shifts the entire terrain of law and order from one of under-standing criminal motivation to one of simply making crime tolerable through systemic co-ordination (see **Chapter 9**). As Feeley and Simon (1992, p. 454) have argued, 'by limiting their exposure to indicators that they can control, managers ensure that their problems will have solutions'. **Managerialism** represents a significant lowering of expectations in terms of what the youth justice system can be expected to achieve. Evaluation comes to rest solely on indicators of internal system performance (McLaughlin, Muncie and Hughes, 2001). The idea of 'joined-up' govern-ment to attack multi-faceted and complex problems (such as youth offend-ing) through multi-agency partnerships employing a broad spectrum of social policy interventions represents a definitive break with traditional methods of public administration. It challenges the specialization of government into discrete areas of functional expertise and, in so doing, defines new objects of governance (Newman, 2001). Youth offending, for example, ceases to be defined only in terms of 'criminality' and subject to the expertise of criminal justice professionals. It also becomes a problem of education, health, employment and, in the argot of New Labour, one of assessing the risks of 'social exclusion' and 'anti-social behaviour' (see **Chapters 7.4 and 9.1**).

In 1996, the Audit Commission published its first report on the youth justice system in England and Wales. Noting that the public services (police, legal aid, courts, social services, probation, prison) spent around £1 billion a year processing and dealing with young offenders, it argued that much of this money was wasted through lengthy and ineffective court procedures. The thrust of the report was a need to shift resources from punitive to preventive measures. It was particularly critical of youth courts: the process of prosecution taking on average four months, costing £2,500 for each young person processed and with half of the proceedings ultimately discontinued, dismissed or discharged. The system, it was argued, had no agreed national strategies and local authorities acted more as an emergency service than as a preventive one. The report recommended the diversion of a fifth of young offenders away from the courts altogether and into alternative programmes (such as Northamptonshire's Mediation and Reparation schemes) – thus saving £40 million annually on costs. In short, the Audit Commission argued that youth justice was inefficient and expensive, with little being done to deal effectively with juvenile nuisance (see Box 8.11).

Box 8.11

Audit Commission and *Misspent Youth*

The present arrangements are failing the young people – who are not being guided away from offending to constructive activities. They are also failing victims – those who suffer from some young people's inconsiderate behaviour, and from vandalism, arson and loss of property from thefts and burglaries. And they lead to waste in a variety of forms, including lost time, as public servants process the same young offenders through the courts time and again; lost rents, as people refuse to live in high crime areas; lost business, as people steer clear of troubled areas; and the waste of young people's potential. Resources need to be shifted from process-ing young offenders to dealing with their behaviour. At the same time, efforts to prevent offending and other antisocial behaviour by young people need to be co-ordinated between the different agencies involved; they should be targeted on deprived areas with high crime rates and piloted and evaluated.

Source: Audit Commission (1996, p. 96).

The Commission's priority was clearly one of 'diversion' through crime preven-tion: partly on the grounds of 'value for money' and partly because of the lack of effectiveness of formal procedures. In congruence with a corporatist model, it advocated the development of multi-agency work with parents, schools and health services acting in tandem with social services and the police. In line with managerialist objectives, the Commission argued that these goals could only be met by a clearer identification of objectives, more rigorous allocation of resources and the setting of staff priorities. The aim was to build a pragmatic strategy to prevent offending rather than wed the system to any particular broad philosophy of justice or welfare. The issue of the causes of offending was side-stepped by the identification of 'risk conditions' (factors that correlate with known offending). In the guise of 'modernization' welfare, justice and rights were eclipsed by the 'imprecise science' of risk assessment and the statutory responsibility to meet performance targets (see **Chapters 1.3, 3.1 and 9.2**). This performance manage-ment agenda prioritized cost-effective measures for the realization of specific outputs (rather than outcomes). It promoted its own 'SMART' targets, that is targets which are 'Specific', 'Measurable', 'Achievable', 'Realistic' and 'Time-tabled' (Audit Commission, 1999).

It is difficult to over-estimate the impact of this logic on the incoming Labour government of 1997. Much of the Audit Commission agenda was subsequently reflected by the *statutory* duty, imposed by the *1998 Crime and Disorder Act*, for local authorities to establish youth offending teams (a partner-ship of social service, police, probation, education and health authorities) to formulate and implement youth justice plans, setting out how youth justice services were to be provided, monitored and funded and how targets for crime reduction could be met in each local authority area. The Act also established a Youth Justice Board (YJB) to monitor the operation of the system, promote good practice and advise the Home Secretary on the setting of national standards. In particular it initiated one of Labour's five key election pledges to introduce *fast-track punishment* for persistent young offenders, by insisting that the time between arrest and sentencing be cut by half. Here Labour was clearly responding to one of the repeated concerns of the Audit Commission (1996, 1998) for more streamlined procedures, better case management and time limits for all criminal proceedings involving young people. The aim was to develop a system that was not only more efficient, but also more cost-effective.

By the late 1990s, all local authorities in England and Wales were also given the *statutory* duty to 'prevent offending by young people'. All aspects of their work have become infused with crime prevention and crime reduction responsibilities. For example, by 2000, all 154 local authorities had formulated and implemented an annual Youth Justice Plan, setting out how youth justice reform was to be funded and put into operation, and had established a YOT (youth offending team), consisting of, on a statutory basis, representatives from each of social services, probation, police, health and education authorities. These agencies were designed to 'pull together' to co-ordinate provision, to ensure each agency acted in tandem and to deliver a range of interventions and programmes that would ensure that young people 'face up to the consequences of their actions'. What were formerly youth *justice* teams (designed to divert young people from court and custody) were replaced by youth *offending* teams (designed to directly intervene in all aspects of criminal, anti-social and disorderly behaviour). In effect, the YOT displaced the statutory child care operations of social services departments (Goldson, 2000b). YOTs have clearly given local inter-agency work a more stable footing but they also operate within targets and guidelines set by the Youth Justice Board. This has issued a series of directives under the auspices of *Key Elements of Effective Practice* and in this respect the system has become both more corporatist and managerialized. YOT work is constantly scrutinized through budgetary planning and auditing for cost and effectiveness. Local Youth Justice Plans enable local agencies to be held to account for their 'success' or 'failure'. Discourses of 'best value', 'fiscal responsibility' and 'cost–benefit' proliferate within commissioning out services, annual performance assessments, targets, audits and statutory limits (Vaughan, 2000; Muncie, 2002 and see Box 8.12). Such measures are then forwarded to the Audit Commission for their consideration of whether public money is being used economically, efficiently and effectively.

In its report *Youth Justice 2004* the Audit Commission (2004) identified various improved performances such as reductions in the time between arrest and court appearance and applauded the fundamental statutory aim of the system being that of prevention. However, it also concluded that the system was becoming over-burdened with minor offences taking up court time, that intensive community programmes were under-resourced and largely ineffective and that too many offenders were still being remanded and sentenced to

| Box 8.12 |

New Labour, new managerialism and youth justice

- Recasting the past as 'failure' in order to clear the ground (despite the 'successes' of the late 1980s in reducing youth crime and custody rates).

- Identifying risk conditions, rather than causes of youth crime.

- Setting statutory time limits from arrest to sentence.

- Establishing performance targets for YOTs.

- Discovering 'what works' via evidence-based research.

- Establishing Youth Justice Board as a central body.

- Establishing YOTs to 'join up' local agencies.

- Establishing statutory obligation on local authorities to 'prevent offending by young people'.

- Establishing means of measuring levels of risk (e.g. by formulating standardized assessment tools).

- Disseminating efficient practice via communication.

Source: Muncie and Hughes (2002, pp. 5–6).

custody. The continuance of elements of authoritarian and racialized injustice were also cited as areas in which 'more could be done'. The YJB annual report for 2006/07 acknowledged that its key targets of having 'fewer first time entrants' in the system and 'reducing offending' were 'at risk' and that a third target of 'reducing the use of custody' was 'highly unlikely to be met'. Further, an independent audit carried out by Solomon and Garside (2008) found that although spending on youth justice since 2000 had increased by 45 per cent, there had been little or no effect on re-offending rates. It concluded that virtually every target relating to education, training, drug abuse, mental health, re-offending rates and reductions in rates of custody had been missed. This suggested that the inter-agency 'joined up' approach might not be working as intended.

Reconstituting Welfare?

Given the developments outlined above, the welfare vs. justice debate may now be considered to be particularly moribund, especially too as neither model has been fully realized in practice and has typically resulted in 'unintended' consequences. However, the remnants of the debate remain with us. Youth justice has evolved into a complex patchwork of processes and disposals, drawing upon welfare and justice, but also inflected with degrees of retribution, rehabilitation, restoration, punishment, prevention and reintegration (see **Chapters 7 and 9**). Each has a constantly shifting presence as political priorities, central directives and local initiatives veer from one position to another. In the circumstances of a 'new punitiveness' since the early 1990s, it is not surprising to find political credibility returning to those who have long sought to reinforce the principle of welfare in the processing of young offenders. Davies (1982), for example, had argued that the failures of welfare were not due to the goals and practices of welfare *per se* but in the main to partial implementation and lack of political commitment. Cullen and Gilbert (1982) have always maintained that welfarism remains an essential route through which the state can be forced to recognize that it has an obligation to care for offenders' welfare and needs. Scraton and Haydon (2002) have argued for the pursuance of policies that are simultaneously based on recognizing welfare need and protecting those needs through children's rights instruments: a welfare-based positive rights agenda.

Certainly in governmental terms 'welfare' has also been used as one legitimation for prioritizing a crime prevention agenda. It has been consistently maintained that there is no contradiction between protecting children in trouble and preventing offending. In policy terms, the framework of *Every Child Matters* includes the aim of preventing crime alongside that of recognizing children's social and personal needs (see **Chapter 7.4**). The 2004 *Children Act* also established the duty of every local authority to form Children's Trusts through which the *Every Child Matters* agenda of health, safety, achievement, well-being and positive contribution was to be delivered through integrated services for *all* children including those in the youth justice system. In organizational terms, part of the remit for youth justice was moved from the Home Office to a new Department for Children, Schools and Families in 2007. In practitioner terms, Burnett and Appleton (2004) and Field's (2007) interviews with YOT members also revealed that the logics of prevention, early intervention and risk assessment were not simply received as punitive or technocratic but were being *subjectively* utilized to maintain welfare as a key aim and to justify the continuing relevance of social work to achieve that aim (see **Chapter 10.4**). For some, such developments can signal a 'socialization of crime policy', enough at least to qualify the 'criminalization of social policy' thesis (see **Chapter 7.4**) (Hughes, 2007; Hughes et al., 2007).

However, in other regards, a distancing of the system – both in England and Wales, and Scotland – from explicit welfare goals is apparent. The minimal intervention ethos of the 1980s has been replaced by a more heavily circumscribed targeting of 'risks for early intervention'. This 'new rehabilitation' is also much more focused on individual responsibility and offender accountability in an attempt to escape the populist condemnation that it is not 'yet another sign' of 'being soft on crime'. The companion document to *Every Child Matters* – titled *Youth Justice: The Next Steps* (Home Office, 2003b) – showed little sign of integrating youth justice into mainstream children's services. Rather, it proposed that any remaining statutory aim to 'take account of welfare' or 'ensure just deserts' be replaced by that of 'preventing offending'. In short, offenders were still to be viewed as offenders first and children (often with serious welfare problems) second. An ongoing debate has also been directed at whether the YJB is most appropriately located in the criminal justice sector at all. Although the reorganization of governmental departments in 2007 shifted the lines of accountability from the Home Office and (partially) to the newly formed Department for Children, Schools and Families, it remained the case that three-quarters of the YJB budget remained in the hands of a (also newly formed) Ministry of Justice in order to finance the juvenile secure estate.

In these ways the justice/welfare debate continues to play itself out in myriad complex and contradictory ways. There is a certain circulatory element to such debates. Welfare and justice are often employed as justificatory devices without either being in any way achieved. The meaning of both remains somewhat illusory. The argument of welfare *versus* justice may also be seriously misplaced given that both have produced highly oppressive outcomes in the past. As a result, Smith (2005) and Allen (2006) have concluded that now is the time to finally move beyond this traditional binary and to rethink the principles of youth justice through a different lens of 'inclusion', 'reconciliation' or 'problem solving'.

■ Summary ■

- The concept of 'need', associated with welfare models of intervention, attempts to address problems either of destitution and delinquency through moral reformation (the nineteenth-century version) or perceived psychosocial disorders through counselling and social work (the 1960s version). It also surfaces obliquely in the alleviating of 'risk conditions' through 'opportunities' and retraining (the current version).

- Justice-based models stress the importance of rights (the liberal version) or just deserts and self-responsibility (the conservative version). In both, intervention is aimed at tackling the offence, rather than its mitigating circumstances.

- Neither welfare (meeting needs) nor justice (responding to deeds) is ever present in pure form. The youth justice system contains elements of both, thus ensuring that a complex, ambiguous and confused *mélange* of policies and practices exists at any one time. Both also have unintended consequences: welfarism leading to over-regulation (particularly of girls); justice leading to the abandonment of 'meeting individual needs' (particularly as appropriated by the right in the 1990s).

- Corporatist and managerial strategies have emerged since the 1970s which appear less interested in 'best interests' or 'protecting rights' and more concerned with achieving cost-effective, pragmatic and tangible outcomes. Wider goals of welfare or justice have become submerged in a more pragmatic and managerial assessment of 'what works'.

- While the welfare versus justice debate may provide a useful starting point to understand youth justice systems, it restricts analysis to the internal machinations of the system itself. We can question how far either ideal can be realized when both remain absent from, or are peripheral to, social relations elsewhere.

study Questions

1   What is the purpose of youth justice?

2   How did concerns for 'welfare' and 'justice' impact on the delivery of youth justice in the UK in the twentieth century?

3   Has welfare been completely removed from modern youth justice systems?

4   To what extent can the introduction of principles of 'justice' into youth justice policy in the 1970s and 1980s be considered a progressive or repressive development?

5   How far have managerial and corporatist techniques delivered a 'new' youth justice in the twenty-first century?

■ ■ Further Reading ■

There are numerous reviews of post-war developments in juvenile and youth justice in England and Wales: Harris and Webb's (1987) *Welfare, Power and Juvenile Justice*, Gelsthorpe and Morris's (1994) chapter 'Juvenile justice 1945–1992', and Pitts's (1988) *The Politics of Juvenile Crime* are all well worth consulting. Hudson's (1987) *Justice through Punishment* provides a radical critique of both welfare and justice strategies.

The Audit Commission's report's *Misspent Youth* (1996) and *Youth Justice 2004* (2004) are clear examples of how managerial solutions can be embedded in youth justice. For critical commentaries on youth justice post-1997 in England and Wales, see Goldson and Muncie's (2006) edited collection *Youth, Crime and Justice*. For critical commentaries on developments in Scotland, see the article by Piacentini and Walters (2006) and the chapter by McAra (2006).

Muncie, Hughes and McLaughlin's edited collection *Youth Justice: Critical Readings* (2002) brings together many of the classic texts with contemporary commentaries. Goldson's *Dictionary of Youth Justice* (2008b) is an invaluable source of information on legislative powers, practice issues and theoretical concerns which does more than most to make sense of the complexity of modern youth justice not just in England and Wales but also Scotland and Northern Ireland.

The journal *Youth Justice: An International Journal* is the only UK-based criminology journal to focus specifically on youth justice issues.

http://www.audit-commission.gov.uk
The site of the Audit Commission providing access to its assessments of youth justice in England and Wales.

http://www.yjb.gov.uk/en-gb/
The site of the youth justice board for England and Wales with access to many of its on-line reports, and details of contemporary powers and procedures.

http://www.homeoffice.gov.uk/crime-victims/reducing-crime/youth-crime/
The Home Office site dedicated to reducing youth crime and improving youth justice.

http://www.youthjusticescotland.gov.uk/
The Youth Justice and Children's Hearings Division site, part of the Children Young People and Social Care Group of the Education Department at the Scottish Executive.

http://www.youthjusticeagencyni.gov.uk/
Site of the youth justice agency in Northern Ireland.

http://www.yjb.gov.uk/en-gb/News/AllWalesYouthOffendingStrategy.htm
The All Wales youth offending strategy.

9

Youth Justice Strategies II: Prevention and Punishment

Overview

Chapter 9 examines:

- the complex of initiatives associated with the 'new' youth justice established in England and Wales in 1998;

- the impact of the statutory requirement that all involved in the youth justice system should aim to 'prevent offending';

- the meaning of evidence-based policy and the principles of 'what works';

- the nature of actuarial justice;

- experiments in restorative justice;

- the use of community-based 'disposals' and the meaning of 'punishment in the community';

- the nature and extent of juvenile incarceration;

- contradictions between preventive and punitive policies and practices;

- the record of the UK in complying with international children's rights directives.

| **key terms** |

actuarialism; bifurcation; cognitive behaviourism; community safety; early intervention; evidence-based policy; punishment in the community; rehabilitation; reparation; responsibilization; restoration; retribution; situational crime prevention; social crime prevention; 'what works'; youth custody

---

Youth justice in England and Wales in the twenty-first century has evolved into a particularly complex state of affairs. It is designed to punish the offender while keeping their welfare paramount. It is at one and the same time about crime prevention and retribution. It makes claims for restoration and reintegration while seeking some of the most punitive measures of surveillance and containment in custodial and community settings. It targets those believed to be 'at risk' as well as the convicted. It is delivered by an ostensibly joined-up series of agencies concerned with health and education as well as criminal justice. It is clouded in layers of rhetoric whereby locking up the young is for their training or controlling their 'cultural space' is for their welfare. Above all, it is the gradual accretion of numerous initiatives that have emerged over two centuries.

But the 'new' has never replaced the old. In the twenty-first century discourses of protection, restoration, punishment, responsibility, rehabilitation, welfare, justice, retribution, diversion, human rights, just deserts and prevention exist alongside each other in some perpetually uneasy and contradictory manner. The perpetual tension between welfare and justice was discussed in **Chapter 8**. This chapter is designed to further unravel this complexity by focussing particular attention on the 'shallow end' (that is, early intervention) and the 'deep end' (that is, incarceration) aspects of the system. Doing so reveals more of the fundamental ongoing tensions within youth justice: that of simultaneously *preventing* and *punishing* behaviour. While the former is forward-looking and designed to anticipate *future* law-breaking, the latter is backward-looking in responding to *past* offences.

Crime Prevention

9.1 The logic that youth justice systems should prevent crime is one of their most long-standing principles (see **Chapter 2**). However, the issue has been given a more focussed and sustained attention from policy-makers and academics alike since the latter decades of the twentieth century. In part, this has been driven by increases in the technological capability to 'harden targets' with 'bolts, locks and barriers', but arguably more significantly by governmental recognition that the institutions of criminal justice are ill equipped to control crime or to rehabilitate offenders on their own. The idea of prevention then has drawn a host of new actors from public and private bodies and from statutory, voluntary, and commercial agencies, into the 'business of crime control'. Multi-agency partnerships have proliferated; local communities, it is argued, have been empowered. This 'preventive turn' has opened up new discourses of 'community safety', 'harm minimization', 'crime and disorder reduction', 'risk management', 'private security' and 'responsibilization' into the crime control arena (Hughes, 2007). The notion of **responsibilization** in particular reflects a shift of primary responsibility for crime prevention and public security away from the state and towards businesses, organizations, individuals, families and communities (Garland, 1996, 2001). Significantly it has developed alongside governments' critique of state dependency and its withdrawal from universal measures of state protection and welfare support. It coalesces with a number of related developments whereby aspects of youth justice have come to reflect market-like conditions and processes; their welfarist core has been eroded; elements of the system have become privatized and access to resources made dependent on acting 'responsibly'.

Two preventive logics, in particular, have come to the fore since the 1980s: *situational* crime prevention and *social* crime prevention.

Situational and Social Crime Prevention

It is widely assumed that most youth crime is opportunistic and that crime rates can be effectively reduced through environmental design, target hardening and situation management. In Britain, the impetus for **situational crime prevention** stemmed from a Home Office research study, *Crime as Opportunity*

(Mayhew et al., 1976), which showed that certain crimes (for example, car theft) could be reduced by the fitting of security devices (such as steering wheel locks). In the following years a series of studies concluded that personal security could be improved by a vast array of risk avoidance measures. But it was not until the early 1980s that the concept of situational prevention was fully realized in practice and political discourse. The reasons for its re-emergence were myriad – the most significant being the clear failure of law enforcement policies to have any effect on crime rates. In England and Wales recorded crime had continued to grow at the rate of about 6 per cent per annum. The rhetoric of 'getting tough' began to look increasingly thin. In tandem, rapidly escalating costs to administer expanded criminal justice systems appeared to deliver a poor cost-effective return. Researchers in the USA and the UK began to look elsewhere to discover what might 'work', including: social and spatial analysis of the places (hot spots) where crime was most likely to occur; and 'defensible space' theorizing which asserted that good architectural design could 'design out' some forms of criminality. The focus on these issues shifted attention away from the personal or social circumstances of the offender and towards the *opportunities* and *circumstances* surrounding the commission of different criminal acts. Underpinning this 'administrative crimi-nology' was rational choice theory (see **Chapter 4.2**). For a crime to occur, it was argued, two events must coincide: the opportunity for the commission of the criminal act must present itself; and the individual must decide that the gains to be had from taking the opportunity outweigh both the chances of being caught and the penalty should s/he be apprehended. Ron Clarke, a former researcher at the UK's Home Office, and Ray Jeffery, an American criminologist, were at the forefront of promoting this pragmatic vision of crime prevention. From Jeffery came the concept of 'crime prevention through environmental design' (CPTED); from Clarke came the notions of rational choice and situa-tional prevention. Clarke (1992) argued that many crimes could be effectively designed out if we take the trouble to adequately protect ourselves and our property. Such an approach to crime prevention has proved to be a remarkable political and commercial success.

These technological and scientific 'solutions' were complemented by techniques of **social crime prevention** and community safety. In general, these placed more emphasis on changing offender behaviour and promoting social inclusion through community engagement. The recognition that situational measures needed the compliance and participation of a wide range of public and private institutions and central and local decision-making bodies and could be carried out through a variety of voluntary agencies and individual action, opened the door for notions of *community crime prevention* to enter the political arena. In England and Wales an interdepartmental circular of 1984 was issued by central government and sent to all chief constables and local authority chief executives encouraging them to co-ordinate their resources in the prevention of crime. Through this initiative the concept of *inter-agency co-operation* was realized. Community crime prevention in England and Wales first materialized in the 1986 Five Towns initiative, the 1987 Safer Cities programme, and in 1991 was redefined as **community safety** through the influential Home Office report *Safer Communities* (the Morgan Report). While the precise constitution of 'communities' remained unclear, the invitation to involve non-criminal justice agencies clearly held the potential to expand the concept of crime prevention into numerous elements of social policy such as housing allocation, welfare rights, employment opportunities, youth clubs and the provision of diversionary activities for young people (see **Chapter 7.4**).

This aspiration of 'socializing criminal justice policy' was also held by the school of left realism also emerging in the 1980s. It argued that the structural factors that give rise to offending – especially relative deprivation – must be acknowledged and confronted, not just ignored. For left realists: 'good jobs with a discernible future, housing estates of which tenants can be proud, community facilities which enhance a sense of cohesion and belonging, a reduction in unfair income inequalities, all create a society which is more cohesive and less criminogenic' (Young, 1994, pp. 115–16, and see **Chapter 4.2**). More specifically, social crime prevention measures tend to prioritise 'early intervention' on the basis that it is better to tackle the causes before crime occurs rather than have to deal with consequences afterwards (Matthews and Young, 1992, p. 102). This might include, for example, schemes targeted at teaching young people the dangers of carrying knives or of using drugs. Through listening to local communities (via the victim survey) left realism was also able to bring attention to the core concerns of working-class communities which typically were directed at anti-social and nuisance as well as criminal behaviours.

Many of left realism's ideas and proposals were taken up by the incoming Labour government of 1997 and reworked so that they complemented those of situational crime prevention. The *1998 Crime and Disorder Act* placed a statutory duty on local authorities, the police, health authorities and probation to work together to reduce problems of crime and disorder in their area. In turn, this coalesced with the reformulation of the purpose of youth justice in England and Wales by defining its statutory aim as the *prevention* of offending. Pre-existing philosophical disputes between care/welfare/protection, on the one hand, and control/justice/punishment on the other were put aside (see **Chapter 8**). In 1999, Crime and Disorder Reduction Partnerships were established to implement programmes on the basis of 'what works' and to mainstream 'best practice'. Disorder reduction became almost synonymous with zero tolerance crusades against 'anti-social youth'. Between 1997 and 2008 a wide range of legislative, policy and practice initiatives precipitated industrial-scale growth in the youth and criminal justice systems of England and Wales (see Box 9.1). The sheer volume and speed of pilot schemes, action plans, targets, 'crackdowns', initiatives and legislative activity have indeed been remarkable. The 'preventive turn' has allowed a raft of initiatives to be targeted at disorderly, anti-social and nuisance behaviour as well as the criminal. It has drawn many aspects of social, health and employment policies into a crime reduction agenda (see **Chapter 7.4**). Collectively these initiatives have been heralded as marking the most radical 'shake-up' of the youth justice system in a century.

Box 9.1

Developments in youth justice legislation, policy and practice, 1998–2008 (England and Wales)

1998 Crime and Disorder Act
Reprimands and final warnings; anti-social behaviour orders; parenting orders; action plan orders; child safety orders; reparation orders; drug treatment and testing orders; detention and training orders # Parenting classes

1999 Youth Justice and Criminal Evidence Act
Referral orders

2000 Criminal Justice and Court Services Act
Exclusion orders; increased penalties for parents of truanting children

2000 Powers of the Criminal Courts (Sentencing) Act
Section 90/91 consolidates 1933 Act: Detention of 10 to17 year olds for more than 2 years; electronic monitoring of 10 year olds

2000 Youth Inclusion Programme
Targeted at those 13 to 16 year olds most 'at risk' of truancy, offending or exclusion

2001 Criminal Justice and Police Act
New offence of 'aggravated truancy'; extended powers to remand in custody; penalty notices for disorder for over-16 year olds

2001 Intensive Supervision and Surveillance Programme
Targeted at serious or persistent offenders either as an element of a supervision order or as part of a detention and training order

2002 Police Reform Act
Interim anti-social behaviour orders

2003 Anti-Social Behaviour Act
Dispersal orders; age restrictions on sale of aerosol paint; fixed penalty notices for low-level disorder; powers to confiscate noisy stereos and televisions

2003 Criminal Justice Act
Extended drug testing to children; extended parenting orders; individual support orders: 'Positive conditions' attached to anti-social behaviour orders; increased sentencing powers: 'extended sentences' and 'detention for public protection'

2004 Children Act
Enacted *Every Child Matters* agenda; established Children's Commissioner for England and Wales

(Continued)

(Continued)

2004 Youth Inclusion and Support Panels
Targeted at 8 to 13 year olds considered 'at risk' of offending

2005 Serious Organised Crime and Police Act
Abolished anonymity of children if an anti-social behaviour order is breached

2005 Clean Neighbourhoods and Environment Act.
Fixed penalty notices for minor 'environmental' disorder for 10 year olds and above

2006 Police and Justice Act
Extended range of agencies that can apply for parenting and anti-social behaviour orders. Extended conditional caution to attach punitive conditions

2006 The Respect Action Plan
Formal advocacy of early intervention to tackle anti-social behaviour

2007 Offender Management Act
Expanded range of secure facilities available to the youth justice board: to be known as 'youth detention accommodation'

2008 Criminal Justice and Immigration Act
Extended the use of conditional cautions; new generic community sentence: the Youth Rehabilitation Order; new powers to tackle anti-social behaviour

2008 Youth Crime Action Plan
A 'triple track' initiative advocating tougher enforcement and punishment, targeted earlier intervention and non-negotiable intensive parenting support

As Hughes (2002) records, the rise of the 'preventive turn' has been exponential and raises the possibility of moving from narrow law and order agendas to more generalized visions of 'harm reduction' in the pursuit of social justice. Yet the vagary of all such terms – crime prevention, crime reduction, community safety, harm minimization – also renders the field open to a continually contested politics. Youth crime prevention remains a poor relation to the dominance of technological surveillance measures which suggest a contrary 'anti-social' world of fortified exclusionary spaces. It also has to work within an authoritarian climate in which recourse to overtly punitive measures of control seem to be increasingly sought after. An obsession with 'prevention' may also simply act to draw all manner of 'nuisances' under official gaze (Hughes et al., 2002).

Pre-emptive Early Intervention

More than anything else early intervention is crucial ... recent advances in our knowledge have offered the promise that we might achieve it. We also now know how to protect people against these risks. We can now be reasonably confident that we can identify likely problems at a very early stage.

(http://www.number-10.gov.uk/output/Page10036.asp)

In 2006, Tony Blair thus announced that criminality could be predicted at a very early age, indeed even pre-birth, and that we now know what works to prevent it. Such ideas are of course by no means new but were given added political impetus by renewed interest in the Cambridge Study of Delinquent Development (see **Chapter 1.3**). The identification of poor child rearing, hyperactivity, low intelligence, harsh or erratic parental discipline, and so on as major risk factors have encouraged numerous authors (Utting, 1996; Sherman et al., 1997; Graham, 1998; Youth Justice Board, 2005; Farrington and Welsh, 2007) to claim that the 'most hopeful' methods to tackle crime and anti-social behaviour are those which involve a series of early interventions (see Box 9.2). The key influence was that of the Perry pre-school programme in Michigan, USA. This experiment began in the 1970s and provided 60 African American 3–5 year olds with high quality nursery education. Their development was compared to a control group who did not have such support. 20 years later, 30 per cent of the experimental group had been arrested at least once compared to 50 per cent of the control group.

Box 9.2

Methods of crime prevention through early intervention

- Home visiting by health professionals to give advice on infant development, nutrition and alcohol and drug avoidance in order to reduce parental child abuse.

- Pre-school 'intellectual enrichment' programmes in nurseries to stimulate thinking and reasoning skills in young children (based on the High/Scope Perry Pre-School Program in Michigan).

- Parenting education programmes.

- Cognitive and social skills training to teach children to consider the consequences of their behaviour.

- Teacher training and anti-bullying initiatives in schools.

Source: Derived from Farrington and Welsh (2007).

It is claimed that this evidence is replicable globally (Farrington, 2000). But it also seems to tell us that if we grant the necessary educational and economic resources to socially and economically deprived families, then their children are likely to benefit. However, when attached to a preoccupation with law and order, it is typically read as the need to discipline 'failing families' (Pitts, 2001, p. 97). The closest equivalent in the UK is the Sure Start programme targeting families with children under the age of 4 in disadvantaged areas. Its impact has been mixed with ethnic minority and 'hard to reach' families being 'difficult to engage' (Burnett, 2007). Further, it continues the ideology that social exclusion can only be tackled in primarily individual and instrumental terms (Clarke, 2006, and see **Chapter 7**).

Low-level disorder and incivilities have always been a major New Labour target. One of the most radical initiatives of its reforming agenda was the availability of new civil orders and powers that can be made other than as a sentence. This 'civilianization of law' is both welfarist and moralizing in tone (Hughes, 2002, p. 129). Child safety orders, local child curfews and anti-social behaviour orders, for example, do not necessarily require either the prosecution or indeed the commission of a criminal offence. *Child safety orders* can be made by a family proceedings court on a child below the age of 10 if that child is considered 'at risk'. Justified as a 'protective' measure, it places the child under the supervision of a social worker or a member of a youth offending team for a period of up to 12 months. The court can specify certain requirements such as attending specified programmes or avoiding particular places and people. Breach may result in the substitution of a care order under the powers of the *1989 Children Act*. In this respect child safety orders further dismantle the relevance of the age of criminal responsibility (at age 10, England and Wales already sets this at a lower level than any other western European country, except Scotland – see **Chapter 10.2**). In addition, local authorities can, after consultation with the police and local community, introduce a *local child curfew* to apply to *all* children under the age of 10 in a specific area. This places a ban on unsupervised children being in a specified area between 9 p.m. and 6 a.m. The reach of such curfews was extended to 15 year olds in 2001, although it remains significant that by 2008 no local authority had ever evoked such a power. The police attempted to do so in Corby, Northants, in 2003 but failed to get local authority backing. A 'voluntary' scheme was introduced in Redruth, Cornwall, in 2008. However, with the introduction of dispersal orders in 2004 (see **Chapter 7.4**), their specific role seemed to be usurped. In 2000, Youth Inclusion Programmes were introduced aimed at 'high risk' under-18 year olds in 110 'high crime' neighbourhoods and designed to promote 'positive attitudes'. By 2008, however, it was unclear if they were implicated in the failure to reduce the number of 'first time entrants' coming into the youth justice system. In 2003, Youth Inclusion and Support Panels were added to this list: here targeting resources and support at a younger age group of 8 to 13 year old 'high-risk' children.

The policy and practice of 'early intervention' are predicated on the notion that crime can be pre-empted by being 'nipped in the bud' through the identification of 'risky' personal or family traits. These may include pregnant teenage mothers (UNBORN BABIES TARGETED IN CRACKDOWN ON CRIMINALITY, *Guardian*, 16 May 2007) or a specified number of 'badly behaved children' (DOCTORS AND SCHOOLS TO SPOT 1000 CHILDREN AT RISK OF TURNING TO CRIME, *Guardian*, 19 March 2008). Such logic appears to be insatiable in identifying 'risk conditions' and behaviours ripe for 'prevention'. Access to welfare or urban regeneration resources often then appears dependent on there being some assumed crime prevention pay-off. Vulnerable children, it seems, have to be identified as potentially criminal before resources will be released for their care. Pre-emptive intervention intensifies the processes of scrutiny and surveillance to which children and families are subjected. It constructs a population of permanent suspects based on a pre-specified number of risks, including low intelligence, poor parenting, impulsive behaviour, family criminality, and so on. The attempt to predict risk takes precedence over the evidence (or lack of it) of offending behaviour (Smith, 2006). Wider nets with thinner mesh can clearly lead to over-prediction and increased criminalization. It is not unknown for risk assessments to produce up to 50 per cent 'false-positive' rates. As Smith (2006) argues, this is no better than tossing a coin. Moves to allow a wider range of bodies (including resident groups, parish councils and community panels) to initiate civil proceedings also allow for an expansion of the means through which criminalization can eventually be secured. Criminal law appears to be increasingly turned to for the resolution of social problems. But an obsession with risk factors and evidence-based analysis fails to address the complex inter-related problems of poverty, racism, urban degeneration and social inequality which may lie behind much anti-social or disorderly behaviour. It also encourages criminalization rather than prevention. Repeated and intensive interventions by formal agencies, whatever their child-centred or punitive rhetoric, 'may be more damaging to young people in the longer term' than applying principles of minimal intervention and maximum diversion (McAra and McVie, 2007, and see **Chapter 8**).

Such processes have been described as involving a significant 'criminalizing of social policy' (see **Chapter 7.4**). Goldson (2002a) put it particularly well:

> To gain access to welfare services, or perhaps more accurately to be 'targeted' by an 'intervention', children and families must be seen to have 'failed' or be 'failing', to be 'posing risk', to be 'threatening'. Prior notions of universality and welfare for *all* children 'in need', have retreated into a context of classification, control and correction where interventions are targeted at the 'criminal', the 'near criminal', the 'possibly criminal', the 'sub-criminal', the 'anti-social', the 'disorderly' or the 'potentially problematic' in some way or another.

The Anti-Social Behaviour Agenda

The concept of anti-social behaviour has typically come to refer to myriad issues such as youths hanging about causing trouble, nuisance neighbours, noise, vandalism, litter, graffiti and drunkenness. Governmental concern over the anti-social rapidly rose to prominence in the 1990s, particularly (and almost exclusively) in the UK. In other countries, such as the USA, where similar concerns have been expressed, legislation has tended to be more specifically targeted, say, at providing for gang injunctions. Rather, in the UK, it has regularly reoccurred as a central governmental motif and appears inextricably bound up with New Labour's politics of crime and disorder (Squires, 2006). Legislating against the anti-social has emerged as much a priority in Ireland, Scotland and Northern Ireland as it has in England and Wales.

During the early 1990s, New Labour's challenge to Conservative dominance in the area of law and order was orchestrated through a distinct 'third way' that would be 'tough on crime and tough on the causes of crime'. In particular, New Labour sought to strengthen the capacity of the criminal justice system to deal with disorder and incivilities as well as more serious crime on the grounds that a 'rising tide of disorder' was blighting neighbourhoods and was itself a precursor to more serious crime. The police and the courts were characterized as impotent to act against 'nuisance' and the 'anti-social', and consequently disorder was indulged in with impunity. Second, at the heart of the agenda was a desire not just to reduce crime and disorder, but to promote a process of 'civil renewal' and 'civic responsibility'. Third, in congruence with Wilson and Kelling's (1982) 'broken windows' thesis, it was widely assumed that failure to adopt 'zero tolerance' policing of minor offending and signs of disorder would encourage the further deterioration and disintegration of already deprived and marginalized communities (see **Chapter 7**).

One of the first official publications that set out New Labour policy specifically in the area of anti-social behaviour was the consultation paper, *A Quiet Life: Tough on Criminal Neighbours*, published two years before they came to power in 1997. Here, the issue was initially constructed in terms of 'neighbours from hell' and demand for legislative action intrinsically connected to housing management and calls from social landlords for stronger powers to use against troublesome tenants (Brown, 2004; Burney, 2005). At the time Conservative proposals for 'probationary' tenancies culminated in new enforcement powers in the 1996 *Housing Act*. New Labour's subsequent proposed new legislative power for dealing with social housing tenants, the *Community Safety Order* (later to be renamed as the anti-social behaviour order), was primarily directed at what was then commonly termed 'anti-social *criminal* behaviour'. The *Anti-social Behaviour Order* (ASBO) was introduced in the flagship *1998 Crime and Disorder Act*. It is a civil (rather than criminal) order but can be made by the police/local authority on anyone over the age of 10 whose behaviour is *thought likely* to cause alarm, distress or harassment. Orders last a minimum of two years. Breach is considered a criminal offence and can be punishable by up to two years imprisonment for juveniles and five years for adults. Further, some local authorities (notably Islington in 1999) began experimenting with *Acceptable Behaviour Contracts* (ABCs) directed at even lower levels of nuisance and targeting those below the age of 10. If so identified, a child or young person must agree to undertake activities to change their behaviour, as formulated by a local youth offending team (YOT) and their parents.

From its inception, legislating against the anti-social has been subject to a barrage of criticism such as its ill-defined nature, its merging of civil and criminal law, its net-widening potential, its criminalization of the non-criminal, the reliance on perceptions rather than proof and its exclusionary effects (Ashworth et al., 1998). While early guidance inferred that ASBOs were intended as measures primarily to be used against adult 'nuisance neighbours', such an assumption was later abandoned. Young people, particularly those living in 'high crime sink' estates gradually became the core target. In Campbell's (2002) Home Office review, 58 per cent were made on under-18 year olds and a further 16 per cent on those aged between 18 and 21. The 'anti-social' became almost synonymous with public perceptions of problems with young people. However, rather than 'nipping crime in the bud' ASBOs served to criminalize non-criminal behaviour. Up to 50 per cent of ASBOs were being breached thereby holding the potential to accelerate routes into custody. In 2000, over half of those sentenced in court for breach received a custodial sentence (Campbell, 2002). ASBOwatch, an organization set up to monitor the use of such orders in England and Wales, reported in 2005 that 45 per cent were made against juveniles, of which 42 per cent were breached and that 46 per cent of those breaching were then given an immediate custodial order. It estimated that around 50 juveniles were being incarcerated through this route every month (www.statewatch.org/asbo/ASBOwatch – accessed July 2005).

The initial take up of ASBOs was, however, fairly slow, and with wide geographical variation (Burney, 2002). In 2001, 350 were issued but rising to 3,440 in 2004 and 4,060 in 2005. Some areas, such as Greater Manchester, appeared to 'trailblaze' the initiative, while in others, such as Dyfed Powys, it was almost ignored (Home Office, 2006). These subsequent rises can in part be explained by renewed governmental effort to keep anti-social behaviour at the head of its campaigning and legislative agenda. In September 2003, the Home Office attempted a 'one day count' of anti-social behaviour which was then extrapolated to estimate that there would be over 13 million instances per year. Teenagers hanging about the streets together with speeding traffic, illegal car parking and rubbish/litter have consistently emerged as the foremost issues identified by those who consider anti-social behaviour to be a problem in their area. The 2003 White Paper – *Respect and Responsibility* (Home Office, 2003a) – extended police and local authority powers to confiscate stereos, to criminalize begging, to give fixed penalties for 'disorderly' 16 and 17 year olds and to ban the sale of spray paints and fireworks to those under 18. Significantly it granted groups other than the police, including private security guards, the power to issue fines. The paper argued that 'fundamentally, anti-social behaviour is caused by a lack of respect for other people'. Moreover, the blame for a large proportion of anti-social behaviour was laid at the door of a small number of 'dysfunctional families' where 'respect is absent'. The *Anti-Social Behaviour Act 2003* that followed heralded the introduction of a further range of enforcement-led interventions including Parenting Contracts, Fixed Penalty Notices and Dispersal Orders (see **Chapter 7**). The police were granted further powers of 'dispersal' to remove under-16 year olds from public places if they 'believe' that a member of the public 'might be' 'intimidated, harassed, alarmed or distressed'. If two or more young people, together in a public place, fail to disperse under the instruction of a police officer, they commit a criminal offence. The 2003 Act also made the parents of children regarded as 'disorderly', 'anti-social' or 'criminally inclined', eligible targets for formal statutory orders (see Box 9.3).

Box 9.3

Powers of the *Anti-social Behaviour Act 2003*

- Fixed penalty fines for a wide range of low level disorders including graffiti, fly-posting and litter. The power to fine held by community safety officers, street wardens, private security guards and others, as well as the police.

- Powers to confiscate noisy stereos and televisions.

- Police power to disperse groups of two or more young people on the street.

- Fines and parenting orders for parents of disorderly children.

- Begging made a recordable offence.

- Ban on airguns and replica guns.

- Ban on selling spray paint to under-16s.

- Local authority powers to close noisy pubs and clubs.

- Media allowed to name 'anti-social' children.

- Kerb crawlers to lose driving licences.

- Community justice 'mini-courts' to deal with low level disorder.

- Closure of 'crack houses' within 48 hours.

Subsequently, the *Serious Organised Crime and Police Act 2005* removed legal safeguards protecting the anonymity of children who breached the terms of their ASBO so that they could be publicly 'named and shamed'. In 2006, a further commitment to encouraging and enforcing 'respect' was rolled out in *The Respect Action Plan*. Elements of this plan were included in the *Police and Justice Act 2006*, including a new mechanism – the 'community call for action' – to allow communities to directly request police action and extending the range of agencies that can be involved in parenting contracts to include housing officers and social landlords. The *Respect Action Plan* was built around notions of 'acceptable behaviour', 'safer, stronger communities' and the need for 'local leadership'. Yet the focus remained almost exclusively on changing the behaviour of young people and improving parenting, by legal enforcement if necessary. Despite a seemingly broad-based agenda of 'respect', a multitude of social problems, including those, for example, related to discrimination, economic disadvantage and social deprivation seemed ignored.

By the end of 2006, over 12,500 ASBOs, and 25,000 acceptable behaviour contracts, had been issued. The first major independent study into the use of ASBOs on young people did, however, raise some serious questions. Research for the Youth Justice Board (2006) looked at those issued to under-18 year olds in ten areas of England and Wales between January 2004 and January 2005. It concluded that while YOT practitioners tended to view ASBOs as having little positive impact on behaviour, police and local authorities typically considered them to be effective (See Box 9.4).

Box 9.4

The use of anti-social behaviour orders

- Wide geographical variation in the use of ASBOs (the most prominent area being Greater Manchester).

- Almost half of the young people (49 per cent) had breached their ASBOs at least once. Breach is a criminal offence.

- 22 per cent of young people given ASBOs are black or Asian – two and a half times the proportion of people from ethnic minorities in England and Wales.

- Many young people did not understand the restrictions placed upon them by their ASBO.

- The overuse of ASBOs has led many youngsters to regard them as a 'badge of honour'.

Source: Derived from Youth Justice Board (2007).

ASBOs have always attracted inordinate controversy and criticism. Sections of the media have delighted in some of their more bizarre applications: such as that issued to a farmer who failed to keep his pigs and geese under control. Campaign groups have brought attention to its inconsistent use and draconian qualities: such as the 14 year old in Manchester who was banned from putting his hood up except in bad weather on the basis that 'his face should be seen and not hidden', or the 13 year old who was banned from using the word 'grass' anywhere in England and Wales (Asboconcern/ NAPO 2005). Academics have argued that such 'precautionary injustice' (Squires and Stephen, 2005) simply 'defines deviance up', with the paradoxical result that public tolerance to nuisance is progressively lowered and public fear of young people significantly increased (Young and Matthews, 2003). Because of its ill-defined and potentially all-encompassing nature (see, for example, Harradine et al., 2004) it is impossible to know if anti-social behaviour is ever going up or down. Moreover it is abundantly clear that it targets the behaviour of the marginalized rather than the anti-social behaviour, say, of those that pollute the environment for profit or are involved in multi-million pound pension swindles (Matthews, 2003). By 2007, a major concern was the high rate of non-compliance with orders. Breach rates were over 60 per cent. Just as significantly, reports started to emerge that ASBOs were no deterrent, rather they were actively sought after as 'badges of honour'. Soon after Blair's departure from Downing Street in 2007 the Respect Taskforce was dismantled. Ten years after their arrival, ASBOs appeared on the brink of failure with ministers urging greater use of (rhetorically less draconian) parenting orders and contracts instead (*Guardian*, 9 May 2008). But attempts to enforce 'respect' also appear locked into a self-perpetuating cycle. The unintended consequence of raising anxiety and fear of the 'disrespectful' is to encourage a greater mistrust not only of 'the irritating' but also of 'difference'.

Risk Management

9.2 Despite the 'successes' of the late 1980s in reducing youth custody (see **Chapter 8.2**), the *1998 Crime and Disorder Act* promised to break with 'past failures' and to open up a new era in youth justice based on the primary aim of *preventing crime* and *disorder*. In place of the pessimistic 'nothing works' paradigm, evidence-based research and the fiscal audit promised to reveal interventions that might 'work' and which might give 'value for money'.

Actuarial Justice, Evidence and 'What Works'

The emergence of the terms 'risk management' and 'evidence-led policy' in criminal and youth justice reflects the growing importance of what has been termed a new penology of **actuarialism**. This shift first took place in the USA in the 1980s in response to demands for more accountability and rationality in correctional policy. Jonathon Simon was one of the first to identify how actuarial assessments of risk were making a radical impact on public and political mentalities (Simon, 1988). The 'old' disciplinary society of correcting and punishing individuals appeared to be challenged by a 'new' risk society in which the primary aim was to identify 'risky populations' on the basis of aggregate data and 'scientifically' informed calculations of future probabilities. For Simon, the ideological power of this 'actuarial risk society' resided in its depoliticization of social problems and its ability to neutralize political and moral resistance. In subsequent analyses, Simon together with Malcolm Feeley (1992; 1994), focused directly on how actuarial logic is capable of radically altering the discourses, objectives and techniques of crime control. For example, the rehabilitative rationales of criminal justice become increasingly challenged by the promise of greater 'scientific certainty' claimed by risk calculation and estimating the statistical probability of offending: akin to insurance tables which predict the likelihood of having a house fire, house flooding or serious illness. Appropriate interventions are modelled on psychological profiling and on predicted levels of current and future 'risk', rather than on assessments of 'need'. Criminal justice shifts its gaze from the individual offender and towards the targeting and managing of specific (pre-criminal) categories of people. Management of these groups is realized through the application of increasingly sophisticated risk assessment technologies and prediction tables. This shift also, of course, enables the system to construct its own measures of success and failure (meeting targets) and to predict its own needs (efficient allocation of resources). Actuarialism logically connects with neo-liberal socio-economic policies that reduce welfare expenditure and produce surplus populations (the underclass) that then have to be contained and controlled. In short, it legitimizes a 'waste management' response to difficult and troubling populations. As Kempf-Leonard and Peterson (2000, p. 78) explain:

> Often called risk and needs classification instruments, these measures are used to assign points to various characteristics of the youth and his or her alleged offense. The points are typically derived from statistical models that identify the relative

importance of each characteristic in predicting the policy outcome of interest ... much in the manner of insurance tables which predict the likelihood of having an automobile collision, house fire or serious illness. The guidelines then provide a classification grid that identifies the suggested juvenile justice intervention within each category of scores.

Offender profiling and risk classification have also been eagerly turned to as a means of overcoming the 'nothing works' pessimism that had pervaded criminal justice, and particularly probation, since the 1970s. Gradually the case has been made that *some* forms of intervention can be successful in reducing *some* re-offending for *some* offenders at *some* times. Much of this 'new optimism' of '**what works**' was generated by the work of the Canadian researchers Ross, Fabiano and Ewles (1988). Their 'reasoning and rehabilitation' project was designed to retrain high risk adult probationers via a cognitive skills training programme. The results showed a recidivism rate reduced by some 50 per cent for those on the programme compared to regular probation. As a result they claimed that some rehabilitation programmes can 'work' remarkably well when properly resourced. In a meta analysis of over 400 research studies on the effectiveness of such 'treatments', Lipsey (1995) claimed that when intervention is focussed around behavioural training or skills issues and sustained over a period of at least six months, then a 10 per cent reduction in re-offending can be expected.

A new 'orthodoxy' of **cognitive behaviourism** claims that highly structured programmes that compel offenders to address their behaviour are capable of success. In turn, this has facilitated the rapid development of highly intensive interventionist approaches, whether directed at preventing crime through 'nipping it in the bud' or at reducing further offending by encouraging 'individual responsibility'. Both are justified by reference to the 'proven' capacity of such treatments to 'work' in risk management terms (see Box 9.5).

Box 9.5

The principles of 'what works'

- Attempt a risk classification and target more intensive programmes at high risk offenders.
- Focus on the specific factors associated with offending.
- Use a structured learning style that requires active participation on the part of the offender.
- Develop high programme integrity.
- Match the level of risk, based on offending history, with the level of intervention.
- Use cognitive-behavioural interventions which help to improve problem solving and social interaction, but which also address and challenge the attitudes, values and beliefs which support offending behaviour.
- Base interventions in the community to facilitate 'real-life' learning.

Source: Derived from Audit Commission (1996), Maguire (1995), Goldblatt and Lewis (1998).

Much contemporary theory and practice in crime prevention, desistance and recidivism then combines techniques of risk calculation backed up by evaluation research with a re-emergent 'rehabilitative' commitment to 'changing people' (see **Chapter 8.3**).

In what has proved to be a hugely influential piece of research, Sherman and colleagues (1997) prepared a report for the US Department of Justice outlining what works, what fails and what might be worth pursuing further in the practice of crime prevention. Based on a review of more than 500 'scientific evaluations' of crime prevention practices, the authors devised lists of successes and failures. For example, they argued that some rehabilitation programmes; early focussed intervention; some prison-based therapeutic community treatments; and the incapacitation of 'high risk' offenders all 'work' to reduce 'crime in the community', while shock probation, Scared Straight programmes, correctional boot camps, juvenile wilderness programs and unstructured counselling do 'not work'. Notwithstanding concerns around the replicability of such results across time and space and the methodological difficulties in measuring what might constitute 'success', their review is now almost universally accepted as incontestable knowledge. It is a lynchpin of **evidence-based policy**.

However, the extent of adoption of the 'scientific evidence' has been somewhat mixed. For example, Sherman et al.'s (1997) report (following the work of developmental criminology – see **Chapter 3**) is clear that early intervention in the form of home visits by health professionals 'works' to prevent the onset of delinquency, while correctional boot camps do 'not work' particularly in preventing recidivism. Ten years after Sherman's report, boot camps in the USA, though reduced in number, still formed a core component of the correctional system in the USA, while many 'welfare' aspects of parental and family support were being cut back. Clearly considerations of what is deemed to 'work' are as much driven by political, economic and ideological imperatives as any adherence to the application of 'science'.

This 'new' paradigm has certainly not been without its critics. Tilley (2003) warns of the methodological and scientific shortcomings of evaluations based on experiments and which are then uncritically employed to inform policy. He suggests the quest for a universal, globally replicable 'what works', is misguided and unachievable. A more 'realist' approach would be to ask the rather more complex and contingent question of 'what works for whom, in what circumstances and contexts, and how?' What works today may not tomorrow. What works with some people in some places will not with others. Indeed attempts to replicate the positive outcomes of the Canadian reasoning and rehabilitation project have not always been successful. An evaluation of cognitive skills programmes for adult male prisoners in Britain between 1996 and 1998 found no difference in reconviction rates for those attending the programme and those who did not (Falshaw et al., 2003). The first evaluation of two prison-based cognitive skills programmes ('Reasoning and Rehabilitation' and 'Enhanced Thinking Skills') for young offenders in England and Wales similarly found that 'programme participation did not have a significant independent effect upon the likelihood of reconviction' (Cann et al., 2006).

'What works' research has indeed been rather inconclusive. It has only rarely been conducted on a scientific basis, using randomized trials (the 'gold standard' for medicine research) and falls into a familiar trap of trying to standardize modes of understanding and intervention which take little note of diverse personal biographies and changing social circumstances. Such research also appears to be used selectively and only when it seems to confirm pre-determined governmental policies. From a practitioner point of view 'what works'-based formulae tend to negate professional autonomy and trap decision-making within an inflexible, technocratic and predetermined ranking of risk (Webb, 2001). Rehabilitation is re-conceptualized primarily in terms of 'risk management' rather than welfare; and treatment is re-legitimized in terms of 'protecting the public' rather than offender support. In a more fundamental sense, social, economic and political issues become redefined as problems to be *managed* rather than issues to be *resolved*.

Smith (2003, p. 137) has in particular queried some of the Youth Justice Board's claims of success. He identifies a relative decline in such 'lenient' disposals as final warnings and fines in favour of community sentences coupled with dramatic rises in custody. Identification of those 'at risk' has contributed to a criminalization of younger and relatively minor offenders against which previously no formal action might have been taken. Above all, Smith casts doubt on the reliability of the statistical reoffending data presented by the YJB. Like is not compared to like and the difficulty remains of isolating any effect specific to a particular intervention without acknowledging wider demographic and socio-economic contexts. It is for this reason that attempts to replicate 'success' from one locality or from one jurisdiction to others have generally failed because the dynamic processes and interactions of change have been overlooked (Crawford and Jones, 1996). The unpredictability, variability and intrinsic complexity of the social and the political militate against crude generality and supposed uniformity. The use of generalized assessment tools to predict population-wide probabilities may create a sense of certainty and reliability but are littered with methodological difficulty and subjective and contested judgements, which in turn places doubt on the desirability and feasibility of devising interventions on the basis of risk identification and risk control (Smith, 2006). The search for standardized risks and the consistently efficient (and cost-effective) practice tends to mean that the dynamics of (unpredictable) personal biographies as well as the relevance of place and the broader context of local opportunities and labour markets are overlooked. (Webster, MacDonald and Simpson, 2006, and see **Chapter 1.3**). 'What works' in some contexts (spatial and temporal) may not 'work' in others. The lives of children and young people involved in youth justice processes are complex and reliance on a generalized 'risk factor paradigm' obscures those complexities.

The discourse of 'what works' is deceptively benign, practical and non-ideological. How could anyone claim to act otherwise and advocate policies that are demonstrable failures? Yet youth justice reform is also clearly driven by assessments of what is politically and publicly popular. In practice, 'what works' is not just a rational, efficient, objective and neutral process; it is also driven by political, institutional and economic imperatives. The political symbolism of toughness may always take precedence over the practical questions of effectiveness and human rights. Pitts (2001), for example, has condemned the 'what works' industry as the subordination of science to governance. Research is used selectively and only when it seems to confirm predetermined governmental policies. This view seems to be reinforced in the way that New Labour often 'rolled out' pilot programmes before any evaluation had been able to report (Wilcox, 2003). Either way, actuarial assessments tend to focus on that which can be measured easily (such as the time interval between arrest and court appearance). That which eludes quantification (such as histories of multiple disadvantage) is ignored. Practice becomes geared to meeting (and manipulating) internal targets rather than responding to the needs and circumstances of offenders (Jones, 2001). It suggests that youth justice work can be value-free and objective, existing in some vacuum outside of social relationships and cultural formations. Evaluation, too, is never a pure science. Most commissioners of evaluation research might want the 'facts', but facts do not speak for themselves. The unpredictability and variability of local contexts and the complexity of the social and the political in general militate against standardization and uniformity. There are no law-like, universal 'best practices' (Goldson, 2001). Further, the clamour for the pragmatic 'quick fix' precludes not only critical research but also policy proposals which might look to the long term and the more fundamentally transformative (Muncie, 2002b). Acknowledgement of social factors, social processes and contextual issues inevitably exposes the limitations of policies based on standardized risk assessment and individualized behavioural change (Kemshall, 2008).

Restorative Justice, Conflict Resolution and Offender Accountability

The development of formalized criminal and youth justice systems has typically witnessed the removal of interpersonal conflict and dispute from the control of those individuals involved and their appropriation by an ever increasing number of state agencies. Writing from an abolitionist perspective, the Norwegian criminologist, Nils Christie (1977), argued that conflicts (now defined as 'crimes' by the state) have been 'stolen' from offenders and victims (who are their rightful 'owners') by the apparatus of criminal justice. This view maintains that orthodox thinking about crime, criminality and crime control is fundamentally flawed because the harms associated with social life cannot, and should not, be regulated by the criminal justice system.

The events, states of mind and behaviours that are criminalized have nothing in common, other than the fact that they have been usurped by the criminal justice system. Social problems, conflicts, harms and antagonisms are an inevitable part of everyday life and their ownership is lost if they are delegated to professionals and legal specialists promising to provide 'expert solutions'. As such, it has been argued that the criminal and youth justice systems are overwhelmingly counter-productive in relation to their objectives. They do not function according to their own claims, whether these be public protection, rehabilitation, retribution, deterrence or prevention. They do not attend to the needs of real people, because they cause unnecessary suffering and offer little influence to those directly involved, whether as victims or perpetrators. They do not protect people from being victimized and cannot control crime.

Amongst more radical writers (such as Christie) efforts were made to imagine forms of justice that would be built on entirely different principles to those operating in Western capitalist societies. Abolitionists argue that we would do better to start with notions of negligence and accidents rather than intent and responsibility. 'Crimes' should be reclassified for what they really are: conflicts, troubles, disputes, problems and harms. Other bodies of law – economic, administrative, environmental, health, labour – rather than criminal law could be drawn on to resolve these dilemmas. Abolition of the apparatuses of the criminal justice system would eliminate the problems specifically generated by the system, such as the fabrication of guilt, the stigmatizing of prisoners, the marginalization and exclusion of certain powerless groups, institutionalized discrimination, the dramatization of conflicts by the mass media, and the reproduction and perpetuation of violence. Abolitionists argue that the agencies of the criminal justice system have a vested interest in making sure that crime remains out of control. Abolition of these expensive and ineffective agencies would also revitalize society by allowing other forms of conflict resolution – redress, restorative justice, peacemaking and community justice – to be imagined and properly resourced. Here the emphasis is not on punishment or legal processes but on opening up communication between offender, victim and community such that the 'dispute' is resolved to everyone's satisfaction. The crucial point for abolitionism is that inclusionary rather than exclusionary means should be utilized to respond to harmful behaviours (Hudson, 1996 pp. 142–5).

Box 9.6

Key elements in restorative justice

- Crime is fundamentally a violation of people and interpersonal relationships.
- Restoration is a continuum of responses to the needs and harms experienced by victims, offenders and communities.
- Maximization of public participation, especially of victims.
- Providing offenders with opportunities and encouragement to understand the harm caused and to make amends.
- Maximization of voluntary participation; minimization of coercion and exclusion.
- Community responsibility to support victims and integrate offenders.
- Mutual agreement and opportunities for reconciliation take precedence over imposed outcomes.
- The prioritization of healing, recovery, accountability and change over punishment.

Source: Derived from Zehr and Mika (1998).

One such form was that of restorative justice. Since the 1980s this has made a remarkable impact on criminal justice in numerous jurisdictions around the world (see **Chapter 10**). The restorative justice movement is a body of work which has gained much momentum in societies which have managed in part to 're-discover', to varying degrees, the systems of justice of their indigenous peoples such as in Canada and New Zealand. Social theologians have also sought to recover traditions of communally based restorative justice when crime is understood as an interpersonal harm rather than as a violation of an abstract legal rule. Some radical advocates have spoken of the potential of replacing legal definitions of crime and formal procedures with processes of reconciling conflicting interests and of healing rifts (De Haan, 1990; Walgrave, 1995). These harms are viewed as creating obligations and liabilities which have to be put right by the parties concerned themselves, with the state and its agents only minimally involved. Supporters of the restorative justice movement argue that the techniques of reintegrative shaming, restitution, mediation and **reparation** work on the conscience of the harm-doer in ways that formal legal procedures cannot (Braithwaite, 1989). Restorative justice holds the potential to restore the 'deliberative control of justice by citizens' and to restore 'harmony based on a feeling that justice has been done' (Braithwaite, 2003, p. 57). There is little doubt too that if taken seriously **restoration** requires a fundamental rethinking of youth justice policy and practice (see Boxes 9.6 and 9.7).

Box 9.7

Restorative and retributive justice compared

Retributive justice	Restorative justice
Crime as law violation; an act against the state	Crime as a harm to individuals and communities
Offender defined by deficits	Offender defined by capacity to repair harm
Focus on establishing guilt/innocence	Focus on problem solving
State-centred	Non-state, community-based
Victims as marginal to decision-making	Victims as central to decision-making
Adversarial	Negotiation and reconciliation
Punishment to deter, prevent or exact retribution	Punishment as ineffective and disruptive of community relations
Exclusion	Re-integration
Justice 'owned' by legal professionals	Public access to justice

The often quoted reference point for youth justice reform is the experience of Family Group Conferences (FGCs) pioneered in New Zealand in 1989 and based on traditional systems of conflict resolution within Maori culture. FGCs involve a professional co-ordinator, dealing with both civil and criminal matters, who calls the young person, their family and victims together to decide whether the young person is 'in need of care and protection' and, if so, what should be provided. The key element of progressive restorative practice is that the offender is not marginalized but accepted as a key contributor to decision-making. It is claimed that their introduction has resulted in an 80 per cent reduction of those in care for welfare or criminal reasons (Morris and Maxwell, 2001). Nearly all FGCs are able to reach agreement and advise an active penalty – usually community work, apologies or reparation. Further, it is argued they act as an effective vehicle for enabling the participation and strengthening of families while respecting the interests of victims (Hudson et al., 1996, p. 234 and see **Chapter 10.3**).

Restorative principles are also said to have informed the police-led cautioning scheme for juveniles established in the Wagga Wagga police district in New South Wales, Australia. There the restoration of juveniles was said to be achieved through processes of 'reintegrative shaming' (Braithwaite, 1989). It was this model that was first imported to England through the establishment of a Restorative Cautioning Unit by Thames Valley Police in Aylesbury in 1995. Two years later it was claimed that of 400 offenders involved, reoffending rates had fallen to as low as 4 per cent, compared to 30 per cent for those who had only received a caution (*Guardian*, 18 October 1997). Young and Hoyle's (2002) subsequent evaluation cast doubt on these figures as no reliable data existed for reconviction following 'old-style' cautioning in Aylesbury. Nevertheless they concluded that exposing offenders to the emotionally charged views of those whom they most care about, such as parents and friends, helped to reduce the likelihood of re-sanctioning by about half. Moreover most offenders, victims and their respective supporters were generally satisfied with the fairness of the process.

Further grounding of elements of restoration in English youth justice was made possible through the introduction of reparation and action plan orders in the *1998 Crime and Disorder Act*, but most significantly in the introduction of *referral orders* and *youth offender panels* following the *1999 Youth Justice and Criminal Evidence Act*. Referral orders in England and Wales are a *mandatory*, standard sentence imposed on (almost) all first-time offenders, no matter how relatively minor the offence, as long as they are under 18 years old, have no previous convictions and plead guilty. Following pilots in 11 areas, they went national in 2002. Offenders are referred to a youth offender panel (made up of local volunteers, family members and a YOT representative) to agree a programme of behaviour to address their offending. Victims are encouraged to attend. There is no provision for legal representation. It is not a formal community sentence but does require a contract to be agreed to last from a minimum of 3 months to a maximum of 12. The programme may include victim reparation, victim mediation, curfew, school attendance, staying away from specified places and persons, participation in specified activities, as well as a general compliance with the terms of the contract for supervision and monitoring purposes. About 30,000 such orders were issued in 2006, constituting approximately 25 per cent of all juvenile community-based sentences. Through such measures it has been claimed that youth justice is in the midst of a potentially radical shift from being exclusionary and punitive to becoming inclusionary and restorative (Crawford and Newburn, 2003; Crawford and Burden, 2005). The Northern Ireland criminal justice review (O'Mahony and Deazley, 2000) has gone somewhat further and ensured that youth conferencing is at the heart of a new 'post-conflict' approach to juvenile justice. (see Box 9.8).

Box 9.8

Restorative youth conferencing in Northern Ireland

Following the Northern Ireland Criminal Justice Review Report of 2000, a National Youth Justice Agency was established to implement a new agenda of youth justice based on diversion, human rights and restorative justice. The Youth Conference Service started to pilot restorative justice in Belfast in 2003. It was extended to the whole of Northern Ireland, on a statutory basis, in 2006.

Youth conferencing seeks not only to encourage young people to recognise the effects of their crime and take responsibility for their actions, but also to devolve power by engaging victim, offender and community in the restorative process. The Youth Conference Service receives referrals from the Public Prosecution Service as a diversion from prosecution or from the courts. It relies on the consent of the offender. The conference discusses ways for the young person to make good the harm caused to the victim and how to stop offending. This plan then becomes a statutory order, monitored by a Youth Conference Co-ordinator. Non-compliance may result in breach action.

When compared to similar schemes internationally, victim participation in conferences was high. A large majority of both offenders and victims preferred the conference over court.

Source: Derived from Campbell et al. (2005).

Critical perspectives on restorative justice have, however, begun to emerge from a number of different avenues. Evaluations of the referral orders, for example, have lauded the more positive lines of communication that have been opened up between offenders, parents, victims and communities, but have lamented its coercive nature, problems of low victim participation, blurred lines of accountability and a general failure to provide offenders with the socio-economic resources necessary for them to develop a 'stake-hold' in community life (Crawford and Newburn, 2003; Gray, 2003). Gelsthorpe and Morris (2002) contend that restorative principles are additions to, rather than core-defining components of, a system that remains built around, and continues to act upon, notions of just deserts, punishment and retribution. There is clear potential for proceedings to be primarily coercive as the child or young person is faced with a panel of adults, none of whom have direct responsibility to promote the 'best interests of the child' (Haines and O'Mahony 2006). Restorative processes also focus their attention on low-level offenders who, through a combination of other measures in crime prevention and pre-emptive early intervention, are being sucked into the system at an increasingly early age. Moreover their informality compromises principles of due process and proportionality. Indeed, rather than offering an alternative to formal processing, restorative justice can be viewed as integral to strategies of risk management in that its primary task can be to sort the 'high risk' from the 'low' (Cunneen, 2003). Within restorative programmes the burden remains on individuals to accept personal responsibility for their actions. This in itself may explain their political popularity. Rather less attention is given to the state and the recognition that it also has a responsibility (within UN conventions and rules – see **Chapter 10**) to its citizens. Notions of individual responsibility rather than those of community empowerment and 'restorative *social* justice' tend to proliferate (White, 2003).

Authoritarianism

9.3 Whatever the progressive intent of welfare and justice and latterly actuarial and restorative justice initiatives, there is contrary evidence to suggest that they have always been embedded in deeper punitive and authoritarian motives. Even at moments of penal reductionism, the young offender institution, detention centre, youth custody centre, borstal, approved school, reformatory or youth prison have formed the cornerstone of youth justice against which all other interventions are measured and assessed (Goldson, 2006). There has also persisted a strong law and order lobby intent on waging a 'moral crusade' against children and young people by maintaining that crime is caused by simple wickedness and that the only real punishment is that which involves incarceration (Scraton, 2008). As a result, every decarcerative reform has been subject to either judicial or political backlash. Governments and policy-makers, it seems, are only prepared to sanction diversion and non-custodial options as long as custody is retained for particular groups of young offenders (Pratt, 1989, p. 244).

The Custodial Sanction

From Borstal to YOI

When the first specialized detention centre for young offenders was formally set up by the *Crime Prevention Act of 1908* at Borstal in Kent, it was heralded as a major liberal breakthrough. The separation of the under-21s from adults in their own closed institutions was seen as a major step towards the training (rather than simply punishment) of the young offender. In the spirit of rehabilitation, borstal 'trainees' were held for between one and three years; the regime was based on strict discipline, hard work and drill; it was directed not at the 'incorrigible' but those of 'criminal habits and tendencies' or those associating with 'persons of bad character'. From the outset it attracted criticism for instituting long periods of confinement – up to three years for offences that would not ordinarily attract more than six months (Radzinowicz and Hood, 1990, p. 389). However, it also claimed a remarkable success in preventing reoffending. The first survey in 1915 reported reconviction rates as low as 27 to 35 per cent.

In 1961, the *Criminal Justice Act* reduced the minimum age for borstal training to 15, and made it easier to transfer young people from approved schools and integrated borstals into the prison system. This integration meant that the training component declined and their regimes became more punitive. The role of borstal as an alternative to prison was undermined, and it was turned instead into a primary punitive institution which acted as a funnel into the prison system. Taylor et al. (1979, p. 65) argued that 'younger and less difficult young people' were increasingly subject to 'tougher punishment'. Partly as a consequence, the reconviction rate which had stayed at 30 per cent throughout the 1930s increased to 70 per cent, suggesting that borstal accentuated forms of behaviour it was designed to suppress. Taylor et al. (1979) described how offers of help were provided inconsistently and arbitrarily withdrawn. Physical and verbal abuse by officers and other inmates was not uncommon. A picture emerged of largely punitive regimes in which retraining was minimal and the possibility of being permanently institutionalized forever present: 'Common humanity, statistical evidence and above all commonsense demand the abolition of the Borstal institution' (Taylor et al., 1979, p. 71).

In 1982, borstals were renamed youth custody centres and in 1988 were included in a wider network of young offender institutions (YOIs). In many respects they now act as mirror images of adult prisons for the young. Following the *1994 Criminal Justice and Public Order Act*, the maximum sentence of detention in a young offender institution was increased from 12 to 24 months. The same Act also introduced secure training orders for 12 to 14 year olds who had been convicted of three or more offences which would be imprisonable in the case of an adult. The *1998 Crime and Disorder Act* abolished these separate sentences and replaced them with a generic detention and training order (DTO). This came into force in April 2000. A DTO can be given to 15 to 17 year olds for any offence considered serious enough to warrant a custodial sentence; and to 12 to 14 year olds who are considered to be 'persistent offenders'. The orders are for between 4 and 24 months. Half of the order is served in the community under the supervision of a social worker, a probation officer or a member of a youth offending team. A custodial sentence of detention (without the training component) is now restricted to those aged 18, 19 and 20. However, for 'grave' crimes, the youth court can pass its jurisdiction to the Crown Court. Under Sections 90–92 of the *Powers of Criminal Courts Act 2000* (which consolidated those of Section 53 of the *1933 Children and Young Persons Act*), a 10–17 year old can be detained for a longer period than the normal maximum of two years, at the discretion of the Home Secretary, either in a local authority secure unit or a prison service establishment. The numbers caught in these powers increased from some 100 in 1992 to over 700 in 2002. In addition, the *Criminal Justice Act 2003* increased sentencing powers of 'extended sentences' and 'detention for public protection' for 65 violent and 88 sexual offences 'specified' as 'dangerous'. It was initially thought these powers would rarely apply to young people, but 240 were so detained in 2005/06.

The Young Offender Institution (YOI) is the main resource of the 'juvenile secure estate'. Approximately 85 per cent of 'juvenile' prisoners are held in YOIs (run by the prison service) with the remainder in Secure Training Centres (STCs) (run by the private sector) and Secure Children's Homes (SCH) (run by local authorities). Between 2000 and 2008 the total number of under-18s in these institutions at any one time ranged from 2,619 (April 2000) to 3,175 (October 2002). The Youth Justice Board is responsible for 'purchasing' places from these three sectors in order to ensure demand is met. Over these years rather more use has been made of prison service and private sector establishments and rather less of those of local authorities (see Box 9.9).

Box 9.9

Under-18 population in secure facilities in England and Wales by type of facility at October 2000–2008

	STC	SCH	YOI	Total
2000	118	303	2394	2815
2001	120	299	2410	2829
2002	149	322	2704	3175
2003	186	311	2315	2812
2004	219	242	2374	2835
2005	252	243	2458	2953
2006	257	223	2516	2996
2007	261	229	2548	3038
2008	235	201	2469	2905

Sources: http://www.yjb.gov.uk/en-gb/yjs/Custody/CustodyFigures/ – accessed 2008 and http://www.howardleague.org/index.php?id=549 – accessed 2008.

All 'young adult' 18 to 20 year old prisoners are normally held in separate YOIs. Since 2000, the Youth Justice Board and the Prison Service have together implemented a programme of substantial reform designed to improve the conditions and treatment of 'juveniles' in penal custody. Institutional regimes must now be based upon clear principles, and the YJB insists that there should be a structured and 'caring' environment in order that 'juvenile' prisoners are kept safe and secure. However, despite such reforms, Her Majesty's Chief Inspector of Prisons continues to raise serious and consistent concerns about the practices and regimes in some YOIs with regard to 'juvenile' and 'young adult' prisoners. In 2003, the privately run YOI at Ashfield was condemned as the worst jail in Britain with bullying endemic and staff having lost effective control (*Guardian*, 5 February 2003). In 2008, prison inspectors in Northern Ireland reported that conditions at Hydebank Wood Young Offenders Centre had *deteriorated* since their previous visit. Noting routine strip searching, intimidation and 20 hour/day lock-ups, the inspectors concluded that 'there can be few custodial settings with so many competing risks and vulnerabilities in one small site' (BBC News, 9 July 2008). The reconviction rates for those released from custody is consistently high, ranging between 60 per cent and 90 per cent. In 2002, the Children's Rights Alliance for England undertook a detailed analysis of the conditions and treatment experienced by juvenile prisoners. The report exposed widespread neglect in relation to physical and mental health; endemic bullying, humiliation and ill-treatment (staff-on-prisoner and prisoner-on-prisoner); racism and other forms of discrimination; systemic invasion of privacy; long and uninterrupted periods of cell-based confinement; deprivation of fresh air and exercise; inadequate educational and rehabilitative provision; insufficient opportunities to maintain contact with family; poor diet; ill-fitting clothing in poor state of repair; a shabby physical environment; and virtually no opportunity to complain and/or make representations. According to the CRAE report (2002), such negative and neglectful processes continue to define the conditions and treatment of many young prisoners in YOI, in England and Wales irrespective of recent reforms.

Girls and young women are particularly ill served by YOIs. Holding girls in wings of adult prisons has long been condemned but despite repeated promises over 25 years to remove all girls from YOI and prison service accommodation, the practice continues. Girls are currently held in separate units at five YOIs. Ironically, it is their small number that means that they appear 'tacked onto' the rest of the system. Because of the few facilities available, girls are often held further from home, again undermining the possibility of restoring family and community ties. In April 2000, 123 girls were held in the secure estate (YOI, STC and SCH) rising to 221 eight years later.

Young Offender Institutions also appear to be riddled with individually and institutionally racist practices. The Commission for Racial Equality (2003) discovered high levels of intimidation, discrimination and failure to protect black prisoners epitomized by the murder of 19 year old Zahid Mubarek in 2000 by his cell mate who was known to the authorities to be a violent racist. In one of the first ethnographic pieces of research to test the impact of the Prison Service's anti-racist policies specifically in YOIs, Wilson and Moore's (2003) interviews of 45 teenage boys vividly describe a daily routine of prison officer verbal abuse. Terms such as 'chimp', 'golliwog', 'nigger', and phrases such as 'when I wipe my arse it looks like you' revealed a deeply imbued racism. Yet each of the three YOIs in this study had officially met their performance targets in race relations. For the boys the work of race relations liaison officers and management teams was an irrelevance. None felt racist incidents were worth reporting, if not for fear of retaliation then because none would be taken seriously.

The critiques of YOIs have been consistent and persistent. A report by the Howard League (1995, p. 67) concluded in much the same terms as Taylor et al.'s (1979) condemnation of the borstal system: 'an approach which concentrates on incarcerating the most delinquent and damaged adolescents, in large soulless institutions under the supervision of staff with no specialist training in dealing with difficult teenage behaviour, is nonsensical and inhumane'. Goldson's (2002c, pp. 159–60) research of the experiences of those subjected to secure and penal regimes, whether in the name of welfare or criminal justice, led him to conclude:

> locking up children is spectacularly ineffective ... children invariably leave prison not only more damaged but also more angry, more alienated, more expert in the ways of crime and more likely to commit more serious offences – in fact more of everything that the children themselves and the community need much less of.

The counterproductive nature of imprisoning children is well known and widely shared. Yet it barely figures in any discussion of a youth justice system which claims to be acting solely on the basis of 'evidence' and 'what works'.

Detention Centres and Boot Camps

Detention centres were introduced by the *Criminal Justice Act of 1948* and enabled the courts to sentence offenders aged 14–21 to short periods of an explicitly punitive regime. This was justified on the grounds that sending young offenders to prison only helped to cement criminal careers, but there is strong evidence that their introduction was also a result of a quid pro quo for the abolition of corporal punishment (Muncie, 1990). Detention centres were established as an 'experiment', but lasted 40 years. Throughout they were dogged by a lack of any precise definition of purpose. Despite significant opposition the only detention centre for girls was opened at Moor Court near Stoke-on-Trent in 1962. It was closed seven years later because military drill and physical education were not considered appropriate in the 'training' of young women.

While detention centres always promised the delivery of a 'short, sharp, shock', in the 1950s and 1960s their regime was not that far removed from that of borstals. In the 1970s, in an effort to appease those who viewed the entire juvenile justice system as too soft, the Home Secretary announced the establishment of two 'experimental' regimes in which 'life will be constricted at a brisk tempo. Much greater emphasis will be put on hard and constructive activities, and discipline and tidiness, on self respect and respect for those in authority ... These will be no holiday camps' (Whitelaw, cited in Thornton et al., 1984, para. 1). The regimes were subsequently evaluated by the Home Office's Young Offender Psychology Unit, which concluded that they had 'no discernible effect on the rate at which trainees were reconvicted' (Thornton et al., 1984, para. 8.21). At one centre (Send, for 14–17 year olds) reconviction rates were 57 per cent both before and after the experiment; at the other (New Hall, for 17–21 year olds), the rate rose from 46 to 48 per cent. Doubt was also expressed as to whether the new tougher regimes were actually experienced as more demanding. Indeed some of the activities, such as drill and physical education, were comparatively popular; more so than the continuous chore of the humdrum work party which they replaced. Despite such findings, the tougher regimes were not abandoned but *extended* to all detention centres. In 1985, the rhetoric and political expediency of the 'short, sharp shock' appeared to take precedence over research evaluation or practical experience (Muncie, 1990, p. 61). The political demand for repressive penal policies repeatedly overshadows logical argument. As Harris (1982, p. 248) commented, 'Punitive and liberal legislation are judged by different criteria, the latter being immediately at risk when it fails to reduce recidivism, but the former, however ineffective, appearing to a society in which to punish wrongdoing seems natural, to contain an intrinsic logic.'

The experiments in 'short, sharp shock' were formally abolished in 1988 but it took only another eight years for their revival. The introduction of American-styled boot camps in 1996–97 ignored all the lessons learnt in the previous 50 years. The origins of the boot camp lie in survival training for US military personnel during the Second World War. They were introduced in the USA from 1983 in response to prison overcrowding and a belief that short periods of retributive punishment would change or deter offending behaviour: 'typically detainees might face pre-dawn starts, enforced shaved heads, no talking to each other, being constantly screamed at by guards, rushed meal times, no access to television and newspapers and a rigorous and abusive atmosphere for 16 hours a day' (Nathan, 1995, p. 2). Such regimes have consistently failed to live up to expectations: the deterrent effect of military training has proved negligible; the authoritarian atmosphere has denied access to effective treatment; there have been occasional lawsuits from inmates claiming that elements of the programme were dangerous and life-threatening; they have failed to reduce prison populations; they distract attention from other policies that may work better; and their popularity relies more on an emotive nostalgia for some mythical orderly past than on effectiveness (Parent, 1995; Simon, 1995).

Despite such warnings, the UK government decided to go ahead. The first boot camp was opened in 1996 at Thorn Cross Young Offenders Institution in Cheshire. But instead of a military-based regime, it employed a 'high-intensity' mixture of education, discipline and training. A second camp, opened at the Military Corrective Training Centre in Colchester in 1997, promised a more spartan regime. Aimed at 17–21 year olds, its open prison conditions, however, excluded the most serious of offenders. The notion, too, of handing criminal cases over to a military authority provoked an avalanche of complaints from virtually all sides of the criminal justice process. Each place cost £850 per week compared to £250 per week in other young offender institutions. Despite these misgivings the New Labour government of 1997 was initially reluctant to move for their abolition for fear of being seen to have gone 'soft' on crime. But eventually pressure from the prison service – on grounds of cost, if not effectiveness – was successful in shutting down the Colchester camp barely 12 months after its opening and when only 44 offenders had gone through its regime. The high-intensity training regime at Thorn Cross, despite a record of relative success in reducing reconviction due to its throughcare, education and employment facilities (Farrington et al., 2002), was closed in 2008 largely because it was deemed not to be 'cost effective'. The rhetoric of 'short, sharp shock' and 'military discipline', however, still prove to be politically popular. In the USA private operators continue to run punitive programmes for juveniles, often paid for by parents seduced by the promise of a 'quick fix solution' and the hope of 'scaring their kids straight'. In the UK a programme designed by the YJB and the Ministry of Defence aims to discipline primary school children who show early signs of disruptive behaviour (*The Independent*, 26 October 2004). In an oft recurring soundbite, in 2006 the Home Secretary advocated enlisting the help of the army to 'discipline young offenders' (*Guardian*, 22 July 2006). And when all else fails the rhetoric of 'bring back national service' is routinely heard (somewhat ignoring that 'military discipline' has also brought allegations of rape, homicide and mass brawls in Cyprus, the bullying and death of recruits in England and systemic torture and abuse in Iraq).

Secure Units

Young offenders may also find themselves subject to incarceration in local authority or privately run secure training centres. During the 1970s almost 500 secure units were introduced in community homes with education, youth treatment centres and in assessment centres. The major argument for expanding prison-like conditions within such settings was that their referrals were more difficult than in the past. Millham et al. (1978) and Cawson and Martell's (1979) research, however, concluded that there was no such significant change. Moreover, because at the time the numbers sent to borstal had increased, those in the residential care system were arguably *less* difficult than previously. Confusion also existed over whether the role of a secure unit was to punish or treat or both, or whether they existed simply because no other 'suitable' disposal was available. Harris and Timms (1993) described the situation as one of 'persistent ambiguity'. In congruence with other custodial disposals, the rate of reoffending was high. Experience of a secure unit also appeared to increase the chance of reoffending for younger children and for those who had not committed offences prior to going in. During the 1980s a number of authorities closed their units partly because of over-provision and partly because of more rigorous conditions attached to gaining a DHSS licence (Harris and Timms, 1993, p. 76). Nevertheless the provision of secure accommodation, not only for offenders but also for runaways, prostitute children and abused suicidal children, rose again in the 1990s to near 300. As Harris and Timms (1993, p. 169) concluded: 'the most potent predictor of high usages of secure accommodation is a local authority's possession of a secure unit'. Any increase in places simply attracts more young people who are considered to be in need of such means of control/protection. Added to this was the proposal, first formally proposed in 1993, just days after the murder of James Bulger, to build five secure training centres for 12–14 year olds to tackle the presumed 'epidemic' of persistent offending, at a cost of between £2,000 and £3,000 per week per child.

Secure Training Centres (STCs) are purpose-built for child offenders – male and female – up to the age of 17. In 2007, there were four centres, all in England, and all run by private operators working under a Private Finance Initiative with the Youth Justice Board. The four centres are: Oakhill in Milton Keynes (opened 2004); Hassockfield in County Durham (opened 1999); Rainsbrook in Rugby (opened 1999) and Medway in Kent (opened 1998). Medway and Rainsbrook are run by Rebound, a subsidiary of Group 4; Oakhill is run by Securicor; and Hassockfield by Premier Custodial Group Ltd. Planning permission to build a fifth centre in Glynneath, Wales, was granted in 2003; whereas plans for a sixth at Brentwood, Essex, were abandoned in 2004. STCs differ from Young Offender Institutions (YOIs) in that they have a higher staff to young offender ratio (a minimum of three staff members to eight 'trainees'), are smaller in size and admit children as young as 12 years old. The regimes in STCs, it is claimed, are more constructive and education-focussed. 'Trainees' are supposedly provided with formal education 25 hours a week, 50 weeks of the year. The existence of STCs is widely assumed to be the root cause of an 800 per cent rise in under-15 year olds being sent to custody in England and Wales between 1992 and 2001.

STCs have proved to be consistently controversial, in particular attracting criticism from the United Nations Committee on the Rights of the Child for enabling the incarceration of children at such a young age. A third of all children in STCs are located over 50 miles away from their homes. Visiting hours are not open. Evaluation of the first two years of Medway found a re-offending rate of 67 per cent. Institutional support following release was notably lacking (Hagell et al., 2000). The turnover rate of staff in STCs is also extremely high. The adequacy of their training has also been consistently questioned in Commission for Social Care Inspection (CSCI) reports. Mounting concern about the suitability of such regimes for particularly young and vulnerable offenders has grown since two child deaths occurred at Rainsbrook and Hassockfield in 2004. The Carlile inquiry was established after 15 year old Gareth Myatt died after being restrained by staff at Rainsbrook STC. He was five feet tall, weighed less than eight stone and was just three days into a 12-month sentence. Lord Carlile's terms of reference were to investigate the use of physical restraint, solitary confinement and forcible strip searching of children in prisons, secure training centres and local authority secure children's homes and to make recommendations. A system of physical interventions known as physical control in care (PCC) was developed in the late 1990s for use in STCs. In 2002, restraint was used on 2,461 occasions; in 2007/2008, it was used on 10,137 occasions. It has been estimated that in each STC restraint is used about twice a day, every day of the year. This suggests routine use of physical control, not a technique of last resort.

In August 2004, 14 year old Adam Rickwood became the youngest person to die in custody in the UK in a restraint-related incident at Hassockfield STC. Labour Peer Lord Judd said at the time, 'there should be no children in prison at all. It is simply not acceptable for a nation of our wealth to say that we cannot make special provision of secure care under local authority administration for youngsters, instead of putting them into the soul-destroying situation of prison' (House of Lords Debates, 9 June 2005). Institutional confinement clearly can compound the ongoing victimization of some of society's most vulnerable youngsters (see **Chapter 5**).

Punitiveness

The *1998 Crime and Disorder Act* may have promised to break with 'past failures' but there is contrary evidence to suggest that the custodial function of youth justice has never been seriously questioned. An ideology of 'popular punitiveness' holds sway, emphasizing the importance of punishing the offender for their wrong-doing in the name of retribution. This strategy is reflected in the doubling of the numbers of young people incarcerated in England and Wales between 1992 and 2002 and the maintenance of a high level of custody throughout the first decade of the twenty-first century. What is often overlooked is that children in custody are routinely drawn from some of the most disadvantaged families and neighbourhoods. They are already likely to have endured family discord and separation, ill health and physical and emotional abuse. The vast majority have been excluded from school and many have had previous contact with care and social services agencies. With high reconviction rates and increasing evidence of inappropriate and brutalizing regimes characterized by racism, bullying, self-harm and suicide, it is clear that child incarceration is an expensive failure. Between 1990 and 2007, 30 children died while in penal custody. YJB targets to reduce the use of custody have never been met. Its use continues apace. As a result a compelling case against **youth custody** has been repeatedly made (see Box 9.10).

Box 9.10

The case against youth custody

- Custody fails to prevent reoffending or to act as an individual deterrent. Around 80 per cent of those sent to youth custody re-offend within a two-year period following release.

- Custody compounds pre-existing disadvantages: almost 30 per cent of boys and 44 per cent of girls have been in care; a quarter have experienced violence in the home; 15 per cent have statements of special educational needs; 80 per cent have been excluded from school.

- A juvenile in custody is making no restitution or reparation to the victim or to the community at large. Custody diverts valuable resources from community-based measures of protection and prevention which appear more successful at preventing reoffending.

- While prisons provide society with immediate 'protection' from the offender, many juveniles sentenced to custody pose no serious risk to the community. About a half have committed non-violent offences but they may become a significantly greater danger on their return.

- Penal custody exacerbates broken links with family, friends, education, work and leisure and causes stigmatization and labelling. Rather than reintegrating young people into the communities where they must learn to live, custody results in further social exclusion.

- Penal custody is not safe: More than 40 per cent of under-18 year olds are officially classified as 'vulnerable'. 30 children have died since 1990; the use of physical restraint techniques is widespread.

Source: Derived from Children's Society (1989, pp. 12–13 and 1993, pp. 45–51); Goldson (2002b); NACRO (2003); Howard League (2008).

The juvenile (under-18) prison population rose from 1,328 in June 1992 to 3,012 in April 2008. It peaked at 3,175 in October 2002 probably as a result then of the street crime initiative to combat mobile phone theft (see **Chapter 1.1**). Over this period there was a notable tendency to incarcerate the under-15s, ethnic minorities and young women. During the 1990s the average sentence length for 15–17 year olds doubled. Ironically such expansion has been explained not only by a greater willingness for magistrates to resort to custody and with longer sentences as a response to the prevailing climate of popular and political punitiveness (*The Independent*, 18 June 2003) but also because the introduction of the DTO with its training component persuaded them this might be a progressive disposal. By making custody appear less harsh, its greater use is encouraged (Goldson, 2002b).

England and Wales now lock up young people at a rate that is five times more than in France, 10 times more than in Italy and 290 times more than in Norway, Sweden and Finland (see **Chapter 10.2**); and often in conditions condemned by the Chief Inspector of Prisons as 'utterly unsuitable' and as 'unworthy of any country that claims to be called civilised' (Children's Rights Alliance, 2002).

Community Payback, Surveillance and Punishment

Despite the resort to incarceration, consistent attempts have been made to devise effective means of dealing with offenders in settings that might avoid the damaging consequences of institutional custody or care. For example, the development of intermediate treatment in the 1970s was initially designed to provide young people 'in need' or 'in trouble' with access to a range of educational, recreational and training opportunities. In the 1980s, this was supplemented by intensive IT programmes justified more explicitly as community-based *alternatives* to custody. Indeed there was some evidence of their success at the time' (see **Chapter 8.2**). This 'anti-custody' ethos was further strengthened in the *1991 Criminal Justice Act* (implemented in October 1992). But it was made contingent on the development of more demanding and rigorously enforced community disposals. There was to be no slackening of control. What then became known as **punishment in the community** was to be achieved through attaching stringent conditions to supervision in the form of electronic monitoring, curfew, community service or residence requirements (Worrall, 1997). The emphasis on *punishment* required a change in focus for the juvenile court and in the practices of probation and social work agencies. For the latter it meant a shift in emphasis away from 'advise, assist, befriend' and towards tightening up the conditions of supervision and surveillance. For the former it meant the abolition of the *juvenile* court (which had previously dealt with criminal and care cases) and the creation of *youth* courts and 'family proceedings' courts to deal with such matters separately. As a result the goal of welfare was effectively removed from youth criminal justice policy (see **Chapter 8.3**).

In 1989, England had already begun experimenting with such US-inspired schemes as electronic monitoring. Despite a faltering start, they have now proliferated (Nellis, 1991). Further in 1995 a Green Paper continued to advocate the further 'strengthening' of the conditions of punishment in the community such that they represented physical hard labour (Home Office, 1995), despite the fact that such a 'strengthening' had apparently already been legislated for in the *1991 Criminal Justice Act*. The *1993 Criminal Justice Act* almost immediately overturned some of the decarcerative principles of the 1991 Act, while the *1994 Criminal Justice and Public Order Act* doubled the maximum sentence of custody within young offender institutions. In addition, the *1997 Crime (Sentences) Act* introduced mandatory minimum sentences for certain offences, extended electronic monitoring to the under-16s as part of a curfew order, and for the first time allowed convicted juveniles to be publicly named if the court was satisfied that it was in the interests of the public to do so.

Despite the formal emphasis on crime prevention, the *1998 Crime and Disorder Act* did little to challenge this punitive mood. Rather it significantly added to the reach and intensity of community-based sentences. The Act added reparation orders, action plan orders and curfew orders to an already long menu of 'community disposals'. In 2001, community rehabilitation orders (previously known as Probation for those aged 16 or over) and community punishment orders (previously known as Community Service for those aged 16 or over) were introduced along with a combination order (community rehabilitation and community punishment). A core element of these may include the use of electronic tags to enforce curfews and order compliance. In 2002, tagging was extended to include 10–15 year olds as part of youth bail conditions or to monitor the community part of a detention and training order. But, as Whitfield (1997) has warned, young people generally have the lowest rates of compliance with tagging orders and high rates of breach may only serve to accelerate the route to custody. Moreover the tag may be used as a status symbol to 'impress friends' rather than acting as a deterrent.

Intensive supervision and surveillance programmes (ISSPs) were launched in 2002 as part of a pilot 'zero tolerance of yob culture' campaign, largely aimed at those 15 and 16 year olds with a prior record of offending and as a last community-based resort before custodial sentencing. They are not a court order as such but can be added to a supervision order, community rehabilitation order or to bail. They typically involve 24-hours-a-day electronic monitoring together with training, offending behaviour work and reparation with the ultimate aim of meeting the YJB target of reducing the number of custodial sentences by 10 per cent. Evaluation of the ISSP, however, found that while there were almost 4,000 cases of ISSP in 2002/03, there was no impact on custody rates. There was a wide variety of programmes depending on access to resource; those targeting 'high risk' offenders and which included a strong rehabilitative (rather than simply punitive focus) proved to be the most successful in reducing reoffending. Even so more than nine out of ten reoffended although their offences were fewer and less serious (Youth Justice Board, 2004). In 2003, a further intensive control and change programme for 18–20 year olds was unveiled combining tagging, curfew, unpaid community work, compensation and work with an assigned mentor. The Director of the National Probation Service enthusiastically declared it to be 'the most restrictive and intensive penalty that probation has yet rolled out. We have very high hopes for this' (*Guardian*, 3 April 2003).

In 2008, the whole system of juvenile community penalties was once more 'reformed' with the announcement of the Youth Rehabilitation Order in the *Criminal Justice and Immigration Act*. This abolished curfew, exclusion, attendance centre, action plan and supervision orders and replaced them with a single community sentence to which a long generic menu of possible 'requirements' might be attached (see Box 9.11).

Box 9.11

The Youth Rehabilitation Order

The Youth Rehabilitation Order (YRO) is a generic community sentence for young offenders and combines a number of existing sentences. It will be the standard community sentence used for the majority of young offenders. It aims to simplify sentencing for young people, while improving the flexibility of interventions.

The YRO represents a more individualized risk and needs-based approach to community sentencing, enabling greater choice from a 'menu' of requirements.

The following requirements can be attached to a YRO:

- Activity Requirement
- Curfew Requirement
- Exclusion Requirement
- Local Authority Residence Requirement
- Education Requirement
- Mental Health Treatment Requirement
- Unpaid Work Requirement (16/17 years)
- Drug Testing Requirement (14 years or over)
- Intoxicating Substance Requirement

- Supervision Requirement
- Electronic Monitoring Requirement
- Prohibited Activity Requirement
- Drug Treatment Requirement
- Residence Requirement (16/17 years)
- Programme Requirement
- Attendance Centre Requirement
- For persistent or serious offenders who would otherwise face custody, extended activity requirements, either Intensive Supervision and Surveillance (based on the current ISSP), and Intensive Fostering, can be attached to YRO.

Source: Adapted from http://www.yjb.gov.uk/en-gb/practitioners/CourtsAndOrders/Criminal JusticeandImmigrationAct/#YRO – accessed June 2008.

A further series of tough 'payback' measures, including more intensive and visible community sentencing (including the wearing of 'offender uniforms'), publication of information on convicted criminals, and the stripping from the probation service of responsibility for community punishment were promoted in the Cabinet Office's 2008 report *Engaging Communities in Fighting Crime*.

Despite this continual pursuance of the more stringent and punitive, community-based interventions have generally had little impact on rates of custody, on their own. Scull (1977) has argued that they are driven more by financial imperatives than from any enlightened desire to decarcerate. They may also act to accelerate routes into custody. In a Canadian study, Hylton (1981) examined the effects of community corrections programmes introduced in Saskatchewan from 1962 to 1979. He concluded that not only did these fail to reduce the size of the prison population, but they actually resulted in a threefold increase in the proportion of persons under formal state control. In the USA, the National Evaluation of the Dein-stitutionalization of Status Offenders project reported that the programmes were so clearly biased to heighten the intake of less serious offenders, that many more were caught up in the referral network than if the project had not been established (Kobrin

Box 9.12

Penal reform and under-18s in secure facilities 1992–2008
England and Wales at 30th June

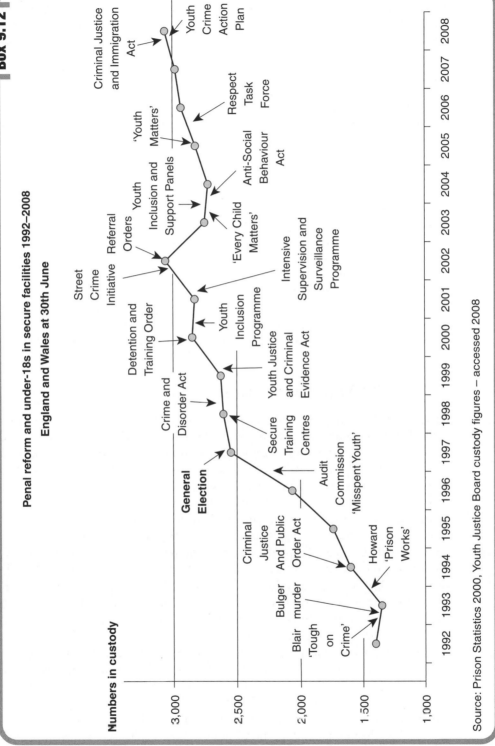

Source: Prison Statistics 2000, Youth Justice Board custody figures – accessed 2008

and Klein, 1983). Hudson (1987, p. 149) commented, it seems as if 'each time a law was reformed or a policy innovation implemented, it came as an addition to the system. New forms of treatment were added; old forms of punishment were retained.' The existence of 'alternatives' also has the effect of instigating a policy of **bifurcation** in which security at the institutional end of the system is hardened and maximized (Bottoms, 1977). The incarcerated come to be viewed as having failed all attempts to reintegrate and are labelled as hardcore, intractable and dangerous. Pursuit of correctional programmes into the community also extends the means of coercive control into non-justice agencies such that probation, housing, education, employment and family services all have a role to play in an extended correctional continuum (see **Chapter 7**). Such practices led Stanley Cohen (1985, p. 62) to ask, 'When do the confines of custody end and those of the community begin?'

Successive Home Secretaries have sought to gain law and order credibility by claiming that existing levels of community supervision and surveillance are a 'soft option'. Custodial and community punishment appear to exist in some symbiosis. If magistrates are to be persuaded to use non-custodial options, it is widely believed that their conditions must be made consistently more punitive. The danger, as frequently voiced, lies in up-tariffing and net widening. If this is the case, then punishment in the community ironically serves to fuel an increase, rather than decline, in the use of the custodial sector. Certainly, any number of community-based and preventive initiatives in England and Wales over the past two decades do not appear to have made an impact on rates of custody (see Box 9.12).

The Abrogation of Rights

Since 1991, the UK (along with 190 other countries) has been a signatory to the 1989 UN Convention on the Rights of the Child (UNCRC). This stresses the importance of incorporating a rights consciousness into juvenile justice by, for example, establishing an age of criminal responsibility relative to developmental capacity, encouraging participation in decision making, providing access to legal representation, protecting children from degrading punishment and ensuring that arrest, detention and imprisonment are measures of last resort. Such principles apply to all those aged under-18 (see **Chapter 10**). In 1995, the UN Committee on the Rights of the Child issued its first comprehensive report on the extent of the UK's implementation of the Convention. It was particularly critical of the low age of criminal responsibility. It also condemned the introduction of secure training centres. There is no European equivalent. It also critiqued the level of child poverty, estimated then to affect over 4 million children in the UK.

The UN Committee reported again in 2002 and reiterated many of these concerns over non-compliance, including: increasing numbers of children in custody (despite decreases in the crime rate); at earlier ages for lesser offences and for longer periods (not as a 'last resort'); custodial conditions that do not adequately protect children from violence, bullying and self-harm (failure to accord with 'best interests') as well as the extremely low age of criminal responsibility and the failure to ban corporal punishment (Monaghan et al., 2003). The Children's Rights Alliance for England (CRAE,

2005) concluded that England and Wales had effectively 'torn up' the UN Convention. Article 6 of the Human Rights Act also provides for the right to a fair trial with legal representation and a right to appeal. The introduction nationwide of referral orders with lay youth offender panels deliberating on 'programmes of behaviour' with no legal representation would appear to be in denial of such rights. Many of the principles of restorative justice that rely on informality, flexibility and discretion sit uneasily against legal requirements for due process and a fair and just trial (Ashworth, 2003). Article 8 confers the right to respect for private and family life and protects families from arbitrary interference. Parenting orders, child curfews and anti-social behaviour orders, in particular, would again appear to be in contempt (Freeman, 2002). Curfews override parental discretion and also seem incompatible with Article 11 of the European Convention on Human Rights, which affirms the right to freedom of peaceful assembly, and Article 14, which bestows such a right to all irrespective of age (Walsh, 2002).

The UK's next periodic report on implementation of the Convention on the Rights of the Child was reviewed by the UN Committee in 2008. In an unprecedented move, the four children's commissioners for England, Scotland, Wales and Northern Ireland submitted their own report to the UN in which they made clear that the UK continues with some 'serious violations' of the Convention (UK Children's Commissioners, 2008). Some of the recurring causes for concern (as they pertain to youth justice) have been identified as:

- *The criminalization and demonization of children*: Successive governments have not only resisted UNCRC calls that the age of criminal responsibility be raised but have introduced a range of civil powers and statutory orders (curfews, child safety orders, ASBOs, and so on) that have targeted, or have been used disproportionately against, under-18 year olds, including in some cases those below the age of 10. As such interventions are 'preventive' they can be applied without either the prosecution or commission of a criminal offence. The UN committee report (2008) explicitly calls for the abolition of ASBOs for children. Pre-emptive intervention may also deliberately comprise public humiliation – for example, through 'naming and shaming' – a practice considered by the European Human Rights Commissioner to be 'entirely disproportionate', 'counter-productive' and in violation of the European Convention on Human Rights (ECHR) (Office of the Commissioner for Human Rights, 2005). The UN Committee (2007) also considers the 'naming and shaming' of young offenders to be a disproportionate interference with the right to privacy. For 'grave' offences children may by-pass the youth justice system altogether and have their cases tried in the 'adult' crown court – a practice again routinely condemned by both the UNCRC and the ECHR for failing to allow the child's full participation in judicial proceedings (Muncie, 2007).

- *Failure to use custody as a last resort*: Age reductions in the detention of young people coupled with increases in maximum sentence have always put the UK at odds with the UNCRC. Custody rates have increased by some 24 per cent since 1997. Such data place England and Wales as one of the most punitive in Western Europe (see **Chapter 10**). Child discrimination is also evident in the maximum six-month custodial sentences for adults versus maximum two-year sentence for equivalent offences for children; the minimum custodial sentence for juveniles is four months whereas adults may be imprisoned for only a few days (Muncie, 2007).

- *Failure to protect children in custody*: The CRAE (2005) notes that the state is not only obliged to refrain from taking life but should take appropriate steps to safeguard life. Between 1998 and 2002, however, there were 1,659 reported incidents of self-injury or attempted suicide by child prisoners in England and Wales. The CRAE also considers that failure of YOTs and prison authorities to identify such children as 'vulnerable' could amount to incompatibility with the UNCRC and the 1998 *Human Rights Act*.

- *Inhuman or degrading treatment*: The treatment of young people in custody has been routinely condemned by children's rights organizations as well as the Prison Inspectorate (Standing Committee for Youth Justice, 2006). The transportation of detained children in adult 'meat wagons' and excessive use of restraint techniques have been recurring matters of concern. For example, it has been estimated that 'pain compliant' techniques were used over 3,000 times in secure training centres between November 2005 and October 2006. In 2008, the Parliamentary Joint Committee on Human Rights, in a review of the use of restraint, concluded that deliberate infliction of pain, through 'distraction' techniques, is in breach of children's human rights.

- *Restricting freedom of association*: In 2004, 'dispersal zones' were established in over 800 areas of the UK. The legality of one such zone in Richmond was successfully challenged by a 15 year old in 2005. The increasing use of ultrasonic devices to disperse young people – their sound is only audible to those under the age of 25 – degrades and discriminates against children rather than treating them with the principles of dignity and respect enshrined in the UNCRC (UN Committee, 2007; 2008).

At the core of the contemporary governance of children seems to be the view that they have already been fully (or over-) endowed with rights. The long-awaited *Youth Crime Action Plan* (HM Government, 2008) made no reference to children's rights at all. Lawbreaking and transgression seem to be used as an excuse for the state to forget that it too has *responsibilities* for the welfare of all of its citizens. Clearly it is possible to claim an adherence to the principle of rights while simultaneously pursuing policies that exacerbate structural inequalities and punitive institutional regimes. It is far from clear how the dismantling of many of the distinctions between youth and adult justice and failure to implement the UNCRC can be construed as acting in a child's 'best interests'.

▉ ▉ Summary ▉

- Contemporary policies and practices of youth justice are complex and complicated. Chapters 8 and 9 have provided a framework of welfare, justice, prevention, and punishment in order to disentangle some of the system's contradictory aims and outcomes.

- As youth justice has developed in response to increases in the influence of those professionals working in the system and also to changes in the broader political climate, it has evolved in a state of constant flux. No one of these approaches has achieved ascendancy. Instead, youth justice has expanded and oscillated to meet a variety of different demands and aspirations. It is an accretion of numerous levels of discourse (see Box 9.13).

Box 9.13

Youth justice discourses

Discourse	Principles
Welfare-paternalism	Youth as deprived. Care, guidance and supervision as the 'paramount consideration'. Focus on needs. Rationale to respond to individual needs.
Liberal justice	Youth as rational actors. The erosion of age considerations by focusing on the gravity of the offence and formulating a proportionate response. Rationale to ensure due process and fairness.
Neo-conservative remoralization	Youth as immoral. Risk assessments to act on the possibility of future crime and on the non-criminal as well as the criminal. Legitimated as crime prevention via early intervention. Rationale to compel social inclusion.
Neo-liberal responsibilization	Youth as irresponsible. Certain individuals, families have a responsibility to transform themselves, increase informal controls and reduce criminal opportunities. Rationale to devolve state responsibility for crime control.
Neo-conservative authoritarianism	Youth as dangerous. The resort to overtly punitive measures to respond to and channel perceptions of public punitiveness for short-term political expediency and electoral gain. Rationale to protect the public.
Managerialism	No particular or specific 'reading' of young. The rewriting of the purpose of youth justice to achieve measurable and cost-effective outcomes that are amenable to audited accounting. Internal system coherence. Rationale to achiieve a pragmatic implementation of policy.
Human rights	Youth as vulnerable to adult power and under-protected. Challenging youth justice to recognize that children can and should participate directly in decisions affecting their lives. Rationale to alleviate harm, abuse, exploitation and social marginalization.

- Progressive practice is forever prey to reactionary overhaul when 'get tough on crime' agendas achieve ascendancy. By the mid-1990s it was claimed that 'prison works' and that specialized detention facilities (secure training centres and boot camps) should be expanded. By 1994, it was noticeable that the numbers in youth custody had once more started to rise: a rise that has never been seriously challenged despite a newfound commitment to crime prevention, risk management and restoration.

- The 'modernization' of youth justice rests on an evidence-led, 'what works' logic in which outputs are to be continually monitored, audited and evaluated. However, this pragmatism coexists with persistently recurring appeals to custody. A constellation of the managerial and the authoritarian is one of the defining fault-lines of twenty-first-century youth justice.

- Youth justice reform is not simply driven by an increase in crime. It is also a reflection of sudden and volatile shifts in political mood in which short-term political gain and the need for the state to assert itself can override all other concerns. The study of youth justice policy and practice ultimately tells us more about social order, the state and political decision-making than it does about the nature of young offending and the most effective ways to respond to it.

 ■ study Questions ■

1   Is the youth justice system the most appropriate place for responding to 'troubled' and 'troublesome' children and young people? Can you imagine any possible viable alternatives?

2   What are the possible dangers of early intervention to 'nip crime in the bud'?

3   What 'evidence' does the youth justice system seem to act upon? What 'evidence' is ignored?

4   Evaluate the view that the importing of principles of restorative justice has only added to the system's inconsistencies and contradictions.

5   Why do welfare, restorative, rights-based and diversionary reforms always appear to be partial, ambiguous and politically contested?

■ ■ **Further Reading** ■

Goldson's edited collection *The New Youth Justice* (2000a), Pitts's *The New Politics of Youth Crime* (2001), Smith's *Youth Justice* (2003, 2nd edition 2007) and Goldson and Muncie's *Youth Crime and Justice* (2006) provide some of the most incisive critiques of recent youth justice reform. Bateman and Pitts's (2005) *The RHP Companion to Youth Justice* is a useful descriptive analysis of all elements of youth justice, particularly in England and Wales. As noted in Chapter 8, Goldson's (2008b) *Dictionary of Youth Justice* also provides a clear introduction to the myriad powers and procedures.

There is a wide literature on all of the specific interventions discussed in this chapter. For the principles of early intervention, see Farrington and Welsh (2007); for the politics of anti-social behaviour legislation, see Burney (2005); for managerialism, see Clarke and Newman (1997); for restorative justice, see Johnstone (2002); for youth custody, see Goldson (2002c; 2008a); for the UK's record in complying with children's rights frameworks, see Scraton and Haydon (2002); UN Committee (2008).

To keep up to date in this fast moving field you should consult the journal *Youth Justice: An International Journal* which carries a *Youth Justice News* section updated three times a year.

http://www.cabinetoffice.gov.uk/
Details governmental initiatives in crime prevention, community safety, social exclusion and criminal justice.

http://www.childrenssociety.org.uk
Site of The Children's Society.

http://www.nacro.org.uk
Site of National Association for the Care and Resettlement of Offenders (NACRO): the principal independent organization in England and Wales working to prevent crime and resettle ex-prisoners. On-line copies of its journal – *Safer Society* – until its final edition in winter 2007/2008 can be accessed at www.safer-society.org.uk.

http://www.nayj.org.uk
Site of key pressure group – National Association for Youth Justice.

http://www.nya.org.uk
Site of National Youth Agency.

http://www.yjb.gov.uk/en-gb/
Site of Youth Justice Board for England and Wales.

http://www.yjb.gov.uk/en-gb/yjs/Custody/CustodyFigures/
Access to the Youth Justice Board's statistics on the juvenile secure estate, from 2000 to present.

http://www.howardleague.org/
The home-site of the UK's leading penal reform agency with a long history of pioneering work in the youth justice field. The weekly 'prison watch', providing regularly updated penal statistics, is particularly useful.

http://www.statewatch.org/asbo/ASBOwatch.html
Site established to monitor the use of anti-social behaviour orders. Provides useful library of media reports on the 'anti-social'.

10

Comparative and International Youth Justice

Chapter 10 examines:

- international developments and global trends in youth and juvenile justice reform;

- national/regional/local configurations in youth and juvenile justice reform;

- the impact of international children's rights frameworks on youth and juvenile justice reform;

- the extent of a global 'punitive turn' in youth and juvenile justice since the 1990s;

- degrees of convergence and divergence in policy and practice across national and regional borders;

- flows of policy from one jurisdiction to another;

- the continuing relevance of 'the local' in youth and juvenile justice practice.

| **key terms** |

children's rights; comparative criminology; convergence; culture of control; globalization; localization; neo-conservatism; neo-liberalism; policy transfer; positive rights; punitive turn; racialization; toleration

---

Understanding the role of globalization in processes of international and national criminal justice reform is in its infancy. At the outset it is worth noting that, while the UK now generally refers to its *youth* justice systems, throughout Europe the term *juvenile* justice is preferred, while the UN advocates the formulation of a *child- centred* criminal justice. Nevertheless there have been some remarkable correspondences in the trajectories of juvenile/youth justice reform particularly across many western societies in the past 40 years. Since the 1970s, welfare models based on meeting individual needs have been seriously challenged or usurped by justice models more concerned with responding to the offence than the offender. By the 1980s, 'justice' had come to take on numerous forms from due process and rights; to 'just deserts' and authoritarian crime control (see **Chapter 8**). In the 1990s, many nation states began experimenting with forms of restorative justice and risk management as a means of re-introducing forms of rehabilitation while holding young people accountable for their actions (see **Chapter 9**). By the twenty-first century juvenile/youth justice had developed into a particularly complex agglomeration of competing and contradictory policies, including retribution, responsibility, rights, restoration and rehabilitation, which simultaneously exhibit strong exclusionary and inclusionary tendencies (Muncie, 2006). These shifts have not been uniform but it appears that few, if any, western societies have been able to ignore their impact. The key issues addressed in this chapter are why did this international trend from welfare to justice to just deserts to restoration and responsibility occur? And with what effects? To do so it assesses the analytical usefulness of the concept of globalization.

The Globalization of Juvenile Justice _____

10.1 The concept of globalization has gradually permeated criminology, but is typically more applied to transnational organized crime, international terrorism and policing than to processes of criminal and juvenile justice reform. Its usefulness in understanding contemporary transformations in systems of youth and juvenile justice is relatively new (Muncie, 2005).

The concept of **globalization** draws attention to a number of interrelated processes: a growing international economic, political, legal and cultural interconnectedness based on advances in technological communications; the removal of trade barriers underpinned by market-led neo-liberal economics and politics; and the formulation of 'universal' directives in international law. Some contend that shifts in political economy, particularly those associated with capital mobility and information exchange, across advanced industrialized countries, have progressively eroded the foundations of redistributive welfare states and severely constrained the range of strategic political strategies and policy options that individual states can pursue (Beck, 2000). The concept of globalization then suggests two inter-related transformations of significance to youth and criminal justice. First, policies are converging worldwide (or at least across the Anglophone global north). A combination of macro socio-economic developments, initiatives in international human rights and accelerations in processes of policy transfer are viewed as symptomatic of a rapid homogenization of policy formation. The necessity of attracting international capital compels governments (if they are to achieve status as modern states) to adopt similar economic, social and criminal justice policies in part aided by geo-political mobility and subsequent policy flows, diffusion and learning. Second, this homogenization, it is contended, is underpinned by a fundamental shift in state/market relations. A loss (or at least a major reconfiguration) of 'the social' is evidenced in the processes whereby neo-liberal conceptions of the market and international capital encourage the formulation of policies based less on principles of social inclusion and more on social inequality, deregulation, privatization, penal expansionism and welfare residualism. In effect, the thesis presages the decline of social democratic reformist politics and projects worldwide (Mishra, 1999). And it is children, as the least powerful members of communities, who are the most likely to routinely feel the brunt of this neo-liberal economic project.

From Welfare to Neo-liberal Governance _____

Numerous authors have argued that since the 1960s penal welfarism has been undermined by the development of forms of **neo-liberalism** or 'advanced' governance (Bell, 1993; Rose, 1996a and b, 2000; Garland, 1996, 2001). This fundamental change in criminal and juvenile justice has been broadly characterized as placing less emphasis on the social contexts of crime and measures of state protection and more on prescriptions of individual/family/community responsibility and accountability. The shift has been captured in the notions of 'responsibilization' (see **Chapter 9**) and 'governing at a distance' (see **Chapter 7**). The delivery of universal welfare provision has been increasingly critiqued for encouraging state dependence, overloading the responsibilities of the state and undermining the ability of individuals to take responsibility for their own actions. 'Old' notions of *social* engineering, *social* benefits, *social* work, and *social* welfare, it is claimed, have been transformed to create responsible and autonomous (i.e. not welfare-dependent) citizens (O'Malley, 2000). A 'loss of the social' thesis suggests a number of interrelated – sometimes contradictory – youth and criminal justice processes that have occurred to varying degrees across most western societies. These include the privatizing of the state sector and the commodifying of crime control; the widening of material inequalities between and within states thus creating new insecurities and fuelling demands for centralized authoritarian law and order strategies; the devolving of responsibility for crime control to individuals, families and communities (as captured in the notion of 'responsibilization'); and the espousing of scientific realism and pragmatic 'what works' responses to crime and disorder in the hope that an image of an 'orderly environment' can be secured which in turn will help to attract further 'nomadic capital'. As global market-led capital becomes apparently out of national control, the state reasserts its authority by creating new sets of 'criminal others' and then attempts to provide protection from such 'threatening and undesirable outsiders' through progressively more authoritarian means. The 'asylum seeker', the 'dangerous foreigner', the 'welfare dependent', the 'work-shy', and the 'morally degenerate', for example, have been typically constructed as prime targets for sustained punitive intervention. The state has been drawn into re-establishing through coercion those very social relations that have been destabilized (or have been made possible) through engagement with globalized free market economics. Poverty is increasingly managed through restrictive 'workfare' and expansive 'prisonfare' (Wacquant, 2008). 'Meeting needs' has been subjugated to 'addressing fears'. Such developments have made a major impact on child and youth populations. It is these populations that have traditionally constituted 'the most intensively governed sector of personal existence' (Rose, 1989, p. 121); they have also endured disproportionate levels of poverty, disempowerment, vulnerability, and victimization (see **Chapter 5**). Any decline in the ability of nation states to deliver protective welfarism will have major repercussions for the state of childhood and youth. Such processes suggest an acceleration of the governance of young people *through* crime and disorder. Adolescent development, such as the transition to adulthood, is redefined as a problem of criminality and disorder rather than as a social policy issue of education, health, welfare and employment (Simon, 1997; 2007). The continual reworking and expansion of youth justice systems; a never-ending stream of legislation apparently dominating all other government concerns; the political use of youth crime as a means to secure electoral gain; the excessive media fascination – both as news and entertainment – with all things 'criminal'; and the obsession with regulation whether through families, schools or training programmes all attest to the disorder attributed to young people as a central motif of governance (Muncie, 2006).

The Punitive Turn

Further homogenization is believed to be encouraged by the spread of **neo-conservatism** and punitive penal policies, particularly from the USA. Wacquant (1999a), for example, noted how law and order talk directed at 'youth', 'problem neighbourhoods', 'incivilities' and 'urban violence' came to increasingly dominate the political and media landscape of the USA in the 1990s. Significantly, he argued, this 'talk' was also in the process of gradually permeating European public debate such that it had begun to provide the framework for any broader political discussions of justice, safety, community and so on. Wacquant detailed how various neo-conservative think tanks, foundations, policy entrepreneurs and commercial enterprises in the USA were able to valorize the diminution of the social or welfare state (in the name of neo-liberal economic competitiveness) and the expansion of a penal or punitive state (in order to deal with the economically excluded). Wacquant recorded how this mentality

> originates in Washington and New York City, crosses the Atlantic to lash itself down in London, and, from there, stretches its channels and capillaries throughout the Continent and beyond ... [such that] one discerns a solid consensus taking shape between the most reactionary segment of the American Right and the self proclaimed avant-garde of the European 'New Left' around the idea that the 'undeserving poor' ought to be brought back under control by the (iron) hand of the state. (Wacquant, 1999a, pp. 322, 333)

Two years later, Garland's analysis of USA/UK policy convergence lent significant weight to this thesis by identifying a new **culture of control** characterized by mass imprisonment, curfews, zero tolerance, naming and shaming, and three strikes legislation which have produced a punitive mentality affecting not only offenders but broader social relations (Garland, 2001). Pratt et al.'s (2005) edited volume was similarly dedicated to analysing (and challenging) the parameters of a 'new punitiveness' capable of crossing international borders. Much of this thesis also resonated directly with the proliferation of law and order politics in the UK, particularly in England since the early 1990s and provided a valuable contextualization for the tangible repenalization of young people who were (and continue to be) subjected to a 'new correctionalism' of intensive pre-emptive intervention and dramatically rising penal populations (see **Chapter 9**).

Numerous published commentaries on juvenile justice, emanating from the USA and various UK and European jurisdictions over the past decade, have lent support to the **punitive turn** thesis. In the UK, the Children's Legal Centre/Y Care International (2006) campaign report, for example, was firmly based on the supposition that 'states all over the world have retained an overwhelmingly punitive response to young offending'. In the USA, juvenile incarceration increased by 43 percent during the 1990s reaching an estimated 105,600 in 2006. From 1989 and until its repeal in 2005, 18 states continued to permit the execution of those who had committed murder at age 16 and 17. Many still retain powers of life imprisonment without parole. At least 2,225 child offenders were serving such a sentence in 2005, 60 per cent of whom were African-American (Human Rights Watch/Amnesty International, 2005). In contrast to the 'best interest' principle underpinning the establishment of the first juvenile court in Chicago in 1899, juvenile justice systems throughout America now give greater weight to punishment as an end in itself. Almost all states have made it easier to transfer young people to the adult system, have created mandatory minimum custody sentences and have undermined the principle of confidentiality by facilitating the sharing of youth defendants' social history among criminal justice, education, health and social service agencies (Amnesty International, 1998; Snyder, 2002; Mears, 2006). The depth of a 'punitive turn' in America in the 1990s is undeniable , although we should also be mindful of distinct state differences and recurrent pressures – economic, moral, pragmatic – to reverse this trend (Krisberg, 2006; Benekos and Merlo, 2008).

But is this mirrored elsewhere? Junger-Tas (2006, p. 505) claims that in Europe the 'main trend in juvenile justice in a number of countries has been more repressive but not necessarily more effective'. Numerous recent developments and state commentaries give this thesis some support. Van Swaaningen (2005) records how a traditional culture of tolerance in Holland has been rapidly dismantled by a vastly expanded and punitive criminal justice state. The number of places of youth detention has tripled since 1990 while early intervention projects, such as STOP, have effectively lowered penal responsibility from 12 to 10 year olds (uit Beijerse and van Swaaningen, 2006). In Belgium, public debate about insecurity and lack of safety has fuelled a fear of youth crime and legitimized police initiatives in curfew and zero tolerance (Put and Walgrave, 2006). Long-standing principles of youth protection also appear threatened by increased resort to referring juvenile offenders to the adult court (van Dijk et al., 2005). The election of Sarkozy in France in 2007 was swiftly followed by a promise that reoffenders aged 16 and above would be treated as adults. Sarkozy's electoral success has been partly explained by his pre-election declaration (at a time of widespread urban disturbances in 2005) that delinquent youths on poor estates were 'scum' that should be 'cleaned out with a hose' (*The Times*, 4 November 2005). In 2008, with regional elections in the offing, Chancellor Merkel in Germany announced plans to introduce boot camps and 'warning shot arrests' particularly for immigrant youth. The issue had come to a head following an attack on a pensioner by two youths – one Greek and one Turkish. She declared that 'we have too many criminal young foreigners' despite statistics showing that crime by non-Germans was in decline and that youth crime had remained stable at around 12% of all crimes for the past 15 years (*Guardian*, 8 January 2008). Commentaries on juvenile justice in Spain have concluded that recent legislative change has in the main devalued principles of 'best interest' in favour of a toughening of responses to young offenders (Rechea Alberola and Fernandez Molina, 2006). The reformed children's court in Ireland (Kilkelly, 2008) and the new youth courts for 16 and 17 year olds in Scotland (Piacentini and Walters, 2006) both tend to fail to recognize the particular needs of young people and operate in a manner more akin to the adult court. This concern also appears capable of crossing traditional political boundaries. In Sweden, alarmism, zero tolerance and increased sanctioning of penal control have become as much at the heart of social democratic as conservative political discourse (Tham, 2001). In the context of a 'return to law and order' (Balvig, 2004), Denmark's long-standing welfare boards, which act instead of court-based systems for young offenders, are also reported to be under threat by more repressive crime control initiatives (Jepsen, 2006). Japan has long enjoyed a reputation of informal, community-based justice, cemented in tradition and reflected in low rates of crime and incarceration.

However, Smith and Sueda's (2008) comparison of the English reaction to the Bulger tragedy and Japan's reaction to murders committed by a 14 year old boy in Kobe revealed some significant similarities. Both set in train legal reforms designed to hold children fully responsible; both were held to signify educational and family failure. Although social reaction in Japan was generally less extreme and vengeful, the similarities did suggest that the 'punitive turn' was more than capable of crossing traditional political and cultural boundaries.

Such commentaries reveal that punitive values associated with retribution, incapacitation, individual responsibility and offender accountability have achieved a political legitimacy to the detriment of traditional principles of juvenile protection and support. Moreover, this is not simply an Anglo-American phenomenon.

Policy Transfer, Flows and Convergence

Policy transfer can be considered as one of the most tangible drivers of such processes. (Wacquant, 1999a; Christie, 2000; Garland, 2001; Jones and Newburn, 2002, 2007; Newburn, 2002a). It has become increasingly common for nation states to look 'worldwide' in efforts to discover 'what works' in preventing crime and to reduce re-offending. Typically this has meant looking to the USA. Certainly, aspects of zero tolerance policing (in France, Australia, Germany, Brazil, Argentina, Ireland), curfews (in Belgium, France, Scotland), electronic monitoring (in Singapore, Canada, Australia, Sweden, Holland, Scotland), scared-straight programmes (in Italy), mandatory sentencing (in Western Australia, Northern Territories) and pre-trial detention as a 'short, sharp, shock' (in Germany, Holland, France) which all originated in the USA have now been 'transported' to many western jurisdictions. They all have, or have had a presence, either practically or rhetorically, in the UK.

However, the possibility of Anglo-American **convergence** tends to dominate the literature on policy transfer (Dolowitz, 2000; Dolowitz and Marsh, 2000; Garland, 2001). And at first sight it seems apposite. In the early days of opposition Labour persistently challenged and condemned the Conservatives' overt transatlantic policy transfers in both social and criminal justice matters. The left of centre preferred to look to Europe. However, after Blair's visit to the USA in 1993, which presaged the new doctrine of 'being tough on crime and tough on the causes of crime', New Labour also shifted its focus from Europe to the New Democratic policies of the USA. Since the mid-1990s, not only compulsory and conditional welfare-to-work (workfare) but also zero tolerance policing, night curfews, electronic tagging, mandatory minimum sentences, drugs czars, the naming and shaming of young offenders, community courts, private prisons, parental sin bins and, for a short period in the 1990s, boot camps have all, in some form, been witnessed in England (see **Chapter 9**). A tough stance on crime and welfare has become the taken-for-granted mantra to achieve electoral success. But as Sparks (2001, p. 165) has put it, there may be inherent difficulties to this type of comparative analysis because of the 'distracting sway of the American case as a pole of attraction'. It tends to drive out historical and cultural difference by assuming that what happens in the USA will always presage comparable developments elsewhere.

The notion of homogenized policy transfer has also been critiqued by those concerned not just with issues of structural convergence/divergence but with the role of 'agency' in the formulation and implementation of specific policies (Jones and Newburn, 2002; Nellis, 2000; Aas, 2007). Detailed empirical examinations of policy-making in different countries reveal important differences in substance and significant differences in the processes through which policy is reformed and implemented. Both O'Donnell and O'Sullivan (2003) and Jones and Newburn (2002), for example, argue that the concept of zero tolerance associated with New York policing reforms in the early 1990s barely survived its import to Ireland and the UK. The strategies adopted by the NYPD were only employed by some minor experiments in mainstream British policing. Its impact has been more on the level of political rhetoric, fuelled by Fianna Fáil in Ireland and by cross-party commitments in the UK to develop more punitively sounding policies that can be widely perceived as being 'tough on crime'. Similarly Nellis's analysis of the transatlantic transfer of electronic monitoring from the USA to England in particular makes clear that the terms 'inspiration' and 'emulation' rather than 'copying' best describe the processes involved.

These lines of enquiry suggest that policy transfer is rarely direct and complete but is partial and mediated through national and local cultures *which are themselves changing at the same time* (Muncie, 2005). Policy transfer can be viewed as simply a pragmatic response where nothing is ruled in and nothing ruled out. Or it can be viewed as symptomatic of juvenile/youth systems that have lost their way and no longer adhere to any fundamental values and principles, whether they are rooted in welfare, punishment, protection or rights. The logic of assuming we can learn 'what works' from others is certainly seductive. It implies rational planning and an uncontroversial reliance on a crime science which is free of any political interference. But it also assumes that policies can be transported and are transportable without cognisance of localized cultures, conditions and the politics of space (Muncie, 2002, and see Section 10.4 below).

International Children's Rights

The 1989 United Nations Convention on the Rights of the Child has established a near global **children's rights** consensus that all children have a right to *protection*, to *participation* and to basic material *provision*. It upholds children's right to life, to be free from discrimination, to be protected in armed conflicts, to be protected from degrading and cruel punishment, to receive special treatment in justice systems and grants freedom from discrimination, exploitation and abuse (see **Chapter 9.3**). The only countries not to have ratified are Somalia and the USA (Somalia has no internationally recognized government; the USA has claimed it cannot ratify while it is considering other rights issues and that it interferes with family autonomy). The Convention builds upon the 1985 UN Standard Minimum Rules for the Administration of Youth Justice (the Beijing Rules) which recognized the 'special needs of children' and the importance of dealing with offenders flexibly. It promoted diversion from formal court procedures, non-custodial disposals and insisted that custody should be a last resort and for minimum periods. In addition, the Rules emphasized the need for anonymity in order to protect children from life-long stigma and labelling. The Convention cemented these themes in the fundamental right that in all legal actions concerning those under the age of 18, the 'best interests of the child shall be a primary consideration'. Further it reasserts the need to treat children differently, to promote their dignity and worth with minimum use of custody and that children should participate in any proceedings relating to them (see Box 10.1).

Box 10.1

United Nations Convention on the Rights of the Child

Article 1
For the purposes of the present Convention, a child means every human being below the age of eighteen years unless under the law applicable to the child, majority is attained earlier.

Article 3
1. In all actions concerning children, whether undertaken by public or private social welfare institutions, courts of law, administrative authorities or legislative bodies, the best interests of the child shall be a primary consideration.

Article 37
States Parties shall ensure that:
(a) No child shall be subjected to torture or other cruel, inhuman or degrading treatment or punishment. Neither capital punishment nor life imprisonment without possibility of release shall be imposed for offences committed by persons below eighteen years of age;

(b) No child shall be deprived of his or her liberty unlawfully or arbitrarily. The arrest, detention or imprisonment of a child shall be in conformity with the law and shall be used only as a measure of last resort and for the shortest appropriate period of time;

(c) Every child deprived of liberty shall be treated with humanity and respect for the inherent dignity of the human person, and in a manner which takes into account the needs of persons of his or her age. In particular, every child deprived of liberty shall be separated from adults unless it is considered in the child's best interest not to do so and shall have the right to maintain contact with his or her family through correspondence and visits, save in exceptional circumstances;

(d) Every child deprived of his or her liberty shall have the right to prompt access to legal and other appropriate assistance, as well as the right to challenge the legality of the deprivation of his or her liberty before a court or other competent, independent and impartial authority, and to a prompt decision on any such action.

Article 40
1. States Parties recognize the right of every child alleged as, accused of, or recognized as having infringed the penal law to be treated in a manner consistent with the promotion of the child's sense of dignity and worth, which reinforces the child's respect for the human rights and fundamental freedoms of others and which takes into account the child's age and the desirability of promoting the child's reintegration and the child's assuming a constructive role in society.

Source: Selected Articles from United Nations Convention on the Rights of the Child (1989).

In 1990, the UN guidelines for the Prevention of Juvenile Delinquency (the Riyadh Guidelines) added that youth justice policy should avoid criminalizing children for their minor misdemeanors. The International Covenant on Civil and Political Rights expressly outlaws capital punishment for under-18s and promotes rehabilitative interventions. The European Convention on Human Rights, first formulated in 1953, provides for the due process of law, fairness in trial proceedings, a right to education, a right to privacy and declares that any deprivation of liberty (including curfews, electronic monitoring and community supervision) should not be arbitrary or consist of any degrading treatment. Further, in 2006, the Commission of the European Communities published its own separate EU strategy on the rights of children affirming the issue as a 'priority' and with the aim of promoting the EU as 'a beacon to the rest of the world'.

Many countries have now used the UN Convention to improve protections for children and have appointed special commissioners or ombudspersons to champion children's rights. Of note has been a raft of legal reforms in Latin America during the 1990s associated with a renewed recognition of a distinctive Latin American affirmation of human rights. Venezuela and Argentina, for example, were key advocates in the formulation of the UN Convention (Carozza, 2003). To establish how far individual states are treating their young in the spirit, if not the word, of the Convention, the United Nations also established a separate Committee which compels nation states to report on their 'progress' and to receive recommendations for further action. The foundational element of international youth justice, it claimed, is that children in 'conflict with the law' deserve to be treated with a respect and dignity that recognizes their vulnerability, immaturity, and their lack of full awareness of the consequences of their behaviour (United Nations Committee on the Rights of the Child, 2007).

Collectively these Conventions and Rules can be viewed as tantamount to a growing legal globalization of juvenile justice.

Comparative Juvenile Justice: Estimating Rates of Custody

10.2 There are relatively few rigorous comparative analyses of youth and juvenile justice. Most provide important case studies of particular jurisdictions but tend to be stronger on the descriptive than the analytical. In many respects this is not surprising. Doing comparative research is fraught with difficulties (Zedner, 1995; Nelken, 1994, 2002).

One of the most obvious places to start in developing a comparative juvenile justice and trying to come to some assessment of a 'global punitive turn' is through examination of the custody statistics collected by national and international bodies. There are various sources, such as the United Nations *Surveys on Crime Trends and the Operations of Criminal Justice Systems* (now in its 10th edition) and The *European Sourcebook of Crime and Criminal Justice* (now in its 3rd edition) which provide estimates (usually as a percentage of total prison population) of the juvenile secure population in various countries at various times. The United Nations Surveys on the Operation of Criminal Justice Systems in 2002, for example, attempted to provide rates of *youth/juvenile* imprisonment per 100,000 of population. These statistics provided a diverse picture of

38.40 per 100,000 in the USA and 18.26 per 100,000 in England and Wales but an almost absence of youth custody in Denmark (0.11/100,000), in Norway (0.07/100,000) and in Belgium (0.02/100,000) (see Box 10.2).

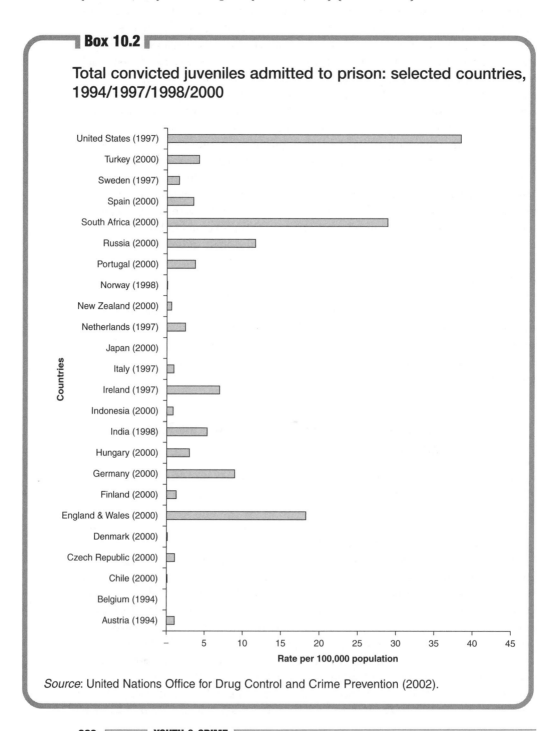

Box 10.2

Total convicted juveniles admitted to prison: selected countries, 1994/1997/1998/2000

Source: United Nations Office for Drug Control and Crime Prevention (2002).

According to these statistics, England and Wales incarcerate young people at a higher *rate* than any other country in Europe; indeed, in the world, only the USA, South Africa, Belize and Swaziland were recorded by the UN as having higher incarceration rates. These particular sources, however, have often proved partial and contradictory with data absent for numerous states (Muncie, 2005). Some, such as Australia and Canada have no entry presumably because they either do not collect such data or declined to respond to the UN's survey. The lack of consistent and reliable data on how many children are incarcerated at any given time is probably symptomatic of the relative lack of importance that some states give to the issue. Even when data are recorded, their use may be of limited comparative value because the age constitution of a 'child', a 'juvenile' or a 'young person' is differentially applied and means different things to different cultures (Malby, 2008). This is clearly apparent in the variance in ages of criminal responsibility across Western countries, ranging from 6 or below in some states in USA, 8 in Scotland to 18 in Belgium (see Box 10.3).

Box 10.3

Variance in ages of criminal responsibility: selected countries

Country	Age
USA	6+ (state variance)
Scotland	8
Australia	10
Switzerland	10 (raised from 7 in 2006)
England and Wales	10 (*doli incapax* abolished 1998)
Northern Ireland	10
Canada	12 (established 1984)
Ireland	12 (from 7 in 2001; to be implemented)
Netherlands	12
Portugal	12
Greece	12
France	13
New Zealand	14
Germany	14
Japan	14 (lowered from 16 in 2000)
Austria	14
Italy	14
Spain	14 (raised from 12 in 2001)
Denmark	15
Finland	15
Norway	15 (raised from 14 in 1990)
Sweden	15
Belgium	18
Luxembourg	18

Further problems with relying solely on UN data appear to be that it is never clear whether the data are based on statistics of 'stock' (numbers on a given date) or 'flow' (numbers admitted during a calendar year). We are never sure whether 'juvenile' always refers to under-18s or to under-21s. Custody data may be of total custodial populations or might only include those under sentence (omitting remands). A key issue in measuring 'juvenile custody' is whether only prison administration facilities are counted, thereby excluding potentially large numbers held in quasi welfare institutions. The *European Sourcebook* (2006, p. 21) acknowledges that 'the lack of uniform definitions of offences, of common measuring instruments and of common methodology makes comparisons between countries extremely hazardous'.

With these warnings in mind the following estimates of penal populations are based on the world prison population list produced by Walmsley initially for the Home Office and latterly for the International Centre for Prison Studies (ICPS) based at Kings College London. Walmsley (2006) estimates that over 9 million people are being held in penal institutions worldwide at any one time. His data do not detail the number of juveniles but this has been estimated at being in the region of one million. Examining the data for 2005–2006 across different regions reveals that the USA has by far the highest penal population with some 738 incarcerated per 100,000 population. The England and Wales rate of 148 places it as the highest in Western Europe. Variance in the willingness of nation states to resort to the custodial option is indeed quite remarkable (see Box 10.4).

These data of course combine adult and juveniles. Arguably the most accurate estimate of rates of *juvenile* incarceration can be derived by combining custody data collected by ICPS and population data gathered by UNICEF (NACRO, 2002; Muncie, 2008). This allows estimates to be made of juvenile custody *rates* per 1000 under-18 population. Such sources confirm the USA as atypical. It easily outstrips the rest with a rate of 1.4/1000. In Western Europe, the Netherlands, England and Wales, and Germany appear the most 'custody prone'. Of note is that England and Wales, France and Italy have roughly equal under-18 populations. But in 2006/7, England and Wales held just under 3,000 under-18 year olds in custody, compared to 619 in France, and 399 in Italy (see Box 10.5).

There are of course good reasons to still remain cautious in 'reading' such statistics. Most worrying is that many countries do not have any reliable statistical record of who they lock up and where. There are no data specifically on under-18 year olds supplied by Portugal and Spain. As a commentary on juvenile justice in Spain noted, 'There is one problem with juvenile justice statistics in our country; there are none' (Rechea Alberola and Fernandez Molina, 2006). When data are collected, it appears rarely done so on a regular basis or on equivalent dates (juvenile custody rates are known to fluctuate widely through the year). Often these *prison* statistics

Box 10.4

World prison populations: highest and lowest rates in different regions, 2005–2006

	Total	Rate per 100,000 population
Africa		
South Africa	157,402	335
Burkina Faso	2,800	23
North America		
USA	2,186,230	738
Canada	34,096	107
South America		
Suriname	1,600	356
Venezuela	19,853	74
Asia		
Singapore	15,038	350
India	332,112	30
Western Europe		
England and Wales	79,861	148
Iceland	119	40
Eastern Europe		
Russia	869,814	611
Turkey	64,458	91
Oceania		
New Zealand	7,620	186
Nauru	3	23

Source: Derived from Walmsley (2006).

exclude those children removed from home on welfare and protection grounds rather than criminal grounds. But what is classified as penal custody in one country may not be in others though regimes may be similar. The existence of specialized detention centres, psychiatric units, training schools, treatment regimes, community homes, reception centres, residential care institutions, closed juvenile care (as in Sweden), reformatories (as in Finland) and secure wards (as in Denmark), may all hold young people against their will but may be excluded from penal statistics.

All of this underlines some of the inherent difficulties of **comparative criminology** and of doing comparative criminological research (see Box 10.6).

Box 10.5

Estimated number and rate of juveniles in penal custody: USA and Western Europe

	Under-18s in custody	Rate per 1000 under-18 population	Increase/decrease over previous four years
USA	105635	1.4	–
Netherlands	2105	0.58	+
England/Wales	2947	0.25	+
Spain	1847 (under-21)	0.24	
Germany	3196	0.22	
Scotland	236	0.21	+
Greece	389	0.20	–
N. Ireland	56	0.12	–
Austria	161	0.10	–
Portugal	122 (under-19)	0.06	
Ireland	56	0.05	–
France	619	0.04	
Italy	399	0.04	–
Switzerland	51	0.03	
Belgium	30	0.01	+
Norway	10	0.009	
Sweden	14	0.007	
Denmark	3	0.002	
Finland	3	0.002	

Sources: Derived from: http://www. unicef. org/statistics/index_countrystats.html and http://www.kcl.ac.uk/depsta/rel/icps/worldbrief/world_brief.html (accessed August 2008)

Notes: USA figure includes those in juvenile correctional facilities as well as state adult jails (as of June 2006) England/Wales figure includes those in STCs and SCHs as well as YOIs (as of May 2008) European figures derived from percentage of total prison populations (at various dates in 2007)

Box 10.6

Methodological and ethical issues in comparative research

- 'Criminological tourism': That is a misreading and oversimplifying of local conditions and cultures. A need to be as critical abroad as we might be at home.

- Linguistic difficulties and differences leave the research open to misinterpretation.

- Similar names given to institutions should not automatically be assumed to have the same function. Official descriptions may mask substantial differences in form, culture and purpose.

- The concepts of both 'crime' and 'youth' are not unitary phenomena. They may be differentially understood and therefore differentially 'measured' according to prevailing political discourse, media interest and legal categorization.

- Attention should always be given to the social and cultural context in which laws are formulated, crime recorded and sentences passed. But conversely a sole focus on localized 'difference' may negate the value of comparative research altogether.

- We must continually ask why comparative research is being undertaken. For what purpose? And by whose asking? Is it simply to record differences and similarities or is it a politically driven exploration of 'what works' which is then uncritically transposed from one cultural context to another?

Source: Derived from Zedner (1995).

National Sovereignty and Cultural Diversity: Comparative Thematics

10.3

Descriptive accounts of, and statistical measures gathered by, particular jurisdictions are useful tools in formative comparative analysis. For example, they suggest that it is only some nation states that can be considered as emulating a US-inspired youth repenalization/ culture of control. Others seem quite content without having any significant resort to penal custody at all. Why this might be the case though remains largely unknown. The following section explores how some widely assumed global trends are being translated and reworked at the 'local' level of the nation state, regional government and particular communities. Six key thematics – repenalization, adulteration, welfare protectionism, restoration, tolerance and rights – are identified (Muncie and Goldson, 2006) and explored to consider how they have been differentially configured and employed.

Repenalization

As we have seen, during the past decade many European countries have witnessed a distinct hardening of attitudes and criminal justice responses to young offending. Walmsley (2006) found in his world prison population list of 211 countries that 73 per cent had recorded *increases* in their total prison populations over the previous five years. There are no comparable regularly produced worldwide or European statistical time series records for under-18s. However according to Council of Europe statistics (European Sourcebook, 2003), England and Wales, The Netherlands, Greece, Germany and Portugal all reported significant *increases* in their daily counts of the numbers of under-18 year olds in prison between 1995 and 2000, while significant *decreases* were reported by Italy and Spain. A monitoring of International Centre for Prison Studies-derived figures between 2004 and 2007 suggested *increases* in the Netherlands (+1,800 since 2004) and England and Wales (+300 since 2004), compared to a *steady (and low)* rate in Denmark, Norway, Sweden, and Finland. It also suggested a movement towards decarceration in other countries such as Ireland, Greece and Italy (Muncie, 2008, and see section below on tolerance).

The Netherlands stands out as an exceptional case of repenalization. Youth prison populations were reduced in the 1970s by limiting penal capacity, emphasizing rehabilitation and supporting a culture of tolerance (Downes, 1988; Komen, 2002). HALT projects that were established in Rotterdam in 1981 and various other social crime prevention initiatives replaced judicial intervention with reparation schemes and advice agencies to improve youth's 'survival skills'. However, there was a dramatic reversal in Dutch penal policy from the mid-1980s onwards. Once heralded as a beacon of tolerance and humanity, Holland embarked on a substantial prison building programme linked to a tendency to expand pre-trial detention and to deliver longer sentences on conviction (Pakes, 2000). In 2002, Dutch city councils gave the police new powers to arbitrarily stop and search without reasonable suspicion in designated areas of 'security risk'. The practice has amounted to the criminalization of poor and black neighbourhoods, targeting in particular Moroccan youth (*Statewatch*, Jan.–Feb., 2003, p. 8). For Pakes (2004a), such shifts are symptomatic of a resurgent law and order discourse which prioritizes security over justice, as epitomized by the remarkable rise of punitive populism often associated with the right-wing politician Pim Fortuyn. Between 1995 and 2001, the number of youth custodial places increased from 900 to 2100.

In Germany, the average number of over-14 year olds in prison increased by 21 per cent during the 1990s (Suhling, 2003).

In Ireland, prison building and expansion have been a notable feature of the 1990s despite falling crime rates (O'Donnell and O'Sullivan, 2003).

In France, in the 1980s, the Mitterand government responded to a series of violent disturbances in Lyon and Marseilles, not by implementing more authoritarian measures, but by developing means of education and vocational opportunity and avenues for local political participation and incorporation. The *Bonnemaison* initiative involved the recruitment of older youth (*animateurs*) to act as paid youth workers with youngsters in the ghetto suburbs. These were connected with residents and local government officials to form crime prevention committees designed to address issues of citizenship and urban redevelopment as well as those of security. It is widely assumed that such strategies, based on local democratic representation, rather than repression, were at least initially successful in achieving a greater integration particularly for children of North African origin (King, 1988, 1991; King and Petit, 1985; Pitts, 1995, 1997). Since the 1980s, however, there is compelling evidence of a greater convergence of French and English crime prevention strategies made up of a patchwork of zero tolerance policing and of situational and social methods (Crawford, 2001; Roche, 2002). The right-wing government of Alain Juppe from 1993 to 1997 prioritized a zero tolerance police-led approach to crime prevention. It is a policy that has crossed the political divide. The socio-economic conditions that produce youth marginalization and estrangement are no longer given central political or academic attention (Bailleau, 1998). Rather concern is directed to migrant children, particularly from Africa, Asia and Eastern Europe who have arrived in search of political asylum and economic opportunity. Special surveillance units have been established to repress delinquency in 'sensitive neighbourhoods', penalties for recidivism have been increased and the deportation of foreigners speeded up (Wacquant, 2001). Since the return to power of the right in 2002, new public safety laws have expanded police powers of search, seizure and arrest, instituted prison sentences for public order offences (such as being disrespectful to those in authority), lowered from 16 to 13 the age at which young offenders can be imprisoned and introduced benefit sanctions for parents of offending children (Henley, 2002). Some commentaries on an Anglophone/France comparison, however, maintain that a culture of French republicanism, driven by 'progressive centre' notions of legal equality and of social *inclusion, solidarity* and *integration,* will ensure more of a lasting rejection of American 'harshness' and 'lack of respect for persons' than seems to be possible or politically acceptable in countries such as England and Wales (Pitts, 2001; Rutherford, 2002; Whitman, 2003).

Such shifts have, in part, been explained with reference to a complex constellation of a break-up of social democratic welfare humanitarianism, the embracing of neo-liberal market-led economies, fears of illegal migrants, changes in labour markets, the emergence of a new moralism of 'zero tolerance' associated with the disciplinary techniques of the free market and a related lowering of the tolerance level for crime and violence. As Junger-Tas (2002; 2004) put it, fear and insecurity fuel demand for a 'norm enforcing system' that is both retributive and interventionist. Governments of many (but not all) persuasions appear to be increasingly turning to law and order as a means of providing symbols of security and to enhance their own chances of electoral support.

'Adulteration'

A shift from welfare to justice-based philosophies has not only opened a door to a consideration of judicial due process but has also allowed justice and rights to be usurped, particularly by political conservatism, as a means of delivering 'just deserts' and enforcing individual responsibility. Retribution and deterrence have taken precedence over positive rights agendas. Special consideration given to young offenders is being undermined in favour of adult-style justice (Fionda, 1998; Bandalli, 2000; Schaffner, 2002). The emphasis has become one of fighting juvenile crime rather than securing juvenile justice (see **Chapter 8.1**).

This thesis is again pertinent to unravelling the contemporary twists and turns of international youth justice reform. In Holland, the conditions governing the possibility of transferring juvenile cases to an adult court have been relaxed. Early intervention projects, such as STOP, have effectively lowered penal responsibility from 12 to 10 year olds (Junger-Tas, 2004). Similarly Canada's 2003 youth justice reforms were based on the core principle that the protection of society be uppermost. The youth court was given the discretion to impose adult sentences on 14 year olds for 'presumptive offences' (Smandych, 2006).

Such 'adulteration' has been most marked in the USA which has witnessed widespread dismantling of special court procedures which had been in place for much of the twentieth century to protect young people from the stigma and formality of adult justice (Feld, 1993). Since the 1980s (but beginning in Florida in 1978) most US states have expanded the charges for which juvenile defendants can be tried as adults in criminal courts, lowered the age at which this can be done, changed the purpose of their juvenile codes to prioritize incapacitation and punishment and resorted to more punitive training and boot camps (Grisso and Schwartz, 2000). A renewed emphasis on public safety (rather than a child's best interests) has also meant that confidentiality has been removed in most states with the names of juvenile offenders made public and in some cases listed on the internet. Equally, in many states, children below the age of 14 and as young as 7 can have their cases waived by the juvenile court and be processed as if they were adult. As Merlo, Benekos and Cook (1997) established, by the mid-1990s at least 23 states had some statutory or legislative waiver provisions in order to facilitate the adjudication of juveniles in adult courts, thereby allowing the possibility of longer and more punitive forms of intervention. As a result, around 200,000 children under 18 are processed as adults each year (Snyder, 2002). Between 1976 and 2004, there were 22 executions of those who had been convicted when they were juveniles. It was only in March 2005 that the US Supreme Court abolished the practice, ruling by a slim majority of 5 to 4 that it accounted to a 'cruel and unusual punishment' (see Section 10.1 above).

Japan has always been considered a model of relative non-punitiveness, accounted for in the context of a tradition of 'maternal protectionism' and a culture of 'amae sensitivity' which prioritizes interdependence over individual accountability. The juvenile offender is deemed as much a victim as a criminal (Morita, 2002). But Japan also appears to be facing a renewed politicization and 'adulteration' of juvenile crime. Whether protectionism can survive cases like the Kobe murders (see Section 10.1 above) and moral panics over school indiscipline, *bosozoku* (high risk car and motorcycle driving) and *enjo kosai* (teenage prostitution) is open to question. The age of criminal responsibility was *lowered* from 16 to 14 in 2000 (Fenwick, 2004).

Welfare Protectionism

The principle that children and young people should be protected from the full weight of 'adult' criminal jurisdiction underpins the concept of welfare in youth justice. For much of the twentieth century most western systems of juvenile justice have sought legitimacy in a rhetoric of child protection and 'meeting needs'. This 'ideal' found a quite remarkable international consensus until at least the 1970s. Child welfare models of juvenile justice have been paramount: beginning with the first juvenile courts established in South Australia in 1895, in Illinois, USA, in 1899 and in England and Canada in 1908, through to the likes of Belgium's *Children's Protection Act* of 1912, France's 1945 edict prioritizing protection and education or Japan's *Juvenile Law of 1948*. Welfare, rehabilitation and 'meeting needs' were the watchwords. But this consensus has been consistently unravelled. In the 1980s, conservative critics argued that the primary function of the youth justice system should be to *control* young offenders rather than to *care* for them. The concept of welfare was widely regarded as evidence that the youth justice system had become too 'soft on crime' (see **Chapter 8.2**).

Two surveys have recently shed some light on the correlation between welfare and penal tolerance/intolerance. In 2006, the Crime and Society Foundation published research exploring the relationship between the proportion of gross domestic product (GDP) devoted to welfare expenditure within 18 western countries, and the local rate of imprisonment (Downes and Hansen, 2006). The report argued that 'welfare aims' have become increasingly marginalized 'as key variables in criminal justice policy and practice', despite evidence that a generous welfare state might enhance perceptions of fairness, social cohesion and stability. Welfare and imprisonment appear inversely related. Countries with higher rates of welfare investment are likely to enjoy lower rates of custody, and vice versa. Those countries – including the UK – with the highest rates of imprisonment, all spend below average proportions of their GDP on welfare; Those with the lowest levels of incarceration (such as Finland, Sweden, Denmark and Belgium – but not Japan) have above average welfare expenditure (see Box 10.7).

Box 10.7

The relationship between welfare spending and rates of imprisonment

Country	Imprisonment rate per 100,000 (15+)	% of GDP on welfare
USA	666	14.6
Portugal	146	18.2
New Zealand	144	21.0
UK	124	20.8
Canada	115	18.0
Spain	112	19.7
Australia	106	17.8
Germany	95	26.0
France	92	28.8
Italy	86	25.1
Netherlands	85	24.5
Switzerland	79	28.1
Belgium	77	24.5
Denmark	63	29.8
Sweden	60	31.0
Finland	54	26.5
Japan	42	14.7

Source: Abbreviated from Downes and Hansen (2006, p. 5).

Child well-being data gathered by UNICEF, published in 2007, looked at 40 indicators including poverty levels, education, safety, drug use, relation with parents within six dimensions (material well-being, health and safety, educational well-being, family and peer relationships, behaviours and risks, subjective well-being) across 21 'rich' countries. The UK and the USA were at the bottom of such a league (see Box 10.8).

▌Box 10.8

Child well-being rankings

Country	Well-being ranking
Netherlands	4.2 (highest well-being ranking)
Sweden	5.0
Denmark	7.2
Finland	7.5
Spain	8.0
Switzerland	8.3
Norway	8.7
Italy	10.0
Ireland	10.2
Belgium	10.7
Germany	11.2
Greece	11.8
Canada	11.8
France	13.0
Portugal	13.7
Austria	13.8
United States	18.0
United Kingdom	18.2 (lowest well-being ranking)

Source: Abbreviated from UNICEF (2007a, p. 2).

It is still possible to find examples of juvenile justice systems where welfare protectionism appears a fundamental rationale. Scotland is a prime example even though it continues to have a high percentage of its prison population dedicated to 16 to 21 year olds. Nevertheless numerous commentators maintain that the hearing system ensures that child welfare considerations hold a pivotal position for younger offenders and provides a credible and stable alternative to the punitive nature of youth justice pursued in many other jurisdictions (McAra and Young, 1997; Bottoms, 2002 and see **Chapter 8.1**).

Belgium, it is claimed, has developed a system that is the 'most deliberately welfare-oriented of all' (Walgrave, 2002 p. 30). The Youth Protection Act 1965 established principles of social protection and judicial protection to apply to all those under the age of 21. With a few exceptions no punishments are available to the under-18s. All judicial interventions for this group are legitimated through an educative and protective, rather than punitive and responsibilizing discourse. In principle, it is the needs of the young person that determine the nature of the intervention. The powers of the youth court which include reprimand, supervision, community service and fostering, however, also allow for placement in a public institution for the purposes of observation and education and in some circumstances those aged 16 or over may have their cases referred directly to an adult court. From March 2003, the temporary placement of juveniles in closed centres run by the federal Ministry of Justice (rather than the Community-run public institutions) has been allowed. For these reasons Walgrave (2002 p. 40) remains suspicious of Belgian welfarism which 'leads not to justice without punishment but punishment without guaranteed justice'. Moreover Walgrave notes a developing politicization of juvenile and street crime in Belgium fuelled by media sensationalism and extremist right-wing vitriol directed at Moroccan and Turkish minorities. Curfews have been introduced as well as the federally run special closed 'detention houses'. Challenges to welfare protectionism appear imminent through a growing emphasis on offender responsibility and accountability (Put and Walgrave, 2006).

Tolerance and Decarceration

According to all of the custodial data that is available to us, the Scandinavian countries appear to stand out as being able to keep youth imprisonment to an absolute minimum and have been able to maintain such toleration throughout the 1990s. Over the past 20 years Italy has also emerged as a significant exemplar of relative decarceration.

The absence of juvenile prisons in Sweden has been accounted for by a political consensus that juvenile sections in adult prisons are highly detrimental to a child's development. Rather, those over 15 who have committed serious crimes are sentenced to closed institutional care. But again the practice is rare. In 2002, 106 young offenders received such a sentence (Meri, 2003). Their regimes are ostensibly run on principles of care, treatment and welfare recognizing that many are also victims of abuse, assault and inadequate care. According to Meri, this welfare approach is, however, underpinned less by unbridled empathy but more by a need to set limits and encourage individual responsibility. Different forms of cognitive behavioural therapy are employed to control anger and aggression; mediation is encouraged where there is a recognizable victim.

Finland made an explicit decision some 40 years ago to abandon its Soviet-style tradition of punitive criminal justice in favour of decarceration and diversion. As a result, the young offender prison population has been reduced by 90 percent since 1960. There has been no associated rise in known offending. This was achieved by a long-term programme of applying indefinite detention to a small number of violent offenders and by suspending imprisonment for a majority of others on the condition that a period of probation was successfully completed. Immediate 'unconditional' sentencing to custody is now a rarity. Prison home leave, early release and family visits are commonplace. There are no specific juvenile courts but 15 to 21 year olds are only imprisoned for the most exceptional reasons. The voluntary acceptance of mediation is used as grounds for the waiving of sentence (Lappi-Seppälä, 1998). In May 2007, there were just three 15 to 17 year olds held in prison (see Box 10.5 above). The Norwegian criminologist, Nils Christie, has argued that this dramatic shift has been made possible by a conscious effort on the part of successive Finnish governments to formulate a national identity closer to that of other Scandinavian states. Certainly it has been made possible by an insistence that elites and experts are better placed to formulate and decide penal policy rather than the whims of public opinion and party politics. Finland's formulation that *good social development policy is the best criminal policy* has indeed been a remarkable 'success'. It has shown that high incarceration rates and tough penal regimes do not control crime. They are unnecessary. Decarceration can be pursued without sacrificing public safety (Lappi-Seppälä, 2006).

Norwegian penal values have also long been read as the epitome of **toleration**. Their juvenile prison population (as of June 2007) stood at 10. There are no dedicated juvenile prisons. One case is indicative. In Trondheim, in 1994, a 5 year old girl was murdered by two 6 year old boys. The exceptionality of this case mirrored that of the murder of James Bulger by two 10 year old boys a year earlier in England. In the seven subsequent years public, media and political outcry remained unabated in the UK, continually dwelling on the 'leniency' of their sentence, their 'privileged' access to specialized rehabilitation and their eventual 'premature' release under a cloak of fearful anonymity. In Norway the murder was always dealt with as a tragedy in which the local community shared a collective shame and responsibility. The boys were never named. They returned to school within two weeks of the event (see **Chapter 1.1**).

Something of a consensus appears to exist in Nordic countries (Iceland, Norway, Sweden, Finland, Denmark) that 'forward-looking' social and educational measures together with mediation take precedence over prosecution and punishment. Compliance with the UN Convention of the Rights of the Child also results in juveniles not being incarcerated with adults and because of an absence of prisons dedicated to juveniles most do not endure penal custody at all (Nordic Working Group, 2001, pp. 147–8). Pitts and Kuula (2006) have, however, argued that 'Scandinavian exceptionalism' might be overstated. For example, Finland's extremely low rate of custody may somewhat mask extensive resort to reformatories and psychiatric units via the youth welfare system. On this basis they estimate that Finland may remove from home and institutionalize more children pro rata than do England and Wales. What is at stake here, though, is the perennially disputed logics of whether troubled and troublesome children are deserving of a 'welfare' or a 'criminal' response.

Italian 'decarceration' has been accounted for by the introduction of new penal laws in 1988 which explicitly stressed penal leniency for juveniles in order not to interrupt educational processes and personal development. It was backed by a widespread cultural attitude which prioritizes the church and the family (rather than formal juvenile justice) as the key agencies of social control. In particular, avoidance of conviction and refusal of punishment are facilitated through the mechanisms of *irrilevanza* (insufficient seriousness), *perdono* (judicial pardon) and *messa alla prova* (pre-trial probation). As a result young people are incarcerated only for a very few serious violent offences (incarceration appears reserved for non-nationals, particularly young Romanis) (Nelken, 2006). While special prisons have been established for minors (*prigione-scuola*), they may be conditionally released at any stage of their sentence. Gatti and Verde's (2002, p. 312) data show a marked decline in the numbers of juveniles entering penal institutions in the late 1980s but some increase during the 1990s following the introduction of reception centres. More fundamentally an Italian cultural tradition of soft paternal authoritarianism has been traditionally linked to low levels of penal repression (Ruxton, 1996; Nelken, 2002). The 'cultural embeddedness' of Catholic paternalism (compared for example to US evangelical Protestantism) may not determine penal policy but provides the parameters in which differential readings of the purpose and meaning of punishment become possible (Melossi, 2000). Young people are more regarded as in need of help and support than requiring of punishment for their misdemeanours.

Restoration

There has been a substantial growth in interest in restorative justice and victim–offender mediation in the past twenty years and restorative techniques have penetrated juvenile justice systems in most western societies. In contrast to processes of 'adulteration' and 'repenalization', restorative justice raises the possibility of less formal crime control and more informal offender/victim participation and harm minimization. These initiatives in part draw upon notions of informal customary practices in Maori, Aboriginal and Native American indigenous populations. A common reference point for youth justice has been the development of family group conferencing pioneered in New Zealand in the late 1980s (see **Chapter 9.2**). Both the United Nations and the Council of Europe have given restorative justice their firm backing. The Council of Europe has recommended to all jurisdictions that mediation should be made generally available, that it should cover all stages of the criminal justice process and, most significantly, that it should be autonomous to formal means of judicial processing. The European Forum for Victim–Offender Mediation and Restorative Justice was established in 2000. Across many parts of Africa, Stern (2001) records renewed interest in solidarity, reconciliation and restoration as the guiding principles for resolving disputes rather than the colonial prison. Arguably the most influential contemporary example of 'restoration' replacing 'retribution' as the guiding principle in achieving 'justice' is South Africa's Truth and Reconciliation Commission, following the abolition of Apartheid. The Commission was charged with investigating past human rights violations, granting amnesty for political crimes and offering reparation to victims. Whatever the political expediency of this strategy (to counter the fear that formal prosecution of sections of the white population would only perpetuate violence), it was clear that it involved a radical re-imagining of the nature of 'justice' and how it could be achieved. The notion that community relations could only be 'healed' through truth telling, forgiveness and acknowledgement of the harm done to past victims was clearly informed by restorative principles. It cemented the idea that lasting peace depended on establishing human rights provisions for long-term reconciliation. The *Child Justice Bill* first considered by the South African government in 2002 is duly influenced by a recognition of children's rights coupled with application of the ideals of restorative justice (Skelton, 2002; van Zyl Smit and van der Spuy, 2004). In 2002, the UN's Economic and Social Council formulated some basic universal principles of restorative justice, including non-coercive offender and victim participation, confidentiality and procedural safeguards. It is clear that restorative justice is no longer marginal but a burgeoning worldwide industry with local projects proliferating across much of Europe, Africa, Canada, the USA and Australasia.

In Europe, Austria has been cited as being at the forefront of such developments. Following its *1988 Juvenile Justice Act*, 50 per cent of cases suitable for prosecution were resolved by out-of-court mediation and by informal negotiations between offender, victim and mediator to achieve reconciliation (Justice, 2000). But throughout Europe the implementation of restorative principles is marked by heterogeneity rather than convergence. In Belgium, Finland and Norway restoration is conceived as an extension of existing welfare, education or rehabilitative strategies. In Norway, victim–offender mediation is used as an *alternative* to judicial processing whereas in most jurisdictions it is integrated into other criminal justice processes. Some systems are victim oriented (Denmark), some (France, Spain) focus on the offender and in others the orientation is mixed. Belgium employs restorative principles at all stages of the judicial process; in France and England and Wales it only operates at an early or pre-trial stage, while in Denmark it is employed at the moment of sentence (Miers, 2001; Tickell and Akester, 2004).

The logic of restoration is that it is designed to resolve conflicts (such as crime) through dialogue and negotiation so that community harmony can be 'restored'. It is, however, far from clear how such outcomes can be achieved when it is co-opted into systems that are otherwise driven by punitive, authoritarian rationales (see **Chapter 9.2**). As has been repeatedly pointed out, there is a clear danger that any form of compulsory restoration may degenerate into a ceremony of public shaming and degradation, precisely because the underlying intent is simply to reinforce (western-inspired) notions of individual responsibility rather than develop those of social justice for indigenous and non-indigenous populations alike (Blagg, 1997; White, 2001; 2003; Bradley et al., 2006). Further, international evaluation research has cast some doubt on whether restorative justice 'works' to reduce recidivism. The results tend to be mixed, but with some reductions in reoffending for young violent offenders. All of this encourages a degree of scepticism and ambivalence towards the claims made for restoration and its future potential to overhaul the injustices of retribution (Daly, 2002). Adapting specific aspects of restorative approaches to particular jurisdictions and in different political climates will also significantly affect their efficacy.

Rights Compliance

Studying the reports of the UN Committee on the Rights of the Child reveals the extent to which international obligations are being ignored or utilized to act in a 'child's best interests' (Muncie, 2008). The UN Committee's 'concluding comments' for the three jurisdictions of the UK and 15 West European states, for example, between 2001 and 2006 noted various positive developments in most jurisdictions, such as:

- introduction of child protection laws;

- acknowledgement of problems of child trafficking, sexual exploitation and the recruitment of children in armed conflict;

- introduction of measures to give children a voice such as through school councils or youth parliaments;

- introduction of legal representation in juvenile court and attempts to divert from court through mediation and restoration.

However, the Committee's general comments published in 2007, together with a report specifically on violence against children in 2006, concluded that implementation of the UNCRC has often been piecemeal and that in juvenile justice reform the issue of children's rights frequently appears as an afterthought (see Box 10.9 and **Chapter 5**).

The UNCRC is persuasive but breach attracts no formal sanction. It may be the most ratified of all international human rights directives but it is also the most violated. Abramson (2006) has concluded that the obligations of the UNCRC are received by many states as 'unwanted'. He notes how disproportionate sentences, insufficient respect for the rule of law, excessive use of custody and *improper use of the juvenile justice system to tackle other social problems*, are widespread.

The recurring issues raised by the UN Committee in relation to children's rights in the UK and Western Europe focus in particular on Sections 37, 39 and 40 of the Convention (see Box 10.1 above). In all of these reports every state (except Norway) is asked to give more consideration to implementing these core principles. Despite almost 20 years to move towards implementation most states appear to have failed to recognize the centrality of such issues as distinctive needs, dignity, humane treatment and so on as core to the realization of children's rights. Arguably, the UN Committee's most critical report was reserved for the UK (see **Chapter 9.3**).

Eight states (Finland, Denmark, Switzerland, Austria, Ireland, UK, Germany, and Portugal) were specifically criticized for failing to separate children from adults in custody or because they are beginning to break down distinctions between adult and juvenile systems allowing for easier movement between the two (as is characteristic of the widely used juvenile transfer to adult court in the USA). The irony is that some states, attempting to comply with the Convention's advocacy of due process, have dismantled existing measures which might have protected children from 'adult justice'.

Box 10.9

Denying children's rights

[M]any States parties still have a long way to go in achieving full compliance with CRC, e.g. in the areas of procedural rights, the development and implementation of measures for dealing with children in conflict with the law without resorting to judicial proceedings, and the use of deprivation of liberty only as a measure of last resort ... The Committee is equally concerned about the lack of information on the measures that States parties have taken to prevent children from coming into conflict with the law. This may be the result of a lack of a comprehensive policy for the field of juvenile justice. This may also explain why many States parties are providing only very limited statistical data on the treatment of children in conflict with the law.

Source: United Nations Committee on the Rights of the Child, 2007, p. 1.

Millions of children, particularly boys, spend substantial periods of their lives under the control and supervision of care authorities or justice systems, and in institutions such as orphanages, children's homes, care homes, police lock-ups, prisons, juvenile detention facilities and reform schools. These children are at risk of violence from staff and officials responsible for their well-being. Corporal punishment in institutions is not explicitly prohibited in a majority of countries. Overcrowding and squalid conditions, societal stigmatization and discrimination, and poorly trained staff heighten the risk of violence. Effective complaints, monitoring and inspection mechanisms, and adequate government regulation and oversight are frequently absent. Not all perpetrators are held accountable, creating a culture of impunity and tolerance of violence against children.

Source: United Nations General Assembly (2006, p. 16).

The report on Germany condemned the increasing number of children placed in detention, especially affecting children of foreign origin, and that children in detention or custody are placed with persons up to the age of 25 years.

The Report on the Netherlands in 2004 expressed concern that custody was no longer being used as a last resort.

In its report on France, the Committee reiterated its concern about legislation and practice which tends to favour repressive over educational measures. It expressed concern about increases in the numbers of children in prison and the resulting worsening of conditions.

Just a significantly 15 (of these 18) jurisdictions were condemned for discriminating against minorities/asylum seekers and having overrepresentations of immigrant and minority groups under arrest or in detention, particularly the Roma and traveller communities (Italy; Switzerland, Finland, Germany, Greece, three UK jurisdictions, Ireland, France, Spain, Portugal), Moroccans and Surinamese (the Netherlands), and North Africans (Belgium, Denmark). This raises a key issue of a fundamental **racialization** of youth justice in Western Europe (Muncie, 2008). Although few nation states collect data on the ethnic background of the juveniles that enter and are processed by their respective systems, there again appears to be a notable emulation of racialized processes and outcomes as witnessed in the USA. In the USA, ethnic minorities make up about a third of all juveniles in the general population but about two-thirds of those in secure detention. In some states almost all cases of juvenile waiver involve minorities. There can be little dispute too that across Europe, ethnic and immigrant groups have been increasingly identified as a threatening 'underclass' deserving only of suspicion, neutralization and exclusion (Wacquant, 1999a). For example, Europe's 8 million Roma, which make up the largest ethnic minority group in the European Union, are widely reported as enduring systematic harassment, discrimination, forced eviction, ghettoization and detention. A poll in Italy in 2008 reported that 68 per cent of Italians wanted to see the country's 150,000 Roma expelled even though many were Italian citizens (*Guardian*, 17 May 2008). In some jurisdictions, such as Switzerland, Austria, Belgium and Italy, over a third of their total prison populations are foreign nationals. Over 100,000 prisoners in EU countries do not have citizenship of the countries in which they are incarcerated. The more punitive elements of juvenile justice do appear to be increasingly used/reserved for the punitive control of primarily immigrant populations.

UN reports confirm that millions of children worldwide continue to live in poverty, have no access to education and are routinely employed in armed conflicts. Street children on every continent continue to endure harassment and physical abuse from the police and many others work long hours in hazardous conditions in flagrant violation of the rights guaranteed to them under the Convention (see **Chapter 5**). Some countries appear to give lip service to rights simply to be granted status as a 'modern developed state' and acceptance into world monetary systems. The pressure to ratify is both moral and economic (Harris-Short, 2003). Abramson's (2000) analysis of UN observations on the implementation of juvenile justice in 141 countries notes a widespread lack of 'sympathetic understanding' necessary for compliance with the UN Convention. He argued that a complete overhaul of juvenile justice is required in 21 countries and that in others torture, inhumane treatment, lack of separation from adults, police brutality, poor conditions in detention facilities, overcrowding, lack of rehabilitation, failure to develop alternatives to incarceration, inadequate contact between minors and their families, lack of training of judges, police, and prison authorities, lack of speedy trial, no legal assistance, disproportionate sentences, insufficient respect for the rule of law and improper use of the juvenile justice system to tackle other social problems, are rife. In addition, there is a notable lack of reliable statistics or documentation as to who is in jail and where they are. Over 30 countries continue to accompany their ratification with reservations. For example, Canada and the UK have issued reservations to Article 37 and the requirement to separate children from adults in detention. The UK – until 2008 – also held a reservation to Article 22 concerning the degree of rights held by children seeking asylum (see **Chapter 5.3**). Many Islamic nations have filed reservations when the Convention appears to be incompatible with Islamic law and domestic legislation (Schabas, 1996).

In many countries it seems abundantly clear that it is possible to claim an adherence to the principle of universal rights while simultaneously pursuing policies which exacerbate structural inequalities and punitive institutional regimes. 'Cultural difference' and the absence of localized human rights cultures preclude meaningful adoption of international agreements (Harris-Short, 2003). The US case is indicative. Violations of the Convention appear built in to aspects of US law which allow for life imprisonment, prosecution in adult courts and which fail to specify a minimum age of criminal responsibility (Campaign for Youth Justice, 2007). Moreover relying on international statements of due process and procedural safeguards may do little to deliver 'justice' on the ground. The development of **positive rights** agendas remains limited (Scraton and Haydon, 2002). Little attention has also been given to the extent to which legal globalization itself is a concept driven by Western notions of individualized justice. Far from opening up challenges to neo-liberalism, rights agendas may simply act to bolster Western notions of *individual freedom* rather than to secure any movement towards global *social justice*. Imperial and postcolonial notions of a barbaric and authoritarian 'global east' or 'global south' are easily perpetuated (Muncie, 2005). It is indicative in itself that of those countries where the UN Committee has identified 'tradition' and 'culture' as impeding implementation, the vast majority are 'non-Western'.

Explaining Diversity

10.4 The most common, popular, indeed political, explanation for international diversity is that it simply reflects differences in rates of juvenile crime, particularly of violent juvenile crime. This assumption has, however, been roundly dismissed. The Council of Europe has long concluded that there is no relation between crime and prison rates: 'High overall crime rates do not necessarily induce high prison rates and vice versa. Neither do high prison rates necessarily induce low overall crime rates and vice versa' (European Sourcebook, 2003, p. 193). Estrada's (2001) study of self report surveys and hospital admission data also concludes that any purported rise in juvenile violence across Europe is probably illusory and more likely to be a politically and media-driven ideological construct paralleling the general shift towards systems of 'just deserts':

> Trends in juvenile crime do not constitute the primary explanation for the rapid rise in the number of youths registered by the criminal justice system during the 1990s. The rise is rather the result in a marked shift in the way society reacts to the actions of young people. (Estrada, 2001, p. 647)

Von Hofer's (2003) comparative study of incarceration in Finland, Sweden and Holland similarly argues that their differences and convergences are best explained as a result of specific political decision making at the level of the nation state. Here again we face something of a paradox: that is an assumption of greater criminal justice intervention across Europe but also an acknowledgement of the centrality of how individual nation states can and do react differently to the 'actions of young people'.

Models of Juvenile Justice

Certain global/neo-liberal readings of criminal justice reform are persuasive that a growing necessity of nation states to attract international capital might compel them to adopt similar economic, social *and* criminal justice policies through which juvenile crime and juvenile justice have become excessively politicized. But it is also clear that there is little homogeneity in how the neo-liberal might be translated into punitive or tolerant values. One widely adopted means employed to illustrate this diversity has been by constructing typologies and models of juvenile justice. Certainly the traditional binaries of 'welfare' and 'justice' are broadly acknowledged as no longer capable of capturing an increasingly complex constellation of competing rationales.

Winterdyk (2002) constructed six models to illustrate international diversity: 'welfare' (e.g. Scotland, France), 'corporate' (e.g. England and Wales), 'modified justice' (e.g. the Netherlands), 'justice' (e.g. Germany), 'crime control' (e.g. the USA) and 'participatory' (e.g. Japan). Cavadino and Dignan (2006) explored patterns in international juvenile justice penality in terms of their relation to differing political economies: such as the 'neo-liberal' (e.g. USA, England and Wales), conservative corporatist (e.g. Germany, Italy, France and the Netherlands), social democratic corporatist (e.g. Sweden, Finland) and oriental corporatist (e.g. Japan) (see Box 10.10).

Such typologies are indeed useful in giving juvenile justice reform some grounding in ideological and material realities but disputes over their accuracy or applicability remain. How, for example, can the apparently vastly different trajectories of juvenile justice in the Netherlands and Italy (see Sections 10.2 and 10.3 above) be explored within such frameworks? 'Snapshot' classificatory models often fail to do justice either to the ways in which systems are always in flux themselves or to the myriad ways in which broad trends can be challenged, reworked, adapted or resisted at the local level (Muncie, 2005).

The Significance of the Local

Individual states continue to jealously guard their own sovereignty and control over law and order agendas. Local implementation of key reforms may also reveal a continuing adherence to some traditional values and a resistance to change. Analyses at the local level, for example, may be better capable of identifying some of the key drivers of less punitive and more progressive policies and practices. For example, we might identify the full incorporation of UNCRC into domestic law (as in Norway); the acknowledgement of children as a deserving case through

Political economies and penal tendencies

Regime types

Neo-liberalism	Conservative corporatism	Social democratic corporatism	Oriental corporatism
Free market, minimalist or residual welfare state	Status-related, moderately generous welfare state	Universalistic, generous welfare state	Private sector-based welfare corporatism, bureaucratic, paternalistic
Individualized, atomised, limited social rights	Conditional and moderate social rights	Relatively unconditional and generous social rights	Quasi-feudal corporatism, strong sense of duty
Right-wing politics	Centrist	Left-wing	Centre-right
High imprisonment rate	Medium	Low	Low
United States	Germany	Sweden	Japan
England and Wales, Australia, New Zealand, South Africa	France, Italy, Netherlands	Finland	

Source: Adapted and abbreviated from Dignan and Cavadino (2007/08, p. 15).

setting the age of criminal responsibility at 15 (as across Scandinavia) or 18 (as in Belgium); a general depoliticization/media desensationalization of the issue of juvenile crime (as in Finland); and the abolition of specific youth prisons (as in Norway and Denmark) as marking some of the foundational elements of a 'principled youth justice' (Goldson and Muncie, 2006). In turn, this might be supported by specific practices such as the Swedish waiver of prosecution/ suspended sentences (Storgaard, 2004); the adoption of the Italian *messa alla prova* (pre-trial probation for all, including the most serious offenders) (Nelken, 2006) or the Finnish insistence that social policy should always come before criminal justice policy (Lappi-Seppälä, 2006). Even then we should acknowledge that just as 'cultures of control' are differentially realized in different contexts, the same applies to anything we might identify as 'progressive'. It is doubtful whether either are simply transferable from one jurisdiction to another. For example, the precise reasons for apparent tolerance in Italy bear little or no relation to that experienced in Scandinavia, being (partly) driven in the former by measures designed to continually postpone or avoid court proceedings (Nelken, 2006) and (partly) driven in the latter by a historical commitment to child welfare (Lappi-Seppälä, 2006).

Whatever the impact of the merging of 'global' neo-liberal economics with neo-conservative politics emanating from the USA (and clearly affecting England and Netherlands), it is also clear that globalization is mediated by distinct national, regional local cultures. The cultural dynamics and institutional constraints of particular localities can empower or dis-empower key professions and enable external policy imperatives to be mediated or resisted (McAra, 2004). Or as Tonry (2001, p. 518) put it, the 'best explanations' for penal severity or tolerance remain 'parochially national and cultural' such that some European countries appear more comfortable with experts, rather than politicians and public opinion, driving penal policy and that those with more extensive social welfare systems continue to foster 'value systems in which crime raises more complex social issues than many politicians in moralistic America believe or will admit' (2001, p. 530). All of this affords a continuing centrality to cultural contingency and local actors in the precise ways in which the global, the national, and the sub-national are activated on the ground. There is something of an unfortunate tendency for many Anglophone academics and policy-makers to assume that general trends in the USA are not only crossing all American states, but are also capable of being transferred internationally. They are not. Because the concept of globalization has been applied predominantly to transformations in Western and Anglophone countries, our understanding of global processes to date might itself also be considered to be peculiarly ethnocentric. Two examples exemplify this divergence. In the USA, juvenile incarceration rates, at the peak of its 'punitive turn' in the late 1990s, varied from 70 per 100,000 juveniles in Vermont to 583 in Louisiana. Mears (2006) accounts for this contrast as reflective of localized cultural mentalities such that juvenile incarceration is used in response to *adult* violent crime and as an extension of *adult* criminal justice policy rather than as anything to do with the behaviour of young people *per se.* Similarly it is becoming increasingly important not to automatically equate England with the rest of the UK. With the establishment of a separate Welsh Assembly, for example, youth policy in Wales appears more concerned with conforming to a UNCRC 'children first' philosophy rather than following an 'offender first' mentality so evident in England (Cross et al., 2003; National Assembly for Wales, 2004; Field, 2007).

The 'catastrophic' images raised by some neo-liberal readings of youth governance may help us to identify significant macro social changes, but are less attuned to resistance to change, to contradictions within neo-liberalism and its often hybrid nature, to the inherent instability of neo-liberal strategies and to the simultaneous emergence of other competing transformational tendencies (Muncie and Hughes, 2002; 'O'Malley 2002). Neo-liberalism not only has a global impact but also, under the rubric of 'governing at a distance', has encouraged the proliferation of 'local solutions' to local problems. To fully understand the workings and influences on juvenile/youth justice we need to be attuned to the twin and contradictory processes of *delocalization* and *relocalization* (Crawford, 2002). The risks and hazards of globalization have simultaneously produced a 'retreat to the local' and nostalgia for tradition and community. The local governance of crime and insecurity is evidenced in the prolific discourses of 'community safety' in the UK and of 'urban security' across Europe (Hughes, 2002). Both are informed by notions of community participation, proactive prevention, informalism, partnership and multi-agency collaboration. What emerges from studies of the actual conduct of governance in particular localities is not uniformity, but diversity. In Australia and the USA, there are wide divergences in custody rates from state to state. In countries such as Spain, Italy, Germany and France, it is indeed difficult to prioritize national developments above widely divergent regional differences, most evident in sentencing disparities. Again, the possibility of identifying coherent and consistent patterns in (youth and juvenile) governance is called into question (Hughes and Edwards, 2002).

Broad governmental mentalities – whether global or national – will also always be subject to **localization**. Policy transfer is rarely neat and complete. Policy is always likely to be reconfigured in local contexts. As Robertson (1996) tried to capture in his notion of the 'glocal', global neo-liberal pressures are always mediated, and can only be realized through national and local identities and sensibilities. For Yeates (2002), a mutually transforming relationship among global and local processes prefigures *plurality* as a driving context for policy implementation. For Aas (2007 p. 12), globalization is beset by 'a complex set of developments with multiple modalities'. Youth justice reform cannot simply be reduced to global economic transformations or to universal legal directives. All such processes are mediated by distinctive national and sub-national cultures and socio-cultural norms when they are activated on the ground. Whatever the rhetoric of government intention, histories of youth justice also tend to be histories of active and passive resistance from pressure groups and from the magistracy, the police and from youth justice workers through which such reform is to be put into practice. There is always a space to be exploited between written and implemented policy. The translation of policy into practice depends on how it is visioned and reworked (or made to work) by those 'on the ground'. As a result, youth justice practice is likely to continue to be dominated by a complex of both rehabilitative 'needs' and responsibilized 'deeds' programmes. Joined up strategic co-operation will often co-exist with sceptical and acrimonious relations at a practitioner level (Liddle and Gelsthorpe, 1994). A continuing social work ethic of 'supporting young people' may well subvert any partnership or national attempt to simply responsibilize the young offender (Souhami, 2007). This is also because many of the 'new' global, neo-liberal targets for intervention – inadequate parenting, low self-esteem, poor social skills, poor cognitive skills – are remarkably similar to those targets identified by a welfare protectionism. Field's (2007) interviews with practitioners in Wales in 2003/04 revealed that the 'punitive turn' often fails to reach down to 'practice cultures' in any direct and determinist fashion (see Box 10.11).

The incongruity between such latent (localized) welfarism and the retributive nature of (national) policy rhetoric may well create some space in which the complex welfare needs of children in trouble can be re-expressed (Goldson, 2000). Equally, there is a growing recognition that securing universal children's rights depends as much (if not more) on grassroots initiatives than on 'agreements' between nation states as epitomized by the UN Convention (Veerman and Levine, 2001). The ill-defined rhetoric of crime prevention can also enable localized social programmes to be re-elevated as those most likely to secure 'community safety'. So, for example, national directives to combat antisocial behaviour through authoritarian and intrusive means can be mediated (subverted?) at the local level through simultaneous efforts to 'work positively with young people' and 'to raise ambition, aspiration and achievement' (Hughes, 2007, p. 133). Even in the USA – reputedly the bastion of conservative neo-liberalism – there are numerous programmes funded by justice departments and run by welfare/police partnerships which appear more concerned with social support (e.g. providing housing, health care, employment opportunities) rather than overt crime control (Mears, 2002). Such reinventions of the social can also be based on long-term and large-scale programmes which address such issues as poverty, powerlessness, discrimination, and so on, which fly in the face of neo-liberal, short-term, 'what works' evaluative, or neo-conservative punitive, agendas. Long-range projects of 'the social' can survive or be reborn (O'Malley, 2000). What is clear is that distinctions need to be made between rhetorical, codified and implemented modes of the policy process (Fergusson, 2007).

In these ways, comparative analysis of juvenile/youth justice can draw attention to a succession of local encounters of complicity and resistance *within* national systems, as well as evaluating the impact of neo-liberal and neo-conservative rationalities and technologies worldwide. Localization ensures that the role of 'agency' is not lost in understanding the processes of international policy flows and transactions. It is an acknowledgement that future comparative analysis must surely focus on how the local and the global intersect differentially in particular contexts rather than assuming that they are mutually exclusive modes of understanding.

▨ ▨ Summary ▨

- Comparative research reveals some fundamental global shifts in juvenile/youth justice, such as the emergence of justice-based principles in the 1970s, risk management in the 1990s and the increasing importance of international conventions and rules. However, it also reveals the USA to be an atypical world case of 'punitiveness' and Scandinavia to be an atypical European case of 'tolerance'.

- Separate systems of justice for children and young people have always been beset by issues of contradiction and compromise. There is compelling evidence that such ambiguity is currently being 'resolved' by a greater governmental resort to neo-conservative punitive and correctional interventions and a neo-liberal responsibilizing mentality in which the protection historically afforded to children is dissolving. This resurgent authoritarianism appears all the more anachronistic when it is set against the widely held commitment to act within the guidelines established by various children's rights conventions. Of note is the United Nations Convention on the Rights of the Child, frequently described as the most ratified human rights convention in the world, but also the most violated.

- The concept of globalization poses some difficult questions for the study of systems of youth justice. Is it synonymous with such competing terms as universalism and transnationalization? Does it signify a wholesale removal of national and international borders or does it conjure up visions that are peculiarly Western? Policy-making in this area has also traditionally been studied with regard to national sovereignty and the independence of the nation state. Indeed, criminal justice remains a powerful icon of sovereign statehood. As a result, youth justice is embroiled not simply in the processes of globalization, but in negotiating its way through a number of diverse and multi-tiered national and local modes of governance.

- Comparative analysis may reveal something of a 'globalized' emergent politicization of the 'youth problem', but also the continuance of a diverse range of 'localized' juvenile justice practices based on informal social control, welfare, diversion, education and social protection. These contrary cases can be used as one basis for reinstating and promoting the broad contours of a juvenile justice based on the 'best interests' of the child and in which the excesses and failures of contemporary punitiveness can be exposed and challenged.

- The idea that global capital is hegemonic and capable of transforming all that it touches is both essentialist and determinist. Relying on a model of US/UK convergence blinds any analysis to the differentiated and differentiating impact of the global. Its effect is neither uniform nor consistent. The empirical 'evidence' of juvenile/youth justice reform does as much to deny than confirm any flattening of national political and cultural difference. The diversity of reform trajectories warns against any attempt to imply homogeneity.

- In every country and in every locality, youth justice appears to be 'made up' through unstable and constantly shifting alliances between the local and the global; through engagements with neo-liberal, neo-conservative and social democratic mentalities; and through the policies and practices of the authoritarian, the retributive, the restorative and the protective. All of these elements jostle with each other to construct a complex multi-modal landscape of youth governance (Muncie, 2006).

■ study Questions ■

1 How useful is the concept of globalization in understanding processes of convergence and divergence in juvenile justice around the world?

2 What evidence is there for a 'punitive turn' in global juvenile justice since the 1980s?

3 How would you explain why some nation states have witnessed a growing intolerance to young offenders while others seem to have been able to reverse such a trend?

4 What is the significance of the 'local' in international juvenile justice reform?

5 What difficulties face the researcher of comparative juvenile justice systems?

■ ■ Further Reading ■

The best introduction to the complexities of crime and crime control in a globalized world is Aas's (2007) *Globalisation and Crime*. However, there are few comparative juvenile justice texts which venture far beyond the descriptive. Tonry and Doob's (2004) *Comparative and Cross-National Perspectives* includes chapters on Canada and New Zealand as well as various European countries and discusses the relevance of welfare, age limitations and the emergence of separate systems. Winterdyk's (2002) edited collection – *Juvenile Justice Systems: International Perspectives* – covers 18 western and non-western countries. Bala et al.'s (2002) *Juvenile Justice Systems* restricts itself to North America, Australasia, and the UK. Junger-Tas and Decker's (2006) *International Handbook of Juvenile Justice* covers 19 North American, Western European and Eastern European countries. It is rare to find comparative texts that do not have an explicit 'Western' focus. Friday and Ren's (2006) *Delinquency and Juvenile Justice Systems in the Non-Western World* is an exception, though again this is primarily a collection of descriptive case studies.

Various comparisons of penal climates in different localities have been carried out, the most thorough being Downes (1988) on the Netherlands and England and Wales. Others include France and England (King, 1991; Pitts, 2001; Crawford, 2002), France, Germany and the USA (Whitman, 2003), Germany and the UK (Lacey and Zedner, 2000), Italy and the USA (Melossi, 2000), Australia and the USA

(O'Malley, 2002), Australia and England (Muncie et al., 1995), England and Scotland (Bottoms, 2002; McAra, 2004) and the USA and Britain (Newburn, 2002a), but not all of these are concerned with juvenile justice, and comparative knowledge of international systems generally remains sketchy and conclusions tentative.

An initial attempt to develop a comparative youth justice in the context of globalization was made by Muncie (2005). Cavadino and Dignan (2006) provide a useful discussion of differing international penal trajectories in terms of political economies. The edited volume by Muncie and Goldson (2006) compares 12 Western jurisdictions by degrees of rights compliance, repenalization, adulteration, tolerance and experiments in restoration and risk management.

⋮ // Web Resources ∟

http://www.un.org/
The main portal for United Nations publications. To initiate more general searches it is of interest that the phrase 'juvenile justice' will open more doors than the term 'youth justice' currently favoured in England.

http://www.unhchr.ch/html/menu3/b/k2crc.htm
The link to the full text of the United Nations Convention on the Rights of the Child.

http://www.unhchr.ch/html/menu3/b/h_comp47.htm
The Riyadh Guidelines.

http://www.unhchr.ch/html/menu3/b/h_comp48.htm
The Beijing Rules.

http://www.unodc.org/unodc/en/data-and-analysis/United-Nations-Surveys-on-Crime-Trends-and-the-Operations-of-Criminal-Justice-Systems.html
A United Nations site based in its Office of Drugs and Crime which provides comparative data on crime and criminal justice trends worldwide. A 10th survey was carried out in 2008 but the latest figures for juvenile incarceration rates are contained in the 8th survey relating to data collected in 2003.

http://www.kcl.ac.uk/depsta/rel/icps/worldbrief/world_brief.html
A site run by the International Centre for Prison Studies based at King's College London which provides regularly updated details of prison populations worldwide, including percentages of juvenile prison populations.

http://www.coe.int/t/e/legal_affairs/legal_co-operation/Prisons_and_alternatives/
The Council of Europe site which publishes annual information on penal and community sanctions: SPACE1 and SPACE2 including estimates of under-18 and 18–21 year old prison populations.

http://www.crin.org/
The Child Rights Information Network (CRIN) is a global network that disseminates information about the Convention on the Rights of the Child and children's rights amongst non-governmental organizations, United Nations agencies, inter-governmental organizations, and educational institutions. The Coordinating Unit is based in London.

http://www.campaignforyouthjustice.org/
American pressure group campaigning for abolition of the practices of treating children as adults.

http://hrw.org/doc/?t=children
Human Rights Watch children's division.

Glossary of Key Terms

A fuller exposition of many of these terms can be found in McLaughlin and Muncie's *The Sage Dictionary of Criminology*, second edition, published by Sage in 2006.

Abolitionism   a rejection of mainstream criminology and criminal justice practices as pernicious and harmful and their replacement with discourse, policy and practices designed to realize social justice

Abuse   any actions or omissions injurious to safety, health and development. In general, child abuse is instigated by adults.

Actuarialism   the classification of populations according to statistical predictors of risk of offending/reoffending (Feeley and Simon, 1992).

Adolescence   a term originating in the eighteenth century to describe the special status of young people undergoing extended periods of educational training. Widely popularized in the twentieth century as a period of emotional upheaval and 'storm and stress' which affects all young people (G.S. Hall, 1905).

'Adulteration'   a dissolving of distinctions between juvenile (child/youth) justice and adult justice.

Aetiology   a term derived from medicine which suggests that the specific causes of crime and deviance can be identified, in much the same way as causes of disease and illness.

Anomie   a social state of 'normlessness' induced when aspirations are incapable of being met because of restricted opportunities (Durkheim, 1897/1952; Merton, 1938).

'Anti-social' control	whereas 'legitimate' social control sets limits to individual action in the interests of the collective, 'anti-social' control mechanisms (such as the deregulation of the market and the curtailing of trade union activity in the 1980s) act to increase social and economic inequality (Carlen, 1996).
Bifurcation	a policy of separating out the treatment of serious offenders from that of minor offenders, with the end result that 'tough' offenders are dealt with by overtly punitive means (Bottoms, 1974).
Bricolage	the reordering and recontexualization of objects to communicate fresh meanings (Lévi-Strauss, 1966).
Carceral society	the notion that, as systems of surveillance increase, forms of control pioneered in the nineteenth-century prison are replicated throughout the social order (Foucault, 1977).
Carnival	the performance of transgression and excess as a part of everyday life and as resistance to conformist rationality (Presdee, 2000).
Cause–effect	the proposition of causal analysis that certain antecedent individual and social factors will invariably and unconditionally have a certain effect.
Child-saving	a term used to describe nineteenth-century philanthropists and reformers who were ostensibly working to remove children from adult forms of criminal jurisdiction (Platt, 1969).
Child soldiers	any person under the age of 18 who is involved in *any* armed conflict in *any* capacity.
Child trafficking	the recruitment, transportation, transfer, harbouring or receipt of under-18 year olds, by any means of threat or deception, for the purpose of exploitation.
Children's rights	respect, protection, dignity and equality as detailed in particular by the United Nations Convention on the Rights of the Child.
Classical Marxism	a theory of history which views social change and social relations (including crime) as the working out of fundamental conflicts between classes rooted within particular economic modes of production (Marx, 1859).

Club cultures	a preferred term to subculture in order to better capture a sense of changing morphology, particularly within the dance cultures of the 1990s (Thornton, 1995).
Cognitive behaviourism	derived from psychology and psychotherapy research and typically employed with offenders through social skills training, role plays, and problem-solving techniques in order to encourage self-reflection and behavioural change (Ross et al., 1988).
Community safety	initially formulated as a more 'social' and 'inclusive' form of crime prevention. By the late 1990s it had been largely supplanted in governmental rhetoric by the term 'crime reduction'.
Comparative criminology	a field of study designed to assess general trends and degrees of convergence and divergence between different variables.
Consumerism	the uninhibited process whereby the market creates an 'endless pursuit of want' including the celebration and commodification of deviant lifestyles and illegal pursuits (Hayward, 2004).
Convergence	A thesis that contends that all modern societies – capitalist or communist – will develop in a similar fashion because of technological and economic imperatives.
Corporate crime	offences committed by business corporations in the furtherance of their own profits.
Corporatism	forming one body with common aims and objectives from previously separate agencies and organizations. Used to describe teams of youth justice workers that emerged in the late 1980s (Pratt, 1989).
Correlational analysis	a statistical technique pioneered in the early twentieth century for quantifying the degree of association between variables.
Counterculture	a term used to describe those youth subcultures which formulate counter-proposals of how the social order should be organized. Usually applied to the protest movements emanating from middle-class, student and bohemian sources in the 1960s (Yinger, 1960).

Crime	conventionally described as a violation of the criminal law, but contested (by some) to include all social injuries and social harms (Michael and Adler, 1933; Hulsman, 1986).
Criminalization	the application of the criminal label to particular 'deviant' behaviours or groups.
Critical criminology	a school of criminology that emerged in the 1970s which examines the deficiencies, absences and closures in existing theories and modes of understanding the concept of 'crime' (Taylor et al., 1975).
Cultural criminology	the study of everyday existences, life histories, music, dance and performances to discover how and why certain cultural forms become criminalized (Ferrell and Sanders, 1995).
Culture of control	the transformation of penal welfarism and expansion of criminal justice systems, particularly in the USA and the UK, characterized by punitiveness, new policing strategies, and an apparatus of prevention and surveillance (Garland, 2001).
Dangerous classes	a nineteenth-century term applied with fear and disgust to those members of the working classes who seemed to pose a threat to order.
Defusion/diffusion	the weakening of subcultural opposition through commercial appropriation (Clarke, 1976).
Delinquency	a term, loosely used, to refer to any kind of youthful misbehaviour.
Demonization	the ascription of negative and pathological labels, epitomized by popular representations of some children as 'feral' or 'evil'.
Depravation	a term used to describe the young as morally corrupt and wicked.
Deprivation	a term used to describe the young as lacking in moral guidance.
Determinism	the proposition that people have no control over their actions and that human action is determined by external forces.

Developmental criminology the study of the relationship between biological, psychological and social factors across the life course. Typically used to identify childhood factors which are assumed to be 'predictive' of future offending (Farrington, 2000).

Deviance a social rather than legal concept to delineate rule-breaking behaviour.

Deviancy amplification the proposition that many of the means designed to control deviant behaviour have the obverse effect of increasing it (Wilkins, 1964).

Difference a concept used to capture a sense of cultural diversity and variability; avoiding the moral connotations of describing any behaviour as deviant, but retaining a tendency to set boundaries between patterns of behaviour in which certain groups can readily be identified as 'differing' from some presumed norm.

Differential association the principle that criminal behaviour is learnt when individuals are exposed, socially and culturally, to pro-criminal rather than anti-criminal values, patterns and association (Sutherland and Cressey, 1970).

Discourse personal, media, political or academic 'talk' and 'writing' about a subject in which knowledges are organized, carried and reproduced in particular ways and through particular institutional practices (Clarke and Cochrane, 1998).

Dispersal of discipline the proposition that means of control pioneered in the prison are now to be encountered in more apparently benign community settings.

Diversionary strategies strategies developed in the youth justice system to prevent young people from committing crime or to ensure that they avoid formal court action and custody if they are arrested and prosecuted.

Doli incapax a principle dating back to the fourteenth century which assumes that under a certain age children are incapable of knowing right from wrong and therefore cannot be held criminally responsible for their actions.

Drift	the proposition that juvenile delinquents are not committed to anti-social behaviour but oscillate between conformity and delinquency (Matza, 1964).
Early intervention	a core policy implication of *developmental criminology* that youth crime can be anticipated in advance and that certain children should be targeted for crime prevention initiatives before an offence has taken place.
Edgework	intense moments of pleasure which accompany the danger and skill of risk taking and breaking boundaries (Lyng, 1990).
Essentialism	the belief that social behaviour is determined and driven by some underlying process or 'essence' as in *genetic determinism* or *positivism* or *classical Marxism*.
Ethnographic research	research which is directed towards in-depth and detailed understandings of the lives and personal meanings of subjects.
Eugenics	a doctrine promoting rejuvenation of the physical stock and moral character of the population by demanding that social undesirables should be isolated or sterilized.
Evidence-based policy	borrowed from medicine, this approach prioritizes the pragmatic formulating of policy and practice on the basis of scientifically robust research.
Exploitation	the use of children by adults as commodities for their own monetary, political or sexual gain.
Extroversion	the proposition that an unreserved or impulsive personality correlates with a higher propensity for criminal behaviour (Eysenck, 1970).
Folk devil	an individual or group who, through stereotyping and scapegoating, comes to be represented as the embodiment of social problems (Cohen, 1973a).
Gang	variously defined, but usually connoting a group of people who persist over time, have rules of membership and an identifiable leadership.

Genetic determinism	a theory which proposes that certain inherited traits predispose certain people towards criminality. Criminals are born (Lombroso, 1876).
Globalization	a contested term but one that draws attention to an increasing homogeneity and convergence of social/criminal justice knowledge and policy and driven in the main by multinational, neo-liberal economics and technologies (Bauman, 1998; Beck, 2000).
Governmentality	the proposition that social order is achieved not through a 'disciplinary society' or by state coercion, but through dynamic relations of power and knowledge to be found in a multitude of institutions (Foucault, 1977).
Hegemonic masculinity	the configuration of gender practice which embodies and guarantees the dominant position of men and the subordination of women (Connell, 1995).
Hegemony	the cultural dynamic by which a group claims and sustains a leading position in social life (Gramsci, 1971).
Hidden crime	those crimes that are not recorded by the official criminal statistics.
Homology	the selection of objects through which style is generated in order to ensure that they 'fit' and form some coherent ensemble (Lévi-Strauss, 1966).
Hooligan	a term originating in the last decade of the nineteenth century, possibly to describe a particular Irish family – the Houlehans – but adopted by the media to refer to any unruly behaviour (Pearson, 1983).
Idealist history	a view of historical change which emphasizes the place of ideas and good intentions and which equates progress with benevolent and humanitarian reform.
Imaginary solutions	the means by which youth subcultures overcome the structural problems of unemployment and disadvantage by expropriating and fetishizing consumption and style.
Interactionism	a school of social science which focuses on the shared meanings that members of a society develop.

Intermediate treatment	a diverse range of community programmes in England and Wales designed to keep young offenders out of court or out of custody. Originating in the early 1970s, they were first directed at those considered 'at risk' of offending. By the mid-1980s, 'intensive' forms were developed as alternatives to custody.
Justice model	the proposition that the principles of proportionality, due process, determinant sentencing and non-discretional decision making should be the central elements of systems of youth justice (von Hirsch, 1976).
Labelling	a sociological approach to crime and deviancy which focuses on the processes whereby social reaction (stereotyping, scapegoating) causes (rather than curtails) further offending (Becker, 1963).
Left realism	a school of criminology that emerged in Britain in the 1980s which claimed to take people's fear of crime seriously. In contrast to critical criminology, it advocates social democratic means of crime control (Lea and Young, 1984).
Localization	the antithesis to globalization which draws attention to the simultaneous proliferation of 'local solutions' to 'local problems'.
Managerialism	a cultural formation and set of ideologies and practices which suggest that the organization of public services is best served by managers, rather than professionals or bureaucrats. It assumes that a pragmatic and perform-ance-centred management will prove an economic, effective and efficient means to solve a wide range of social and economic problems (Clarke et al., 1994).
Marginalization	the proposition that changes in the labour market have acted to push some young people to the periphery of the social order by preventing their transition to social and economic independence.
Maternal deprivation	a theory that proposes that juvenile crime is caused by the separation of children from their mothers (Bowlby, 1946).
Modernity	a period from industrialization to the 1970s in which it was assumed that social problems could be addressed through positivist science and rationality.

Moral panic	a concept that implies that the social reaction to certain phenomena is out of proportion to the scale of the problem, but performs a vital function for the state in distracting attention from more deep-seated problems and in acting as a means by which moral boundaries can be reactivated (Young, 1971; Cohen, 1973a).
Neo-conservatism	political doctrine emerging in the USA in the 1970s which stressed the importance of a strong state, particularly in foreign policy.
Neo-liberalism	an economic and political doctrine which emphasizes deregulated market competition and minimal state intervention.
Neo-tribe	a 'post-subcultural' term to signify the more fluid structure, states of mind, appearance and form of contemporary youth lifestyles (Maffesoli, 1996). Most typically applied to dance-music cultures.
Net widening	the process whereby attempts to prevent crime inadvertently draw more subjects into the criminal justice system (Austin and Krisberg, 1981).
Night-time economy	the transformation of city spaces, particularly since the commercialization of club culture, as centres of marketable and mainstream hedonism, excess and excitement.
Official statistics	statistical data compiled by the police and the courts and routinely published by the Home Office as indices of the extent of crime.
Perishing classes	a nineteenth-century term used originally by Mary Carpenter to distinguish the destitute (and worthy of philanthropic support) from the 'dangerous' (and worthy only of punishment).
Persistent offending	the recurring notion that a small group of offenders make up a disproportionate part of the 'crime problem'.
Policy transfer	the processes whereby policies and discourse originating in one nation state flow to and are reconfigured in another.
Positive rights	when applied to young people, a political programme designed to protect individual human rights within a protectionist and welfare framework.

Positivism

a theory that emerged in the early nineteenth century which argues that social relations can be studied scientifically using methods derived from the natural sciences. In criminology it straddles biological, psychological and sociological disciplines in an attempt to isolate key causes of crime.

Postmodernism

an intellectual movement which challenges faith in science as a foundational principle for the structuring of society and is sceptical of any grand theory's attempt to discover the 'truth'. In contrast to modernism, it is prepared to accept doubt, uncertainty and relativism.

Protective factors

the antithesis of 'risk factors': that is those elements of family and social circumstance that appear to prevent (re-)offending.

Punishment in the community

a strategy developed in the 1980s, that community-based sentences would only be effective (popularly and politically) if they became more punitive.

Punitive turn

an extension of means of punishment that rely on an intolerance and a vindictive infliction of pain, originating in the main from the USA in the 1980s.

Pyrrhic defeat

the proposition that failures in criminal justice to reduce crime recreate particular images of crime and criminals and deflect attention from the crimes of the powerful. Failure yields such benefits for those in positions of power that it amounts to a success (Reiman, 2007).

Racialization

a process whereby specific groups of people are construed as a 'type' by referring to a limited number of their physical or cultural attributes.

Rational choice

in contrast to positivism, the proposition that has come to some prominence since the 1980s that offenders make rational decisions about which crimes to commit and where, according to the available opportunities (Cornish and Clarke, 1986).

Recording of crime	the selective act of the police making a record that a crime has occurred.
Reformation	the reform of offenders through punishment in the hope they will come to realize their own moral shortcomings.
Rehabilitation	the reform of offenders through various treatment methods whereby they can be retrained and re-educated.
Relative deprivation	a concept, latterly associated with left realism, by which it is argued that it is not absolute deprivation or poverty that causes crime, but perceptions of deprivation or injustice (Lea and Young, 1984).
Reparation	a strategy employed in the criminal justice system whereby an offender pays compensation to, or acknowledges their wrongdoing in the presence of, the victim.
Reporting of crime	the selective act of the public informing the police that a crime has been committed.
Representation	the process whereby knowledge and understanding of social phenomena are constructed by how they are (re)presented by public bodies and institutions (media, governments, academics).
Repressive welfare	the expansion of indefinite means of youth surveillance, treatment and control under the guise that it is for 'their own good' (Hudson, 1987).
Rescue	part of the rhetoric of nineteenth-century juvenile justice: the intention of removing children from the 'vices' of the street.
Resistance	the means by which subordinate cultures and youth subcultures are able to 'win space' from a hegemonic dominant culture (Clarke et al., 1976).
Responsibilization	strategies for holding offenders responsible for their own actions and for encouraging communities to be more active in crime control (Garland, 1996).
Restoration	a philosophy and practice of bringing offenders, victims and communities together in order to repair harms, reconcile conflicts and heal rifts (Zehr and Mika, 1998).

Retribution	the philosophy that vengeance should be sought and offenders punished for acts they have committed in the past.
Revisionist history	in contrast to *idealist history*, revisionist history analyses historical change not as progress but as evidence of a strengthening of state power through which 'problem populations' can be identified and criminalized.
Right realism	a school of criminology that emerged in the 1970s which was less interested in discovering the causes of crime and more in developing effective means for its control (Wilson, 1975).
Risk factors	as used by *developmental criminology*, those characteristics (such as abuse, large family size, criminal parents) that longitudinal and quantitative research suggests will produce negative outcomes such as an increase in the likelihood of future offending.
Risk society	the proposition that in the late twentieth century the certainties of industrialism and science have collapsed and been replaced by a series of local, global and individualized conditions of risk (Beck, 1992).
Self report studies	a means of assessing the extent of crime by asking people directly whether they are perpetrators.
Semiology	a branch of linguistics concerned with the 'reading' of signs and symbols.
Situational crime prevention	a policy of preventing crime by making targets harder to hit, such as improving household security, redesigning housing estates and increasing means of surveillance.
Social capital	loosely defined but usually referring to the range of resources, bonds and networks available to different individuals and communities. Viewed by many as a neo-liberal inspired concept which masks issues of historical and material class inequalities.
Social constructionism	a perspective that begins with exploring assumptions associated with the labelling of things and emphasizes the importance of social expectations in the analysis of taken-for-granted and apparently natural social processes (Clarke and Cochrane, 1998).

Social control	an ill-defined term which has been used to describe all means through which conformity might be achieved – from infant socialization to incarceration (Cohen, 1985).
Social crime	the proposition that some crime is committed simply for self and family survival.
Social crime prevention	a policy of preventing crime by targeting anti-social behaviour and those considered 'at risk' as well as known offenders. Includes programmes to open up educational opportunities, improve parenting skills and provide wider access to sports/leisure facilities.
Social disorganization	a concept that implies that certain communities have no stable values and lack effective means of social control (Shaw and McKay, 1942).
Social exclusion	a broad concept that refers not simply to the way in which the poor are marginalized from the economic mainstream, but which emphasizes isolation from relationships and sources of identity.
Social harm	a replacement concept to that of 'crime' which recognizes those serious and injurious practices that are not recognized in legal and state definitions (Hillyard and Tombs, 2007).
Social inclusion	often used as the obverse of social exclusion, and typically conceived as referring to policies that aspire to prevent 'exclusion' through anti-poverty, equal opportunity, urban regeneration, parenting support, education, training and community safety initiatives.
Somatotyping	a means of measuring variations in body types according to which certain physiological features have been claimed to be causative of delinquency (Sheldon, 1949).
State control	a radical perspective on social control which contends that the primary source of control lies with the state and that all forms of deviancy control have become increasingly centralized (Cohen, 1985).
Status frustration	the end result of judging working-class children by middle-class standards. Working-class youth who find themselves at the bottom of the status hierarchy find a 'solution' to their lack of formal status by achieving status through delinquent means (Cohen, A., 1955).

Status offence   violation of formal or informal rules which are applied only to certain sections of society. The focus is less on the offence itself and more on who commits it. In the USA such status offences as being incorrigible, truant or sexually precocious apply only to children.

Strain   a social structural condition whereby certain pressures are exerted on people to engage in non-conformist behaviour, for example, because of disjunctures between culturally defined goals and available means to achieve such goals (Merton, 1938).

Style   the means by which subcultures are able to express their 'resistance' (Clarke, 1976).

Subculture   first used by anthropologists, Cohen (1955) applied it to the study of delinquency to connote a set of values that differed from the mainstream or dominant culture. Subsequently used by Clarke et al. (1976) to explore correspondences and divergencies between youth and their class-based 'parent' cultures.

Toleration   the acknowledgement that non-intervention may be less socially damaging than repression.

Transcarceration   a reworking of Foucault and Cohen's radical perspective on social control, to stress the fluidity of the correspondences between, and the cross-institutional dynamics of, the help-control complex, whereby delinquents are constantly shifted between agencies of correction, probation, welfare and mental health (Lowman et al., 1987).

Transgression   a preferred term to 'deviance' to signify elements of boundary crossing and transcendence in rule breaking.

Underclass   first used in America to describe the economically marginalized. Subsequently reworked to describe those who are dependent on state benefits, either as morally bankrupt, workshy scroungers and thus 'undeserving' (Murray, 1990) or as the victims of recession, deprivation and political marginalization (Mann, 1991).

Victim blaming   holding those suffering from neglect, poverty, abuse, exploitation or crime, as being (at least in part) responsible for their own suffering. Frequently used to divert attention away from the social structural contexts of individual behaviour.

Victim surveys	a means of measuring the extent of crime by asking the public to recall any crimes committed against them which may not have been recorded in the official statistics.
Victimization	the social, economic, political and personal processes associated with being recognized as a victim.
Violence	any abuse of individual and collective well-being and rights though typically employed in media and political discourse to refer to visible physical harm as recognized in criminal law.
Waywardness	similar to 'delinquency', an elastic concept but applied particularly in the early twentieth century to fears for the increasing independence of girls. Its power lay in its imprecision (Cox, 2003).
Welfare model	the proposition that the principles of meeting needs, wide judicial discretion, informalism and treatment should be the central elements of systems of youth justice (Cullen and Gilbert, 1982).
'What works'	An ethos developed as a response to the negative 1970s message that 'nothing works' in order to legitimize certain interventions designed to reduce offending – typically associated with cognitive behavioural methods in probation.
Youth	an ill-defined and variable period of the life-span between infancy and adulthood.
Youth custody	a variety of institutions designed for the reform and/or punishment of children, juveniles and young people, ranging from the reformatories, industrial schools and Parkhurst prison of the nineteenth century; the borstals, approved schools, community homes, detention centres, youth custody centres, secure units and boot camps of the twentieth century; to the young offender institutions and secure training centres of the twenty-first century.
Zero tolerance	an intensive community policing strategy pioneered in New York in the mid 1990s whereby minor offences and incivilities are targeted, on the assumption that more serious offending will be curtailed as a result (Dennis, 1997).
Zone in transition	run-down inner-city areas which produce stable patterns of delinquency even when their populations change.

References

Aas, K.F. (2007) *Globalization and Crime,* London, Sage.

Abrams, M. (1959) *The Teenage Consumer*, London, Press Exchange.

Abramson, B. (2000) *Juvenile Justice: The 'Unwanted Child' of State Responsibilities. An Analysis of the Concluding Observations of the UN Committee on the Rights of the Child, in Regard to Juvenile Justice from 1993 to 2000*, International Network on Juvenile Justice/Defence for Children International. www.defence-for-children.org

Abramson, B. (2006) 'Juvenile justice: the unwanted child', in Jensen, E. and Jepsen, J. (eds) *Juvenile Law Violators, Human Rights and the Development of New Juvenile Justice Systems*, Oxford, Hart.

Agnew, R. (1992) 'Foundation for a general strain theory of crime and delinquency', *Criminology*, vol. 30, no. 1, pp. 47–87.

Aichhorn, A. (1925) *Wayward Youth*, reprinted 1955, New York, Meridian.

Ainsworth, P. (2000) *Psychology and Crime: Myths and Reality*, London, Longman.

Alcock, P. and Harris, P. (1982) *Welfare, Law and Order*, London, Macmillan.

Allen, R. (1990) 'Punishing the parents', *Youth and Policy*, no. 31, pp. 17–20.

Allen, R. (1991) 'Out of jail: the reduction in the use of penal custody for male juveniles 1981–88', *Howard Journal*, vol. 30, no. 1, pp. 30–52.

Allen, R. (2006) *From Punishment to Problem Solving: A New Approach to Children in Trouble*, London, Centre for Crime and Justice studies.

Amnesty International (1998) *Betraying the Young: Children in the US Justice System*, AI Index AMR 51/60/98.

Anderson, D. (ed.) (1992) *The Loss of Virtue: Moral Confusion and Social Disorder in Britain and America*, London, Social Affairs Unit.

Anderson, S., Kinsey, R., Loader, I. and Smith, C. (1994) *Cautionary Tales: Young People, Crime and Policing in Edinburgh*, Aldershot, Avebury.

Ariès, P. (1962) *Centuries of Childhood*, London, Cape.

Armstrong, D. (2004) 'A risky business? Research, policy, governmentality and youth offending', *Youth Justice*, vol. 4, no. 2, pp. 100–16.

Armstrong, D., Hine, J., Hacking, S., Armaos, R., Jones, R., Klessinger, N. and France A. (2005) *Children, Risk and Crime: The On Track Youth Lifestyles Surveys*, Home Office Research Study no. 278, London, Home Office.

Arthur, R. (2005) 'Punishing parents for the crimes of their children', *The Howard Journal of Criminal Justice*, vol. 44, no. 3, pp. 233–53.

Asboconcern/NAPO (2005) *ASBOs: An Analysis of the First Six Years*, London, NAPO.

Ashworth, A. (2003) 'Is restorative justice the way forward for criminal justice?', in McLaughlin, E. et al. (eds) *Restorative Justice: Critical Issues*, London, Sage.

Ashworth, A., Gardner, J., Morgan, R., Smith, A., Von Hirsch, A. and Wasik, M. (1998) 'Neighbouring on the oppressive: the government's Anti-Social Behaviour Order proposals', *Criminal Justice*, vol. 16, no. 1, pp. 7–14.

Asquith, S. (1983) 'Justice, retribution and children', in Morris, A. and Giller, M. (eds) *Providing Criminal Justice for Children*, London, Edward Arnold.

Asquith, S. (ed.) (1996b) *Children and Young People in Conflict with the Law*, London, Jessica Langley.

Association of County Councils, Association of Metropolitan Authorities, Association of Directors of Social Service, National Association for the Care and Resettlement of Offenders and Association of Chief Officers of Probation (1996) *National Protocol for Youth Justice Services*, London, Association of Metropolitan Authorities.

Audit Commission (1996) *Misspent Youth: Young People and Crime*, London, Audit Commission.

Audit Commission (1998) *Misspent Youth '98: The Challenge for Youth Justice*, London, Audit Commission.

Audit Commission (1999) *Safety in Numbers: Promoting Community Safety*, London, Audit Commission.

Audit Commission (2004) *Youth Justice 2004: A Review of the Reformed Youth Justice System*, London, Audit Commission.

Audit Scotland (2002) *Dealing with Offending by Young People*, Edinburgh, Auditor General.

Auletta, K. (1982) *The Underclass*, New York, Random House.

Aust, R., Sharp, C. and Goulden, C. (2002) *Prevalence of Drug Use: Key Findings from the 2001/2002 British Crime Survey*, Findings, no. 182, London, Home Office.

Austin, J. and Krisberg, B. (1981) 'Wider, stronger and different nets: the dialectics of criminal justice reform', *Journal of Research in Crime and Delinquency*, vol. 18, no. 1, pp. 165–96.

Aye Maung, N. (1995) *Young People, Victimization and the Police*, Home Office Research Study no. 140, London, HMSO.

Back, L. (1996) *New Ethnicities and Urban Culture*, London, UCL Press.

Bagguley, P. and Mann, K. (1992) 'Idle, thieving bastards? Scholarly representations of the underclass', *Work, Employment and Society*, vol. 6, no. 1, pp. 113–26.

Bailey, S., Thornton, L. and Weaver, A. (1994) 'The first 100 admissions to an adolescent secure unit', *Journal of Adolescence*, vol. 17, pp. 207–20.

Bailey, V. (1987) *Delinquency and Citizenship: Reclaiming the Young Offender 1914–1948*, Oxford, Clarendon.

Bailleau, F. (1998) 'A crisis of youth or of juridicial response?', in Ruggiero, V., South, N. and Taylor, I. (eds) *The New European Criminology*, London, Routledge.

Bala, N., Hornick, J., Snyder, H. and Paetsch, J. (eds) (2002) *Juvenile Justice Systems: An International Comparison of Problems and Solutions*, Toronto, Thompson.

Ball, R. and Curry, D. (1995) 'The logic of definition in criminology: purposes and methods for defining "gangs"', *Criminology*, vol. 33, no. 2, pp. 225–45.

Balvig, F. (2004) 'When law and order returned to Denmark', *Journal of Scandinavian Studies in Criminology and Crime Prevention*, vol. 5, no. 2, pp. 167–87.

Bandalli, S. (1998) 'Abolition of the presumption of *Doli Incapax* and the criminalisation of children', *The Howard Journal*, vol. 37, no. 2, pp. 114–23.

Bandalli, S. (2000) 'Children, responsibility and the New Youth Justice', in Goldson, B. (ed.) *The New Youth Justice*, Lyme Regis, Russell House.

Banks, M., Bates, I., Breakwell, G., Bynner, J., Emler, N., Jamieson, L. and Roberts, K. (1992) *Careers and Identities*, Buckingham, Open University Press.

Barton, A., Corteen, K., Scott, D. and Whyte, D. (2007) *Expanding the Criminological Imagination: Critical Readings in Criminology*, Cullompton, Willan.

Batchelor, S. (2001) 'The myth of girl gangs', *Criminal Justice Matters*, no. 43, pp. 26–7.

Bateman, T. (2006) 'Youth crime and justice: statistical "evidence", recent trends and responses', in Goldson, B. and Muncie, J. (eds) *Youth Crime and Justice*, London, Sage.

Bateman, T. and Pitts, J. (eds) (2005) *The RHP Companion to Youth Justice*, Lyme Regis, Russell House.

Bauman, Z. (1993) *Postmodern Ethics*, Oxford, Blackwell.

Bauman, Z. (1997) *Postmodernity and its Discontents*, Oxford, Blackwell.

Bauman, Z. (1998) *Globalization: The Human Consequences*, Cambridge, Polity.

Bazemore, G. and Walgrave, L. (eds) (1999) *Restorative Juvenile Justice: Repairing the Harm of Youth Crime*, Monsey, NY, Criminal Justice Press.

Beck, U. (1992) *Risk Society: Towards a New Modernity*, London, Sage.

Beck, U. (2000) *What is Globalization?* Cambridge, Polity.

Becker, H. (1963) *Outsiders*, New York, Free Press.

Becker, H. (1967) 'Whose side are we on?', *Social Problems*, vol. 14, no. 3, pp. 239–47.

Beinart, S., Anderson, B., Lee, S. and Utting, D. (2002) *Youth at Risk? A National Survey of Risk Factors, Protective Factors and Problem Behaviour among Young People in England, Scotland and Wales*, London, Communities That Care/Joseph Rowntree Foundation.

Beirne, P. and Messerschmidt, J. (1991) *Criminology*, Fort Worth, TX, Harcourt Brace Jovanovich.

Bell, V. (1993) 'Governing childhood: neo-liberalism and the law', *Economy and Society*, vol. 22, no. 3, pp. 390–403.

Belsey, A. (1986) 'The New Right, social order and civil liberties', in Levitas, R. (ed.) *The Ideology of the New Right*, Cambridge, Polity.

Belson, W.A. (1975) *Juvenile Theft: The Causal Factors*, London, Harper & Row.

Benekos, P. and Merlo, A. (2008) Juvenile justice: the legacy of punitive policy', *Youth Violence and Juvenile Justice*, vol. 6, no.1, pp. 28–46.

Bennett, A. (1999) 'Subcultures or neo-tribes? Rethinking the relationship between youth, style and musical taste', *Sociology*, vol. 33, no. 3, pp. 599–617.

Bennett, A. (2000) *Popular Music and Youth Culture: Music, Identity and Place*, New York, St Martins Press.

Bennett, A. and Kahn-Harris, K. (eds) (2004) *After Subculture: Critical Studies in Contemporary Youth Culture,* Basingstoke, Palgrave Macmillan.

Bennett, T., Holloway, K. and Williams, T. (2001) *Drug Use and Offending: Summary Results of the First Year of the New-ADAM Research Programme*, Home Office Research Study no. 236, London, Home Office.

Bianchi, H. (1986) 'Pitfalls and Strategies of Abolition' in Bianchi, H. and van Swaaningen, R. (eds) *Abolitionism: Towards a Non-Repressive Approach to Crime*, Free University Press, Amsterdam.

Bircham, E. and Charlton, J. (eds) (2001) *Anti-capitalism: A Guide to the Movement*, London, Bookmarks.

Blagg, H. (1997) 'A just measure of shame?: Aboriginal youth and conferencing in Australia', *British Journal of Criminology*, vol. 37, no. 4, pp. 481–501.

Blagg, H., Pearson, G., Sampson, A., Smith, D. and Stubbs, P. (1988) 'Interagency co-ordination: rhetoric and reality', in Hope, T. and Shaw, M. (eds) *Communities and Crime Reduction*, London, HMSO.

Blanch, M. (1979) 'Imperialism, nationalism, and organised youth', in Clarke, J., Critcher, C. and Johnson, R. (eds) *Working Class Culture*, London, Hutchinson.

Bland, N. and Read, T. (2000) *Policing Anti-social Behaviour*, Police Research Series no. 123, London, Home Office.

Bonger, W. (1916) *Criminality and Economic Conditions*, Chicago, Little, Brown.

Boswell, G. (1995) *Violent Victims*, London, Prince's Trust.

Bottomley, K. and Pease, K. (1986) *Crime and Punishment: Interpreting the Data*, Milton Keynes, Open University Press.

Bottoms, A. (1974) 'On the decriminalization of the juvenile court', in Hood, R. (ed.) *Crime, Criminology and Public Policy*, London, Heinemann.

Bottoms, A. (1977) 'Reflections on the renaissance of dangerousness', *Howard Journal*, vol. 16, no. 2, pp. 70–96.

Bottoms, A. (1995) *Intensive Community Supervision for Young Offenders*, Cambridge, Institute of Criminology.

Bottoms, A. (2002) 'The divergent development of juvenile justice policy and practice in England and Scotland', in M. Rosenheim et al. (eds) *A Century of Juvenile Justice*, Chicago, University of Chicago Press.

Bottoms, A. and Wiles, P. (1992) 'Explanations of crime and place', in Evans, D.J., Fyle, N.R. and Herbert, D.T. (eds) *Crime, Policing and Place*, London, Routledge.

Bowlby, J. (1946) *Forty-four Juvenile Thieves*, London, Baillière, Tindall and Cox.

Bowling, B. (1999) *Violent Racism: Victimisation, Policing and Social Context*, revised edn, Oxford, Oxford University Press.

Bowling, B. and Phillips, C. (2002) *Racism, Crime and Justice*, London, Longman.

Box, S. (1981) *Deviance, Reality and Society*, 2nd edn, London, Holt, Rinehart & Winston.

Box, S. (1983) *Power, Crime and Mystification*, London, Tavistock.

Box, S. (1987) *Recession, Crime and Punishment*, London, Macmillan.

Bradley, T., Tauri, J. and Walters, R. (2006) 'Demythologising youth justice in Aotearoa/New Zealand', in Muncie, J. and Goldson, B. (eds) *Comparative Youth Justice*, London, Sage.

Braithwaite, J. (1989) *Crime, Shame and Reintegration*, Cambridge, Cambridge University Press.

Braithwaite, J. (2003) 'Restorative justice and a better future', in McLaughlin, E. et al. (eds) *Restorative Justice: Critical Issues*, London, Sage.

Brake, M. (1980) *The Sociology of Youth and Youth Subcultures*, London, Routledge.

Brake, M. (1990) 'Changing leisure and cultural patterns among British youth', in Chisholm, L., Büchner, P., Kruger, H-H. and Brown, P. (eds) *Childhood, Youth and Social Change*, London, Falmer.

Brake, M. and Hale, C. (1992) *Public Order and Private Lives*, London, Routledge.

Brantingham, P.J. and Brantingham, P.L. (1984) *Patterns of Crime*, New York, Macmillan.

Bray, R.A. (1911) *Boy Labour and Apprenticeship*, London, Constable.

Brinkley, I. (1997) 'Underworked and underpaid', *Soundings*, no. 6, pp. 161–71.

Brown, A. (2004) 'Anti-Social Behaviour, Crime Control and Social Control', *Howard Journal of Criminal Justice*, vol. 43, no. 2, pp. 203–11.

Brown, B. (1986) 'Women and crime: the dark figures of criminology', *Economy and Society*, vol. 15, no. 3, pp. 355–402.

Brown, D. and Hogg, R. (1992) 'Law and order politics – left realism and radical criminology: a view from down under', in Matthews, R. and Young, J. (eds) *Issues in Realist Criminology*, London, Sage.

Brown, I. and Hullin, R. (1992) 'A study of sentencing in the Leeds Magistrates' Courts: the treatment of ethnic minority and white offenders', *British Journal of Criminology*, vol. 32, no. 1, pp. 41–53.

Brown, S. (1998) *Understanding Youth and Crime: Listening to Youth?*, Buckingham, Open University Press.

Brown, S. (2003) *Crime and Law in Media Culture*, Buckingham, Open University Press.

Brown, S. (2005) *Understanding Youth and Crime: Listening to Youth?*, 2nd edn, Maidenhead, Open University Press.

Brunson, R. and Miller, J. (2006) 'Gender, race and urban policing: The experience of African American youths', *Gender and Society,* vol. 20, no. 4, pp. 531–52.

Bull, R. and Green, J. (1980) 'The relationship between physical appearance and criminality', *Medicine, Science and the Law*, vol. 20, no. 2, pp. 79–83.

Bullock, K. and Tilley, N. (2002) *Shootings, Gangs and Violent Incidents in Manchester*, Crime Reduction Series Paper 13, London, Home Office.

Burbach, R., Nunez, O. and Kagarlistsky, B. (1997) *Globalization and its Discontents*, London, Pluto.

Burchell, G., Gordon, C. and Miller, P. (eds) (1991) *The Foucault Effect: Studies in Governmentality*, Hemel Hempstead, Harvester.

Burchill, J. and Parsons, T. (1978) *The Boy Looked at Johnny*, London, Pluto.

Burgess, P.K. (1972) 'Eysenck's theory of criminality: a new approach', *British Journal of Criminology*, vol. 12, no. 1, pp. 74–82.

Burke, T. (1996) *Policing and the Public: Findings from the 1994 British Crime Survey*, Research Findings, no. 28, London, Home Office.

Burnett, R. (2007) 'Nipping crime in the bud: developmental research and intervention in infancy', *Criminal Justice Matters*, no. 69, pp. 14–15.

Burnett, R. and Appleton, C. (2004) *Joined up Youth Justice*, Dorset, Russell House.

Burney, E. (2002) 'Talking tough, acting coy: what happened to the Anti-Social Behaviour Order?', *Howard Journal*, vol. 41, no. 5, pp. 469–84.

Burney, E. (2005) *Making People Behave: Antisocial Behaviour, Politics and Policy*, Cullompton, Willan.

Burt, C. (1925) *The Young Delinquent*, London, University of London Press.

Cain, M. (ed.) (1989) *Growing Up Good*, London, Sage.

Cain, M. (1990) 'Towards transgression: new directions in feminist criminology', *International Journal of the Sociology of Law*, vol. 18, no. 1, pp. 1–18.

Callaghan, G. (1992) 'Locality and localism: the spatial orientation of young adults in Sunderland', *Youth and Policy*, no. 39, pp. 23–33.

Campaign for Youth Justice (2007) *Jailing Juveniles: The Dangers of Incarcerating Youth in Adult Jails in America*, www.campaignforyouthjustice.org.

Campbell, A. (1981) *Girl Delinquents*, Oxford, Blackwell.

Campbell, A. (1984) *The Girls in the Gang*, Oxford, Blackwell.

Campbell, A. and Muncer, S. (1989) 'Them and us: a comparison of the cultural context of American gangs and British subcultures', *Deviant Behaviour*, vol. 10, pp. 271–88.

Campbell, B. (1993) *Goliath: Britain's Dangerous Places*, London, Methuen.

Campbell, C., Devlin, R., O'Mahony, D., Doak, J., Jackson, J., Corrigan, T. and McEvoy, K. (2005) *Evaluation of the Northern Ireland Youth Conference Service*, NIO Research and Statistical Series: Report No. 12, Belfast.

Campbell, S. (2002) *A Review of Anti-social Behaviour Orders*, Home Office Research Study no. 236, London, Home Office.

Cann, J., Falshaw, L. and Friendship, C. (2006) 'Understanding what works: accredited cognitive skills programmes for young offenders', *Youth Justice*, vol. 5, no. 3, pp. 165–79.

Carlen, P. (1992) 'Criminal women and criminal justice: the limits to and potential of feminist and left realist perspectives', in Matthews, R. and Young, J. (eds) *Issues in Realist Criminology*, London, Sage.

Carlen, P. (1996) *Jigsaw: A Political Criminology of Youth Homelessness*, Buckingham, Open University Press.

Carlile, Lord A. (2006) *An Independent Inquiry into the Use of Physical Restraint, Solitary Confinement and Forcible Strip Searching of Children in Prisons, Secure Training Centres and Local Authority Secure Children's Homes*, London, Howard League for Penal Reform.

Carozza, P. (2003) 'From conquest to constitutions: retrieving a Latin American tradition of the idea of human rights', *Human Rights Quarterly*, vol. 25, no. 2, pp. 281–313.

Carpenter, M. (1853) *Juvenile Delinquents, Their Condition and Treatment*, London, Cash.

Carrabine, E., Iganski, P., Lee, M., Plummer, K. and South, N. (2004) *Criminology: A Sociological Introduction*, London, Routledge.

Carrington, B. and Wilson, B. (2002) 'Global club cultures: cultural flows and late modern dance music culture', in Cieslik, M. and Pollock, G. (eds) *Young People in Risk Society*, Aldershot, Ashgate.

Carrington, K. and Hogg, R. (eds) (2002) *Critical Criminology: Issues, Debates, Challenges*, Cullompton, Willan.

Casburn, M. (1979) *Girls Will be Girls*, London, WRRCP.

Case, S. (2007) 'Questioning the "evidence" of risk that underpins evidence-led youth justice interventions', *Youth Justice: An International Journal*, vol. 7, no. 2, pp. 91–106.

Cashmore, E. (1979) *Rastaman: The Rastafarian Movement in England*, London, Allen & Unwin.

Cashmore, E. (1997) *The Black Culture Industry*, London, Routledge.

Cashmore, E. and Troyna, B. (eds) (1982) *Black Youth in Crisis*, London, Allen & Unwin.

Caspi, A., McClay, J., Moffit, T., Mill, J., Martin, J., Craig, I., Taylor, A. and Poulton, R. (2002) 'Role of genotype in the cycle of violence in maltreated children', *Science*, vol. 297, no. 5582, pp. 851–4.

Cavadino, M. and Dignan, J. (2006) *Penal Systems: A Comparative Approach*, London, Sage.

Cawson, P. and Martell, M. (1979) *Children Referred to Closed Units*, DHSS Research Report, no. 5, London, DHSS.

CCCS (Centre for Contemporary Cultural Studies) (1980) *Fads and Fashions*, London, Social Science Research Council/Sports Council.

Chambliss, W. (1975) 'Towards a political economy of crime', *Theory and Society*, vol. 2, pp. 149–70.

Chesney-Lind, M., Skelden, R. and Joe, K. (1996) 'Girls, delinquency and gang membership', in Huff, C.R. (ed.) *Gangs in America*, 2nd edn, London, Sage.

Chibnall, S. (1977) *Law and Order News*, London, Tavistock.

Children's Legal Centre (CLC) (1982) *Locked Up in Care*, London, CLC.

Children's Legal Centre/Y Care International (2006) *Youth Justice in Action: Campaign Report*, London, Y Care International.

Children's Rights Alliance (2002) *Rethinking Child Imprisonment*, London, Children's Rights Alliance.

Children's Rights Alliance for England (2002) *State of Children's Rights in England*, London, CRAE.

Children's Rights Alliance for England (2005) *State of Children's Rights in England*, London, CRAE.

Children's Society (1989) *Penal Custody for Juveniles: The Line of Least Resistance*, London, Children's Society.

Children's Society (1993) *A False Sense of Security*, London, Children's Society.

Christiansen, K.O. (1977) 'A review of studies of criminality among twins', in Mednick, S. and Christiansen, K.O. (eds) *Biosocial Bases of Criminal Behaviour*, New York, Gardner.

Christie, N. (1977) 'Conflicts as property', *British Journal of Criminology*, vol. 17, no. 1, pp. 1–15.

Christie, N. (1986) 'The ideal victim', in Fattah, E. (ed.) *From Crime Policy to Victim Policy: Reorienting the Justice System*, London, Macmillan.

Christie, N. (2000) *Crime Control as Industry*, 3rd edn, London, Routledge.

Chunn, D. and Gavigan, S. (1988) 'Social control: analytical tool or analytical quagmire?', *Contemporary Crises*, vol. 12, no. 2, pp. 107–24.

Ciba Foundation Symposium (1996) *Genetics of Criminal and Antisocial Behaviour*, Chichester, Wiley.

Clarke, G. (1990) 'Defending ski jumpers: a critique of theories of youth subcultures', in Frith, S. and Goodwin, A. (eds) *On Record*, London, Routledge.

Clarke, J. (1975) *The Three R's: Repression, Rescue and Rehabilitation*, Birmingham, Centre for Contemporary Cultural Studies, University of Birmingham.

Clarke, J. (1976) 'Style', in Hall, S. and Jefferson, T. (eds) *Resistance through Rituals*, London, Hutchinson.

Clarke, J. (1984) 'Young, gifted and highly dangerous: media images of youth', unpublished paper, Milton Keynes, Faculty of Social Sciences, The Open University.

Clarke, J. (1985a) 'Managing the delinquent: the Children's Branch of the Home Office 1913–30', in Langan, M. and Schwarz, B. (eds) *Crises in the British State 1880–1930*, London, Hutchinson.

Clarke, J. (1985b) 'Whose justice? The politics of juvenile control', *International Journal of the Sociology of Law*, vol. 13, no. 4, pp. 405–21.

Clarke, J. (2000) 'A world of difference? Globalisation and the study of social policy', in Lewis, G., Gewirtz, S. and Clarke, J. (eds) *Rethinking Social Policy*, London, Sage.

Clarke, J. (2005) 'New Labour's citizens: activated, empowered, responsibilised, abandoned?' *Critical Social Policy*, vol. 25, no. 4, pp. 447–63.

Clarke, J. and Cochrane, A. (1998) 'The social construction of social problems', in Saraga, E. (ed.) *Embodying the Social: Constructions of Difference*, London, Routledge/Open University.

Clarke, J., Cochrane, A. and McLaughlin, E. (eds) (1994) *Managing Social Policy*, London, Sage.

Clarke, J., Hall, S., Jefferson, T. and Roberts, B. (1976) 'Subcultures, cultures and class: a theoretical overview', in Hall, S. and Jefferson, T. (eds) *Resistance through Rituals*, London, Hutchinson.

Clarke, J. and Jefferson, T. (1973) *The Politics of Popular Culture*, Birmingham, Centre for Contemporary Cultural Studies Occasional Paper, University of Birmingham.

Clarke, J. and Newman, J. (1997) *The Managerial State*, London, Sage.

Clarke, K. (2006) 'Childhood, parenting and early intervention: a critical examination of the Sure Start national programme', *Critical Social Policy*, vol. 26, no. 4, pp. 699–721.

Clarke, R. (ed.) (1992) *Situational Crime Prevention: Successful Case Studies*, Albany, NY, Harrow and Heston.

Clarke, R. and Sinclair, I. (1974) 'Toward more effective treatment evaluation', *Collected Studies in Criminological Research*, vol. 12, pp. 55–82, Strasbourg, Council of Europe.

Cloonan, M. (1995) 'I fought the law: popular music and British obscenity law', *Popular Music*, vol. 14, no. 3, pp. 349–63.

Cloward, R. and Ohlin, L. (1961) *Delinquency and Opportunity: A Theory of Delinquent Gangs*, London, Routledge & Kegan Paul.

Cockburn, C. (1987) *Two-Track Training: Sex Inequalities and the YTS*, London, Macmillan.

Coffield, F., Borrill, C. and Marshall, S. (1986) *Growing up at the Margins*, Milton Keynes, Open University Press.

Coffield, F. and Gofton, L. (1994) *Drugs and Young People*, London, Institute for Public Policy Research.

Cohen, A. (1955) *Delinquent Boys: The Culture of the Gang*, Chicago, Chicago Free Press.

Cohen, N. (2003) '661 new crimes – and counting', *New Statesman*, 7 July.

Cohen, P. (1972) *Subcultural Conflict and Working Class Community*, Working Papers in Cultural Studies, no. 2, Birmingham, Centre for Contemporary Cultural Studies, University of Birmingham.

Cohen, P. (1979) 'Policing the working class city', in NDC/CSE, *Capitalism and the Rule of Law*, London, Hutchinson.

Cohen, P. (1982) 'School for dole', *New Socialist*, no. 3, pp. 43–7.

Cohen, P. (1986) *Rethinking the Youth Question*, Post-16 Education Centre, Working Paper no. 3, London, Institute of Education.

Cohen, P. (1997a) 'The same old generation game?', *Criminal Justice Matters*, no. 28, pp. 8–9.

Cohen, P. (1997b) *Rethinking the Youth Question*, London, Macmillan.

Cohen, P. (2000) 'In the country of the blind: youth studies and cultural studies in Britain', in Pickford, J. (ed.) *Youth Justice: Theory and Practice*, London, Cavendish.

Cohen, S. (1968) 'The politics of vandalism', *New Society*, 12 December, pp. 872–4.

Cohen, S. (1967) 'Mods, rockers and the rest: Community reactions to juvenile delinquency', *Howard Journal of Criminal Justice,* vol. 12, pp. 121–30.

Cohen, S. (1973a) *Folk Devils and Moral Panics: The Creation of Mods and Rockers*, London, Paladin.

Cohen, S. (1973b) 'The failures of criminology', *The Listener*, 8 November, pp. 622–5.

Cohen, S. (1973c) 'Property destruction: motives and meanings', in Ward, C. (ed.) *Vandalism*, London, Architectural Press.

Cohen, S. (1979) 'The punitive city: notes on the dispersal of social control', *Contemporary Crises*, vol. 3, no. 4, pp. 341–63.

Cohen, S. (1980) 'Symbols of trouble', Introduction to *Folk Devils and Moral Panics*, 2nd edn, Oxford, Martin Robertson.

Cohen, S. (1985) *Visions of Social Control*, Cambridge, Polity.

Cohen, S. (1987) 'Taking decentralization seriously: values, visions and policies', in Lowman, J., Menzies, R.J. and Palys, T.S. (eds) *Transcarceration: Essays in the Sociology of Social Control*, Aldershot, Gower.

Cohen, S. (1988) *Against Criminology*, New Brunswick, NJ, Transaction Publishers.

Cohen, S. (1989) 'The critical discourse on "social control": notes on the concept as a hammer', *International Journal of the Sociology of Law*, vol. 17, pp. 347–57.

Cohen, S. (1993) 'Human rights and crimes of the state: the culture of denial', *Australian and New Zealand Journal of Criminology*, vol. 26, no. 2, pp. 97–115.

Cohen, S. (1994) 'Social control and the politics of reconstruction', in Nelken, D. (ed.) *The Futures of Criminology*, London, Sage.

Cohen, S. (1998) 'Intellectual scepticism and political commitment: the case of radical criminology', in Walton, P. and Young, J. (eds) *The New Criminology Revisited*, Basingstoke, Macmillan.

Cohen, S. (2001) *States of Denial*, Cambridge, Polity.

Cohen, S. (2002) *Folk Devils and Moral Panics*, 3rd edn, London, Routledge.

Cohen, S. and Scull, A. (eds) (1983) *Social Control and the State: Historical and Comparative Essays*, Oxford, Martin Robertson.

Coleman, C. and Moynihan, J. (1996) *Understanding Crime Data*, Buckingham, Open University Press.

Coleman, J.C. (1980) *The Nature of Adolescence*, London, Methuen.

Coles, B. (1995) *Youth and Social Policy*, London, UCL Press.

Collin, M. (1997) *Altered State*, London, Serpent's Tail.

Commission for Racial Equality (2003) *Racial Equality in Prisons*, London, CRE.

Connell, R.W. (1987) *Gender and Power*, Cambridge, Polity.

Connell, R.W. (1995) *Masculinities*, Cambridge, Polity.

Corby, B. (1997) 'The mistreatment of young people', in Roche, R. and Tucker, S. (eds) *Youth in Society*, London, Sage/Open University.

Cornish, D. and Clarke, R. (eds) (1986) *The Reasoning Criminal*, New York, Springer-Verlag.

Corrigan, P. (1976) 'Doing nothing', in Hall, S. and Jefferson, T. (eds) *Resistance through Rituals*, London, Hutchinson.

Corrigan, P. (1979) *Schooling the Smash Street Kids*, London, Macmillan.

Coward, R. (1994) 'Whipping boys', *Guardian, Weekend*, 3 September, pp. 32–5.

Cowie, J., Cowie, V. and Slater, E. (1968) *Delinquency in Girls*, London, Heinemann.

Cox, P. (2003) *Gender, Justice and Welfare: Bad Girls in Britain 1900–1950*, Basingstoke, Palgrave.

Cox, P. and Shore, H. (eds) (2002) *Becoming Delinquent: British and European Youth 1650–1950*, Aldershot, Ashgate.

Craig, G., Gaus, A., Wilkinson, M., Skrivankova, K. and McQuade, A. (2007) *Contemporary Slavery in the UK*, York, Joseph Rowntree Foundation.

Craine, S. and Coles, B. (1995) 'Alternative careers: youth transitions and young people's involvement in crime', *Youth and Policy*, no. 48, pp. 6–27.

Crawford, A. (1997) *The Local Governance of Crime: Appeals to Community and Partnership*, Oxford, Clarendon Press.

Crawford, A. (2001) 'The growth of crime prevention in France as contrasted with the English experience', in Hughes, G., McLaughlin, E. and Muncie, J. (eds) *Crime Prevention and Community Safety: New Directions*, London, Sage.

Crawford, A. (2002) 'The governance of crime and insecurity in an anxious age: the trans-European and the local', in Crawford, A. (ed.) *Crime and Insecurity: The Governance of Safety in Europe*, Cullompton, Willan.

Crawford, A. and Burden, T. (2005) *Integrating Victims in Restorative Youth Justice*, Bristol, Policy Press.

Crawford, A. and Jones, M. (1996) 'Kirkholt revisited: some reflections on the transferability of crime prevention initiatives', *Howard Journal*, vol. 35, no. 1, pp. 21–39.

Crawford, A., Jones, T., Woodhouse, T. and Young, J. (1990) *Second Islington Crime Survey*, London, Middlesex Polytechnic.

Crawford, A. and Lister, S. (2007) *The Use and Impact of Dispersal Orders*, Bristol, Policy Press/Joseph Rowntree Foundation.

Crawford, A. and Newburn, T. (2003) *Youth Offending and Restorative Justice*, Cullompton, Willan.

CRE (Commission for Racial Equality) (1992) *Juvenile Cautioning – Ethnic Monitoring in Practice*, London, CRE.

Creighton, S. (2004) *Prevalence and Incidence of Child Abuse: International Comparisons*, London, NSPCC Research Department.

Crookes, T. (1979) 'Sociability and behaviour disturbance', *British Journal of Criminology*, vol. 19, no. 1, pp. 60–6.

Cross, N., Evans, P. and Minkes, J. (2003) 'Still children first? Developments in youth justice in Wales', *Youth Justice*, vol. 2, no. 3, pp. 151–62.

Crowley, A. (1998) *A Criminal Waste: A Study of Child Offenders Eligible for Secure Training Centres*, London, Children's Society.

Cullen, F. and Gilbert, K. (1982) *Reaffirming Rehabilitation*, Cincinnati, Anderson.

Cunneen, C. (2003) 'Thinking critically about restorative justice', in McLaughlin, E. et al. (eds) *Restorative Justice: Critical Issues*, London, Sage/OU.

Cunneen, C. and White, R. (2002) *Juvenile Justice: Youth and Crime in Australia*, Melbourne, Oxford University Press.

Cunningham, H. (1995) *Children and Childhood in Western Society since 1500*, Harlow, Longman.

Currie, E. (1985) *Confronting Crime: An American Challenge*, New York, Pantheon.

Currie, E. (1993) *Reckoning: Drugs, the Cities and the American Future*, New York, Hill & Wang.

Daly, K. (2002) 'Restorative justice: the real story', *Punishment and Society*, vol. 4, no. 1, pp. 55–79.

Damer, S. (1977) 'Wine Alley: the sociology of the dreadful enclosure', in Carson, W. and Wiles, P. (eds) *The Sociology of Crime and Delinquency in Britain*, vol. 2, Oxford, Martin Robertson.

Davies, B. (1982) 'Juvenile justice in confusion', *Youth and Policy*, vol. 1, no. 2, pp. 33–6.

Davies, P., Francis, P. and Jupp, V. (2000) *Victimization: Theory, Research and Policy*, Basingstoke, Macmillan.

Davies, S. (1987) 'Towards the re-moralisation of society', in Loney, M. (ed.) *The State or the Market*, London, Sage.

Davis, J. (1990) *Youth and the Condition of Britain*, London, Athlone.

Davis, M. (1990) *City of Quartz*, London, Verso.

Davis, M. and Bourhill, M. (1997) '"Crisis": the demonisation of children and young people', in Scraton, P. (ed.) *'Childhood' in 'Crisis'?*, London, UCL Press.

Davis, N.Z. (1971) 'The reasons of misrule: youth groups and charivaris in sixteenth century France', *Past and Present*, no. 50, pp. 41–75.

Day Sclater, S. and Piper, C. (2000) 'Remoralising the family – family policy, family law and youth justice', *Child and Family Law Quarterly* vol. 12, no. 2, pp. 135–51.

Deakin, J. (2006) 'Dangerous people, dangerous places: the nature and location of young people's victimisation and fear', *Children and Society*, vol. 20, no. 5, pp. 376–90.

Dean, M. (1999) *Governmentality: Power and Rule in Modern Society*, London, Sage.

De Haan, W. (1990) *The Politics of Redress*, London, Unwin Hyman.

De Haan, W. (1991) 'Abolitionism and crime control: a contradiction in terms', in Stenson, K. and Cowell, D. (eds) *The Politics of Crime Control*, London, Sage.

DeMause, L. (1976) *The History of Childhood: The Evolution of Parent–Child Relationships as a Factor in History*, London, Souvenir Press.

Dennis, N. (1993) *Rising Crime and the Dismembered Family*, London, Institute of Economic Affairs.

Dennis, N. (ed.) (1997) *Zero Tolerance: Policing a Free Society*, London, Institute of Economic Affairs.

Dennis, N. and Erdos, G. (1992) *Families without Fatherhood*, London, Institute of Economic Affairs.

DHSS (Department of Health and Social Security) (1981) *Offending by Young People: A Survey of Recent Trends*, London, DHSS.

Dickie, D. (1979) 'The social work role in Scottish juvenile justice', in Parker, M. (ed.) *Social Work and the Courts*, London, Edward Arnold.

Dignan, J. and Cavadino, M. (2007/08) 'Penal policy in comparative perspective', *Criminal Justice Matters*, no. 70, pp. 15–16.

Dingwall, R., Eekelaar, J.M. and Murray, T. (1984) 'Childhood as a social problem', *Journal of Law and Society*, vol. 11, no. 2, pp. 207–32.

Ditchfield, J. (1976) *Police Cautioning in England and Wales*, Home Office Research Study, no. 37, London, HMSO.

Ditton, J. and Duffy, J. (1983) 'Bias in the newspaper reporting of crime news', *British Journal of Criminology*, vol. 23, no. 2, pp. 159–65.

Dolowitz, D. (ed.) (2000) *Policy Transfer and British Social Policy: Learning from the USA?*, Buckingham, Open University Press.

Dolowitz, D. and Marsh, D. (2000) 'Learning from abroad: the role of policy transfer in contemporary policy making', *Governance*, vol. 13, no. 1, pp. 5–24.

Donzelot, J. (1979) *The Policing of Families*, London, Hutchinson.

Dorn, N. and South, N. (1982) *Of Males and Markets*, Research Paper no. 1, London, Middlesex Polytechnic.

Downes, D. (1966) *The Delinquent Solution*, London, Routledge & Kegan Paul.

Downes, D. (1988) *Contrasts in Tolerance*, Oxford, Oxford University Press.

Downes, D. and Hansen, K. (2006) 'Welfare and punishment: the relationship between welfare spending and imprisonment', *Briefing No. 2*, London, Crime and Society Foundation.

Downes, D. and Rock, P. (1982) *Understanding Deviance*, Oxford, Clarendon.

Drakeford, M. and Butler, I. (2007) 'Everyday tragedies: justice, scandal and young people in contemporary Britain', *Howard Journal*, vol. 46, no. 3, pp. 219–35.

Dugdale, R. (1910) *The Jukes*, New York, Putnam.

Dunkel, F. (1991) 'Legal differences in juvenile criminology in Europe', in Booth, T. (ed.) *Juvenile Justice in the New Europe*, Social Services Monographs, Sheffield, University of Sheffield.

Dunning, E., Murphy, P. and Williams, J. (1988) *The Roots of Football Hooliganism*, London, Routledge.

Durkheim, E. (1895/1964) *The Rules of Sociological Method*, reprinted 1964, New York, Free Press.

Durkheim, E. (1897/1952) *Suicide*, reprinted 1952, London, Routledge.

Dyhouse, C. (1981) *Girls Growing Up in Late Victorian and Edwardian England*, London, Routledge.

Einstadter, W. and Henry, S. (1995) *Criminological Theory*, Fort Worth, TX, Harcourt Brace.

Empey, L. (1982) *American Delinquency: Its Meaning and Construction*, Chicago, Dorsey.

Emsley, C. (1996) 'The origins and development of the police', in McLaughlin, E. and Muncie, J. (eds) *Controlling Crime*, London, Sage/Open University.

Ericson, R.V. (1991) 'Mass media, crime, law and justice', *British Journal of Criminology*, vol. 31, no. 3, pp. 219–49.

Ericson, R.V. and Haggerty, K.D. (1991) 'Governing the young', in Smandych, R. (ed.) *Governable Places*, Ashgate, Aldershot.

Erikson, E. (1968) *Identity, Youth and Crises*, London, Faber & Faber.

Esbensen, F.A. and Huizinga, D. (1991) 'Juvenile victimisation and delinquency', *Youth and Society*, vol. 23, no. 2, pp. 202–28.

Estrada, F. (2001) 'Juvenile violence as a social problem', *British Journal of Criminology*, vol. 41, pp. 639–55.

Etzioni, A. (1995) *The Spirit of Community*, London, Fontana.

European Sourcebook of Crime and Criminal Justice Statistics (2003) 2nd edn, WODC, Den Haag.

European Sourcebook of Crime and Criminal Justice Statistics (2006) 3rd edn, WODC, Den Haag.

Eysenck, H. (1970) *Crime and Personality*, London, Paladin. First published 1964.

Falshaw, L. (2005) 'The link between a history of maltreatment and subsequent offending behaviour', *Probation Journal*, vol. 52, no. 4, pp. 423–34.

Falshaw, L., Browne, K.D. and Hollin, C.R. (1996) 'Victim to offender: a review', *Aggression and Violent Behavior*, no. 1, pp. 389–404.

Falshaw, L., Friendship, C., Travers, R. and Nugent, F. (2003) *Searching for What Works: An Evaluation of Cognitive Skills Programmes*, Home Office Research Findings No. 206, London, Home Office.

Farrington, D. (1994) 'Human development and criminal careers', in Maguire, M., Morgan, R. and Reiner, R. (eds) *The Oxford Handbook of Criminology*, Oxford, Clarendon.

Farrington, D. (1996) *Understanding and Preventing Youth Crime*, Social Policy Research Findings, no. 93, York, Joseph Rowntree Foundation.

Farrington, D. (2000) 'Explaining and preventing crime: the globalisation of knowledge', *Criminology*, vol. 38, no. 1, pp. 1–24.

Farrington, D. (2002) 'Developmental and risk-focused prevention', in Maguire, M., Morgan, R., and Reiner, R. (eds) *The Oxford Handbook of Criminology*, 3rd edn, Oxford, Oxford University Press.

Farrington, D. (2003) 'Key results from the first 40 years of the Cambridge Study in delinquent development', in Thornberry, T. and Krohn, M. (eds) *Taking Stock of Delinquency*, New York/Kluwer.

Farrington, D. (2007) 'Childhood risk factors and risk-focused prevention', in Maguire, M., Morgan, R., and Reiner, R. (eds) *The Oxford Handbook of Criminology*, 4th edn, Oxford, Oxford University Press.

Farrington, D., Barnes, G. and Lambert, S. (1996) 'The concentration of offending in families', *Legal and Criminological Psychology*, vol. 1, pp. 47–63.

Farrington, D. and Dowds, E. (1985) 'Disentangling criminal behaviour and police reaction', in Farrington, D. and Gunn, J. (eds) *Reactions to Crime*, Chichester, Wiley.

Farrington, D. and Welsh, B. (2007) *Saving Children from a Life of Crime*, Oxford, Oxford University Press.

Farrington, D. and West, D. (1990) 'The Cambridge study in delinquent development', in Kerner, H.J. and Kaiser, G. (eds) *Criminality: Personality, Behaviour and Life History*, Berlin, Springer-Verlag.

Farrington, D. et al. (2002) *Evaluation of Two Intensive Regimes for Young Offenders*, Home Office Research Study, No. 239, London, Home Office.

Fass, P.S. (1977) *The Damned and the Beautiful*, New York, Oxford University Press.

Feeley, M. and Simon, J. (1992) 'The new penology', *Criminology*, vol. 30, no. 4, pp. 449–74.

Feeley, M. and Simon, J. (1994) 'Actuarial justice: the emerging new criminal law' in Nelken, D. (ed.) *The Futures of Criminology*, London, Sage.

Feeley, M. and Simon, J. (2007) 'Folk devils and moral panics: an appreciation from North America', in Downes, D. et al. (eds) *Crime, Social Control and Human Rights: Essays in Honour of Stanley Cohen*, Cullompton, Willan.

Feilzer, M. and Hood, R. (2004) *Differences or Discrimination?*, London, Youth Justice Board.

Feld, B. (1993) 'Criminalizing the American juvenile court' in Tonry, M. (ed.) *Crime and Justice: An Annual Review of Research*, vol. 17, Chicago, Chicago University Press.

Felson, M. (1998) *Crime and Everyday Life*, 2nd edn, Thousand Oaks, CA, Pine Forge Press.

Fenwick, M. (2004) 'Youth crime and crime control in contemporary Japan' in C. Sumner (ed.) *The Blackwell Companion to Criminology*, Oxford, Blackwell.

Fergusson, R. (2002) 'Rethinking youth transitions: policy transfer and new exclusions in New Labour's New Deal', *Policy Studies*, vol. 23, no. 3/4, pp. 173–90.

Fergusson, R. (2007) 'Making sense of the melting pot: multiple discourses in youth justice policy', *Youth Justice: An International Journal*, vol. 7, no. 3, pp. 179–94.

Fergusson, R., Pye, D., Esland, G., McLaughlin, E. and Muncie, J. (2000) 'Normalised dislocation and new subjectivities in post-16 markets for education and work', *Critical Social Policy*, vol. 20, no. 3, pp. 283–306.

Ferrell, J. (1996) *Crimes of Style: Urban Graffiti and the Politics of Criminality*, Boston, Northeastern University Press.

Ferrell, J. (1997) 'Youth, crime and cultural space', *Social Justice*, vol. 24, no. 4, pp. 21–38.

Ferrell, J. (1998) 'Criminological Verstehen: inside the immediacy of crime', in Ferrell, J. and Hamm, M. (eds) *Ethnography at the Edge*, Boston, Northeastern University Press.

Ferrell, J. (1999) 'Cultural criminology', *Annual Review of Sociology*, vol. 25, pp. 395–418.

Ferrell, J. (2001) *Tearing Down the Streets: Adventures in Urban Anarchy*, Basingstoke, Palgrave.

Ferrell, J., Hayward, K, Morrison, W. and Presdee, M. (eds) (2004) *Cultural Criminology Unleashed*, London, Glasshouse Press/Cavendish.

Ferrell, J. and Sanders, C.R. (eds) (1995) *Cultural Criminology*, Boston, Northeastern University Press.

Ferri, E. (1901) *Criminal Sociology*, Boston, Little, Brown.

Field, S. (2007) 'Practice cultures and the "new" youth justice in (England and) Wales', *British Journal of Criminology*, vol. 47, no. 2, pp. 311–30.

Finn, D. (1983) 'The youth training schemes: a new deal?', *Youth and Policy*, vol. 1, no. 4, pp. 16–24.

Finn, D. (1987) *Training without Jobs*, London, Macmillan.

Fionda, J. (1998) 'The age of innocence?: The concept of childhood in the punishment of young offenders', *Child and Family Law Quarterly*, vol. 10, no. 1, pp. 77–87.

Fionda, J. (2005) *Devils and Angels: Youth Policy and Crime*, Oxford, Hart.

Fitzgerald, M. (1993) *Ethnic Minorities and the Criminal Justice System*, Royal Commission on Criminal Justice, Research Study no. 20, London, HMSO.

Fitzgerald, M. and Hale, C. (1996) *Ethnic Minorities, Victimisation and Racial Harassment*, Home Office Research Study no. 154, London, Home Office.

Flood-Page, C., Campbell, S., Harrington, V. and Miller, J. (2000) *Youth Crime: Findings from the 1998/99 Youth Lifestyles Survey*, Home Office Research Study, no. 209, London, Home Office.

Forrester, D., Chatterton, M. and Pease, K. (1988) *The Kirkholt Burglary Prevention Project*, Crime Prevention Unit, paper no. 13, London, HMSO.

Foster, J. (1990) *Villains*, London, Routledge.

Foucault, M. (1977) *Discipline and Punish*, London, Allen Lane.

Foucault, M. (1991) 'Governmentality', in Burchell, G., Gordon, C. and Miller, P. (eds) *The Foucault Effect: Studies in Governmentality*, Hemel Hempstead, Harvester.

Francis, P. (2007) 'Young people, victims and crime', in Davies, P., Francis, P. and Greer, C. (eds) *Victims, Crime and Society*, London, Sage.

Franklin, B. and Petley, J. (1996) 'Killing the age of innocence: newspaper reporting of the death of James Bulger', in Pilcher, J. and Wagg, S. (eds) *Thatcher's Children*, London, Falmer.

Freeman, D. (1983) *Margaret Mead and Samoa*, Cambridge, MA, Harvard University Press.

Freeman, M. (2002) 'Children's rights ten years after ratification', in Franklin, B. (ed.) *The New Handbook of Children's Rights*, London, Routledge.

Freud, A. (1952) 'Adolescence', *Psychoanalytical Study of the Child*, vol. 13, pp. 255–78.

Friday, P. and Ren, X. (eds) (2006) *Delinquency and Juvenile Justice Systems in the Non-Western World*, Monsey, New York, Criminal Justice Press.

Frith, S. (1978) 'The punk bohemians', *New Society*, 9 March, pp. 353–56.

Frith, S. (1983) *Sound Effects: Youth, Leisure and the Politics of Rock*, London, Constable.

Frith, S. (1984) *The Sociology of Youth*, Ormskirk, Causeway.

Frith, S. and McRobbie, A. (1978) 'Rock and sexuality', *Screen Education*, vol. 29, pp. 3–19.

Frost, N. and Stein, M. (1989) *The Politics of Child Welfare*, Hemel Hempstead, Harvester Wheatsheaf.

Furlong, A. and Cartmel, F. (1997) *Young People and Social Change*, Buckingham, Open University Press.

Fyvel, T.R. (1961) *The Insecure Offenders: Rebellious Youth in the Welfare State*, London, Chatto & Windus.

Garland, D. (1985) *Punishment and Welfare: A History of Penal Strategies*, Aldershot, Gower.

Garland, D. (1990) *Punishment and Modern Society*, Oxford, Oxford University Press.

Garland, D. (1996) 'The limits of the sovereign state: strategies of crime control in contemporary society', *British Journal of Criminology*, vol. 36, no. 4, pp. 445–71.

Garland, D. (1997) '"Governmentality" and the problem of crime', *Theoretical Criminology*, vol. 1(2), pp. 173–214.

Garland, D. (2001) *The Culture of Control*, Oxford, Oxford University Press.

Garland, D. and Young, P. (eds) (1983) *The Power to Punish: Contemporary Penality and Social Analysis*, Aldershot, Gower.

Garrett, P.M. (2002) '"Encounters in the new welfare domains of the Third Way": social work, the Connexions agency and personal advisers', *Critical Social Policy*, vol. 22, no. 4, pp. 596–618.

Garrett, P.M. (2007) 'Sinbin solutions: the pioneer projects for problem families and the forgetfulness of social policy research', *Critical Social Policy*, vol. 27, no. 2, pp. 203–30.

Gartside, P. (1997) 'By-passing politics? The contradictions of "DIY culture"', *Soundings*, no. 6, pp. 198–208.

Gatrell, V. (1990) 'Crime, authority and the policeman-state', in Thompson, F.M.L. (ed.) *Cambridge Social History of Britain 1750–1950*, vol. 3, Cambridge, Cambridge University Press.

Gatti, U. and Verde, A. (2002) 'Comparative juvenile justice: an overview of Italy', in Winterdyk, J. (ed.) *Juvenile Justice Systems: International Perspectives*, 2nd edn, Toronto, Canadian Scholars Press.

Gelder, K. (ed.) (2005) *The Subcultures Reader*, 2nd edn, London, Routledge.

Gelder, K. and Thornton, S. (eds) (1997) *The Subcultures Reader*, London, Routledge.

Gelsthorpe, L. (1984) 'Girls and juvenile justice', *Youth and Policy*, no. 11, pp. 1–5.

Gelsthorpe, L. and Morris, A. (1994) 'Juvenile justice 1945–1992', in Maguire, M., Morgan, R. and Reiner, R. (eds) *The Oxford Handbook of Criminology*, Oxford, Clarendon.

Gelsthorpe, L. and Morris, A. (2002) 'Restorative justice: the last vestiges of welfare?', in Muncie, J., Hughes, G. and McLaughlin, E. (eds) *Youth Justice: Critical Readings*, London, Sage.

Gelsthorpe, L. and Sharpe, G. (2006) 'Gender, youth crime and justice' in B. Goldson and J. Muncie (eds) *Youth Crime and Justice: Critical Issues*, London, Sage.

Ghate, D. and Ramella, M. (2002) *Positive Parenting: The National Evaluation of the Youth Justice Board's Parenting Programme*, London, Youth Justice Board.

Giddens, A. (1991) *Modernity and Self Identity*, Cambridge, Polity.

Gill, K. (1985) 'The Scottish hearings system', *Ajjust*, no. 5, pp. 18–21.

Gill, O. (1977) *Luke Street: Housing Policy, Conflict and the Creation of the Delinquency Area*, London, Macmillan.

Gillespie, M. and McLaughlin, E. (2003) *Media and the Shaping of Public Knowledge and Attitudes towards Crime and Punishment,* Rethinking Crime and Punishment Research Briefing, London, Esmée Fairbairn Foundation.

Gilling, D. and Barton, A. (1997) 'Crime prevention and community safety: a new home for social policy?', *Critical Social Policy*, vol. 17, no. 1, pp. 63–83.

Gillis, J.R. (1974) *Youth and History*, London, Academic Press.

Gillis, J.R. (1975) 'The evolution of juvenile delinquency in England 1890–1914', *Past and Present*, no. 67, pp. 96–126.

Gilroy, P. (1987a) 'The myth of black criminality', in Scraton, P. (ed.) *Law, Order and the Authoritarian State*, Milton Keynes, Open University Press.

Gilroy, P. (1987b) *There Ain't No Black in the Union Jack*, London, Hutchinson.

Gilroy, P. (1993) *The Black Atlantic*, London, Verso.

Gilroy, P. and Lawrence, P. (1988) 'Two tone Britain: white and black youth and the politics of anti-racism', in Cohen, P. and Bains, H.S. (eds) *Multi-Racist Britain*, London, Macmillan.

Ginsberg, N. (1985) 'Striking back for the empire', *Critical Social Policy*, vol. 12, pp. 127–30.

Glueck, S. and Glueck, E. (1950) *Unravelling Juvenile Delinquency*, New York, Harper & Row.

Goddard, H. (1927) *The Kallikak Family: A Study in the Heredity of Feeble-mindedness*, London, Macmillan.

Goldblatt, P. and Lewis, C. (eds) (1998) *Reducing Offending*, Home Office Research Study, no. 187, London, HMSO.

Golding, W. (1954) *Lord of the Flies*, London, Faber and Faber.

Goldson, B. (1997a) 'Children, crime, policy and practice: neither welfare nor justice', *Children and Society*, vol. 11, no. 2, pp. 77–88.

Goldson, B. (1997b) 'Children in trouble: state responses to juvenile crime', in Scraton, P. (ed.) *'Childhood' in 'Crisis'?*, London, UCL Press.

Goldson, B. (1999) 'Youth (In)justice: contemporary developments in policy and practice' in Goldson, B. (ed.) *Youth Justice: Contemporary Policy and Practice*, Aldershot, Ashgate.

Goldson, B. (ed.) (2000a) *The New Youth Justice*, Lyme Regis, Russell House.

Goldson, B. (2000b) 'Children in need or young offenders?', *Child and Family Social Work*, vol. 5, pp. 255–65.

Goldson, B. (2001) 'A rational youth justice?', *Probation Journal*, vol. 48, no. 2, pp. 76–85.

Goldson, B. (2002a) 'New Labour, social justice and children: political calculation and the deserving–undeserving schism', *British Journal of Social Work*, vol. 32, pp. 683–95.

Goldson, B. (2002b) 'New punitiveness: the politics of child incarceration', in Muncie, J., Hughes, G. and McLaughlin, E. (eds) *Youth Justice: Critical Readings*, London, Sage.

Goldson, B. (2002c) *Vulnerable Inside: Children in Secure and Penal Settings*, London, The Children's Society.

Goldson, B. (2006) 'Penal custody: intolerance, irrationality and indifference', in Goldson, B. and Muncie, J. (eds) *Youth Crime and Justice*, London, Sage.

Goldson, B. (2008a) 'Child incarceration: institutional abuse, the violent state and the politics of impunity', in Scraton, P. and McCulloch, J. (eds) *The Violence of Incarceration*, London, Routledge.

Goldson, B. (ed.) (2008b) *Dictionary of Youth Justice*, Cullompton, Willan.

Goldson, B. and Chigwada-Bailey, R. (1999) '(What) justice for black children and young people?', in Goldson, B. (ed.) *Youth Justice: Contemporary Policy and Practice*, Aldershot, Ashgate.

Goldson, B. and Coles, D. (2005) *In the Care of the State? Child Deaths in Penal Custody in England and Wales*, London, INQUEST.

Goldson, B. and Jamieson, J. (2002) 'Youth crime, the parenting deficit and state intervention: a contextual critique', *Youth Justice*, vol. 2, no. 2, pp. 82–99.

Goldson, B., Lavalette, M. and McKechnie, J. (eds) (2002) *Children, Welfare and the State*, London, Sage.

Goldson, B. and Muncie, J. (2006a) 'Rethinking youth justice: comparative analysis, international human rights and research evidence', *Youth Justice*, vol. 6, no. 2, pp. 91–106.

Goldson, B. and Muncie, J. (eds) (2006b) *Youth Crime and Justice: Critical Issues*. London: Sage.

Goldson, B. and Peters, E. (2000) *Tough Justice*, London, The Children's Society.

Goode, E. and Ben-Yehuda, N. (1994) *Moral Panics: The Social Construction of Deviance*, Oxford, Blackwell.

Goodey, J. (2001) 'The criminalization of British Asian youth', *Journal of Youth Studies*, vol. 4, no. 4, pp. 429–50.

Goodey, J. (2005) *Victims and Victimology: Research, Policy and Practice*, Harlow, Pearson/Longman.

Goring, C. (1913) *The English Convict*, London, HMSO.

Gottfredson, M.R. and Hirschi, T. (1990) *A General Theory of Crime*, Stanford, CA, Stanford University Press.

Graham, J. (ed.) (1990) *Crime Prevention Strategies in Europe and America*, Helsinki, Institute for Crime Prevention and Control.

Graham, J. (1998) 'What works in preventing criminality', in Goldblatt, P. and Lewis, C. (eds) *Reducing Offending*, Home Office Research Study, no. 187, London, HMSO.

Graham, J. and Bowling, B. (1995) *Young People and Crime*, Home Office Research Study, no. 145, London, HMSO.

Gramsci, A. (1971) *Selection from the Prison Notebooks*, London, Lawrence & Wishart.

Gray, P. (2003) *An Evaluation of the Plymouth Restorative Justice Programme*, University of Plymouth, Department of Social Policy and Social Work.

Gray, P. (2005) 'The politics of risk and young offenders' experiences of social exclusion and restorative justice', *British Journal of Criminology*, vol. 45, no. 6, pp. 938–57.

Gray, P. (2007) 'Youth justice, social exclusion and the demise of social justice', *The Howard Journal*, vol. 46, no. 4, pp. 401–16.

Green, D. and Parton, A. (1990) 'Slums and slum life in Victorian England', in Gaskell, S.M. (ed.) *Slums*, Leicester, Leicester University Press.

Greenberg, D. (1977) 'Delinquency and the age structure of society', *Contemporary Crises*, vol. 1, no. 2, pp. 189–224.

Griffin, C. (1985) *Typical Girls?* London, Routledge.

Griffin, C. (1993) *Representations of Youth*, Cambridge, Polity.

Griffith, P. (2002) 'Juvenile delinquency in time', in Cox, P. and Shore, H. (eds) *Becoming Delinquent*, Aldershot, Ashgate.

Grisso, T. and Schwartz, R.G. (eds) (2000) *Youth on Trial*, Chicago, University of Chicago Press.

Hagan, J. and McCarthy, B. (1998) *Mean Streets: Youth Crime and Homelessness*, Cambridge, Cambridge University Press.

Hagell, A. and Newburn, T. (1994) *Persistent Young Offenders*, London, Policy Studies Institute.

Hagell, A., Hazel, N. and Shaw, C. (2000) *Evaluation of Medway Secure Training Centre*, London, Home Office.

Haines, K. and Drakeford, M. (1998) *Young People and Youth Justice*, Basingstoke, Macmillan.

Haines, K. and O'Mahony, D. (2006) 'Restorative approaches, young people and youth justice', in Goldson, B. and Muncie, J. (eds) *Youth Crime and Justice*, London, Sage.

Hale, C., Hayward, K., Wahidin, A. and Wincup, E. (2005) *Criminology*, Oxford, Oxford University Press.

Hall, G.S. (1905) *Adolescence: Its Psychology and Its Relations to Physiology, Anthropology, Sociology, Sex, Crime, Religion and Education*, New York, Appleton.

Hall, S. (1969) 'The hippies: an American moment', in Nagel, J. (ed.) *Student Power*, London, Merlin.

Hall, S. (1978) 'The treatment of football hooliganism in the press', in Ingham, R. (ed.) *Football Hooliganism*, London, Inter-Action.

Hall, S. (1980) *Drifting into a Law and Order Society*, London, Cobden Trust.

Hall, S. (1988) 'New ethnicities', in Donald, J. and Rattansi, A. (eds) *'Race', Culture and Difference*, Milton Keynes, Sage/Open University.

Hall, S. (1992) 'The question of cultural identity', in Hall, S., Held, D. and McGrew, T. (eds) *Modernity and Its Futures*, Cambridge, Polity/Open University.

Hall, S. (1997) 'The terms of change', *New Ethnicities*, no. 2, University of East London. pp. 7–8.

Hall, S. and Jefferson, T. (eds) (1976) *Resistance through Rituals: Youth Subcultures in Post-war Britain*, London, Hutchinson.

Hall, S., Clarke, J., Critcher, C., Jefferson, T. and Roberts, B. (1975) *Newsmaking and Crime*, Occasional Paper, Birmingham Centre for Contemporary Cultural Studies, University of Birmingham.

Hall, S., Critcher, C., Jefferson, T., Clarke, J. and Roberts, B. (1978) *Policing the Crisis: Mugging, the State and Law and Order*, London, Macmillan.

Hall, S. and Scraton, P. (1981) 'Law, class and control', in Fitzgerald, M., McLennan, G. and Pawson, J. (eds) *Crime and Society*, London, Routledge/Open University.

Hammersley, R., Khan, F. and Ditton, J. (2002) *Ecstasy and the Rise of the Chemical Generation*, London, Routledge.

Hancock, L. (2001) *Community, Crime and Disorder*, Basingstoke, Palgrave.

Hancock, L. (2004) 'Criminal justice, public opinion, fear and popular politics', in Muncie, J. and Wilson, D. (eds) *Student Handbook of Criminal Justice and Criminology*, London, Cavendish.

Hargreaves, D.H. (1967) *Social Relations in a Secondary Modern School*, London, Routledge & Kegan Paul.

Harman, C. (2000) 'Anti-capitalism: theory and practice', *International Socialism*, no. 88.

Harradine, S., Kodz, J., Lemetti, F. and Jones, B. (2004) *Defining and Measuring Anti-social Behaviour*, Development and Practice Report 26, London, Home Office.

Harris, R. (1982) 'Institutionalised ambivalence: social work and the Children and Young Persons Act 1969', *British Journal of Social Work*, vol. 12, no. 3, pp. 247–63.

Harris, R. and Timms, N. (1993) *Secure Accommodation in Child Care*, London, Routledge.

Harris, R. and Webb, P. (1987) *Welfare, Power and Juvenile Justice*, London, Tavistock.

Harris-Short, S. (2003) 'International human rights law: imperialist, inept and ineffective? Cultural relativism and the UN Convention on the Rights of the Child', *Human Rights Quarterly*, vol. 25, no. 1, pp. 130–81.

Hartless, J., Ditton, J., Nair, G. and Phillips, S. (1995) 'More sinned against than sinning: a study of young teenagers' experience of crime', *British Journal of Criminology*, vol. 35, no. 1, pp. 114–33.

Hay, C. (1995) 'Mobilisation through interpellation: James Bulger, juvenile crime and the construction of a moral panic', *Social and Legal Studies*, vol. 4, no. 2, pp. 197–223.

Haydon, D. and Scraton, P. (2000) '"Condemn a little more, understand a little less": the political context and rights implications of the domestic and European rulings in the Venables–Thompson case', *Journal of Law and Society*, vol. 27, no. 3, pp. 416–48.

Hayek, F.A. (1983) *Knowledge, Evolution and Society*, London, Adam Smith Institute.

Hayward, K. (2002) 'The vilification and pleasures of youthful transgression', in Muncie, J., Hughes, G. and McLaughlin, E. (eds) *Youth Justice: Critical Readings*, London, Sage.

Hayward, K. (2004) *City Limits: Crime, Consumer Culture and the Urban Experience*, London, Glasshouse.

Healy, W. and Bronner, A. (1936) *New Light on Delinquency and its Treatment*, New Haven, CT, Yale University Press.

Hebdige, D. (1976a) 'The meaning of mod', in Hall, S. and Jefferson, T. (eds) *Resistance through Rituals*, London, Hutchinson.

Hebdige, D. (1976b) 'Reggae, rastas and rudies', in Hall, S. and Jefferson, T. (eds) *Resistance through Rituals*, London, Hutchinson.

Hebdige, D. (1979) *Subculture: The Meaning of Style*, London, Methuen.

Hebdige, D. (1981) 'Skinheads and the search for white working class identity', *New Socialist*, vol. 1, September/October, pp. 38–41.

Hebdige, D. (1988) *Hiding in the Light*, London, Comedia.

Heidensohn, F. (1985) *Women and Crime*, London, Macmillan.

Hendrick, H. (1990) *Images of Youth: Age, Class and the Male Youth Problem 1880–1920*, Oxford, Clarendon.

Hendrick, H. (1997) 'Constructions and reconstructions of British childhood: an interpretative survey, 1800 to the present', in James, A. and Proat, A. (eds) *Constructing and Reconstructing Childhood*, 2nd edn, Basingstoke, Falmer.

Henry, S. and Milovanovic, D. (1994) 'The constitution of constitutive criminology: a postmodern approach to criminological theory', in Nelken, D. (ed.) *The Futures of Criminology*, London, Sage.

Henry, S. and Milovanovic, D. (1996) *Constitutive Criminology*, London, Sage.

Herrnstein, R.J. and Murray, C. (1994) *The Bell Curve*, New York, Basic Books.

Hester, S. and Eglin, P. (1992) *A Sociology of Crime*, London, Routledge.

Hetherington, K. (1998) 'Vanloads of uproarious humanity: New Age travellers and the utopics of the countryside', in Skelton, T. and Valentine, G. (eds) *Cool Places: Geographies of Youth Cultures*, London, Routledge.

Hill, J. and Wright, G. (2003) 'Youth, community safety and the paradox of inclusion', *The Howard Journal*, vol. 42, no. 3, pp. 282–97.

Hillyard, P., Pantazis, C., Tombs, S. and Gordon, D. (2004) *Beyond Criminology: Taking Harm Seriously*, London, Pluto.

Hillyard, P. and Tombs, S. (2007) 'From "crime" to social harm?' *Crime, Law and Social Change*, Vol. 48, pp. 9–25.

HM Government (2008) *Youth Crime Action Plan*, London, Ministry of Justice.

Hobbs, D. (1997) 'Criminal collaboration: youth gangs, subcultures, professional criminals and organized crime', in Maguire, M., Morgan, R. and Reiner, R. (eds) *The Oxford Handbook of Criminology*, 2nd edn, Oxford, Clarendon.

Hoffman, A. (1968) *Revolution for the Hell of It*, Chicago, Dial Press.

Holdaway, S. et al. (2001) *New Strategies to Address Youth Offending: The National Evaluation of the Pilot Offending Teams*, Research Directorate Occasional Paper, no. 69, London, Home Office.

Hollands, R. (1990) *The Long Transition: Class, Culture and Youth Training*, Basingstoke, Macmillan.

Hollands, R. (1995) *Friday Night, Saturday Night: Youth Cultural Identification in the Post-Industrial City*, Newcastle, University of Newcastle Press.

Hollands, R. (2002) 'Divisions in the dark; youth cultures, transitions and segmented consumption spaces in the night time economy', *Journal of Youth Studies*, vol. 5, no. 2, pp. 153–71.

Hollin, C. (1989) *Psychology and Crime*, London, Routledge.

Home Office (1927) *Report of the Departmental Committee on the Treatment of Young Offenders*, (The Molony Committee), Cmnd 2831, London, HMSO.

Home Office (1968) *Children in Trouble*, Cmnd 3601, London, HMSO.

Home Office (1990) *Crime, Justice and Protecting the Public*, Cmnd 965, London, HMSO.

Home Office (1991) *Safer Communities: The Local Delivery of Crime Prevention through the Partnership Approach* (The Morgan Report), London, HMSO.

Home Office (1995) *Strengthening Punishment in the Community*, London, HMSO.

Home Office (1997a) *Tackling Delays in the Youth Justice System*, London, HMSO.

Home Office (1997b) *Preventing Children Offending*, Cmnd 3566, London, HMSO.

Home Office (1997c) *Tackling Youth Crime: A Consultation Paper*, London, HMSO.

Home Office (1997d) *No More Excuses: A New Approach to Tackling Youth Crime in England and Wales*, Cmnd 3809, London, HMSO.

Home Office (2003a) *Respect and Responsibility: Taking a Stand against Anti-Social Behaviour*, Cmnd 5778, London, HMSO.

Home Office (2003b) *Youth Justice: The Next Steps*, London, Home Office.

Home Office (2006) 'Antisocial Behaviour Orders: statistics', http://www.crimereduction. homeoffice.gov.uk/asbos/asbos02a.xls

Home Office, DES, DE, DHSS and Welsh Office (1984) *Crime Prevention* (Circular 8/1984), London, HMSO.

Honwana, A. (2006) *Child Soldiers in Africa*, Philadelphia, PA, University of Pennsylvania Press.

Hood, R. (1992) *Race and Sentencing: A Study in the Crown Court*, Oxford, Clarendon.

hooks, bell (1994) *Outlaw Culture: Resisting Representations*, New York, Routledge.

Hooton, E. (1939) *Crime and the Man*, Cambridge, MA, Harvard University Press.

Hopkins Burke, R. (2001) *An Introduction to Criminological Theory*, Cullompton, Willan.

Hough, M. (1996) *Drugs Misuse and the Criminal Justice System: A Review of the Literature*, Home Office Drugs Prevention Initiative Paper, no. 15, London, HMSO.

Hough, M., Jacobson, J. and Millie, A. (2003) *The Decision to Imprison,* London, Prison Reform Trust.

Hough, M. and Mayhew, P. (1983) *The British Crime Survey: First Report*, Home Office Research Study, no. 16, London, HMSO.

Hough, M. and Roberts, J. (1998) *Attitudes to Punishment*, Home Office Research Study, no. 179, London, HMSO.

Hough, M. and Roberts, J. (2004) *Youth Crime and Youth Justice: Public Opinion in England and Wales*, Bristol, Policy Press.

Howard League (1995) *Banged Up, Beaten Up, Cutting Up*, London, The Howard League for Penal Reform.

Howard League (1999) *Protecting the Rights of Children*, London, The Howard League for Penal Reform.

Howard League (2007) *Children as Victims: Child-sized Crimes in a Child-sized World*, London, Howard League for Penal Reform.

Howard League (2008) *Growing Up, Shut Up Factsheet*, London, Howard League for Penal Reform.

Hudson, A. (1988) 'Boys will be boys: masculinism and the juvenile justice system', *Critical Social Policy*, no. 21, pp. 30–48.

Hudson, B. (1984) 'Femininity and adolescence', in McRobbie, A. and Nava, M. (eds) *Gender and Generation*, London, Macmillan.

Hudson, B. (1987) *Justice through Punishment*, London, Macmillan.

Hudson, B. (1989) 'Discrimination and disparity: the influence of race on sentencing', *New Community*, vol. 16, no. 1, pp. 23–34.

Hudson, B. (1996) *Understanding Justice*, Buckingham, Open University Press.

Hudson, J., Morris, A., Maxwell, G. and Galaway, B. (1996) *Family Group Conferences*, Annandale, Australia, Federation Press.

Huff, R. (1996) *Gangs in America*, 2nd edn, London, Sage.

Hughes, G. (1991) 'Taking crime seriously: a critical analysis of new left realism', *Sociology Review*, vol. 1, no. 2, pp. 18–23.

Hughes, G. (1996) 'Communitarianism and law and order', *Critical Social Policy*, vol. 16, no. 4, pp. 17–41.

Hughes, G. (1998) *Understanding Crime Prevention: Social Control, Risk and Late Modernity*, Buckingham, Open University Press.

Hughes, G. (2002a) 'Crime and disorder partnerships: the future of community safety?', in Hughes, G., McLaughlin, E. and Muncie, J. (eds) *Crime Prevention and Community Safety: New Directions*, London, Sage.

Hughes, G. (2002b) 'Plotting the rise of community safety', in Hughes, G. and Edwards, A. (eds) *Crime Control and Community*, Cullompton, Willan.

Hughes, G. (2007) *The Politics of Crime and Community*, Basingstoke, Palgrave Macmillan.

Hughes, G. and Edwards, A. (eds) (2002) *Crime Control and Community: The New Politics of Public Safety*, Cullompton, Willan.

Hughes, G., Leisten, R. and Pilkington, A. (1998) 'Diversion in a culture of severity', *Howard Journal*, vol. 37, no. 1, pp. 16–33.

Hughes, G., McLaughlin, J. and Muncie, J. (2002) 'Teetering on the edge: the futures of crime control and community safety', in Hughes, G., McLaughlin, E. and Muncie, J. (eds) *Crime Prevention and Community Safety: New Directions*, London, Sage.

Hughes, N., Mason, P. and Prior, D. (2007) 'The socialisation of crime policy?: Evidence from the national evaluation of the Children's Fund', in Roberts, R. and McMahon, W. (eds) *Social Justice and Criminal Justice*, London, Centre for Crime and Justice Studies.

Hulsman, L. (1986) 'Critical criminology and the concept of crime', *Contemporary Crises*, vol. 10, no. 1, pp. 63–80.

Human Rights Watch (1997) *Racist Violence in the United Kingdom*, New York, Human Rights Watch.

Human Rights Watch (1999) *Promises Broken: An Assessment of Children's Rights on the 10th Anniversary of the Convention of the Rights of the Child*, www.hrw.org/campaigns/crp/promises.

Human Rights Watch/Amnesty International (2005) *The Rest of their Lives: Life without Parole for Child Offenders in the United States*, New York, Human Rights Watch.

Humphries, S. (1981) *Hooligans or Rebels?* Oxford, Blackwell.

Humphries, S. (1994) 'Yesterday's yobs, today's grandfathers', *Independent*, 31 October, p. 21.

Hunt, A. (1991) 'Postmodernism and critical criminology', in McClean, B. and Milovanovic, D. (eds) *New Directions in Critical Criminology*, Vancouver, University of Vancouver Press.

Hutson, S. and Liddiard, M. (1994) *Youth Homelessness: The Construction of a Social Issue*, London, Macmillan.

Hyland, T. and Musson, D. (2001) 'Unpacking the New Deal for young people: promise and problems', *Educational Studies*, vol. 27, no. 1, pp. 55–67.

Hylton, J. (1981) 'Community corrections and social control: the case of Sastkatchewan, Canada', *Contemporary Crises*, vol. 5, no. 2, pp. 193–215.

Jacques, M. (1973) 'Trends in youth culture: some aspects', *Marxism Today*, vol. 17, no. 9, pp. 268–80.

James, A. and James, A. (2001) 'Tightening the net: children, community and control', *British Journal of Sociology*, vol. 52, no. 2, pp. 211–28.

James, A. and Jenks, C. (1996) 'Public perceptions of childhood criminality', *British Journal of Sociology*, vol. 47, no. 2, pp. 315–31.

Jankowski, M. (1991) *Islands in the Street: Gangs and American Urban Society*, Berkeley, CA, University of California Press.

Jefferson, T. (1976) 'Cultural responses of the Teds', in Hall, S. and Jefferson, T. (eds) *Resistance through Rituals*, London, Hutchinson.

Jefferson, T. (1997) 'Masculinities and crime', in Maguire, M., Morgan, R. and Reiner, R. (eds) *The Oxford Handbook of Criminology*, 2nd edn, Oxford, Clarendon.

Jefferson, T. (2002) 'For a psychosocial criminology', in Carrington, K. and Hogg, R. (eds) *Critical Criminology*, Cullompton, Willan.

Jefferson, T., Sim, J. and Walklate, S. (1992) 'Europe, the Left and criminology in the 90s', in Farrington, D. and Walklate, S. (eds) *Offenders and Victims: Theory and Policy*, London, British Society of Criminology/ISTD.

Jeffery, C.R. (1978) 'Criminology as an interdisciplinary behavioural science', *Criminology*, vol. 16, no. 2, pp. 149–69.

Jeffs, T. and Smith, M. (1994) 'Young people, youth work and a new authoritarianism', *Youth and Policy*, no. 46, pp. 17–32.

Jeffs, T. and Smith, M. (1996) 'Getting the dirtbags off the streets – curfews and other solutions to juvenile crime', *Youth and Policy*, no. 53, pp. 1–14.

Jeffs, T. and Spence, J. (2000) 'New Deal for young people', *Youth and Policy*, no. 66, pp. 34–61.

Jenkins, R. (1983) *Lads, Citizens and Ordinary Kids*, London, Routledge.

Jenkins, S. (1987) 'Crime soars – or does it?', *Sunday Times*, 22 March, p. 25.

Jenks, C. (1996) *Childhood*, London, Routledge.

Jepsen, J. (2006) 'Juvenile justice in Denmark: from social welfare to repression', in Jensen, E. and Jepsen, J. (eds) *Juvenile Law Violators, Human Rights and the Development of New Juvenile Justice Systems*, Oxford, Hart.

Jewkes, Y. (2004) *Media and Crime*, London, Sage.

Johnstone, G. (2002) *Restorative Justice: Ideas, Values and Debates*, Cullompton, Willan.

Jones, D. (2001) 'Misjudged youth: a critique of the Audit Commission's reports on youth justice', *British Journal of Social Work*, vol. 31, no. 1, pp. 57–79.

Jones, J. and Newburn, T. (2002) 'Policy convergence and crime control in the USA and the UK', *Criminal Justice*, vol. 2, no. 2, pp. 173–203.

Jones, T., Maclean, B. and Young, J. (1986) *The Islington Crime Survey*, Aldershot, Gower.

Jordan, B. (1996) *Poverty: A Theory of Social Exclusion*, Cambridge, Polity.

Jubb, R. (2003) *Youth Victimisation: A Literature Review*, London, NACRO.

Junger-Tas, J. (2002) 'The juvenile justice system: past and present trends in western society', in Weijers, I. and Duff, A. (eds) *Punishing Juveniles*, Oxford, Hart.

Junger-Tas, J. (2004) 'Youth justice in the Netherlands', in Tonry, M. and Doob, A. (eds) *Youth Crime and Youth Justice*, Chicago, University of Chicago Press.

Junger-Tas, J. (2006) 'Trends in International Juvenile Justice: What Conclusions Can be Drawn?', in J. Junger-Tas and Decker, S. (eds) *International Handbook of Juvenile Justice*. Dordrecht: Springer.

Junger-Tas, J. and Decker, S. (2006) (eds) *International Handbook of Juvenile Justice*, Dordrecht, Springer.

Jupp, V., Davies, P. and Francis, P. (1999) 'The features of invisible crimes', in Davies, P., Francis, P. and Jupp, V. (eds) *Invisible Crimes*, Basingstoke, Macmillan.

Justice (2000) *Restoring Youth Justice: New Directions in Domestic and International Law and Practice*. London, Justice.

Kalra, V., Fieldhouse, E. and Alam, S. (2001) 'Avoiding the New Deal', *Youth and Policy*, no. 72, pp. 63–79.

Karmen, A. (1990) *Crime Victims: An Introduction to Victimology*, Pacific Grove, CA, Brooks Cole.

Karstedt, S. (2001) 'Comparing cultures, comparing crime: challenges, prospects and problems for a global criminology', *Crime, Law and Social Change*, vol. 36, no. 3, pp. 285–308.

Katz, J. (1988) *Seductions of Crime: Moral and Sensual Attractions in Doing Evil*, New York, Basic Books.

Katz, J. (2000) 'The gang myth', in Karstedt, S. and Bussman, K.D. (eds) *Social Dynamics of Crime and Control*, Oxford, Hart.

Keane, J. (1997) 'Ecstasy in the unhappy society', *Soundings*, no. 6, pp. 127–39.

Keith, M. (1993) *Race, Riots and Policing*, London, UCL Press.

Kemp, A. and Rugg, J. (2001) 'Young people, housing benefit and the risk society', *Social Policy and Administration*, vol. 35, no. 6, pp. 688–700.

Kempf-Leonard, K. and Petersen, E. (2000) 'Expanding the realms of the new penology: the advent of actuarial justice for juveniles', *Punishment and Society*, vol. 2, no. 1, pp. 66–97.

Kemshall, H. (2008) 'Risk, rights and justice: understanding and responding to youth risk', *Youth Justice: An International Journal*, vol. 8, no. 1, pp. 21–37.

Kerouac, J. (1957) *On the Road*, reprinted 1972, Harmondsworth, Penguin.

Kettle, M. (1982) 'The racial numbers game in our prisons', *New Society*, 30 September, pp. 535–7.

Kilkelly, U. (2008) 'Youth courts and children's rights: the Irish experience', *Youth Justice: An International Journal*, vol. 8, no. 1, pp. 39–56.

Killeen, D. (1992) 'Leaving home', in Coleman, J.C. and Warren Adamson, C. (eds) *Youth Policy in the 1990s*, London, Routledge.

Kimmel, C. and Roby, J. (2007) 'Institutionalized child abuse: the use of child soldiers', *International Social Work*, vol. 50, no. 6, pp. 740–54.

King, M. (1988) *How to Make Social Crime Prevention Work: The French Experience*, London, NACRO.

King, M. (1989) 'Social crime prevention à la Thatcher', *Howard Journal*, vol. 28, no. 4, pp. 291–312.

King, M. (1991) 'The political construction of crime prevention: a contrast between the French and British experiences', in Stenson, K. and Cowell, D. (eds) *The Politics of Crime Control*, London, Sage.

King, M. (1995) 'The James Bulger murder trial: moral dilemmas and social solutions', *International Journal of Children's Rights*, vol. 3, no. 2, pp. 167–87.

King, M. and Petit, M.-A. (1985) 'Thin stick and fat carrot: the French juvenile system', *Youth and Policy*, no. 15, pp. 26–31.

King, P. (1998) 'The rise of juvenile delinquency in England 1780–1840: changing patterns of perception and prosecution', *Part and Present*, no. 160, pp. 116–66.

King, P. (2002) 'A brief history of panic', *Safer Society*, no. 13, pp. 8–10.

King, P. (2006) *Crime and Law in England, 1750–1840*, Cambridge, Cambridge University Press.

King, P. and Noel, J. (1993) 'The origins of the problem of juvenile delinquency: the growth of juvenile prosecutions in London in the late eighteenth and early nineteenth centuries', in *Criminal Justice History*, vol. 14, Westport, CT, Greenwood.

Klein, D. (1973) 'The etiology of female crime', *Issues in Criminology*, vol. 8, no. 2, pp. 3–30.

Klein, N. (2001) 'Farewell to the "end of history"', in Panitch, L. and Leys, C. (eds) *Socialist Register 2002*, London, Merlin.

Kobrin, S. and Klein, M. (1983) *Community Treatment of Juvenile Offenders: The DSO Experiments*, London, Sage.

Komen, M. (2002) 'Dangerous children: juvenile delinquency and judicial intervention in the Netherlands, 1960–1995', *Crime, Law and Social Change*, vol. 37, pp. 379–401.

Krisberg, B. (2006) 'Rediscovering the juvenile justice ideal in the United States', in Muncie, J. and Goldson, B (eds) *Comparative Youth Justice*, London, Sage.

Krisberg, B. and Austin, J. (1993) *Reinventing Juvenile Justice*, London, Sage.

Lacey, N. and Zedner, L. (2000) 'Community and governance: a cultural comparison', in Karstedt, S. and Bussman, K-D. (eds) *Social Dynamics of Crime and Control*, Oxford, Hart.

Lacombe, D. (1996) 'Reforming Foucault: a critique of the social control thesis', *British Journal of Sociology*, vol. 47, no. 2, pp. 333–52.

Laming, H. (2003) *The Victoria Climbié Inquiry*, Cm 5730, London, Home Office.

Landau, S. and Nathan, G. (1983) 'Selecting delinquents for cautioning in the London metropolitan area', *British Journal of Criminology*, vol. 23, no. 2, pp. 128–49.

Lappi-Seppälä, T. (1998) *Regulating the Prison Population*, Research Communications no. 38, Helsinki, National Research Institute of Legal Policy.

Lappi-Seppälä, T. (2006) 'Finland: A model of tolerance?' in Muncie, J. and Goldson, B. (eds) *Comparative Youth Justice*, London, Sage.

Lauritsen, J., Sampson, R. and Laub, J. (1991) 'The link between offending and victimisation among adolescents', *Criminology*, vol. 29, no. 2, pp. 265–92.

Lea, J. and Young, J. (1984) *What Is To Be Done about Law and Order?*, Harmondsworth, Penguin.

Lees, S. (1986) *Losing Out: Sexuality and Adolescent Girls*, London, Hutchinson.

Leffert, N. and Petersen, A. (1995) 'Patterns of development during adolescence', in Rutter, M. and Smith, D. (eds) *Psychosocial Disorders in Young People*, Chichester, Wiley.

Lemert, E. (1951) *Social Pathology*, New York, McGraw-Hill.

Lemert, E. (1967) *Human Deviance, Social Problems and Social Control*, Englewood Cliffs, NJ, Prentice-Hall.

Leonard, E. (1982) *Women, Crime and Society*, London, Longman.

Lerman, P. (1975) *Community Treatment and Social Control*, Chicago, University of Chicago Press.

Lévi-Strauss, C. (1966) *The Savage Mind*, London, Weidenfeld & Nicolson.

Levitas, R. (1996) 'The concept of social exclusion and the new Durkheimian hegemony', *Critical Social Policy*, vol. 16, no. 1, pp. 5–20.

Levitas, R. (1998) *The Inclusive Society? Social Exclusion and New Labour*, London, Macmillan.

Liddle, M. and Gelsthorpe, L. (1994) *Crime Prevention and Inter-Agency Co-operation*, Crime Prevention Unit, Paper no. 53. London, Home Office.

Liddle, M. and Solanki, A.R. (2002) *Persistent Young Offenders: Research on Individual Backgrounds and Life Experiences*, NACRO Research Briefing no. 1, London, NACRO.

Lilly, R., Cullen, F. and Ball, R. (1989) *Criminological Theory: Context and Consequences*, London, Sage.

Lincoln, S. (2004) 'Teenage Girls' Bedroom Culture: Codes Versus Zones', in A. Bennett and K. Kahn-Harris (eds) *After Subculture*, Basingstoke, Palgrave Macmillan.

Lipsey, M. (1995) 'What do we learn from 400 research studies on the effectiveness of treatment with juvenile delinquents?', in McGuire, J. (ed.) *What Works: Reducing Reoffending*, London, Wiley.

Lipsitz, G. (1994) 'We know what time it is: race, class and youth culture in the nineties', in Ross, A. and Rose, T. (eds) *Microphone Fiends: Youth Music and Youth Culture*, London, Routledge.

Livingstone, S. (1996) 'On the continuing problem of media effects', in Curran, J. and Gurevitch, M. (eds) *Mass Media and Society*, 2nd edn, London, Arnold.

Lloyd, C., Mair, G. and Hough, M. (1994) *Explaining Reconviction Rates: A Critical Analysis*, Home Office Research Findings, no. 12, London, HMSO.

Loader, I. (1996) *Youth, Policing and Democracy*, London, Macmillan.

Lockyer, A. and Stone, F. (eds) (1998) *Juvenile Justice in Scotland: Twenty Five Years of the Welfare Approach*, Edinburgh, T. & T. Clark.

Lombroso, C. (1911) *Crime: Its Causes and Remedies,* Boston, Little Brown.

Lombroso, C. (1876) *L'Uomo Delinquente*, Milan, Hoepli.

Loney, M. (1981) 'Making myths', *Youth in Society*, June, pp. 10–11.

Lowman, J., Menzies, R.J. and Palys, T.S. (eds) (1987) *Transcarceration: Essays in the Sociology of Social Control*, Aldershot, Gower.

Lusignan, R. (2007) 'Risk assessment and offender–victim relationship in juvenile offenders', *International Journal of Offender Therapy and Comparative Criminology*, vol. 51, no. 4, pp. 433–43.

Lyng, S. (1990) 'Edgework: a social psychological analysis of voluntary risk taking', *American Journal of Sociology*, vol. 95, no. 4, pp. 851–86.

MacDonald, R. (ed.) (1997) *Youth, the 'Underclass' and Social Exclusion*, London, Routledge.

MacDonald, R. and Marsh, J. (2005) *Disconnected Youth? Growing up in Britain's Poor Neighbourhoods*, Basingstoke, Palgrave.

MacLean, B. (1991) 'In partial defense of socialist realism', *Crime, Law and Social Change*, vol. 15, pp. 213–54.

Maffesoli, M. (1996) *The Time of the Tribes*, London, Sage.

Magarey, S. (1978) 'The invention of juvenile delinquency in early nineteenth century England', *Labour History* (Sydney), vol. 34, pp. 11–25.

Malby, S. (2008) 'Juvenile justice and the United Nations survey on crime trends and criminal justice systems' in K. Aromaa and M. Heiskanen (eds) *Crime and Criminal Justice Systems in Europe and North America 1995–2004*, Helsinki, HEUNI.

Malek, B. (1997) 'Not such tolerant times', *Soundings*, no. 6, pp. 140–51.

Mann, K. (1991) *The Making of an English 'Underclass'?*, Milton Keynes, Open University Press.

Marcuse, H. (1964) *One-Dimensional Man*, London, Routledge.

Marcuse, H. (1972) *An Essay on Liberation*, Harmondsworth, Penguin.

Marsh, P. (1977) 'Dole queue rock', *New Society*, 20 January, pp. 112–14.

Martin, C. (1997) *The ISTD Handbook of Community Programmes for Young and Juvenile Offenders*, Winchester, Waterside.

Martinson, R. (1974) 'What works? – questions and answers about prison reform', *The Public Interest*, no. 35, pp. 22–54.

Marx, K. (1859) Preface to *A Contribution to the Critique of Political Economy*, reprinted in Marx and Engels (1968) *Selected Works*, London, Lawrence & Wishart.

Marx, K. (1865) *Theories of Surplus Value*, reprinted 1964, London, Lawrence & Wishart.

Marx, K. and Engels, F. (1848) *Manifesto of the Communist Party*, reprinted 1952, Moscow, Progress.

Mason, D. (2001) *Building Safer Communities for Children*, London, NSPCC.

Matthews, R. (1987a) 'Taking realist criminology seriously', *Contemporary Crises*, vol. 11, pp. 371–401.

Matthews, R. (1987b) 'Decarceration and social control: fantasies and realities', in Lowman, J., Menzies, R.J. and Palys, T.S. (eds) *Transcarceration: Essays in the Sociology of Social Control*, Aldershot, Gower.

Matthews, R. (2003) 'Enforcing respect and reducing responsibility: a response to the White Paper on anti-social behaviour', *Community Safety Journal*, vol. 2, no. 4, pp. 5–8.

Matthews, R. and Trickey, J. (1996) *Drugs and Crime: A Study amongst Young People in Leicester*, Leicester, Centre for the Study of Public Order.

Matthews, R. and Young, J. (eds) (1992) *The New Politics of Crime and Punishment*, Cullompton, Willan.

Matza, D. (1964) *Delinquency and Drift*, New York, Wiley.

Mawby, R. (1979) 'The victimization of juveniles: a comparative study of three areas of publicly owned housing in Sheffield', *Journal of Crime and Delinquency*, vol. 16, no. 1, pp. 98–114.

Mawby, R. and Walklate, S. (1994) *Critical Victimology*, London, Sage.

May, D. (1977) 'Delinquent girls before the courts', *Medical Science Law*, vol. 17, no. 2, pp. 203–10.

May, M. (1973) 'Innocence and experience: the evolution of the concept of juvenile delinquency in the mid-nineteenth century', *Victorian Studies*, vol. 17, no. 1, pp. 7–29.

Mayer, C. (2008) 'Britain's mean streets', *Time*, 26 March.

Mayhew, H. (1861) *London Labour and London Poor*, vol. 1, London, Griffin, Bohn & Co.

Mayhew, P., Clarke, R., Sturman, A. and Hough, M. (1976) *Crime as Opportunity*, Home Office Research Study, no. 34, London, HMSO.

Mayhew, P., Mirrlees-Black, C. and Maung, N.A. (1994) *Trends in Crime: Findings from the 1994 British Crime Survey*, Home Office Research Findings, no. 14, London, HMSO.

Mayhew, P. and White, P. (1997) *The 1996 International Crime Victimisation Survey*, Home Office Research and Statistics Directorate, Research Findings, no. 57, London, HMSO.

McAra, L. (2004) 'The cultural and institutional dynamics of transformation: youth justice in Scotland, England and Wales', *Cambrian Law Review*, vol. 35, pp. 23–54.

McAra, L. (2006) 'Welfare in crisis? Key developments in Scottish youth justice', in Muncie, J. and Goldson, B. (eds) *Comparative Youth Justice*, London, Sage.

McAra, L. and McVie, S. (2005) 'The usual suspects? Street life, young people and the police', *Criminal Justice*, vol. 5, no. 1, pp. 5–36.

McAra, L. and McVie, S. (2007) Youth justice? The impact of system contact on patterns of desistance from offending', *European Journal of Criminology*, vol. 4, no. 3, pp. 315–45.

McAra, L. and Young, P. (1997) 'Juvenile justice in Scotland', *Criminal Justice*, vol. 15, no. 3, pp. 8–10.

McCaghy, C. (1976) *Deviant Behaviour*, London, Macmillan.

McGhee, J., Waterhouse, L. and Whyte, B. (1996) 'Children's hearings and children in trouble', in Asquith, S. (ed.) *Children and Young People in Conflict with the Law*, London, Jessica Langley.

McGuigan, J. (1992) *Cultural Populism*, London, Routledge.

McGuire, J. (ed.) (1995) *What Works: Reducing Reoffending*, London, Wiley.

McKay, G. (1996) *Senseless Acts of Beauty: Cultures of Resistance since the Sixties*, London, Verso.

McKay, G. (ed.) (1998) *DIY Culture: Party and Protest in Nineties Britain*, London, Verso.

McLaughlin, E., Fergusson, R., Hughes, G. and Westmarland, L. (eds) (2003) *Restorative Justice: Critical Issues*, London, Sage/Open University.

McLaughlin, E. and Muncie, J. (1993) 'Juvenile delinquency', in Dallos, R. and McLaughlin, E. (eds) *Social Problems and the Family*, London, Sage/Open University.

McLaughlin, E. and Muncie, J. (1994) 'Managing the criminal justice system', in Clarke, J., Cochrane, A. and McLaughlin, E. (eds) *Managing Social Policy*, London, Sage.

McLaughlin, E. and Muncie, J. (1999) 'Walled cities: surveillance, regulation and segregation', in Pile, S., Brook, C. and Mooney, G. (eds) *Unruly Cities?*, London, Routledge.

McLaughlin, E., Muncie, J. and Hughes, G. (2001) 'The permanent revolution: New Labour, new public management and the modernization of criminal justice', *Criminal Justice*, vol. 1, no. 3, pp. 301–18.

McLaughlin, E., Muncie, J. and Hughes, G. (eds) (2003) *Criminological Perspectives: Essential Readings*, 2nd edn, London, Sage.

McMahon, M. (1990) 'Net-widening: vagaries in the use of a concept', *British Journal of Criminology*, vol. 30, no. 2, pp. 121–49.

McNeish, D. (1996) 'Young people, crime, justice and punishment', in Roberts, H. and Sachdev, D. (eds) *Young People's Attitudes*, Ilford, Barnardo's.

McQuail, D. (1993) *Media Performance*, London, Sage.

McQueen, R. (1990) 'The prospects for left realist criminology in Australia', *The Critical Criminologist*, vol. 2, no. 2, pp. 9–10, 13–15.

McRobbie, A. (1978) 'Working class girls and the culture of femininity', in Centre for Contemporary Cultural Studies, *Women Take Issue*, London, Hutchinson.

McRobbie, A. (1980) 'Settling accounts with subcultures: a feminist critique', *Screen Education*. no. 34, pp. 37–49.

McRobbie, A. (1991) *Feminism and Youth Culture*, London, Macmillan.

McRobbie, A. (1994) *Postmodernism and Popular Culture*, London, Routledge.

McRobbie, A. and Garber, J. (1976) 'Girls and subcultures', in Hall, S. and Jefferson, T. (eds) *Resistance through Rituals*, London, Hutchinson.

McRobbie, A. and Nava, M. (eds) (1984) *Gender and Generation*, London, Macmillan.

McRobbie, A. and Thornton, S. (1995) 'Rethinking moral panic for multi-mediated social worlds', *British Journal of Sociology*, vol. 46, no. 4, pp. 559–74.

Mead, G.H. (1934) *Mind, Self and Society*, Chicago, University of Chicago Press.

Mead, M. (1928) *Coming of Age in Samoa*, New York, Morrow.

Mears, D. (2002) 'Sentencing guidelines and the transformation of juvenile justice in the 21st century', *Journal of Contemporary Criminal Justice*, vol. 18, no. 1, pp. 6–19.

Mears, D. (2006) 'Exploring state-level variation in juvenile incarceration rates', *The Prison Journal*, vol. 86, no. 4, pp. 470–90.

Measham, F., Newcombe, R. and Parker, H. (1994) 'The normalisation of recreational drug use amongst young people in the north-west of England', *British Journal of Sociology*, vol. 45, no. 2, pp. 287–311.

Measor, L. and Squires, P. (2000) *Young People and Community Safety*, Aldershot, Ashgate.

Mednick, S.A., Gabrielli, W. and Hutchings, B. (1987) 'Genetic factors in the etiology of criminal behaviour', in Mednick, S., Moffit, T. and Stack, S. (eds) *The Causes of Crime: New Biological Approaches*, Cambridge, Cambridge University Press.

Mednick, S. and Volavka, J. (1980) 'Biology and crime', in Morris, N. and Tonry, M. (eds) *Crime and Justice*, vol. 2, Chicago, University of Chicago Press.

Melly, G. (1972) *Revolt into Style*, Harmondsworth, Penguin.

Melossi, D. (2000) 'Translating social control: reflections on the comparison of Italian and North American cultures', in Karstedt, S. and Bussman, K-D. (eds) *Social Dynamics of Crime and Control*, Oxford, Hart.

Meri, T. (2003) *Prison is no place for a child*, www.sweden.se

Mérigeau, M. (1996) 'Legal frameworks and interventions', in McCarney, W. (ed.) *Juvenile Delinquents and Young People in Danger in an Open Environment*, Winchester, Waterside.

Merlo, A., Benekos, P. and Cook, W. (1997) 'Waiver and juvenile justice reform: widening the punitive net', *Criminal Justice Policy Review*, vol. 8, no. 2–3, pp. 145–68.

Merton, R. (1938) 'Social structure and anomie', *American Sociological Review*, vol. 3, pp. 672–82.

Merton, R. (1957) *Social Theory and Social Structure*, New York, Free Press.

Messerschmidt, J.W. (1993) *Masculinities and Crime*, Lanham, MD, Rowman & Littlefield.

Michael, J. and Adler, M. (1933) *Crime, Law and Social Science*, New York, Harcourt Brace Jovanovich.

Miers, D. (2001) *An International Review of Restorative Justice*, Crime Reduction Research Series Paper no. 10, London, Home Office.

Miles, S. (2000) *Youth Lifestyles in a Changing World*, Buckingham, Open University Press.

Miller, J. (1998) *Last One Over the Wall: The Massachusetts Experiment in Closing Reform Schools*, 2nd edn, Columbus, OH, Ohio State University Press.

Miller, P. and Plant, M. (1996) 'Drinking, smoking and illicit drug use among 15 and 16 year olds in the United Kingdom', *British Medical Journal*, vol. 313, pp. 344–7.

Millett, K. (1970) *Sexual Politics*, New York, Doubleday.

Millham, S., Bullock, R. and Hosie, R. (1978) *Locking Up Children*, London, Saxon House.

Ministry of Justice (2007) *Statistics on Race and the Criminal Justice System 2006*, www.justice.gov.uk/publications/raceandcjs.htm

Mirrlees-Black, C., Budd, T., Partridge, S. and Mayhew, P. (1998) *The 1998 British Crime Survey: England and Wales*, Home Office Statistical Bulletin, issue 21/98, London, HMSO.

Mirrlees-Black, C., Mayhew, P. and Percy, A. (1996) *The 1996 British Crime Survey*, Home Office Statistical Bulletin, issue 19/96, London, HMSO.

Mirza, H.S. (1992) *Young, Female and Black*, London, Routledge.

Mishra, R. (1999) *Globalisation and the Welfare State*, Cheltenham, Edward Elgar.

Mizen, P. (1995) *The State, Young People and Youth Training*, London, Mansell.

Mizen, P. (2003) 'Tomorrow's future or signs of a misspent youth?', *Youth and Policy*, no. 79, pp. 1–18.

Mizen, P. (2004) *The Changing State of Youth*, Basingstoke, Palgrave.

Mizen, P. (2006) 'Work and social order: the new deal for the young unemployed', in Goldson, B. and Muncie, J. (eds) *Youth Crime and Justice*, London, Sage.

Monaghan, G., Hibbert, P. and Moore, S. (2003) *Children in Trouble: Time for Change*, London, Barnardo's.

Mooney, J. (2003) 'It's the family, stupid', in Matthews, R. and Young, J. (eds) *The New Politics of Crime and Punishment*, Cullompton, Willan.

Morgan, D. (1981) 'Youth call-up: social policy for the young', *Critical Social Policy*, vol. 1, no. 2, pp. 101–10.

Morgan, J. and Zedner, L. (1992) *Child Victims*, Oxford, Clarendon.

Morgan, P. (1978) *Delinquent Fantasies*, Aldershot, Temple Smith.

MORI (2002) *Youth Survey: Summary*, London, Youth Justice Board.

Morita, A. (2002) 'Juvenile justice in Japan: a historical and cross-cultural perspective', in Rosenheim, M., Zimring, F., Tanenhaus, D. and Dohrn, B. (eds) *A Century of Juvenile Justice*, Chicago, University of Chicago Press.

Morris, A. (1974) 'Scottish juvenile justice: a critique', in Hood, R. (ed.) *Crime, Criminology and Public Policy*, London, Heinemann.

Morris, A. and Giller, M. (1987) *Understanding Juvenile Justice*, London, Croom Helm.

Morris, A., Giller, H., Geach, H. and Szwed, E. (1980) *Justice for Children*, London, Macmillan.

Morris, A. and Maxwell, G. (eds) (2001) *Restorative Justice for Juveniles*, Oxford, Hart.

Morris, A. and McIsaac, M. (1978) *Juvenile Justice?*, London, Heinemann.

Morris, T. (1957) *The Criminal Area: A Study in Social Ecology*, London, Routledge.

Morrison, W. (1995) *Theoretical Criminology: From Modernity to Post-Modernism*, London, Cavendish.

Muggleton, D. and Weinzierl, R. (eds) (2003) *The Post-Subcultures Reader*, Oxford, Berg.

Muncie, J. (1984) *The Trouble with Kids Today: Youth and Crime in Post-War Britain*, London, Hutchinson.

Muncie, J. (1987) 'Much ado about nothing? The sociology of moral panics', *Social Studies Review*, vol. 3, no. 2, pp. 42–7.

Muncie, J. (1990) 'Failure never matters: detention centres and the politics of deterrence', *Critical Social Policy*, no. 28, pp. 42–7.

Muncie, J. (1997) 'Investing in our future', *Criminal Justice Matters*, no. 28, pp. 4–5.

Muncie, J. (1998) 'Reassessing competing paradigms in criminological theory', in Walton, P. and Young, J. (eds) *The New Criminology Revisited*, Basingstoke, Macmillan.

Muncie, J. (1999a) 'Institutionalized intolerance: youth justice and the 1998 Crime and Disorder Act', *Critical Social Policy*, vol. 19, no. 2, pp. 147–75.

Muncie, J. (1999b) *Youth and Crime: A Critical Introduction*, 1st edn, London, Sage.

Muncie, J. (2000a) 'Decriminalizing criminology', in Lewis, G., Gewirtz, S. and Clarke, J. (eds) *Rethinking Social Policy*, London, Sage.

Muncie, J. (2000b) 'Pragmatic Realism? Searching for criminology in the New Youth Justice', in Goldson, B. (ed.) *The New Youth Justice*, Lyme Regis, Russell House.

Muncie, J. (2001) 'The construction and deconstruction of crime', in Muncie, J. and McLaughlin, E. (eds) *The Problem of Crime*, 2nd edn, London, Sage.

Muncie, J. (2002a) 'A new deal for youth?: Early intervention and correctionalism', in Hughes, G., McLaughlin, E. and Muncie, J. (eds) *Crime Prevention and Community Safety: New Directions*, London, Sage.

Muncie, J. (2002b) 'Policy transfers and what works: some reflections on comparative youth justice', *Youth Justice*, vol. 1, no. 3, pp. 27–35.

Muncie, J. (2003a) 'Juvenile justice in Europe: some conceptual, analytical and statistical comparisons', *Childright*, no. 202, pp. 14–17.

Muncie, J. (2003b) 'Youth, risk and victimisation', in Davies, P., Francis, P. and Jupp, V. (eds) *Victimisation: Theory, Research and Policy*, Basingstoke, Palgrave Macmillan.

Muncie, J. (2004) *Youth and Crime*, 2nd edn, London, Sage.

Muncie, J. (2005) 'The globalisation of crime control: the case of youth and juvenile justice', *Theoretical Criminology*, vol. 9, no. 1, pp. 35–64.

Muncie, J. (2006) 'Governing young people: coherence and contradiction in contemporary youth justice', *Critical Social Policy*, vol. 26, no. 4, pp. 770–93.

Muncie, J. (2007) 'The responsibilised child', *Safer Society*, no. 32, pp. 2–4.

Muncie, J. (2008) 'The punitive turn in juvenile justice: cultures of control and rights compliance in western Europe and the USA', *Youth Justice: An International Journal*, vol. 8, no. 2, pp. 107–21.

Muncie, J., Coventry, G. and Walters, R. (1995) 'The politics of youth crime prevention', in Noaks, L., Maguire, M. and Levi, M. (eds) *Contemporary Issues in Criminology*, Cardiff, University of Wales Press.

Muncie, J. and Fitzgerald, M. (1981) 'Humanizing the deviant', in Fitzgerald, M., McLellan, G. and Pawson, J. (eds) *Crime and Society*, London, Routledge/Open University.

Muncie, J. and Goldson, B. (2006) 'England and Wales: the new correctionalism', in Muncie, J. and Goldson, B. (eds) *Comparative Youth Justice: Critical Issues*, London, Sage.

Muncie, J. and Hughes, G. (2002) 'Modes of youth governance: political rationalities, criminalisation and resistance', in Muncie, J., Hughes, G. and McLaughlin, E. (eds) *Youth Justice: Critical Readings*, London, Sage.

Muncie, J., Hughes, G. and McLaughlin, E. (2002) *Youth Justice: Critical Readings*, London, Sage.

Muncie, J. and McLaughlin, E. (eds) (2001) *The Problem of Crime*, 2nd edn, London, Sage/Open University.

Muncie, J., McLaughlin, E. and Langan, M. (eds) (1996) *Criminological Perspectives: A Reader*, London, Sage/Open University.

Mungham, G. and Pearson, G. (eds) (1976) *Working Class Youth Culture*, London, Routledge & Kegan Paul.

Murdock, G. and McCron, R. (1973) 'Scoobies, skins and contemporary pop', *New Society*, 29 March, pp. 690–2.

Murdock, G. and McCron, R. (1976) 'Youth and class: the career of a confusion', in Mungham, G. and Pearson, G. (eds) *Working Class Youth Culture*, London, Routledge & Kegan Paul.

Murdock, G. and Troyna, B. (1981) 'Recruiting racists', *Youth in Society*, November, pp. 9–10.

Murphy, R. and Roe, S. (2007) *Drug Misuse Declared: Findings from the 2006/07 British Crime Survey*, Home Office Statistical Bulletin 18/07, London, TSO.

Murray, C. (1984) *Losing Ground*, New York, Basic Books.

Murray, C. (1990) *The Emerging Underclass*, London, Institute of Economic Affairs.

Murray, C. (1994) *Underclass: The Crisis Deepens*, London, Institute of Economic Affairs.

Murray, C. (2000) 'Baby beware', *Sunday Times*, February 13th.

Musgrove, F. (1964) *Youth and the Social Order*, London, Routledge.

Myrdal, G. (1964) *Challenge to Affluence*, London, Victor Gollancz.

NACRO (1993) *Community Provision for Young People in the Youth Justice System*, London, NACRO.

NACRO (1995) *Family Group Conferencing*, NACRO Briefing Paper, September, London, NACRO.

NACRO (2002) 'Europe and the use of custody', *Youth Crime Briefing*, December, London, NACRO.

NACRO (2003) *A Failure of Justice: Reducing Child Imprisonment*, London, NACRO.

NACRO (2008) 'Some facts about children and young people who offend – 2006', *Youth Crime Briefing*, March, London, NACRO.

NAJC (New Approaches to Juvenile Crime) (1993) *Creating More Criminals*, Briefing Paper no. 1, June, London, NAJC.

Nathan, S. (1995) *Boot Camps: Return of the Short Sharp Shock*, London, Prison Reform Trust.

National Assembly for Wales (2004) *Children and Young People: Rights to Action*, Cardiff, Welsh Assembly.

National Audit Office (NAO) (2002) *The New Deal for Young People*, 28 February, HC639, London.

National Research Institute of Legal Policy (1998) *Regulating the Prison Population*, Research Communications no. 38, Helsinki, NRILP.

Nayak, A. (2003) *Race, Place and Globalisation; Youth Cultures in a Changing World*, Oxford, Berg.

Nelken, D. (1989) 'Discipline and punish: some notes on the margin', *Howard Journal*, vol. 28, no. 4, pp. 245–54.

Nelken, D. (1994) 'Whom can you trust? The future of comparative criminology', in Nelken, D. (ed.) *The Futures of Criminology*, London, Sage.

Nelken, D. (2002) 'Comparing criminal justice', in M. Maguire et al. (eds) *The Oxford Handbook of Criminology*, 3rd edn, Oxford, Oxford University Press.

Nelken, D. (2006) 'Italian juvenile justice: tolerance, leniency and indulgence', *Youth Justice*, vol. 6, no. 2, pp. 107–28.

Nellis, M. (1991) 'The electronic monitoring of offenders in England and Wales', *British Journal of Criminology*, vol. 31, no. 2, pp. 165–85.

Nellis, M. (2000) 'Law and order: the electronic monitoring of offenders', in Dolowitz, D. (ed.) *Policy Transfer and British Social Policy*, Buckingham, Open University.

Nellis, M. (2002) 'Community justice, time and the new National Probation Service', *The Howard Journal*, vol. 41, no. 1, pp. 59–86.

Neustatter, A. (1998) 'Kids – what the papers say', *Guardian*, 8 April, pp. 8–9.

Neville, R. (1971) *Playpower*, London, Paladin.

Newburn, T. (1996) 'Back to the future? Youth crime, youth justice and the rediscovery of "authoritarian populism"', in Pilcher, J. and Wagg, S. (eds) *Thatcher's Children*, London, Falmer.

Newburn, T. (2002a) 'Atlantic crossings: policy transfer and crime control in the USA and Britain', *Punishment and Society*, vol. 4, no. 2, pp. 165–94.

Newburn, T. (2002b) 'Young people, crime and youth justice', in Maguire, M., Morgan, R. and Reiner, R. (eds) *The Oxford Handbook of Criminology*, 3rd edn, Oxford, Oxford University Press.

Newburn, T. (2007) *Criminology*, Uffculme, Willan.

Newburn, T. and Jones, T. (2007) 'Symbolising crime control: reflections on zero tolerance', *Theoretical Criminology*, vol. 11, no. 2, pp. 221–43.

Newburn, T. and Stanko, E. (eds) (1994) *Just Boys Doing Business?* London, Routledge.

Newman, J. (2001) *Modernising Governance*, London, Sage.

Nicholas, S., Kershaw, C. and Walker, A. (2007) *Crime in England and Wales 2006/07*, Home Office Statistical Bulletin, London, TSO.

Nordic Working Group on Youth Crime (2001) *Youth Crime in the Nordic Countries*, Haaksbergen, De Lindeboom Publishers.

Norrie, K. (1997) *Children's Hearings in Scotland*, Edinburgh, Sweet and Maxwell.

Norris, C. and Armstrong, G. (1999) *The Maximum Surveillance Society: The Rise of CCTV*, Oxford, Berg.

NSPCC (2002) *Child Abuse in Britain*, London, NSPCC.

NSPCC (2003) *Child Killings in England and Wales*, London, NSPCC.

O'Brien, M. (2005) 'What is cultural about cultural criminology?' *British Journal of Criminology*, vol. 45, no. 5, pp. 599–612.

O'Donnell, I. and O'Sullivan, E. (2003) 'The politics of intolerance – Irish style', *British Journal of Criminology*, vol. 43, no.1, pp. 41–62.

O'Mahony, D. and Deazley, R. (2000) *Juvenile Crime and Justice: Review of the Criminal Justice System in Northern Ireland*, Research Report no. 17, Belfast, Northern Ireland Office.

O'Malley, P. (1992) 'Risk, power and crime prevention', *Economy and Society*, vol. 21, no. 3, pp. 252–75.

O'Malley, P. (2000) 'Criminologies of catastrophe?: Understanding criminal justice on the edge of the New Millennium', *Australian and New Zealand Journal of Criminology*, vol. 33, no. 2, pp. 153–67.

O'Malley, P. (2002) 'Globalising risk?: Distinguishing styles of neo liberal criminal justice in Australia and the USA', *Criminal Justice*, vol. 2, no. 2, pp. 205–22.

O'Malley, P. and Mugford, S. (1994) 'Crime, excitement and modernity', in Barak, G. (ed.) *Varieties of Criminology*, Westport, CT, Praeger.

Oakley, A. (1972) *Sex, Gender and Society*, New York, Harper & Row.

Office of the Commissioner for Human Rights (2005) *A Report by Mr Alvaro Gil-Robles, Commissioner for Human Rights, on his Visit to the United Kingdom, 4th–12th November 2004*, Strasbourg, Council of Europe.

Osborne, R. (1995) 'Crime and the media: from media studies to post-modernism', in Kidd-Hewitt, D. and Osborne, R. (eds) *Crime and the Media*, London, Pluto.

Osgerby, B. (1998) *Youth in Britain since 1945*, Oxford, Blackwell.

Owen, R. and Sweeting, A. (2007) *Hoodie or Goodie? The Link between Violent Victimisation and Offending in Young People*, London, Victim Support.

Pakes, F. (2000) 'League champions in mid table: on the major changes in Dutch prison policy', *Howard Journal*, vol. 39, no. 1, pp. 30–9.

Pakes, F. (2004a) 'The politics of discontent: the emergence of a new criminal justice discourse in the Netherlands', *Howard Journal*, vol. 43, no. 3, pp. 284–98.

Pakes, F. (2004b) *Comparative Criminal Justice*, Cullompton, Willan.

Palmer, T. (1971) *The Trials of OZ*. London, Blond & Briggs.

Parent, D. G. (1995) 'Boot camps failing to achieve goals', in Tonry, M. and Hamilton, K. (eds) *Intermediate Sanctions in Over-Crowded Times*, Boston, MA, Northeastern University Press.

Park, R. and Burgess, E. (1925) The City, Chicago, University of Chicago Press.

Parker, H. (1974) *View from the Boys*, Newton Abbot, David & Charles.

Parker, H. (1996) 'Alcohol, young adult offenders and criminological cul-de-sacs', *British Journal of Criminology*, vol. 36, no. 2, pp. 282–98.

Parker, H., Aldridge, J. and Measham, F. (1998) *Illegal Leisure: The Normalisation of Adolescent Recreational Drug Use*, London, Routledge.

Parker, H., Casburn, M. and Turnbull, D. (1981) *Receiving Juvenile Justice*, Oxford, Blackwell.

Parker, H., Jarvis, G. and Sumner, M. (1987) 'Under new orders: the redefinition of social work with young offenders', *British Journal of Social Work*, vol. 17, no. 1, pp. 21–43.

Parker, H. and Measham, F. (1994) 'Pick 'n' mix: changing patterns of illicit drug use amongst 1990s adolescents', *Drugs: Education, Prevention and Policy*, vol. 1, no. 1, pp. 5–13.

Parker, H., Measham, F. and Aldridge, J. (1995) *Drugs Futures: Changing Patterns of Drug Use amongst English Youth*, Research Monograph no. 7, London, ISDD.

Parker, H. and Newcombe, R. (1987) 'Heroin use and acquisitive crime in an English community', *British Journal of Sociology*, vol. 38, no. 3, pp. 331–48.

Parker, H., Newcombe, R. and Bakx, K. (1988) *Living with Heroin, Milton Keynes*, Open University Press.

Parker, H., Williams, L. and Aldridge, J. (2002) 'The normalisation of "sensible" recreational drug use', *Sociology*, vol. 36, no. 4, pp. 941–64.

Parkin, F. (1968) *Middle Class Radicalism*, Manchester, Manchester University Press.

Parsons, T. (1942) 'Age and sex in the social structure of the United States', *American Sociological Review*, vol. 7, pp. 604–16.

Patrick, J. (1973) *A Glasgow Gang Observed*, London, Methuen.

Pearce, F. and Tombs, S. (1992) 'Realism and corporate crime', in Matthews, R. and Young, J. (eds) *Issues in Realist Criminology*, London, Sage.

Pearson, G. (1975) 'Vandals in the park', *New Society*, 9 October, p. 69.

Pearson, G. (1976) 'Paki-bashing in a north-east Lancashire cotton town', in Mungham, G. and Pearson, G. (eds) *Working Class Youth Culture*, London, Routledge & Kegan Paul.

Pearson, G. (1983) *Hooligan: A History of Respectable Fears*, London, Macmillan.

Pearson, G. (1985) 'Lawlessness, modernity and social change: a historical appraisal', *Theory, Culture & Society*, vol. 2, no. 3, pp. 15–35.

Pearson, G. (1987) *The New Heroin Users*, London, Batsford.

Pearson, G. (1991) 'Drug-control policies in Britain', in Tonry, M. (ed.) *Crime and Justice: A Review of Research*, vol. 14, Chicago, University of Chicago Press.

Pearson, G. (1993–94) 'Youth crime and moral decline: permissiveness and tradition', *The Magistrate*, December/January, pp. 190–2.

Pearson, G. (1994) 'Youth, crime and society', in Maguire, M., Morgan, R. and Reiner, R. (eds) *The Oxford Handbook of Criminology*, Oxford, Clarendon.

Percy, A. (1998) *Ethnicity and Victimisation: Findings from the 1996 British Crime Survey*, Home Office Statistical Bulletin, issue 6/98, London, HMSO.

Percy-Smith, B. and Weil, S. (2002) 'New Deal or raw deal? Dilemmas and paradoxes of state interventions into the youth labour market', in Cieslik, M. and Pollock, G. (eds) *Young People in Risk Society*, Aldershot, Ashgate.

Percy-Smith, J. (ed.) (2000) *Policy Responses to Social Exclusion*, Buckingham, Open University Press.

Perri, 6., Jupp, B., Parry, H. and Lasky, K. (1997) *The Substance of Youth: The Place of Drugs in Young People's Lives*, York, Joseph Rowntree Trust.

Peters, L. (2005) *War is No Child's Play: Child Soldiers from Battlefield to Playground*, Occasional Paper no. 8, Geneva, Centre for the Democratic Control of Armed Forces (DCAF).

Piacentini, L. and Walters, R. (2006) 'The politicization of youth crime in Scotland and the rise of the "Burberry Court"', *Youth Justice*, vol. 6, no. 1, pp. 43–60.

Pinchbeck, I. and Hewitt, M. (1973) *Children in English Society*, vol. 2, London, Routledge.

Pinheiro, P. S. (2006) *World Report on Violence Against Children*, Geneva: United Nations.

Pitts, J. (1988) *The Politics of Juvenile Crime*, London, Sage.

Pitts, J. (1992) 'The end of an era', *Howard Journal*, vol. 31, no. 2, pp. 133–49.

Pitts, J. (1995) 'Public issues and private troubles: a tale of two cities', *Social Work in Europe*, vol. 2, no. 1, pp. 3–11.

Pitts, J. (1997) 'Youth crime, social change and crime control in Britain and France in the 1980s and 1990s', in Jones, H. (ed.) *Towards a Classless Society*, London, Routledge.

Pitts, J. (1999/2000) 'New youth justice, new youth crime', *Criminal Justice Matters*, no. 38, pp. 24–5.

Pitts, J. (2001) *The New Politics of Youth Crime: Discipline or Solidarity?*, Basingstoke, Palgrave.

Pitts, J. and Kuula, T. (2006) 'Incarcerating young people: an Anglo-Finnish comparison', *Youth Justice*, vol. 5, no. 3, pp. 147–64.

Platt, A. (1969) *The Child Savers*, Chicago, University of Chicago Press.

Platt, A. and Takagi, P. (1977) 'Intellectuals for law and order: a critique of the new realists', *Crime and Social Justice*, no. 8, pp. 1–16.

Plummer, K. (1979) 'Misunderstanding labelling perspectives', in Downes, D. and Rock, P. (eds) *Deviant Interpretations*, Oxford, Martin Robertson.

Pollock, L. (1983) *Forgotten Children: Parent–Child Relations from 1500 to 1900*, Cambridge, Cambridge University Press.

Polsky, N. (1971) *Hustlers, Beats and Others*, Harmondsworth, Penguin.

Porteous, M.A. and Colston, N.J. (1980) 'How adolescents are reported in the British Press', *Journal of Adolescence*, vol. 3, pp. 197–207.

Porter, R. (1996) 'The history of the "drugs problem"', *Criminal Justice Matters*, no. 24, pp. 3–4.

Pratt, J. (1983) 'Reflections on the approach of 1984: recent developments in social control in the UK', *International Journal of the Sociology of Law*, vol. 11, pp. 339–60.

Pratt, J. (1986) 'Diversion from the juvenile court', *British Journal of Criminology*, vol. 26 no. 3, pp. 212–33.

Pratt, J. (1989) 'Corporatism: the third model of juvenile justice', *British Journal of Criminology*, vol. 29, no. 3, pp. 236–54.

Pratt, J. (1999) 'Governmentality, neo-liberalism and dangerousness', in Smandych, R. (ed.) *Governable Places: Readings on Governmentality and Crime Control*, Aldershot, Ashgate.

Pratt, J., Brown, D., Brown, M., Hallsworth, S. and Morrison, W. (eds) (2005) *The New Punitiveness*, Cullompton, Willan.

Presdee, M. (1994) 'Young people, culture and the construction of crime: doing wrong versus doing crime', in Barak, G. (ed.) *Varieties of Criminology*, Westport, CT, Praeger.

Presdee, M. (2000) *Cultural Criminology and the Carnival of Crime*, London, Routledge.

Puffer, J. (1912) *The Boy and His Gang*, Boston, Houghton Mifflin.

Put, J. and Walgrave, L. (2006) 'Belgium: from protection to accountability', in Muncie, J. and Goldson, B. (eds) *Comparative Youth Justice*, London, Sage.

Quetelet, M.A. (1842) *A Treatise on Man*, Edinburgh, Chambers.

Quinney, R. (1970) *The Social Reality of Crime*, Boston, Little, Brown.

Qvortrup, J., Bardy, M., Sgritta, G. and Wintersberger, H. (eds) (1994) *Childhood Matters*, Aldershot, Avebury.

Radzinowicz, L. and Hood, A. (1990) *The Emergence of Penal Policy*, Oxford, Clarendon.

Ramsay, M. (1997) *Persistent Drug-Misusing Offenders*, Home Office Research Findings, no. 50, London, HMSO.

Ramsay, M., Baker, P., Goulden, C., Sharp, C. and Sandi, A. (2001) *Drug Misuse Declared in 2000: Results from the British Crime Survey*, Home Office Research Study, no. 224, London, Home Office.

Ramsay, M. and Percy, A. (1996) *Drug Misuse Declared: Results of the 1994 British Crime Survey*, Home Office Research Findings, no. 33, London, HMSO.

Ramsay, M. and Spiller, J. (1997) *Drug Misuse Declared in 1996: Key Results from the British Crime Survey*, Home Office Research Findings, no. 56, London, HMSO.

Rechea Alberola, C. and Fernandez Molina, E. (2006) 'Continuity and change in the Spanish juvenile justice system', in Junger-Tas, J. and Decker, S. (eds) *International Handbook of Juvenile Justice*, Dordrecht, Springer.

Redhead, S. (1990) *The End of the Century Party*, Manchester, Manchester University Press.

Redhead, S. (1993) *Rave Off: Politics and Deviance in Contemporary Youth Culture*, Aldershot, Avebury.

Reiman, J. (2007) *The Rich get Richer and the Poor get Prison*, 8th edn; first published 1979, Boston, Pearson.

Reiner, R. (2002) 'Media made criminality', in Maguire, M., Morgan, R. and Reiner, R. (eds) *The Oxford Handbook of Criminology*, 3rd edn, Oxford, Oxford University Press.

Release (1997) *Drugs and Dance Survey: An Insight into the Culture*, London, Release.

Report of Committee into Juvenile Delinquency (1816) *Committee for Investigating the Alarming Increase of Juvenile Delinquency in the Metropolis*, London, Dove.

Rex, J. and Moore, R. (1967) *Race, Community and Conflict*, London, Oxford University Press for the Institute of Race Relations.

Rice, M. (1990) 'Challenging orthodoxies in feminist theory: a black feminist critique', in Gelsthorpe, L. and Morris, A. (eds) *Feminist Perspectives in Criminology*, Milton Keynes, Open University Press.

Riddell, P. (1989) *The Thatcher Effect*, Oxford, Blackwell.

Ritchie, J. (2000) 'New Deal for young people: participants' perspectives', *Policy Studies*, vol. 21, no. 4, pp. 301–12.

Roberts, H. and Sachdev, D. (eds) (1996) *Young People's Social Attitudes*, Ilford, Barnado's.

Roberts, K. (1995) *Youth and Employment in Modern Britain*, Oxford, Oxford University Press.

Roberts, K. and Parsell, G. (1994) 'Youth cultures in Britain: the middle class take-over', *Leisure Studies*, vol. 13, no. 1, pp. 33–48.

Robertson, R. (1996) 'Glocalisation: Time–space and homogeneity–heterogeneity', in Featherstone, M., Lash, S. and Robertson, R. (eds) *Global Modernities*, London, Sage.

Roche, J. and Tucker, S. (eds) *Youth in Society*, London, Sage/Open University.

Roche, S. (2002) 'Toward a new governance of crime and insecurity in France', in Crawford, A. (ed.) *Crime and Insecurity: The Governance of Safety in Europe*, Cullompton, Willan.

Rock, P. and Cohen, S. (1970) 'The teddy boys', in Bogdanor, V. and Skidelsky, R. (eds) *The Age of Affluence*, London, Macmillan.

Rodger, J. (2006) 'Antisocial families and withholding welfare support', *Critical Social Policy*, vol. 26, no.1, pp. 121–43.

Rose, N. (1989) *Governing the Soul*, London, Routledge.

Rose, N. (1996a) 'Governing "advanced" Liberal democracies', in Barry, A., Osborne, T. and Rose, N. (eds) *Foucault and Political Reason*, London, UCL Press.

Rose, N. (1996b) 'The death of the social? Refiguring the territory of government', *Economy and Society*, vol. 25, no. 3, pp. 327–46.

Rose, N. (1999) *Powers of Freedom: Reframing Political Thought*, Cambridge, Cambridge University Press.

Rose, N. (2000) 'Government and control', *British Journal of Criminology*, vol. 40, pp. 321–39.

Rose, N. and Miller, P. (1992) 'Political power beyond the state: problematics of government', *British Journal of Sociology*, vol. 43, no. 2, pp. 173–205.

Rose, T. (1994) 'A style nobody can deal with: politics, style and the post-industrial city in hip hop', in Ross, A. and Rose, T. (eds) *Microphone Fiends*, New York and London, Routledge.

Roshier, B. (1973) 'The selection of crime news by the press', in Cohen, S. and Young, J. (eds) *The Manufacture of News*, London, Constable.

Ross, R., Fabiano, E. and Ewles, C. (1988) 'Reasoning and rehabilitation', *International Journal of Offender Therapy and Comparative Criminology*, vol. 32, pp. 29–33.

Roszak, T. (1971) *The Making of a Counter-Culture*, London, Faber & Faber.

Rowbotham, J., Stevenson, K. and Pegg, S. (2003) 'Children of misfortune', *Howard Journal*, vol. 42, no. 2, pp. 107–22.

Rowbotham, S. (1973) *Women's Consciousness, Man's World*, Harmondsworth, Penguin.

Rubin, J. (1970) *Do It!*, New York, Simon & Schuster.

Ruggerio, V. (1997) 'Trafficking in human beings: slaves in contemporary Europe', *International Journal of the Sociology of Law*, vol. 25, pp. 231–44.

Runciman, W.G. (1966) *Relative Deprivation and Social Justice*, London, Routledge.

Rush, P. (1992) 'The government of a generation: the subject of juvenile delinquency', *Liverpool Law Review*, vol. 14, no. 1, pp. 3–41.

Russell, C. (1917) *The Problem of Juvenile Crime*, Oxford, Oxford University Press.

Rutherford, A. (1986) *Growing Out of Crime*, Harmondsworth, Penguin.

Rutherford, A. (1989) 'The mood and temper of penal policy: curious happenings in England during the 1980s', *Youth and Policy*, no. 27, pp. 27–31.

Rutherford, A. (1992) *Growing out of Crime: The New Era*, Winchester, Waterside.

Rutherford, A. (1993) *Criminal Justice and the Pursuit of Decency*, Oxford, Oxford University Press.

Rutherford, J. (1997) 'Young Britain', *Soundings*, no. 6, pp. 112–25.

Rutherford, A. (2002) 'Youth justice and social inclusion', *Youth Justice*, vol. 2, no. 2, pp. 100–107.

Rutter, M. and Giller, H. (1983) *Juvenile Delinquency: Trends and Perspectives*, Harmondsworth, Penguin.

Rutter, M., Giller, H. and Hagell, A. (1998) *Anti-social Behaviour by Young People*, Cambridge, Cambridge University Press.

Rutter, M., Graham, P., Chadwick, O. and Yule, W. (1976) 'Adolescent turmoil: fact or fiction?', *Journal of Child Psychology and Psychiatry*, vol. 17, pp. 35–56.

Rutter, M. and Smith, D. (eds) (1995) *Psychosocial Disorders in Young People*, Chichester, Wiley.

Ruxton, S. (1996) *Children in Europe*, London, NCH Action for Children.

Said, E. (1991) *Orientalism*, Harmondsworth, Penguin.

Sanders, B. (2005) *Youth Crime and Youth Culture in the Inner City*, London, Routledge.

Sanders, C.R. and Lyon, E. (1995) 'Repetitive retribution: media images and the cultural construction of criminal justice', in Ferrell, J. and Sanders, C. (eds) *Cultural Criminology*, Boston, MA, Northeastern University Press.

Saraga, E. (2001) 'Dangerous places: the family as a site of crime', in Muncie, J. and McLaughlin, E. (eds) *The Problem of Crime*, 2nd edn, London, Sage/Open University.

Save the Children UK (2007) *The Small Hands of Slavery*, London, Save the Children.

Saville, J. (1957) 'The welfare state: an historical approach', *New Reasoner*, vol. 3, pp. 5–24.

Schabas, W. (1996) 'Reservations to the Convention on the Rights of the Child', *Human Rights Quarterly*, vol. 18, no. 4, pp. 472–91.

Schaffner, L. (2002) 'An age of reason: paradoxes in the US legal construction of adult-hood', *International Journal of Children's Rights*, vol. 10, pp. 201–32.

Schlesinger, P. and Tumber, H. (1994) *Reporting Crime: The Media Politics of Criminal Justice*, Oxford, Clarendon.

Schwartz, M. and Dekeseredy, W. (1991) 'Left realist criminology: strengths, weaknesses and the feminist critique', *Crime, Law and Social Change*, vol. 15, no. 1, pp. 51–72.

Schwendinger, H. and Schwendinger, J. (1970) 'Defenders of order or guardians of human rights', *Issues in Criminology*, no. 7, pp. 72–81.

Scott, A. (1990) *Ideology and the New Social Movements*, London, Unwin Hyman.

Scottish Consortium on Crime and Criminal Justice (2000) *Rethinking Criminal Justice in Scotland*, Edinburgh, Scottish Consortium.

Scottish Executive (2003) *Youth Court Feasibility Project Group Report*, Edinburgh, Scottish Executive.

Scraton, P. (ed.) (1987) *Law, Order and the Authoritarian State*, Milton Keynes, Open University Press.

Scraton, P. (1997a) 'Whose "childhood"? What "crisis"?', in Scraton, P. (ed.) *'Childhood' in 'Crisis'?*, London, UCL Press.

Scraton, P. (ed.) (1997b) *'Childhood' in 'Crisis'?* London, UCL Press.

Scraton, P. (2007) *Power, Conflict and Criminalisation*, Abingdon, Routledge.

Scraton, P. (2008) 'The Criminalisation and punishment of children and young people', *Current Issues in Criminal Justice*, vol. 20, no. 1, pp. 1–13.

Scraton, P. and Chadwick, K. (1991) 'The theoretical and political priorities of critical criminology', in Stenson, K. and Cowell, D. (eds) *The Politics of Crime Control*, London, Sage.

Scraton, P. and Haydon, D. (2002) 'Challenging the criminalisation of children and young people: securing a rights based agenda', in Muncie, J., Hughes, G. and McLaughlin, E. (eds) *Youth Justice: Critical Readings*, London, Sage.

Scruton, R. (1980) *The Meaning of Conservatism*, Harmondsworth, Pelican.

Scull, A. (1977) *Decarceration*, Englewood Cliffs, NJ, Prentice-Hall.

Seddon, T. (2006) 'Drugs, crime and social exclusion: social context and social theory in British drugs-crime research', *British Journal of Criminology*, vol. 46, no. 4, pp. 680–703.

Segal, L. (1990) *Slow Motion: Changing Masculinities, Changing Men*, London, Virago.

Sellin, T. (1938) *Culture, Conflict and Crime*, New York, Social Science Research Council.

Shacklady Smith, L. (1978) 'Sexist assumptions and female delinquency', in Smart, C. and Smart, B. (eds) *Women, Sexuality and Social Control*, London, Routledge.

Shallice, A. and Gordon, P. (1990) *Black People, White Justice? Race and the Criminal Justice System*, London, Runnymede.

Sharma, A. (1996) 'Sounds oriental: the (im)possibility of theorizing Asian musical cultures', in Sharma, S., Hutnyk, J. and Sharma, A. (eds) *Dis-orienting Rhythms*, London, Zed.

Sharma, S., Hutnyk, J. and Sharma, A. (eds) (1996) *Dis-orienting Rhythms: The Politics of the New Asian Dance Music*, London, Zed.

Shaw, C.R. (1929) *Delinquency Areas*, Chicago, University of Chicago Press.

Shaw, C.R. and McKay, H.D. (1942) *Juvenile Delinquency and Urban Areas*, Chicago, University of Chicago Press.

Sheldon, W. (1949) *Varieties of Delinquent Youth*, New York, Harper.

Sherman, L., Gottfredson, D., MacKenzie, D., Eck, J., Reuter, P. and Bushway, S. (1997) *Preventing Crime: What Works, What Doesn't, What's Promising*, Washington, DC, US Department of Justice.

Shore, H. (1999) *Artful Dodgers: Youth and Crime in Early Nineteenth Century London*, London, Royal Historical Society.

Shore, H. (2000) 'The idea of juvenile crime in 19th century England', *History Today*, vol. 50, no. 6, pp. 21–7.

Shore, H. (2002) 'Reforming the juvenile: gender, justice and the child criminal in nineteenth century England', in Muncie, J., Hughes, G. and McLaughlin, E. (eds) *Youth Justice: Critical Readings*, London, Sage.

Sibley, D. (1995) *Geographies of Exclusion*, London, Routledge.

Sim, J., Scraton, P. and Gordon, P. (1987) 'Crime, the state and critical analysis', in Scraton, P. (ed.) *Law, Order and the Authoritarian State*, Milton Keynes, Open University Press.

Simmons, C. and Wade, W. (1984) *I Like to Say What I Think*, London, Kogan Page.

Simmons, J. and Dodd, T. (2003) *Crime in England and Wales 2002/2003*, Home Office Statistical Bulletin, London, Home Office.

Simon, J. (1988) 'The ideological effects of actuarial practices', *Law and Society Review*, vol. 22, no. 4, pp. 771–800.

Simon, J. (1995) 'The boot camp and the limits of modern penality', *Social Justice*, vol. 22, no. 2, pp. 25–48.

Simon, J. (1997) 'Governing through crime', in Friedman, L. and Fisher, G. (eds) *The Crime Conundrum*, Boulder, CO, Westview.

Simon, J. (2001) 'Entitlement to cruelty: neo Liberalism and the punitive mentality in the United States', in Stenson, K. and Sullivan, R. (eds) *Crime, Risk and Justice*, Cullompton, Willan.

Simon, J. (2007) *Governing through Crime: How the War on Crime Transformed American Democracy and Created a Culture of Fear*, New York, Oxford University Press.

Singer, S. (1996) *Recriminalising Delinquency*, Cambridge, Cambridge University Press.

Sivanandan, A. (1976) 'Race, class and the state: in black experience in Britain', *Race and Class*, vol. 17, no. 4, pp. 347–68.

Skelton, A. (2002) 'Restorative justice as a framework for juvenile justice reform: a South African perspective', *British Journal of Criminology*, vol. 42, no. 3, pp. 496–513.

Skelton, T. and Valentine, G. (eds) (1998) *Cool Places: Geographies of Youth Cultures*, London, Routledge.

Smandych, R. (ed.) (1999) *Governable Places: Readings on Governmentality and Crime Control*, Aldershot, Ashgate.

Smandych, R. (ed.) (2001) *Youth Justice: History, Legislation and Reform*, Toronto, Harcourt.

Smandych, R. (2006) 'Canada: repenalisation and young offenders' rights', in Muncie, J. and Goldson, B. (eds) *Comparative Youth Justice*, London, Sage.

Smart, C. (1976) *Women, Crime and Criminology*, London, Routledge.

Smart, C. (1989) *Feminism and the Power of Law*, London, Routledge.

Smart, C. (1990) 'Feminist approaches to criminology or postmodern woman meets atavistic man', in Morris, A. and Gelsthorpe, L. (eds) *Feminist Perspectives in Criminology*, Buckingham, Open University Press.

Smith, D. (1990) 'Juvenile delinquency in Britain in the First World War', in *Criminal Justice History*, vol. 11, Westport, CT, Meckler.

Smith, D. (2000) 'Learning from the Scottish juvenile justice system', *Probation Journal*, vol. 47, no. 1, pp. 12–17.

Smith, D. and Gray, S. (1983) *Police and People in London*, London, Policy Studies Institute.

Smith, D. and Sueda, K. (2008) 'The killing of children by children as a symptom of national crisis: reactions in Britain and Japan', *Criminology and Criminal Justice*, vol. 8, no. 1, pp. 5–25.

Smith, D.J. (2004) *The Links between Victimisation and Offending*, Edinburgh Study of Youth Transitions and Crime, Research Digest No. 5. Edinburgh: University of Edinburgh.

Smith, G. (2002) 'Remorseless young predators: the bottom line of "caging children"', in Strickland, R. (ed.) *Growing up Postmodern*, Lanham, MD, Rowman and Littlefield.

Smith, R. (2003) *Youth Justice: Ideas, Policy, Practice*, Cullompton, Willan.

Smith, R. (2005) 'Welfare vs justice again!', *Youth Justice*, vol. 5, no. 1, pp. 3–16.

Smith, R. (2006) 'Actuarialism and early intervention in contemporary youth justice', in Goldson, B. and Muncie, J. (eds) *Youth Crime and Justice*, London, Sage.

Smith, S. (1973) 'The London apprentices as seventeenth-century adolescents', *Past and Present*, no. 61, pp. 149–61.

Smith, S.J. (1984) 'Crime in the news', *British Journal of Criminology*, vol. 24, no. 3, pp. 289–95.

Smithies, E. (1982) *Crime in Wartime: A Social History of Crime in World War II*, London, Allen & Unwin.

Snyder, H. (2002) 'Juvenile crime and justice in the United States of America', in Bala, N., Hornick, J., Snyder, H. and Paetsch, J. (eds) *Juvenile Justice Systems: An International Comparison of Problems and Solutions*, Toronto, Thompson.

Social Exclusion Unit (SEU) (2001) *Preventing Social Exclusion*, London, HMSO.

Social Exclusion Unit (SEU) (2002) *Young Runaways*, London, HMSO.

Solomon, E. and Garside, R. (2008) *Ten Years of Labour's Youth Justice Reforms: An Independent Audit*, London, Centre for Crime and Justice Studies.

Solomos, J. (1988) *Black Youth, Racism and the State*, Cambridge, Cambridge University Press.

Souhami, A. (2007) *Transforming Youth Justice: Occupational Identity and Cultural Change*, Cullompton, Willan.

Sparks, R. (2001) 'Degrees of estrangement: the cultural theory of risk and comparative penology', *Theoretical Criminology*, vol. 5, no. 2, pp. 159–76.

Spergel, I. (1992) 'Youth gangs: an essay review', *Social Service Review*, vol. 66, pp. 121–40.

Spitzer, S. (1975) 'Toward a Marxian theory of deviance', *Social Problems*, vol. 22, no. 5, pp. 638–51.

Springhall, J. (1977) *Youth, Empire and Society*, London, Croom Helm.

Springhall, J. (1983–84) 'The origins of adolescence', *Youth and Policy*, vol. 2, no. 3, pp. 20–4.

Springhall, J. (1986) *Coming of Age: Adolescence in Britain 1860–1960*, London, Gill & Macmillan.

Squires, P. (2006) 'New Labour and the politics of antisocial behaviour', *Critical Social Policy*, vol. 26, no. 1, pp. 144–68.

Squires, P. and Stephen, D. (2005) *Rougher Justice: Antisocial Behaviour and Young People*, Cullompton, Willan.

Stack, J.A. (1992) 'Children, urbanisation and the chances of imprisonment in mid-Victorian England', *Criminal Justice History*, vol. 13, Westport, CT, Greenwood.

Stafford, A. (1982) 'Learning not to labour', *Capital and Class*, no. 17, pp. 55–77.

Standing Committee for Youth Justice (2006) *Still Waiting for Youth Justice*, London, SCYJ.

Stanko, E.A. (1994) 'Challenging the problem of men's individual violence', in Newburn, T. and Stanko, B. (eds) *Just Boys Doing Business?*, London, Routledge.

Stanko, E.A. and Hobdell, K. (1993) 'Assault of men: masculinity and male victimisation', *British Journal of Criminology*, vol. 33, no. 3, pp. 400–15.

Stansill, P. and Mairowitz, D.Z. (1971) *BAMN: Outlaw Manifestos and Ephemera 1965–70*, Harmondsworth, Penguin.

Stedman-Jones, G. (1971) *Outcast London*, Oxford, Clarendon.

Stedman-Jones, G. (1977) 'Class expression versus social control? A critique of recent trends in the social history of "leisure"', *History Workshop Journal*, no. 4, pp. 162–70.

Steinert, H. (1986) 'Beyond Crime and Punishment', *Contemporary Crises*, vol. 10, no. 1, pp. 21–38.

Stenson, K. (2000) 'Crime control, social policy and liberalism', in Lewis, G. et al. (eds) *Rethinking Social Policy*, London, Sage.

Stenson, K. and Factor, F. (1994) 'Youth work, risk and crime prevention', *Youth and Policy*, no. 45, pp. 1–15.

Stenson, K. and Sullivan, R. (eds) (2001) *Crime, Risk and Justice*, Cullompton, Willan.

Stern, V. (2001) 'An alternative vision: criminal justice developments in non-Western societies', *Social Justice*, vol. 28, no. 3, pp. 88–104.

Stevens, P. and Willis, C. (1979) *Race, Crime and Arrests*, Home Office Research Study, no. 58, London, HMSO.

Stewart, G. and Tutt, N. (1987) *Children in Custody*, Aldershot, Avebury.

Storgaard, A. (2004) 'Juvenile justice in Scandinavia', *Journal of Scandinavian Studies in Criminology and Crime Prevention*, vol. 5, no. 2, pp. 188–204.

Straus, M. (1994) *Beating the Devil out of Them: Corporal Punishment in American Families*, New York, Lexington.

Straw, J. (1998) 'New approaches to crime and punishment', *Prison Service Journal*, no. 116, pp. 2–6.

Straw, J. and Michael, A. (1996) *Tackling the Causes of Crime: Labour's Proposals to Prevent Crime and Criminality*, London, Labour Party.

Sugarman, B. (1967) 'Involvement in youth culture, academic achievement and conformity', *British Journal of Sociology*, vol. 18, pp. 151–64.

Suhling, S. (2003) 'Factors contributing to rising imprisonment figures in Germany', *The Howard Journal*, vol. 42, no. 1, pp. 55–68.

Sumner, C. (ed.) (1990) *Censure, Politics and Criminal Justice*, Buckingham, Open University Press.

Sumner, C. (1994) *The Sociology of Deviance: An Obituary*, Buckingham, Open University Press.

Surette, R. (1998) *Media, Crime and Criminal Justice*, Belmont, CA, Wadsworth.

Sutherland, E. (1939) *Principles of Criminology*, Philadelphia, PA, Lippincott.

Sutherland, E. and Cressey, D. (1970) *Criminology*, 8th edn, Philadelphia, PA, Lippincott.

Sykes, G.M. and Matza, D. (1957) 'Techniques of neutralisation: a theory of delinquency', *American Sociological Review*, vol. 22, pp. 664–70.

Tame, C. (1991) 'Freedom, responsibility and justice: the criminology of the New Right', in Stenson, K. and Cowell, D. (eds) *The Politics of Crime Control*, London, Sage.

Tannenbaum, F. (1938) *Crime and the Community*, New York, Columbia University Press.

Taylor, H. (1998a) 'The politics of the rising crime statistics of England and Wales 1914–1960', *Crime, History and Societies*, vol. 2, no. 1, pp. 5–28.

Taylor, H. (1998b) 'Rationing crime: the political economy of criminal statistics since the 1850s', *Economic History Review*, vol. 3, pp. 569–90.

Taylor, I. (1971) 'Soccer consciousness and soccer hooliganism', in Cohen, S. (ed.) *Images of Deviance*, Harmondsworth, Penguin.

Taylor, I. (1981a) 'Crime waves in post-war Britain', *Contemporary Crises*, no. 5, pp. 43–62.

Taylor, I. (1981b) *Law and Order: Arguments for Socialism*, London, Macmillan.

Taylor, I. (1992) 'Left Realist criminology and the free market experiment in Britain', in Young, J. and Matthews, R. (eds) *Rethinking Criminology: The Realist Debate*, London, Sage.

Taylor, I. (1999) *Crime in Context: A Critical Criminology of Market Societies*, Cambridge, Polity.

Taylor, I., Evans, K. and Fraser, P. (1996) *A Tale of Two Cities*, London, Routledge.

Taylor, I. and Wall, D. (1976) 'Beyond the skinheads: comments on the emergence and significance of the glam rock cult', in Mungham, G. and Pearson, G. (eds) *Working Class Youth Culture*, London, Routledge & Kegan Paul.

Taylor, I., Walton, P. and Young, J. (1973) *The New Criminology*, London, Routledge.

Taylor, I., Walton, P. and Young, J. (eds) (1975) *Critical Criminology*, London, Routledge.

Taylor, L. (1971) *Deviance and Society*, London, Michael Joseph.

Taylor, L., Lacey, R. and Bracken, D. (1979) *In Whose Best Interests?*, London, Cobden Trust/Mind.

Tham, H. (2001) 'Law and order as a leftist project?: The case of Sweden', *Punishment and Society*, vol. 3, no. 3, pp. 409–26.

Thane, P. (1981) 'Childhood in history', in King, M. (ed.) *Childhood, Welfare and Justice*, London, Batsford.

Thompson, E.P. (1963) *The Making of the English Working Class*, Harmondsworth, Penguin.

Thornton, D., Curran, C., Grayson, D. and Holloway, V. (1984) *Tougher Regimes in Detention Centres*, London, HMSO.

Thornton, S. (1995) *Club Cultures: Music, Media and Subcultural Capital*, Cambridge, Polity.

Thorpe, D.H., Smith, D., Green, C.J. and Paley, J.H. (1980) *Out of Care: The Community Support of Juvenile Offenders*, London, Allen & Unwin.

Thrasher, F. (1927) *The Gang*, Chicago, University of Chicago Press.

Tickell, S. and Akester, K. (2004) *Restorative Justice: The Way Ahead*, London, Justice.

Tierney, J. (1980) 'Political deviance: a critical commentary on a case study', *Sociological Review*, vol. 28, no. 4, pp. 829–50.

Tierney, J. (1996) *Criminology: Theory and Context*, Hemel Hempstead, Prentice-Hall/Harvester Wheatsheaf.

Tifft, L. (1995) 'Social harm definitions of crime', *The Critical Criminologist*, vol. 7, no. 1, pp. 9–13.

Tilley, N. (2003) 'The rediscovery of learning: crime prevention and scientific realism', in Hughes, G. and Edwards, A. (eds) *Crime Control and Community*, Cullompton, Willan.

Tonge, J. (1999) 'New packaging, old deal? New Labour and employment policy innovation', *Critical Social Policy*, vol. 19, no. 2, pp. 217–32.

Tonry, M. (2001) 'Symbol, substance and severity in western penal policies', *Punishment and Society*, vol. 3, no. 4, pp. 517–36.

Tonry, M. and Doob, A. (eds) (2004) *Youth Crime and Youth Justice: Comparative and Cross-national Perspective*: Crime and Justice volume 31, Chicago, Chicago University Press.

Uit Beijerse, J. and van Swaaningen, R. (2006) 'The Netherlands: penal welfarism and risk management', in Muncie, J. and Goldson, B. (eds) *Comparative Youth Justice*, London, Sage.

UK Children's Commissioners (2008) *Report to the UN Committee on the Rights of the Child*, London, 11 Million, NICCY, SCCYP, Children's Commissioner for Wales.

UK Government (1999) *Convention on the Rights of the Child: Second Report to the UN Committee on the Rights of the Child by the United Kingdom*, London, HMSO.

UNICEF (2006) *Behind Closed Doors: The Impact of Domestic Violence on Children*, New York, UNICEF.

UNICEF (2007a) *Child Poverty in Perspective: An Overview of Child Well-Being in Rich Countries,* Innocenti Research Centre, Report Card 7, New York/Geneva.

UNICEF (2007b) *Rights Here; Rights Now: Recommendations for Protecting Trafficked Children*, London, UNICEF.

United Nations (1989) *The United Nations Convention on the Rights of the Child*, New York, United Nations.

United Nations (1996) *Promotion and Protection of the Rights of Children: Impact of Armed Conflict on Children* (the Machel Report) A/51/150, New York, United Nations.

United Nations Committee on the Rights of the Child (2007) *Children's Rights in Juvenile Justice*, 44th Session General Comment, No. 10, CRC/C/GC/10, Geneva, United Nations.

United Nations Committee on the Rights of the Child (2008) *Consideration of Reports submitted by States Parties under Article 44 of the Convention: United Kingdom of Great Britain and Northern Ireland*, 49th Session, CRC/C/GBR/CO/4, Geneva, United Nations.

United Nations General Assembly (2006) *Report of the Independent Expert for the United Nations on Violence against Children*, 61st Session, A/61/299, Geneva, United Nations.

United Nations Office for Drug Control and Crime Prevention (2002) *The Seventh Survey on Crime Trends and the Operations of Criminal Justice Systems*, www.odccp.org/odccp/crime-cicp-survey-seventh.html.

Urwick, E.J. (ed.) (1904) *Studies of Boy Life in Our Cities*, London, Dent.

Utting, D. (1996) *Reducing Criminality among Young People: A Sample of Relevant Programmes in the UK*, Home Office Research Study, no. 161, London, HMSO.

Vague, T. (1997) *Anarchy in the UK: The Angry Brigade*, Edinburgh, AK Press.

Valier, C. (2002) *Theories of Crime and Punishment*, Harlow, Longman/Pearson Education.

Van den Haag, E. (1975) *Punishing Criminals*, New York, Basic Books.

Van Dijk, C., Nuytiens, A. and Eliaerts, C. (2005) 'The referral of juvenile offenders to the adult court in Belgium', *Howard Journal*, vol. 44, no. 2, pp. 151–66.

Van Dijk, J., Van Kesteren, J. and Smit, P. (2007) *Criminal Victimisation in International Perspective: Key Findings from the 2004–2005 ICVS and EU ICS*, The Hague, Ministry of Justice.

Vaneigem, R. (2001) *The Revolution of Everyday Life*, London, Rebel Press.

Van Kesteren, J., Mayhew, P. and Nieuwbeerta, P. (2001) *Criminal Victimisation in Seventeen Industrialised Countries: Key Findings from the 2000 International Crime Victims Survey*, The Hague: Ministry of Justice.

Van Swaaningen, R. (1997) *Critical Criminology: Visions from Europe*, London, Sage.

Van Swaaningen, R. (2005) 'Public safety and the management of fear', *Theoretical Criminology*, vol. 9, no. 3, pp. 289–305.

Van Zyl Smit, D. and van der Spuy, E. (2004) 'Importing criminological ideas in a new democracy: recent South African experiences', in Newburn, T. and Sparks, R. (eds) *Criminal Justice and Political Cultures: National and International Dimensions of Crime Control*, Cullompton, Willan.

Vaughan, B. (2000) 'The government of youth: disorder and dependence', *Social and Legal Studies*, vol. 9, no. 3, pp. 347–66.

Veerman, P. and Levine, H. (2001) 'Implementing children's rights on a local level', *International Journal of Children's Rights*, vol. 8, pp. 373–84.

Viding, E., Blair, R.J.R., Moffitt, T. and Plomin, R. (2005) 'Evidence for the substantial genetic risk for psychopathy in 7 year olds', *Journal of Child Psychology and Psychiatry*, vol. 46, no. 6, pp. 592–97.

Vigil, J. (1988) *Barrio Gangs: Street Life and Identity in Southern California*, Austin, TX, University of Texas Press.

Vold, G. and Bernard, T. (1986) *Theoretical Criminology*, 3rd edn, Oxford, Oxford University Press.

Von Hentig, H. (1948) *The Criminal and His Victim*, New Haven, CT, Yale University Press.

Von Hirsch, A. (1976) *Doing Justice: The Choice of Punishments*, New York, Hill & Wang.

Von Hofer, H. (2003) 'Prison populations as political constructs: the case of Finland, Holland and Sweden', *Journal of Scandinavian Studies in Criminology and Crime Prevention*, vol. 4, pp. 21–38.

Wacquant, L. (1999a) 'How penal commonsense comes to Europeans', *European Societies*, vol. 1, no. 3, pp. 319–52.

Wacquant, L. (1999b) 'Suitable enemies: foreigners and immigrants in the prisons of Europe', *Punishment and Society*, vol. 1, no. 2, pp. 215–22.

Wacquant, L. (2001) 'The penalization of poverty and the rise of neo-liberalism', *European Journal on Criminal Policy and Research*, vol. 9, pp. 401–12.

Wacquant, L. (2008) 'Ordering insecurity: Social polarisation and the punitive upsurge', *Radical Philosophy Review*, vol. 11, no. 1, pp. 9–27.

Waddington, P.A.J. (1986) 'Mugging as a moral panic: a question of proportion', *British Journal of Sociology*, vol. 32, no. 2, pp. 245–59.

Waiton, S. (2001) *Scared of the Kids! Curfews, Crime and the Regulation of Young People*, Sheffield, Sheffield Hallam Press.

Waldo, G. and Dinitz, S. (1967) 'Personality attributes of the criminal', *Journal of Research in Crime and Delinquency*, vol. 4, no. 2, pp. 185–201.

Walgrave, L. (1995) 'Restorative justice for juveniles: just a technique or a fully fledged alternative?', *Howard Journal*, vol. 34, no. 3, pp. 228–49.

Walgrave, L. (2002) 'Juvenile justice in Belgium', in Winterdyk, J. (ed.) *Juvenile Justice Systems: International Perspectives*, 2nd edition, Toronto, Canadian Scholars Press.

Walgrave, L. and Mehlbye, J. (eds) (1998) *Confronting Youth in Europe: Juvenile Crime and Juvenile Justice*, Copenhagen, Institute of Local Government Studies.

Walker, M. (1983) 'Some problems in interpreting statistics relating to crime', *Journal of the Royal Statistical Society Series A*, no. 146, part 3, pp. 282–93.

Walker, M. (1988) 'The court disposal of young males, by race, in London in 1983', *British Journal of Criminology*, vol. 28, no. 4, pp. 441–60.

Walker, M., Jefferson, T. and Seneviratne, M. (1990) *Ethnic Minorities, Young People and the Criminal Justice System*, ESRC Project no. E06250023, Centre for Criminological and Socio-Legal Studies, University of Sheffield.

Walklate, S. (1989) *Victimology: The Victim and the Criminal Justice Process*, London, Unwin Hyman.

Walklate, S. (1995) *Gender and Crime: An Introduction*, Hemel Hempstead, Prentice-Hall/Harvester.

Walklate, S. (2001) *Gender, Crime and Criminal Justice*, Cullompton, Willan.

Walklate, S. (2007) *Imagining the Victim of Crime*, Maidenhead, Open University Press.

Wallace, C. (1987) *For Richer, for Poorer: Growing up in and out of Work*, London, Tavistock.

Walmsley, R. (2006) *World Prison Population List*, 7th edn, London, International Centre for Prison Studies.

Walsh, C. (2002) 'Curfews: no more hanging around', *Youth Justice*, vol. 2, no. 2, pp. 70–81.

Walsh, C. (2008) 'The Mosquito: a repellent response', *Youth Justice: An International Journal*, vol. 8, no. 2, pp. 122–33.

Walters, R. and Woodward, R. (2007) 'Punishing "Poor Parents" – "Respect", "responsibility" and parenting orders in Scotland', *Youth Justice*, vol. 7, no. 1, pp. 5–20.

Walton, P. and Young, J. (eds) (1998) *The New Criminology Revisited*, Basingstoke, Macmillan.

Waterhouse, L., McGhee, J., Whyte, B., Loucks, N., Kay, H. and Stewart, R. (2000) *The Evaluation of Children's Hearings in Scotland*, vol. 3, *Children in Focus*, Edinburgh, Scottish Executive.

Webb, S. (2001) 'Some considerations on the validity of evidence based practice in social work', *British Journal of Social Work*, vol. 31, no. 1, pp. 57–79.

Webster, C. (1997) 'The construction of British "Asian" criminality', *International Journal of the Sociology of Law*, vol. 25, pp. 65–86.

Webster, C. (2006) 'Race', youth crime and justice', in Goldson, B. and Muncie, J. (eds) *Youth Crime and Justice*, London, Sage.

Webster, C. (2007) *Understanding Race and Crime*, Maidenhead, Open University Press.

Webster, C., MacDonald, R. and Simpson, M. (2006) 'Predicting criminality? Risk factors, neighbourhood influence and desistance', *Youth Justice*, vol. 6, no. 1, pp. 7–22.

Webster, C., Simpson, D., MacDonald, R., Abbas, A., Cieslik., M., Shildrick, T. and Simpson, M. (2004) *Poor Transitions: Social Exclusion and Young Adults*, Bristol, Policy Press.

Weijers, I. (1999) 'The double paradox of juvenile justice', *European Journal on Criminal Policy and Research*, vol. 7, no. 3, pp. 329–51.

Weinberger, B. (1993) 'Policing juveniles: delinquency in late nineteenth and early twentieth century Manchester', *Criminal Justice History*, vol. 14, Westport, CT, Greenwood.

Weiner, M.J. (1990) *Reconstructing the Criminal: Culture, Law and Policy in England, 1830–1914*, Cambridge, Cambridge University Press.

West, D. (1967) *The Young Offender*, Harmondsworth, Penguin.

West, D. and Farrington, D. (1973) *Who Becomes Delinquent?*, London, Heinemann.

West, D. and Farrington, D. (1977) *The Delinquent Way of Life*, London, Heinemann.

Westergaard, J. (1965) 'The withering away of class: a contemporary myth', in Anderson, P. and Blackburn, R. (eds) *Towards Socialism*, London, Fontana.

White, R. (1990) *No Space of Their Own: Young People and Social Control in Australia*, Cambridge, Cambridge University Press.

White, R. (2001) 'Social justice, community building and restorative strategies', *Contemporary Justice Review*, vol. 3, no. 1, pp. 55–72.

White, R. (2003) 'Communities, conferences and restorative social justice', *Criminal Justice*, vol. 3, no. 2, pp. 139–60.

White, R. and Haines, F. (2000) *Crime and Criminology*, 2nd edn, Oxford, Oxford University Press.

Whitfield, D. (1997) *Tackling the Tag*, Winchester, Waterside.

Whitman, J. (2003) *Harsh Justice: Criminal Punishment and the Widening Divide between America and Europe*, New York, Oxford University Press.

Whyte, B. (2000) 'Youth justice in Scotland', in Pickford, J. (ed.) *Youth Justice: Theory and Practice*, London, Cavendish.

Whyte, W.F. (1943) *Street Corner Society*, Chicago, University of Chicago Press.

Widdicombe, S. and Wooffitt, R. (1995) *The Language of Youth Subcultures*, Hemel Hempstead, Harvester.

Wikström, P-O. and Butterworth, D. (2006) *Adolescent Crime: Individual Differences and Lifestyles*, Cullompton, Willan.

Wikström, P-O. and Loeber, R. (2000) 'Do disadvantaged neighbourhoods cause well adjusted children to become adolescent delinquents?' *Criminology*, vol. 38, no. 4, pp. 1109–1142.

Wilcox, A. (2003) 'Evidence based youth justice?, *Youth Justice*, vol. 3, no. 1, pp. 19–33.

Wilkins, L. (1964) *Social Deviance*, London, Tavistock.

Wilkinson, C. (1995) *The Drop-Out Society: Young People on the Margin*, Leicester, Youth Work Press.

Williams, K.S. (1994) *Textbook on Criminology*, 2nd edn, London, Blackstone.

Williams, P. and Dickinson, J. (1993) 'Fear of crime: read all about it?', *British Journal of Criminology*, vol. 33, no. 1, pp. 33–56.

Williamson, H. (1993) 'Youth policy in the United Kingdom and the marginalization of young people', *Youth and Policy*, no. 40, pp. 33–48.

Williamson, H. (1997) 'Status zero youth and the underclass', in MacDonald, R. (ed.) *Youth, the 'Underclass' and Social Exclusion*, London, Routledge.

Willis, P. (1977) *Learning to Labour*, London, Saxon House.

Willis, P. (1978) *Profane Culture*, London, Chatto & Windus.

Willis, P. (1990) *Common Culture,* Buckingham, Open University Press.

Willmott, P. (1966) *Adolescent Boys of East London*, London, Routledge.

Wills, A. (2007) 'Historical myth-making in juvenile justice policy', www.historyandpolicy. org/papers

Wilson, D. and Moore, S. (2003) *Playing the Game: The Experiences of Young Black Men in Custody*, London, Children's Society/Community Fund.

Wilson, D., Sharp, C. and Patterson, A. (2006) *Young People and Crime: Findings from the 2005 Offending, Crime and Justice Survey*, Home Office Statistical Bulletin, London, TSO.

Wilson, J.Q. (1975) *Thinking about Crime*, New York, Vintage.

Wilson, J.Q. and Herrnstein, R.J. (1985) *Crime and Human Nature*, New York, Simon & Schuster.

Wilson, J.Q. and Kelling, G. (1982) 'Broken windows', *Atlantic Monthly*, March, pp. 29–38.

Wincup, E., Buckland, G. and Bayliss, R. (2003) *Youth Homelessness and Substance Use*, Home Office Research Study, no. 258, London, HMSO.

Winlow, S. and Hall, S. (2006) *Violent Night: Urban Leisure and Contemporary Culture*, Oxford, Berg.

Winterdyk, J. (ed.) (2002) *Juvenile Justice Systems: International Perspectives*, 2nd edn, Toronto, Canadians Scholars Press.

Wolfe, T. (1969) *The Electric Kool-Aid Acid Test*, New York, Bantam.

Wood, M. (2005) *The Victimisation of Young People: Findings from the Crime and Justice Survey 2003*, Home Office Research Findings, no. 246, London, Home Office.

Worden, R., and Myers, S. (1999) 'Police Encounters with Juvenile Suspects', *Report to the National Research Council's Panel on Juvenile Crime: Prevention, Treatment and Control*. Washington, DC, US Government Printing Office.

Wordes, M. and Nunez, M. (2002) *Our Vulnerable Teenagers: Their Victimization, its Consequences, and Directions for Prevention and Intervention*, Oakland, CA, NCDD/Washington, DC, NCVC.

Worrall, A. (1997) *Punishment in the Community*, Harlow, Longman.

Worrall, A. (1999) 'Troubled or troublesome? Justice for girls and young women', in Goldson, B. (ed.) *Youth Justice: Contemporary Policy and Practice*, Aldershot, Ashgate.

Worrall, A. (2001) 'Girls at risk? Reflections on changing attitudes to young women's offending', *Probation Journal*, vol. 48, no. 2, pp. 86–92.

Wyn, J. and White, R. (1997) *Rethinking Youth*, London, Sage.

Yablonsky, L. (1968) *The Hippie Trip*, New York, Pegasus.

Yeates, N. (2002) 'Globalisation and social policy: from global neo-liberal hegemony to global political pluralism', *Global Social Policy*, vol. 2, no. 1, pp. 66–91.

Yinger, J.M. (1960) 'Contraculture and subculture', *American Sociological Review*, vol. 55, pp. 625–35.

Young, A. (1996) *Imagining Crime*, London, Sage.

Young, J. (1971) *The Drugtakers*, London, Paladin.

Young, J. (1974) 'Mass media, drugs and deviance', in Rock, P. and McKintosh, M. (eds) *Deviance and Social Control*, London, Tavistock.

Young, J. (1975) 'Working class criminology', in Taylor, I., Walton, P. and Young, J. (eds) *Critical Criminology*, London, Routledge.

Young, J. (1979) 'Left idealism, reformism and beyond', in Fine, B., Kinsey, R., Lea, J., Picciotto, S. and Young, J. (eds) *Capitalism and the Rule of Law*, London, Hutchinson.

Young, J. (1986) 'The failure of criminology: the need for a radical realism', in Young, J. and Matthews, R. (eds) *Confronting Crime*, London, Sage.

Young, J. (1990) 'Asking questions of Left Realism', *Critical Criminologist*, vol. 2, no. 2, pp. 1–2, 10.

Young, J. (1992) 'Ten points of realism', in Young, J. and Matthews, R. (eds) *Rethinking Criminology: The Realist Debate*, London, Sage.

Young, J. (1994) 'Incessant chatter: recent paradigms in criminology', in Maguire, M., Morgan, R. and Reiner, R. (eds) *The Oxford Handbook of Criminology*, Oxford, Clarendon Press.

Young, J. (1999) *The Exclusive Society*, London, Sage.

Young, J. (2002) 'Critical criminology in the 21st century: critique, irony and the always unfinished', in Carrington, K. and Hogg, R. (eds) *Critical Criminology*, Cullompton, Willan.

Young, J. (2003) 'Winning the fight against crime? New Labour, populism and lost opportunities', in Matthews, R. and Young, J. (eds) *The New Politics and Crime and Punishment*, Cullompton, Willan.

Young, J. (2007) *The Vertigo of Late Modernity*, London, Sage.

Young, J. and Matthews, R. (2003) 'New Labour, crime control and social exclusion', in Matthews, R. and Young, J. (eds) *The New Politics and Crime and Punishment*, Cullompton, Willan.

Young, R. and Hoyle, C. (2002) *An Evaluation of the Implementation and Effectiveness of an Initiative in Restorative Cautioning*, Findings no. 542, York, Joseph Rowntree Foundation.

Youth Justice Board (2004) *ISSP: The Initial Report*. London: Youth Justice Board.

Youth Justice Board (2005) *Risk and Protective Factors*, London, Youth Justice Board.

Youth Justice Board (2006) *Antisocial Behaviour Orders*, London Youth Justice Board.

Youth Justice Board (2007) *Groups, Gangs and Weapons*, London, Youth Justice Board.

Zedner, L. (1991) *Women, Crime and Custody in Victorian England*, Oxford, Clarendon.

Zedner, L. (1994) 'Child Victims', in Jones, I.G. and Williams, G. (eds) *Social Policy, Crime and Punishment*, Cardiff, University of Wales Press.

Zedner, L. (1995) 'Comparative research in criminology' in Noaks, L., Levi, M. and Maguire, M. (eds) *Contemporary Issues in Criminology*, Cardiff, University of Wales Press.

Zehr, H. and Mika, H. (1998) 'Fundamental concepts of restorative justice', *Contemporary Justice Review*, vol. 1, pp. 47–55.

Index

Glossary definitions are indicated by an asterisk (*) before the page number, e.g. abolitionism, *391.

families *cont.*
  as factor in crime/delinquency, 6, 26, 57, 76
  and genetic determinism, 90–1
  lack of discipline, 64, 71, 143
  and poverty, 27, 49, 50, 263
  privacy and abuse of children, 174
  and welfare of children, 49–50
Family Group Conferences (FGCs), 328–9, 375
Farrington, D., 26, 27, 29, 115, 116
Farrington, D. *et al*, 91
Farrington, D. and Welsh, B., 315, 348
fast-tracking, 300
fear of crime, 7–8, 12, 13, 15, 140
  reflecting social reality, 148
  of Victorians, 53
fear of youth, 4, 9, 11
Feeley, M. and Simon, J., 298
Feilzer, M. and Hood, R., 295
feminist criminology, 135–8, 157
  and anti-criminology, 136–7
Ferrell, J., 220, 259
Ferrell, J. *et al*, 227
Ferrell, J. and Sanders, C.R., 227
Ferri, Enrico, 88
festival days: rowdy behaviour, 63, 189
Field, S., 384, 385
final warnings, 257, 313
Finland, 368, 376
  decarceration and diversion, 373–4
Finn, D., 243
Five Towns initiative, 311
Fixed Penalty Notices, 259
Flood-Page, C. *et al*, 41
folk devils, 9, 127, *396
football hooliganism, 127–8
Foster, J., 28
Foucault, Michel, 56, 235–8, 242, 270
France, 357, 365, 368–9, 370, 378
Francis, P., 171
Franklin, B. and Petley, J., 6, 8
free action, adaptive to social conditions, 123
free will, 87, 88, 93, 112, 142–3
freedom of choice, 289
freedom and discipline, 141
Freeman, Derek, 98
Freud, Anna, 94
Freud, Sigmund, 94
Friday, P. and Ren, X., 387
function of crime in society, 101
Furlong, A. and Cartmel, F., 245, 253, 269
further education, 245

gangs, 9, 32–5, 67, 68–9, *396
  membership in Britain, 33–5
  and subcultures, 110, 111, *404
Garland, D., 75, 237, 356
Gatti, U. and Verde, A., 375

Gelder, K. and Thorton, S., 227
Gelsthorpe, L. and Morris, A., 304, 330
gender, 29–32, 135–8
  and class, 32, 138
  and delinquency, 285–6
  and state/social control, 235
  see also boys; feminist criminolgy; masculinity;
    women/girls
generation gap, 191
genetic determinism, 90–3, 115, *397
  and enviromental factors, 91
  and personality, 95–7, 115
Germany, 357, 365, 367, 368, 384
Gillis, J., 66, 67, 69, 72–3
Gilroy, P., 215, 216
Gilroy, P. and Lawrence, P., 202
Girl Guides, 73
girls *see* women/girls
Girls' Guildry, 73
global justice movement, 209–10
globalization, 354, *397
globalization of juvenile justice, 354–61
  and localised cultures, 383–6
  policy transfer, 358–9, 383, 384, *399
  punitive turn, 355–8
  and rights of children, 359–61
  welfare to neo-liberal governance, 354–5
Glueck, S. and Glueck, E., 89
Goldblatt, P. and Lewis, C., 323
Goldson, B., 176, 295, 317, 334–5, 348
Goldson, B. and Coles, D., 177
Goldson, B. and Muncie, J., 304, 348
Goode, E. and Ben-Yehuda, N., 129
Goodey, J., 185
Goring, C., 88–9, 90, 91
Gottfredson, M.R. and Hirschi, T., 142–3
governance, 239–42
  new modes of, 241
governmentality, 237, 240, *397
Graham, J. and Bowling, B., 24, 25, 36, 41
Gramsci, A., 192
Greece, 367, 368
Green, D. and Parton, A., 61
Greenberg, D., 111
group identification, 127
group violence, 34, 126–7
Guardian, 6, 18, 260–1
Guerry, 100
gun crime, 34, 35

Hagan, J. and McCarthy, B., 111
Hale, C. *et al*, 116
Hall, Granville Stanley, 66, 67, 94
Hall, S., 6, 215–16
Hall, S. *et al*, 127, 158, 200, 201, 235
Hall, S. and Jefferson, T., 193, 227
HALT, 368

Hancock, L., 107
Hargreaves, D.H., 191
harm reduction, 314
Harris, R., 335–6
Harris, R. and Timms, N., 337
Harris, R. and Webb, P., 286, 304
Hay, C., 7
Hayek, F.A., 141
Hayward, K., 212
health, 72
Healy, W. and Bronner, A., 95
Hebdige, D., 193, 194, 227
hegemonic masculinity, 138, *397
Hendrick, H., 71, 81
heroin, 38
HerrnsteinR.J. and Murray, C., 92
hidden crime, 18, 25, *397
Hillyard, P. *et al*, 158
hip-hop, 217
hippies, 203–5, 219
Hollands, R., 212
Homeless Act 2002, 251
homelessness, 248–51
    and criminalization, 251–3
homocides, 34, 35, 36, 172
homology, 194, 211, *397
Honwana, A., 181, 182
hooligans, 64, 68–70, *397
Hooton, E., 89, 90
Hopkins Burke, R., 116
Hough, M. and Roberts, J., 41
Housing Act 1980, 249
Housing Act 1996, 318
housing estates, 106, 249
housing shortage, 249
Howard Association on Juvenile
    Offenders, 69
Howard League, 166, 167–8, 334, 349
Hudson, A., 286
Hudson, B., 282, 295–6, 304
Hughes, G., 242, 314
human evolution, 66, 89
Human Genome Project, 93
human rights, 347
Human Rights Watch, 181, 389
Humphries, S., 46, 75–6
Hutson, S. and Liddiard, M., 250
hybridity, 215–19
Hylton, J., 342

idealist history, 45–6, *397
identity crisis, 94
illegitimacy, 145–6
imaginary solutions, 193, *397
incarceration *see* youth custody
independence of youths, 66
Independent, 14, 15, 18

individual positivism, 86–100
    criticism, 99
    genetics, 90–3
    and personality, 93–7
    physiology, 88–90
    and sociological positivism, 102
individual responsibility, 354–5
individualism, 107, 108, 355
Industrial Schools Act 1857, 59
industrial training, 70
inequality, 266
    see also class; poverty
infanticide, 48
innocence of children, 5–9, 49, 57
institutional care, 29, 273–4, 285, 292
    abuse of children in, 175–8
intelligence and criminality, 92
intensive supervision and surveillance
        programmes (ISSPs), 313, 341
inter-agency co-operation, 311
interactionism, 122–3, 122–4, *397
intermediate treatment, 278, 293, 340, *398
International Centre for Prison Studies (ICPS),
        364, 368
international comparisons, 361–9
    adulteration, 369–70
    ages of criminal responsibility, 363
    child well-being, 372
    diversity, 380–6
    ethnic minorities, 379
    immigrants and asylum *see*kers, 378–9
    lack of data, 363
    local cultures and practices, 382–6
    models of juvenile justice, 381–2
    racialization, 379
    repenalization, 367–9
    restoration, 375–6
    rights of children, 377–80
        denial of rights, 377–8
    tolerance and decarceration, 373–5
    total convicted juveniles, 362
    welfare protectionism, 370–3
    welfare spending and rates of imprisonment, 371
    world regions: highest and lowest custody
        rates, 364–5
    youth custody, 365–6, 367–8
international crime surveys, 169
International Crime Victimization Survey
        (ICVS), 169
intervention, 312, 314–17
interventions, 77
introversion, 95, 96
Ireland, 357, 368
Irish children, criminalization of, 61
Islington Crime Survey, 148
Italy, 365, 368, 373, 379, 384
    decarceration, 374–5